SPACE LAW: A CASE STUDY FOR THE PRACTITIONER

Space Law:
A Case Study
for the Practitioner

Implementing a Telecommunications Satellite Business Concept

by

Pamela L. Meredith

and

George S. Robinson

MARTINUS NIJHOFF PUBLISHERS

DORDRECHT / BOSTON / LONDON

ISBN 9041106472

Published by Martinus Nijhoff Publishers,
P.O. Box 163, 3300 AD Dordrecht, The Netherlands.

Sold and distributed in the U.S.A. and Canada
by Kluwer Academic Publishers,
101 Philip Drive, Norwell, MA 02061, U.S.A.

In all other countries, sold and distributed
by Kluwer Academic Publishers Group,
P.O. Box 322, 3300 AH Dordrecht, The Netherlands.

Printed on acid-free paper

Printed in the Netherlands

Dedications

"For my mother Liv Overvoll, husband James Rohacik and son Andrew Rohacik —"

Pamela L. Meredith
Washington, D.C. 1992

"For Doris, Ann, George and Whitson —"

George S. Robinson
Warrenton, Virginia 1992

Table of Contents

Preface

When preparations for space activities began several decades ago, international accords and national laws began to evolve that, hopefully, would anticipate the consequences of these activities and provide some order to their unfolding. As a body of applicable principles and rules, they were referred to as "space law." In fact, they were of little use to the average practicing attorney.

In the last several years, however, space-related technology has developed with surprising rapidity, allowing ever-increasing exploitation of space for scientific, military and commercial purposes. Additional rules and laws have been adopted to regulate the conduct of such activities. Consequently, space law now constitutes a body of international rules and agreements, as well as domestic laws and regulations, that frequently are of routine use in a lawyer's daily practice.

SPACE LAW: A CASE STUDY FOR THE PRACTITIONER: *Implementing a Telecommunications Satellite Business Concept* concentrates on the law governing commercial space ventures, commercial telecommunications satellite projects, in particular. This focus was selected because the telecommunications satellite industry is by far the most mature of all the commercial space industries with a commensurate body of law governing it. Helpful extrapolations, nevertheless, can be made to other commercial space ventures and, to some extent, even to civil non-commercial and military space projects. Many of the same types of regulatory processes and private law transactions discussed in this book also pertain to the implementation of these projects.

This text describes the legal actions lawyer and client must take to provide for the construction, launching and operation of a privately-owned telecommunications satellite. Among such legal actions are ensuring that a client's project is consistent with the cardinal principles of international space law, securing national authorizations and international clearances and completing transactions for the construction, launching and insurance of the satellite.

A step-by-step approach to legal actions was adopted to help make this book a practical, easy-to-use reference for implementing a space business concept. It is designed to assist lawyers in private practice, government attorneys, corporate legal counsel, entrepreneurial executives and teachers and students of space law. It may serve as a desk-top manual for attorneys, as well as executives who wish to know, either in depth or at a glance, what legal actions may be required to initiate and pursue a proposed space business. The majority of available reference books on space law are historical recountings and iterations of treaties, conventions and domestic legislation relating to international and national space activities. Very little is available in the way of practical guidance for the attorney.

Both international and national laws and regulations pertaining to space projects are discussed. Legal regimes in the United States are emphasized over domestic legal frameworks in other countries since more space-related laws and regulations have been adopted and contracts entered into in America than in any other nation. Moreover, the practice of commercial space law is much more widespread and varied in the United States than in any other nation. However, lawyers, business executives and government officials in other countries also will find this information invaluable since the vast majority of the world's commercial space business still is generated in, through, or by private and public sector interests in the United States. Moreover, two decades of United States experience with regulating commercial space activities may also prove to be a useful resource upon which foreign governmental regulators may draw. United States regulatory provisions may serve either as models for other countries, or, indeed, as examples which should be avoided.

Acknowledgements

The authors wish to express their appreciation to friends and colleagues who have contributed to or otherwise assisted in the preparation of this book. Some individuals deserve special mention: Michael G. Aceto, Kristin Alden, Richard R. Colino, James G. Ennis, William D. English, Eric J. Gertler, Douglas A. Heydon, Brien G.R. Hughes, Ronald J. Lepkowski, Peter D. Nesgos, Milton L. Smith, Franceska O. Schroeder and Rachel B. Trinder.

To "[illegible]" Bill English, a real [illegible] man (as was his father), and a true adventurer, [illegible] A.O., of course, my cousin. His father & my uncle [illegible] to [illegible] to the [illegible] ([illegible] type) without [illegible] a key. All my best, and good luck

Bill English

List of Acronyms Most Used

ABM	Anti-ballistic missile
ASAT	Anti-satellite satellite
CCIR	Comité consultatif international des radio-communications
CNES	Centre National d'Etudes Spatiales
COPUOS	Committee on the Peaceful Uses of Outer Space
DARPA	Defense Advance Research Project Agency
ESA	European Space Agency
EUTELSAT	European Telecommunications Satellite Organization
FCC	Federal Communications Commission
ICBM	Inter-continental ballistic missile
IFRB	International Radio Frequency Board
INMARSAT	International Maritime Telecommunications Satellite Organization
INTELSAT	International Telecommunications Satellite Organization
ITAR	International Traffic in Arms Regulations
ITU	International Tele communication Union
MPM	Multilateral Planning Meetings
NASA	National Aeronautics and Space Administration
NASDA	National Space Development Agency of Japan
PTT	Post, Telephone and Telegraph Administration
RARC	Regional Administrative Radio Conference
U.N.	United Nations
USTR	United States Trade Representative
WARC	World Administrative Radio Conference

Introduction

January 14, 1992

Dear Space Lawyer:

We understand that you have been retained by a private company seeking to implement a space business venture. Enclosed is a book we believe will be immensely helpful to you and your client, as well as others who might be involved in your client's space business venture.

SPACE LAW: A CASE STUDY FOR THE PRACTITIONER: *Implementing a Telecommunications Satellite Business Concept* provides a step-by-step guide to legal actions which are necessary to place a commercial satellite in orbit. While the focus of this text is on a satellite telecommunications business concept, useful extrapolations can be made to other space projects, such as satellite remote-sensing and space transportation, since many of the same types of legal steps are necessary also to engage in these activities.

The book describes seven legal actions and considerations that are key to the implementation of your client's commercial telecommunications satellite project: 1) determining the implications of the cardinal principles of international space law for your client's project; 2) obtaining the necessary national governmental authorizations to construct, launch and operate your client's satellite; 3) securing protection from harmful radio interference to your client's satellite transmissions through the procedures of the International Telecommunication Union (ITU); 4) coordinating your client's satellite operation with those of the International Telecommunications Satellite Organization (INTELSAT) and other similar international organizations; 5) assessing and managing the risks of damage and liability your client faces during satellite manufacturing, launching and operation; 6) concluding an agreement for launching of your client's satellite; and 7) procuring insurance to protect your client against the risks of loss and liability.

Usually, it takes about six years to complete the steps just outlined. Obtaining the necessary licenses and permissions from the appropriate national authority(ies) often can be extremely time-consuming. Moreover, the manufacturing of the satellite takes considerable time, e.g., between thirty and thirty-six months for an average geostationary telecommunications satellite. Also contributing to the long lead-time for satellite projects are the difficulties often experienced in the efforts to obtain financing. Indeed, financial may not be possible in some cases. After all, the capital investment required to construct two average geostationary telecommunications satellites and to launch and insure one of them is in the neighborhood of $400 million. Several U.S. entrepreneurial, start-up companies, which received authorizations from the United States Federal Communications Commission to construct, launch and operate satellite systems in the 1980s, have since abandoned their plans due to lack of capital, after expending considerable effort. Even some large, established companies decided not to pursue their planned satellite ventures for failure to attract investment partners.

Given the desire to minimize the project implementation time, the relative timing of the necessary legal steps is critical. Already at the business planning stage, you should consider the implications of the cardinal principles of international space law for your client's project. For example, legislative or regulatory initiatives may be necessary to ensure compliance with international space law that could delay your client's project. Such legislation and regulations may be required in the country where your client intends to operate its satellite business in order for that country to conform with the fundamental principle of international law requiring government authorization and supervision of private space activities. See Chapter 2.

As soon as your client's satellite system and services have been conceptualized, a business plan completed, and the cardinal principles of international law have been considered, it is time to request authorization (license) from the appropriate national authority to launch and operate the satellite. In the United States, a satellite construction permit is required, as well. Only a handful of countries have designated licensing authorities and adopted regulatory regimes for the authorization of telecommunications satellites or other space activities. Where such rules do not exist, and where existing laws pertaining to related activities are not sufficiently broad in scope and purpose to encompass satellites, it may become necessary for your client to encourage and influence executive and/or legislative processes required to establish rules or other mechanisms whereby its project may be officially sanctioned. As noted, obtaining an authorization can be a lengthy process. Surprisingly, perhaps, even in the United States, where private satellite authorizations already are a relatively routine matter, it still takes two-to-three years on average to obtain the requisite permits and licenses. See Chapter 3.

Registration in the International Telecommunication Union's (ITU) Master International Frequency Register of the frequencies to be used by your client is essential to protect its satellite transmissions from harmful radio interference from other satellite operations. Since the ITU is an intergovernmental organization, only a State or governmental agency —

typically, a governmental agency in charge of telecommunications in the country from whose territory your client's satellite will be operated — can initiate and complete the procedures leading to ITU registration. However, your client must monitor the process and be prepared to supply the technical information required for submission to the ITU. The process of obtaining ITU registration may take anywhere from ten months to four years, and can be started as soon as the governmental entity handling the matter is confident that an authorization will be granted for your client's satellite system, or some other satellite system with the same or similar technical characteristics. In the United States, in order to expedite the process, the Federal Communications Commission often initiates the process while applications for satellite authorizations are still pending. See Chapter 4.

Coordination must take place with INTELSAT and other international organizations that operate commercial telecommunications satellites and to whose satellite transmissions your client's satellite operations could cause harmful radio interference. Again, since these are public international organizations, your client cannot initiate or carry out the coordination process, but must rely on a governmental entity to do so. The coordination process can be initiated as soon as your client's satellite system has been authorized, and will go on in parallel with the ITU procedures since the interference issues to be resolved are similar. If the services your client is proposing are the same as the core services provided by any of these commercial international organizations, then so-called "economic harm" coordination will be necessary, as well, to ensure that your client's operation does not deprive significantly the organization of business. Such coordination may result in certain restrictions on your client's competing service in order to protect the organization's revenue base. See Chapter 5.

When national authorizations to construct, launch and operate the satellite have been secured and international coordination efforts are under way, but before any transactions for the construction, launch or insurance of the satellite have been completed, it is time to pause for risk assessment and risk management. Several risks face your client during the implementation of the satellite project. Policies and laws may change jeopardizing your client's governmental authorization (political risk). Your client's innovative satellite design may result in an in-orbit failure (technical risk). Market projections may not materialize (market risk). Perhaps calling most specifically for legal talent in their management are the risks of damage and liability that face your client during satellite construction, launch and operation. For example, the satellite may be destroyed during launching; it may malfunction in orbit with consequent loss of revenue and perhaps even liability to your client's customers who do not receive service; and the satellite may cause damage to persons and property on the ground and subject your client to third party liability. In varying degrees, these risks can be managed through risk minimization techniques, contractual risk allocation and insurance. In the United States, certain risk allocation solutions are mandated by law pertaining to the contract with the launch company for launching of your client's satellite. See Chapter 6.

One attractive risk management solution to consider involves contracting with the satellite manufacturer for a "turn-key" satellite system. The turn-key concept implies that the manufacturer delivers the satellite to your client in orbit in an operational condition, with the manufacturer assuming the risk of loss or damage to the satellite during launching. Traditionally, the transfer of risk to the satellite owner has taken place at the time of launch, which means that your client would bear the risk during launching, the most precarious phase of the satellite project implementation. A few manufacturers now offer turn-key systems. If a turn-key arrangement cannot be negotiated, your client should consider insurance for the launch. Requests for proposals to build the satellite, and negotiations with the manufacturer, should begin as soon as possible after the necessary national construction permits and authorizations have been secured, considering the time it takes to manufacture the satellite. Preliminary discussions with manufacturers may, of course, take place before such time. See Chapter 6.4.1.

When negotiations for the manufacture of the satellite have been completed and the satellite purchase contract signed, it is time to initiate the procurement of launch services. While the majority of launch providers are found in the United States, commercial launch services are offered also by European, Soviet and Chinese companies or entities. The launch contracts offered by major launch providers today are remarkably similar in terms of the items they address and particularly with respect to risk allocation. For example, they generally contain interparty waivers stipulating that each party shall be responsible for the damage it sustains during launch activities, and provide for "flow-down" of the waivers to the parties' respective contractors and subcontractors which participate in launch activities. Launch contracts usually also provide that the launch company shall take out third party liability insurance also protecting your client as an additional insured under the policy. Most launch contracts offered by today's commercial launch providers can trace their origins to the United States National Aeronautics and Space Administration's (NASA) Space Shuttle standard commercial launch contract, crafted in the early 1980s when NASA dominated the commercial space launch arena. See Chapters 6. and 7.

Insurance is an option if, after pursuing risk minimization techniques and contractual risk allocation with the satellite manufacturer and the launch company, risks of loss or liability still remain which your client may not want to assume. Four general categories of space insurance coverage exist: pre-launch, launch, in-orbit and third party liability insurance. Coverage options are available within each of these general categories. As an alternative to procuring insurance, your client can self-insure, that is, assume the risk. While self-insurance may be an attractive option for relatively large organizations operating several satellites, it usually is not a solution for an entrepreneurial, start-up company the entire future of which depends on the successful launch of one satellite. Another important factor in the consideration of whether to buy insurance is the premium amount. Premium rates especially for launch insurance fluctuate, and the incentive to buy insurance is greater, of course, the lower the premium rate (see Chapter 8.)

Finally, you will note that the book refers to space activities and related laws and policies of the former Union of Soviet Socialist Republics. The book manuscript was completed for publication while the status of the Soviet Union was still quite unsettled and the complexion, indeed, the immediate fate, of the newly-established Commonwealth of Independent States was far from clear. Although about five space agencies seem to be emerging from the political and economic chaos of an unraveled Soviet Union, it is expected that some time will pass before the former U.S.S.R. space program will develop precise and dependable guidelines upon which space entrepreneurs and free market investors can rely with confidence. Since it is clear the unfolding political process will continue for some time, the publisher agreed with us not to change references to the Soviet Union's space program, policies, contracts and agreements as set forth in the text, other than in occasional footnotes, until the political and economic characteristics of the program have settled and restabilized somewhat.

As you can see from this summary, we are providing the reader with current "hands-on" advice that incorporates some of the jurisprudential underpinnings of space law, but which focuses on how to implement your client's satellite project in an orderly and logical, sequential fashion (see figure 1). We hope this book will be of help to you, and wish you success and personal satisfaction in your space law practice. The regime of commercial space law is poised for rapid development, along with the commercial undertakings being formulated and pursued by States, organizations and the new generation of space entrepreneurs!

Sincerely,

The Authors

Figure 1

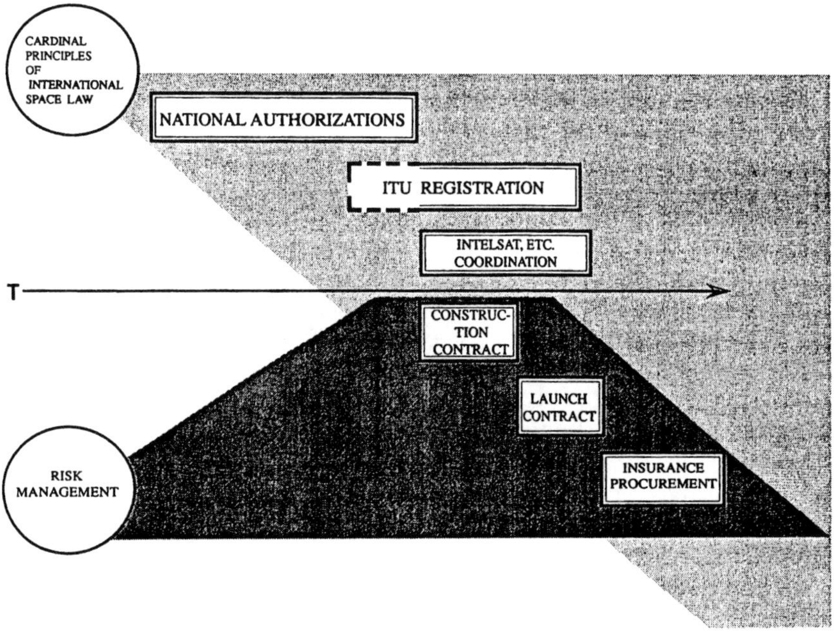
CARDINAL
PRINCIPLES
OF
INTERNATIONAL
SPACE LAW
NATIONAL AUTHORIZATIONS
ITU REGISTRATION
INTELSAT, ETC.
COORDINATION
T
CONSTRUC-
TION
CONTRACT
LAUNCH
CONTRACT
RISK
MANAGEMENT
INSURANCE
PROCUREMENT

1. The Practice of Commercial Space Law

Brief descriptions of space law, the commercial space industry to which it in part applies, and the nature of the practice of space law are provided in this Chapter. The purpose is to introduce the subjects, concepts and terms of space law and business, and to touch upon some of the basic issues confronting the space law practitioner. More extensive discussions of the legal actions required to initiate and maintain a space business are provided in Chapters 2. through 8. The reader who already is familiar with the subjects of space law and business may wish to refer directly to the Chapter of specific interest.

1.1. What is Space Law?

DESCRIPTION. Space law can be described rather loosely as the law applicable the other to space activities. As such, space law includes international agreements, treaties, conventions, customary international law, resolutions, declarations and memoranda of understanding, as well as national laws, executive orders, administrative regulations and judicial decisions that control or otherwise influence the conduct of activities in space.[1] Certain transactions relating to space operations, such as satellite launch contracts, have become so standardized that they, too, can be considered part of an evolving body of space law.

Although all legal instruments that control or influence space activities in broad terms may be referred to as space law, there is variation in their relative degrees of "space uniqueness." Some international agreements and domestic laws were adopted specifically to regulate space activities and are, therefore, quite "space unique." Examples include the United Nations space treaties, such as the Treaty on Principles Governing the Activities of States in the Exploration and Use of Outer Space, Including the Moon and Other Celestial Bodies (Outer Space Treaty);[2] the Agreement Relating to the International Telecommunications Satellite Organization (INTELSAT Agreement);[3] the United States Communications Satellite Act of 1962;[4] the United States Commercial Space Launch Act of 1984;[5] the Swedish Act on Space Activities of 1982;[6] and the United Kingdom Outer Space Act of 1986.[7] Also, satellite launch agreements may be included in this body of space unique law.

Other international agreements and national laws have been amended or modified to apply also to space activities. These include, for example, the International Telecommunication Union (ITU) Radio Regulations,[8] which were amended when the ITU assumed jurisdiction over space communication;[9] the British Cable and Broadcasting Act of 1984,[10] Parts 25 and 100 of Title 47 of the United States Code of Federal Regulations,[11] which have been amended to include provisions for telecommunications satellites; and Chapter 10 of Title 35 of the United States Code, which was amended to extend United States patent law to inventions made in space.[12]

Then, there are other rules of international law, as well as domestic laws and regulations, that were not adopted or modified to regulate space activities, yet they apply, nevertheless, because they embrace space activities as secondary or incidental to their purposes. In other words, a partic-

---

1. In S. Gorove, STUDIES IN SPACE LAW: ITS CHALLENGES AND PROSPECTS (1977) [hereinafter cited as Gorove, STUDIES IN SPACE LAW], at 41, the author describes space law in the following fashion:

   > [domestic legislation, executive orders, administrative and judicial decisions may deal with various aspects of the problems arising out of man's activities in outer space. Similarly, international treaties, conventions, agreements, understandings, as well as customary international law, along with resolutions and declarations of the United nations and other international organizations, decisions of international tribunals and writings of highly qualified publicists may provide authoritative or auxiliary sources . . . .

   In the very early days of space law, certain scholars suggested that space law represented an entirely new and separate legal regime that did not fit within the bounds of traditional international and domestic law. This view was repudiated in the mid-1960s. *See* B. Cheng, The *Legal Regime of Airspace and Outer Space: The Boundary Problem: Functionalism Versus Spatialism,* 5 ANNALS of AIR & SPACE L. 323, 328 (1980) (providing that "there is no such thing as an independent legal system known as space law freewheeling in outer space"). Reflecting what seems to be the prevailing view among legal scholars today, Cheng describes space law as "merely a functional classification of those rules of international law and of [domestic] law relating to outer space, natural and man-made objects in outer space, astronauts and man's activities in outer space or affecting outer space." *Id.*

   The following books and annual compendia provide space law introductions, overviews and topical discussions: S. Gorove, STUDIES IN SPACE LAW, *supra;* A.S. Piradov, CURRENT PROBLEMS: INTERNATIONAL SPACE LAW (Moscow, 1976); C.Q. Christol, THE MODERN INTERNATIONAL LAW OF OUTER SPACE (1984); N.C. Goldman, AMERICAN SPACE LAW: INTERNATIONAL AND DOMESTIC (1988); G.H. Reynolds & R.P. Merges, OUTER SPACE: PROBLEMS OF LAW AND POLICY (1989); ANNALS OF AIR & SPACE L. (Ed. M. Matte, Institute & Center of Air & Space Law, McGill University); and COLLOQUIUMs ON THE L. OF OUTER SPACE (International Institute of Space Law, International Astronautical Federation).
2. Done Jan. 27, 1967, *entered into force* Oct. 10, 1967, T.I.A.S. 6347.

ular space activity, or aspect of a space business endeavor, is part of a larger category that the law is intended to regulate. Examples of such legal instruments include the Charter of the United Nations,[13] customary international law concerning international liability for damage, the United States Communications Act of 1934[14] (which applies to satellites since they are considered "radio stations"), and general principles of contract and tort law. Indeed, these laws and legal principles are not at all "space unique," and it may seem far-fetched to refer to them as space law, even when they are applied specifically to space operations.

EXAMPLES OF SPACE LAW INSTRUMENTS. Definitions and classifications of space law are not of immediate and paramount importance to the space law practitioner. Rather, a firm grasp of existing rules and criteria that apply to, or might impact upon, a client's space project is what matters to the practitioner. Depending upon the nature and characteristics of a client's project, the attorney should be knowledgeable about the types of laws referred to below, and also be able to answer the kinds of business-related questions which bring them into play.

UNITED NATIONS TREATIES. Four treaties have been promulgated under the auspices of the United Nations that embody certain cardinal principles of space law applicable to all space projects and programs:[15] the Outer Space Treaty;[16] Agreement on the Rescue of Astronauts, the Return of Astronauts and the Return of Objects Launched Into Outer Space (Rescue and Return Agreement);[17] Convention on International

---

3. Done Aug. 20, 1971, *entered into force* Feb. 12, 1973. T.I.A.S. 7532. *See also* Operating Agreement Relating to the International Telecommunications Satellite Organization [hereinafter cited as INTELSAT Operating Agreement] (concerning in particular the financial principles governing the International Telecommunications Satellite Organization (INTELSAT)). The above dates and cite apply.
4. 47 U.S.C. §§ 701-757 (1988).
5. 49 U.S.C. §§ 2601-2623 (1988).
6. 1962: 963. The Act is supplemented by a decree, Decree on Space Activities (1982: 1069). *See* J Reifarth, *Nationale Weltraum Gesetze in Europa, 36* ZEITSCHRIFT FUR LUFT UND WELTRAUMRECHT 11 (1987) (describing the Act).
7. 1 Current L. Stat. Annot. 38-1, para. 1 (1986).
8. *Final Acts,* World Administrative Radio Conference (1979), done Sept. 24-Dec. 6, 1979, *entered into force* Jan. 1, 1982 [hereinafter cited as *Final Acts,* WARC-79].
9. The ITU for the first time allocated frequencies for space operations in 1959. *See* Chapter 4.2. (providing a history of ITU frequency allocations for satellite services).
10. Cable and Broadcasting Act, 1984, ch. 46.
11. Title 47 is entitled "Telecommunications." Parts 25 and 100 of this Title have been amended to include provisions governing telecommunications satellites.
12. 35 U.S.C. § 105 (1988).
13. *Done* June 26, 1945, *entered into force* Oct. 24, 1945, E.A.S. 236, 3 *Bevans 697.*.
14. 47 U.S.C. §§ 151-701 (1988).

Liability for Damage Caused by Space Objects (Liability Conventio-n);[18] and Convention on Registration of Objects Launched Into Outer Space (Registration Convention).[19]

The kinds of questions raised by these treaties include, for example, whether the legal framework in the country where your client resides meets the requirements of Article VI of the Outer Space Treaty, which mandates authorization and supervision of private space activities by a nation State. In other words, do licensing and regulatory provisions exist through which the government can authorize and supervise your client's space project in accordance with Article VI? Additionally, does the country authorizing your client's space project maintain a national space registry as required under the Registration Convention, or will registration of your client's spacecraft in a foreign registry be necessary? What are the implications of foreign registration? Furthermore, what is your client's indirect exposure to liability considering the government/State's international liability under the Liability Convention?

INTERNATIONAL REGULATION OF TELECOMMUNICATIONS SATELLITES. Several international agreements, treaties, conventions and resolutions specifically regulate telecommunications satellites. Chief among these are the Radio Regulations promulgated by the International Telecommunication Union.[20] Questions, such as whether your client can use a particular radio frequency band to provide the proposed telecommunications satellite service and what measures have to be taken to obtain protection from radio interference, are in part answered by the ITU Radio Regulations. Furthermore, a number of agreements have been concluded for the establishment of international satellite operating organizations, such as the International Telecommunications Satellite Organization (INTELSAT),[21] the International Maritime Satellite Organization (INMARSAT)[22] and others. Questions brought into play by these agreements

---

15. *See* Chapter 2. (discussing the cardinal principles of space law). A fifth agreement, entitled Agreement Governing the Activities of States on the Moon and Other Celestial Bodies, *done* Dec. 18, 1979, *entered into force* Jul. 12, 1984. U.N.G.A. Res. 34/68, Dec. 5, 1979 [hereinafter cited as the Moon Treaty], is not included in the list, below, since only very few countries have ratified the agreement, not including the major spacefaring nations, *i.e.*, the United States, the Soviet Union, Japan, France, India, the U.K. and China.
16. Outer Space Treaty, *supra* note 2.
17. *Done* Apr. 2, 1968, *entered into force* Dec. 3, 1968. T.I.A.S. 6599.
18. *Done* Mar. 29, 1972, *entered into force* Sept. 1, 1973. T.I.A.S. 7762.
19. *Done* Jan. 14, 1975, *entered into force* Sept. 15, 1976, T.I.A.S. 8480.
20. *Final Acts*, WARC-79, *supra* note 8. The International Telecommunication Union (ITU) Radio Regulations are revised periodically at ITU Administrative Radio Conferences. *See* Chapter 4.2. (providing a history of ITU Administrative Radio Conferences). The last general revision took place in 1979.
21. INTELSAT Agreement, *supra* note 3.
22. Convention of the International Maritime Satellite Organization, done September 3, 1976, *entered into force* July 16, 1979, T.I.A.S. 9605

relate to whether, and to what extent, your client's satellite operation must be coordinated with those of INTELSAT and INMARSAT to avoid technical interference and business deprivation.

NATIONAL REGULATION OF TELECOMMUNICATION SATELLITES. Domestic laws and regulations have been promulgated in the United States and other countries for licensing and regulation of privately-operated telecommunications satellites,[23] and may provide answers to your client's questions, such as whether it can commence construction of a satellite without government authorization? What are the procedures and criteria for obtaining a satellite construction permit and an operating license? How are the criteria usually interpreted and applied? Is the financial condition of a company a consideration in the determination of whether to grant a construction permit or an operating license? What is the time-frame for obtaining all the necessary authorizations? Sometimes, laws and regulations provide little guidance on the application of criteria and on time-frames. Instead, the practitioner must refer to past experience.

TELECOMMUNICATIONS SATELLITE-RELATED CONTRACTS. Transactions pertaining to telecommunications satellites, such as satellite purchase contracts, satellite launch services agreements, satellite insurance policies and transponder lease agreements, are critical components of a space lawyer's practice.[24] Certain fairly standardized provisions contained in these transactional instruments and established industry practices can help answer your client's questions regarding, for example, the manufacturer's liability for damage to the satellite during construction and for lost earnings due to satellite malfunction in orbit, as well as the launch provider's liability for loss of the satellite during launching. Your client also may want to know the relative time-frames for commencing and completing negotiations of the various transactions that must be consummated for a space operation to materialize.

INTERNATIONAL REGULATION OF LAUNCH SERVICES. International regulation of launch services is emerging. A series of memoranda of

---

23. For example, in the U.S., the Communications Act of 1934, as amended, 47 U.S.C. §§ 151-701 (1988), the Communications Satellite Act of 1962, as amended, 47 U.S.C. §§ 701-757 (1988), and their implementing regulations, 47 C.F.R. Part 25, entitled "Satellite Communications," and Part 100, entitled "Direct Broadcast Satellite Service," provide for licensing and regulation of privately-owned and operated telecommunications satellites.

24. For example, launch contracts have become fairly standardized. In particular, risk allocation provisions appearing in launch contracts offered by major launch providers in business today are remarkably similar. *See* Chapters 6., 7. and 8. (concerning transactions pertaining to the manufacture, launching and insurance of a satellite). *See also* P.L. Meredith, *Risk Allocation Provisions in Commercial Launch Contracts*, XXXIV COLLOQUIUM ON THE L. OF OUTER SPACE, 264 (1991) (comparing risk allocation provisions found in five commercial launch agreements).

agreements concerning the launching of United States-manufactured satellites on the Chinese Long March vehicle were concluded by the United States and China in 1989, addressing pricing, technology transfer and liability issues (see Chapter 7.1.). Negotiations are now underway between the United States Trade Representative and the European Space Agency to establish "rules of the road" for Arianespace and U.S. launch companies with regard to subsidies and unfair trading practices. Later, the trade talks may be extended to include other countries, as well.

NATIONAL REGULATION OF LAUNCH VEHICLES. In the U.S., legislation has been enacted and implemented with respect to licensing and regulation of privately-owned and operated launch vehicles and "space ports."[25] These rules establish criteria and procedures for licensing, and provide answers to questions, such as whether your client needs a license simply to launch just a sounding rocket. Does your client need a license to participate in a space port project in a foreign country, or to launch a vehicle from the territory of a foreign country? Does a state government (within the United States) need authorization from the Federal Government to operate a launch port? If your client is a satellite company, need it concern itself with the licensing of the launch vehicle?

LAUNCH VEHICLE-RELATED CONTRACTS. Private transactions pertaining to space transportation, such as launch services agreements and agreements for the use of government and private launch facilities are evolving, although no private launch facility is yet in operation. Your client may ask whether a launch provider normally would agree to bear the risk of damage to the satellite and to third parties. If your client is a private U.S. or a foreign launch port operator, does the United States Air Force Model Agreement,[26] providing for the use of U.S. government launch facilities by private launch companies, serve as an acceptable model?

REGULATION OF REMOTE-SENSING SATELLITES. International and domestic laws and regulations exist for commercial satellite remote-sensing. International law addresses the issue of whether a person, business, or nation has the right to "sense" by satellite (remote-sensing) the territory and resources of a foreign country and, if so, what rights the sensed State has in the data and information gathered.[27] In the United States, laws have been adopted and implemented which regulate the licensing and operation of privately-owned, remote-sensing satellites.[28]Your client may want to know the procedures and criteria for obtaining a license to operate a satellite and market satellite images or data. Perhaps your client has heard that the U.S. government can censor certain information in the interest of "national security" and is concerned about the impact such a measure would have on its business. Moreover, are there

25. Commercial Space Launch Act of 1984, as amended, 49 U.S.C. §§ 2601-2623 (1988), and its implementing regulations, Commercial Space Transportation; Licensing Regulations, 14 C.F.R. Parts 400-499 (1990).

26. Department of the Air Force Model Expendable Launch Vehicle Commercialization Agreement, Revision Two, May 12, 1989.

restrictions with respect to the degree of resolution used to obtain images from the satellite? Is there an obligation to distribute satellite data on a non-discriminatory basis? Assuming your client is a foreign company intending to establish a marketing and sales office in the United States, would it be subject to U.S. law?

TRANSACTIONS CONCERNING MATERIALS PROCESSING. Although no rules have been adopted to regulate specifically materials processing and microgravity research in space, several transactions have been consummated between private parties and government agencies, or brokers for such agencies, providing access to space. For example, several companies have entered into joint endeavor agreements with NASA to fly their experiments on the NASA Space Shuttle.[29] Your client may ask about the criteria and procedures for obtaining such agreements. Your client may wonder, also, whether restrictions apply to the placement of experiments on foreign space stations. Some United States companies already have contracted with Payload Systems, Inc. of Cambridge, Massachusetts, which arranges for the placement of microgravity-gravity experiments on the Soviet space station *Mir.*

EXPORT RESTRICTIONS. Export laws, regulations and policies exist concerning transfer to foreign countries of spacecraft, their component parts and related technical data.[30] Typically, at issue may be whether

---

27. *See* Principles Relating to Remote Sensing of the Earth from Outer Space, U.N.G.A. Res. 41/65 Dec. 3, 1986 (adopted without a vote) (permitting remote-sensing of the territory of a foreign State, provided, however, that the sensed State shall have access to "primary data" on a "non-discriminatory basis" and at "reasonable cost." *Id.,* art. XII). The sensed State also shall have access to "analyzed information" that is "available" and in the "possession of any State." *Id.* The latter phrase may be interpreted to mean that analyzed information owned by a private company is not subject to the access requirement. "Primary data" means "those raw data that are acquired by remote sensors borne by a space object and that are transmitted or delivered to the ground from space by telemetry in the form of electromagnetic signals, by photographic film, magnetic tape or other means." *Id.,* art. I(b). "Analyzed information" means "the information resulting from the interpretation of processed data, inputs of data and knowledge from other sources." *Id.,* rt. I(d). "Processed data" means "the products resulting from the processing of primary data, needed in order to make such data usable." *Id.,* art I(c). The Resolution applies only to civil and commercial satellite remote-sensing, and not to military reconnaissance or surveillance. *Id.,* art I(a).
28. Land Remote-Sensing Commercialization Act of 1984, 15 U.S.C. §§ 4201-4292 (1988), and its implementing regulations, Licensing of Private Remote-Sensing Space Systems, 15 C.F.R. Part 960 (1990).
29. *See e.g.* Master Joint Endeavor Agreement Between National Aeronautics and Space Administration and The Minnesota Mining and Manufacturing Company for the Commercial Use of Space in the Area of Organic Science and Polymer Science, (Dec. 5, 1986) (concerning access to NASA Space Shuttle flights for Minnesota Mining and Manufacturing Company's experiments).

export laws prohibit the launching of your client's satellite by a foreign launch vehicle from a facility in a foreign country. Under certain circumstances, the required export license for the satellite simply may not be granted. Furthermore, with regard to transfer of launch-related technology, an interesting, and somewhat esoteric, controversy developed over the participation in a management role in a launch project planned at Cape York, N.S.W., Australia, of a division of United Technologies Corporation of Hartford, Connecticut.[31] United Technologies will need an export license under United States law to participate in this project. However, since the Cape York project contemplates the use of Soviet launch vehicles, the license will be contingent upon an agreement between the United States and Soviet Union limiting the latter's commercial launch activities elsewhere.

---

30. In the U.S., the transfer of technology is controlled by one of two statutes, depending upon the classification of the technology: Either the Export Administration Act, 50 U.S.C. §§ 768-799 (1988), and its implementing regulations, Export Administration Regulations, 15 C.F.R. §§ 121-130 (1990), if the technology comes under the jurisdiction of the Department of Commerce, or the Arms Export Control Act, 22 U.S.C. §§ 2751-2796 (1988), and its implementing regulations, the International Traffic in Arms Regulations (ITAR), 22 C.F.R. §§ 121-130 (1990), if the technology falls within the jurisdiction of the Department of State. Most spacecraft and their component parts, as well as related services and technical data, fall within the Department of States' jurisdiction, and are subject to ITAR regulation. This is because they are considered "defense articles" and, consequently, they are included in the United States Munitions List, which is administered by the Department of State. The Munitions List is set forth in 22 C.F.R. § 121.1 (1990). Category VIII of that list concerns spacecraft, including communications satellites and launch vehicles, and their component parts; Category XVIII concerns related technical data; and Category XIX concerns related services. The significance of being subject to Department of State jurisdiction, rather than Department of Commerce jurisdiction, is that different considerations apply in the evaluation of the export license application. United States foreign policy and national security interests are overriding concerns in licensing items on the Munitions List, while the promotion of U.S. industry and trade is the principal consideration in the licensing of items subject to Department of Commerce jurisdiction (*i.e.*, items on the Commodity Control List). The likelihood of obtaining a license also is greater if the commodity is included in the Commodity Control List.

    The export of certain space-related technology to particular countries may be proscribed outright as a matter of law or policy: *See e.g.* Departments of Commerce, Justice and State, the Judiciary, and Related Agencies Appropriations Act of 1992, Pub. L. No. 102-140 § 608, 105 Stat. 782, (1991) (restricting the export of U.S.-made satellites to China for launch on the Long March vehicle). *See* also 50 U.S.C. App. § 2404 (1988) (providing the President with the authority to restrict the export of certain technologies for national security reasons).

31. The project is still at a very preliminary stage.

TAX CONSIDERATIONS. As with any other business, tax considerations can be critical also to space ventures.[32] For example, will income from your client's space project be considered foreign source income, and how does foreign sourcing affect foreign tax credit?[33] Moreover, tax treatment of potential lenders and investors in your client's space project is of great importance with respect to financing. For example, U.S. banks and financial institutions provide financing for satellite operations through transponder sale and lease-back arrangements, which entitle them to take advantage of the Accelerated Cost Recovery System, a depreciation method permitting the cost of the satellite to be recovered over a predetermined recovery period that is shorter than the satellite's income-producing life.[34]

INTELLECTUAL PROPERTY LAW. Intellectual property law relevant to spacecraft and space projects has developed some very interesting twists, and invite such questions as whether certain information revealed in transactions can be protected by trade secret or proprietary data agreements. Moreover, are inventions made wholly in space patentable?[35] What are the copyright implications of your client's planned satellite television or remote-sensing business?

FINANCING. Space project financing is replete with legal considerations. From a financing perspective, space ventures typically are characterized as high-risk, capital-intensive projects with long lead-times, often involving a single asset (e.g. the satellite). The selection of sources and methods of financing, as well as the structuring of, a space venture must reflect these characteristics. Further, sources and methods of financing usually depend on the structure of the venture, and *vice versa*. Also, tax considerations impact financing decisions and may determine, for example, whether your client's space venture is organized as a limited partnership, a Chapter "S" Corporation, or a joint venture. (A Chapter "S" Corporation is not subject to Federal income tax as a corporation; rather, each shareholder must account for its *pro rata* share of the corporation's income or loss). Further, restrictions on foreign investment also may have to be explored. In the United States, for example, severe limitations on foreign ownership i.e., equity investment, apply to satellite companies that are characterized as broadcasters or common carriers (see Chapter 3.2.3.). Furthermore, your client also should be aware of the intricate interplay that sometimes exists between government authorization of a

---

32. Previously, space projects were somewhat at a disadvantage under the Internal Revenue Code (I.R.C.) based on the premise that space activities were not conducted within the geographical limits of the U.S. For example, research credit was not available to a company doing research in space since Section 30(d)(1) of the Internal Revenue Code, I.R.C.§ 30(d)(1) (1988), defined qualified research to exclude research conducted outside the U.S. *See* J.V. Baird, *Space Commercialization and the Federal Income Tax* 51 J. AIR L. & COM., 897, 921 (1986) (discussing tax-related issues peculiar to an entrepreneurial start-up space platform company and its materials processing customers).

space project and its financing. Often, both are interdependent and neither may be possible to abtain separately![36]

ENVIRONMENTAL REGULATION. Environmental regulation of space projects is emerging. In the United States, for example, every private launch company must conduct an environmental impact evaluation as a condition of a license to operate a launch vehicle.[37] This also is true for satellite Earth station construction in certain cases.[38] In the future, rules may be adopted that require space operators to minimize the generation of debris from their space missions. Such rules might require satellite operators to boost geostationary satellites into higher so-called "graveyard" orbits and to re-enter low-Earth orbit satellites through controlled maneuvers. Launch companies also could be required to ensure re-entry of their rocket upper stages. Alternatively, venting of excess propellants

---

33. "Except as provided in regulations, any income derived from space or ocean activity (A) if derived by a United States person, shall be sourced in the United States, and (B) if derived by a person other than a United States person, shall be sourced outside the United States," I.R.C.§ 863(d)(1) (1988). Space and ocean activity is defined to include "any activity conducted in space . . . ." I.R.C.§ 863(d)(2)(A) (1988). According to a Senate Finance Committee Report accompanying the Tax Reform Act of 1986, Pub.L. 99-514, reprinted in 917 CCH STANDARD FED. TAX REP., para. 27,000, at 49,206 (1990), "space and ocean activities" include the following space activities: "performance and provision of services in space . . . the leasing of equipment, including spacecraft located in space . . . the licensing of technology or other intangibles for the use in space . . . and manufacturing of property in space. Also . . . underwriting income from the insurance of risks on activities conducted in space . . . ." Query: Are the provision of domestic telecommunications and remote-sensing satellite services, the lease of satellite transponders, licensing of space technology, materials processing in space, and underwriting of, *e.g.*, satellite launch risks, considered "space and ocean activities? Pursuant to I.R.C.§ 863(d)(2)(B) (1988), certain space activities are not considered "space or ocean activities." These include "(i) any activity giving rise to transportation income as defined in section 863(c) and (ii) any activity giving rise to international communications income as defined in subsection (e)(2) . . . ." These activities are subject to special sourcing rules. *See* I.R.C.§§ 863(c)(1)-(2) and 863(e)(1) (1988) (concerning sourcing of transportation and international communications income, respectively). Transportation income is defined as income derived from or in connection with "(A) the use of . . . a vessel or aircraft, or (B) the performance of services directly related to the use of a vessel or an aircraft," I.R.C.§ 863(c)(3) (1988). Query: Is space launch service-related income considered transportation income? International communications income is defined to include "all income derived from the transmission of communications and data from the United States to any foreign country . . . or from any foreign country . . . to the United States," I.R.C.§ 863(e)(2) (1988). Space and ocean income previously was considered foreign source income. *See* C. Kelly, *Taxing Space and Ocean Activities*, TAX NOTES (Special Rep.) (Nov. 16, 1987) (discussing the consequences of taxation of income from space operations as income sourced in the U.S.).

remaining in the upper stage rocket bodies could be required, thereby reducing the risk of explosions that generate large amounts of space debris.[39]

PRESENT AND FUTURE PERSPECTIVES. Presently, and for the foreseeable future, the practice of space law will be largely Earth-oriented since most space technologies currently employed have only terrestrial applications. Satellites, for example, are employed to facilitate communications between and among points on Earth, or they are used to collect data about Earth's resources, geographical contours, or weather patterns. Materials processing in space is still at the experimental stage, and for quite some time pharmaceuticals and other products, even if they are manufactured or refined in space, will be marketed primarily for use on Earth.

In the future, as technology and economic conditions allow, long-duration and permanent habitats or manufacturing facilities in space will

---

34. I.R.C.§ 168 (1988). In addition, the financial institution will receive lease payments for the satellite, as well as the residual value, if any, after the lease term expires. The Investment Tax Credit has been repealed.
35. In 1990, the application of U.S. patent law was extended to inventions in space, 35 U.S.C. § 105 (1988). Section 105 provides that
    (a) Any invention made, used or sold in outer space on a space object or component thereof under the jurisdiction or control of the United States shall be considered to be made, used or sold within the United States for purposes of this title, except with respect to any space object or component thereof that is specifically identified and otherwise provided for by an international agreement to which the United States is a party, or with respect to any space object or component thereof that is carried on the registry of a foreign state in accordance with the Convention on Registration of Space Objects Launched into Outer Space [and] (b) Any invention made, used or sold in outer space on a space object or component thereof that is carried on the registry of a foreign state in accordance with the Convention on Registration of Space Objects Launched into Outer Space, shall be considered to be made, used or sold within the United States for purposes of this title if specifically so agreed in an international agreement between the United States and the state of registry." *Id.*
36. For example, in order to obtain a license to operate a domestic fixed satellite in the U.S., a company must demonstrate "current financial ability" to meet the estimated cost of the satellite construction, launch and one-year operation, 47 C.F.R. § 25.391 (1990). *See* Chapter 3.2.5. (describing financial qualifications requirements imposed on applicants for satellite systems by the U.S. Federal Communications Commission). A financial institution asked to provide capital for a satellite project may require that the company first obtain a license before committing the funds.
37. *See* 14 C.F.R. § 415.33 (1990) (requiring U.S. launch companies to submit environmental information to the U.S. Department of Transportation's Office of Commercial Space Transportation, which is responsible for licensing and regulation of launch vehicles).
38. *See* 47 C.F.R. Part 1 (1990) (requiring an environmental impact statement to the United States Federal Communications Commission prior to the construction of a certain Earth station).

become a reality. This situation will pose entirely new legal problems for the space lawyer. More attention will have to be focused on the governance of space societies, including how to structure legal regimes to reflect relations between habitat societies and their financial underwriters, as well as among the different habitat societies and among the inhabitants of individual space communities. Biomedical research on humans functioning in the synthetic and alien life-support environment of space suggests that traditional legal sources, methodologies, standards and institutions may not always be applied effectively to space societies. New laws reflecting unique space habitat conditions, including the special needs and values of the space inhabitants, will have to be fashioned, perhaps primarily by the space inhabitants, themselves.[40]

1.2. The Commercial Space Industry

DEFINITION. The commercial space industry refers primarily to entities *conducting* commercial space activities but also includes spacecraft manufacturers, resellers, financiers, and insurance brokers and underwriters, all of which play vital roles in the implementation of any space project. Three general categories of space activities have been commercialized to date: 1) satellite telecommunications, 2) satellite remote-sensing and 3) space transportation. With a twenty-five year history, the telecommunications satellite industry is by far the most mature. The commercial space transportation and remote-sensing satellite industries are still in their infancy, with substantial commercial undertakings dating only to the late 1980s.

NON-COMMERCIAL SPACE OPERATIONS. The three types of space activities that have been commercialized also are pursued on a non-commercial basis, by governments for government use. For example, military establishments and civilian government agencies in the United States and the Soviet Union operate communications satellites, reconnaissance and surveillance satellites (compare remote-sensing) and space transportation systems. Moreover, communications satellites are operated, for example, by the Indian government's Department of Space, Telecommunicaciones de Mexico, Empressa Brasileira de Telecommunicaciones and Deutsche Bundespost, among others.

Non-commercial space operations comprise other kinds of activities,

---

39. For example, on October 4, 1990, the rocket body of a Chinese CZ-4 launch vehicle fragmented while in a circular (850-900 km) sun-synchronous orbit. The vehicle was launched on September 3, 1990, and successfully deployed one satellite and two balloons. *See Breakup in Review — Fengyun 1-2 Rocket Body,* 4 ORBITAL DEBRIS MONITOR 6 (ed. D.S. McKnight, 1991).
40. *See* G.S. Robinson, *Astronauts and a Unique Jurisprudence: A Treaty for Spacekind,* 7 HASTINGS INT'L & COMP. L. REV. 483 (1984), and G.S. Robinson & H.M. White, ENVOYS OF MANKIND (1987) (concerning the law applicable to space communities).

as well. Space science and exploration, including planetary missions, and space programs with unique military applications, such as anti-satellite satellite testing or deployment, do not lend themselves to commercialization. Only governments are likely to invest in these types of projects, although space exploration conceivably has the potential of being commercialized as a tourist attraction toward the latter part of the next Century, or perhaps sooner.

MEANING OF "COMMERCIALIZATION." The essential ingredient in the concept of commercialization is the sale/purchase of products and services in the open market, albeit a very limited sector of the market. Although "commercialization" traditionally has had a private enterprise connotation, at least in the United States, the term refers both to private and government initiated space projects. Indeed, several governments now are in the business of providing commercial space services. For example, the Soviet Union, through the government agency Glavkosmos, and China, through the State-owned Great Wall Industry Corporation, offer commercial launch services.[41] In Australia, the government-owned corporation Aussat Pty. Ltd. provides telecommunications satellite services on a commercial basis.[42] So does Telesat Canada, a corporation which is about fifty percent owned by the Canadian Government.[43]. Arianespace S.A. of Evry, France, which provides commercial launch services in the world market, offers an interesting blend of government and private sector ownership.[44]

REASONS FOR GOVERNMENT INVOLVEMENT IN SPACE ACTIVITIES. Motivations vary for government involvement in space activities. Often, government participation in space endeavors is simply a logical extension of government ownership of the national industrial base and telecommunications and transportation infrastructures at the terrestrial level. Government involvement may reflect an institutionalized philosophy

---

41. The U.S. National Aeronautics and Space Administration (NASA) provides very limited commercial transportation services on the Space Shuttle. It only is allowed to launch payloads that require the unique characteristics of the Space Shuttle, or whose launching otherwise is required in the national security interest or foreign policy interest of the U.S., *United States Launch Strategy,* National Security Decision Directive 254 (Dec. 27, 1986), stated in the National Aeronautics and Space Administration Authorization Act, Fiscal Year 1991, Pub. L. 101-611, sec. 112 (1990).
42. The Australian government is in the process of reshaping that country's telecommunications industry by introducing competition and privatizing existing, government-owned telecommunications carriers, including Aussat Pty. Ltd. Initial expressions of interest were sought by January 11, 1991, and, as contemplated then, the sale of Aussat is scheduled to be completed by December 1991.
43. Bell Canada and Telecom Canada each own 25% of the stock. Privatization of Telesat is imminent. *See* Telesat Canada Reorganization and Divestiture Act (Bill C-38), tabled in the House of Commons, Oct. 23, 1991, which is likely to become law.

of excluding private sector participation in certain types of activities considered to be of national importance. Not only socialist States, but also many social democracies subscribe to such policies. Sometimes, though, government participation in space activities has simple, practical, economic explanations. For example, in small, or so-called lesser-developed, countries only governments can afford the enormous capital investments associated with space projects.

Telecommunications present a special case of government involvement. In nearly every country in the world, the responsibility for telecommunications traditionally has been vested in a government agency. Such agencies are generally referred to as "PTTs," an acronym for post, telegraph and telephone administration. For the most part, satellite telecommunications have been treated no differently. As satellite technology became available, PTTs were placed firmly in charge of this new means of communication. Recently, however, a wave of liberalization and deregulation has swept across Europe, Australia and parts of Asia, increasingly allowing private industry to provide telecommunications equipment and services, including certain types of satellite telecommunications services. Private telecommunications satellite enterprises now exist in the United States, the United Kingdom, Luxembourg, Hong Kong and Japan. Privatization of Telesat Canada, as well as of the Australian Aussat, is imminent.

The United States is unique with respect to private sector — and lack of government — involvement in commercial space activities in general, and satellite telecommunications in particular.[45] Indeed, seven private U.S. companies presently own and operate about thirty telecommunications satellites, and more than half a dozen private companies provide, or hope

---

44. The shares of Arianespace are divided among thirty-six leading European aerospace and electronics companies, thirteen major banks and the French space agency, Centre National d'Etudes Spatiales (CNES). French shareholders hold approximately 59%, and include Aerospatiale, Air Liquide, Comsip Entreprise, Crouzet, Deutsch, Intertechnique, Matra, SAFT, Credit Lyonnais, Banque Vernes, Societe Generale, Banque de Paris et des Pays Bas and CNES. German shareholders hold approximately 20%, and include Dornier, MBB/ERNO, MA Bayerische Vereinsbank A.G., Dresdnerbank, Westdeutsche Landesbank Girocentrale. Belgian shareholders hold approximately 4%, and include ETCA, Fabrique Nationale and SABCA. British, Spanish, Danish Swedish, Swiss and Irish corporations and financial institutions share the remaining stock. Most of these shareholders are controlled by their respective governments through part or outright ownership. Arianespace was formed March 26, 1980, to market the Ariane launch vehicle. Ariane launch vehicle technology is developed by the European Space Agency (ESA), and Arianespace markets the launch vehicles pursuant to a May 15, 1981, agreement.
45. NASA provides commercial launch services to a limited extent.*See supra* note 41 (describing the kinds of commercial payloads NASA may launch on the Space Shuttle).

to provide, launch services on a commercial basis.

COMMERCIAL INDUSTRY PLAYERS. When examining the commercial space industry more closely, a categorization of the various players is helpful. As mentioned above, the space industry, in a broad sense, is comprised not only of spacecraft operators, but also of spacecraft manufacturers, resellers, financiers and insurance brokers and underwriters. Some large financial institutions and insurance brokers and underwriters have specialized departments or personnel for dealing with space enterprises.

SPACECRAFT MANUFACTURERS. World-wide, there presently are about a dozen major commercial spacecraft manufacturers. Some are privately owned and some are wholly or partly state owned.[46] A majority of these spacecraft manufacturers are located in the United States, and they are all private companies. GE Astro Space Division of Princeton, New Jersey, Space Systems/Loral Corporation (formerly Ford Aerospace & Communications Corporation) of Palo Alto, California, and Hughes Space and Communications Group of El Segundo, California, are the three major U.S. commercial satellite manufacturers.[47] Major U.S. commercial launch vehicle manufacturers include Martin Marietta Corporation of Bethesda, Maryland, General Dynamics Corporation of Falls Church, Virginia, and McDonnell Douglas Corporation of St. Louis Missouri.

Among the large spacecraft manufacturers in other countries are British Aerospace PLC., Space & Communications Division of Stevenage, Herts, England; Spar Aerospace Ltd., Satellite & Communications Group of Mississauga in Ontario, Canada; MBB/ERNO Raumfahrttechnik GmBH of Bremen, Germany;[48] Aerospatiale, Space and Strategic Systems Division of Mureaux, France; Marconi Space Systems Ltd. of Portsmouth, England; Matra Space of Velizy Vilacoublay, France; and Mitsubishi Heavy Industries, Ltd. of Tokyo, Japan.

Multinational teaming arrangements are not uncommon, especially among companies competing to build satellites for international organizations or third-world countries.[49] Hughes and British Aerospace, for

46. In addition to the large "prime" contractors, dozens of companies make spacecraft components and subcomponents and serve as subcontractors to the larger companies.

47. Manufacturers of smaller classes of commercial satellites include Fairchild Space & Defense Corporation of Germantown, Maryland; Ball Corporation, Space Systems Division, of Boulder, Colorado; and Lockheed Missiles and Space Company of Sunnyvale, California.

48. Messerschmitt-Boelkow-Blohm (MBB) is part of the German aerospace conglomerate, Deutsche Aerospace, which was formed by Daimler Benz GmbH in 1989, and which also includes Dornier, Telefunken System und Technik GmbH and others.

49. For example, Matra of France teamed with Spar Aerospace of Canada in competing for a contract to build the Brasilsat-satellite for Empressa Brasileira de Telecommunicaciones, S.A. The team offered technology transfer incentives, as well. However, Hughes Aircraft, a competitor, was selected. *Communications Daily/*, Sept. 5, 1990, at 7.

example, head a team for the construction of the second-generation satellites for the International Maritime Satellite Organization (INMARSAT). At a Council meeting at Cannes, France, on July 25, 1990, INMARSAT decided to award a contract for the third generation satellites to a team of GE Astro and Marconi Space Systems.

SPACECRAFT OPERATORS. Spacecraft operators in business today include telecommunications satellite operators, remote-sensing satellite operators and launch vehicle operators. Some of these spacecraft operators are private companies, and some are state or government agencies or entities with mixed private and government ownership. Satellite telecommunication[50] is by far the most common type of commercial space operation.

TELECOMMUNICATIONS SATELLITE OPERATORS. The history of commercial satellite telecommunications dates back to April 6, 1965, when INTELSAT's "Early Bird," the first commercial satellite, was launched. INTELSAT is an international organization charged with operating satellites and making international telecommunications satellite capacity available on a commercial basis. (See Chapter 5.1.1.). The organization is headquartered in Washington, D.C., in the United States, and now has 121 members. Over the years, INTELSAT has contracted for the manufacture and launch of a total of approximately fifty satellites, fifteen of which are currently in operation.

Almost a decade passed after INTELSAT's pioneering step before other entities entered the commercial satellite market. Telesat Canada launched ANIK 1-A on November 9, 1972. Several private U.S. companies launched their satellites in 1974 and the following years (see Chapter 3.1.1.). In the late 1970s, additional international commercial satellite operating organizations were formed, including INMARSAT, based in London, England, and the European Telecommunications Satellite Organization (EUTELSAT), based in Paris, France.[51] However, these organizations did not have satellites launched until the 1980s and 1990s. EUTELSAT's first satellite was launched in 1983. INMARSAT has leased satellite capacity for many years on satellites owned and operated by others (see Chapter

---

50. Satellite telecommunications refers to the use of satellites for a variety of communications, broadcasting, navigation and position-location purposes. *See* Chapter 4.1., note 11 (providing the definition of "telecommunications" adopted by the International Telecommunication Union). The majority of commercial satellites in operation today are used for 1) television program transmission or distribution, 2) private voice, data and video networks, and 3) international telephony via the public-switched network.

51. Other regional organizations include the Arab Corporation for Space Communications (ARABSAT), based in Tunis, Tunisia, for communications between the Arab League nations; PALAPA, based in Jakarta, Indonesia, which serves Indonesia, Malaysia and the Philippines, among other countries in the region; and INTERSPUTNIK for the Soviet Union and the former East Block countries.

5.1.2.). It launched its own first satellite in October 1990. The last and present decades, have also witnessed several private, semi-private and state-owned commercial satellite companies situated in Luxembourg, France, the United Kingdom, Australia, Hong Kong and Japan.

The largest concentration of commercial telecommunications satellite operators still is found in the United States. Seven private companies own and operate some thirty satellites for communications within the United States, including Hughes Communications Galaxy, Inc. of Los Angeles, California, GE American Communications of Princeton, New Jersey, Communications Satellite Corporation (Comsat) of Washington, D.C., AT&T Communications, Inc. of North Bedminster, New Jersey, GTE Spacenet Corporation of McLean, Virginia and Contel American Satellite Company of Rockville, Maryland (the latter two of which recently have merged).[52] Satellites operated by these companies serve two major functions: 1) distribute television programming to cable operators and television network affiliate stations, and 2) provide privately-owned, special-purpose communications networks, including very small aperture terminal (VSAT) networks within the United States.[53] Only one company, Alpha Lyracom Space Communications of Greenwich, Connecticut, doing business as Pan American Satellite, provides international communications, i.e., between the United States and South America and Europe. The company's only satellite is used for occasional television transmissions and private communications networks between the United States and these foreign locations.

Only a handful of private, commercial telecommunications satellite operators exist outside the United States. British Satellite Broadcasting Company of London, England, launched its first broadcasting satellite "Marco Polo" in 1990. The satellite is used to broadcast programming for direct reception by individual households with home receiving equipment. Société Européenne des Satellites of Luxembourg operates communications satellites called "ASTRA," the first of which was launched December 1988. Transponders on these satellites being leased for television program distribution throughout Europe. Rupert Murdoch, for example, leases transponders for his four-channel Sky Television, a program distribution service for cable operators and individual households with receiving equipment. A merger between Mr. Murdoch's Sky Television and operations of British Satellite Broadcasting Company recently was consummated. Japan Communications Satellite Company of Tokyo, Japan, a private international consortium of Hughes, Itoh and Mitsui, operates two communications satellites designated "JC-Sat," and offers transponders for sale or long-term lease. Japan Space Communications Corporation of Tokyo, Japan, is another international consortium also representing Japa-

52. GTE and Contel ASC completed a merger in 1991.

53. These satellites are classified by the United States Federal Communications Commission as "domestic fixed satellites." *See* Chapter 3.1.1. (providing the regulatory history of domestic fixed satellites).

nese and U.S. interests. Asia Satellite Telecommunications Company, Ltd., of Hong Kong, a commercial consortium of Cable and Wireless, Hutchison Whampoa Ltd. and China International Trust and Investment Company, launched "ASIA-Sat" in 1990. Other commercial satellite companies, either wholly or partly government owned, include Telesat Canada of Ontario, Canada, and Aussat, Pty of Sydney, N.S.W., Australia. Privatization is imminent for both.

As noted, above, several international organizations own and operate satellites on a commercial basis. Chief among them is INTELSAT, which operates a fifteen-satellite system for global telephony, television relay and other communications services.[54] With sixty-three member States, INMARSAT operates two and leases capacity on eight satellites for maritime and aeronautical communications.[55] EUTELSAT operates four satellites mainly for television program distribution in Europe, and has twenty-eight members.[56]

TELECOMMUNICATIONS SATELLITE BROKERS. Brokers and resellers of satellite capacity are common in the American telecommunications satellite industry and are emerging also in other countries as a result of deregulation of the telecommunications services in those countries. Brokers typically arrange for "time," or transmission capacity, on particular satellites for customers who, for example, wish to conduct a teleconference, transmit or receive certain programming, or have a private communications network installed. Resellers buy satellite capacity from the satellite operator, often at a discount, and then resell it to users. Typically, brokers and resellers provide added service features, such as Earth stations and associated ground equipment. For example, some even offer "turn key" services, such as for teleconferencing. Resale may represent an interim stage in a company's business plan, the final aim of which ultimately is to own and operate a satellite. Resale is a means of building experience and a customer base. This approach was chosen by American Satellite Company, which provided resale services for several years before launching its own satellite in 1985.

NEW TRENDS IN SATELLITE TELECOMMUNICATIONS. Four trends in satellite telecommunications deserve special mention. One involves the use of so-called "lightsats," which are smaller and lighter satellites with less communications capacity. Interest in such satellites has increased recently because they are less expensive to build, launch and insure, and may offer a flexible solution for countries or entities with lesser communications requirements.[56] Moreover, the United States Defense Advanced Research Project Agency (DARPA) has been promoting the concept for military communications, and several United States satellite manufacturers and operators are now proposing commercial applications.[57]

---

54. *See* Chapter 5.1.1. (describing INTELSAT).
55. *See* Chapter 5.1.2. (describing INMARSAT).
56. *See* Chapter 5.1.3. (describing EUTELSAT).

A second emerging trend is toward low-Earth orbit satellites. Currently, all commercial telecommunications satellites are located in the geostationary orbit, a circular orbit in the plane of Earth's equator, 35,786 km from the surface of Earth. In this orbit, satellites are stationary in relation to a specific geographical area of coverage on Earth. Due to increasing saturation of the geostationary orbit, coupled with the high cost of launching satellites to this orbit, among other reasons, at least nine private companies have sought authorizations from the United States Federal Communications Commission to operate low-Earth orbit telecommunications satellite systems consisting of multiple lightsats. For example, Motorola, Inc., through its wholly-owned subsidiary Motorola Satellite Communications, Inc. of Chandler, Arizona, is proposing a constellation of seventy-seven satellites in seven polar orbits. The system is referred to as "IRIDIUM." An orbital altitude of about 765 km has been proposed for the IRIDIUM system. Also, INMARSAT has expressed an interest in a low-Earth orbit satellite system.

A third trend is toward mobile communications and radiodetermination satellite services. Until now, commercial satellite operations have been almost exclusively of the "fixed" type, meaning that transmit and receive Earth stations have been installed on the ground or on stationary objects. Mobile communications and radiodetermination (navigation and position-location) satellite services contemplate objects in motion, including vehicles, ships and aircraft. American Mobile Satellite Corporation of Washington, D.C., a consortium of eight U.S. companies, was authorized in 1989 to launch three geostationary satellites for an unspecified variety of land, maritime and aeronautical mobile services. Also, in the U.S., the nine low-Earth orbit satellite applicants mentioned above are proposing to offer mobile and radiodetermination-type services.[58]

A fourth trend is toward placing special-purpose "packages" on a host satellite. Geostar Corporation of Washington, D.C., pioneered this concept in 1987 when it placed radiodetermination (position-location) equipment on a GTE Spacenet domestic fixed satellite. This approach allowed Geostar to provide interim radiodetermination satellite service to help gain experience and build a customer base for its dedicated satellite service scheduled to begin in the mid 1990s. Despite its prudent approach in this respect, Geostar encountered other difficulties, which caused the company to file for bankruptcy in May 1991.

SATELLITE REMOTE-SENSING OPERATORS. The commercial remote-sensing satellite industry is still in its infancy. So far, only two private companies, Earth Observation Satellite Corporation (EOSAT) of Lan-

---

57. The term "lightsat" often is used for satellites weighing less than 1000 kg. Applications are pending before the U.S. Federal Communications Commission for authorizations to launch lightsats. *See* Chapter 3.1.6. (describing some of these applicants and their satellite systems).

58. *See* Chapter 3.1.6. (describing some of these applicants and their proposed services).

ham, Maryland, and Spot Image S.A. of Toulouse, France, operate remote-sensing satellites and sell satellite images and data. The data is used for purposes of Earth resource and geographical mapping, crop and pollution monitoring, urban planning, newsgathering, law enforcement and more. EOSAT is a joint venture of General Electric and Hughes Aircraft Company, which is owned by General Motors. It was formed in 1984 to market data from the two government-owned, remote-sensing satellites Landsat 4 and Landsat 5, and to provide next generation remote-sensing satellites. Spot Image S.A was formed in July 1982 to market remote-sensing data from the SPOT satellites. The satellites were developed by the French government agency Centre National d'Etudes Spatiales, and launched in 1986 and 1990, respectively. Spot Image Corporation of Reston, Virginia, a subsidiary of the French company, was formed in December 1982 to market data within the United States. The Soviet Union is attempting to enter the commercial satellite remote-sensing market, as well, through the efforts of the government agency Soyuskarta and its United States marketing agent, Space Commerce Corporation of Houston, Texas.

Using the data supplied by EOSAT and Spot Image, a so-called value-added (or reseller) industry has emerged. Value-added companies, such as Barringer Geoservices, Inc. of Golden, Colorado, KRS Remote Sensing of Landover, Maryland, and Earth Satellite Corporation of Chevy Chase, Maryland, process, manipulate, enhance, interpret and otherwise "add value" to satellite data in order to make satellite data usable to customers with special needs. For example, an oil company may wish to obtain a geological analysis to assist in the determination of whether to proceed with oil exploration at a targeted site.

LAUNCH VEHICLE OPERATORS. Most of the commercial launch vehicle operators are located in the United States. Three major U.S. aerospace companies, which are also launch vehicle manufacturers, operate the vehicles for commercial customers. These companies include Martin Marietta Commercial Titan, Inc. of Denver, Colorado, General Dynamics Commercial Launch Services, Inc. of San Diego, California, and McDonnell Douglas Astronautics Company of Huntington Beach, California. Moreover, a number of small entrepreneurial companies offer launch services for smaller-class payloads: EER Systems Corporation's Space Services Division of Vienna, Virginia, Orbital Sciences of Fairfax, Virginia, American Rocket Company of Camarillo, California, and Microspace International of Herndon, Virginia. NASA plays a limited role in the commercial launch market. It is restricted to launching commercial payloads that require the unique characteristics of the NASA Space Shuttle, or that otherwise would serve the national security or foreign policy interests of the United States.[59] (See Chapter 7.1. for further description of the com-

59. *United States Launch Strategy*, National Security Decision Directive, *supra* note 41.

mercial launch industry).

Commercial launch vehicle operators in other countries include Arianespace of Evry, France; the Soviet Union, through its government agency Glavkosmos and U.S. marketing agent, Space Commerce Corporation of Houston, Texas; and China, through the Great Wall Industry Corporation. Arianespace's stockholders comprise the French space agency Centre National d'Etudes Spatiales, European aerospace companies, banks and other financial institutions, many of which are government owned or controlled. Arianespace has captured over fifty percent of the global commercial launch market.

The United States government has been concerned with foreign launch services competition for quite some time. Its concern is twofold: first, private U.S. launch companies cannot compete against government-sponsored corporations or agencies which subsidize their launch services prices and offer unrelated incentives (such as technology transfer); second, the U.S. is concerned about potential transfer of technology in conjunction with the launching of U.S.-made satellites on foreign vehicles. Transfer of certain technical data is inevitable to accomplish integration of the payload with the launch vehicle. To allay these concerns, among others, the U.S. concluded three memoranda of agreement with China in 1988, limiting the latter's access to the U.S. commercial launch market. Negotiations also are under way between the United States Trade Representative, Department of Commerce, and the European Space Agency to establish "rules of the road" with respect to marketing of Arianespace and U.S. commercial launch services.[60] Furthermore, the U.S. is attempting to restrict Soviet commercial launch activities to a space port project in Cape York, Australia, which contemplates the use of Soviet launch vehicles. As a matter of policy, the U.S. presently prohibits the launching of U.S.-manufactured satellites on Soviet and Chinese launch vehicles (see Chapter 7.1.).

SPACE PORT OPERATORS. No commercial "space port" is yet in operation. U.S. private launch companies still are using U.S. military launch sites and facilities. To a limited extent, agreements exist also for the use of NASA's Wallops Island launch facility on the Atlantic coast of Virginia. Commercial space ports are being planned, however, in Florida, Hawaii, Virginia and Alaska, as well as at Andoya in the north of Norway, and Cape York Peninsula, Australia, among other places. Of these, the Florida space port project appears to be most advanced at this time. The

---

60. In 1985, Transpace Carriers Inc., which was under contract to McDonnell Douglas to market the Delta commercial launch vehicle, filed a complaint with the United States Trade Representative (USTR), alleging unfair trading practices on the part of Arianespace. After a review by the USTR, President Ronald Reagan concluded that Arianespace's practices were not unreasonable or substantially different from U.S. practices supporting the NASA Space Shuttle, the primary U.S. commercial launch vehicle at the time. 50 Fed. Reg. 29631 (1985). *See also supra* note 41 (concerning the commercial use of the Space Shuttle today).

Cape York project has encountered several hurdles, including the withdrawal of its major investor and protests from environmental interest groups.

MATERIALS PROCESSING. Materials processing in space was not included in the above discussion of commercial space industries since this technology is still in an embryonic research stage. Several U.S. pharmaceutical companies, such as Johnson & Johnson, E.I. Du Pont de Nemours & Company, Shering-Plough, The Eli Lilly Company, as well as other types of companies and institutions, including the Minnesota Mining and Manufacturing Company, the U.S. National Bureau of Standards and the University of Alabama, have placed materials processing experiments on the NASA Space Shuttle. Moreover, Payload Systems, Inc. of Cambridge, Massachusetts, has brokered arrangements for U.S. companies and universities to place materials processing payloads on the Soviet space station, *Mir*, including launching to *Mir* by a Soviet launch vehicle. A European consortium, Intospace of Bremen, West Germany, serves a similar function for European markets, and reportedly has arranged for microgravity experiments on the Chinese Long March launch vehicle, as well.

Although the research, so far, has not lead to commercial production, materials processing and space manufacturing have the potential of becoming the largest commercial space industry. The greatest impediment to the advancement of the industry is the current high cost of space transportation, which cannot be passed on realistically to the consumer. Materials processing in space is attractive because the unique attributes of space, such as microgravity, near vacuum conditions and the absence of convection, make homogeneous crystal growth and impurities separation techniques possible that often are costly and difficult, if at all possible, to replicate on Earth.

SPACE PLATFORMS. Another potentially large commercial space industry, yet in the research or design, development and testing phases, involves the use of various space platform, module and container concepts for materials processing and manufacturing, either free-flying, docked with, or contained within, space shuttles or space stations. This industry will likely develop hand-in-glove with the materials processing industry since the latter provides the customer base for the former.

The platform concepts currently being explored and developed vary. Space Industries, Inc. of Houston, Texas, has proposed a free flying, pressurized module known as the "Industrial Space Facility." It would be launched and serviced by the NASA Space Shuttle. The company currently is one of three participants in the NASA-sponsored Commercial Experiment Transporter (COMET) program. Space Industries and Westinghouse Electric Corporation have developed the non-pressurized "Free Flyer" consisting of a service module and a reentry vehicle, designed for experiments in space. Spacehab, Inc. of Washington, D.C., has obtained an agreement with NASA making the agency an "anchor tenant" for a proposed pressurized cargo module to be placed inside the NASA Space Shuttle cargo bay. Interrelated problems of the high cost of space transportation and the difficulty of obtaining customer commitments and financing are slowing the development of this industry.

FINANCIAL INSTITUTIONS. Insurance brokers and underwriters, venture capitalists, banks and other financial institutions play vital roles in launching a space business. Often, such organizations have special departments, offices, or personnel designated to deal specifically with insurance and financing of space ventures. For example, in the United States, Willis Corroon Inspace of Bethesda, Maryland, Johnson & Higgins Space Systems Group in New York, Marsh & McLennan Aviation of New York and Alexander & Alexander, also of New York, are especially equipped to broker satellite insurance.

These brokers work closely with their British counterparts, e.g., Lloyd's brokers, such as Leslie Godwin, Ltd., Grawlay Warren, Ltd., Willis, Faber & Dumas, Ltd., and others[61] (see Chapter 8.3.). A large percentage of the insurance capacity committed for satellites is provided by British underwriters. Chief among them are the Merret-Dixie and Ariel syndicates. Among the major U.S. underwriting managers are U.S. Aviation Insurance Group and International Technology Underwriters (see Chapter 8.3.).

Financing for space projects may derive from several sources. Venture capital often provides the initial funding for start-up space businesses. Usually, additional financing is needed, given the large capital investment generally required for space projects. For example, to construct two average, state-of-the-art geostationary telecommunications satellites and launch and insure one of them requires an investment on the order of $400-million. Major U.S. banks, such as Citibank and Chemical Bank, as well as financial services subsidiaries of large American corporations, provide loans to satellite operators. It is not uncommon for such financial institutions to acquire satellite transponders in sale-lease-back arrangements. Such transactions benefit the satellite operator because it receives the sales proceeds, and benefits the bank because it receives rental payments, tax advantages and the residual value of the satellite, if any, when the lease term expires. Satellite manufacturers and launch providers also may play a role in the financing by taking equity positions in the satellite company, or by deferring payments until the satellite is operational and produces revenues.

Strategic investors are very important in the context of space project

61. Consolidations and International joint ventures have been prevalent in the insurance industry during 1990 and 1991. For example, Corroon & Black Corporation of New York merged with London-based Willis, Faber & Dumas. Crawley, Warren & Company, Ltd. of London, England, Le Blanc de Nicolay Reassurance of Paris, France, and Frank Crystal & Co. of New York have formed a joint venture called International Space Brokers, Inc., based in Rosslyn, Virginia.

financing. These are investors with an interest in the success of the business beyond the return on investment, such as a satellite receiving equipment manufacturer investing in a satellite project which contemplates the use of receiving equipment manufactured by that investor. Moreover, foreign investment is emerging as a solution to financing of U.S. space projects. For example, Spacehab, Inc. has attracted substantial Japanese investment for its pressurized module, described above. Orion Satellite Corporation of Rockville, Maryland, which recently received authorizations for a satellite providing trans-Atlantic communications, formed a limited partnership, which includes foreign limited partners. Finally, a somewhat unusual and quite celebrated case of satellite financing involves Pan American Satellite Company of Greenwich, Connecticut, for which a wealthy individual, the company's founder, provided much of the necessary capital.

1.3. Space Law Practice Today

THE LAWYER'S ROLE. The authors of this book recognize that the role and functions of the attorney may differ from one society to the next. What may be the lawyer's domain in one country may in part be the responsibilities of special counselors, brokers, administrators, judges, or especially empowered citizens or government officials in another. Variations in the roles, functions and importance attributed to the lawyer are due to differences in perception of the law, itself, and its purpose in society, as well as to differences in legal traditions, judicial systems and even the ideological or philosophical foundations of societies. Much of the discussion, below, has direct reference to United States attorneys and legal practice, mainly because space law practice is more developed there than in any other country.

WHO PRACTICES SPACE LAW? The practice of space law is limited to the following space projects undertaken by governments and private individuals or entities: 1) commercial space projects, which are undertaken by the private sector, as well as governments (separately or jointly), and 2) civil non-commercial, including scientific, and military space programs initiated by governments. Government projects or programs, whether they are civil or military, and to the extent they have legal implications, often are dealt with by government attorneys. Outside counsel may be consulted for certain particular aspects of a project. For example, NASA occasionally retains private law firms to handle patent and trademark matters.

Legal issues raised by private commercial space ventures are the subject of corporate and private law practice. Typically, a corporation, which is planning to initiate, or is engaging in, a space project, depending on the size of the company, will handle certain matters "in-house" and contract out the remaining to one or more private law firms. The in-house counsel is responsible for the selection and management of outside counsel. The latter is intended to supplement, not replace, the former and to be part of the company legal "team."

Government attorneys also become involved with private commercial space ventures, i.e., from a regulatory perspective. Staff attorneys in government regulatory agencies handle licensing and other regulatory aspects of private commercial space ventures. For example, attorneys at the United States Federal Communications Commission become involved when a satellite company applies for a license to construct and operate a satellite, and lawyers with the Department of Transportation's Office of Commercial Space Transportation may become involved when a launch company applies for a license.

SATELLITE TELECOMMUNICATIONS PRACTICE. By far, the largest and most profitable area of *private* pace law practice today relates to telecommunications satellites and associated businesses, such as Earth station and satellite network operations and program distribution via satellite. In fact, these activities have generated a fair amount of space law business for private law firms over the last two decades. In the United States, a relatively large number of private law firms are engaged in the practice of one or more facets of telecommunications satellite-related law, and their clients may include, for example, satellite manufacturers, satellite owner/operators, transponder owners or lessees and Earth station operators, as well as satellite financiers and insurers. Also in Europe, private law firms increasingly are being engaged to advise and represent clients engaged in satellite related activities. Space law practices are emerging in other continents, as well, albeit on a much smaller scale.

CONFLICTS OF INTEREST. Conflicts of interest considerations sometimes limit the number and kinds of satellite-related businesses a law firm may represent. For instance, the same law firm cannot represent two different communications satellite operators that are targeting the same market. However, it would not necessarily be unethical for a law firm to represent two communications satellite companies that provide different types of services. In the latter situation, no conflict exists because promoting one company's interest does not adversely affect the other company; the companies are competing neither at the regulatory level (e.g., for orbital locations and associated frequencies), nor at the business level (e.g., for market share). Following this line of reasoning, it may be equally proper for a firm to represent a satellite operator and a reseller or transponder owner at the same time although not with respect to the same satellite.

LEGAL ADVICE. Providing legal representation to, or otherwise advising, a client planning to operate a telecommunications satellite typically might involve

- advising your client at the business planning stage concerning, for example, the type of business entity that would be most advantageous from regulatory, tax and financing perspectives;

- ensuring that your client's proposed project complies with the cardinal principles of international space law as embodied in the United Nations-promulgated space treaties (Chapter 2.);
- obtaining government authorizations for your client, including construction permits and operating licenses for the satellite(s) and Earth stations (Chapter 3.);
- securing international protection of your client's frequency assignment and orbital location through the International Telecommunication Union (ITU) (Chapter 4.);
- ensuring successful coordination of your client's satellite operation with INTELSAT, INMARSAT and/or EUTELSAT, as appropriate (Chapter 5.);
- negotiating an operating agreement with a foreign PTT, or other authorized entity, in the event your client intends to provide communications to and from a foreign country (Chapter 3.1.4. and 6.5.1.);
- advising your client on risk management and satellite insurance matters (Chapters 6. and 8.);
- negotiating a satellite purchase contract with a manufacturer to build the satellite for your client (Chapter 6.4.1.);
- negotiating an agreement for the launching of your client's satellite (Chapters 6. and 7.);
- negotiating an agreement for the sale or lease of satellite transponders to a user or a financial institution; and
- advising on export regulatory matters.

WHAT KINDS OF LAW FIRMS HAVE TELECOMMUNICATIONS SATELLITE-RELATED PRACTICES? In the United States, law firms serving telecommunications satellite businesses tend to be those with an existing and substantial communications practice. These firms may be specialized "boutique" communications law firms or large multi-service area law firms, i.e., "department stores." In any event, a background in traditional communications law, as it applies to common carriers or broadcasters, is essential for providing competent advice to a telecommunications satellite client on domestic and international regulatory matters, such as obtaining authorizations from the United States Federal Communications Commission to operate the satellite and international frequency protection through the International Telecommunication Union.

It is not uncommon for satellite companies to retain two or more law firms to handle different, and even the same, aspects of their business. One firm may advise on the regulatory requirements. A second firm may be retained to deal with the transactional aspects of the business, such as satellite or launch procurement. If a satellite company faces litigation, it might hire a firm specializing in this work.

As noted previously, satellite companies, depending upon size and corporate structure, often handle many legal matters through the services of in-house counsel. For example, a satellite company may engage a Washington, D.C., law firm to handle the satellite licensing process, the interaction with the Federal Communications Commission and the preparation of documents to be submitted to the International Telecommunication Union, while letting its corporate legal staff deal with the satellite procurement, launch service and other related transactions.

OTHER SPACE LAW PRACTICE. Many of the legal actions referred to, above (page 31-32), as necessary to implement a telecommunications satellite business concept, are equally relevant to other commercial space projects. For example, licensing is a prerequisite to operating a remote-sensing satellite and a launch vehicle, although the licensing criteria and procedures, as well as the government agencies involved, differ. Furthermore, satellite and launch procurements also are necessary in the case of remote-sensing satellites. Risk allocation and insurance considerations are essential to any space project, although risk management options and solutions may vary from one type of project to the next.

SPACE LAW ENTHUSIASTS. In some large American law firms, it is not uncommon to find one or two partners devoted to commercial space law, and thus spending a fair amount of time on legal work for commercial space clients. These services often are provided on the basis of subsidized fees, or even in exchange for shares in a start-up company. In the latter circumstance, lawyers tend to believe that assistance to fledgling space companies ultimately will translate into a viable and growing industry with a commensurate growth of a space law practice.

Artist rendering of Telstar 4(AT&T).
Provided courtesy of GE Astro-Space Division.

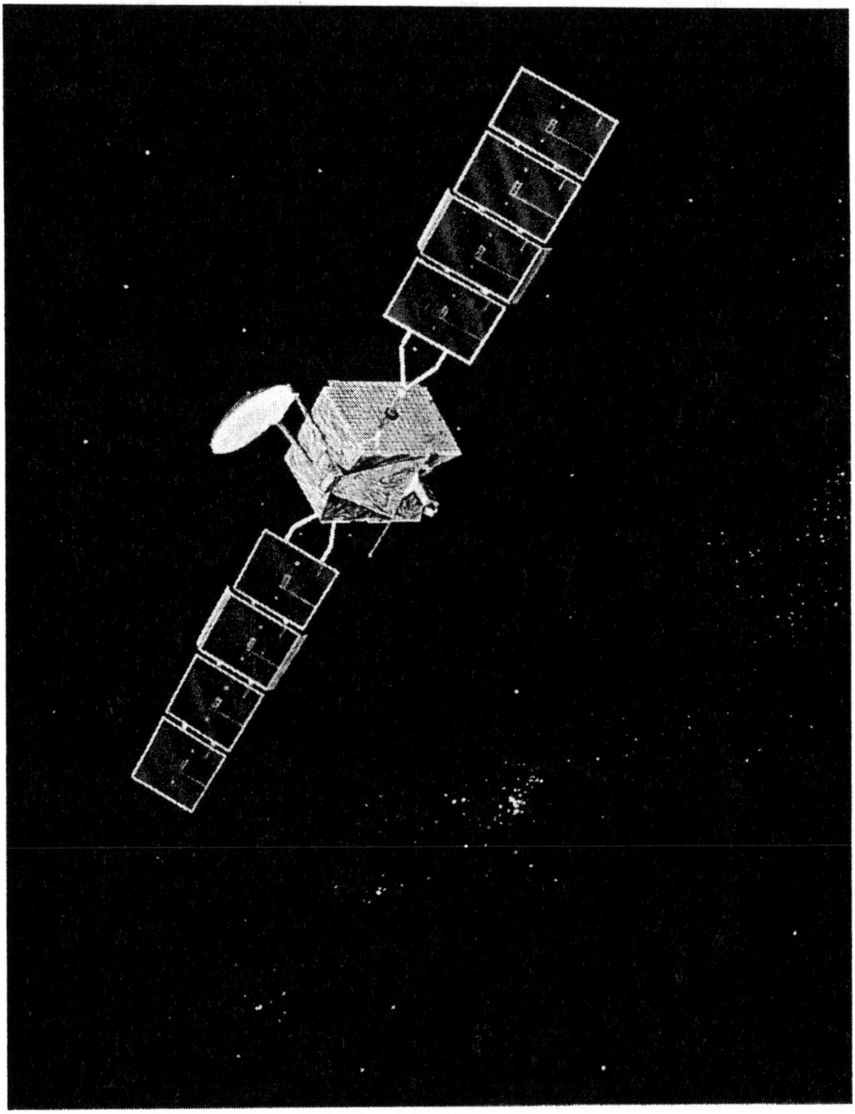

Artist rendering of Astra 1B.
Provided courtesy of GE Astro-Space Division.

2. Implications of the Cardinal Principles of International Space Law for Your Client's Project

Seven cardinal, or fundamental, principles of international space law, and their implications for private commercial telecommunications satellite operators, are discussed in this Chapter. It is important to consider these principles and their implications at a relatively early stage of a satellite project since they may influence the strategy for obtaining national authorizations (Chapter 3.), as well as risk management solutions (Chapter 6.) and the choice of launch provider (Chapter 7.). Knowledge of these principles also provides a background for understanding the International Telecommunication Union's special concern for the interests of Third World countries when discharging its frequency allocation and registration responsibilities (Chapter 4.) and, indeed, the general geopolitical climate in which the International Telecommunications Satellite Organization (INTELSAT) emerged (Chapter 5.).

2.1. The Cardinal Principles of International Space Law

THE SPACE TREATIES. Certain fundamental principles of international law apply to all space projects, whether military or civilian, and whether commercially undertaken by governments or the private sector. These cardinal principles are embodied in four international agreements[1] promulgated under the auspices of the United Nations: Treaty on Principles Governing the Activities of States in the Exploration and Use of Outer Space, Including the Moon and Other Celestial Bodies (Outer Space Treaty);[2] Agreement on the Rescue of Astronauts, the Return of Astronauts and the Return of Objects Launched Into Outer Space (Rescue and Return Agreement);[3] Convention on International Liability for Damage Caused by Space Objects (Liability Convention);[4] and Convention on Registration of Objects Launched Into Outer Space (Registration Convention).[5] The treaties were formulated by the United Nations Committee on the Peaceful Uses of Outer Space (COPUOS), the principal forum for international space law-making.[6]

The provisions of these space treaties are vague and broad. Although, in theory, they are legally binding, some are so vaguely formulated that the purported legal principle cannot be relied upon to protect a client's position. Such provisions reflect more the spirit and intent of the treaty than a definitive and arguable principle of law. A typical example of such a provision is found in Article I of the Outer Space Treaty, which declares that the exploration and use of space shall be "carried out for the benefit and in the interests of all countries . . . ."[7] Other provisions are somewhat more precise. For example, Article VI of the Outer Space Treaty stipulates that the activities of private entities in space shall "require authorization and continuing supervision by the appropriate State Party to the Treaty."[8]

SEVEN CARDINAL PRINCIPLES. Despite the ambiguities and lack of precision in legal definitions suffered by many of the provisions of the space treaties, at least seven fundamental, or cardinal, principles emerge that reflect a universally recognized spirit and intent underlying those treaties:

1) the right to use space without appropriating it;
2) the obligation to use space for peaceful purposes;
3) State responsibility for activities of private citizens in space;
4) the requirement for registration of objects launched into space;
5) retention of jurisdiction and control over objects launched into space;
6) retention of ownership of objects launched into space; and

---

1. A fifth treaty, Agreement Concerning the Activities of States on the Moon and Other Celestial Bodies, U.N.G.A. Res. 34/68, Dec. 5, 1979, [hereinafter cited as Moon Treaty] *done* Dec. 18, 1979, *entered into force* Jul. 12, 1984, is of little significance in the context of commercial telecommunications satellite projects based on current technology since it does not apply to activities in Earth orbit. The provisions of the Moon Treaty apply to the Moon and "other celestial bodies within the solar system, *other than the Earth* . . ." and to the "orbits around or other trajectories to or around" the Moon and other celestial bodies to which the treaty applies (emphasis added). *Id.*, art. 1, paras. 2, 3. Celestial bodies typically refer to planets and their moons, as well as to asteroids and comets. The U.S. and most other industrialized nations have not signed or ratified the Moon Treaty, particularly because it calls for "equitable sharing by all States Parties in the benefits derived from . . . resources [on the Moon and other celestial bodies]," *id.*, art. XI, para. 7(d), and because the treaty contemplates the establishment of an international regime to govern the exploitation and distribution of those resources. *Id.*, art. XI, para. 5.
2. *Done* Jan. 27, 1967, *entered into force* Oct. 10, 1967. 18 U.S.T. 2410, T.I.A.S. 6347.
3. *Done* Apr. 2, 1968, *entered into force* Dec. 3, 1968. 19 U.S.T. 7570, T.I.A.S. 6599.
4. *Done* Mar. 29, 1972, *entered into force* Sept. 1, 1972. 24 U.S.T. 2389, T.I.A.S. 7762.
5. *Done* Mar. 29, 1972, *entered into force* Sept. 1, 1972. 24 U.S.T. 2389, T.I.A.S. 7762.

7) international liability for damage caused by space objects.

Although these principles of public international law are not necessarily applicable directly to private entities, they nevertheless affect private undertakings in space. Typically, certain obligations under the treaties may be passed on to private entities through domestic legislation and regulation. For example, private operators of spacecraft may be subjected to authorization requirements and supervision under a country's domestic laws and regulations implementing Article VI of the Outer Space Treaty. This provision requires that private space activities be authorized and supervised by a State. On the other hand, where laws and regulations do not exist that are sufficient to satisfy Article VI, your client proposing to engage in space operations may have to encourage their adoption.

UNLIKELY TO BAR THE IMPLEMENTATION OF A SATELLITE PROJECT. It is unlikely that the space treaties will present obstacles to the implementation of a commercial satellite project, or any other commercial space project, that cannot be overcome. Actions needed to overcome obstacles, such as the passage of domestic legislation or regulation, may delay a project, though.

Over the years, controversies have arisen over the rights of satellite operators to engage in various space activities, consistent with the space treaties. These controversies generally have placed the Western industri-

---

6. COPUOS became a permanent committee of the United Nations General Assembly in 1959. U.N.G.A Res. 1472 (XIV), Dec. 12, 1959. COPUOS has 53 members, and has established a Legal Subcommittee and a Technical Subcommittee. Since 1962, COPUOS' practice when formulating treaties or resolutions has been to attempt to reach agreement by consensus (a compromise between unanimity and majority vote). Once COPUOS reaches consensus on the text of an international agreement or resolution, the matter is referred to the First Committee of the United Nations General Assembly, and then to the United Nations General Assembly, itself, for a vote. If an agreement is approved by the General Assembly, it is opened for signature by member States. Signatory States are then free to ratify the agreement pursuant to their respective internal procedures for ratification. When the requisite number (normally specified in the agreement) of ratifications has been deposited with the Secretary General of the United Nations, the Agreement will enter into force and become legally binding on all Parties to the Agreement. Declarations and resolutions are not legally binding, but often take on a moral force by which States supporting a resolution often feel morally bound. It is important to note that certain principles set forth in a treaty may evolve into customary international law, in which case they become binding also on non-parties to a treaty. *See e.g. infra* note 17 (concerning the principle of airspace sovereignty) and note 26 (concerning State responsibility for private space activities). Three elements must be present for customary international law to exist: consistent State practice, *opinio juris* (a good faith belief by States that the practice is legal) and time (the practice must go on over time). *See* M.N. Shaw, INTERNATIONAL LAW (1986), at 59-81 (discussing customary international law as a source of international law). A recent trend in international law deemphasizes the time element.

alized world in confrontation with the Third World and occasionally the former Soviet Union and East block countries. While some of these controversies persist, such as that concerning the claim of several Equatorial countries to portions of the geostationary orbit above their respective territories (Bogota Declaration, see Chapter 2.2.), most have been resolved in ways that are largely favorable to the commercial satellite operator. Even the claim by the Equatorial States to the geostationary orbit is considered by the overwhelming majority of spacefaring nations, as well as many other countries, to lack serious merit.

2.2. The Right to Use Space Without Appropriating It

RIGHT TO USE SPACE. The right to use, but not appropriate, space flows from Articles I and II of the Outer Space Treaty. Article I asserts that "[o]uter space, including the Moon and other celestial bodies, shall be free for exploration and use by all States . . . ."[9] Deploying, testing and operating a telecommunications satellite in orbit around the Earth for the purpose of relaying radio signals from one point on Earth to another represent uses of space consistent with the Outer Space Treaty. Other conforming uses include: remote-sensing of Earth from satellites in space for purposes of resource or geographical mapping, crop or pollution monitoring, urban planning, law enforcement, and more; the passage through space of launch vehicles and other transportation systems; the establishment of space stations, i.e., relatively large, long-duration, permanently manned orbiting structures for space-related research, manufacturing, or the like;[10] and military surveillance and reconnaissance. Although Article I literally confers the right to use space upon "all States," there is no doubt that the right extends also to private entities, such as corporations and private international consortia.

IN THE INTERESTS OF ALL COUNTRIES. Article I qualifies the permissible uses of space. The use shall be "for the benefit and in the interests of all countries, irrespective of their degree of economic and scientific development . . ."[11] and "without discrimination of any kind, on a basis of equality . . . ."[12] Obviously, this provision does not require industrial coun-

---

7. Outer Space Treaty, art. I, para. 1.
8. *Id.*, art. VI.
9. *Id.*, art. I, para. 2.
10. Some Western legal scholars hold that even the exploitation of resources, *e.g.*, minerals mining on the Moon, constitutes an acceptable "use." *See e.g.* C.Q. Christol, THE MODERN INTERNATIONAL LAW OF OUTER SPACE (1984) [hereinafter cited as Christol, THE MODERN INTERNATIONAL LAW], at 40 (claiming that resource exploitation is a permitted use of space). *See also* S. Gorove, STUDIES IN SPACE LAW: ITS CHALLENGES AND PROSPECTS (1977) [hereinafter cited as Gorove, SPACE LAW], at 51 (discussing the meaning of "freedom" and "exploration and use").
11. Outer Space Treaty, art. I, para. 1.

tries to share satellite technology with Third World countries, or a commercial satellite operator to donate satellite capacity. It has, however, influenced principles and rules for sharing of the geostationary orbit and associated radio frequencies adopted by the International Telecommunication Union (ITU). The ITU is an intergovernmental organization in charge of managing the radio frequency spectrum and all satellite operators must have their geostationary locations and their radio frequencies coordinated through the ITU (see Chapter 4.). The lesser-developed countries have invoked the Outer Space Treaty to compel the adoption by the ITU of rules that will guarantee them equitable access to the geostationary orbit in the future when they are ready to launch satellite systems.[13] Their concern was that unrestricted use of this orbit by the industrialized countries would lead to saturation of the orbit, thereby precluding "late-comers" from launching their satellite systems. For private satellite operators, the guarantee of equitable access in its various manifestations provided to Third World countries sometimes implies operational limitations and constraints on the satellite services that may be provided.[14]

NO APPROPRIATION. Article II of the Outer Space Treaty prohibits territorial conquest, colonization, or other acts of appropriation of space. Specifically, this provision proscribes "national appropriation [of space] by claim of sovereignty, by means of use or occupation, or by any other means." [15] It is now well settled in international law that the deployment of a telecommunications satellite in a fixed location in the geostationary orbit does not amount to an appropriation of space. Based on the premise that its occupation of an orbital location is neither permanent nor exclusive, a geostationary satellite is deemed merely to be using space. Geostationary telecommunications satellites typically have a ten-year design lifetime, after which the orbital location may be used by others.[16] Moreover, two satellites may occupy the same orbital location, provided they operate on different frequencies or serve separate geographical areas.

NO AIRSPACE-OUTER SPACE BOUNDARY. Interestingly enough,

---

12. *Id.*, art. I, para. 2.
13. *See e.g.* Chapter 4.2. (describing the various ITU World and Regional Administrative Radio Conferences at which Third World interests have been have influenced decision-making).
14. *See e.g.* Chapter 4.3. (describing broadcasting satellite service allotment plans). These plans designate orbital locations and prescribe satellite coverage areas, signal power and other satellite design and operating parameters for countries operating (or private entities authorized by such countries to operate) broadcasting satellites in the 12/14 GHz band in ITU Regions 1 and 3 (roughly Europe, Africa and Asia).
15. Outer Space Treaty, art. II.
16. Some government agencies, international organizations and private companies now boost their geostationary satellites into higher, so-called "graveyard," orbits at the end of the satellites' useful lives, a practice that avoids debris-crowding in the geostationary orbit, but which is not required either by international or domestic laws at this time.

"space," or "outer space," has yet to be defined legally. No legal boundary has been drawn separating airspace from space. The significance of a definitional, if not a scientific, boundary is evident from the fact that two completely different legal regimes apply to airspace and space. Airspace is sovereign to the subjacent State,[17] and space is *res communes*, i.e., free for use by everyone and not subject to appropriation by anyone.[18] For many years, the United Nations Committee on the Peaceful Uses of Outer Space has attempted to resolve the boundary issue in conjunction with the Bogota Declaration;[19] so far, without result. The stalemate on the boundary issue is due mainly to the divergent positions of the United States and the Soviet Union. While the latter favors an arbitrary boundary at the altitude of 110 km, coupled with innocent passage for launch vehicles below this altitude, the United States considers a legal boundary to be premature.[20] Its view is that a boundary is not necessary now and would serve to stifle technological development.

2.3. The Obligation to Use Space for Peaceful Purposes Only

Article IV of the Outer Space Treaty governs the use of space by the military. The provision is not of paramount importance to the private, commercial, telecommunications satellite operator. It is included in this overview, nevertheless, because it reflects a fundamental principle of space law, and because the private commercial satellite operator should be aware of the rights attributed to military spacecraft which, after all, share the same orbital environment.

---

17. Convention on International Civil Aviation (Chicago Convention), *done* at Chicago, Dec. 7, 1944, *entered into force* Apr. 4, 1947, T.I.A.S. 1591. Art. I, provides that "the contracting States recognize that every State has complete and exclusive sovereignty over the airspace above its territory." Although the Chicago Convention has nearly universal adherence, it is important to note that the principle of airspace sovereignty exists as a rule of customary international law, regardless of the Chicago Convention and, therefore, is binding also on non-Parties to the convention. The convention merely affirmed the principle of airspace sovereignty. *See* G.W. Lupton, CIVIL AVIATION LAW (1935); J.C. Cooper, EXPLORATIONS IN AEROSPACE LAW (1966); J.C. Cooper, *Backgrounds of International Public Air Law*, Y.B. of AIR & SPACE L. 3 (1965), D.H.N. Johnson, RIGHTS IN AIRSPACE (1965); and T.H. Wolcott, AERONAUTICAL LAW (1978) (discussing the concept of airspace sovereignty). *See also* Gorove, SPACE LAW, *supra* note 10, at 7 (discussing the upward extent of airspace sovereignty).
18. Outer Space Treaty, arts. I and II. The concept of *res communes* derives from civil law and refers to "things" common to all; that is, those things which are used and enjoyed by every one, even in single parts, but never can be exclusively acquired as a whole, *e.g.*, light and air, BLACK'S LAW DICTIONARY 1173 (5th ed. 1979). *See* Christol, THE MODERN INTERNATIONAL LAW, *supra* note 10, at 286 (discussing *res communes* in the context of the notion of "common heritage of mankind").

PERMITTED MILITARY USES. Certain military uses of space are permitted. Indeed, the U.S. and Soviet military forces are the major users of space today, primarily for purposes of communications, reconnaissance and surveillance. These particular uses are consistent with the provisions of the Outer Space Treaty. Military reconnaissance and surveillance by satellite are also condoned, and even encouraged, as part of the verification regimes permitted by bilateral arms control agreements between the U.S. and the Soviet Union.[21]

PROSCRIBED MILITARY USES. Certain military uses are specifically prohibited. Nuclear weapons and other weapons of mass destruction (e.g., biological weapons) may not be placed in orbit around Earth, installed on celestial bodies, or stationed in space in any other manner.[22] Additional restrictions apply to the use of the Moon and other celestial bodies. These can only be used for non-aggressive purposes.[23] Moreover, the testing of weapons or the establishment of military bases on the Moon or other celestial bodies is specifically prohibited.

ASAT AND ABM SYSTEMS. Testing and deployment in Earth orbit of anti-satellite satellites (ASATs) and anti-ballistic missile (ABM) systems that destroy enemy satellites or missiles on impact, rather than through nuclear explosions, are consistent with Article IV of the Outer Space Treaty. However, the deployment of an ABM system is proscribed by the Treaty Between the United States of America and the Union of Soviet Socialist Republics on the Limitation of Anti-Ballistic Missile Systems (ABM Treaty).[24] It should be noted that intercontinental ballistic missiles

---

19. For years, the boundary issue has been one of a handful of items on the agenda of the U.N. COPUOS. It is now listed under the heading "Matters Relating to the Definition and Delimitation of Outer Space and to the Character and Utilization of the Geostationary Orbit, Including Consideration of Ways and Means to Ensure the Rationale and Equitable Use of the Geostationary Orbit Without Prejudice to the Role of the International Telecommunication Union." Report of the Committee on the Peaceful Uses of Outer Space to the United Nations General Assembly, 46 U.N.G.A. Supp. (No.20), U.N. Doc. A/45/20 (1991). The United Nations' attempt to resolve the boundary issue has been clouded to some extent by the so-called Bogota Declaration. On December 3, 1976, at a meeting in Bogota, Columbia, eight equatorial countries, including Brazil, Columbia, Congo, Equador, Indonesia, Kenya, Uganda and Zaire, issued a declaration laying claim to sectors of the geostationary orbit above their respective territories. No rights were claimed to the space in-between sovereign airspace and the geostationary orbit. The Bogota Declaration provides in part:

    > Equatorial countries declare that the geostationary synchronous orbit is a physical fact linked to the reality of our planet because its existence depends exclusively on its relation to gravitational phenomena generated by the Earth, and that is why it must not be considered part of outer space. Therefore, the segments of the geostationary synchronous orbit are part of the territory over which Equatorial States exercise their national sovereignty . . . .

    The Bogota Declaration is recited in Cheng, The Legal Regime, *infra* note 20. The Bogota Declaration has been dismissed by most countries.

(ICBMs) are not considered as falling within the jurisdiction of the Outer Space Treaty since they do not complete a full orbit around Earth.

2.4. State Responsibility for Activities of Private Citizens in Space

INTERNATIONAL RESPONSIBILITY FOR PRIVATE SPACE ACTIVITIES. States bear international responsibility for the activities in space of private individuals and entities within their jurisdiction, as well as for governmental agencies.[25] Article VI of the Outer Space Treaty provides that States "shall bear international responsibility for national activities in space . . . whether such activities are carried out by governmental agencies or by non-governmental entities . . . ."[26] Non-governmental entities include private corporations, consortia, firms, foundations and other private organizations, as well as individuals. Governmental agencies include executive departments, such as the United States Department of Defense, as well as agencies, such as the United States National Aeronautics and Space Administration (NASA), the French Centre National d'Etudes Spatiales (CNES) and the National Space Development Agency of Japan (NASDA).

In permitting the activities of private entities in space, on the condition that a State bear international responsibility, Article VI represents a compromise between the divergent positions previously held by the United States and the Soviet Union. During the negotiations leading to the Outer Space Treaty, the Soviet Union initially opposed private enterprise in space and argued, instead, that only nation States should be allowed to conduct space activities, a view reflecting the ideological and philosophical underpinnings of the Soviet society. Not surprisingly, the United

---

20. *See* B. Cheng, *The Legal Regime of Airspace and Outer Space: The Boundary Problem: Functionalism Versus Spatialism: The Major Premise,* V ANNALS OF AIR & SPACE L. 323 (1980) (discussing the U.S. and Soviet positions, as well as a third approach, the functionalist.) [hereinafter cited as Cheng, The Legal Regime].
21. Interim Agreement Between the United States of America and Union of Soviet Socialist Republics on Certain Measures With Respect to the Limitation of Strategic Offensive Arms, *signed* May 26, 1972, *entered into force* Oct. 3, 1972, 944 U.N.T.S. 0 [hereinafter cited as SALT I], art. V, para. 1, provides that "[f]or the purpose of providing assurance of compliance with the provisions of this Interim Agreement, each Party shall use national technical means of verification at its disposal . . . ." The reference to "national technical means" is a reference to reconnaissance and surveillance from space.
22. States Parties to the Outer Space Treaty "undertake not to place in orbit around the Earth any objects carrying nuclear weapons or any other kinds of weapons of mass destruction, install such weapons on celestial bodies, or station such weapons in outer space in any other manner." Outer Space Treaty, art. IV, para. 1.

States, which promotes private enterprise as a fundamental principle, held the opposite view.

TWO ASPECTS OF INTERNATIONAL RESPONSIBILITY. International responsibility for private space activities has two aspects: 1) a State is responsible in the sense that it may be held liable for any damage caused by private sector space activities (vicarious liability); and 2) a State is responsible for assuring that private sector activities are carried out in conformity with the provisions of the Outer Space Treaty. The first aspect of responsibility is merely alluded to in Article VI of the Outer Space Treaty, and becomes clearer in the context of international liability, discussed in Chapter 2.8. The second aspect of responsibility is spelled out in Article VI, which provides that "States Parties to the Treaty shall bear international responsibility . . . for assuring that national activities are carried out in conformity with provisions set forth in the present Treaty."

AUTHORIZATION AND CONTINUED SUPERVISION. As a corollary to State responsibility for private space activities, States are required to subject to "authorization and continuing supervision"[27] non-governmental entities that engage in space activities under their jurisdiction. No guidance is provided in international space law with regard to the nature and scope of the authorization and supervision required. For example, does a letter from an appropriate governmental authority granting your client permission to launch and operate a satellite satisfy the requirement for "authorization" within the meaning of Article VI? Or must an authorization, to be acceptable, be the culmination of a more extensive and elaborate licensing process involving the application of laws and regulations? Moreover, can supervision be arranged *ad hoc*, or is the promulgation of regulations required? What kind of supervision is envisaged by the Treaty? Is supervision required only to ensure consistency with the provisions of the Outer Space Treaty, or is additional regulation contemplated? Additional regulation might pertain to the safety and business, as well as national security, aspects of private space activities. These questions are not answered clearly by the Outer Space Treaty or any other space treaty, or the official records of their respective negotiating histories.

NATIONAL IMPLEMENTATION. The few States that have authorized

---

23. The Moon and other celestial bodies shall be used "exclusively for peaceful purposes." *Id.*, art. IV, para. 2. The term "peaceful" has been interpreted to mean "non-aggressive" rather than non-military. *See* Gorove, SPACE LAW, *supra* note 10, at 85-94; S.H. Lay & H. Taubenfeld, THE LAW RELATING TO ACTIVITIES OF MAN IN SPACE (1970), at 25; and D. Goedhuis, THE CHANGING LEGAL REGIME OF AIR AND OUTER SPACE (1978), at 27 (supporting the position that "peaceful" means non-aggressive). However, certain military uses of the celestial bodies are specifically prohibited, including the establishment of military bases, installations and fortifications, military testing and the conduct of military maneuvers. Outer Space Treaty, art. IV, para. 2. Military personnel and equipment may be used for scientific research. *Id.*

private space activities to date have tended to consider it an internal matter for sovereign nations to determine what form the authorization and supervision should take. For example, the United States, one of the few countries having authorized private activities in space, has adopted three fairly elaborate regimes for authorization (licensing) and supervision (regulation) of private commercial telecommunications satellites, private space transportation systems and private remote-sensing space systems.[28] All three regulatory regimes establish criteria and procedures for obtaining a license, but impose only a minimum of restrictions essential to ensuring compliance with U.S. treaty obligations, and to safeguard the United States national security, public safety and other public interests. Very little, if any, business restrictions have been imposed on the three types of private space activities. For example, market entry, service offerings and prices are unrestricted with only minor exceptions.

Licensing regimes for private space activities that are much more rudimentary and general in nature exist in a few other countries. Since these licensing regimes are far less detailed, the same set of licensing provisions often apply to all kinds of space activities. For example, Section 2 of the Swedish Act on Space Activities of 1982[29] provides that "space activities," which it defines broadly to include the launching and operation of a telecommunications satellite, as well as all other space activities, may not be carried out from Swedish territory "without a license" from the National

---

24. *Signed* May 26, 1972, *entered into force* Oct. 3, 1972, T.I.A.S. 7503. *See* P.L. Meredith, *The Legality of a High-Technology Missile Defense System: The ABM and Outer Space Treaties*, 78 AM. J. INT'L L. 418 (1984) (discussing the legality of space-based ABM systems). *See also* Statement of Abraham D. Sofaer, Legal Advisor, U.S. Department of State, on the interpretation of the ABM Treaty with respect to future ABM systems based on new technologies, *Before the Subcommittee on Arms Control, International Security, and Science of the House Committee on Foreign Affairs* (Oct. 22, 1985) (proposing a broad interpretation of the ABM Treaty that would allow for the development and testing, but not deployment, of futuristic ABM systems). *See further* analysis by the Committee on International Arms Control and Security Affairs, Association of the Bar of the City of New York, *The Anti-Ballistic Missile Treaty Dispute*, 43 REC. OF THE ASS'N. OF THE BAR OF THE CITY OF N.Y. 300 (1988) (concerning the dispute on narrow versus broad interpretation of the ABM Treaty).
25. Outer Space Treaty, art. VI. Where the activities are carried out by an international organization, international responsibility shall be borne both by the organization and by the member States. Id. *See* Convention on International Liability for Damage Caused by Space Objects, *supra* note 4, art. XXII (providing for direct liability for international organizations, if certain conditions are met).
26. Outer Space Treaty, art. VI. In B. Cheng, *The Commercial Development of Space: The Need for New Treaties*, 19 J. SPACE L. 17, 21 (1991), the author suggests that this provision may have entered the "realm of general international law binding on all States."

Board for Space Activities pursuant to the Decree on Space Activities.[30] The United Kingdom Outer Space Act of 1986 applies to persons "(a) launching or procuring the launch of a space object, (b) operating a space object, [and engaged in] (c) any activity in outer space,"[31] and a license from the Secretary of State under this Act is required if your client is a United Kingdom national, a Scottish firm, or a body incorporated under the law of any part of the United Kingdom.[32]

In countries where specific licensing regimes have been adopted for space activities, compliance with Article VI of the Outer Space Treaty usually will not present an issue. On the other hand, where no such licensing regimes exist, creativity, skill and political connections may have to be employed to find a way in which the country where your client is situated can authorize and supervise your client's space activities in compliance with Article VI.[33] In some cases, existing laws adopted to regulate terrestrial activities are sufficiently broad in scope and purpose to encompass space activities, as well. Where such laws cannot be found, your client should encourage the introduction and enactment of the necessary legislation.[34] In States where decree, rather than legislation, is the primary means of governing the activities of private citizens, your client should seek to influence the appropriate governmental authority to issue a decree.

EXAMPLES OF SITUATIONS WHERE EXISTING LAW HAS BEEN SUFFICIENT. When examining existing law in an attempt to identify provisions broad enough in scope and purpose to encompass your client's proposed telecommunications satellite venture, statutes governing radio and telecommunications provide a starting point. For example, when private companies first proposed to operate telecommunications satellites in the United States in the late 1960s, they sought authorization pursuant to the Communications Act of 1934.[35] This Act applies to radio, telephony

---

27. Outer Space Treaty, art. VI, which provides that private space activities shall require authorization and supervision by the "appropriate State Party to the Treaty." No definition or explanation is provided of what constitutes the appropriate State. In cases where more than one State, theoretically, has jurisdiction over your client's space project, based on generally recognized principles of national jurisdiction, such as nationality and locus of operation, article VI offers no guidance for selecting the appropriate State. It appears that this selection is left to States sponsoring or otherwise controlling the activities of a private party. *See* K.H. Bockstiegel, *Reconsideration of the Legal Framework for Commercial Space Activities*, XXXIII IISL 3, 5 (1990) (suggesting that the "appropriate" State should be interpreted to mean the State of nationality). *See also* B. Reijnen, *International Law and Business in Space — In Europe*, XXXIII IISL 68, 70 (1990) (suggesting that the State of registry might be considered the "appropriate" State). The significance of the determination of the appropriate State becomes more clear in the context of international liability for private space activities; the State which is internationally responsible for a private entity also is internationally liable for damages. *See* Chapter 2.8, below (describing international liability).

and other types of telecommunications. The United States Federal Communications Commission, which is the implementing authority for the Communications Act, concluded in 1970 that the Act applies also to telecommunications satellites since they fall within the definition of "radio station," which is precisely what the Communications Act was intended to regulate. The Federal Communications Commission stated:

> 3. The 1934 Act, which directs the Commission to provide "a rapid, efficient, Nation-wide and world-wide wire and radio communications service" (47 U.S.C.§§151), applies to all "interstate and foreign communication by wire or radio and all interstate and foreign transmission of energy by radio, which originates and/or is received within the United States" and to "the licensing and regulating of all radio stations" (47 U.S.C.§ 152(a)). A license from the Commission is required for all radio stations except government-owned stations (47 U.S.C.§ 301, 303, 305, 307, 308 and 309). By definition, "radio station" is "a station equipped to engage in radio communications or radio transmission of energy" (47 U.S.C.§ 153(k)). "Communication by radio" is defined to include "all instrumentalities, facilities, apparatus, and services" incidental to "the transmission by radio of writing, signs, signals, pictures, and signs of all kinds" (47 U.S.C.§ 153(b)), and

---

28. *See*, for telecommunications satellites, the Communications Act of 1934, 47 U.S.C. §§ 151-609 (1988), the Communications Satellite Act of 1962, 47 U.S.C. §§ 701-757 (1988) and implementing regulations, 47 C.F.R. Parts 25 and 100 (1990); for space transportation systems, the Commercial Space Launch Act of 1984, 49 U.S.C. §§ 2601-2623 (1988) and its implementing regulations, 14 C.F.R. Parts 400-499 (1990); and for remote-sensing space systems, the Land Remote-Sensing Commercialization Act of 1984, 15 U.S.C. §§ 4201-4292 (1988) and its implementing regulations, 15 C.F.R. Part 960 (1990) (establishing licensing and regulatory regimes).
29. 1982: 963.
30. 1982: 1069. *See* J. Reifarth, *Nationale Weltraum Gesetze in Europa*, 36 ZEITSCHRIFT FUR WELTRAUMRECHT 11 (1987) (describing the Act)
31. U.K. Outer Space Act of 1986, 1 Current L. Stat. Annot. 38-1, sec. 1.
32. *Id.*, sec. 2.
33. For a U.S. lawyer, this situation may arise, for example, if a U.S. client company enters into a joint venture with a foreign company and the joint venture is incorporated in a foreign country for the purpose of operating a telecommunications satellite from that country; and, also, the joint venture seeks certain advice from the U.S. lawyer.
34. For example, Societe Europeenne des Satellites of Luxembourg (a private company created to operate satellites for broadcasting in Europe) received authorization and financial guarantees by the State of Luxembourg through legislation: Projet de loi autorisant le Governement à accorder une garantie de l'Etat dans l'intérêt du financement du systéme des satellites GDL, No. 2972, Chambre des Deputés, Session ordinaire 1985-1986.
35. 47 U.S.C. §§ 151 600 (1988).

> "transmission of energy by radio" similarly includes both such transmission and "all instrumentalities, facilities, and services incidental to such transmission" (47 U.S.C.§ 153(d)). These all-inclusive definitions *clearly include [private] satellite and earth-station facilities* used for communication or transmission of energy by radio, which originates or is received in the United States.
>
> 4. The Commission's jurisdiction under the plain language of the 1934 statute to license and regulate domestic satellite facilities is not affected by the circumstance that the radio transmission involves stations located in space and a new technology not explicitly mentioned in that Act. *California Interstate Telephone Co. v. Federal Communications Commission*. 328 F.2d. 556 (C.A.D.C.). Section 303(g) directs the Commission to "study new uses of radio, provide for experimental uses of frequencies, and generally encourage the larger and more effective use of radio in the public interest" (47 U.S.C.§ 303(g)). The policy underlying this section was stated during the Congressional hearings on the 1934 Act. "Our supremacy in radio cannot be maintained except by active encouragement and development of its use. Its possibilities are almost untouched today . . . Who knows what future developments may bring." Hearing on H.R. 8310 before the House Committee on Interstate and Foreign Commerce, 73. Cong., 2d Sess., p. 21.
>
> . . .
>
> 5. The Act has been uniformly construed as granting broad powers to the Commission which do not depend on a specific reference to service, technology, or practice in the Statute. In *National Broadcasting Company v. United States,* 319 U.S. 190, 217, 219, the Supreme Court stated with respect to the Commissions comprehensive powers over newly developing instrumentalities of radio communications:
>
>> The avowed aim of the Communications Act of 1934 was to secure the maximum benefit of radio to all people in the United States. To that end Congress endowed the Communications Commission with comprehensive powers to promote and realize the vast potentialities of radio.[36]

Based on the decision that it has authority under the Communications Act, the Federal Communications Commission has authorized more than fifty privately owned telecommunications satellites pursuant to this Act. (See Chapter 3.).

---

36. Emphasis added. *Establishment of Domestic Communication-Satellite Facilities by Non-Governmental Entities,* 22 F.C.C. 2d 86 (1970), Appx. C, entitled "Memorandum on Legal Issues," at paras. 3-5.

In some cases, telecommunications statutes may contain language that appears to exclude their application to your client's satellite project, although close scrutiny may reveal that such is not the case. For example, the licensing provision appearing in the British Telecommunications Act of 1984[37] provides that "a person who runs a telecommunications system *within* the United Kingdom shall be guilty of an offence unless he is authorized to run the system by a license granted under section 7 below."[38] At first glance, the phrase "within the United Kingdom" appears to preclude the application of the Act to satellites since they are located in space and are not, strictly speaking, telecommunications systems run within the United Kingdom. However, as pointed out by the U.K. Department of Trade and Industry, telecommunications satellites fall within the ambit of the above-quoted licensing provision since the *ground station* (whether it be a sophisticated ground station or a simple receiver dish) necessary to communicate with the satellite is a telecommunications system within the meaning of the Act, the operation in the United Kingdom of which requires a license.[39]

WHERE SEVERAL EXISTING LAWS APPLY. As opposed a scenario where existing laws appear to be, or actually are, too narrow to encompass your client's proposed space activity, a situation is possible in which a multitude of different, and at times conflicting, laws appear to govern. This was the situation facing Space Services, Inc. of Houston, Texas, an entrepreneurial start-up company seeking United States Government permission in 1982 to conduct a test space launching of its commercial launch vehicle "Conestoga" from United States territory. At that time, legislation pertaining specifically to launch vehicles had not yet been adopted. However, several United States Federal government agencies claimed to have at least indirect or potential jurisdiction over the launching.[40] A decision was made[41] to rely on the Department of State's authority under the Arms Export Control Act[42] as the umbrella authority for licensing of Space Services, Inc. This represented an interim solution allowing the U.S. government to discharge its international obligations to authorize and supervise private space activities, pending the adoption of a launch licensing regime. Space Services, Inc.'s launching request was then granted.[43]

This episode, involving Space Services, Inc. and the bureaucratic tangle of rules and regulations confronting it, precipitated a process that in the words of E. Jason Steptoe, then an attorney with the Department of Transportation, "compelled the Government to give more rigorous definition to the amorphous concepts of 'authorization' and 'supervision' of private commercial space activities by U.S. nationals."[44] The process culminated in the designation of the Department of Transportation (DOT) as the lead agency responsible for licensing and regulation of launch vehi-

---

37. British Telecommunications Act of 1984, sec. 5.
38. Emphasis added.
39. Letter from D.C.B. Morris, United Kingdom Department of Trade and Industry, to P.L. Meredith (May 2, 1986).

cles and the adoption of the Commercial Space Launch Act of 1984.[45] The DOT established an Office of Commercial Space Transportation with authority to formulate implementing regulations, including licensing procedures, and to carry out the actual licensing of private commercial launch vehicles.

2.5. The Requirement to Register Objects Launched Into Space

REGISTRATION REQUIREMENT. Registration of objects launched into space, including satellites, launch vehicles and other spacecraft, is a requirement for States Parties to the Registration Convention.[46] The Convention provides for two types of registers: national registries to be maintained by States,[47] and one international, master register to be maintained by the Secretary General of the United Nations.[48] Whenever a State Party to the Registration Convention launches an object into space, it must 1) make an entry in its own national registry reflecting the launch;[49] and 2) furnish information on the launched object to the United Nations Secre-

---

40. The following agencies claimed to have jurisdiction over one or more aspects of Space Services' proposed launch: The Department of State, Office of Munitions Control, which grants Temporary Export License of Unclassified Defense Articles pursuant to the Arms Export Control Act, 22 U.S.C. § 2778 (1988) and its implementing regulations, International Traffic in Arms Regulations, 22 C.F.R. § 121.01. (Munitions List) (1990); the Department of Transportation (DOT), Federal Aviation Administration (FAA), which grants exemption for rocket travel through U.S. airspace pursuant to the Federal Aviation Act of 1958, 49 U.S.C. §§ 1341-1359 (1988) and its implementing regulations, Federal Aviation Regulations, 14 C.F.R. Parts. 1-199 (1990); the U.S. Coast Guard (under the DOT), which has jurisdiction over water traffic within three miles of any launch site or trajectory pursuant to the Ports and Waterways Safety Act, 33 U.S.C. § 1225 (1988); the Materials Transportation Bureau (also under the DOT), which grants exemptions from regulations for transport of hazardous materials pursuant to 46 U.S.C. § 144 (1988); the Federal Communications Commission, which controls the use of radio frequencies pursuant to the Communications Act of 1934, 47 U.S.C. §§ 151-609 (1988); the Department of Commerce, which grants export license if the payload is classified under the Commodity Control List pursuant to the Export Administrations Act of 1979, 50 U.S.C. §§ 758-799 (1988) and its implementing regulations, Export Administration Regulations, 15 C.F.R. Parts 368-399 (1990); the National Aeronautics and Space Administration, which provides advice on flight safety requirements pursuant to the National Aeronautics and Space Act of 1958, as amended, 42 U.S.C. § 2473 para. 209 (1988); and the Department of Defense, which reviews launch proposals relative to the transfer of technology under the Arms Export Control Act, *supra*, *See* J.R. Myers, *Federal Government Regulation of Commercial Operations Using Expendable Launch Vehicles*, 12 J. SPACE L. 40 (1984) (describing the jurisdiction of each of these agencies in the context of commercial launch vehicle licensing).

tary General for purposes of registration in the international register maintained by the U.N. or by the Secretary General.[50] At least six States and one international organization maintain national registries.[51] The contents of a national registry and the conditions under which it is maintained are for each State maintaining a registry to decide.[52]

NATIONAL REGISTRATION. The requirement for registration in a national registry applies to the "launching State,"[53] which is defined to include the "State which launches or procures the launching of a space object" and the "State from whose territory or facility a space object is launched."[54] Of course, situations do occur where more than one State falls within the definition of "launching State" with respect to a single space object. Typically, one State, or an entity within such a State, may launch a satellite for another State, or entity within such a State. Both States then qualify as launching States of the satelite.[55] In this and other cases of multiple launching States, only one State may register the space object, i.e. serve as the State of registry.[56] The launching States shall "jointly determine which one of them shall register the object . . . ."[57] The State on whose national registry an object launched into space is carried becomes the "State of registry,"[58] and is entitled to exercise jurisdiction and control over the object carried on its registry[59] (see Chapter 2.6.).

If the State authorizing your client to operate a satellite does not maintain a national registry, either it can establish one or it can conclude an agreement with another launching State that the latter will carry the satellite on its national registry.[60] Your client should understand the consequences of foreign registration; that is, the foreign country will have jurisdiction and control over your client's satellite, unless an agreement has been concluded between the foreign State and the State authorizing your client to launch the object that the latter shall retain jurisdiction and control.[61]It is interesting to note, also, that "flag-of-convenience" registra-

---

41. Recommendation made by the Senior Interagency Group on Space, operating under the aegis of the National Security Council.
42. 22 U.S.C. §§ 2751-2796 (1988).
43. E.J. Steptoe, *United States Government Licensing of Commercial Space Activities by Private Enterprise*, XXVII IISL 191, 193 (1984).
44. *Id.*, at 192.
45. 49 U.S.C. §§ 2601-2823 (1988).
46. Convention on Registration of Objects Launched Into Outer Space, *supra* note 5.
47. Registration Convention, art. II, para. 1.
48. *Id.*, art. III, para. 1.
49. *Id.*, art. II, para. 1.
50. *Id.*, art. IV.
51. *Application of the Convention on Registration of Objects Launched into Outer Space*, Report by the Secretary General, U.N. Doc. A/AC.105/382 (1987), at 2.
52. Registration Convention, art. II, para. 3.
53. *Id.*, art. II, para. 1.
54. *Id.*, art. I(a)..

tion, which is common maritime practice, is not acceptable for space operations. The State of registry must be a "launching State," that is, one of the participants in the launching.[62]

INTERNATIONAL REGISTRATION. The State of Registry has a duty to furnish information for entry in an international register maintained by the United Nations Secretary General.[63] It must do so "as soon as practicable" after the launching.[64] The information to be provided shall include the name(s) of the launching State(s), the location of the launch, a designator of the space object, orbital parameters, and the function of the object. Andrew J. Young, in *A Decennial Review of the Registration Convention,*[65] offers an example of information Canada submitted to the United Nations Secretary General in 1986 on the communications satellite ANIK, owned and operated by Telesat Canada of Ottawa, Ontario.

---

55. Complex situations involving registration can arise when several States participate in intergovernmental cooperative space projects. An example is presented by the permanently-manned international Space Station *Freedom*, a cooperative program involving the United States, Canada, Japan and nations that are members of the European Space Agency (ESA). These countries participate as sovereign States, as well as through their national space agencies, or through ESA in the case of the European countries. Each agency will contribute specific elements of the modular Space Station scheduled for launch in the late 1990s. For example, the U.S. will contribute the habitat module and the structural framework for the Station, and Canada will contribute a so-called Mobile Servicing System. The various contributions are specified in the Agreement Among the Government of the United States of America, Governments of Member States of the European Space Agency, the Government of Japan, and the Government of Canada on Cooperation in the Detailed Design, Development, Operation, and Utilization of the Permanently Manned Civil Space Station, *done* 1988 [hereinafter cited as the Space Station Agreement] and in more detail in a series of bilateral Memoranda of Understanding between implementing agencies or executive departments of these countries. The Space Station Agreement is not yet in force. A provisional agreement has been concluded among the parties allowing them to act as if it were in force.

    During the negotiations of the Space Station Agreement, the issue of registration of the Space Station received considerable attention. Basically, three options were available: 1) one country could register the entire Space Station on its national registry as one space object and have jurisdiction and control over the entire Space Station; 2) one country could register the entire Space Station on its national registry and the parties could agree on a formula for sharing jurisdiction and control; and 3) each party could register as space objects the flight elements it provides and retain jurisdiction and control over such flight elements. The third option was selected. Space Station Agreement, *supra*, art. 5. Reasons for this selection include national pride and prestige considerations, as well as the fact that the Space Station is modular with clearly separate elements to be provided by different States parties and to be launched at different times.

Name of launching country:	Canada
Designator:	Anik D-2
Date of launch:	November 8, 1984
Location of Launch:	Cape Canaveral United States of America
Launch vehicle:	STS-Space Shuttle
Nodal Period:	Geostationary
Inclination:	-
Apogee:	-
Perigee:	-
Longitude:	111.5 degrees West
Frequencies and transmitter powers:	Table attached
Purpose:	Telecommunications
Operating entity:	Telesat Canada

The requirements for international registration of information have been criticized for being too vague, thus rendering the international register incomplete, unreliable and, for most purposes, useless. It is largely up to each State of registry to determine what kind of information to provide, as well as when to submit it. As might be expected, information has been particularly sparse with respect to the function of the space object, especially regarding military missions.

HOW THE REGISTRATION REQUIREMENTS AFFECT PRIVATE OPERATORS. Registration, pursuant to the Registration Convention, is an international legal obligation imposed upon States Parties to that Convention. Nonetheless, private space operators, such as your client, may be required as a matter of domestic law to supply the information necessary

---

56. Registration Convention, art. II, para. 2.
57. *Id.,* art. II, para. 2.
58. *Id.,* art. I(c). *See infra* note 62 (defining "State of Registry").
59. Outer Space Treaty, art. VIII, which provides that the "[a] State Party to the Treaty on whose registry an object launched into outer space is carried shall retain jurisdiction and control over such object . . . ."
60. Foreign registration may occur, *e.g.,* where the State whose satellite is being launched is not a Party to the Registration Convention.
61. Outer Space Treaty, art. VIII. *See supra* note 59 (quoting the relevant provision). Such agreements are permitted under Registration Convention art. II, para. 2.
62. Registration Convention, Article II, paragraph 1, provides that "the launching State shall register. . . ." Further, Article I(c) provides that the term "State of Registry" means "a launching State on whose registry an object is carried in accordance with Article II."
63. *Id.,* art. IV
64. *Id.*
65. A.J. Young, *A Decennial Review of the Registration Convention,* XI ANNALS OF AIR & SPACE L. 287 (1986), reciting U.N. Doc. ST/SG/SER.E/137 (1986).

for purposes of registration. For example, United States private commercial launch companies must submit to the U.S. Department of Transportation's Office of Commercial Space Transportation (which licenses private launch operators) information about the vehicle and the payload (typically a satellite), if American, for purposes of the Registration Convention.[66]

2.6. Jurisdiction and Control Over Objects Launched Into Space

THE STATE OF REGISTRY GENERALLY HAS JURISDICTION AND CONTROL. As a general rule, the State of registry exercises jurisdiction and control over an object launched into space. Article VIII of the Outer Space Treaty provides that "[a] State Party to the Treaty on whose registry an object launched into outer space is carried shall retain jurisdiction and control over such object . . . while in outer space . . . ." [67] In other words, the State of registry, usually the State authorizing the launching and operation of the satellite (see Chapter 2.5.), may apply and enforce its own civil and criminal laws with respect to your client's satellite while it is in space.[68]

WHERE A STATE OTHER THAN THE STATE OF REGISTRY HAS JURISDICTION AND CONTROL. Article II of the Registration Convention

---

66. Commercial Space Transportation; Licensing Regulations, 14 C.F.R. § 415.10 (1990). Section 415.10(a) provides that "[i]n accordance with Article IV of the Convention on Registration of Objects Launched Into Outer Space, each [launch company] is responsible for registering all objects placed in space in the course of conducting activities authorized by the license, except for objects owned by a foreign entity. Registration of objects owned by a foreign entity is the responsibility of that foreign entity." Section 415.10(b) provides that

> [e]ach licensee shall, within thirty days after launch, submit to the Office the following information concerning any vehicle or other object it has launched into outer space: (1) The international designator of the space object(s);
> 2) Date and location of launch;
> (3) Basic programmed orbital parameters, including:
> (i) Nodal period,
> (ii) Inclination
> (iii) Apogee
> (iv) General function of the space object.

Section 7 of the U.K. Outer Space Act of 1986, 1 Current L. Stat. Annot. 38-1, sec. 7, requires the Secretary of State to maintain a register in which there "shall be entered . . . such particulars of such space objects as the Secretary considers appropriate to comply with the international obligations of the United Kingdom." Under Section 4 of the Swedish Act on Space Activities of 1982, 1982: 963, *supra* note 30, the National Board of Space Activities is required to keep a register of the space objects for which Sweden is considered to be the launching State in accordance with the definition in Article I of the Registration Convention. In both cases, it would seem that the private party is required to provide the necessary information.

allows launching States to agree that a State other than the State of registry shall have jurisdiction and control over a space object.[69] This provision offers a means to avoid the problematic consequences of foreign registration. Absent an agreement to the contrary, registration of your client's satellite on a foreign registry would subject your client's satellite to the laws and control of a foreign country.[70] Despite the fact that the foreign jurisdiction arguably may not be far-reaching, affecting only the satellite's presence in space and not its business applications on Earth,[71] foreign jurisdiction still may have undesirable consequences concerning, for example, transponder sales. Potential customers may hesitate to buy transponders, and financial institutions may be reluctant to execute transponder sale lease-back transactions, or to provide loans to transponder purchasers, when the satellite (the collateral) is subject to foreign jurisdiction.

Furthermore, where a foreign State exercises jurisdiction and control, a potential exists for conflict between laws applied, or actions taken, pursuant to jurisdictional authority and those applied or taken in accordance with the obligation to supervise the private space activity (Chapter 2.4.).[72]No incident has yet forced a practical consideration of the conflict and required a legal resolution.

2.7. Ownership of Space Objects in Space and Upon Return to Earth

OWNERSHIP IS NOT AFFECTED BY PRESENCE IN SPACE. Ownership of an object, typically a satellite, does not change as a result of its being launched into space, being present in space, or upon returning to Earth. Article VIII of the Outer Space Treaty provides that "[o]wnership of objects launched into outer space . . . and their component parts, is not affected by their presence in outer space . . . or by their return to the Earth."[73] This means that in countries which recognize private ownership, a satellite owner would retain ownership of the satellite while it is in space, and upon its retrieval and return to Earth. Ownership can be defined as a collection of rights to use and enjoy property, including the right to convey title.[74]

THE SIGNIFICANCE OF OWNERSHIP IN SPACE. The ownership rule is significant in that it allows the owner not only to use the satellite for its intended purpose, or in any other manner not inconsistent with the laws and regulations of the country having jurisdiction over the satellite operation, but also to sell, lease, mortgage and otherwise dispose of the satellite, including its transponders, while in space. Transponder sales and leases to users are common, particularly in the United States[75] and

67. Outer Space Treaty, art. VIII. The principle of jurisdiction and control complements the principle of international responsibility for national space activities, Outer Space Treaty, art. VI, discussed in Chapter 2.4.

Europe.[76] Transponder sales also may occur in the context of satellite financing as part of a sale lease-back transaction. In such an arrangement, the satellite owner transfers to a bank or financial institution legal title (ownership) to one or more transponders, receives the sales proceeds in return, and then leases the transponders for a fixed term, usually equal to the design life of the satellite. The financial institution receives lease payments, tax benefits in the form of accelerated depreciation (see Chapter 1.1.) and the residual value of the satellite, if any, at the end of the lease term. Moreover, in cases of secured lending, the satellite may serve as collateral, which, upon default, will revert to the financial institution having the security interest.

DURATION OF OWNERSHIP. Article VIII of the Outer Space Treaty does not limit ownership to *operational* space objects. Rather, it appears that ownership extends beyond the useful life of a satellite, that is, when that satellite is no longer operational.[77] Ownership also does not cease if the satellite malfunctions in orbit, or even if the satellite does not reach its proper orbit because of a failed launching. As a consequence, satellite

---

68. *See* Gorove, SPACE LAW, *supra* note 10, at 141 (discussing criminal jurisdiction in space). In 1982, Section 7 of the United States Crimes and Criminal Procedures Act of 1948, 18 U.S.C. § 7 (1988) was amended to provide for the extension of United States criminal jurisdiction to

    [a]ny vehicle used or designed for flight or navigation in space and on the registry of the United States pursuant to the Treaty on Principles Governing the Activities of States in the Exploration and Use of Outer Space, Including the Moon and Other Celestial Bodies and the Convention on Registration of Objects Launched into Outer Space, while that vehicle is in flight, which is from the moment when all external doors are closed on Earth following embarkation until the moment when one such door is opened on Earth for disembarkation or in the case of a forced landing, until the competent authorities take over the responsibility for the vehicle and persons and property aboard.

    In 1990, the United States extended its patent law jurisdiction to inventions in space. A new Section 105, entitled "Inventions in Outer Space," was added to Title 35 of the United States Code, providing that

    (a) any invention, made, used or sold in outer space on a space object or component thereof under the jurisdiction or control of the United States shall be considered to be made, used or sold within the United States for purposes of this title except with respect to any space object or component thereof that is specifically identified and otherwise provided for by an international agreement to which the United States is a party, or with respect to any space object or component thereof that is carried on the registry of a foreign state in accordance with the Convention on the Registration of Objects Launched into Outer Space.

    (b) Any invention made, used or sold in outer space on a space object or component thereof that is carried on the registry on a foreign state in accordance with the Convention on Registration of Objects Launched into Outer Space, shall be considered to be made, used or sold within the United States for purposes of this title if specifically so agreed in an international agreement between the United States and the state of registry.

    See P.L. Meredith, *Status of the "Patents in Space Legislation" in Congress*, 17 J. SPACE L. 163 (1989) (discussing the legislation).

insurance underwriters sometimes provide in their satellite launch insurance policies for transfer to the insurers, at their option, of title to the satellite that failed to reach orbit or that malfunctioned in orbit and for which a claim has been paid in full. For example, one insurance policy provides: "Upon Payment of a Total or Constructive Total Loss under this Policy, the Insured agrees, upon the request of the Insurers, to transfer the title to the Satellite to the Insurers."

In a precedent-setting and celebrated incident, two communications satellites, WESTAR and PALAPA, owned respectively by Western Union and the Government of Indonesia, were left to drift in useless, low-Earth orbits when their perigee kick motors failed to boost them to geostationary altitude. The satellites were destined for the geostationary orbit. Both satellites had been launched and deployed, as planned, into low-Earth orbits by the NASA Space Shuttle. The perigee kick motors attached to each satellite were to take over from there. Both satellites were insured, and the insurers treated each one as a complete loss. Proceeds were paid under the insurance policies to the owners of the satellites, i.e., Western Union Telegraph Company and the Government of Indonesia. The insurers, which obtained title to the satellites, then arranged for their "rescue." NASA agreed to use its Space Shuttle for retrieval of the two satellites. Hughes Aircraft, the satellite manufacturer, agreed to refurbish them. The rescue mission was carried out successfully in November 1984, and the satellites were later sold by the insurers: The WESTAR satellite, for exam-

---

69. Registration Convention, art. II, para. 2.
70. Outer Space Treaty, art. VIII.
71. The limitation is logical in view of the purpose of the Outer Space Treaty, which is to govern the activities of States in the use of space, and also considering the language of article VIII of the Outer Space Treaty, which refers to an object's presence in space ("while in outer space"). Foreign jurisdiction and control over your client's satellite typically could refer to positioning and station-keeping in the geostationary orbit, or the use of any other orbit, as well as end-of-life disposal measures.
72. Outer Space Treaty, art. VI.
73. *Id.*, art. VIII.
74. BLACK'S LAW DICTIONARY 997 (5th ed. 1979).
75. Hughes Communications, Inc., a subsidiary of Hughes Aircraft Company, of El Segundo, California, pioneered the transponder sales concept in the early 1980s. *See Domestic Fixed Satellite Transponder Sales, 90* F.C.C.2d 1238 (1982) (providing for authorizations by the U.S. Federal Communications Commission of transponder sales). Currently, several U.S. satellite operators either sell or long-term lease transponders on their satellites. Transponder owners include, *e.g.*, Home Box Office, American Broadcasting Company, Public Broadcasting Service and USA Today, to mention a few.
76. Société Européennes des Satellites, a private Luxembourg company, leases transponders on its ASTRA satellite to private parties, and the European Telecommunications Satellite Organization (EUTELSAT) leases transponders on its satellites to EUTELSAT Signatories.

ple, was purchased by Asia Satellite Telecommunications Company of Hong Kong and re-launched on the Chinese Long March vehicle on April 7, 1990.

SALVAGE. A yet unsettled area of the law concerns salvage of space objects.[78] Under maritime law, private[79] vessels or property on navigable waters that have been abandoned are subject to salvage by anyone who in good faith takes possession of the property as a salvor. A vessel is considered to be abandoned if those in charge of it have deserted it, without hope on their part of recovering it, and without the intention of returning to it. The abandonment may arise from an accident or necessity, or from voluntary dereliction. The salvor is entitled to a salvage reward if the ship is conveyed to shore.[80] Legal title to the vessel does not transfer to the salvor; it remains with the original owner.[81]

Similar principles have not been adopted for space, although some legal scholars have suggested the application of maritime law by analogy.[82]For example, one might argue that a satellite has been abandoned when it has ceased its operational functions at the end of life, when it malfunctions, or when it fails to reach its proper orbit because of a failed launching: *Provided* that tracking, telecommand and control functions have ceased *and* the owner fails within a reasonable period of time to take action to retrieve or otherwise control the satellite, or the owner indicates that no such actions will be taken.[83]

2.8. International Liability for Damage Caused by Space Objects

INTERNATIONAL LIABILITY IN GENERAL. The Outer Space Treaty, Article VII, as well as the Liability Convention,[84] imposes international liability for third party damage caused by space objects authorized or operated by States Parties to these agreements. Absolute liability, i.e., liability

---

77. For example, the U.S. National Aeronautics and Space Administration transferred ownership to the Smithsonian Institution of the Viking I Lander (still located on Mars). G.S. Robinson, *Artifacts, Abandonment, Salvage . . . And the Jolly Roger in Space,* II SAN FRAN. ST. U. BUS. J. 65 (1990). The transfer indicates that NASA believed that it retained ownership of a space object beyond its useful life.

78. The reason is, of course, that the ability to carry out salvage operations is limited. Presently, only the United States Space Shuttle can be used to recover space objects, and that only in low-Earth orbit under certain conditions.

79. There is no equivalent international recognition of salvage of public ships. Article XIV of the Brussels Convention on Salvage of 1910 (to which the United States and the Soviet Union are parties) excludes government ships. R.G. Hall, *Comments on Salvage and Removal of Man-made Objects from Outer Space,* COMMENTARIES BASED ON VOLS. I-XV OF THE COLLOQUIA ON THE L. OF OUTER SPACE, 153, 156 (Ed. M. D. Schwartz, 1976) [hereinafter cited as Hall, Comments on Salvage].

regardless of fault, applies if damage has occurred to the surface of Earth or to an aircraft in flight. The liability is fault-based for damage to another space object in airspace or in space.

INTERNATIONAL LIABILITY MAY AFFECT PRIVATE OPERATORS. As a private commercial telecommunications satellite operator, your client cannot be held liable directly under the Outer Space Treaty or the Liability Convention since these are international agreements binding upon States, as such. Only the State, which authorized and therefore is internationally responsible for your client's satellite operation, can be held directly liable under these agreements (see Chapter 2.4.). Nevertheless, the financial burden ultimately may come to rest upon your client. For example, as a domestic law matter, a State may hold your client responsible in whole or in part for damage resulting from its space activities and require it to indemnify the State for any damages awarded pursuant to the Liability Convention. A State may even require that your client obtain third party liability insurance and name the government as an additional insured under the policy.[85] For these reasons, a grasp of the international liability provisions also is important for the private space operator.

THE OUTER SPACE TREATY. Article VII of the Outer Space Treaty provides that

> [e]ach State Party to the Treaty that launches or procures the

---

80. Maritime salvage has been defined as the "compensation allowed to persons by whose assistance a ship or her cargo has been saved, in whole or in part, from impending peril on the sea or in recovering such property from actual loss, as in cases of shipwreck, derelict or recapture." *The Blackwell*, 77 U.S.1 (1870), recited in H. DeSaussure, *The Application of Maritime Salvage to the Law of Outer Space*, XXIV IISL 128 (1985) [hereinafter cited as DeSaussure, The Application of Maritime Salvage]. The salvage may be 1) voluntary, where compensation is dependent upon success, 2) contractual, or 3) quasi-contractual, where an agreement to pay is implied. It is the category of voluntary salvage that has provided so much of the admiralty law on this subject and which has yet to be considered directly for application by analogy in space. *Id.*, at 128.
81. Hall, Comments on Salvage, *supra* note 79, at 156.
82. *See* Hall, Comments on Salvage, *supra* note 79; DeSaussure, The Application of Maritime Salvage, *supra* note 80, at 127; R. M. Jarvis, *The Space Shuttle Challenger and the Future Law of Outer Space Rescues*, 20 THE INT'L LAW. J. 591 (1986); and R.M. Jarvis, *Space Salvage: A Proposed Treaty Amendment to the Agreement on the Rescue of Astronauts, the Return of Astronauts, and the Return of Objects Launched Into Space*, 25 VA. J. INT'L L. 965 (1986) (discussing maritime salvage in the context of space objects).
83. Such a rule does not appear to conflict with Article VIII of the Outer Space Treaty, which provides that space objects or component parts "found beyond the limits of the State Party to the Treaty on whose registry they are carried shall be returned to that State Party . . . ." *See also* Rescue and Return Agreement, *supra* note 3, art. V, para. 3 (providing for return to the "launching authority").

> launching of an object into outer space . . . and each State Party from whose territory or facility an object is launched, is internationally liable for damage to another State Party to the Treaty or to its natural or juridical persons by such object or its component parts on the Earth, in air space or in outer space . . . .[86]

This provision merely declares that certain States participating in launch activities shall be held liable in the event of damage. It does not specify the circumstances under which liability attaches, nor does it indicate whether the liability is absolute or fault-based. A definition of "damage" also is lacking.

THE LIABILITY CONVENTION. The Liability Convention elaborates and expands on the liability provision of the Outer Space Treaty. It clarifies to some extent the conditions that must exist for liability to attach. It also defines "damage," provides a measure of damages or awards, and sets forth a claims procedure. The Liability Convention broadens the basis of recovery in certain respects. For example, while it is unclear whether the drafters of the Outer Space Treaty envisaged absolute liability, it explicitly was made a cause of action under the Liability Convention. Further, while the Outer Space Treaty covers only physical damage, the Liability Convention imposes liability for certain forms of non-physical damage (e.g., damage resulting from radiation), as well. In other respects, the Liability Convention may offer a narrower basis for recovery. For example, it only applies when damage is caused by a "space object". The Outer Space Treaty applies when damage is caused by an "object launched into outer space." While the precise meaning of "space object" is unclear, this term probably is narrower than "objects launched into outer space". Consequently, recovery may be possible under the Outer Space Treaty in certain cases where it is precluded under the Liability Convention. Furthermore, under the Liability Convention, damage caused elsewhere than on the surface of the Earth must be caused to a "space object". Under the Outer Space Treaty, it is sufficient that damage is caused to "another State Party". Because recoveries under the Liability Convention and the Outer Space Treaty are not entirely congruent, a State which has suffered damage or whose private citizens have suffered damage due to space activities, should claim under both treaties, as well as under general international law.

ABSOLUTE OR FAULT LIABILITY. The Liability Convention imposes absolute or fault-based liability depending upon where the damage

---

84. Convention on International Liability for Damage Caused by Space Objects, *supra* note 4. It is interesting to note that in many languages, the terms "responsibility" and "liability" are one and the same. This situation often confuses the discussion of international responsibility and international liability. *See* G. Schwarzenberger, INTERNATIONAL LAW (1957), at 562-656, and N.M. Shaw, INTERNATIONAL LAW (1986), at 406-435 (providing general discussions of international liability).

occurs. Under Article II a launching State is "absolutely liable to pay compensation for damage caused by its space object on the surface of the Earth or to an aircraft in flight."[87] Article III imposes liability based on fault "[i]n the event of damage being caused elsewhere than on the surface of the Earth to a space object of one launching State. . . by a space object of another launching State . . . ."[88]

ABSOLUTE LIABILITY. For geostationary telecommunications satellites, the risk of damage to the surface of Earth or an aircraft in flight, for all practical purposes, is present only during the pre-deployment phase, that is, during the launching phase or, because of a failed launching, if the satellite is left to drift in an unintended, low-Earth orbit with a risk of re-entry. Once the satellite has reached its location in the geostationary orbit, 37,786.1 km above the surface of Earth, the risk of re-entry into Earth's atmosphere and consequent damage to persons and property on Earth is extremely remote; virtually non-existent. On the other hand, satellites (whether they are used for telecommunications or for other purposes) in low-Earth orbits may have a greater risk of orbital decay and uncontrolled atmospheric re-entry, depending on the orbital altitude, even after successful deployment. Even though, in most incidents of uncontrolled reentry, the friction of the atmosphere will cause the spacecraft to disintegrate

---

85. This is true in the U.S. where a scheme for third-party liability risk-sharing between private launch vehicle operators, the insurance community and the Federal government has been enacted, *i.e.,* the Commercial Space Launch Act Amendments of 1988 [hereinafter cited as 1988 Amendments], 49 U.S.C. § 2615 (1988). Under the 1988 Amendments, the launch vehicle operator is required to demonstrate financial responsibility or obtain third party liability insurance in an amount determined by the Secretary of Transportation (the Office of Commercial Space Transportation by delegated authority), 49 U.S.C. § 2615(a)(1)(A) (1988). The maximum amount of insurance a private operator can be required to take out with respect to a particular launch is $500,000,000, or the maximum liability insurance available in the world market at a reasonable price if that is less. *Id.* In the past, the requirements have been set at varying sums less than half of this amount, depending on the size of the vehicle. *See* Chapter 6.5.2. (describing the risk-allocation regime outlined in this note, as well as the insurance required). The private launch operator is required to name the Federal government, as well as the customer (typically, the satellite owner, your client), as additional insureds under the insurance policy. 49 U.S.C. § 2615(a)(2) (1988). Third party claims exceeding the insured amount are covered by the Federal government up to $1.5 billion exceeding the insured amount. 49 U.S.C. § 2615(b)(1)(A), (B) (1988). Under Section 6 of the Swedish Act on Space Activities of 1982, 1982: 963, *supra* note 30, private entities are required to indemnify the Swedish state for payment on claims pursuant to the Liability Convention. Under Section 5(2)(f) of the United Kingdom Outer Space Act of 1986, 1 Current L. Stat. Annot. 38-1, sec 5(2)(f), a license to engage in a private space activity may require "the licensee to insure himself against liability incurred in respect of damage or loss suffered by third parties, in the United Kingdom, or elsewhere, as a result of activities authorized under the license."

and burn up, there are instances where spacecraft parts and debris have reached the Earth's surface.[89]

Only once has a formal claim for damage been presented pursuant to Article II of the Liability Convention. In January 1979, Canada claimed $6 million for alleged damage caused when radioactive debris from the de-orbited Soviet nuclear-powered ocean surveillance satellite *Cosmos 954* had scattered over large areas of Canadian territory in January 1978. Canada sought compensation from the Soviet Union for expenses Canada had incurred in connection with a search and clean-up operation undertaken to remove pieces of radioactive debris from a largely uninhabited 24,000 square kilometer area of the North-West Territories. At first, the Soviet Union rejected the claim and argued, among other points, that Canada had suffered no "damage" within the meaning of the Liability Convention and, therefore, could not recover damages (see discussion of "damage," below). Nevertheless, a settlement was reached in November 1980. The Soviets agreed to pay $3 million, or half of Canada's claim, without acknowledging liability under the Convention.[90]

FAULT LIABILITY. Article III of the Liability Convention contemplates a situation where two spacecraft collide in space. At present, the risk of collision between operational satellites deployed either in the geostationary or low-Earth orbits is not great. However, the risk will increase particularly as the low-Earth orbit environment becomes steadily crowded. The likelihood of a collision between two spacecraft during launching also is remote at present. More realistic is a scenario where a satellite is hit by a piece of space debris and becomes functionally impaired or disabled as a result. As discussed at greater length, below, depending on the circumstances giving rise to the incident and the kind of debris involved, the Liability Convention might not apply in such a case. If it does in fact apply, identification of the tortfeasor may prove to be extraordinarily difficult, if

---

86. Outer Space Treaty, art. VII.
87. Liability Convention, art. II.
88. *Id.*, art. III.
89. On July 11, 1979, the orbiting laboratory SKYLAB reentered the atmosphere and debris landed in the Western part of Australia. SKYLAB was a joint program between NASA and the European Space Research Organization (ESRO). *See* Agreement for a Cooperative Program Concerning the Development, Procurement and Use of a Space Laboratory in Conjunction with the Space Shuttle System, With Memorandum of Understanding Between the National Aeronautics and Space Administration and the European Space Research Organization, *done* Aug. 14, 1973, *entered into force* Aug. 14, 1973, T.I.A.S. 7722 (providing the legal framework for the SKYLAB project). ESRO and the European Space Vehicle Launcher Development Organization (ELDO) were merged and became the European Space Agency, which was established in April 1975. *See* Convention for the Establishment of the European Space Agency, *done* Apr. 15, 1975, *entered into force* Oct. 30, 1980, 14 I.L.M. 864, (providing for the constitution of ESA). The reentry of the Soviet *Cosmos 954* satellite is described in the text.

not impossible.

Article III provides that liability for damage occurring to spacecraft elsewhere than on the surface of Earth shall be based on fault, but offers no definition of "fault." Also, the negotiating history of the Liability Convention fails to elucidate the drafters' understanding of the term, and the precise meaning of this standard is unclear. While it is generally recognized that fault refers to negligence,[91] or *culpa* in civil law, the degree of negligence or culpa required for liability to attach is uncertain. For example, is simple, ordinary, or gross negligence (*levissima, levis* or *lata culpa* in civil law) required to invoke Article III? Even if a standard of fault could be established, the need to prove fault would present yet another obstacle to recovery under this provision. Since no case has ever been brought under Article III, the fault standard has never been tested.

It is important to note that the fault of a private entity will be imputed to the State which authorized the particular space activity in much the same way as an employee's negligent conduct is imputed to the employer under the doctrine of *respondeat superior*. However, unlike an employer's liability, the State's liability is not affected by the fact that the private space operating entity may have acted outside the scope of its authorization: The State is responsible under Article VI of the Outer Space Treaty, regardless of whether the private space operating entity acted within the scope of its authorization.

DEFINITIONS. Article I of the Liability Convention defines four basic terms that are critical to the understanding and application of Articles II and III: "damage," "launching," "launching State" and "space object." While they are helpful in some respects, the definitions nevertheless leave many questions unanswered as to their precise meaning.

DAMAGE. Damage is defined as "loss of life, personal injury or other impairment of health; or loss of or damage to property of States or of persons, natural or juridical, or property of international intergovernmental

---

90. *See* C. Q. Christol, *International Liability for Damage Caused by Space Objects*, 74 AM. J. INTL. L. 346 (1980); S. Gorove, *Cosmos 954: Issues of Law and Policy*, 6 J. SPACE L. 137 (1978); P.C. Haanapel, *Some Observations on the Crash of Cosmos 954*, 6 J. SPACE L. 148 (1978); E. Galloway, *Nuclear Powered Satellites: The U.S.S.R. Cosmos 954 and the Canadian Claim*, 12 AKRON L. REV. 401 (1979); M.L. Berlin, *After the Fall; An Analysis of the Canadian Legal Claims for Damage Caused by Cosmos 954*, 27 MC.GILL L. J. 676 (1982); and L.H. Legault & A. Farand, *Canada's Claim for Damage Caused by the Soviet Cosmos 954 Satellite*, Paper presented at ABA Forum Committee on Air & Space Law, Lake Buena Vista, Fla. (1st annual forum, Feb. 23-25, 1984) (providing factual background on and legal analyses of, the *Cosmos 954* incident).

91. Negligence is the failure to do something which a reasonable man, guided by those ordinary considerations which ordinarily regulate human affairs, would do, or the doing of something a reasonable man would not do. Negligence refers to the legal delinquency that results whenever a man fails to exhibit the care which he ought to exhibit, whether it be slight, ordinary or great, BLACK'S LAW DICTIONARY 930-1 (5th ed. 1979).

organizations."[92] While direct damage (harm, loss, or injury) is covered by the Convention, it is not clear whether, or to what extent, *indirect* damage is covered. For example, if your client's satellite is damaged by another spacecraft, or debris from another spacecraft, rendering the satellite useless or functionally impaired, the loss of the satellite represents direct damage and is clearly recoverable under the Liability Convention, provided the conditions for liability otherwise are met. Your client's lost revenues as a result of the loss of use of the satellite, on the other hand, represent indirect damage, and it is uncertain whether these will be compensated.

According to some legal scholars, no indication is given by the Liability Convention as to whether claims will lie for indirect damage.[93] The matter was discussed only briefly by the United Nations Committee on the Peaceful Uses of Outer Space during the negotiations leading to the Convention. No formal agreement was reached on whether indirect damage should be included, although the majority felt that the issue could be dealt with as claims arose.[94] Other legal authors have argued that the Convention can be interpreted to include recovery for indirect, or consequential, damages.[95]

It also is not clear whether *moral* damage (pain, suffering and humiliation) is covered under the Liability Convention. The issue received relatively little attention during the negotiations leading to the Convention and was not resolved. It may be argued that the reference in the definition of damage to "personal injury or other impairment of health" is sufficiently broad to cover moral damage, as well; particularly if the passage is interpreted in light of the definition of "health" offered by the World Health Organization as "a state of complete physical, mental and social well being."[96]

Despite initial opposition by the Soviet Union, it was agreed during the Convention negotiations and drafting that damage in the form of nuclear radiation should be covered under the Liability Convention, provided it

---

92. Liability Convention, art. I(a).

93. W.F. Foster, *The Convention on International Liability for Damage Caused by Space Objects*, 10 CANADIAN Y.B. OF INT'L L. 137, 141-142 (1972), and N.M. Matte, AEROSPACE LAW (1977), at 157.

94. N.M. Matte, AEROSPACE LAW, *supra* note 93, at 157.

95. *See e.g.* Christol, THE MODERN INTERNATIONAL LAW, *supra* note 10, at 97 (offering this view). In a legal analysis of the *Cosmos 954* incident, P.C. Haanapel argued that if the scattering of radioactive debris in Canadian territory could not be considered "damage" under the Liability Convention, which was the Soviet contention, then the *clean-up expenses* incurred by Canada should be considered indirect damage and recoverable under the Convention. P.C Haanapel, *Some Observations on the Crash of the Cosmos 954*, *supra* note 90.

96. *See* Gorove, SPACE LAW, *supra* note 10, at 125 (making this argument). *See also* Christol, THE MODERN INTERNATIONAL LAW, *supra* note 10, at 97-100 (discussing moral damage).

results in "loss of life, personal injury or other impairment of health; or loss of or damage to property . . . ."[97] In the *Cosmos 954* incident, Canada claimed that it had suffered "damage to property" because of the radioactive nature of the debris. In its Statement of Claim presented to the Soviet Union January 23, 1979, Canada defined the damage it had suffered as "the deposit of hazardous radioactive debris from the satellite throughout a large area of Canadian territory, and the presence of that debris in the environment rendering that part of Canada's territory unfit for use . . . ."[98] The Soviet Union, although it did not object to the applicability of the Convention to nuclear damage, argued that Canada had suffered no "damage" within the meaning of the Convention since no actual damage was caused to the largely uninhabited territory.[99]

Legal scholars appear to agree that damage in the form of radio interference or jamming is not covered by the Liability Convention.[100] Potential problems of radio interference usually are resolved prior to launching of a satellite, during the frequency coordination process conducted within the regulatory framework established by the International Telecommunication Union (see Chapter 4.3.), as well as the national authorization process (see Chapter 3.2.). The Liability Convention also provides no recourse for damage involving intentional radio interference, jamming, or signal piracy occurring after the satellite has been launched.

LAUNCHING STATE. "Launching State" is defined as a State that launches or procures the launching of a space object, or a State from whose territory or facility the space object is launched.[101] Ascertaining the launching State is important since that State is subject to liability under the Liability Convention, as well as the Outer Space Treaty. Theoretically, a situation could arise where four different States might qualify as launching States: one State (or entity authorized by it) performs the launching for a second State (or entity authorized by it), which has procured the launching, and the launching takes place from the territory of a third State, with a launching facility belonging to a fourth State (or entity authorized by it). In practice, however, launchings generally involve only one or two States. This is true even when, for example, a French Ariane rocket launches a satellite owned by a U.S. company from a launching facility located in French Guiana.[102] It is noteworthy that the country where the launch vehicle or the payload is manufactured is irrelevant to the identification of launching States, unless, of course, the manufacturer

---

97. B. Cheng, *International Liability for Damage Caused by Space Objects,* 1 MANUAL ON SPACE L. 83, 115 (1979).
98. Canada, Statement of Claim (Jan. 23, 1979), I.L.M. 899 (1979).
99. *See generally supra* note 90 (listing articles discussing the Canadian claim and the Soviet response in the *Cosmos 954* case).
100. *See* discussions in S. Gorove, SPACE LAW, *supra* note 10, at 125, and C.Q. Christol, *International Liability for Damage Caused by Space Objects, supra* note 90, at 354.
101. Liability Convention, art. I(c). Compare Outer Space Treaty, art. VII.

also procures the launch. Recently, a few satellite manufacturers started offering so-called "turn-key" satellite systems, which implies that the manufacturer delivers the satellite to the customer in orbit and, consequently, is responsible for purchasing launch services (see Chapter 6.4.1.). Traditionally, delivery of the satellite has taken place on the ground, before launch.

When two or more launching States are involved, joint liability will apply for resulting damage.[103] Further, when these launching States can be considered participants in a "joint launching," they are severally, as well as jointly, liable.[104] A joint launching occurs when two or more States jointly launch a spacecraft. A State from whose territory or facility the spacecraft is launched, if it is different from the State that carries out the launch, always is considered a party to the joint launching.[105] It is unclear whether the State procuring the launch is considered a party to a joint launching within the meaning of the Liability Convention.[106]

The distinction between joint liability, on the one hand, and joint and several liability, on the other, is significant. In a situation where two launching States merely are jointly liable, the launching State which is being sued can insist that the other launching State be joined in the suit. Where two launching States are jointly and severally liable, the fact that the States also are severally liable means that the claimant State has the option of bringing an action against only one of the launching States or jointly against both, since both States are liable for the full amount. The claimant State cannot obtain the full amount from both States, however. States participating in a joint launching may agree as between (among) themselves on how to apportion the liability.[107] Such an agreement would not affect the rights of a claimant State to pursue its available remedies.

LAUNCHING. An attempted, but unsuccessful, launching is still considered a launching.[108] Consequently, if a launch vehicle and its payload were to explode shortly after lift-off, with explosion debris causing damage on the surface of Earth, the Liability Convention would apply, provided the injured third parties are not nationals of the launching State,

---

102. The Ariane launch vehicle was developed by the European Space Agency, but is now operated by Arianespace, a French company whose stockholders include banks and financial institutions of a number of European countries, as well as the French Centre National d'Etudes Spatiales (CNES). French Guiana is French territory, and the launching facility belongs to Arianespace. *See* Chapter 7.1. (describing Arianespace and other launch companies).
103. Liability Convention, arts. II and III.
104. *Id.*, art. V, para. 1
105. *Id.*, art. V, para. 3.
106. No mention is made in article V of the Liability Convention of the State procuring the launch. *See* Christol, THE MODERN INTERNATIONAL LAW, *supra* note 10, at 114, and B. Cheng, *International Liability for Damage Caused by Space Objects*, *supra* note 97, at 120 (discussing the implications of this omission).

foreign nationals participating in the launching, or foreign nationals invited by the launching State.[109] It is unclear precisely how far an attempt to launch a vehicle must have advanced to be considered an "attempted launching." For example, in the event of an "on-the-pad abort," would the intentional ignition of a launch vehicle's first stage engines constitute an attempted launching? This question may not have much practical significance since the situation contemplated is unlikely to bring the Liability Convention into play. This is true because damage in this situation likely will result to the parties mentioned above and to which the convention does not apply.

SPACE OBJECT. As noted, above, the Liability Convention imposes liability for damage caused by a "space object." The Liability Convention defines such an object to include "component parts of a space object as well as its launch vehicle and parts thereof."[110] While satellites, planetary probes and launch vehicles seem obvious examples of space objects, it is not precisely clear at what point in time they become space objects. For example, does the satellite become a space object when mated to the launch vehicle when there has been intentional ignition of the launch vehicle first stage engines, or at launch vehicle lift-off? The above reasoning with respect to attempted launchings applies here, as well.

An issue that has received much attention recently relates to whether *space debris* [111] can be considered a "space object" within the meaning of the Liability Convention. The issue was never formally addressed by the drafters of the Convention.[112] It is unclear, therefore, what, if any, kinds of space debris are covered under the Liability Convention.[113] For example, can spent rocket bodies (launch vehicle upper stages) or inactive payloads, such as non-operational satellites, be considered space objects with the consequence that damage caused by them is actionable under the Liability Convention? Moreover, can a lens cap discarded during the deployment of a satellite, or a minute piece of debris traceable to the explosion of an upper stage, be considered a space object within the meaning of the Lia-

107. Liability Convention, art. V, para. 2, which provides that the participants in a joint launching may conclude agreements among themselves with regard to the apportionment of the liability, but such agreements are without prejudice to the right of the claimant State to seek the entire compensation from any one of the launching States. Under a Memorandum of Agreement on Liability for Satellite Launches Between the Government of the United States of America and the Government of the Peoples Republic of China, 1988, art. IV, the Parties agreed that the government of the Peoples' Republic shall compensate the United States for any amounts for which it may be held liable under the Liability Convention, the Outer Space Treaty, or other applicable law. At the time, China was not a party to the Liability Convention.

108. Liability Convention, art. I(b).

109. *Id.*, art. VII(a), (b).

110. *Id.*, art. I(d). *See* B. Cheng, *International Liability for Damage Caused by Space Objects*, *supra* note 97, at 116-117 (suggesting that the concept of 'space object' is temporal).

bility Convention? Arguments in favor can certainly be made, and no doubt will be made, by lawyers advising client States whose spacecraft are damaged by debris. In most cases where damage is caused by space debris, however, the major difficulties will involve the identification of the tortfeasor and establishment of proximate causation. To date, no operational spacecraft has been reported to have been functionally impaired, or damaged, by space debris, although NASA has evidence that its Space Shuttle has been hit by small pieces of debris. As orbital environments become more crowded, however, incidents of damage are bound to happen.

THE LIABILITY CONVENTION APPLIES TO STATES. Only States can sue or be sued under the Liability Convention and the Outer Space Treaty;[114] private parties cannot. Accordingly, if your client, a private satellite operator, has caused actionable damage, it cannot be sued under either of these agreements. Moreover, only a State which may be considered a launching State with respect to your client's satellite can be sued. This would include the State which authorized your client's satellite operation, as the "procuring" State, if not the State conducting the launch, as well as any other launching State.As a private party, your client also cannot invoke these international agreements in the event it has suffered damage. Tort claims can be pursued, of course, in national courts under national laws, subject to relevant conflicts-of-law rules. Moreover, a State that has paid an award for damage caused by a private party may seek indemnification from the private party.

CLAIMS PROCEDURES. Claims for compensation under the Liability Convention must be presented through diplomatic channels.[115] The stat-

---

111. According to the Report on Orbital Debris by Interagency Group (Space) for the United States National Security Council (Feb. 1989), at 3, 6-8, approximately 7,000 objects in Earth orbit larger than ten centimeters currently are being tracked by the U.S. Space Command of the United States Air Force. Only 5% of these objects represent operational spacecraft. The remainder constitutes space debris of one form or another, falling into one of four general categories: 1) operational debris (12%), which includes objects intentionally discarded as a routine matter during satellite launching, deployment and operation, such as separation devices, lens caps, empty propellant tanks, and payload shrouds; 2) spent and intact rocket bodies (14%); 3) inactive payloads (20%), which, typically, includes satellites that have reached the end of their useful lives; and 4) fragmentation debris (49%), which may result from a collision or explosion. All known collisions between unfragmented spacecraft to date have been deliberate, conducted, *e.g.*, as part of anti-satellite satellite (ASAT) testing. Several spent rocket bodies are known to have exploded as a result of residual fuel causing overpressurization. *See* P.L. Meredith, *Legal Implementation of Orbital Debris Mitigation Measures: A Survey of Options and Approaches*, 6 AM. U.J. OF INT'L L. & POLICY 203, 204, note 1 (1991) (providing an example of a break-up of a rocket body due to an explosion, citing *Breakup in Review — Fengyun 1-2 Rocket Body*, 4 ORBITAL DEBRIS MONITOR 6 (ed. D.S. McKnight, 1991).

ute of limitation is one year.[116] The negotiations between the governments of Canada and the Soviet Union following the *Cosmos 954* incident illustrate the claims procedure required by the Liability Convention. On February 28, 1978 (approximately one month after the incident occurred on January 24, 1978), the Canadian Department of External Affairs officially notified Soviet authorities of Canada's intention to submit a claim. A claim was presented on January 23, 1979. Three rounds of diplomatic negotiations ensued before a final settlement was reached: in Ottawa March 1980, in Moscow June 1980 and, finally, in Ottawa in November 1980. Again, although settlement was reached and compensation awarded, the Soviet Union never acknowledged liability under the Liability Convention.

Exhaustion of local remedies in the launching State is not required, although the claimant State is not barred from pursuing the claim through the judicial system of the former.[117] Claims may not be pursued simultaneously in the judicial system of the Claimant State and under the Convention with respect to the same damage.[118]

If, after one year of diplomatic negotiations pursuant to the Convention, no settlement has been reached, the Parties concerned must establish a Claims Commission at the request of either Party.[119] The Commission shall be composed of three members: one appointed by the launching State, one by the claimant State, and the third member to be chosen jointly by the first two members.[120] If the Parties agree, the decision of the Commission shall be final and binding; otherwise, the decision shall have the nature of a recommendation.[121]

DAMAGES. Article XII of the Liability Convention provides a formula for computing damages, that is, the compensation the launching State shall be liable to pay. Such compensation

---

112. *See* H.A. Baker, *Liability for Damage Caused in Outer Space by Space Refuse,* XIII ANNALS OF AIR & SPACE L. 183 (1988) (discussing what classes of space debris are covered by the Liability Convention). *See also* H.A. Baker, *Space Debris: Law and Policy in the United States,* 60 U. Colo. L. Rev. 55 (1989), and SPACE DEBRIS, LEGAL AND POLICY IMPLICATIONS (1989).Query: Would space debris be considered an "object launched into space" and therefore covered by the Outer Space Treaty?
113. H.A. Baker, *Liability for Damage Caused in Outer Space by Space Refuse, supra* note 112.
114. *See* Liability Convention, art. VIII (listing the various States which may bring suit under the Convention).
115. *Id.,* art. IX.
116. *Id.,* art. X.
117. *Id.,* art. X.
118. *Id.,* art. XI, para. 2.
119. *Id.,* art. XIV.
120. *Id.,* art. XV.
121. *Id.,* art. XIX, para 2.

> shall be determined in accordance with international law and the principles of justice and equity, in order to provide such reparation in respect of the damage as will restore the person, natural or juridical, State or international organization on whose behalf the claim is presented to the condition which would have existed if the damage had not occurred.[122]

The requirement to restore the victim to the condition which would have existed were it not for the damage (the principle of *restitutio in integrum*) reflects customary international law and judicial precedent.[123] On the other hand, the reference to "justice and equity" is novel in international law. "Equity" is used here, not in the Anglo-American legal sense of the word, but rather as a reference to moral justice. Arguably, it allows for taking into account "all principles [of law] which are just and equitable."[124] The drafters of the Convention included the phrase "justice and equity" to allow the standards used in assessing damages to be drawn from the laws of the claimant State, as well as to reflect common sense, or *ex aequo et bono.*[125] The compensation shall be paid in the currency of the claimant State, unless that State prefers the currency of the defendant State.[126]

WHERE DAMAGE IS CAUSED TO NATIONALS OF THE LAUNCHING STATE. It is important to note that the Convention does not apply in situations where damage is caused to nationals (citizens and entities under the jurisdiction) of the launching State,[127] since, in essence, this would imply the irony of a claim being brought by a launching State against itself. For example, if a privately-operated launch vehicle with your client's satellite on board explodes shortly after lift-off in State A and causes damage to persons and property in State A cities near the launch site, injured persons and property are not covered under the Convention with respect to State A. Assuming that your client's satellite is authorized in State B, they would, however, be covered with respect to the State B,

---

122. *Id.,* art. XII. In computing the damages, one should keep in mind that the Convention is victim-oriented as reflected by the provision of the Preamble of the Liability Convention which calls for "the prompt payment . . . of a full and equitable measure of compensation to victims . . . ."
123. In *Chorzow Factory,* 1928 P.C.I.J., ser. A, No. 17, the International Court of Justice held that the function of international tort law is to restore the injured person to the condition which would have existed absent the injury. *See* G. Schwarzenberger, INTERNATIONAL LAW (1957), at 654-655 (discussing the *Chorzow Factory* case in the context of reparations). *See also Corfu Channel,* 1949 I.C.J. 23 (concerning Albania's duty to make reparations for failing to prevent a disaster resulting from mine fields laid with Albania's actual or presumed knowledge in that country's territorial waters).
124. N.M. Matte, AEROSPACE LAW, *supra* note 93, at 169.
125. *Id.,* citing U.N. Doc. A/AC.105/C.2/SR 162 (1971).
126. Liability Convention, art. XIII.
127. *Id.,* art. VII.

provided they were not nationals of State B. State B is liable since it procured the launch and, therefore, is a launching State, as well.

NOT UNDER THE DOMAIN OF THE LIABILITY CONVENTION. Left entirely to domestic law are the relationships between a State and the private entities authorized by it to engage in space activities. The Liability Convention does not attempt to regulate the conditions imposed upon private parties with respect to liability: for example, whether they must agree to indemnify the State, purchase liability insurance with the State named as an insured, and/or demonstrate financial responsibility. A few countries have adopted legislation concerning the liability of private entities.[128]

128. Legislation governing the interrelationship between the government and private entities engaged in space activity exists in some countries. *See supra* note 85 (providing examples of such legislation) and Chapter 6.5.2. (discussing the applicable United States legislation).

3. Obtain Permission from a National Authority: The United States Federal Communications Commission (FCC) as an Example

GOVERNMENT AUTHORIZATION IS REQUIRED. In order to place in orbit and operate a satellite, your client must first receive an authorization (permit or license) from a national government. As discussed in Chapter 2.4., above, private sector activities in space are subject to the authorization and continuous supervision by a nation State.

A few countries have designated government departments or agencies and established legal regimes for authorizing space activities. Where regulators and legal frameworks are in place for authorizing satellite operations, your client must follow the procedures and meet the criteria prescribed. In that case, at least to some degree, the response to your client's licensing request will be relatively predictable. Although, when novel satellite service concepts are proposed that challenge established rules and categories, the outcome may be uncertain, despite the existence of a licensing regime.

Where no governmental authority has been designated to be responsible for the authorization of space activities, and where no legal regime for satellite licensing exists, your client's approach must be planned carefully. If the political system and prevailing economic philosophy in the country where your client intends to operate its satellite allow for a private telecommunications satellite venture, your client has several options. The most prudent approach might be to submit a license request to the national governmental body in charge of telecommunications in the hope and anticipation that this body's authority is sufficiently broad to cover satellite telecommunications, as well.

AUTHORIZATION OF TELECOMMUNICATIONS SATELLITES IN THE U.S. In the United States, private ownership of telecommunication facilities and private telecommunications service offerings, satellites and satellite facilities and services included, are actively promoted and encouraged. Indeed, it is only through private sector initiatives that telecommunication is available to the public in that country. The United States Federal Communications Commission, an independent agency charged with regulating radio and wire communications, has authorized private telecommunications satellites for almost two decades. Authorizations from the Federal Communications Commission is a prerequisite to building a satellite and launching and operating it from United States territory. Over the years, the Federal Communications Commission has developed policies and regulations setting forth criteria and procedures for obtaining such authorizations.

Because the authorization process for private telecommunications satellites (and all other spacecraft, for that matter) is more mature in the United States than in any other country, the ensuing discussion focuses exclusively on the Federal Communications Commission and its licensing and regulation of telecommunications satellites. These regulatory policies may serve as models for other countries in the process of privatizing their telecommunications industries, or, indeed, in some cases, as examples to be avoided.

3.1. Categories of Private Commercial Telecommunications Satellite Services Authorized by the Federal Communications Commission

OVERVIEW OF FCC SATELLITE AUTHORIZATIONS. Private commercial telecommunications satellite operations authorized by the Federal Communications Commission (FCC or Commission) to date fall into five categories listed in the order they were first authorized: domestic fixed satellite service, direct broadcasting satellite service, radiodetermination satellite service, international fixed satellite ("separate systems")[1] service and mobile satellite service. (See sections 3.1.1. - 3.1.5. of this Chapter for descriptions of the services). Satellites used or intended to provide these kinds of services are geostationary, i.e., they occupy a location in the geostationary orbit, a circular orbit in the plane of Earth's equator 35,786.1 km from the Earth's surface, in which the satellites are stationary relative to a specific geographic area of coverage on Earth.[2]

The Commission authorized the first private commercial telecommunications satellites in 1973,[3] and has since authorized several dozens of

1. Separate systems" is a term borrowed from Section 201(a)(6) of the Communications Satellite Act of 1962, as amended, 47 U.S.C. § 721(a)(6) (1988), and indicates that the international fixed satellites operated by U.S. private companies are separate from the satellite constellation owned and operated by the International Telecommunications Satellite Organization (INTELSAT). *See* Chapter 3.1.4. (describing separate systems).
2. The satellite appears stationary because it revolves around Earth at a velocity and direction matching the planet's rotation.
3. *See infra* notes 24-27 (listing these authorizations).

them. About thirty of these satellites are in operation today and are owned by seven different private companies. With minor exceptions, all of the satellites currently in operation are used to provide *fixed* satellite service. (The exceptions refer to Qualcomm, Inc. of San Diego, California, which uses capacity on fixed satellites for mobile services, and to some fixed satellite operators that provide "quasi" direct broadcasting satellite service (see Chapter 3.1.2.)). Moreover, with the exception of the "separate system" operated by Alpha Lyracom Space Communications of Greenwich, Connecticut, doing business as Pan American Satellite Company, all satellites in operation today are used for *domestic* fixed satellite service. Pan American Satellite Company provides international fixed satellite service. Holders of authorizations in other categories of satellite services either have delayed the implementation of their projects due to inadequate financing or a perceived lack of a market for the proposed satellite service, or they simply have not reached the operational stage of their project implementation. For example, their authorizations may have just been granted.

REQUESTS FOR NEW SATELLITE AUTHORIZATIONS. Challenging the FCC's established satellite service categories are several new applications pending that propose a variety of multiple-small-satellite systems in low-Earth orbit to provide a combination of mobile and radiodetermination-type services, as well as other novel service concepts.[4] For example, Motorola, Inc. is planning a constellation of seventy-seven satellites ("Iridium") in seven low-Earth polar orbits. Before Motorola's, or any other application, can be granted the Commission must find suitable radio frequencies in which the proposed satellites can operate. The FCC also must determine whether the "public interest," the "touchstone" for FCC authorizations, would be served by permitting the new satellite services, and whether the applicant is legally, technically and financially qualified.

3.1.1. Domestic Fixed Satellite Service

DEFINITION. The Commission's Rules define fixed satellite service as "[a] radiocommunication service between Earth stations at specified fixed points when one or more satellites are used . . . ."[5] *Domestic* fixed satellite service indicates service to and from points within United States territory, including Hawaii, the Virgin Islands and Puerto Rico.[6] The definition of "fixed satellite-service" appearing in the Commission's Rules was modeled

---

4. Other new satellite service concepts being proposed include "digital radio broadcasting satellite service" and "generic satellite service."

5. 47 C.F.R. § 25.201(b) (1990), defining fixed satellite service as

> [a] radiocommunication service between Earth stations at specified fixed points when one or more satellites are used; in some cases this service includes satellite-to-satellite links, which may also be effected in the inter-satellite service; the fixed satellite service may also include feeder links for other space radiocommunication services.

upon a definition adopted by the International Telecommunication Union at a World Administrative Radio Conference in 1971,[7] which contemplated the transmission of satellite signals between two very large Earth stations at specified fixed points, e.g., for telephone transmissions.[8] The definition does not accurately reflect the services being provided under the label "fixed satellite service" in the United States today.

SERVICES PROVIDED TODAY. Domestic fixed satellite services in the United States today primarily involve 1) program distribution to cable operators or local television stations, 2) very small aperture terminal

---

6. Beginning in 1981, the Commission in more than 200 cases has authorized domestic fixed satellite operators to provide *incidental* services to transborder locations, *i.e.*, locations in Canada, Mexico, the Caribbean and certain other countries in Central an South America. The Commission refers to such incidental satellite service as "transborder service." *See infra* note 143 (listing important transborder service authorizations) and accompanying text (explaining these authorizations). The Commission will authorize transborder service if: 1) the International Telecommunications Satellite Organization (INTELSAT) cannot provide the service; or 2) it would be clearly uneconomical or impractical to use the INTELSAT system. *Transborder Satellite Video Services,* 88 F.C.C. 2d 258 (1981) [hereinafter cited as Transborder I]. *See* Chapters 3.1.4., 5.1.1. and 5.2.1. (describing INTELSAT). These criteria were formulated in a Letter from James L. Buckley, Undersecretary of State, to Mark S. Fowler, FCC Chairman, (Jul. 23, 1981) [hereinafter cited as the Buckley Letter] and have since been applied by the Commission. Transborder satellite services authorized by the Commission fall into two categories: 1) one-way receive-only and 2) two-way communications services. The Commission routinely authorizes one-way, receive-only (typically, television program distribution) services. Usually, these services already are provided within the U.S. and can be extended to transborder locations easily. The Commission reasons that, although INTELSAT can provide these services, it would be "clearly uneconomical or impractical" to use INTELSAT. Transborder I, *supra.* With respect to two-way transborder services, a distinction appears to have been established between transborder services to Canada and Mexico, on the one hand, and those to other countries, on the other. Since INTELSAT traditionally has not provided cross-border services between the U.S. and Canada and the U.S. and Mexico (they have been provided through terrestrial links), the Commission has been inclined to authorize them. *See Satellite Business Systems,* 88 F.C.C. 2d 195 (1981) (permitting extension of an already-established two-way network) and *American Satellite Company,* 88 F.C.C. 2d 178 (1981) (authorizing a new two-way service). However, when the Commission attempted to extend transborder authorization to International Teleport and American Satellite Company for an entirely new, two-way communications service to Jamaica on the grounds that it would be "uneconomical and impractical" to use INTELSAT, *Teleport International, Ltd. and American Satellite Company,* 2 F.C.C. Rcd 4149 (1987) and 1 F.C.C. Rcd. 101 (1986), the court vacated the decision, *Communications Satellite Corp v. FCC,* 836 F.2d 623 (1988). The court concluded that the Commission had failed to provide adequate explanation for why it would be "uneconomical and impractical" to use INTELSAT.

(VSAT) network services, and 3) specialized private network services. Program distribution involves one-way transmission of video signals from the premises of a program producer (e.g., Home Box Office) or a television network (e.g., American Broadcasting Company) via satellite to cable heads or network affiliate stations for retransmission to the public through cable or terrestrial broadcast stations. Earth stations at the receiving locations normally have antenna sizes of 3-4 meters in diameter. Programmers and television networks typically own or lease satellite transponders for this purpose. Transponders are units on the satellite that receive, shift frequency, amplify and retransmit radio signals. An average geostationary satellite has twenty-four transponders.

VSAT networks are used by large corporations and organizations to connect a central location, e.g., a headquarters office, with hundreds and sometimes thousands of field sites, such as retail outlets. Small Earth stations with antennas 1-2 meters in diameter are installed at the field sites, and a somewhat larger Earth ("hub") station is required at the central location. Satellites are used to connect central and field locations, allowing for data, voice and video distribution and/or two-way transmission. Hundreds of VSAT networks are currently installed in the United States, some of them sharing hub Earth stations. The major VSAT service providers are Hughes Network Systems, AT&T Tridom, GTE Spacenet and Scientific Atlanta. The VSAT users typically do not own satellite responders.

Specialized networks refer to private communications networks that use non-standard transmission formats, usually higher data rates. Antennas larger than those employed in VSAT networks generally are required. For example, Dow Jones & Co., Inc. employs a specialized network, *inter alia,* for the purposes of printing the Wall Street Journal in several locations throughout the United States. The company owns a total of three transponders on the SPACENET 3 and WESTAR 5 satellites, which are operated respectively by GTE Spacenet Corporation of McClean, Virginia, and Hughes Communications, Inc. of El Segundo, California.

FREQUENCY BANDS. The Commission's Rules require that domestic fixed satellite operations take place in certain frequency bands allocated for fixed satellite service.[9] Domestic fixed satellite operations to date generally have taken place in the following frequency bands: 3700-4200 MHz (space-to-Earth) and 5925-6425 MHz (Earth-to-space), often referred to as the "4/6 GHz band" or "C-band;" or in the 11.2.-11.7 GHz (space-to-Earth) and 14.0-14.5 GHz (Earth-to-space), often referred to as the "10/14 GHz

7. *See* Chapter 4.3.1., note 14 (quoting the current International Telecommunication Union's (ITU) definition of "fixed satellite service," which reflects somewhat more closely the services being provided under the label of "fixed satellite service" today).
8. When a definition of "fixed satellite service" was first adopted by the ITU, international telephone signal transmissions between national "gateway" Earth stations operated by national telecommunications administrations or operating entities (or other designated entities) were contemplated.

band" or "Ku-band."

HISTORY: 1965-1970. Over a quarter century has passed since September 21, 1965, when American Broadcasting Company, Inc. (ABC) became the first private company to apply to the FCC for authority to operate a domestic satellite system.[10] ABC requested authorization for a fixed satellite system to be used for television program distribution purposes.[11] The Company proposed to use the 3700-4200 MHz and 5925-6425 MHz frequency bands for transmission of network programming from Earth stations in New York and California, via satellite, to ABC-owned and affiliate stations throughout the United States. ABC later abandoned its application. Today, the company owns or leases transponders on satellites owned and operated by others and uses these transponders for program distribution purposes.

ABC's pioneering application raised novel issues never before considered, and led the Commission to institute an inquiry regarding the operation of satellites by "non-governmental entities." A *Notice of Inquiry*[12] was adopted on March 2, 1966, requesting comments from interested parties.[13]The principal issues raised in the inquiry were: 1) whether any legal

---

9. 47 C.F.R. § 25.202(a)(1) (1990) provides that the following frequency bands may be used for fixed satellite service:

Space-to-Earth	*Earth-to-space*
3700-4200 MHz	5925-6425 MHz
10.95-11.2 GHz	14.0-14.5 GHz
11.2 -11.7 GHz	27.5-29.5 GHz
17.7-19.7 GHz	29.5-30.0 GHz
19.7-20.0 GHz	

Some of these frequency bands are shared co-equally with other radiocommunications services, and some are available only for international fixed satellite service, 47 C.F.R. § 25.202(a)(1) (1990). Precise frequencies and bandwidths of emission will be assigned on a case-by-case basis. *Id.* The frequencies listed above conform to the Table of Frequency Allocations contained in Article 8 of the ITU Radio Regulations. *See* Chapter 4.1. (explaining ITU frequency allocations). It may be possible to provide domestic fixed satellite service in other frequency bands. 47 C.F.R. § 202(b) (1990).

10. Research and amateur satellite proposals had been made prior to that date

11. *See Establishment of Domestic Communications Satellite Facilities by Non-Governmental Entities,* 22 F.C.C. 2d 86 (1970) [hereinafter cited as Domsat I], Appx. B., entitled "Background and Summary of Comments of the Parties" (describing ABC's proposal).

12. *Establishment of Domestic Communications Satellite Facilities by Non-Governmental Entities,* 31 Fed. Reg. 3507 (1966), which was specifically concerned with the use of satellite facilities for "private or specialized" purposes, services ABC had proposed, rather than authorization of common carrier operations. In a Supplemental Notice of Inquiry issued later that year, the Commission broadened the scope of its inquiry to include common carrier operations, as well, *Establishment of Domestic Communications Satellite Facilities by Non-Governmental Entities,* 31 Fed. Reg. 13763 (1966).

constraints existed on the Commission's power to authorize the construction and operation of non-governmental communications satellite facilities for domestic use; 2) whether the "public interest" would be served by authorizing such satellites; 3) in what manner the Commission should authorize non-governmental satellite operations (e.g., monopoly or multiple entry); and 4) whether it would be technically feasible to accommodate the space services proposed. During the time of the inquiry, additional satellite applications were filed.

1970-1973. A *Report and Order*, entitled *Establishment of Domestic Communication-Satellite Facilities by Non-governmental Entities* [14] (hereinafter Domsat I), adopted March 20, 1970, concluded the inquiry.[15] The Commission determined that it had legal authority under the Communications Act of 1934[16] to authorize non-governmental domestic satellites (satellites were considered to be "radio stations," which the Commission was created to regulate),[17] and that the authority was not constrained by the Communications Satellite Act of 1962,[18] or by United States treaty obliga-

---

13. At the same time, the Commission returned ABC's application without prejudice to appropriate refiling in light of the outcome of the inquiry.
14. 22 F.C.C. 2d 86 (1970).
15. Since ABC's first application in 1965, that company had refiled its application and several other companies, too, had applied to operate satellite systems, proposing a variety of different service offerings. AT&T proposed an integrated "Space-Earth Communications System" to meet anticipated growth in future long-distance communications demand. The Ford Foundation called for a "Broadcasters' Non-Profit Service Corporation" to operate a satellite system for the transmission of commercial and non-commercial television and radio programming. The Communications Satellite Corporation (Comsat) sought to operate a multi-purpose satellite system and to act as a carrier for television networks and other users. In 1967, Comsat submitted an additional proposal for a pilot demonstration program for satellite communications in conjunction with the newly-created Public Broadcasting Corporation. In February 1967, President Lyndon Johnson proposed legislation that later became the Public Broadcasting Act of 1967, 47 U.S.C. §§ 390-399B (1988). In 1969, General Electric Company (GE) proposed a satellite system for data and other record message and video point-to-point transmissions. Furthermore, the Executive Branch, had intervened during this time to ensure consistency with the Communications Satellite Act of 1962, as amended, 47 U.S.C. §§ 701-735 (1988), and United States obligations under the Agreement Relating to the International Telecommunications Satellite Organization, 1971, T.I.A.S. 7532. January 23, 1970. *See* Memorandum from Peter Flanigan, Assistant to the President of the United States, to Dean Burch, FCC Chairman (Jan. 23, 1970). *See* Domsat I, *supra* note 11, Appx. B, entitled "Background and Summary of Comments of the Parties" (providing a transcript of the letter).
16. 47 U.S.C. §§ 151-613 (1988).
17. *See* Domsat I, *supra* note 11, Appx. C, entitled "Memorandum on Legal Issues" (explaining why the Commission had the authority under the Communications Act of 1934 to authorize satellites).

tions. The Commission further concluded that the public interest would be served by an "open entry" approach to satellite authorizations, i.e., allowing multiple satellite operators to be licensed. Rather than authorizing a monopoly provider, or attempting to prescribe ownership arrangements for satellite systems, or even the manner and type of service to be provided, the Commission promised to entertain applications from any technically, financially and legally qualified entity proposing specialized or multi-purpose services to be provided on a common carrier or other basis.[19] The "open entry" policy adopted by the Commission was supported by a finding that multiple satellite systems could be accommodated from a technical feasibility perspective.

Although Domsat I paved the way for the authorization of privately-owned satellite systems, such as those proposed by ABC and other companies that had filed applications in the meantime,[20] it did not, itself, grant the satellite applications. Instead, it established licensing procedures and criteria and invited applicants to submit, or resubmit, applications. Seven companies, or teams of companies, responded with applications: Western Union Telegraph Company (Western Union); Hughes Aircraft Company and operating companies of GTE Service Corporation (Hughes/GTE); Western Tele-Communications, Inc.; Communications Satellite Corporation and American Telephone and Telegraph Company (Comsat/AT&T); MCI Lockheed Satellite Corporation (MCI Lockheed); Communications Satellite Corporation; and Fairchild Industries.

Prior to authorizing any of these companies, the Commission initiated a rule-making proceeding concerning the possible adverse effects on the satellite market of entrants, such as AT&T and Comsat, which already held dominant positions in the telecommunications service market. The concern was that these companies would be able to cross-subsidize competitive satellite services with revenues from their monopoly services.[21] The proceeding culminated in a *Second Report and Order*[22] issued in 1972 (hereinafter Domsat II), which placed certain restrictions on Comsat's and

18. 47 U.S.C. §§ 701-757 (1988). The Communications Satellite Corporation (Comsat), created by the Communications satellite Act of 1962 to be the United States participant in INTELSAT, had argued that the Communications Satellite Act of 1962 superseded or restricted the Commission's powers under the Communications Act of 1934, thus requiring any domestic satellite system to be authorized to Comsat, alone.

19. The Commission noted that public interest judgments could best be rendered in conjunction with specific proposals for satellite systems. The basic criterion for FCC authorization of any radio service is that the proposed service be in the public interest. *See* Chapter 3.2.4. (describing the public interest criterion).

20. *See, supra* note 15 (listing the applicants and describing their proposed services).

21. AT&T held a monopoly on long-distance telephone service, and Comsat was the only U.S. entity allowed to provide international satellite communications. Furthermore, AT&T was a major shareholder in Comsat.

AT&T's entries into the satellite market.[23]

1973-1980. Satellite construction permits and operating licenses were granted to several companies beginning in 1973. Western Union Telegraph Company was authorized to construct three satellites in 1973,[24] and to launch one of them, WESTAR I, in 1974.[25] Other initial licensees included Comsat and AT&T,[26] GTE Satellite Corporation,[27]RCA Global Communications[28] and Satellite Business Systems.[29]

1980-1983. By 1980, nine satellites were in orbit.[30]Three of these satellites were operated by Western Union, three by Comsat for use by AT&T and GTE Satellite Corporation, two by RCA Global Communications, and one by Satellite Business Systems. In 1980, authorizations were granted to these companies for additional satellites,[31]as well as to two new entrants: Hughes Communications, Inc. and Southern Pacific Communications Company.[32]

In 1980, the Commission was able to grant all requests for domestic

---

22. *Establishment of Communications-Satellite Facilities by Non-Governmental Entities,* 35 F.C.C. 2d 844 (1972) [hereinafter cited as Domsat II], *recon. in part,* 38 F.C.C. 2d 665 (1972) [hereinafter cited as Domsat III].
23. The Commission restricted the kinds of telecommunications services AT&T could provide via satellite to its regular and wide area telephone services and AUTOVON, a private line service for the Department of Defense, and disallowed a proposed AT&T/Comsat lease arrangement whereby Comsat would own and operate the satellite and AT&T would lease all the transponders. AT&T was given the option of owning and operating its own satellites or leasing transponders under tariff from Comsat or any other carrier. Comsat would have to elect between pursuing its multi-purpose application or serving AT&T. Selecting the latter, however, Comsat would be required to operate as a carrier's carrier pursuant to tariff, and to provide some capacity for use by other carriers, as well. The restrictions were motivated by a concern that AT&T and Comsat would not otherwise compete in the provision of specialized domestic telecommunications services and that any other arrangement would give Comsat an unfair competitive advantage *vis à vis* other satellite operators.
24. *Western Union Telegraph Company,* 38 F.C.C. 2d 1197 (1973), 40 F.C.C. 2d 1123 (1973) and 41 F.C.C. 2d 379 (1973).
25. *Western Union Telegraph Company,* 47 F.C.C. 2d 274 (1974).
26. *Comsat General Corporation,* 42 F.C.C. 2d 677 (1973), 45 F.C.C. 2d 444 (1974) and 59 F.C.C. 2d 344 (1976). *American Telephone & Telegraph Company,* 42 F.C.C. 2d 654 (1973), 48 F.C.C. 2d 674 (1974) and 61 F.C.C. 2d 139 (1976).
27. *GTE Satellite Corporation,* 43 F.C.C. 2d 1141 (1973) and 57 F.C.C. 2d 147 (1975).
28. *RCA Global Communications Inc.,* 56 F.C.C. 2d 660 (1975), 56 F.C.C. 2d 1066 (1975) and 74 F.C.C. 2d 531 (1979).
29. *Satellite Business Systems, Inc.* 62 F.C.C. 2d 997 (1977) *aff'd. sub nom United States V. FCC,* 652 F. 2d 72 (D.C. Cir. 1980).
30. *Assignment of Orbital Locations to Space Stations in the Domestic Fixed Satellite Service,* 84 F.C.C. 2d 584, 587 (1981), *modified* 44 F.C.C. 2d 129 (1983) [hereinafter cited as 1980 Assignment Order].

fixed satellites and to find orbital locations for these satellites based on a combination of three- and four-degree orbital separation between satellites. The Commission realized, however, that the orbital arc usable by U.S. domestic satellite operators[33] was fast becoming saturated, and that it would have to reduce spacing to two degrees to accommodate applicants in the future. Consequently, a rulemaking was instituted in October 1981,[34] which culminated in *Licensing of Space Stations in the Domestic Fixed Satellite Service and Related Revisions of the Rules and Regulations*[35] (hereinafter Two-Degree Spacing Order), adopting a policy of reduced spacing between satellites.[36]

1983-1985. Based on its then newly-adopted, reduced spacing policy, the Commission was able to authorize the construction of nineteen new domestic fixed satellites and the launch of nineteen new and previously constructed satellites in 1983.[37] Except for three newcomers, i.e., Rain-

---

31. *Comsat General Corporation*, 64 F.C.C. 2d 547 (1981); *GTE Satellite Corporation*, 64 F.C.C. 2d 562 (1981); *RCA American Communications, Inc.* 84 F.C.C. 2d 633 (1981); and *Western Union Telegraph Company*, 86 F.C.C. 2d 196 (1981).
32. *Hughes Communications, Inc.* 84 F.C.C. 2d 578 (1981) and *Southern Pacific Communications Company*, 84 F.C.C. 2d 650 (1981).
33. With current technology, only a limited segment of the geostationary orbit (64-143 degrees West Longitude) is usable by U.S. domestic satellite operators, since only from orbital locations in this segment of the arc will the satellite beams cover most of the United States. *See Assignment of Orbital Locations to Space Stations in the Domestic Fixed Satellite Service*, 3 F.C.C. Rcd 6972 (1988) [hereinafter cited as 1988 Assignment Order] (providing the current FCC orbital deployment plan).
34. *Licensing of Space Stations in the Domestic Fixed Satellite Service and Related Revisions of Part 25 of the Rules and Regulations*, 88 F.C.C. 2d 318 (1981).
35. 93 F.C.C. 2d 1260 (1983).
36. The Two-Degree Spacing Order, *supra* note 35, prescribed reduced spacing between satellites and also more stringent Earth station standards to avoid interference as a consequence of reduced spacing. The Commission ordered that two-degree spacing be implemented immediately with respect to new satellites in the 12/14 GHz band, and that a phased approach apply to satellites in the 4/6 GHz band, with a combination of 3, 2.5, and 2 degree spacing as a transitional arrangement to uniform two-degree spacing. A gradual implementation in the 4/6 GHz band was necessary to minimize the need for modifications of existing Earth station equipment and to allow Earth station operators several years to amortize and upgrade facilities. About one dozen satellites and thousands of licensed Earth stations were operating in this frequency band. By contrast, only three satellites and few Earth stations were operating in the 12/14 GHz band at the time. Two-Degree Spacing Order, *supra* note 35, at para. 4.
37. *Assignment of Orbital Locations to Space Stations in the Domestic Fixed Satellite Service*, 94 F.C.C. 2d 121 (1983), *recon.* FCC 84-32 (February 2, 1984), *further recon.* FCC 84-184 (May 15, 1984) [hereinafter cited as 1983 Assignment Order].

bow, Inc., United States Satellite, Inc. and Advanced Business Communications, Inc., which received conditional licenses, all of the licensees were companies with satellites already in orbit.

In 1983, for the first time, the Commission began to scrutinize the financial qualifications of applicants. The Commission was concerned that entrepreneurial, start-up companies, like Rainbow Satellite, United States Satellite and Advanced Business Systems would not be able to obtain the necessary financing to proceed promptly with the construction and launch of their satellites and that these companies would "tie up" scarce orbital locations without being able to make use of them. There also was a concern that the applications of these three companies might be speculative, that is, intended only to secure valuable orbital resources. Consequently, the Commission conditioned the authorizations of the three companies on their ability to arrange financing for their proposed satellite systems within a period of six months.[38] None of the companies met the deadline and their authorizations were declared null and void. Prior to 1983, all satellite applicants had been large, established companies, or the subsidiaries or joint ventures of such companies, whose financial qualifications were never in doubt.

The conditional licensing experiment, involving Rainbow Satellite, United States Satellite and Advanced Business Communications, and particularly the fact that all three companies failed to obtain financing, confirmed the Commission's suspicion that start-up companies without major corporate backers are unlikely to secure the necessary capital to establish domestic fixed satellite systems in a timely fashion. It prompted the Commission to adopt a Rule that would disqualify domestic fixed satellite applicants unless they could show that they had sufficient financial resources to proceed expeditiously with the construction, launch and operation of a satellite immediately upon authorization.[39]

1985-1988. In 1985, the Commission disposed of the largest number of satellite applications ever before it. A total of eighty-five applications for new and replacement satellites, construction permits and launch and operating licenses, had been filed by twenty-one separate entities. Uncertainty about the future availability of scarce orbital locations and the Commission's methods for allocating them caused existing satellite operators and entrepreneurial newcomers, alike, to attempt to secure orbital space. For the first time, the Commission was faced with a situation in which the number of applications exceeded the number of available orbital locations. Applying its new financial qualifications test, however, the Commission was able to eliminate a sufficient number of financially "unqualified"[40] applicants so as to accommodate the remaining.[41]

1988-Present. In 1988, the Commission authorized the construction of

38. *Rainbow Satellite, Inc.* 94 F.C.C. 2d 437 (1983), *United States Satellite Systems, Inc.*, 94 F.C.C. 2d 462 (1983), and *Advanced Business Communications, Inc.*, 94 F.C.C. 2d 1 (1983).

39. 47 C.F.R. § 25.391(b), (c) (1990).

thirteen additional satellites and the launch of nine satellites, as well as the construction and launch of ten replacement satellites.[42] All applications were granted since all applicants met the Commission's financial and other standards. They included Alascom, Inc., AT&T, Contel ASC, GE American Communications, Inc., GTE Spacenet Corporation, Hughes Communications Galaxy, Inc. and National Exchange Satellite, Inc.[43] Orbital assignments were based on uniform two-degree spacing in the 4/5 and 11/14 GHz bands, respectively, in a segment of the geostationary orbit ranging from 143 to 64[44]degrees West Longitude.[45]

The domestic fixed satellite-service industry has matured to a state of relative equilibrium. A handful of large companies are firmly established in the satellite market as suppliers of capacity on satellites they own and operate. Their customers range from transponder owners or lessees, such as Cable News Network, Public Broadcasting Corporation, USA Today and Dow Jones & Co., to middlemen, such as Keystone Communications and Hughes Network Systems, a subsidiary of Hughes Communications, which arrange for satellite capacity and install VSAT networks for other service takers or users. From time to time, these satellite owners will have

---

40. Since they were intended to eliminate applications of unqualified applicants, the financial standards became quite controversial. Entrepreneurial start-up companies argued that they were not given a fair chance. Some argued that the Commission should apply the less stringent financial test applied in *Ultravision Broadcasting,* 1 F.C.C. 2d 544 (1965), or a "due diligence" standard which was applied in the direct broadcasting satellite service, *Development of Regulatory Policy in Regard to Direct Broadcast Satellites for the Period Following the 1983 World Administrative Radio Conference,* 90 F.C.C. 2d 676 (1982). National Exchange, Inc., a company whose application was denied for lacking financial qualifications, also attacked the Commission's financial standards on procedural grounds, alleging that the Commission had violated the Administrative Procedure Act, 5 U.S.C. § 500 (1988) *National Exchange, Inc.,* 1 F.C.C. Rcd 682 (1986). *See* Chapter 3.2.5. (describing financial standards for satellite applicants) and Chapter 3.2.13. (describing National Exchange's attempt to have reversed the Commission's decision on its application). On the other hand, established satellite companies, as well as the FCC, itself, contended that stringent financial rules were necessary to prevent speculative applications and to ensure that valuable orbital locations were not left unused.
41. *See Licensing Space Stations in the Domestic Fixed Satellite Service,* 58 Rad. Reg. 2d 1267 (1985) [hereinafter cited as 1985 Licensing Order] (describing the FCC authorizations). It has been suggested that the fixed satellite service business has become an oligopoly of a few large established companies, Unpublished Paper by J. Swaim, American University, Washington College of Law, entitled "Domestic Fixed Satellite Service: Closing the Door on Open Entry," May 1990.
42. 1988 Assignment Order, *supra* note 33.
43. Satellite Transponder Leasing Corporation was transferred to Hughes Communications Galaxy, Inc., in 1990, *International Business Machines,* 5 F.C.C. Rcd 1655 (1990). *See* Chapter 3.2.11. (describing the transfer).

to replace their satellites, but it is unlikely that they will increase satellite capacity substantially. Instead, market expansion is expected for mobile communications and position-location-type satellite services. Consequently, these services are the focus of the FCC regulatory activity today (see Chapter 3.1.6.).

3.1.2. Direct broadcasting satellite Service

DEFINITION. The Commission's Rules define direct broadcasting satellite service as

> [a] radio communications service in which signals transmitted or retransmitted by space stations are intended for direct reception by the general public. In direct broadcast satellite service the term "direct reception" shall encompass both individual reception and community reception.[46]

The central phrase in this definition is "intended for direct reception by the general public."[47] While fixed satellites sometimes are used also for broadcasting (or program distribution), the broadcasts usually are not

---

44. Pursuant to bilateral agreements between the United States and Canada, and the United States and Mexico, satellites owned or authorized by Canada and Mexico occupy orbital locations in the central portion of the arc from 105-121 degrees West Longitude. Moreover, in 1988, the Commission adopted a policy of arc segmentation designating the 75-79 and 132-136 degrees West Longitude segments of the geostationary orbit as the "high power density arc." *GE American Communications, Inc.*, 3 F.C.C. Rcd 6871 (1988). This means that satellites operating at higher power levels will be assigned orbital locations in the high power density arc to prevent interference to low-powered satellites. The policy was modified. *Modification of Space Station Authorization of GE American Communications*, 54 Fed. Reg. 5483 (1988).
45. 1988 Assignment Order, *supra* note 33. *Assignment of Orbital Locations to Space Stations in the Domestic Fixed Satellite Service*, 5 F.C.C. Rcd 179 (1990), made certain changes to the orbital assignments pursuant to requests by licensees.
46. 47 C.F.R. § 100.3 (1990). The definition was modeled upon that adopted for "broadcasting satellite-service" by the International Telecommunication Union at an Extraordinary World Administrative Radio Conference in 1963 and modified at a World Administrative Radio Conference in 1971. *See* Chapter 4.2. (discussing these definitions).
47. The requirement that service be rendered to the "general public" does not preclude subscription service, that is, a satellite service in which only subscribers equipped with special decoder devices are able to receive the program signals. However, subscription service is not considered broadcasting in the FCC regulatory sense. *Subscription Video*, 2 F.C.C. Rcd 1001 (1987) *aff'd. sub nom National Association of Better Broadcasting v. FCC*, 849 F.2d 665 (D.C. Cir. 1988). Indeed, it is believed that, at least initially, direct broadcasting satellite operators or their customers will provide subscription services.

intended for *direct* reception by the general public, but rather for reception, for example, by cable operators for retransmission to the general public (see Chapter 3.1.1.). "Back-yard" receiving dishes currently installed are used for incidental reception of program signals in the fixed satellite-service. Such reception is legal and quite commonplace in the United States and several other countries today. By contrast, direct broadcasting satellite signals are intended primarily for direct reception by the general public. Licensees in the direct broadcasting satellite service are required to use powerful satellites to allow for reception by small, inexpensive receiving dishes suitable for mounting on a roof-top, balcony, etc.[48] By contrast, since the satellites that fixed satellite operators use are subject to power limitations, larger receiving dishes are necessary.

The Commission traditionally has required that licensees in the direct broadcasting satellite service have as their primary objective the provision of direct-to-home video entertainment and information.[49] The Commission considered taking a less restrictive view of the use of direct broadcast satellites in certain orbital locations for ancillary or additional services, but decided to maintain its previous position.[50]

NO U.S. DIRECT BROADCASTING SATELLITE IN OPERATION. Although several companies have received authorizations to construct, launch and operate direct broadcasting satellites, none has yet been launched. A perceived lack of a market for the service, due to a proliferation of cable offerings, the fact that cheaper lower-power fixed satellites may be used to provide broadcasting-type services, and the consequent lack of interest in the financial community are contributing factors. The partnership, "Sky Cable," formed in February 1989 by Hughes Communications, NBC, Cablevision and Rupert Murdock's News Corporation to launch a direct broadcasting satellite with 108 channels in 1993,[51] promised a brighter future for direct satellite broadcasting in the United States. However, it now appears certain that the venture will not materialize. Recently, United States Satellite Broadcasting Company (USSB) and Hughes Communications agreed to join together in launching one direct broadcasting satellite with eleven television channels for Hughes and five channels for USSB. Several foreign countries have direct broadcasting satellites already in operation.[52]

FREQUENCIES AND ORBITAL LOCATIONS. The Commission has

---

48. *United States Satellite Broadcasting Company, Inc.* 1 F.C.C. Rcd 977, 979 (1986).
49. *Id. See also United States Broadcasting Satellite Company, Inc.*, 2 F.C.C. Rcd 3642 (1987) (concerning the use of the satellites for other purposes than video program distribution).
50. *See Potential Uses of Certain Orbital Allocations by Operators in the Direct Broadcast-Satellite Service* [hereinafter cited as Potential Uses], 4 F.C.C. Rcd 6306 (1989) (discussing the use of direct broadcast satellites for applications other than video program distribution). *See* Potential Uses, *supra*, 6 F.C.C. 2d 2581 (1991) (reversing this policy.)

designated the 12.2 - 12.7 GHz (space-to-Earth) and 17.3.-17.8 GHz (Earth-to-space) frequency bands for use by direct broadcasting satellite service.[53] Orbital locations are fixed for this service as a result of a regional arrangement with Canada and other countries in the Americas.[54] Eight orbital locations were made available for use by U.S. companies: 175, 166, 157 and 148 degrees West Longitude in the Western orbital arc, and 119, 110, 101 and 61.5 degrees West Longitude in the Eastern orbital arc.[55] With present technology, each orbital location allows for a total of thirty-two channels. However, with signal compression techniques now being explored, many more channels likely will be available in the future.

HISTORY. Direct broadcasting satellite service became a regulatory concern of the FCC in the mid-1970s. In these early years, however, the Commission's attention focused on international frequency allocations for direct broadcasting satellites. The prospect of direct satellite broadcasting had generated both interest and concern in the international community because of the enormous potential inherent in the new technology.[56] Direct broadcasting satellites would be capable of beaming television program signals directly into every home equipped with a parabolic receiving antenna 20 to 30 cm in diameter. At the time, United States satellite companies, television networks and station owners, program producers and entrepreneurs were just beginning to recognize the commercial potential

---

51. *See DBS: The Next Generation,* BROADCASTING, Feb. 25, 1990, at 27-31, 55 (describing the proposed venture). Cablevision operates cable services in about eleven states and has approximately 1.5 million subscribers. Lewn and Landler, *Four Stars Team Up to Launch Sky Cable,* BUSINESS WEEK, Mar. 5, 1990, at 29. Hughes Communications, a subsidiary of Hughes Aircraft, is the largest supplier and operator of commercial satellites in the world, and also the holder of an FCC license to construct and operate direct broadcasting satellites. NBC, a subsidiary of General Electric, offers considerable programming experience, and Rupert Murdoch's News Corporation owns TV Guide and Harper & Row Publishers, potential marketing sources for Sky Cable.
52. For example, British Satellite Broadcasting Company of the United Kingdom operates the "Marco Polo" satellite. Deutsche Bundespost operates two "TV-Sat" satellites. Teledifusion France operates two "TDF" satellites.
53. 47 C.F.R. § 100.1, 13(b) (1990). Section 100.13(b) of the Commission's Rules, 47 C.F.R. § 100.13(b) (1990), refers to a regional agreement concerning direct broadcasting satellite service in the Western hemisphere reached at the International Telecommunication Union (ITU) Regional Administrative Radio Conference for the Planning in Region 2 of the Broadcasting Satellite Service in the Frequency Band 12.2-12.7 GHz and Associated Feeder Links in the 17.3-17.8 GHz Band (1983). *See* Chapter 4.2. (describing ITU Administrative Radio Conferences). This agreement designated frequencies and orbital locations for direct broadcasting satellite service to countries in the Americas. It is up to each country to allocate these resources further, *e.g.* to private entities.
54. *Id.*

of this technology.

Responding to a growing domestic interest in direct broadcasting satellites over the next few years, the Commission instituted an inquiry on November 3, 1980,[57] concerning policies for licensing and regulation of such systems. Shortly thereafter, on December 17, 1980, Satellite Television Corporation (STC), a subsidiary of the Communications Satellite Corporation (Comsat), became the first company to apply for authority to establish a direct broadcasting satellite system in the United States. About six months later, the Commission adopted a *Notice of Proposed Policy Statement and Rulemaking,*[58] proposing criteria and procedures for the authorization of direct broadcasting satellites. Thirteen additional applications were filed in response.

The rulemaking culminated in a *Report and Order*[59] (hereinafter DBS

---

55. From positions in the Western arc, the satellite coverage area is limited to the Western part of the United States. However, three positions in the Eastern arc, 119, 110 and 101 degrees, offer coverage of the continental United States (CONUS). Coverage of the Western part of the U.S. is marginal from the fourth Eastern position, at 61.5 degrees. Until 1989, the Commission authorized two orbital locations (one in the Western arc and one in the Eastern arc) for each direct-broadcast satellite licensee to transmit complementary signals to each half of the United States. The combined use of these orbital locations would allow the satellite operator to reach the entire CONUS. In *Continental Satellite Corporation,* 5 F.C.C. Rcd 7421 (1989), the Commission revised this orbital assignment policy, authorizing instead full-CONUS service from the three Eastern orbital locations that permit such coverage. Several advantages are offered by full CONUS authorization from one location. One satellite, instead of two, could be used to accomplish full CONUS direct broadcasting satellite service, provided satellites can be built sufficiently powerful. Even if such satellites are not technically feasible and co-location of two satellites is necessary, "there is some efficiency involved in designing and building multiple satellites (possibly including back-up capacity) in similar configurations from the same orbital location." *Continental Satellite Corporation, supra.* Furthermore, operation from one location reduces the cost of ground equipment. The Commission also pointed out that the use of a direct broadcast channel from the Eastern locations for full CONUS service "would preempt the use of western location channels — in effect the same Western location channel that would otherwise have been used to complement the Eastern location channel if it were used for half-CONUS service." *Id.* Consequently, the Commission instituted a rulemaking with respect to the possible uses of these "surplus" Western channels. Potential Uses, *supra* note 50.
56. *See* Chapter 4.2. (explaining why direct broadcasting satellites were a concern to developing countries, as well as authoritarian States).
57. *Inquiry Into the Development of Regulatory Policy in Regard to Direct Broadcast Satellites for the Period Following the 1983 Regional Administrative Radio Conference,* 45 Fed. Reg. 72719 (1980).
58. *Inquiry Into the Development of Regulatory Policy in Regard to Direct Broadcast Satellites for the Period Following the 1983 Regional Administrative Radio Conference,* 86 F.C.C. 2d 719 (1981).

Report and Order) issued on June 23, 1982, which designated frequencies and established licensing policies for direct broadcasting satellites. As was the case with domestic fixed satellite service, discussed above, the Commission also adopted an "open entry" approach to direct broadcasting satellite licensing, welcoming any legally, technically and financially qualified applicant for authorization to operate a direct broadcasting satellite system.

In a separate order, adopted November 4, 1982,[60] the Commission authorized[61] seven companies to construct direct broadcasting satellites. All but two of these companies (United States Satellite Broadcasting Company, Inc. and Dominion Video Satellite, Inc.) later surrendered their authorizations or had them cancelled.[62] For example, Comsat's Satellite Television Corporation abandoned its plans in November 1984 when it failed to attract financial partners to share the cost of developing the satellite system. In certain respects, Comsat's case is typical.

Several direct broadcasting satellite authorizations have since been issued.[63] Currently, the following companies hold authorizations for direct broadcasting satellite systems: Advanced Communications, Continental Satellite Corporation, Direct Broadcast Satellite Corporation, Directsat Corporation, Dominion Video Satellite, Inc., EchoStar Satellite Corporation, Hughes Communications, Inc., and United States Satellite Broadcasting Company, Inc.

The DBS Report and Order, which designated frequencies and adopted licensing policies for direct broadcasting satellites, and the ensuing satellite authorizations were not issued without controversy. Terrestrial broadcasters felt threatened by potential competition in the market place and, among other interest groups, argued that 1) the Commission lacked the legal authority to authorize *non-local* television services, such as direct broadcasting satellite service;[64] 2) direct broadcasting satellite service would reduce the amount of quality programming produced by local television stations because their revenues would decline in competition with

---

59. *Inquiry Into the Development of Regulatory Policy in Regard to Direct Broadcast Satellites for the Period Following the 1983 Regional Administrative Radio Conference*, 90 F.C.C. 2d 676 (1982) [hereinafter cited as DBS Report and Order].
60. *CBS, Inc.*, 92 F.C.C. 2d 64 (1982).
61. The authorizations were conditional. *See* Chapter 3.2.3. (explaining the two-step procedure for authorizing direct broadcasting satellite applicants).
62. *See, however, United States Satellite Broadcasting Company, Inc.*, 3 F.C.C. Rcd 6858 (1987) (granting extensions of time to United States Satellite Broadcasting Company and Dominion when these companies were unable to meet the milestone schedules specified in their respective construction permits). Under the original schedules, the satellites were required to be in operation by December 1988.
63. *See e.g. RCA Communications, Inc.*, Mimeo No.7115, *released* September 19, 1985, and *Continental Satellite Corporation, supra* note 55 (granting authorizations to groups of applicants).

satellite services;[65] and 3) the Commission's flexible regulatory approach, specifically that of exempting from traditional FCC broadcast regulation customers of direct broadcasting satellite common carriers, was legally wrong and not in the public interest.[66] Moreover, terrestrial microwave operators,[67] which were forced to give up their frequencies in the 12.2-12.7 GHz band to accommodate the new satellite service, protested that fact and argued that direct broadcasting satellite operators should pay the costs incurred in relocating microwave operations from frequencies then being used.[68] All of the arguments were rejected by the Commission.[69]

Court battles ensued. In *National Association of Broadcasters v. Federal Communications Commission,*[70] the court upheld the Commission's conclusion that it had authority to authorize non-local broadcasting, but vacated that part of the DBS Report and Order that exempted from broadcast regulation customers of direct broadcasting satellite common carriers. The court held that the Commission, by exempting such customers from broadcast regulation under the Communications Act, had departed from its declared policy and definition of what constitutes "broadcasting" and, thus, had engaged in "forbidden statutory experimentation."[71] Said

---

64. The controversy centered on Section 307(b) of the Communications Act of 1934, 47 U.S.C. § 307(b) (1988), which provides that

> [i]n considering applications for licenses . . . the Commission shall make such distribution of licenses, frequencies, hours of operation, and of power among the several States and communities as to provide a fair, efficient, and equitable distribution of radio service to each of the same.

Citing *FCC v. Pottsville Broadcasting Company,* 309 U.S. 134 (1940), the Commission countered that it had broad discretion to "select the means by which it will implement the statutory directive to 'provide fair, efficient, and equitable distribution of radio service' across the nation." DBS Report and Order, *supra* note 59, at 686.

65. DBS Report and Order, *supra* note 59, at 686-689.
66. *Id.,* at 709. *See National Association of Broadcasters v. FCC,* 740 F.2d 1190 (D.C. Cir. 1984), and *National Association of Better Broadcasting v. FCC, supra* note 47 and accompanying text (discussing the Commission's regulatory treatment of customers of direct broadcasting satellite common carriers).
67. Terrestrial microwave operators provided a variety of private, industrial, transportation and safety-related fixed communications services in the frequency bands sought for direct broadcasting satellites. *See* DBS Report and Order, *supra* note 59, at 699-704 (discussing accommodation of these operators).
68. *Id.,* at 694.
69. Citing *FCC v. Sanders Brothers Radio Station,* 309 U.S.470 (1940) and *Carroll Broadcasting Company v. FCC,* 258 F.2d 440 (D.C. Cir. 1958), the Commission countered that it is required to consider the economic effect of a new service on existing broadcasters only if there is "strong evidence that a significant net reduction in service to the public will result" which, it concluded, was not the case. DBS Report and Order, *supra* note 59, at 689.
70. 740 F.2d 1190 (D.C. Cir. 1984).

the court, in an arrangement where a customer leases capacity from a direct broadcasting satellite common carrier, "someone — either the lessee or the satellite owner — is broadcasting" and must be regulated as such.[72] The court found that the Commission, "without reasoned explanation," had departed from a long adhered to policy of looking to the *content* of the broadcast (whether the programming had mass appeal) as the critical factor in determining what constitutes broadcasting.[73] The Commission later remedied this defect in the DBS Report and Order by formally adopting a new policy establishing the *technology* employed in the distribution of video signals as the relevant factor in deciding what constitutes "broadcasting."[74] The court upheld this policy in *National Association of Better Broadcasting* v. *Federal Communications Commission*.[75]

3.1.3. Radiodetermination Satellite Service

DEFINITION. The Commission's Rules define radiodetermination satellite service as a "radiocommunication service for the purpose of radiodetermination involving the use of one or more [satellites]."[76] Radiodetermination is defined as the "determination of the position, velocity and/or other characteristics of an object, or the obtaining of information relating to these parameters, by means of the propagation of the radio waves."[77] Essentially, radiodetermination satellite service is a combination of position-location and navigation services provided via satellite to mobile users on land, at sea, or in the air. Although the Commission has not authorized voice communications as part of this service, it does allow for ancillary message capability,[78] meaning that users can send short, non-voice, incidental, alphanumeric messages, for example, to an individual whose position has been located.[79]

RADIODETERMINATION SERVICES TODAY. No dedicated radiodetermination satellite, i.e., one dedicated *exclusively* for radiodetermination satellite service, is yet in operation. Geostar Corporation of Washington, D.C., among others, received FCC permission in 1986 to launch and operate three such satellites. The company contracted with GE Astro Space Division, Princeton, New Jersey, for construction of the satellites.[80] Until its bankruptcy filing in May 1991, Geostar was offering "interim" position

71. *Id.*
72. *Id.*
73. *Id.*
74. *Subscription Video, supra* note 47.
75. 849 F.2d 665 (D.C. Cir. 1988). (Neither this court, nor the FCC has determined which one of the parties must be classified as a broadcaster).
76. 47 C.F.R. § 25.201 (1990).
77. 47 C.F.R. § 2.1 (1990).
78. 47 C.F.R. § 25.392(b) (1990).
79. Radiodetermination must be the primary service. If the message service were primary, the service, in essence, would be a mobile satellite service. *See Radiodetermination Satellite* Licensing Order, *infra* note 94, para. 21.

location services through the use of radiodetermination equipment "packages" placed on two domestic fixed "host" satellites owned and operated by GTE Spacenet Corporation.[81] Qualcomm, Inc. of San Diego, California, is offering two-way mobile data communications services with radiodetermination-type applications, also using a GTE Satellite Corporation satellite.[82] While Geostar employed frequency bands designated for radiodetermination services, Qualcomm is using a portion of the domestic fixed satellite service band in which mobile service is permitted. Potential future providers in the radiodetermination satellite service market include American Mobile Satellite Corporation[83] of Washington, D.C., and several applicants for low-Earth orbit satellite systems, e.g., Motorola Satellite Communications, Inc. of Chandler, Arizona, Starsys, Inc. of Washington, D.C., and a subsidiary of Orbital Sciences Corporation of Fairfax, Virginia. See Chapter 3.1.5-6.

FREQUENCIES. According to the Commission's Rules, the frequencies available for use in the radiodetermination satellite service are: 1610-1626.5 MHz (individual user-to-satellite) and 2483.5-2500 MHz (satellite-to-individual user). In addition, certain fixed satellite service bands may be used for links between radiodetermination satellites and control facilities on Earth since these communications essentially are of a fixed type, i.e., 5117-5183 MHz (satellite-to-central ground control facility) and 6525-6541.5 MHz (ground control facility to satellite).[84]

HISTORY. The regulatory history of radiodetermination satellites dates back to March 31, 1983, when Geostar Corporation, an entrepreneurial, start-up company, became the first to apply for authorization to construct and operate three satellites for position-location and navigation.[85] Geostar also filed a petition for rulemaking since new FCC Rules and frequency allocations would be necessary in order to grant its application.[86] Responding to Geostar's filings, the Commission adopted a *Notice of Pro-*

---

80. *See Geostar Corporation*, 60 Rad. Reg.2d 1725 (1986) [hereinafter cited as Geostar Authorization] (authorizing Geostar Corporation's service).
81. Prior to the company's bankruptcy in May 1991, the trucking industry represented by far the largest market for Geostar's services. Some seventeen-hundred trucks were equipped with devices that allowed the trucking company headquarters to keep track of each truck at all times and to exchange brief digital messages with individual truck drivers.
82. *See Qualcomm, Inc.* 4 F.C.C. Rcd 1543 (1989) (authorizing Qualcomm's service).
83. *See* Chapter 3.1.5. (describing mobile satellite service). In *Aeronautical Radio, Inc. v. FCC*, 928 F.2d 428 (D.C. Cir. 1991), the court ruled that the Commission had not provided adequate justification for requiring mobile satellite applicants to form a consortium, *i.e.*, American Mobile Satellite Corporation. *See* Chapter 3.1.5. (providing the history of mobile satellite authorization).
84. 47 C.F.R. § 25.202(a)(2) (1990). Allocations in the 5117-5199 MHz band were changed to 5150-5216 MHz during the International Telecommunication Union's World Administrative Radio Conference on Mobile Services in 1987. *See* Chapter 4.2. (discussing the results of this Conference).

posed Rulemaking[87] (hereinafter Notice) on July 12, 1984, suggesting allocations in three frequency bands,[88] as well as licensing rules for radiodetermination satellite service. To expedite the start of the new service, which the Commission had concluded promised great benefit to the public,[89] the Commission decided to conduct the licensing proceeding concurrently with the rulemaking proceeding. Usually, the Commission completes a rulemaking before commencing the adjudicatory, i.e., licensing, process (see Chapter 3.2.8.). Favoring competition as the best way to serve the public interest (again, the "touchstone" for FCC authorizations), the Commission proposed a policy of "multiple entry" in the radiodetermination satellite service; an approach to which it had adhered in the domestic fixed satellite and broadcasting satellite services, as well. In other words, the Commission proposed permitting more than one entity to provide radiodetermination satellite services on a competitive basis. The Commission suggested that the Geostar system design be used as a baseline for all other systems since that design would allow several radiodetermination satellite operators to provide service within the allocated frequency bands.[90] The Commission noted, however, that it would consider applications proposing incompatible designs if they were shown by the applicant to be superior and allow for multiple entry.[91]

Responding to the Commission's call for multiple entry, three other

---

85. Ancillary digital message capability was proposed as an additional feature. Geostar submitted "Supplemental Information" on August 20, 1983, "Additional Information" on September 29, 1984, and a "Geostar Satellite System Compendium of Application and Technical Information" on April 5, 1985.
86. Ancillary digital message capability was proposed as an additional feature. Geostar submitted "Supplemental Information" on August 20, 1983, "Additional Information" on September 29, 1984, and a "Geostar Satellite System Compendium of Application and Technical Information" on April 5, 1985.
87. *Amendment of the Commission's Rules to Allocate Spectrum for, and to Establish Other Rules and Policies Pertaining to, a Radiodetermination Satellite Service,* 49 Fed. Reg. 36512 (1984) [hereinafter cited as Radiodetermination Satellite Notice].
88. The Notice proposed to allocate the following frequency bands for radiodetermination satellite service: 1610-1626.5 MHz (individual user-to-satellite), 2483.5-2500 MHz (satellite-to-individual user), 5117-5183 MHz (satellite-to-central control ground facility). Television auxiliary broadcast stations and private radio services (such as police, fire and local government radio services) occupied the 2483.5-2500 MHz band. The other two bands were allocated to aeronautical radio navigation. Sharing arrangements were proposed. In addition, the Commission proposed that the 6525-6541.5.MHz band, currently allocated for domestic fixed satellite service, be used for the link from the control ground facility to the satellite. In essence, this link was a fixed satellite-type communication.
89. Geostar Corporation initially emphasized the potential safety aspects of its proposed new service. Geostar radiodetermination satellite applications included air traffic control (aeronautical position location), search and rescue operations, crime control, and more.

companies (in addition to Geostar) filed satellite applications: McCaw Space Technologies, Inc., MCCA American Radiodetermination Corporation and Omninet Corporation. The two former companies conformed their proposals to the Geostar baseline design. Omninet proposed an incompatible design, involving a hybrid mobile/radiotermination satellite concept that would not allow for multiple entry in the radiodetermination satellite service. Omninet later amended its application to comply with the Geostar baseline design.

On July 25, 1985, the Commission adopted a *Report and Order*[92] (Allocation Order) finalizing the frequency allocations proposed in the Notice.[93] The Commission adopted a *Second Report and Order* (Licensing Order)[94] on April 22, 1985, establishing licensing policies and procedures for radiodetermination satellite systems. The Commission then granted the applications of Geostar, McCaw Space Technologies Corporation, MCCA American Radiodetermination Corporation and Omninet Corporation.[95] All but Geostar later informed the Commission that they did not intend to pursue their proposals, which left Geostar as the sole entrant in the radiodetermination satellite business. However, in May 1991, Geostar filed for bankruptcy.

3.1.4. International Fixed Satellite Service: "Separate Systems" Operations as Distinguished from Transborder Service

DEFINITION. The Commission's Rules define fixed satellite service as "[a] radiocommunication service between Earth stations at specified fixed points, when one or more satellites are used . . . ."[96] See Chapter 3.1.1.,

---

90. Geostar proposed a "random access, time division multiplex" baseline design that contemplated a spread spectrum scheme in which users transmit at the same time and at the same frequency, but separate their signals by modulating them with unique pseudo-random number code sequences. The baseline design did not, however, specify modulation characteristics, power level, and coding schemes. *See* Radiodetermination Satellite Notice, *supra* note 87, at paras. 32-39. *See also* Radiodetermination Satellite Licensing Order, *infra* note 94, at para. 9, note 18 (describing the spread spectrum technique).
91. Radiodetermination Satellite Notice, *supra* note 87, at para 34.
92. *Amendment of the Commission's Rules to Allocate Spectrum for, and to Establish Other Rules and Policies Pertaining to, Radiodetermination Satellite Service,* 50 Fed. Reg. 39101 (1985) [hereinafter cited as Radiodetermination Satellite Allocation Order], *recon.* 104 F.C.C. 2d 637 (1987).
93. The Commission also amended certain sections of Parts 74, 90 and 94 of its regulations to reflect the reallocation in the 2483.5-2500 MHz band and to provide for the grandfathering of certain stations in those bands.
94. *Amendment of the Commission's Rules to Allocate Spectrum for, and to Establish Other Rules and Policies Pertaining to, Radiodetermination Satellite Service,* 51 Fed. Reg. 18444 (1986) [hereinafter cited as Radiodetermination Satellite Licensing Order].
95. Geostar Authorization, *supra* note 80.

entitled "Domestic Fixed Satellite Service," for further description of fixed satellite service. Licensees in the international fixed satellite service are restricted to international service offerings, although the Commission does allow for the provision of domestic services on an ancillary basis, provided the primary thrust of the service is international.[97] "Ancillary" domestic services has been defined by the Commission to mean those that are "reasonably related to use of the facilities for international communications."[98] Fixed satellite systems owned by private U.S. companies and that are intended primarily for international communications are referred to by the Commission as "separate systems."[99] Services provided by separate systems must be distinguished from "transborder services," which contemplate the use of U.S. domestic fixed satellites[100] for incidental[101]service to neighboring countries.[102]

FREQUENCIES. These frequency bands have been set aside by the Commission specifically for international fixed satellite service: 10.95 -11.2 GHz and 11.46-11.7 GHz (space-to-Earth).[103] The 14.0 -14.5 GHz band, which is used for Earth-to-space communications in the domestic fixed satellite service, is available also to international fixed satellite operators.[104] International fixed satellite operations are permitted also in other parts of the 11/12 GHz band, as well as in the 4/6 GHz band allocated for fixed satellite service. See Chapter 3.1.1.

INTERNATIONAL ORGANIZATIONS. Several international organizations today own and operate satellite systems for international fixed satellite service (see Chapter 5.).[105] Chief among them is the International Telecommunications Satellite Organization (INTELSAT), a hybrid intergovernmental and commercial organization (see Chapter 5.1.1.), of which the United States and 120 other countries are members.[106] INTELSAT launched its first satellite "Early Bird" on April 6, 1965, and now has fifteen satellites in orbit. Through a designated entity, the Communications

---

96. *See supra* note 5 (defining fixed satellite service).
97. *Establishment of Satellite Systems Providing International Communications*, 61 Rad. Reg. 2d 649 (1986) [hereinafter Separate Systems Reconsideration Order].
98. *Id.*
99. *See supra* note 1 (providing an explanation of the term "separate systems").
100. Domestic fixed satellite service is defined in Chapter 3.1.1.
101. The satellite must be intended primarily for service within the United States.
102. Neighboring countries include Canada, Mexico and countries in the Caribbean and Central and South America that are within the domestic satellite footprint. *See supra* note 6 (providing the criteria for transborder service authorizations).
103. 47 C.F.R. § 25.202(a)(1), note 2 (1990).
104. *Id.*
105. Apart from INTELSAT, these include the European Telecommunications Satellite Organization (EUTELSAT), the Arab Corporation for Space Communications (ARABSAT) and the INTERSPUTNIK International System and Organization for Space Communications.

Satellite Corporation (Comsat), the United States contributes to the financing and participates in the management of the INTELSAT space segment.[107]

COMSAT. Comsat was created by the Communications Satellite Act of 1962, as amended[108] (Satellite Act),[109] as a corporation "for profit [not to be] an agency or establishment of the United States Government."[110] Initially, much of Comsat's stock was held by major international telephone and record carriers, such as AT&T and RCA Global Communications. These carriers have since divested themselves of most of their Comsat stock holdings making shares available for public trading. Comsat is subject to FCC licensing and common carrier regulation,[111] as well as to FCC oversight on certain financial matters, such as the issuance of shares[112] and participation in INTELSAT space segment procurement.[113]

DIRECT ACCESS TO INTELSAT. In the United States, Comsat holds a monopoly on access to the INTELSAT satellites, which means that Comsat

---

106. INTELSAT was established as an interim organization in 1964 by Agreement Establishing Interim Arrangements for a Global Commercial Communications Satellite System and Special Agreement. T.I.A.S. No. 5646. Eleven countries were Members of interim INTELSAT, and Comsat served as the manager of the satellite system. In 1973, INTELSAT was established in its current form by Agreement Relating to the International Telecommunications Satellite Organization "INTELSAT." T.I.A.S. 7532 [hereinafter INTELSAT Agreement]. INTELSAT's prime objective was to continue "on a definitive basis the design, development, construction, establishment, operation and maintenance of the space segment of the global commercial telecommunications satellite system . . . ." *Id.*, art. II(a). Comsat no longer serves exclusively as the manager of the satellite system. *See* Chapter 5.1. (describing INTELSAT and its functions).
107. Comsat was created for the purpose of participating in the planning, procurement, operation, management and ownership of a global satellite system, *i.e.*, INTELSAT, 47 U.S.C. § 735 (a)(1) (1988).
108. 47 U.S.C. § 701-757 (1988). In 1978, the Communications Satellite Act was amended to provide also for U.S. participation in the International Maritime Satellite Organization (INMARSAT), which was established to provide international maritime mobile communications. Comsat is the designated instrument for U.S. participation also in this organization. 47 U.S.C. § 751-757 (1988). INMARSAT was established by the Convention of the International Maritime Satellite Organization and Operating Agreement. 1976, T.I.A.S. 9605. *See* Chapter 5.1.2. (describing INMARSAT and its functions).
109. The purpose of the Satellite Act was to provide for, and facilitate the participation of, the United States in the establishment of a "commercial communications satellite system, as part of an improved global communications network" (later to be known as INTELSAT). 47 U.S.C. § 701(a) (1988).
110. 47 U.S.C. § 731 (1988).
111. *Id.*, § 741. See *also* 47 U.S.C. § 721(c) (1988) (concerning the Commission's regulatory authority over Comsat).
112. 47 U.S.C. § 721(c)(8) (1988).
113. *Id.*, § 721(c)(1).

is the sole supplier of INTELSAT space segment capacity, and that any person or entity seeking transmission via INTELSAT satellites, to or from an Earth station in the United States, must contract with Comsat. Comsat's monopoly position has been challenged repeatedly by U.S. carriers and users desiring to access INTELSAT directly, primarily for cost-saving purposes (Comsat marks up INTELSAT's charges), but the Commission has always allowed Comsat to retain its monopoly position.[114]

AUTHORIZED USERS. Traditionally, only so-called "authorized users," that is, international service and record carriers, such as AT&T, Western Union International, RCA Global Communications and ITT World Communications, were permitted to contract with Comsat for INTELSAT space segment capacity, and Comsat could not serve end-users directly.[115] Comsat operated exclusively as a "common carrier's common carrier." Over time, however, the "authorized user" policy has been modified substantially,[116] allowing Comsat to offer service directly to end-users and permitting all licensed operators of Earth stations accessing the INTELSAT system to obtain INTELSAT capacity through Comsat.[117]

INTELSAT EARTH STATIONS. Initially, all Earth stations used for communications via the INTELSAT system were owned and operated by a consortium known as the Earth Station Ownership Committee (ESOC), consisting of Comsat (50%) and international service carriers, such as AT&T, ITT World Communications, RCA Global Communications and

---

114. *Regulatory Policies Concerning Direct Access to INTELSAT Space Segment for U.S. International Service Carriers,* Notice of Inquiry, 90 F.C.C. 2d 1446 (1982); and Report and Order, 97 F.C.C. 2d 296 (1984) *aff'd. sub nom Western Union International, Inc. v. FCC,* 804 F.2d 1280 (D.C. Cir. 1986). The direct access issue was discussed briefly in *Establishment of Satellite Systems Providing International Communications,* 101 F.C.C. 2d 1046 (1985) [hereinafter cited as Separate Systems Order], at para. 221. However, the Commission concluded that no change in policy was warranted. On January 9, 1990, the Commission dismissed a petition for rulemaking by the National Telecommunications and Information Administration (NTIA), requesting the Commission to authorize competitive access to INTELSAT by carriers and users. *Petition to Consider Authorizing Competitive Access by Carriers and Users to the INTELSAT Space Segment for the Provision of Customized International Communications Services,* FCC 90-6, *released* Jan. 11, 1990. The Commission listed these developments among others as justifying the dismissal of NTIA's petition: 1) the permissions to establish separate systems, Separate Systems Order, *supra;* 2) the introduction of fiber optic technology, *American Telephone and Telegraph Company,* 98 F.C.C. 2d 440 (1984) (TAT-8 Decision), Mimeo No. 1794 (Common Carrier Bureau Jan. 7, 1986) and 4 F.C.C. Rcd 1129 (1988), *erratum* 4 F.C.C. Rcd 1136 (1989) (TAT-9 decision); and 3) the authorizations of private fiber optics cable systems, including *Tel-Optic Limited,* 100 F.C.C. 2d 1033 (1985).

115. *Authorized Entities and Authorized Users Under the Communications Satellite Act of 1962,* 4 F.C.C. 2d 421 (1966), *recon in part* 6 F.C.C. 2d 593 (1967) [hereinafter cited as Authorized User I].

Western Union International (50%).[118] In 1984, the Commission provided for the dissolution of ESOC, and for individual carriers, or groups of carriers, to build and operate their own INTELSAT Earth stations.[119] Today, common carriers, private (non-common) carriers, and users may be licensed to operate INTELSAT transmit/receive Earth stations.[120]

"SEPARATE SYSTEMS" IN OPERATION TODAY. As noted, in FCC regulatory parlance, the term "separate system" is used to describe international fixed satellite systems that are operated by private U.S. companies. The term was borrowed from a passage in the Satellite Act, which provides that the United States shall rely on INTELSAT, "except where a separate communications satellite system is required . . . ."[121] So far, only one separate system is in operation. Alpha Lyracom, doing business as Pan American Satellite (PanAmSat), operates one satellite for communications to and from several countries in South America and Europe. The company plans to expand its satellite operations, and currently has applications on file with the Commission for additional satellites. Orion Satellite Corporation (Orion) recently received all the necessary FCC and other regulatory approvals to provide trans-Atlantic service,[122] but has yet to launch a satellite. Several other companies have received preliminary approvals from the FCC to establish separate systems, but their plans have been delayed for lack of financing, among other reasons.[123]

HISTORY OF SEPARATE SYSTEMS AUTHORIZATIONS. The regula-

---

116. *See Spanish International Network*, 70 F.C.C. 2d 2127 (1978) (authorizing Spanish International Network to take end-to-end service directly from Comsat for purposes of international television transmissions); *Proposed Modifications of the Commission's Authorized User Policy Concerning Access to the Satellite Services of the Communications Satellite Corporation*, First Report and Order, 90 F.C.C. 2d 1394 (1982), *vacated and remanded ITT World Communications, Inc. v. FCC*, 725 F.2d 732 (D.C. Cir. 1984); Second Report and Order, 100 F.C.C. 2d 177 (1985), *recon. denied* 59 Rad. Reg.2d 213 (1985) [hereinafter collectively cited as Authorized User II] (allowing non-carrier users to lease "basic satellite transmission capacity" directly from Comsat; and Comsat, through a separate subsidiary, to provide switched and other services directly to end-users).
117. Authorized User II, *supra* note 116, Second Report and Order, at para. 21.
118. *Amendment of Part 25 of the Commission's Rules and Regulations With Respect to Ownership and Operation of Initial Earth Stations in the United States for Use in Connection With the Proposed Global Commercial Communication Satellite System*, 5 F.C.C. 2d 812 (1966).
119. *Modification of Policy on Ownership and Operation of U.S. Earth Stations that Operate with the INTELSAT Global Communications System*, *Report and Order*, 100 F.C.C. 2d 250 (1984) [hereinafter cited as Earth Station Ownership Order]. *See also Modification of Policy on Ownership and Operation of U.S. Earth Stations that Operate with the INTELSAT Global Communications System*, Notice of Inquiry, 90 F.C.C 2d 1458 (1982) and Notice of Proposed Rulemaking, 97 F.C.C. 2d 444 (1984) (concerning the evolution of Earth station ownership policy).

tory history of separate systems began on March 11, 1983, when Orion became the first private company to apply to the FCC to establish a satellite system for trans-Atlantic communications. Orion's application immediately became controversial since it challenged an almost twenty-year monopoly on global satellite communications held by INTELSAT.[124] What made Orion's application particularly controversial was the company's proposal to compete with INTELSAT in the trans-Atlantic market, the organization's most lucrative.[125] The stage was set for a protracted and acrimonious legal and policy debate involving the President and the Congress of the United States, as to whether the U.S. should authorize separate systems.

Shortly after Orion's application was filed with the Commission, the Executive Branch of the government intervened. In a joint letter, dated

---

120. In authorizing Earth stations, the Commission makes a distinction based on the type of satellite service to be provided. Applications for Earth stations to provide so-called international business service (IBS), *i.e.*, dedicated private-line service and television service are granted in a routine fashion, *i.e.*, upon a showing of legal, technical and financial qualifications. Earth Station Ownership Order, *supra* note 119, at 265. *See e.g. GE American Communications, Inc.*, 5 F.C.C. Rcd 898 (1990), *GTE Spacenet Corporation*, 4 F.C.C. Rcd 5026 (1989) and *American Satellite Company*, 3 FCC Rcd 6787 (1988) (authorizing these companies to operate Earth Stations for those types of services in connection with the INTELSAT satellite system). Applications for multi-purpose stations, which are used to provide international public-switched services, are examined closely, to determine whether the operation of the Earth stations will result in technical interference and/or economic harm to existing stations that might outweigh the public interest in the proposed new stations. Earth Station Ownership Order, *supra* note 119. In 1986, the Commission deregulated *receive-only* Earth stations operating with the INTELSAT satellite system to provide INTELNET service. *Deregulation of receive-Only Satellite Earth Stations Operating with the INTELSAT Global Communications Satellite System*, FCC 86-214, May 19, 1986. INTELNET is an international digital data service involving the use of very small aperture terminals (VSATs) and a central "hub" station. In 1988, the Commission decided that all private, *i.e.*, non-common, carriers may be licensed to operate transmit/receive Earth stations with the INTELSAT satellite system. *Licensing Under Title II of the Communications Act of 1934, as amended, of Private Transmit/Receive Earth Stations Operating With the INTELSAT Global Communications Satellite System* (Declaratory Ruling), 3 F.C.C. Rcd 1585 (1988). Reuters U.S., Inc., which provides news, photo and information to newspapers and financial institutions world-wide, had requested this ruling as it intended to build a transmit/receive Earth station for use with the IBS and INTELNET services it was leasing from Comsat.
121. 47 U.S.C. § 721(a)(6) (1988).
122. *Orion Satellite Corporation*, 5 F.C.C. Rcd 4937 (1990) and 6 F.C.C. Rcd 4201 (1991). *See Orion Satellite Corporation*, Mimeo No. 6871, *released* Sept. 6, 1985, and 101 F.C.C. 2d 1302 (1986) (authorizing Orion in a preliminary fashion).

April 6, 1983, the U.S. Departments of State and Commerce requested that the Commission refrain from taking final action on the application until the Executive Branch was given the opportunity to study its implications with regard to the national security and foreign policy interests of the United States.[126] A determination is required by the President of the United States under the Satellite Act that separate systems are "required in the national interest."[127] The Executive Branch also was concerned that the authorization of private companies to compete with INTELSAT might be perceived in the international community as an abrogation of the long-time U.S. commitment to INTELSAT.

During the time of the Executive Branch review, four additional separate systems applications were filed with the Commission: International Satellite, Inc., on August 12, 1983; RCA American Communications, Inc., on February 13, 1984; Cygnus Satellite Corporation on March 7, 1984; and Pan American Satellite Corporation on May 31, 1984. Financial Satellite

---

123. *International Satellite, Inc.,* 101 F.C.C. 2d 1201 (1985); *Pan American Satellite Corporation,* 101 F.C.C. 2d 1318 (1986); *Cygnus Satellite Corporation,* Mimeo No. 0362, *released* Oct. 22, 1985; and *Financial Satellite Corporation,* FCC 86-13, *released* Jan. 15, 1986. In *RCA American Communications, Inc.,* 101 F.C.C. 2d 1342 (1985), RCA was granted authority to modify an existing domestic fixed satellite authorization. *See also International Satellite, Inc. and Financial Satellite Corporation,* 5 F.C.C. Rcd 35 (1990) (granting these two companies extensions which were required since they failed to meet implementation milestones specified in their authorizations)

124. The challenge was significant since INTELSAT and its Signatory Comsat had become rigid, inflexible and, to a degree, non-service minded. These characteristics are typical of a monopoly service provider.

125. INTELSAT would be at a competitive disadvantage due to a requirement to average charges on its high and low density communications routes pursuant to Article V(d) of the INTELSAT Agreement, *supra* note 106. In other words, INTELSAT is required to subsidize charges on low density routes with revenues from high density routes, such as the trans-Atlantic and, therefore, may not have the flexibility to lower prices on these routes when faced with competition.

126. Letter from David J. Markey, Assistant Secretary-Designate for Communications and Information, Department of Commerce, and Diana Lady Dougan, Coordinator, International Communications and Information Policy, Department of State, to Mark S. Fowler, FCC Chairman (Apr. 6, 1983).

127. Communications Satellite Act of 1962, sec. 202(a)(6), 47 U.S.C. § 701(d) (1988), *cf.* sec. 102(d), 47 U.S.C. § 721(a)(6) (1988). Section 102(d) provides that "[i]t is not the intent of Congress by this Act . . . to preclude the creation of additional communications satellite systems if required to meet unique governmental needs or if otherwise required in the national interest." Section 201(a)(6) provides that "[t]he President shall . . take all necessary steps to insure the availability and appropriate utilization of the communications satellite system for general governmental purposes except where a separate communications satellite system is required to meet unique governmental needs, or is otherwise required in the national interest."

Corporation filed an application on May 17, 1985, i.e., after the Executive Branch review had been completed.

The Executive Branch review culminated in a *Presidential Determination,*[128] signed by President Ronald Reagan on November 28, 1984, that separate systems were "required in the national interest" within the meaning of the Satellite Act.[129] On that same day, the U.S. Departments of State and Commerce, in a joint letter, informed the Commission of the criteria necessary to ensure fulfillment of the United States' obligations *vis à vis* INTELSAT.[130] The criteria were designed to protect INTELSAT, and would require separate systems companies, prior to final FCC authorization, to obtain operating agreement(s)[131] from an appropriate authority in one or more foreign countries to which the international service would be provided and, together with such foreign authority(ies), enter into technical and economic coordination with INTELSAT under Article XIV(d) of the INTELSAT Agreement.[132] Moreover, separate systems operators would have to restrict their service offerings to sale or long-term lease of transponders or satellite capacity for communications that are not interconnected with the public-switched network.[133] The latter requirement was intended to protect INTELSAT's core business, since the major portion of INTELSAT's revenues derives from international public-switched network communications. The requirement to refrain from interconnection with the public-switched network is now being eliminated.

The *Presidential Determination* paved the way for the Commission to proceed with a rulemaking to determine the public interest benefits of separate systems and establish criteria and procedures for evaluating separate systems applications. A *Notice of Inquiry and Proposed Rulemaking*[134] was adopted on December 19, 1984, instituting the rulemaking and soliciting comments on the applications, as well as the criteria proposed

128. Presidential Determination No. 85-2. 49 Fed. Reg. 46987 (1984).

129. *See supra* note 127 (quoting provisions from the Satellite Act which provide that separate systems are permitted if they are required in the United States national interest)

130. Letter from George P. Shultz, Secretary of State, and Malcolm Baldridge, Secretary of Commerce, to Mark S. Fowler, Chairman, FCC (Nov. 28, 1984). The policy grounds for the Presidential Determination were set forth in *A White Paper on New International Satellite Systems* (issued Feb. 8, 1985) [hereinafter cited as White Paper], which had been prepared by the Senior Interagency Group on International Communication and Information. The White Paper was incorporated in the FCC proceeding concerning separate systems and added to FCC C.C. Docket No. 84-1299, Report No. I-4032, Feb. 11, 1985.

131. The purpose of an operating agreement is to allow for communications to and/or from Earth stations in a foreign country.

132. *See supra* note 106 (providing full title of the INTELSAT Agreement).

133. The public-switched network refers to the communications network for public message and record traffic, including telephony, telex and facsimile that may be accessed by the public through, *e.g.*, a telephone apparatus. Private networks can be accessed only by private parties.

by the Executive Branch.[135] Comments were generally favorable. Proponents of separate systems pointed out that competition in the international satellite service market would increase consumers' service selections,[136] reduce rates[137] and stimulate technological innovation, as had been the case in the domestic fixed satellite service. Among other points, the opponents argued that the establishment of separate systems would reflect unfavorably upon the United States in the international community, and might even lead to the demise of INTELSAT.[138]

In a *Report and Order* adopted July 25, 1985[139] (hereinafter Separate Systems Order), the Commission concluded that it would be in the public interest to authorize separate systems with the restrictions recommended by the Executive Branch. The Commission then proceeded to issue conditional authorizations to the applicants on file.[140] On reconsideration, the Commission affirmed the general conclusions reached in the Separate Systems Order while adopting minor modifications to the proposed restrictions on separate system service offerings.[141] The Commission's separate systems policy later became law, providing that it is United States policy to promote separate systems as long as they are technically compatible with the INTELSAT satellite system, and that significant economic harm to the organization can be avoided.[142]

DISTINGUISH "TRANSBORDER SERVICE." The Commission distinguishes separate systems operations from so-called "transborder services." While separate systems are satellites specifically intended for international communications, transborder services are provided via domestic fixed satellites (authorized for domestic service), and only to neighboring countries. Because a domestic satellite coverage area cannot

---

134. *Establishment of Satellite Systems Providing International Communications,* 50 Fed. Reg. 1570 (1985).
135. *See* White Paper, *supra* note 130 (explaining the criteria).
136. Since INTELSAT is required in its charter to serve all countries in the world indiscriminately, (INTELSAT Agreement, *supra* note 106, arts. I and V(d)), the organization does not always have the flexibility to meet customers' specialized needs.
137. It was believed that INTELSAT and Comsat would be forced to reduce their rates in order to be competitive.
138. Initially Comsat, as the U.S. Signatory to INTELSAT, opposed the separate systems. *See* Chapter 5.1. (explaining the meaning of "Signatory" in the INTELSAT context). Later, Comsat was required to conform its position with that of the U.S. Government. Comsat's strategy then shifted to one of advocating strict interpretation of the restrictions on separate systems recommended by the Executive Branch in the White Paper, *supra* note 130.
139. Separate Systems Order, *supra* note 114.
140. *See supra* notes 122 and 123 (listing these authorizations).
141. Separate Systems Reconsideration Order, *supra* note 97, *further reconsideration,* 1 F.C.C. Rcd 439 (1986).
142. 1986-87 Foreign Relations Act, Pub. L. No. 99-93, § 146, 99 Stat. 405, 425-26 (1985).

be tailored to fit the United States borders precisely, considerable satellite signal "spillover" inevitably occurs into neighboring countries, such as Canada or Mexico, the Caribbean and Central America, depending on the orbital location of the satellite. The Commission allows domestic satellite operators to take advantage of the spillover effect to offer incidental program distribution and two-way communications services to countries within the domestic satellite coverage area.[143]

The critical factor in determining whether a proposed satellite service will be processed by the Commission in the "separate systems" or "transborder" category appears to be whether the foreign country is within the coverage area of a domestic satellite. In *RCA American Communications,*[144] the Commission considered and granted under its separate systems policy RCA's applications to modify a domestic fixed satellite under construction to add international beams for service to Europe and Africa. These countries were not within the domestic fixed satellite coverage area. On the other hand, the Commission considered under its transborder policy an application by Teleport International and American Satellite Company to use the latter's domestic satellite for two-way communications service between the U.S. and Jamaica. The Commission noted that the fact that Jamaica was not contiguous to the United States was of no consequence, as long as it falls within the domestic satellite's footprint.[145] The

143. *Transborder Satellite Video Services,* 88 F.C.C. 2d 258 (1981) (Transborder I); *Eastern Microwave, Inc.,* Mimeo No. 2617, *released* Mar. 1, 1983 (Transborder II); *American Telephone and Telegraph Company,* Mimeo No. 6119, *released* Aug. 24, 1983 (Transborder III); *Bonneville Satellite Corporation,* Mimeo No. 1554, *released* Dec. 29, 1983 (Transborder IV); *Western Union Telegraph Company,* Mimeo No. 3286, *released* Apr. 4, 1984 (Transborder V); *Eastern Microwave, Inc.,* Mimeo No. 6425, *released* Sept. 11, 1984 (Transborder VI); *Western Union Telegraph Company,* Mimeo No. 3643, *released* Apr. 8, 1985 (Transborder VII); *American Satellite Company,* Mimeo No. 7299, *released* Sept. 30, 1985 (Transborder VIII); *RCA Communications, Inc.,* Mimeo No. 2578, *released* Feb. 14, 1986 (Transborder IX); *AT&T,* 1 F.C.C. Rcd 72 (1986) (Transborder XI); *RCA American Communications,* 2 F.C.C. Rcd 1869 (1987) (Transborder XII); and *GTE Spacenet Corporation,* 2 F.C.C. Rcd 2477 (1987) (Transborder XIII). The Commission's transborder policy was upheld in *Communications Satellite Corporation v. FCC,* 836 F.2d 623 (D.C. Cir. 1988). *See* C.W. Derrick, *Competition versus Cooperation: The D.C. Circuit Referees the Transborder Policy,* 14 N.C. J. OF INT'L L. & COMMERCIAL REG. 315 (1989) (discussing the case). *See supra* note 6 (describing the criteria for transborder service authorization).

144. 101 F.C.C. 2d 1342 (1985).

145. *Teleport International and American Satellite Company,* 1 F.C.C. Rcd 101, 104 (1986). While vacating the Commission's decision for other reasons, the court in *Communications Satellite Corporation v. FCC, supra* note 143, concluded that the Commission properly had considered the application under its transborder policy. *See also* Teleport International and American Satellite CompanyTeleport International and American Satellite Company, 2 F.C.C. Rcd 4149 (1987) (implementing the court's decision)

Commission's reasoning was endorsed by the court in *Communications Satellite Corporation* v. *Federal Communications Commission.*[146] The distinction between separate systems and transborder services is important because different licensing procedures and criteria apply. Generally, it is easier to obtain a permission to provide transborder service.

3.1.5. Mobile Satellite Service

DEFINITION: Mobile satellite-service is defined in the Commission's Rules as "[a] radiocommunications service: (1) between mobile earth stations and one or more space stations, or between space stations used by this service; or (2) between mobile earth stations by means of one or more space stations."[147] The Commission's rules contemplate three kinds of mobile satellite services: aeronautical, maritime and land mobile. In aeronautical mobile satellite service, Earth stations are located on-board aircraft;[148] in maritime mobile satellite service, Earth stations are located on-board ships;[149] and in land mobile satellite service, Earth stations are located on land.[150] Aeronautical mobile satellite service has two components: safety-related aeronautical mobile satellite service (AMSS(R)), for air safety and traffic control, i.e. communications concerning the speed, altitude and location of an aircraft; and non-safety-related aeronautical mobile satellite service (AMSS), involving airline business and passenger communications. The generic term "mobile satellite service," used by the Commission, encompasses all three, i.e., maritime, aeronautical and land mobile satellite-services.

MOBILE SATELLITE-SERVICE TODAY. The International Maritime Satellite Organization (INMARSAT) provides mobile communications services to the international maritime community via a combination of INMARSAT-owned satellites and satellites leased from INTELSAT, Comsat and the European Space Agency[151] (see Chapter 5.1.2.). More than 10,000 ships and off-shore facilities use the INMARSAT satellite system. Recently, aeronautical services were introduced by INMARSAT.[152] Like INTELSAT, INMARSAT is a hybrid intergovernmental and commercial organization. Sixty-four States are members, including the United States. Comsat also is the designated U.S. participant (Signatory) in this organization.[153]

On May 31, 1989, the Commission authorized a consortium of eight companies called American Mobile Satellite Corporation (AMSC)[154] to

146. 863 F.2d 623 (D.C. Cir. 1988).

147. 47 C.F.R. § 2.1 (1990), listing in alphabetical order definitions of radio telecommunications services.

148. *Id.*

149. *Id.*

150. *Id.*

151. *See* Chapter 5.2.1., note 77 and accompanying text (describing the INMARSAT space segment).

construct, launch and operate three dedicated mobile satellites[155] to provide a variety of land, maritime and aeronautical mobile satellite services.[156] With its first satellite not due for launching until 1993, AMSC sought and received permission from the FCC to begin interim service by leasing mobile satellite capacity from INMARSAT.[157] At least two other companies, Aeronautical Radio Inc., and IDB Communications Group, Inc., plan to lease INMARSAT capacity for this purpose.[158] A recent court decision concerning the legality of the Commission's Rules and policies leading to the establishment of AMSC has added some uncertainty to the company's future,[159] although it is likely that AMSC will continue to exist, possibly with additional participants.

Qualcomm, Inc. of San Diego, California, has provided mobile satellite

---

152. *See* INMARSAT Convention, *supra* note 108 (establishing INMARSAT). The INMARSAT Convention was amended in 1985 to allow INMARSAT to provide aeronautical mobile satellite services in addition to maritime mobile satellite service, which the organization initially was created to provide. The amendment entered into force October 13, 1989. At the organization's Sixth Extraordinary General Assembly Meeting, January 15-17, 1989, the INMARSAT Convention was amended again to allow for the provision of land mobile satellite services.
153. 47 U.S.C. § 752 (1988).
154. The companies that make up American Mobile Satellite Corporation are Hughes Communications Mobile Satellite Services, Inc., MCCA American Satellite Service Corporation, McCaw Space Technologies, Inc., Mobile Satellite Corporation, Satellite Mobile Telephone Company, Skylink Corporation and Transit Communications, Inc.
155. *Amendment of Parts 2, 22 and 25 of the Commission's Rules to Allocate Spectrum for, and to Establish Other Rules and Policies Pertaining to, the Use of Radio Frequencies in a Land Mobile Satellite Service for the Provision of Various Common Carrier Services,* 4 F.C.C. Rcd. 6041 (1989) [hereinafter cited as AMSC Authorization Order]. *See* J.D. Thomas, *International Aspects of Mobile Satellite Services,* 43 FED. COM. L. J. 45 (1990) (discussing American Mobile Satellite Corporation)
156. AMSC was authorized to provide *generic* mobile satellite services (including land, maritime and aeronautical). In addition, AMSC was permitted to provide certain fixed satellite services, such as rural telephone. *See* AMSC Authorization Order, *supra* note 155, at 6047 (describing the kinds of services AMSC has been authorized to provide).
157. *Communications Satellite Corporation and American Mobile Satellite Corporation Request for Interim Waiver of Section 2.106 of the Commission's Rules to Provide AMSS(R) and MSS Services in the Maritime Bands 1530-1544 MHz and 1626.5-1645.5 MHz,* 5 F.C.C. Rcd 4117 (1990). AMSC must obtain INMARSAT satellite services through Comsat since Comsat is the only entity which can access INMARSAT, *see* 47 U.S.C. § 752 (1988) (providing Comsat with monopoly access with respect to maritime mobile services) and *Provision of Aeronautical Services Via the INMARSAT System,* 4 F.C.C. Rcd 6072 (1989) (concerning aeronautical mobile satellite services directly through INMARSAT)

service, using GTE Spacenet Corporation's domestic fixed satellite capacity, since 1989.[160] Geostar Messaging Corporation, a subsidiary of Geostar Corporation, which had applied to provide a new digital mobile satellite service,[161] no longer is a potential, future contender in light of the bankruptcy of the parent company. For a description of low-Earth orbit mobile satellite systems applications currently on file with the FCC, see Chapter 3.1.6.

FREQUENCIES. The Commission has assigned the following frequency band for generic mobile satellite service for use by AMSC (see Chapter 5.1.2. concerning INMARSAT's operating frequencies):

Space to Earth	*Earth to Space*
1545.0 - 1549.5 MHz	11.7 - 11.8 GHz*
1646.5 - 1651.0 MHz	14.0 - 14.1 GHz*
1549.5 - 1558.5 MHz	10.70 - 10.95 GHz**
	13.00 - 13.15 GHz**
	13.20 - 13.25 GHz**[162]

*) at 101 degrees West longitude

**) at 62 and 139 degrees West longitude

On March 5, 1990, the Commission proposed allocating an additional 33 MHz spectrum for generic mobile satellite service in the bands: 1530-1544 MHz (space-to-Earth) and 1626.5-1645.5 MHz (Earth-to-space).[163] In part, the Commission was responding to a petition for rulemaking filed by Geostar Messaging Corporation on July 16, 1986, requesting that spectrum be allocated for a new digital land mobile satellite service that company had applied to provide.[164] If these bands are, in fact, allocated, an opportunity is presented for potential new mobile satellite service providers to apply for the use of these bands.[165]

HISTORY OF THE AMSC AUTHORIZATION. The regulatory history of

158. Also these companies must obtain satellite capacity from Comsat. *See supra* note 157 (concerning legal authority for Comsat's monopoly access).

159. *See Aeronautical Radio, Inc. v. FCC, supra* note 83 (providing that the Commission's criteria and procedure for establishing AMSC was improper).

160. *Qualcomm Inc.*, 4 F.C.C. Rcd 1543 (1989).

161. Geostar Messaging Corporation proposed to use the 1530-1544 and 1626.5-1645.5. MHz bands, and requested a domestic allocation to this effect. *See Amendment of Part 2 of the Commission's Rules to Allocate Spectrum for mobile satellite Services in the 1530-1544 MHz and 1626.5-1645.5 MHz Bands,* 5 F.C.C. Rcd. 1255 (1990) [hereinafter cited as Geostar Messaging Rulemaking] (discussing Geostar's application).

the AMSC dates back to 1984, when a *Notice of Proposed Rulemaking*[166] (hereinafter Notice) was adopted in response to a petition for rulemaking by the National Aeronautics and Space Administration (NASA),[167] as well as subsequent mobile satellite systems applications. The Notice proposed frequency allocations and licensing policies for mobile satellite-service. It generated enormous interest due to the great commercial potential perceived to be inherent in mobile satellite technology. This technology was touted by some as allowing for the first time a truly universal, uninterrupted "cellular" telephone service. Twelve companies filed applications to establish mobile satellite systems to exploit this new technology.[168]

In 1986, the Commission issued a *Report and Order,* (Allocation Order)[169] allocating frequencies for mobile satellite service. Later that

---

162. AMSC Authorization Order, *supra* note 155. In the 1545.0-1549.5 and 1646.5-1651.0 MHz bands, safety-related aeronautical mobile satellite service (AMSS(R)) will have primary status and generic mobile satellite service, including non-safety aeronautical services (air passenger communications), will have secondary status. All mobile satellite traffic will have co-primary status in the 1549.5-1558.5 MHz bands. However, AMSS(R) will have priority and real time preemptive access in the entire band, which means that all mobile satellite services must yield access to the spectrum on an "as needed" basis to AMSS(R). Services in co-primary status have an equal right to use the spectrum, whereas a service in a secondary allocation cannot cause, or claim protection from, interference to or from a service with primary status. A controversy developed early in the mobile satellite proceeding concerning the use for non-safety related communications purposes of spectrum allocated to AMSS(R). The International Telecommunication Union (ITU) Radio Regulations, Final Acts, World Administrative Radio Conference, Geneva, 1979 [hereinafter cited as WARC-79], art. 50, No. 3630, prohibit other than safety-related communications in such bands. The United States is a party to the International Radio Regulations. U.S. frequency allocations in the mobile satellite service are not identical to allocations set forth in the ITU Radio Regulations, Table of Frequency Allocations. Non-conforming national allocations are permitted, provided that harmful interference does not result, ITU Radio Regulations (WARC-79), art. 6, No. 342. While the Commission's Rules make allocations to a *generic* mobile satellite service, the ITU Radio Regulations provide *separate* allocations to land, maritime and aeronautical mobile satellite services. The U.S. believes generic allocations in the mobile satellite service will facilitate the commercial implementation of this service. The U.S. proposed generic allocations at the ITU World Administrative Radio Conference on Mobile Radio Services, Geneva, 1987. The U.S. proposal was rejected. Consequently, the U.S. took the following reservation:

> The United States, in view of the fact that the Conference has unduly restricted allocations for mobile satellite services in the bands 1530-1559 MHz and 1626.5-1660.5 MHz, states its intention to utilize these bands in the way most appropriate to safety, its particular mobile satellite services requirements recognizing the priority of AMSS(R) and maritime safety requirements.

Statement No. 58, *Final Protocol,* World Administrative Radio Conference on Mobile Services, Geneva, 1987.

year, a *Second Report and Order* (Licensing Order)[170] was issued, establishing general licensing policies and paving the way for the authorization of mobile satellite applications. The Licensing Order provided that only one mobile satellite system should be licensed to use the entire bandwidth of frequencies allocated for mobile satellite service, and that the license would be granted to a consortium comprising all qualified and willing applicants for mobile satellite systems. To demonstrate qualification and willingness, each applicant was required to 1) place $5 million in an escrow account as a contribution towards the consortium, and 2) join with the other applicants in developing an ownership structure for the consortium, as well as a technical proposal for the satellite system.[171]

Eight companies contributed $5 million, formed a consortium known as American Mobile Satellite Corporation (AMSC), and submitted a joint application to the Commission. The application was granted on August 4, 1989.[172] AMSC was authorized to provide an unspecified variety of

---

163. Geostar Messaging Rulemaking, *supra* note 161.
164. The service proposed by Geostar Messaging Corporation was for low bit rate data and voice communications.
165. Geostar Messaging Rulemaking, *supra* note 61, at 1258.
166. *Amendment of Parts 2, 22, and 25 of the Commission's Rules to Allocate Spectrum for, and Establish Other Rules and Policies Pertaining to, the Use of Radio Frequencies in a Land Mobile Satellite Service for the Provision of Various Common Carrier Services,* 50 Fed. Reg. 8149 (1985) [hereinafter cited as Mobile Satellite Notice].
167. As part of an advanced telecommunications satellite technology research program, NASA had taken an interest in the development of a mobile satellite communications system in collaboration with Canada. Initially, NASA proposed to use the UHF frequency band, which engendered much opposition (especially from cellular telephone operators, which wanted to be able to expand their operations into the UHF bands in question) and served to delay the commercial implementation of mobile satellite service in the United States. In the mid-1980s, former NASA engineers who had participated in the NASA mobile satellite research program left that agency to form private mobile satellite companies. *See supra* note 154 (listing the companies, some of which were formed by former NASA engineers).
168. *See supra* note 154 (listing these companies).
169. *Amendment of Parts 2, 22 and 25 of the Commission's Rules to Allocate Spectrum for, and Establish Other Rules and Policies Pertaining to, the Use of Radio Frequencies in a Land Mobile Satellite Service for the Provision of Various Common Carrier Services,* 2 F.C.C. Rcd 1825 (1986) [hereinafter cited as Mobile Satellite Allocation Order].
170. *Amendment of Parts 2, 22 and 25 of the Commission's Rules to Allocate Spectrum for, and to Establish Other Rules and Policies Pertaining to, the Use of Radio Frequencies in a Land Mobile Satellite Service for the Provision of Various Common Carrier Services,* 2 F.C.C. Rcd 485 (1987) [hereinafter cited as Mobile Satellite Licensing Order].
171. *Id.*
172. AMSS Authorization Order, *supra* note 155.

mobile satellite services on a common carrier basis, and was permitted to use the entire bandwidth then allocated by the Commission for domestic mobile satellite service in the U.S. The Commission noted that, as a practical matter, it was precluded from authorizing additional mobile satellite systems in those frequency bands.[173] Three companies, Global Land Mobile Satellite, Inc., Globesat Express and Mobile Satellite Service, Inc., had their applications dismissed for failure to contribute $5 million to the consortium.

In the meantime, on April 14, 1987, Aeronautical Radio, Inc. (ARINC), a provider of communications services for airlines, which did not wish to become part of the mobile satellite consortium, filed an application to construct and operate a global *aeronautical* mobile communications satellite system to provide a variety of safety-related, as well as business and passenger, communications services for airlines. ARINC contemplated a constellation of six satellites operating in the frequency bands 1548-1555 MHz, 1649-1656.5 MHz, 5200-5208 MHz, 6450-6458 MHz, 1544-1555 MHz and 1645.5-1646.5. To justify the frequency allocations, ARINC presented its service as an AMSS(R)-type service. The Commission dismissed ARINC's application, however, on the grounds that 1) it conflicted with the Commission's spectrum allocation policies adopted in the Licensing Order, 2) passenger communications services could not be provided within the scope of AMSS(R) and 3) ARINC was not financially qualified to construct and operate the proposed system.[174]

ARINC and the three companies whose applications had been dismissed for failure to contribute $5 million to the mobile satellite consortium (Global Land Mobile Satellite, Globesat Express and Mobile Satellite Service) appealed the Commission's decisions on April 16, 1990, challenging the dismissal of their applications. Albeit for different reasons, ARINC, as well as Global, Globesat and Mobile, claimed that the Commission's Rules were arbitrary and capricious, and that the Commission had violated its statutory obligations by failing to hold comparative hearings when faced with mutually exclusive applications.[175] *Aeronautical Radio, Inc.* v. *Federal Communications Commission*[176] was decided on March 19, 1991. The court denied ARINC's appeal, but reversed the dismissals of Global's, Globesat's and Mobile's applications. In the case of the latter three companies, the court noted that "the Commission has not provided an adequate justification for its abandonment of the hearing approach..."[177] By ruling invalid the Commission's Rules that led to the

173. *Id.*, at 6048.

174. *Aeronautical Radio, Inc.*, 2 F.C.C. Rcd 5990 (1987) [hereinafter cited as Arinc Dismissal Order], *recon denied*, 4 F.C.C. Rcd 6067 (1989), *aff'd. Aeronautical Radio, Inc. v. FCC, supra* note 83.

175. Under *Ashbacker Radio Corp. v. FCC*, 326 U.S. 327 (1945), applications that are mutually exclusive cannot be dismissed without a hearing. *See infra* note 362 and accompanying text (describing mutual exclusivity).

176. 928 F.2d 428 (1991).

establishment of American Mobile Satellite Corporation, the court added some uncertainty to the future of the consortium and mobile satellite service in the United States in the near future. It is likely that a solution will be found whereby AMSC will be able to continue to exist, possibly with the participation also of Globesat Express, Global Land Mobile Satellite and Mobile Satellite Service. The Commission recently issued a tentative decision in reaction to the court's remand order allowing for the consortium to continue.

3.1.6. Non-Geostationary Satellites for Mobile Communications and Radiodetermination Satellite Services

At present, half a dozen or so satellite applications are pending before the FCC for low-Earth orbit satellite systems intended for mobile and radiodetermination satellite services. The Commission has separated the low-Earth orbit satellite applications into two groups, based on the operating frequencies sought by the applicants. One group of applicants contemplates the use of the 148-149 MHz band[178] for up-link transmissions and the 137-138 MHz band for down-link transmissions. This group includes Orbital Communications Corporation of Fairfax, Virginia, Starsys, Inc. of Washington, D.C., LEOSAT Corporation also of Washington, D.C., and Volunteers in Technical Assistance (VITA) of Arlington, Virginia. The other group proposes to use various frequencies above 1 GHz, including the 1610-1626.5 MHz band, currently allocated for radiodetermination satellite service. This group includes Motorola Satellite Communications, Inc. of Chandler, Arizona,[179] Ellipsat Corporation of Washington, D.C.,[180] Constellation Communications, Inc. of Herndon, Virginia,[181] Loral Qualcomm Satellite Services, Inc. of Palo Alto, California (the company was formed by Space Systems/Loral Corporation and Qualcomm, Inc.) and TRW, also of California.

For example, Starsys is proposing a constellation of twenty-four satellites distributed randomly in circular orbits at between fifty and sixty degree inclinations at an altitude of 1300 km.[182] The system is referred to

---

177. *Id.*
178. However, Starsys, Inc. requests the use of the 148.0-149.411 MHz band in the event the use of non-spread spectrum techniques is required by the FCC, *Starsys, Inc.,* 5 F.C.C. Rcd 4660 (1990). *See supra* note 90 (explaining the meaning of spread spectrum techniques). In this decision, the Commission accepted Starsys' application for filing
179. The company is a wholly owned subsidiary of Motorola, Inc. of Schaumburg, Illinois.
180. Ellipsat Corporation is an entrepreneurial start-up company.
181. Microspace International, Inc. of Herndon, Virginia, (*see* Chapter 7.1.) holds a substantial investment share in Constellation Communications, Inc. Both are entrepreneurial start-up companies.
182. *Starsys, Inc.* Application to the FCC, File No. 33-DSS-P-90, May 4, 1990 [hereinafter cited as Starsys Application], Executive Summary, at 2.

as "STARNET." The satellites will have five-year design lives.[183] Starsys claims that between ten and twenty million subscribers can be served through the STARNET system.[184] The company proposes to provide the following services: two-way non-voice messaging using hand-held calculator-size terminals and allowing for interconnection with the public-switched telephone network; position-determination anywhere in the world; emergency alert services for safety of life and property; environmental monitoring services to reduce pollution; mobile property and construction equipment management services for anti-theft purposes; automatic vehicle pollutant emission level monitoring; biosensor monitoring for telemedicine applications; home remote control; and judicial system locating service.[185]

Motorola Satellite Communications is proposing a constellation of seventy-seven satellites in seven polar orbits (with eleven satellites in each orbit) at an altitude of approximately 765 km.[186] The satellite system, referred to as "IRIDIUM," is intended to provide radiodetermination satellite services in the United States and two-way digital voice and data communications between portable hand-held units globally.[187] Interconnection with the public-switched network[188] is contemplated.[189] The voice component of the IRIDIUM system is similar to existing cellular telephone systems, except in reverse.[190] While in the case of cellular telephone systems, a static set of cells serves a large number of mobile units, IRIDIUM's cells will move at a speed of about 7.4 km per second while mobile units remain relatively still.[191] Inter-satellite links are proposed for the IRIDIUM system,[192] permitting international communications.[193] The feasibility of international communications through inter-satellite links will depend on agreements with foreign telecommunications administrations.[194]

The Commission has accepted for filing the applications of the above-

---

183. *Id.*
184. *Id.*
185. *Id.*, at 4.
186. *Motorola Satellite Communications, Inc.*, Application to the FCC, File Nos. 9-DSS-P-91, CSS-91-010, Dec. 3, 1990, Executive Summary [hereinafter cited as Motorola Application], at 2.
187. FCC Public Notice, Report No. DS-1068, *released* Apr. 1, 1991 [hereinafter cited as Motorola Acceptance for Filing] accepting for filing the application of Motorola Satellite Communications.
188. The public-switched network refers to the public telephone network, which is accessible by the general public through a telephone apparatus.
189. Motorola Application, *supra* note 186, at 2.
190. *Id.*
191. *Id.*
192. *Id.*
193. To a limited extent (limited by technical feasibility of inter-satellite links), Motorola Satellite Communications can provide international communications bypassing terrestrial public-switched networks.

mentioned companies and initiated pleading cycles involving comments and reply comments on the applications (see Chapter 3.2.8.).[195] Rulemakings and licensing proceedings will follow.[196] It is currently uncertain how the Commission will act on the applications. Much depends on frequency allocation decisions taken at the upcoming 1992 International Telecommunication Union (ITU) World Administrative Radio Conference (WARC-92) (see Chapter 4.2.).[197] The services proposed by the applicants cannot be provided consistent with current frequency allocations, and many applicants have asked the Commission to request allocations at the ITU conference that would make possible their proposed operations.[198] Most likely, compromises will be reached at WARC-92 which will provide sufficient allocations to pave the way for FCC authorizations of some, if not all, of the applicants.

For example, with regard to frequency allocations above 1 GHz, the United States position at WARC-92 will be to allocate the 1610-1626.5 MHz band co-equally to radiodetermination satellite service and mobile satellite service, and to upgrade radiodetermination satellite service to primary status. Today, the 1610-1626.5 MHz band is allocated to radiodetermination satellite service globally; the allocation is primary in the United States and, with a few exceptions, secondary elsewhere in the world. If the U.S. position prevails, or an acceptable compromise is reached, operations such as those proposed by Motorola will become possible. INMARSAT and Canada (which is planning a geostationary mobile satellite system), among others, oppose the U.S. position, claiming that they need the 1616.5-1626.5 MHz band for their mobile satellite services. These parties also seek the 1515-1525 MHz band as a companion up-link band. The low-Earth orbit applicants will provide down-links and up-links in the 1610-1626 MHz band. Although INMARSAT is not a member of the ITU (only nation States can be members) and, therefore, has observer status only, the organization still exerts considerable influence over the positions of its member States. See Chapter 4.1.

An additional quandary facing the FCC, with respect to applicants seeking authorizations in frequency bands above 1 GHz, is that their service proposals are not technically compatible. In other words, all of the

---

194. In order to provide international telecommunications services, Motorola Satellite Communications must first obtain operating agreements, *supra* note 131, with foreign telecommunications administration.

195. *See Starsys, Inc., supra* note 178, and Motorola Acceptance for Filing, *supra* note 187 (accepting these applications for filing).

196. *See* Chapter 3.2.8. (explaining the procedures for FCC processing of satellite applications).

197. Frequency allocations for satellite systems, such as those proposed by Motorola Satellite Communications and Starsys, are on the agenda for the upcoming World Administrative Radio Conference in 1992. *See* Chapter 4., Attachment A (transcribing the agenda).

198. *See e.g.* Starsys Application, *supra* note 182, at IV-3.

applications cannot be granted. As noted previously, the Commission generally favors multiple entry and, therefore, will seek to avoid a situation where only one of the applications can be granted. It is possible that the FCC will conduct comparative hearings although satellite applicants have never been subjected to comparative hearings. It also is possible that the Commission will impose stringent criteria, which would exclude some applicants. It is less likely that the Commission will require applicants to form a consortium as it did in the case of AMSC (Chapter 3.1.5.).

3.2. Licensing and Regulation of Private Commercial Telecommunications Satellites by the Federal Communications Commission

In order to build, launch and operate a telecommunications satellite in the United States, a construction permit, a launch authorization and an operating license first must be obtained from the United States Federal Communications Commission, an independent agency created by the United States Congress to regulate telecommunications, including radio communications (see Chapter 3.2.3.). Construction permits, launch authorizations and operating licenses are granted pursuant to the Communications Act of 1934, as amended.[199] The operative phrase for FCC authorization is the "public interest" (see Chapter 3.2.4.). To obtain any satellite authorization, a company must be found by the Commission to be legally, technically and financially qualified (see Chapter 3.2.5.). A written application must be submitted to the Commission, including the requisite filing fee (see Chapter 3.2.5.-3.2.7.). The Commission processes satellite applications, usually in groups, and grants them if it determines that the applicants are technically, financially and legally qualified and that the proposed service will serve the public interest (see Chapter 3.2.8.-3.2.10.). Construction permits and licenses may be modified (see Chapter 3.3.11.) and transferred (see Chapter 3.2.12.), subject to FCC approval. Companies whose applications for construction permits or licenses, or whose requests for modification or transfer of permits or licenses, have been turned down may resort to administrative or judicial review (see Chapter 3.2.13.).

3.2.1. FCC Functions and Composition

CREATION AND JURISDICTION. The Federal Communications Commission[200] is an independent[201] regulatory agency created by the Communications Act of 1934 to regulate[202] interstate and foreign

199. 47 U.S.C. §§ 151-613 (1988).

200. The FCC's predecessor was the Federal Radio Commission, established by the Radio Act of 1927. *See* B.Schwartz, *The Economic Regulation of Business and Industry: A Legislative History of U.S. Regulatory Agencies* (Vol. IV, 1973) (providing a legislative history of the Communications Act of 1934).

communications[203] by wire and radio.[204] The FCC assumed regulatory jurisdiction over satellites in the early 1970s, in accordance with its legislative mandate under the Communications Act to regulate "interstate and foreign communications . . . by radio,"[205] as well as "radio stations."[206] A satellite was found by the Commission to be a "radio station," as defined in the Communications Act,[207] and satellite telecommunications were considered communications by radio. Therefore, the Commission concluded that licensing and regulation of satellite operations were encompassed by its regulatory responsibility under the Communications Act.[208]

COMMISSIONERS. The Commission is composed of five Commissioners appointed by the President of the United States, with the advice and consent of the United States Senate.[209] One of the Commissioners is designated by the President as Chairman.[210] Only three of the five Commissioners may be members of the same political party.[211] Normally, one Commissioner is appointed or reappointed on a rotating basis each year for a term of five years,[212] and the terms are staggered to limit political control. The Commission is located at 1919 M Street, N.W., in Washington D.C. It meets at least once a month and its meetings generally are open to the public. Several Washington, D.C. law firms that have substantial com-

---

201. *See* H. Shooshan and E. Krasnow, *Congress and the Federal Communications Commission: Continuing the Contest for Power,* COM. & ENTERTAINMENT L. J., 619, 620 (1987) (discussing how the Congress over the last decade has taken a more active role in overseeing and exerting control over the FCC).
202. The FCC is not a provider of telecommunications services or equipment. In the U.S., these functions are left entirely to private parties.
203. Compare the jurisdiction of the International Telecommunication Union (ITU), Chapter 4.1., and the definition of "telecommunication" in the ITU Radio Regulations. *See* Chapter 4.1., note 11 (providing a definition of "telecommunication").
204. Section 151 of the Communications Act of 1934, 47 U.S.C. § 151 (1988) provides that "[f]or the purpose of regulating interstate and foreign commerce in communication by wire and radio . . . there is hereby created a Commission to be known as the 'Federal Communications Commission,' which shall be constituted as hereinafter provided, and which shall execute and enforce the provisions of this Act." Title I of the Communications Act, 47 U.S.C. §§ 151-156 (1988), and Part 0 of its implementing regulations, entitled "Commission Organization," 47 C.F.R. Part 0 (1990), contain rules about the Commission's composition and functioning.
205. 47 U.S.C. § 152(a), *cf.* § 151 (1988).
206. 47 U.S.C. § 152(a) (1988).
207. *See* 47 U.S.C. § 153(k) (1988) (defining "[r]adio station").
208. *See* Domsat I, *supra* note 11, Appx. C, entitled "Memorandum on Legal Issues," at para. 3 (explaining why the Commission concluded that it had jurisdiction over communications satellites).
209. 47 U.S.C. § 154(a) (1988).
210. *Id.*
211. 47 U.S.C. § 154(b)(5) (1988).
212. 47 C.F.R. § 0.1 (1988).

munications practices have arranged for closed-circuit television reception in their offices of Commission meetings.

STAFF UNITS. The Commission maintains a large staff organized into eight offices and four bureaus.[213] The bureaus, in turn, are separated into divisions and branches. With the exception of direct broadcasting satellites, which are handled by the Mass Media Bureau, and amateur satellites, which are dealt with by the Private Radio Bureau, applications for all other types of satellites, so far, have been processed by the Common Carrier Bureau. For historical reasons, this apparent procedural idiosyncrasy exists even though most satellite operators today are not common carriers[214] and, strictly speaking, fall within the jurisdiction of the Private Radio Bureau. Since all the early satellite operators were common carriers, the Common Carrier Bureau, particularly its Satellite Radio Branch, gained substantial experience and expertise in licensing and regulating satellites and, therefore, the Common Carrier Bureau simply assumed jurisdiction also over so-called private carrier satellite operations. Within the Common Carrier Bureau, the Satellite Radio Branch processes applications (see Chapter 3.2.8.) and handles certain other regulatory matters for all types of telecommunications satellites, with the exception of the international fixed satellites, which fall within the jurisdiction of the International Facilities Division.[215] Of the other principal Commission staff units, the Office of Engineering and Technology deserves special mention since it is responsible for frequency allocations. Whenever a new or additional frequency allocation is requested for a particular satellite service, that Office administers the matter. However, as noted in Chapter 4., the Office of Engineering and Technology usually acts within the framework of the Table of Frequency Allocations appearing in Article 8 of the Radio Regulations adopted by the International Telecommunication Union. (See Chapter 4.1.).

DELEGATION. The Commission has broad discretion to delegate decision-making authority to its staff.[216] However, in particularly important matters, such as licensing of satellites or rulemakings, the Commission generally makes the decisions, itself. Administrative review of actions taken by delegated authority pursuant to Section 5(c) of the Communications Act[217] is always conducted by the Commission. The staff undertakes the preparatory work leading up to formal Commission decisions, and the Commission usually relies on the recommendation of its staff in technical as well as routine administrative matters. In less important cases, particu-

---

213. *See* 47 C.F.R. § 0.5 (1990) (listing the principal staff units). *See also* 47 U.S.C. § 155(b) (concerning organization of staff units).
214. *See infra* note 233 and accompanying text (explaining the common carrier concept).
215. Until 1980, the Satellite Radio Branch and International Facilities Division were united as the International Satellite Branch.
216. 47 U.S.C. § 155(c) (1988); 47 C.F.R. § 0.201 (1990).
217. 47 U.S.C. § 155(c)(4) (1988).

larly when significant policy issues are not involved, decision-making authority is often delegated to bureaus or branches. For example, decisions on requests for modification or assignment of a satellite construction permit or operating license at times are left to the Common Carrier Bureau.

DECISION AND POLICY MAKING. As is generally true of any regulatory agency, the FCC has the option of implementing its policies through rulemaking or adjudication. A rulemaking seeks to resolve more general, and often prospective, issues. It is the process for formulating, amending, or repealing a rule, which governs the treatment of all similarly situated applicants.[218] For example, the Commission generally will use a rulemaking to establish legal, technical and financial qualification requirements for satellite applicants. Adjudication is the procedure for determining individual or specific rights or duties, and culminates in an "order." For example, licensing of a satellite company is considered adjudication.

3.2.2. Petition for Rulemaking

If your client plans to provide a satellite service that does not fit within an already established FCC satellite service category, such as domestic fixed satellite service, radiodetermination satellite service, or direct broadcasting satellite service (see Chapter 3.1.), or if your client plans to use frequencies not previously used for the service it plans to provide, your client should petition the Commission for a rulemaking.[219] The petition should propose frequency allocations and/or the formulation of rules (criteria and procedures) pursuant to which your client's planned satellite operation can be authorized and should state why authorizations pursuant to such rules would serve the public interest. The Commission may respond with a Notice of Inquiry or a Notice of Proposed Rulemaking, initiating the rulemaking proceeding. The rulemaking proceeding may culminate in a Rule, paving the way for the Commission to authorize your client's planned satellite operation.

---

218. 5 U.S.C. § 551(5) (1988).

219. Rulemaking proceedings are commenced by the Commission either on its own initiative, or on the basis of a petition for rulemaking. 47 C.F.R. § 1.411 (1990). Any interested person may petition for rulemaking. 47 C.F.R. § 1.401(a) (1990). Two alternative procedures exist for rulemaking under the Administrative Procedure Act: the "informal" and the "formal." The informal procedure, requires that 1) a notice of proposed rulemaking be published, 2) an opportunity be given for interested parties to submit comments, and 3) the final rule include a concise statement of basis and purpose. 5 U.S.C. § 553 (1988). On the other hand, the formal procedure requires a hearing with an examiner and cross-examination. 5 U.S.C. §§ 556-157 (1988). All rulemakings concerning satellites have been of the informal kind. In the event a final Rule is adopted, the court has required that the Rule be a "logical outgrowth" of its rulemaking proposal. *United Steel Workers of America v. Marshall,* 647 F.2d 1189, 1221 (D.C. Cir. 1980), *cert. denied* 452 U.S. 913 (1981).

3.2.3. Requirement for FCC Authorizations

Before your client can construct, launch, or operate a telecommunications satellite, it must first apply for and receive from the Commission a construction permit, a launch authorization and an operating license. These authorization requirements apply equally to all commercial telecommunications satellites, including domestic fixed satellites,[220] radiodetermination satellites,[221] direct broadcasting satellites,[222] mobile satellites,[223] international fixed satellites ("separate systems")[224] and low-Earth orbit mobile satellites,[225] among other non-established categories.

It is important to note that an FCC launch authorization does not confer any right on your client to launch or operate a launch vehicle; it merely allows for your client's satellite to be launched on a U.S. or foreign launch vehicle of its choice, subject, of course, to legal and policy restrictions. See Chapter 7.1., describing launch vehicle options. If your client's satellite is being launched on a launch vehicle operated by a private U.S. company, then that company must apply for and receive a launch license from the Department of Transportation's Office of Commercial Space Transportation, pursuant to the Commercial Space Launch Act of 1984, as amended.[226]

CONSTRUCTION PERMIT. Before your client can obtain a license to operate the satellite, it must have secured a permit to build the satellite. The Communications Act provides that "[n]o license shall be issued . . . for the operation of any station, unless a permit for construction has been granted by the Commission."[227] The rationale behind the requirement for a construction permit is that it precludes a situation where the Commission is presented with a *fait accompli,* i.e., an already constructed radio station (satellite), for which the Commission would have difficulty denying

---

220. *See supra* note 5 and accompanying text (defining domestic fixed satellite service).
221. *See supra* note 46 and accompanying text (defining direct broadcasting satellite service).
222. *See supra* notes 76 and 77 and accompanying text (defining radiodetermination satellite service).
223. *See supra* notes 147-50 and accompanying text (defining mobile satellite service).
224. *See supra* note 96 and accompanying text, as well as note 1 (defining separate systems).
225. *See* Chapter 3.1.6 (describing low-Earth orbit mobile satellite systems for which FCC authorizations are being sought). This is a new service category not previously authorized by the FCC. Another new service is referred to as digital radio broadcasting satellite service. On May 18, 1990, Satellite CD Radio, Inc. of Washington, D.C., requested authorization to construct, launch and operate two geostationary satellites to provide nation-wide digital, CD quality radio services in the 1470-1530 MHz band.
226. 49 U.S.C. §§ 2601-2623 (1988).
227. 47 U.S.C. § 319(a) (1988).

an operating license because of the amount invested in the construction.

Your client can apply to have the construction permit requirement waived.[228] A waiver should be considered if your client wishes to proceed rapidly toward the implementation of a satellite project, for example, if a "window" of business opportunity may otherwise close.[229] In practice, the Commission is unlikely to grant a waiver to begin construction of the satellite unless it is reasonably certain that it later will grant an operating license. If the Commission does grant a waiver, however, it generally specifies that the construction will take place at the risk of the permittee, in the event the Commission should decide not to grant a license.

OPERATING LICENSE. The Communications Act of 1934 provides that "[n]o person shall use or operate any apparatus for the transmission of energy or communications or signals by radio . . . except under and in accordance with this Act and with a license . . . ."[230] Because a telecommunications satellite is an apparatus for the transmission of communications signals by radio, your client will require a license to operate it.

LAUNCH AUTHORIZATION. Naturally, the Communications Act of 1934 does not mention launch authorization, since telecommunications satellites were not contemplated by the drafters of that Act. The requirement for a launch authorization is stipulated, however, in the Commission's Rules, which state that with regard to all satellites, "a launch authorization must be applied for and granted before a space station may be launched and operated in orbit."[231] The term "space station" sometimes is used by the Commission and usually is synonymous with "satellite."

COMMON CARRIER CERTIFICATION. If your client plans to operate as a common carrier, certification as a common carrier may be necessary pursuant to Section 214 of the Communications Act,[232] in addition to the authorizations discussed above. A common carrier is one which holds

---

228. 47 U.S.C. § 319(d) (1988).

229. For example, Starsys, Inc., in its May 4, 1990, application to establish a low-Earth orbit mobile satellite system (described in Chapter 3.1.6.) requested a waiver pursuant to Section 319(d), 47 U.S.C. § 319(d), to begin construction. Starsys Application, *supra* note 182, Executive Summary, at 8.

230. 47 U.S.C. § 301 (1988).

231. 47 C.F.R. § 25.113 (d) (1990).

232. 47 U.S.C. § 214 (1988). This section provides that "[n]o [common carrier] shall undertake the construction of a new line or of an extension of any line, or shall acquire or operate any line, or extension thereof, or shall engage in transmission over or by means of such additional or extended line, unless and until there shall first have been obtained from the Commission a certificate that the present and future public convenience and necessity [so] require . . . ." *Id.* However, Section 214 certification is not required for common carriers that have been forborne, *i.e.*, exempted. *See infra* note 235 (explaining the meaning of forbearance in this context). Nevertheless, an application for a satellite operating license should state whether the applicant proposes to be a common carrier.

itself out to the public for hire on non-discriminatory terms.[233] The significance of common carrier certification is that, in principle, service regulation under Title II of the Communications Act applies. Title II controls the terms and conditions under which service may be provided to customers and requires tariff filings.[234] Most satellite common carriers have been exempted from Title II regulation, however, based on considerations of market economics.[235]

ALTERNATIVE CLASSIFICATIONS. Satellite operators that are not common carriers may be classified as "private carriers," "broadcasters," or "non-broadcasters,"[236] depending on the nature of the services they provide. Private carriers, or non-common carriers as they often are called, offer service to selected customers on individualized, negotiated terms and are not subject to common carrier regulation.[237] A transponder ven-

---

233. 47 U.S.C. § 153(h) (1988), defining common carrier as "any person engaged as a common carrier for hire, in interstate or foreign communication by wire or radio or in interstate or foreign radio transmission of energy . . . ." In *National Association of Regulatory Utility Commissioners v. FCC,* 525 F.2d 630, 641 (D.C. Cir. 1976) *cert. denied,* 425 U.S. 992 (1976), the court embellished upon the definition as follows:

> Implicit in the common carrier concept is that the carrier undertakes to carry for all people indifferently.'. . . . This does not mean a given carrier's service must practically be available to the entire public. One may be a common carrier though the nature of the service rendered is sufficiently specialized as to be of possible use to only a fraction of the total population. And business may be turned away either because it is not of the type normally accepted or because the carrier's capacity has been exhausted. But a carrier will *not* be a common carrier where its practice is to make individualized decisions, in particular cases, whether and on what terms to deal.

The court established a two-part test for determining whether a service is provided on a common carrier basis: 1) whether there is or should be a legal compulsion to serve the public indiscriminately; and 2) whether there are reasons inherent in the nature of the service that would require indiscriminate service to the public. *Id.,* at 642.

234. *See* 47 U.S.C. §§ 201-203 (1988) (concerning charges, discriminatory practices and tariffs).

235. Based on their power in the marketplace, including the ability to sustain prices above cost, the Commission distinguishes between "dominant" and "non-dominant" common carriers. Non-dominant carriers either are subject to streamlined Title II regulation or have been forborne, *i.e.,* exempted from Title II regulation. Dominant carriers are subject to the full panoply of Title II regulations. With the exception of AT&T, which is still considered dominant, all satellite common carriers are now considered non-dominant. *See Policy and Rules Concerning Rates for Competitive Common Carrier Services and Facilities Authorizations Therefor,* First Report and Order, 85 F.C.C. 2d 1 (1980); Second Report and Order, 91 F.C.C. 2d 59 (1982); Fourth Report and Order, 95 F.C.C. 2d 554 (1983); Fifth Report and Order, 98 F.C.C. 2d 1191 (1984); and Sixth Report and Order, 99 F.C.C. 2d 1020 (1985); *MCI Telecommunications Corporation v. FCC,* 765 F.2d 1186 (D.C. Cir. 1985) (providing for deregulation of satellite and other common carriers).

dor is a typical example of a private carrier. Broadcasters are those who or which engage in the "dissemination of radiocommunication intended to be received by the public, directly or by intermediary relay stations."[238] Based on the transmission and reception technologies employed, the Commission in *Video Subscription Service*[239] determined that direct broadcasting satellite service provided on a subscription basis is not "broadcasting."[240] Consequently, an entity engaged in such activity is a non-broadcaster. Broadcasters are subject to regulation under the Communications Act, primarily with respect to the content of their programming and access to the broadcasting facilities.[241]

Not all of these service classifications are available to each type of satellite operator. fixed satellite operators have the option of serving their customers on a common carrier basis; selling or leasing transponders on individualized, negotiated terms, in which case they are private carriers; or using their fixed satellites in a quasi broadcasting mode (see Chapter 3.1.2.), in which case they are broadcasters.[242] Direct broadcasting satellite operators have the option of being classified as common carriers, private carriers, broadcasters or non-broadcasters, or some combination thereof.[243] Radiodetermination satellite operators may operate as private carriers, although common carrier status probably is not precluded.[244]

236. The distinction between common carriers and broadcasters is fundamental to the Communications Act. *See* 47 U.S.C. § 153(h) (defining common carriers to exclude broadcasters). The Act is divided into Titles II and III, traditionally applying to common carriers and broadcasters, respectively. New technologies, such as satellites, have made the distinction somewhat obsolete since both Titles II and III sometimes apply. Private carriers are not defined in the Communications Act, nor are they subject to service regulation under Title II of the Act, although they do require a construction permit and operating license under Title III. Non-broadcasters also are not defined in the Act. *See infra* notes 238 and 239 and accompanying text (explaining the non-broadcaster concept).
237. *Id.*
238. 47 U.S.C. § 153(o) (1988).
239. 2 F.C.C. Rcd 1001 (1987).
240. *National Association of Better Broadcasting v. FCC,* 849 F.2d 665 (D.C. Cir. 1988) upheld this decision.
241. *National Association of Better Broadcasting v. FCC,* 849 F.2d 665 (D.C. Cir. 1988) upheld this decision.
242. *See Domestic fixed satellite Transponder Sales,* 90 F.C.C. 2d 1238 (1982) *aff'd sub nom, Wold Communications v. FCC,* 735 F.2d 1465 (D.C. Cir. 1984) (authorizing transponder sales). *See also Martin Marietta Communications Systems, Inc.,* 60 Rad. Reg.2d 779 (1986) (providing for routine licensing of transponder sales). A domestic fixed satellite operator engaging in "broadcasting," as defined in the Communications Act, will be classified as a broadcaster and subjected to broadcast regulation. *See United States Satellite Broadcasting, Inc. v. FCC,* 740 F.2d 1190 (D.C. Cir. 1984) (reversing the Commission's decision that a fixed satellite operator engaged in direct-to-home program distribution is not a broadcaster).

Separate systems operators are precluded from common carrier operations.[245] American Mobile Satellite Corporation, which was authorized as a *de facto* monopoly mobile satellite operator, is required to be a common carrier.[246]

WRITTEN APPLICATION. To obtain a satellite construction permit, a launch authorization and an operating license, your client must submit a written application to the FCC.[247] As a practical matter, construction permit, launch authorization and operating license, as well as common carrier certification, may be requested simultaneously in the same application. A typical opening statement of a telecommunications satellite application might say that "XYZ Satellite Corporation hereby requests authority pursuant to Sections 308, 809 and 319 of the Communications Act of 1934, as amended, to construct, launch and operate a satellite system consisting of . . . ." The content of the satellite application is discussed in Chapter 3.2.6.

3.2.4. The "Public Interest" Test

A STATUTORY REQUIREMENT. In order to receive an authorization from the Commission, your client must meet the "public interest" test. In other words, your client's application must demonstrate, and the Commission must find, that the service your client is proposing to provide will serve the public interest. The Communications Act specifies that the Commission "shall determine . . . whether the public interest, convenience, and necessity will be served by the granting of such application . . . ."[248] If the Commission makes a favorable determination, it "shall grant such appli-

---

243. DBS Report and Order, *supra* note 59, at 708-709, *aff'd in part National Association of Broadcasters v. FCC,* 740 F.2d 1190 (D.C. Cir. 1984). The court upheld the Commission's decision with respect to classifications of satellite service operators. However, it struck down the portion of the Commission's decision exempting customers of direct broadcasting satellite common carriers from broadcasting regulation. The court said that in such a relationship, someone must be the broadcaster. In *Video Subscription Services, supra* note 74, the Commission changed its policy concerning the criteria for determining whether a person satisfies the definition of "broadcasting." *National Association of Better Broadcasting v. FCC, supra* note 40, affirmed this decision. *Video Subscription Services,* 4 F.C.C. Rcd 4948 (1989) implemented the court's holding.
244. Radiodetermination Satellite Licensing Order, *supra* note 94, at para. 26.
245. Separate Systems Order, *supra* note 139; Separate Systems Reconsideration Order, *supra* note 97, at para. 7.
246. Mobile Satellite Licensing Order, *supra* note 170, at para. 34.
247. 47 U.S.C. § 308(a) (1988). *See* 47 C.F.R. § 25.116 (concerning amendments to the application).
248. 47 U.S.C. § 309(a) (1988). The phrase "public interest, convenience and necessity" has become an anachronism which often is referred to only as the "public interest."

cation."[249]

CRITERIA. The Commission has stated that the "basic touchstone" for deciding whether the public interest will be served is its mandate in Section 1 of the Communications Act to regulate "interstate . . . commerce in communication by wire and radio so as to make available, so far as possible, to all people of the United States a rapid, efficient, Nationwide . . . wire and radio communication service with adequate facilities at reasonable charges . . . ."[250] In practice, the Commission looks to see whether your client's proposed service will benefit the public, or some segment of the public (e.g., a particular user group), in the form of improved service, lower rates, increased service options, or innovative service offerings. More general considerations sometimes are factored in, as well, such as the national security interest of the United States and prospects for improvement in the U.S. trade balance.

EVALUATION. The public interest evaluation of your client's satellite application will differ, depending on whether the proposed service falls within an established FCC category (see Chapter 3.1.). If your client is applying within an established service category, it usually will meet the public interest test *ipso facto*. This is because the Commission will have determined during the rulemaking proceeding establishing the service class within which your client is applying that the particular category of service is in the public interest. On the other hand, if your client is proposing a new satellite service, or an established service in new frequency bands and the Commission has not previously considered the public interest in a rulemaking, the Commission will consider the public interest as a matter of first impression in the context of the application. Therefore, this application will receive closer-than-normal scrutiny.

PUBLIC INTEREST STATEMENT. Your client should, of course, demonstrate in its application that it meets the public interest standard.[251] A satellite application should always contain a public interest statement. Illustrative of the contents of a public interest statement are those appearing in the applications of International Satellite, Inc. (ISI) and Financial Satellite Corporation (FINANSAT). In 1983 and 1985, ISI and FINANSAT, respectively, applied for authority to construct, launch and operate satellites for the provision of customer-premise-to-customer-premise trans-Atlantic satellite service in competition with INTELSAT. These applicants, among others, were requesting authority in a new satellite service category, namely, the international fixed satellite service ("separate systems"). Excerpts from the ISI application provide that

> [t]he ability to provide a direct link by satellite from customer

---

249. *Id.*

250. 47 U.S.C. § 151 (1988). *See* Domsat I, *supra* note 11, at para. 20 (offering this statement).

251. The Commission has stated that it makes public interest determinations in the context of individual applications, Domsat I, *supra* note 11, at para. 20.

> location to customer location will substantially reduce the cost to wideband users since double hops or lengthy expensive landline extensions can be eliminated. Moreover, ISI believes that by offering space segment capacity with unique capability at competitive rates and on innovative terms, it will stimulate new regional satellite uses which would otherwise not be developed or would be much delayed in development. The ISI proposal also advances important U.S. goals with respect to trade in telecommunications services and helps to assure that an independent regional satellite system in the Atlantic region is of U.S. origin.
>
> ISI recognizes that there are special foreign policy dimensions to international satellite service. ISI intends to develop a market which INTELSAT has not in the past served and cannot serve using existing spacecraft or those now in the construction phase. . . . Finally, recognizing again the special responsibilities of the U.S. as reflected in U.S. foreign policy, ISI will make the equivalent of one transponder . . . available free of cost to the United Nations.[252]

FINANSAT's application provides in part that

> [t]he preceding section of this application demonstrates that FINANSAT's proposed satellite services will provide significant private operational, technical and economic benefits to its transponder purchasers and lessees. For example, grant of FINANSAT's application will result in the widespread distribution of inexpensive micro earth stations on customer premises, thus eliminating the need for less efficient and more expensive terrestrial facilities and providing overall cost savings to users. Operational reliability will be increased due to the fewer number of transmission links involved in international transmissions. Moreover, FINANSAT's proposal will result in improved transmission quality and the elimination of multiple terrestrial and international satellite hops required to access existing INTELSAT earth stations and satellites. In short, by allowing the purchase or lease of FINANSAT's transponders on a long-term basis, financial and business customers will be able to implement a wide array of private international communications networks specifically tailored to their requirements.[253]

ISI's and FINANSAT's applications subsequently were conditionally granted (see Chapter 3.1.4.). Neither of these companies has yet launched

---

252. *International Satellite, Inc.*, Application to the FCC, File No. CSS-83-004-P(LA) Aug. 12, 1983, at 7-8.

253. *Financial Satellite Corporation*, Application to the FCC, FCC File No. CSS-85-004-P(LA) May 17, 1985, at 32-33.

a satellite system, mainly because of difficulties in obtaining financing and "landing rights" in foreign countries.[254]

Below is an excerpt from the public interest statement contained in the application of Starsys, Inc., filed May 4, 1990. Starsys requested authorization for a low-Earth orbit multi-satellite system ("STARNET") for the purpose of two-way mobile communications and position-location (see Chapter 3.1.6.).[255] The Commission has never before considered or authorized such a satellite system. Starsys' public interest statement provides in part that

> [t]he STARNET system applied for herein will serve the public interest in several different and important ways. It will save lives, protect property, help safeguard the environment, and monitor persons on probation and parole. The system will also improve the efficiency of American business, especially in the transport sector, thereby enhancing American competitiveness in the global economy. The STARNET system will also serve the national interest in developing a free and open global market in telecommunications services. In so doing, Applicant's technology is also helping to provide an infrastructure for greater global economic integration."[256]

3.2.5. FCC Requirements for Applicant Qualifications and Satellite System Design

In addition to meeting the public interest test described in Chapter 3.2.4., your client must demonstrate in its satellite application that it satisfies the legal, financial and technical qualifications requirements prescribed by the Commission.[257] As part of the technical qualification requirement, your client must show that its proposed satellite system is consistent with FCC satellite design specifications.[258] Pursuant to the Communications Act, the Commission has the authority to "prescribe the qualifications of station operators . . . [c]lassify radio stations . . . [p]rescribe the nature of the service . . . [r]egulate the kind of apparatus to be used . . . [and] [a]ssign bands of frequencies . . . ."[259]

LEGAL QUALIFICATIONS. Legal qualifications primarily refer to the character and ownership of the applicant company, your client, and the people or organizations controlling it. The Commission will consider whether your client, or a person or entity controlling it, has been con-

---

254. "Landing rights" refer to the rights to transmit satellite signals to and/or from the territory of a foreign country and are conferred by operating agreements, *supra* note 131, with foreign telecommunications entities.

255. Starsys Application, *supra* note 182, at III-1.

256. *Id.*

257. 47 U.S.C. § 308(b) (1988).

258. *Id.*

259. 47 U.S.C. §§ 303(l)(1), (a), (b), (f), (e) (1988).

victed of any felony or found guilty by any court of unlawfully monopolizing or attempting to monopolize radio communications directly or indirectly, through the control of manufacture or sale of radio apparatus, exclusive traffic arrangement, or other unfair method of competition. Questions concerning the applicant's character are posed in FCC Form 430, entitled "Common Carrier and Satellite Radio Licensee Qualification Report," which must be completed and submitted with every satellite application (see Chapter 3.2.6.).

With regard to ownership, no foreign government or representative thereof may own a controlling interest in your client's company, since foreign governments and their representatives are prohibited from obtaining a radio (including satellite) license from the FCC.[260] This restriction applies equally to all types of satellite operators, including domestic fixed satellite, direct broadcasting satellite, radiodetermination satellite, separate systems and mobile satellite operators, regardless of whether they are common carriers, private carriers, broadcasters, or non-broadcasters.

Additional ownership restrictions apply if your client is classified as a common carrier or a broadcaster.[261] Broadcaster and common carrier licenses may not be granted to 1) aliens or representatives of aliens;[262] 2) foreign corporations;[263] 3) corporations of which any officer or director is an alien, or of which more than 20% of the capital stock is owned or voted by aliens or their representatives, a foreign government or its representatives, or by any foreign corporation;[264] and 4) corporations directly or indirectly controlled by a corporation where 25% of the directors are aliens, or 20% of the capital stock is owned or voted by aliens or their representatives, a foreign government or its representatives, or by a foreign corporation;[265] except that in the latter case, the Commission may in its discretion issue a license.[266]

Fixed satellite operators are subject to these alien ownership restric-

---

260. 47 U.S.C. § 310(a) (1988). *See Orion Satellite Corporation,* 5 F.C.C. Rcd. 4937 (1990) 6 F.C.C. Rcd 4201 (1991) (establishing that Orion's limited partnership arrangement involving foreign partners satisfies the requirements of this section). *See also Hughes Communications, Inc.,* 94 F.C.C. 2d 866 (1983) (permitting foreign ownership of satellite transponders).

261. 47 U.S.C. § 310(b) (1988). *See* R.W. Gavillet and J.M. Foehrkolb, *Structuring Foreign Investments in FCC Licensees Under Section 310(b) of the Communications Act,* 27 CAL. W.L. REV. 7 (1991) (discussing innovative solutions to foreign ownership problems).

262. 47 U.S.C. § 310(b)(1) (1988).

263. *Id.,*. § 310(b)(2).

264. 47 U.S.C. § 310(b)(3) (1988).

265. *Id.,* § 310(b)(4). Controlling interest appears to be viewed by the FCC as 50% or more. *See William S. Paley,* 1 FCC Rcd. 1025, 1026 (1986), *recon. denied,* 2 FCC Rcd. 2274 (1987), *aff'd. sub nom. Fairness in Media v. FCC,* 851 F.2d. 1500 (D.C. Cir. 1988), *cert. denied* 488 U.S. 293 (1988) (concerning controlling interest in transfer of control cases).

266. 47 U.S.C. § 310(b)(4) (1988).

tions only if they are classified as common carriers or broadcasters. Separate alien ownership rules are set forth in the Commission's Rules for direct satellite broadcasters,[267] but it appears that direct broadcasting satellite operators are subject to these restrictions only if they are classified as broadcasters or common carriers. Accordingly, a direct broadcasting satellite operator who is a private carrier or non-broadcaster, would not be subject to the restrictive alien ownership requirements discussed above. Radiodetermination satellite operators authorized to date have been private carriers and, therefore, not subject to additional alien ownership restrictions. Separate systems operators also are not subject to these restrictions since they are required to be private carriers.[268] American Mobile Satellite Corporation, the sole mobile satellite licensee, is subject

---

267. 47 C.F.R. § 100.11 (1990) provides that "[a]n authorization for operation of a station in the Direct Broadcast Satellite Service . . . shall not be granted to or held by any a) . . . alien or representative of any alien; b) . . . foreign government or the representative thereof; c) . . . corporation organized under the laws of any foreign government; d) . . . corporation of which any officer or director is an alien; e) . . . corporation of which more than one-fifth of the capital stock is owned of record or voted by aliens or their representatives or by a foreign government or representative thereof or by any corporation organized under the laws of a foreign country; f) . . . corporation directly or indirectly controlled by any other corporation of which any officer or more than one-fourth of the directors are aliens if the Commission finds that the public interest will be served by the refusal or revocation of such license; or g) . . . corporation directly or indirectly controlled by any other corporation of which more than one-fourth of the capital stock is owned of record or voted by aliens, their representative, or by a foreign government or representatives thereof, or by any corporation organized under the laws of a foreign country, if the Commission finds the public interest will be served by the refusal or revocation of such license." No distinction appears to have been made as to whether the licensee is a broadcaster. On the other hand, the alien ownership restrictions in the Communications Act apply only to broadcasters and common carriers. The Act overrides the FCC Rules.
With regard to *concentration* of ownership and *cross-ownership* of direct broadcasting satellite operations, the Commission did not restrict the number of channels that may be owned or controlled by any one entity, nor did it limit control and ownership of direct broadcast satellites by other media groups. DBS Report and Order, *supra* note 59, at 711-712. *See also Continental Satellite Corporation*, 4 F.C.C. Rcd 6292, 6299 (1989) (concluding that the involvement in direct broadcast satellite service by Tele-Communications, Inc. (TCI) through a subsidiary, Tempo Satellite, Inc., was not barred despite TCI's substantial cable system holdings).

268. In *Orion Satellite Corporation, supra* note 260, the Commission determined that international separate systems applicants are not subject to 47 U.S.C. § 310(b) alien ownership restrictions because they are private carriers, and because nothing in the Separate Systems Order, *supra* note 139, or the White Paper, *supra* note 130, indicates that stricter ownership requirements are warranted.

to the additional restrictions since it is required to be a common carrier.

FINANCIAL QUALIFICATIONS. Financial qualifications refer to your client's ability to secure sufficient funds to proceed with the construction, launch and operation of the proposed satellite system. Requirements for financial qualifications vary from one category of satellite service to the next. They are tightly drawn and narrowly interpreted for domestic fixed satellite applicants, and in varying degrees the requirements are more relaxed for applicants in other services.

Domestic fixed satellite applicants must demonstrate at the time of the application that they have "current financial ability" to meet 1) estimated costs of the proposed construction and/or launch of the satellite and related expenses and 2) estimated operating expenses for one year after launch of the proposed satellite.[269] The rationale behind this stringent financial requirement, which virtually precludes entrepreneurial start-up companies from obtaining a license in the domestic fixed satellite service, is to limit applicants in a service for which orbital locations and frequencies are scarce due to saturation.

Applicants in the radiodetermination satellite service, on the other hand, need only show financial preparedness to assume the costs and liabilities of constructing, launching and operating the satellite system. The Commission requires that "applicants [to] demonstrate that sufficient funds are *or will be* available to meet the cost of constructing, launching and operating the system for one year."[270] It justifies the more lenient financial standard by the fact that there is sufficient spectrum to accommodate several additional applicants, and the authorization of an applicant which is unable to finance the system will not preclude the granting of another application.

In the broadcasting satellite service, financial scrutiny is not applied at all, initially. Instead, applicants are granted conditional authorizations and required to proceed with "diligence" in constructing and launching their satellite systems.[271] To observe the "diligence" requirement, a holder of a conditional authorization must 1) begin construction, or complete contracting for construction, of the satellite within one year of the grant of the construction permit and 2) place the satellite in operation within six years of the grant of the construction permit.[272] The first due diligence requirement has been interpreted strictly;[273] the second requirement, more leniently.[274]

---

269. 47 C.F.R. § 25.140(b) (1990). *See also Licensing of Space Stations in the Domestic Fixed Satellite Service and Related Revisions of Part 25 of the Rules and Regulations,* 54 Rad. Reg.2d 577 (1983) [hereinafter cited as Two Degree Spacing Order] (adopting strict financial standards as FCC policy prior to codification).
270. Emphasis added. Radiodetermination Satellite Licensing Order, *supra* note 94, at para. 24.
271. 47 C.F.R. § 100.19(b) (1990).
272. *Id.*

International fixed satellite, or separate systems, applicants must meet a two-step financial qualifications test.[275] The first step merely requires a showing in the application of certain cost estimates and sources of funding.[276] Upon such showings, a conditional construction permit will be granted that does not allow for satellite construction to begin. Rather, it allows the holder to proceed with obtaining operating agreements with foreign authorities for transmissions to and/or from such countries. INTELSAT coordination also may begin at this stage (see Chapters 3.1.4. and 5.2.1.).

The second step of the financial qualifications test, which may begin before or after coordination with INTELSAT has been completed, and which must be completed within one year after the conditional permit is granted, requires a showing of current financial ability to meet the cost of construction, launch and one year of operation of the proposed satellite(s),[277] i.e., the same standard adopted for domestic fixed satellite applicants. Upon such a showing, construction of the satellite may begin. However, if at that time coordination with INTELSAT has not yet been completed, construction takes place at your client's own risk in the event that the Commission does not grant a license to operate the satellite system. Such a license will be granted only after the INTELSAT coordination has been completed.[278]

---

273. Permittees which have not contracted for construction within a year of the grant have had their authorizations cancelled. *United States Satellite Broadcasting Company, Inc.*, 3 F.C.C. Rcd 6858 (1988). *See RCA American Communications, Inc.*, 62 Rad Reg.2d 554 (1987) (cancelling authorizations of three direct broadcasting satellite permittees which did not meet the first due diligence test).

274. In granting extensions to United States Satellite Broadcasting Company, Inc. and Dominion Video Satellite, Inc., which were not able to meet the December 1988 deadline for having their satellites in operation, the Commission looked to the totality of the circumstances. It stated: "[t]he totality of circumstances — those efforts made and those not made, the difficulties encountered and those overcome, the rights of all parties, and the ultimate goal of service to the public — must be considered in making the determination in these cases," *United States Satellite Broadcasting Company, supra* note 273, at 6859. Extensions of authorizations to United States Satellite Broadcasting Company and Dominion Video satellite were justified, said the Commission, based on the "prevailing circumstances" and the fact that their failure to comply "reveals no lack of capability and commitment." *Id.*, at 6860.

275. Separate Systems Order, *supra* note 139, at para. 235.

276. The applicant must show 1) the estimated cost of construction and launch of the proposed satellite(s) and any other expenses, 2) the estimated expenses for a one-year operation of the proposed satellite(s) and 3) the source, or potential sources, of funding, as well as the identity of the financiers and letters of interest. *Id.*

277. Separate Systems Reconsideration Order, *supra* note 97, at para. 39.

278. *Id.*, at para. 8.

No general financial standard has been adopted for the mobile satellite service. In the case of American Mobile Satellite Corporation, a consortium whose formation was ordered by the Commission (see Chapter 3.1.5), each partner was required to contribute $5 million initially as seed money. The Court of Appeals (D.C. Cir.) reversed the Commission on this point, however, and said the a performance-based or other evidence of ability to meet the $5 million requirement should have sufficed (see Chapter 3.1.5.).

TECHNICAL QUALIFICATIONS. Technical qualifications concern the technical characteristics of the proposed satellite system, as well as the ability of the applicant to operate it. Your client must demonstrate in the satellite application that it meets the satellite design and performance requirements prescribed by the Commission for the proposed service and that it has or intends to hire technically qualified personnel.

The Commission has always applied a "minimalist" approach to technical regulation of satellite systems, affording satellite licensees maximum flexibility in designing their satellite systems and selecting the satellite services they wish to provide. The Commission imposes only such technical requirements as are required for consistency with the International Telecommunication Union's Radio Regulations (see Chapter 4.1.) and to achieve the Commission's own overarching regulatory goals, such as ensuring efficient use of the orbit and spectrum resource and fostering competition in the satellite service market. See Chapter 3.2.9.

Specific design and performance requirements vary from one kind of satellite service to the next. For example, as noted in Chapter 3.1., different frequency bands have been designated for each category of satellite services. Your client's application must show that the proposed satellite system will use the frequencies allocated for the satellite service in which your client intends to operate. Moreover, if your client is applying for a license in the domestic fixed satellite service, it must show that the proposed satellite is compatible with two-degree orbital spacing,[279] which requires certain satellite system design and operational measures to avoid harmful interference to other satellite operators.[280] Furthermore, if your client seeks to operate a radiodetermination satellite system, its application must demonstrate that the proposed satellite system is compatible

279. 47 C.F.R. § 25.140(a) (1990), referring to Two Degree Spacing Order, *supra* note 269.

280. Two Degree Spacing Order, *supra* note 269, at para. 69, note 67. Satellite systems must employ at least present state-of-the-art design. This means that they must be capable of full frequency reuse in each frequency band, as well as station-keeping tolerance of +/- 0.1 degree or better, *id.* Full frequency reuse refers to the capability of a satellite design to provide at least the same transmission capacity between equivalent Earth stations as a 4/6 GHz satellite with 24 transponders, with 36 MHz bandwidths and 8 Watt solid state amplifiers. At 12/14 GHz, equivalent characteristics would be 20 transponders with 48 MHz bandwidth and 20 Watt amplifiers, *id.*

with previously licensed radiodetermination satellite systems.[281] These are examples, only, and do not constitute an exhaustive list of technical design and performance standards.

3.2.6. Content of the Satellite Application

STATUTORY REQUIREMENT. The Communications Act provides that all applications for radio station (including satellite) licenses

> shall set forth such facts as the Commission by regulation may prescribe as to the citizenship, character, and financial, technical, and other qualifications of the applicant to operate the station; the ownership and location of the proposed station and of the stations, if any, with which it is proposed to communicate; the frequencies and the powers desired to be used; .... the purposes for which the station is to be used; and such other information as [the Commission] may require.[282]

FCC REGULATION. FCC regulations specify the information to be contained in an application for the satellite construction permit, launch authorization and/or operating license.[283] These regulations explicitly are made applicable to domestic fixed satellites, radiodetermination satellites, mobile satellites and international fixed satellites, i.e., the established FCC satellite categories, but apply equally to applications in non-established categories. Different and very general Rules apply to the content of applications for direct broadcasting satellite authorizations.[284] In practice, however, direct broadcasting satellite applications, to the extent practicable, also will conform to the requirements applicable to other satellite services, as described below.

MORE THAN ONE SATELLITE. If your client seeks authority for more than one satellite, it should file one comprehensive "systems application,"

---

281. 47 C.F.R. § 25.141(a), (f) (1990). The Commission adopted a baseline design, based on Geostar Corporation's satellite design, with which all radiodetermination satellite systems must be compatible (in order to allow multiple entry in this service). *See* Radiodetermination Satellite Notice, *supra* note 87, at para. 33 (proposing and describing the baseline design) and Radiodetermination Satellite Licensing Order, *supra* note 94, at paras. 8-9 (adopting and describing the baseline design).
282. 47 U.S.C. § 308(b) (1988).
283. 47 C.F.R. § 25.114 (1990), entitled "Applications for Space Station Authorizations." The requirements for information set forth in this section were modeled on those found in *Filing of Applications for New Space Stations in the Domestic Fixed Satellite Service*, 93 F.C.C. 2d 1260 (1983), Appx. B, [hereinafter cited as Domestic Fixed Satellite Processing Order]. The information requirements in the Domestic Fixed Satellite Processing Order applied only to domestic fixed satellites, but in practice applicants in other services also complied with them.
284. 47 C.F.R. § 100.13 (1990).

which describes in narrative and technical detail the entire satellite system, your client's legal, technical and financial qualifications, and why the proposed service will serve the public interest.[285] Separate applications should be filed for each satellite, stating the particulars of that satellite and associated ground equipment, and incorporating the systems application by reference.

CONSULT AN ENGINEER. Because of the technical nature of some of the information required in the satellite application, your client must consult an engineer. Several engineering firms and independent consultants, particularly in the Washington, D.C., area, have combined engineering and FCC regulatory expertise, and can assist your client in preparing the information required for the application. The attorney and engineer should work together to make sure that all the necessary technical information is provided and that statements made in all sections of the application are consistent.

APPLICATION OUTLINE. The Commission's Rules impose no particular form requirement for satellite applications. In other words, as long as your client's application contains the pertinent information and satisfies the Commission's basic requirements regarding paper size, margins, etc.,[286] it is free to organize the application in the manner it pleases. It is prudent, nevertheless, to follow an outline that parallels the sequence of the information requirements set forth in the Commission's Rules.[287] This has the advantage of presenting the Commission with a format with which it is familiar. Also, it is easier to check whether all the information requirements have been complied with. A suggested outline is set forth, below. (A transmittal letter should accompany the application).

SYSTEMS APPLICATION

I. BASIC INFORMATION ABOUT THE APPLICANT
The following information must be included (and can be provided briefly at the first page of the application):
Name, post office address and telephone number of the applicant.
Name, address and telephone number of the person(s), including counsel, to whom inquiries or correspondence should be directed.
Type of authorization requested (e.g. construction permit, launch authorization, operating license, or modification of an authorization.

II. SUMMARY OF APPLICATION

III. TABLE OF CONTENTS

---

285. *Id.*, § 25.114 .
286. *Id.*, § 1.49.
287. *Id.*, § 25.114.

IV. INTRODUCTION

Your client may want to include brief descriptions of the proposed satellite system and services (highlights), as well as its prior experience, if any. Reasons why its application should be granted also could be provided here.

V. THE APPLICANT

If your client has experience with satellite operations or related technologies, or if its corporate parent or affiliates have such experience, a special section describing this experience may be warranted.

VI. TECHNICAL INFORMATION: SATELLITE SYSTEM DESIGN AND OPERATIONS

The following information must be included:

OVERVIEW. General descriptions of overall system, facilities, operations and services.

FREQUENCIES. Radio frequencies and polarization plan (including beacon, telemetry, and telecommand functions), center frequency and polarization of transponders (both receiving and transmitting frequencies), emission designators and allocated bandwidth of emission, final amplifier output power (identify any net losses between output of final amplifier and input of antenna and specify the maximum EIRP for each antenna beam), identification of which antenna beams are connected or switchable to each transponder and TT&C function, receiving system noise temperature, the relationship between satellite receive antenna gain pattern and gain-in-temperature ratio and saturation flux density for each antenna beam (may be indicated on antenna gain plot), the gain of each transponder channel (between output of receiving antenna and input of transmitting antenna) including any adjustable gain step capabilities, and predicted receiver and transmitter channel filter response characteristics.

ORBITAL LOCATION. Orbital location, or locations if alternatives are proposed or requested for the satellite, the factors which support such an orbital assignment, the range of orbital locations from which adequate service can be provided, and the basis for determining that range of orbital locations, and a detailed explanation of all factors that would limit the orbital arc over which the satellite could adequately serve its expected users.

SATELLITE ANTENNA GAIN. Predicted satellite antenna gain contour(s) for each transmit and each receive antenna beam and nominal orbital location requested. These contour(s) should be plotted on an area map at 2 dB intervals down to 10 dB below the peak value of the parameter and at 5 dB intervals between 10 dB and 20 dB below the peak value, with the peak value and sense of polarization clearly specified.

EARTH STATIONS. Estimated number and geographic distribution of Earth stations, and description of proposed arrangements for access to the system between the premises of the users and the Earth stations for domestic fixed satellites only.

SERVICES. A description of the types of services to be provided, the estimated demand for these services, and the areas and entities to be served, including a description of the transmission characteristics and performance objectives for each type of proposed service, details of the link noise budget, typical or baseline Earth station parameters, modulation parameters and overall link performance analysis (including an analysis of the effect of each contributing noise and interference source). An estimate of transponder capacity under each of the proposed operating conditions must be supplied.

SERVICE TO ALASKA AND HAWAII. A detailed description of the capabilities, if any, of each proposed domestic satellite to provide service to Alaska, Hawaii, and/or Puerto Rico/Virgin Islands.

STATION KEEPING. Accuracy at which the orbital inclination, the antenna axis altitude, and longitudinal drift will be maintained.

POWER FLUX DENSITY. Calculation of power flux density levels within each coverage area and of the energy dispersal, if any, needed for compliance with Section 25.208 of the Commission's Rules, 47 C.F.R. 25.208 (1990), which specifies power flux density limits.

TT&C. Arrangements for tracking, telemetry and control.

THE SATELLITE. Physical characteristics of the satellite, including weight and dimensions, detailed mass (on the ground and in orbit) and power (beginning and end of life) budgets, and estimated operational lifetime and reliability of the satellite and the basis for that estimate.

LAUNCH VEHICLE. Launch vehicle and arrangements for procuring launch services.

> If your client is applying for additional or replacement satellites, its application also must include:
>
> HISTORY. Detailed information on the historical use of the system, transponder-by-transponder and on a year-by-year basis, together with a projection of the types and amounts of services, including restoral and protection requirements, for each additional satellite on a year-by-year and transponder-by-transponder basis over the estimated lifetime of the satellite(s).

Depending on the kind of satellite your client is proposing, additional requirements for technical information may apply as follows:

ADDITIONAL TECHNICAL INFORMATION. If your client is applying in the domestic fixed satellite service, additional requirements are set forth in Section 25.140 of the Commission's Rules, 47 C.F.R. §

25.140 (1990), which refers to *Licensing of Space Stations in the Domestic Fixed Satellite Service and Related Revisions of Part 25 of the Rules and Regulations,* 54 Rad. Reg. 2d 577 (1983), concerning compatibility with two-degree spacing. If your client is applying in the radiodetermination satellite service, the application must comply with additional requirements set forth in 47 C.F.R. § 25.141 (1990) concerning compatibility with other radiodetermination satellite systems. If your client is applying in the international fixed satellite service, requirements are set forth in *Establishment of Satellite Systems Providing International Communications,* 50 Fed. Reg. 42266 (Oct. 10, 1985), *recon.* 61 Rad. Reg. 2d 849 (1986), *further recon* 1 F.C.C. Rcd 439 (1986). If your client is applying in the direct broadcasting satellite service, see *Inquiry Into the Development of Regulatory Policy in Regard to Direct Broadcasting Satellites for the Period Following the 1983 Administrative Radio Conference,* 90 F.C.C. 2d 676 (1922), and 47 C.F.R. § 100.21 (1990).

TECHNICAL QUALIFICATIONS. The application also should state that your client is technically qualified to operate the satellite system, and why.

VII. FINANCIAL QUALIFICATIONS OF THE APPLICANT

Your client's application must contain the following information:

COSTS AND REVENUES. A detailed schedule of the estimated investment costs and operating costs for the proposed system by year, including annual depreciation, maintenance and operating costs, and the basis upon which such costs are calculated. Estimated annual revenue requirements should be provided in detail on a year-by-year basis over the estimated design lifetime of the satellite, including any pre-operational period.

FINANCIAL QUALIFICATIONS. Detailed information demonstrating the financial qualifications of the applicant to construct and launch the proposed satellite.

Because the financial qualification requirements vary from one service to another (see Chapter 3.2.5.), the information requirements vary accordingly. If your client is applying to operate a domestic-fixed satellite, it must provide the information required by Section 25.140(b)-(c) of the Commission's Rules, 47 C.F.R. § 25.140(b)-(c) (1990). If your client is applying to operate an international fixed satellite ("separate system"), it must provide the financial information required by *Establishment of Satellite Systems Providing International Communications,* 101 F.C.C. Rcd 1046 (1985), *recon.* 61 Rad. Reg. 2d 849 (1986), *further recon* 1 F.C.C. Rcd 439 (1986). If your client is applying to operate a radiodetermination satellite, its application must show that it meets the requirements specified in *Amendment to the Commission's Rules to Allocate Spectrum for, and to Establish Other Rules and Policies Pertaining to, Radiodetermination Satellite Service,* 54 Fed. Reg. 18444 (1986). If your client is applying in the direct broadcasting satellite service, see 47 C.F.R. § 100.19(b) (1990).

VII. LEGAL QUALIFICATIONS

Your client's application must include the following information:

OWNERSHIP. Description of the ownership of the applicant and information on its directors and officers, as necessary, to show compliance with Section 310(a) of the Communications Act, 47 U.S.C. § 310(a) (1988), concerning alien ownership.

SERVICE CLASSIFICATION. A clear and detailed statement of whether the satellite will be operated on a common carrier basis, or whether non-common carrier transactions are contemplated. If non-common carrier transactions are proposed, describe the nature of the transactions and specify the number of transponders to be offered on a non-common carrier basis.

PUBLIC INTEREST STATEMENT. A public interest statement in support of the grant.

MILESTONES. Dates by which satellite construction will be commenced and completed, launch date, and estimated date of placement into service of the satellite.

WAIVER. A waiver as required by Section 304 of the Communications Act, 47 U.S.C. § 304 (1988), with respect to "any claim to the use of any particular frequency or of the electromagnetic spectrum."

FORM 430. Form 430 (License Qualification Report).

VIII. ADDITIONAL CONSIDERATIONS

Depending on the type of satellite service your client is proposing, additional requirements may apply to the content of the satellite application. Such requirements would appear in Section 140 of the Commission's Rules, 47 C.F.R. § 140 (1990), for domestic fixed satellites; Section 141 of the Commission's Rules, 47 C.F.R. § 141 (1990), for radiodetermination satellites; *Establishment of Satellite Systems Providing International Communications,* 50 Fed. Reg. 42266 (Oct. 10, 1985), *recon.* 61 Rad. Reg. 2d 849 (1986), *further recon.* 1 F.C.C. Rcd 439 (1986), for international fixed satellites (separate systems); *Amendment of Parts 2, 22 and 25 of the Commission's Rules to Allocate Spectrum for, and Establish Rules and Policies Pertaining to, the Use of Radio Frequencies in a Land Mobile Satellite Service for the Provision of Various Common Carrier Services,* 2 F.C.C. Rcd 485 (1987), for mobile satellites; and Part 100 of the Commission's Rules, 47 C.F.R. Part 100 (1990), for direct broadcasting satellites.

APPENDICES

Typically, support materials in the form of detailed technical or financial information or showings appear in appendices, e.g., information for purposes of advance publication by the International Telecommunication Union (see Chapter 4.3.), letters of support from financial institutions and Annual Reports. Forms that must be filed with the application, such as Form 430, may be appended, as well.

INDIVIDUAL APPLICATION

If your client is requesting authorization for more than one satellite, it must submit individual applications for each satellite, as well. Only information pertaining to the particular satellite will have to be provided. Individual applications should incorporate the comprehensive systems application by reference.

3.2.7. Fees for Satellite Applications

Fees for satellite applications were introduced in 1987.[288] The following filing fees apply as of May 1990: $2,000.00 for each application for construction permit; $70,000.00 for each application for launch and operating authority; $500.00 for requests for temporary authority or waiver of prior construction permit; $5,000.00 for each application to modify or transfer a construction permit or operating license; and $1,000.00 for each amendment to the application.[289] The fees were introduced to make applicants pay for the processing of their own applications in order to ease the fiscal burden imposed on the FCC. An important side effect of the fees is that they deter speculative applications.[290] What these fees have led to in practice, however, is an increasing tendency to apply initially only for the satellite construction permit, rather than construction permit, launch authorization and operating license because of the cost associated with the latter.

3.2.8. Processing of the Satellite Application

The Commission recently codified Rules for processing of satellite applications,[291] and the reader may refer to them for further detail. A general description of the processing of satellite applications is provided here.

ACCEPTING THE APPLICATION FOR FILING. As soon as your client's satellite application has been received by the FCC, it will be routed to

---

288. *Establishment of a Fee Collection Program to Implement Provisions of the Consolidated Omnibus Budget Reconciliation Act of 1985,* 2 F.C.C. Rcd 947 (1987).

289. Federal Communications Commission, Common Carrier Services, Fee Filing Guide, at 26-27, available from the Federal Communications Commission's Satellite Radio Branch

290. As initially introduced, the fees were contemplated for large geostationary satellites. Controversies developed when the Commission sought to apply the same fees to each of dozens of small satellites in constellations recently proposed to the Commission. *See* Chapter 3.1.6. (describing these applications).

the appropriate bureau, division, or branch for initial review. If the application falls within an established FCC satellite service category, does not raise novel issues, and is otherwise complete, i.e., containing all the necessary information (see Chapter 3.2.6.), the Commission will issue a public notice announcing the "acceptance for filing" of your client's application. Essentially, this means that the Commission has conducted a cursory review of the application and agrees to consider it. An application proposing a satellite service which does not fit within an established FCC category, seeks to use a new frequency band, or otherwise raises novel issues, sometimes is "tendered for filing" before it is accepted for filing. This simply means that the Commission acknowledges receipt of the application. Acceptance of an application for filing can occur within a few weeks after submission of the application, but normally takes several months. An application that is not complete will be dismissed; but usually may be resubmitted in complete form.

COMMENTS AND OPPOSITIONS TO THE APPLICATION. After your client's application has been accepted for filing, a period of time will be allowed for comments and "petitions to deny." Typically, companies whose existing or planned satellite businesses stand to lose by a proposed new satellite system will file opposing comments (and even petitions to deny), while those that stand to gain, typically a customer, will submit comments in support. Initial comments or petitions to deny are due within thirty days after the public notice announcing the acceptance of the satellite application for filing. Ten days are allowed for responses to the initial comments, including "oppositions" to petitions to deny. A further five days is allowed for reply comments by the party that filed the original petition. The Commission may extend these deadlines, and is likely to do so, for example, when an application proposes a non-established service category.

CUT-OFF DATES: ADDITIONAL APPLICATIONS. If no other applications for satellites in a particular service (domestic fixed-, radiodetermination-, direct broadcasting-, *et cetera,* satellite service) are on file at the time your client's application is received, the Commission may invite other parties to file applications to be considered in conjunction with your client's application. It will establish a "cut-off" date for filing of such applications. Generally, the cut-off date is set 60-120 days following the issuance of the notice of invitation to file, depending on whether the satellite service for which authorization is sought is new or fits within an established category. At the expiration of the cut-off period, the Commission will accept for filing the additional applications, provided, of course, that they, too,

---

291. 47 C.F.R. § 25.150-6 (1990). While the processing rules are detailed and explanatory in some respects, they are lacking and ambiguous in others. For example, can the Commission return an application after it has been accepted for filing, *i.e.,* if the application later is found to be defective in accordance with the Commission's Rules Section 25.150, 47 C.F.R. § 25.150 (1990), does not answer that question.

are complete. The acceptance for filing of these applications triggers the same pleading cycle as described for your client's application, above. The practice of establishing cut-off dates allows the Commission to consider applications in groups, rather than disposing of them individually as they are received by the Commission.[292]

WHEN A RULEMAKING IS NECESSARY. Applications proposing new types of satellite services or the use of parts of the spectrum not previously used for the proposed service, usually are preceded or accompanied by a petition for rulemaking (see Chapter 3.2.2.). If the Commission chooses to initiate a rulemaking, it may postpone further action on the application, pending the completion of the rulemaking. A rulemaking begins with a "Notice of Inquiry" or a "Notice of Proposed Rulemaking" and may lead to the adoption of a Rule. It can take several years and may delay considerably the introduction of your client's satellite service.[293] Under certain circumstances, however, the Commission may agree to process the satellite application concurrently with the rulemaking, in which

---

292. The Commission instituted group processing in the domestic fixed satellite service in 1980 to improve procedural efficiency, and to ensure that applications that were mutually exclusive would receive comparative evaluations. *Assignment of Orbital Locations in the Domestic Fixed Satellite Service*, 84 F.C.C. 2d 584, 585 (1980).

293. In addition, action on a satellite application may be postponed pending the outcome of an Executive Branch review. On a few occasions, foreign policy and international legal implications of the proposed satellite systems have been such that the Executive Branch of the Government has intervened and requested the Commission to refrain from further action on a satellite application until certain extant issues were resolved. Such intervention occurred, *e.g.*, on April 6, 1983, after Orion Satellite Corporation (Orion) proposed to launch a satellite system for trans-Atlantic communications in competition with the International Telecommunications Satellite Organization (INTELSAT). *See* Letter from David J. Markey, Assistant Secretary-Designate for Communications and Information, Department of Commerce, and Diana Lady Dougan, Coordinator, International Communications and Information Policy, Department of State, to Mark S. Fowler, Chairman, FCC (Apr. 6, 1983) (requesting that the FCC refrain from further action on Orion's application). *See also* Separate Systems Order, *supra* note 139, at para. 12 (discussing the letter and background). Since Orion was requesting authorization for a satellite system for international communications, a Presidential Determination was necessary under the Communications Satellite Act of 1962, as amended, 47 U.S.C. § 701(d) (1988), that Orion's proposed system was "required in the national interest." Moreover, the Executive Branch of the United States Government was responsible for ensuring consistency with U.S. obligations under the INTELSAT Agreement, *supra* note 106. *See* Chapter 3.1.4. (describing the circumstances surrounding Orion's application). Executive Branch intervention also occurred when transborder satellites were first proposed in 1982, *Transborder Video Services*, 88 F.C.C. 2d 558 (1981), and when domestic fixed satellites were first considered in 1970, Domsat I, *supra* note 11, at para. 4 and Appx. B, at para. 49.

case less delay is likely.

EXAMINATION OF APPLICATIONS. When the pleading cycle has ended, i.e., when comments, oppositions and replies have been filed for a group of applications to be considered concurrently, the evaluation of the satellite applications can begin. Applications will be examined in light of 1) the applicable legal, technical and financial criteria, which may vary from one kind of satellite service to the next (see Chapter 3.2.5.), 2) public interest considerations, and 3) opposing and supporting comments filed. Never in the evaluation of satellite applications has the Commission resorted to comparative hearings.[294] Through clever application, perhaps even manipulation, of the criteria for licensing, the Commission has been able to prevent the occurrence of the type of situation which gives rise to comparative hearing rights. In *Ashbacker Radio Corp. v. Federal Communications Commission,*[295] the Supreme Court provided that whenever the grant of one radio station application would require the denial of another, mutual exclusivity exists that gives rise to comparative hearing rights. By applying strict qualification criteria to satellite applicants,[296] and by resorting to creative solutions when necessary,[297] the Commission always has been able to eliminate a sufficient number of applications to be able to authorize all *qualified* applicants.[298]

AN EXAMPLE OF APPLICATION PROCESSING. The regulatory process involving Geostar Corporation illustrates the pleading cycle and FCC actions described above. On March 31, 1983, Geostar filed a petition for rulemaking to establish a new satellite service, i.e., a radiodetermination

---

294. The Communications Act provides that when mere examination of the application does not support a finding that the proposed service will serve the public interest, the Commission "shall . . . designate the application for hearing. 47 U.S.C. § 309(e) (1988). In *Ashbacker Radio Corp. v. FCC,* 326 U.S. 327, 333 (1945), the Supreme Court provided that "where two bona fide applications are mutually exclusive the grant of one without hearing of both . . ." is improper. The Supreme Court has recognized, however, that the right to a hearing created pursuant to 47 U.S.C. § 309(e) is not absolute. In *United States v. Storer Broadcasting Co.,* 351 U.S. 192, 202 (1956), the Supreme Court stated that it does not "read the hearing requirement . . . as withdrawing from the power of the Commission the rulemaking authority necessary for orderly conduct of its business . . . ."

295. 326 U.S. 327 (1945). *See* 47 C.F.R. § 25.155 (1990) (providing the Commission's interpretation of mutual exclusivity between satellite applications).

296. For example, when the number of applications in the fixed satellite service increased to a point where the Commission no longer could accommodate all of them, the Commission first responded by reducing orbital spacing between satellites in the U.S. portion of the geostationary arc. Two Degree Spacing Order, *supra* note 269. The U.S. portion of the orbit refers to the portion of the orbit that is suitable for use by U.S. satellite operators since satellites placed within this portion have footprints covering the United States. Next, the Commission responded by adopting and enforcing stringent financial criteria. 47 C.F.R. § 25.140(b), (c) (1990).

satellite service, which never before had been considered by the Commission. At the same time, Geostar applied for authority to operate a radiodetermination satellite system. On September 7, 1984, the Commission issued a Notice of Proposed Rulemaking (NPRM),[299] proposing to allocate certain segments of the radio spectrum for radiodetermination satellite service. The release of the NPRM was accompanied by a public notice accepting Geostar's application for filing and inviting other applications for concurrent consideration. The Commission decided to conduct the licensing and rulemaking proceedings in parallel. Several new applications, as well as extensive comments, were filed in response to the NPRM and Geostar's satellite application.[300] Three parties petitioned to deny Geostar's application. All of the petitions were denied. Finding that the public interest would be served by the establishment of radiodetermination satellite service, the Commission issued a *Report and Order*[301] on July 25, 1985, allocating the frequencies for radiodetermination satellite service requested by Geostar. In a *Second Report and Order,*[302] released May 8, 1986, the Commission set forth policies and Rules governing radiodetermination satellite service. It then proceeded, by separate actions on August 1, 1986, to grant Geostar's and other satellite applications on file.[303]

---

297. When presented with a situation where it was unable to accommodate all applicants in the mobile satellite service, the Commission ordered the applicants to form a consortium. *See* Mobile Satellite Licensing Order, *supra* note 170 (establishing ownership rules for the consortium). The Commission then proceeded to authorize American Mobile Satellite Corporation, a consortium of eight companies created pursuant to the Commission's request, AMSC Authorization Order, *supra* note 155. On March 19, 1991, the court ruled invalid the consortium, stating that "the Commission has not provided an adequate justification for its abandonment of the hearing approach in this case," *i.e.*, when it required applicants to form a consortium rather than holding comparative hearings among the applicants on their respective proposals. *Aeronautical Radio, Inc. v. FCC,* 928 F.2d 428 (1991), at 450. The Commission attempted to remedy the defect. *Amendments of Parts 2, 22 and 25 of the Commission's Rules to Allocate Sprectrum for and to Establish Other Rules and Policies Pertaining to the Use of Radio Frequencies in a Land Mobile Satellite Service,* Tentative Decision, 6 F.C.C. Rcd 4900 (1991), Final Decision, 1992 FCC LEXIS 122.

298. The Commission has stated repeatedly that requests by two applicants for the same orbital location do not give rights to comparative hearings. *See e.g.* 1980 Assignment Order, *supra* note 30, and 1988 Assignment Order, *supra* note 33 (providing that conflicting requests by applicants for the same orbital location do not give rise to comparative hearing rights).

299. Radiodetermination Satellite Notice, *supra* note 87.

300. *See* Chapter 3.1.3. (describing these applicants).

301. Radiodetermination Satellite Allocation Order, *supra* note 92.

302. Radiodetermination Satellite Licensing Order, *supra* note 94.

303. *Geostar Corporation,* 60 Rad. Reg.2d 1725 (1986) [hereinafter cited as Geostar Authorization].

3.2.9. FCC Licensing Approach and Philosophy

Since the beginning of its regulatory experience with satellites in the early 1970s, the FCC has adhered to a policy of "open entry."[304] In other words, the Commission basically has authorized every legally, technically and financially qualified satellite applicant to the extent it has been technically feasible to do so. Technical feasibility primarily refers to the availability of orbit and spectrum resources. The open entry policy, or licensing approach, which has prevailed in all the satellite service categories, is rooted in a fundamental Commission philosophy that competition, rather than regulation, including entry, service and satellite system design restrictions, will serve the public interest, which, of course, is the Commission's licensing mandate. The basic premise of this philosophy is that the market place will eliminate service providers that do not serve the public interest, and will reward and retain those which do.

3.2.10. Authorization to Construct, Launch and Operate the Satellite and Conditions of the Authorization

TIME FRAME. Obtaining a satellite authorization can be a lengthy process. Several years (perhaps two or three, and sometimes more) may pass from the time your client's satellite application is first filed to the actual granting of authorization(s) to construct, launch and operate the satellite(s). This is particularly true if your client proposes a new service, the authorization of which may require a protracted rulemaking. For example, the first application in the radiodetermination satellite service (before this was an established service category), which was filed by Geostar Corporation in March 1983, was not granted until August 1986.[305] Similarly, Orion Satellite Corporation filed the first application in the international fixed satellite service in March 1983, and its application was granted in September 1985, following Executive Branch and Congressional interventions, as well as an FCC rulemaking.[306] Orion's 1985 authorization was only preliminary. Its final authorization was not received until 1991. However, this delay was occasioned in large part by Orion's own financing efforts.

SINGLE OR CONSOLIDATED AUTHORIZATIONS. For some types of satellite services, the granting of a construction permit, launch authorization and operating license is consolidated; for others, it is a two-step pro-

---

304. *See* Domsat I, *supra* note 11 (establishing the Commission's open entry policy), and *Satellite Business Systems*, 52 F.C.C. 2d 997 (1977) and the 1980 Assignment Order, *supra* note 30 (enforcing the open entry policy). Regarding the Commission's general philosophy of fostering competition in the market place through an open entry policy, *see* D.I. Baker, *Competition and Regulation: Charles River Bridge Recrossed*, 60 CORNELL L. REV. 159 (1975) (discussing competition as an alternative to regulation).
305. Geostar Authorization, *supra* note 303
306. *Orion Satellite Corporation*, Mimeo No. 6871, *released* Sept. 6, 1985.

cess. Domestic fixed satellite applicants are granted all the necessary authorizations concurrently, while applicants in the direct-broadcast and international fixed satellite services first receive conditional authorizations.[307] Applications for more than one satellite generally are disposed of simultaneously. If an authorization has been granted for the use of a satellite as a ground spare only, separate authorizations will be needed later to launch and operate that satellite. As noted previously, because of the high fees required for a satellite operating license many applicants nowadays elect to apply only for a construction permit, initially.

MILESTONE SCHEDULE. Included in the typical satellite authorization is a "milestone" schedule specifying the dates by which the construction of the satellite must be started and completed, and by which the launching must take place. Often, the Commission requires that construction be started, or that a contract for construction be signed, approximately one year from the date of the authorization. With regard to domestic fixed- and mobile satellites, the Commission has required that construction be completed over a period of three years and that launching take place within one year thereafter. Satellite licensees are required to file semi-annual progress reports.

When the Commission authorized American Mobile Satellite Corporation (AMSC) to construct, launch and operate three mobile satellites, the Commission included the milestone schedule in the company's license (released August 4, 1989), as set forth below:

> It is further ordered that unless extended by the Commission for good cause shown, each of the authorizations shall become null and void in the event the [satellites] are not constructed, launched and successfully placed into operation in accordance with the technical parameters and terms and conditions of the authoriza-

---

307. Pursuant to the Communications Act, "no license shall be issued . . . for the operation of any station unless a permit for its construction has been granted by the Commission." 47 U.S.C. § 319(a). Nothing in the Act, however, prohibits the Commission from issuing a construction permit and operating license simultaneously and, in 1980, the Commission adopted a consolidated approach to authorization of satellite applicants in the domestic fixed satellite service. 1980 Assignment Order, *supra* note 30. In this order the Commission stated that "[t]he authorization process for a domestic fixed satellite has generally occurred in three distinct phases: (1) issuance of a construction permit; (2) grant of launch authority and tentative orbital assignment; and (3) grant of operating authority under both Title II and Title III of the [Communications] Act . . . Based on our experience with this three-step approach, we believe some reexamination of its efficacy is needed at this time . . . The uncertainties which initially justified this bifurcated approach have been substantially resolved." Consequently, a consolidated approach was adopted after almost one decade of licensing in the domestic fixed satellite service. Licensing processes in the other satellite services have not reached the same stage of maturity.

tion by the following dates, as certified in writing to the Commission by the licensee:

[Satellite]	Construction	Construction	Launched
AMSC-1	July 1990	January 1993	July 1993
AMSC-2	July 1991	January 1994	July 1994
AMSC-3	July 1991	January 1994	July 1994[308]

The Commissions's Rules provide that "[a]n authorization to construct and/or to launch a space station becomes null and void if the construction is not begun or is not completed, or if the space station is not launched and positioned at its assigned orbital location and operations commenced in accordance with the station authorization, by the respective date(s) specified in the authorization."[309] In practice, however, the Commission often considers these milestone dates more as guidelines than absolute deadlines.

EXTENSION. A request for extension supported by good cause is necessary if your client is unable to meet a milestone. (This is a request for modification, see Chapter 3.2.11.). In *United States Satellite Broadcasting Company, Inc.,*[310] the Commission considered certain factors beyond a company's control to constitute "good cause." Among these causes were the need for entirely new transmission and reception equipment and the related need for an entire direct broadcasting satellite industry infrastructure to be established. The Commission granted a request for extension of time to complete construction. The Commission also noted that the need for the extension was not due to the lack of capability and commitment by the company.[311] However, the Commission has stated that in the domestic fixed satellite service, an uncertain business climate, in itself, does not warrant an extension.[312] Neither does the failure to obtain financing for

---

308. AMSC Authorization Order, *supra* note 155. at 6060. With a slight variation in time schedule, a milestone provision was included in *GTE Spacenet Corporation,* Order and Authorization, 3 F.C.C. Rcd 6986 (1988). GTE Spacenet operates "GSTAR" and "Spacenet" satellites, and the authorization sets forth the following milestone schedule:

Satellite	*Construction Commenced*	*Construction Completed*	*Launched*
GSTAR IV	[in progress]	August 1989	Feb. 1990
Spacenet IR	March 1990	March 1993	May 1993
Spacenet IIR	May 1990	May 1993	Sept.1993
Spacenet IIIR	Jan. 1991	Jan. 1994	spare
GSTAR IR	March 1991	March 1994	June 1994.

309. 47 C.F.R. § 25.202(d) (1990).
310. 3 F.C.C. Rcd 6858 (1988).
311. *Id.,* at 6860.
312. *AT&T,* 2 F.C.C. Rcd 4431 (1987); and *MCI Communications Corporation,* 2 F.C.C. Rcd 233 (1987).

the domestic fixed satellite service.[313]

WHAT RIGHTS DOES THE LICENSE CONVEY? Essentially, a license to operate a satellite entitles your client to use a particular orbital location and specific radio frequencies for a limited period of time. License terms generally have been ten years, except in the direct broadcasting satellite service where a five year license term is the maximum allowed under the Communications Act.[314] The license term begins to run when the satellite is declared operational in orbit. Note, also, that the Commission may require a licensee to relocate its satellite to another orbital position during the license term on a thirty-day notice.[315]

NO GUARANTEE OF SATELLITE REPLACEMENT. Although it repeatedly has been urged to do so by satellite operators, the Commission has consistently refused to guarantee a renewal of their licenses for replacement satellites in the same orbital locations, primarily because such assurances would limit the Commission's flexibility to adopt new orbital assignment policies (e.g., closer orbital spacing between satellites). Satellite operators whose customers (e.g., cable operators and VSAT network owners) have invested in expensive ground equipment pointed at satellites at particular orbital locations have asked the Commission to guarantee that they can continue to serve their customers from the same orbital locations. Although, the Commission has refused to give outright guarantees, it has stated that "[w]hen the location is available for assignment to a satellite with the technical characteristics of the proposed replacement satellite, we will generally authorize the replacement satellite in the same location."[316]

---

313. Two Degree Spacing Order, *supra* note 269, at 579, note 62. Extensions were granted in the international fixed satellite service, *International Satellite, Inc.*, 5 F.C.C. Rcd 35 (1990).

314. 47 U.S.C. § 307(c) (1988); 47 C.F.R. § 25.120 (1990). In the past, the ten year license term has coincided with the design-life of an average geostationary telecommunications satellite. Sometimes, however, satellites remain functional beyond their design lives, in which case a request for extension of a license term becomes necessary. Increasingly, satellites have longer design-lives, as well.

315. Typically, a satellite authorization will provide that the licensee must re-locate the satellite at the Commission's request. *See e.g. GTE Spacenet Corporation*, 3 F.C.C. Rcd 6986 (1988) (stating that the assignments of orbital locations are "subject to change by summary order of the Commission on 30 days notice and do not confer any permanent right to use the orbit and spectrum"). The Rule is codified in 47 C.F.R. § 25.202(d) (1990).

316. 1988 Assignment Order *supra* note 33, at para. 31. The Commission cited *Licensing of Space Stations in the Domestic Fixed Satellite Service*, 50 Fed. Reg. 3607 (1985).

3.2.11. Modification of Construction Permit, Launch Authorization and Operating License

REQUEST FOR MODIFICATION. As a holder of a satellite construction permit, launch authorization and/or operating license, your client may apply to the Commission for modification of such authorizations. The application must be in writing, pursuant to the same provisions of the Communications Act under which the authorization was requested initially. The content of the application for modification should conform to the requirements for the application for the original authority (Chapter 3.2.6.), although only the items for which the information will change need be included. The Act provides that "[t]he Commission may grant construction permits and station licenses, or modifications . . . thereof, only upon written application therefor . . . ."[317] If your client also holds a common carrier certification, a request for modification under Title II of the Communications Act also may be necessary.[318]

WHEN IS A MODIFICATION GRANTED? Requests to modify the technical design and operation of the satellite are quite common and generally are granted if the proposed modification is consistent with the Commission's Rules, serves the public interest, and is not detrimental to other satellite operations. With regard to modification of construction permits, the Commission has stated that

> [g]iven the two to three year construction period for a satellite, the Commission often receives requests from licensees to modify the technical design of their satellites while they are being built. *If the proposed modification does not present any significant interference problems and is otherwise consistent with the Commission's policies, it is generally granted.* [319]

EXAMPLES OF MODIFICATIONS. Typically, satellite construction permittees or licensees apply to modify the satellite beam coverage, increase satellite power,[320] add equipment, re-locate a satellite in orbit, extend a deadline, e.g., for commencement of satellite construction (see Chapter 3.2.10.), or change certain satellite performance characteristics or operating parameters. For example, on June 29, 1989, AT&T applied to modify its TELSTAR 401 and 402 domestic fixed satellites to include switchable spot-beam[321] capability. The Commission granted the application based on a determination that the proposed modification would serve the public interest. It noted that switchable spot-beams would allow AT&T

---

317. 47 U.S.C. § 308(a) (1988); 47 C.F.R. § 25.117(a) (1990).

318. 47.U.S.C. § 214 (1988).

319. Emphasis added. *American Telephone & Telegraph Company,* 5 F.C.C. Rcd 1184 (1990).

320. *See e.g., Hughes Communications Galaxy, Inc.,* 5 F.C.C. Rcd 1653 (1990) (granting a request by Hughes to use 16 Watt amplifiers rather than the 10 Watt amplifiers previously authorized).

to "provide better service to its customers in Hawaii, with no significant impact on its other customers or on adjacent satellite operations."[322]

In another example, the Commission granted GTE Spacenet Corporation's request in 1989 for modification of the construction permit for its GSTAR III satellite to allow for a radiodetermination satellite service receive-only antenna to be placed on the satellite.[323] The radiodetermination equipment was to be used by Geostar Corporation. The Commission noted that the inclusion of the additional equipment would not significantly affect operating characteristics of GTE Spacenet's domestic fixed satellite and, furthermore, it would allow for early access to interim radiodetermination satellite service, a service the Commission considered to be in the public interest.

In another 1989 decision, the Commission authorized Comsat General Corporation to operate four satellites, already in orbit, with a modified inclination of up to five degrees above or below the equatorial plane of the Earth.[324] The modified orbit inclination was intended to extend the operational lives of the satellites and is accomplished by a satellite control technique developed by Comsat and referred to as the "Comsat maneuver." Modification of Comsat's operating licenses would serve the public inter-

---

321. A spot beam is an antenna beam that covers a small portion of the satellite's general service area. The general service area is the total area covered by the satellite, *e.g.* for U.S. domestic satellites, the service area typically could be the contiguous United States, Alaska and Hawaii. A spot beam might, for example, cover Alaska, Hawaii, the Eastern part, or the Western part of the continental United States. The advantage of a spot beam is that it focuses the satellite power on a limited portion of the service area, with the result that the satellite signal is stronger and smaller transmit and receive dishes are required. Switchable spot-beams allow the satellite operator to switch between spot-beam coverage areas on ground command.

322. *AT&T, supra* note 319, at para. 8. AT&T had been authorized one year earlier to construct, launch and operate Telstar 401 and 402, each satellite with twenty-four C-band transponders with a 36 MHz bandwidth. *AT&T,* 3 F.C.C. Rcd 6980 (1988). Under that authorization, the C-band coverage area of the satellites would include the contiguous United States, Alaska, Hawaii, Puerto Rico and the U.S. Virgin Islands. Maximum edge-of-coverage equivalent isotropic radiated power (EIRP) would be 35.0 dBW. AT&T proposed to modify the satellites so that six of the C-band transponders on each satellite could be used for switchable spot-beams covering either Hawaii or the contiguous United States on ground command. The modification proposal contemplated that the Hawaii spot-beam would have a nominal EIRP of 40.0 dBW. No opposition to AT&T's application was filed.

323. *GTE Spacenet Corporation,* Mimeo No. 829, *released* Aug. 15, 1988. *See also GTE Spacenet Corporation,* Mimeo No. 5171, *released* June 16, 1986, and *GTE Spacenet Corporation,* 1 F.C.C. Rcd 1163 (1986) (authorizing the company to include radio determination equipment on previous occasions).

324. *Comsat General Corporation,* 4 F.C.C. Rcd 3820 (1989) (granting an application for modification of COMSTAR D-2 and D-4, SBS-1 and SBS-2 domestic fixed satellite licenses).

est, the Commission concluded, "because the public will benefit from the extended useful lives of these older satellites with no accompanying detriment."[325]

Furthermore, the Commission granted GTE Spacenet's application for a new orbital location for its GSTAR IV satellite, which was co-located with GSTAR III at that time.[326] The Commission granted the application pursuant to a provision of its own Rules, which provides that a qualified applicant may be assigned one additional orbital location in a frequency band if its in-orbit satellites are essentially filled and it has no more than two orbital locations for previously authorized, but unlaunched, satellites.[327] GTE Spacenet was found to have satisfied these conditions.

In 1988, the Commission denied a request by Contel ASC that the orbital location for its unlaunched ASC-2 satellite be reassigned from 83 to 99 degrees West Longitude.[328] Contel ASC had requested the modification of its license to allow its own ASC-2 satellite to replace Western Union's WESTAR IV satellite at the latter's end-of-life. Contel ASC owned nine transponders on WESTAR IV and wished to be able to continue service uninterrupted to its customers. It estimated that repointing of customers' antennas otherwise would cost a total of more than $10 million and would take at least one year to accomplish. Instead of granting ASC's request, however, the Commission proceeded to grant Western Union the right to launch a replacement satellite for Westar IV at 99 degrees. (Western Union's satellite authorizations had been assigned in the meantime to Hughes Communications). In denying Contel ASC's request and accommodating Western Union, the Commission reasoned that, in order to promote predictability and stability in the satellite market, it is important to protect the enormous investment in the satellite system made by the *licensee* (i.e., Western Union). The Commission noted that "[a]doption of a policy that would permit satellite customers (such as Contel ASC) to require licensees to move from their existing orbital locations could add to investor risks and discourage investment [in new satellite systems]."[329]

3.2.12. Transfer of Control

FCC APPROVAL IS REQUIRED. A satellite construction permit or an operating license cannot be transferred or assigned without prior approval from the Commission. The Communications Act provides that

> [n]o construction permit or station license, or any rights thereunder, shall be transferred, assigned, or disposed of in any manner, voluntary or involuntary, directly or indirectly, or by transfer of control of any corporation holding such permit or license, to any

325. *Id.*
326. *GTE Spacenet Corporation,* 3 F.C.C. Rcd 6986 (1988).
327. 47 C.F.R. § 25.140(g) (1990).
328. *American Satellite Company,* 3 F.C.C. Rcd 6969 (1988).
329. *Id.,* at para. 11.

> person except upon application to the Commission and upon finding by the Commission that the public interest . . . will be served thereby.[330]

According to the Commission's Rules concerning satellites, transfers of control requiring FCC approval "shall include any and all transactions that (1) change the party controlling the affairs of the licensee, or (2) affect any change in the controlling interest in the ownership of the licensee, including changes in legal and equitable ownership."[331] It is the transfer of *control* over the FCC authorized activities and satellite that triggers the requirement for Commission approval.

Transfer or assignment of a construction permit or an operating license may occur 1) by assignment from the permittee/licensee (assignor) to a new party (assignee), or 2) as part of the transfer of control of the permittee/licensee corporation (transferor) to a new corporation (transferee). An example of the former situation is where a permit/license holder agrees to sell to another company its satellite operations, including the satellites, and to assign pertinent authorizations. The satellite may be in orbit or under construction, or construction may not even have started. This is an example of voluntary transfer. An example of involuntary transfer is where the permit/license holder has declared bankruptcy, and permits and licenses are acquired by a new company at an auction. For instance, Geostar Corporation's construction permits and operating licenses for three dedicated radiodetermination satellites were auctioned in December 1991, after that company had declared bankruptcy in May of the same year.

An example of a situation in which satellite authorizations are transferred as part of a change in corporate control is where a company holding construction permits and operating licenses is acquired by another company. The acquiring company cannot obtain or make use of the authorizations without the Commission's prior approval.

RATIONALE. One rationale behind the rule requiring FCC approval for assignments to take place is to ensure that whoever holds a construction permit or license, and thus controls the satellite, is legally, technically and financially qualified and continues to serve the public interest. Another rationale is to prevent trafficking in licenses since these convey rights to use valuable resources, free of charge, such as the radio spectrum and geostationary orbit, which constitute the "public trust."

MUST FILE AN APPLICATION. To obtain FCC approval for a transfer or assignment of a permit or a license, your client must first file an application.[332] In fact, a joint application should be filed by the transferor and transferee, or assignor and assignee. Applications are disposed of by the

---

330. 47 U.S.C. § 310(d) (1988); 47 C.F.R. § 25.118(a) (1990). If your client is a common carrier subject to Title II regulation, approval also is required pursuant to 47 U.S.C. § 214 (1988).

331. 47 C.F.R. § 25.118(b) (1990).

Commission "as if the proposed transferee or assignee were making an application under Section 308 for the permit or license in question."[333] In other words, the Commission considers whether the transferee/assignee meets the legal, financial and technical qualification requirements applicable to the given satellite service, as well as whether the public interest test is met.[334] The Commission is required to weigh potential anti-trust consequences against other public interest factors.[335] Pursuant to the Clayton Act, the Commission must consider whether the effect of the proposed transaction will tend "substantially to lessen competition . . . or to create a monopoly."[336] In the past, antitrust implications often have presented the most controversial issues with respect to the transfer of satellite authorizations, while the qualifications of the transferees/assignees usually have not been at issue.[337]

EXAMPLES OF TRANSFERS OF CONTROL. Since it first authorized domestic fixed satellites in the early 1970s, the Commission has approved a number of transfers. For example, the Commission approved the acquisition by GTE of all the stock of Southern Pacific Satellite Company in 1983;[338] by Contel of American Satellite Company in 1985;[339] by MCI of Satellite Business Systems in 1986;[340] and by Hughes Communications Galaxy, Inc. of Satellite Transponder Leasing Corporation in 1990.[341] Moreover, it granted requests for assignments of satellite authorizations

---

332. 47 U.S.C. § 310(d) (1988). *See* 47 C.F.R. § 25.118(c), (d) (1990) (stating requirements that certain forms be submitted with the application). Form 702, entitled "Application for Consent of Assignment of Radio Station Construction Permit or License for Stations in Services Other than Broadcast," is required for assignment of a permit/license. *Id.* Form 704, entitled "Application for Consent to Transfer of Control," is required for transfer of control of the corporation holding the permit/license. *Id.*
333. 47 U.S.C. § 310(d) (1988).
334. *Id.*
335. *United States v. FCC*, 652 F.2d 72, 88 (D.C. Cir. 1980).
336. 15 U.S.C. § 18 (1988). *See also* 15 U.S.C. § 21 (1988) (concerning the Commission's authority to enforce the antitrust provisions).
337. So far, transferees/assignees have tended to be large, established companies, some already owning and operating satellites, themselves. *See Application of GTE Corporation and Southern Pacific Company for Consent to Transfer Control of Southern Pacific Communications Company and Southern Pacific Satellite Company*, 94 F.C.C. 2d 235 (1983) [hereinafter cited as GTE Acquisition], paras. 38-40 (discussing anticompetitiveness considerations in connection with a satellite transfer).
338. GTE Acquisition, *supra* note 337.
339. *Application for Approval of the Transfer of Control of American Satellite Company*, Slip Opinion (Common Carrier Bureau) *released* Oct. 16, 1985 (1985 FCC LEXIS 2433).
340. *Application for Consent to Transfer of Control of Satellite Business Systems from IBM Corporation to MCI Communications Corporation*, Slip Opinion (Common Carrier Bureau) *released* Feb. 14, 1986 (1986 FCC LEXIS 3963) [hereinafter cited as MCI Acquisition].

in connection with the sale of satellites to Hughes Communications Galaxy, Inc. by Western Union Corporation in 1988.[342]

GTE Corporation and Southern Pacific Company sought FCC permission to transfer control of Southern Pacific Satellite Company, and its domestic fixed satellite licenses and service authorizations, to GTE pursuant to Sections 212, 214 and 310(d) of the Communications Act.[343] The Commission authorized the transfer in 1983, noting that GTE was legally, technically and financially qualified to operate the satellites, and that the transfer of licenses and authorizations would serve the public interest.[344]. The transfer raised substantial antitrust issues, however, and certain restrictions were imposed on GTE's corporate structure as conditions of the approval.

Further, in 1986, the Commission approved the transfer of control of Satellite Business Systems (SBS), including satellite authorizations held by it, to MCI Communications Corporation (MCI) from International Business Machines (IBM).[345] The Commission noted that MCI's legal, technical and financial qualifications were not in question, and concluded that the transaction was in the public interest. At the time of the transfer, SBS was a partnership of three companies (Information Satellite Corporation, BCI Satellite, Inc. and Aetna Diversified Technologies). IBM, directly or indirectly, controlled the outstanding stock of the former two companies. The transfer of control would involve conveyance by IBM of its interest in SBS to MCI by exchanging the stock of the companies making up the SBS partnership in return for approximately 17% of MCI's issued and outstanding stock. SBS was to continue to do business as a partnership between MCI and Aetna Diversified Technologies. [346]

In yet another decision, Western Union Corporation was authorized in 1988 to assign licenses and authorizations held in connection with the

---

341. *IBM Corporation and Hughes Communications Galaxy, Inc, Satellite Transponder Leasing Corporation,* 5 F.C.C. Rcd 1655 (1990).

342. *Western Union Corporation and Hughes Communications Galaxy, Inc.,* 3 F.C.C. Rcd 6792 (1988) (regarding transfer of three "WESTAR" satellites) [hereinafter cited as Hughes Acquisition].

343. 47 U.S.C. §§ 212, 214 and 310(d) (1988).

344. GTE Acquisition, *supra* note 337. At the time of the transfer, Southern Pacific Satellite Company was a wholly-owned subsidiary of Southern Pacific Company. The transfer was intended as part of the acquisition by GTE of two of Southern Pacific Company's subsidiaries, Southern Pacific Satellite Company and Southern Pacific Communications Company. Southern Pacific Satellite Company was authorized by the Commission to build three domestic fixed satellites, for which it had contracted with RCA Corporation, and to launch two of them in 1984. GTE Corporation, to which the transfer of Southern Pacific Satellite Company's licenses was being sought, also was authorized to construct three domestic fixed satellites, and to operate two of them in orbit. GTE is a holding company, and its satellite authorizations were held by the operating company GTE Satellite Corporation

345. MCI Acquisition, *supra* note 340.

WESTAR satellite system to Hughes Communications Galaxy, Inc.[347] Hughes had agreed to purchase from Western Union the WESTAR satellite system consisting of the three operational satellites WESTAR-III, IV and V, as well as the fully constructed, but unlaunched WESTAR VI, to replace WESTAR III. Under the purchase agreement, Hughes also would acquire the tracking, telemetry and control facility in order to enable it to control the satellites and assume all other licensee responsibilities, and continue uninterrupted service to Western Union's customers.

TRANSPONDER SALES. It is interesting to note that the sale of a transponder on a satellite does not constitute a transfer of control of a radio station under the Communications Act.[348] This holding by the Commission is premised upon the notion that the entire satellite, rather than each individual transponder, constitutes a radio station whose operation is subject to a license. The Commission reasoned that it is the satellite operator, rather than the transponder owner, that exercises control over the satellite (radio station) in the sense that only the satellite operator can discharge the licensee's responsibilities. Only the satellite operator has control over the maintenance of attitude and orbital position, the electrical power necessary to operate the transponders, and all other tracking and telemetry functions.

PERCENTAGE SALES. Even the purchase of a percentage of the satellite will not require FCC approval, provided the seller (licensee) retains control over the satellite. For example, the acquisition by American Satellite Company in 1981 of 20% interest in the WESTAR IV and V satellites, which was to be reflected in the ownership of discrete transponders, did not require transfer of control authorization.[349]

SALE LEASE-BACK TRANSACTIONS. Again, based on the premise that the buyer does not obtain control over the satellite, a sale lease-back transaction executed solely for financial purposes is not subject to Commission approval.[350] In such transactions, the satellite operator typically sells all or some satellite transponders to a bank or other financial institution, and then leases them back. These transactions, which normally take

---

346. The transaction involved the transfer of authorizations to construct, launch and operate SBS 7 and 8, and to construct SBS-9. Other satellites, including SBS 4, 5 and 6, were to remain with IBM to be operated by a newly formed, wholly-owned subsidiary called Satellite Transponder Leasing Corporation. Public Notice, *released* Nov. 6, 1985, DS-463. In 1989, the latter three satellites were sold to Hughes. *See supra* note 341 (concerning this transfer). *See Satellite Business Systems*, 98 F.C.C. 2d 762 (1984) (regarding the history on SBS ownership).

347. Hughes Acquisition, *supra* note 342.

348. *Domestic fixed satellite Transponder Sales*, 90 F.C.C. 2d. 1238 (1982), at paras. 46-49.

349. *Western Union Telegraph Company and American Satellite Company*, 86 F.C.C. 2d 196 (1981).

350. Hughes Acquisition, *supra* note 342.

place after the satellite has been placed in orbit, have benefits for the financial institution, as well as the satellite operator. The latter receives the sales proceeds, in exchange for a promise to make lease payments to the financial institution, and retains control over the satellite. The financial institution becomes title owner of the satellite, receives tax benefits in the form of accelerated depreciation, and becomes entitled to the residual value of the satellite, if any, when the lease term expires.

ASSUMPTION OF ASSIGNORS'S LIABILITIES. When a satellite is sold and a license to operate it is assigned, the buyer/assignee may or may not assume obligations under seller/assignor's other contracts, such as with transponder owners. For example, when operating licenses for three of Western Union Corporation's WESTAR satellites were assigned to Hughes Communications Galaxy, Inc., in 1988, in connection with the sale of these satellites, obligations under the transponder purchase contracts between Western Union and Contel ASC (ASC), and Western Union and Public Broadcasting Corporation (PBC), were not assumed by Hughes.[351] ASC and PBS had urged the Commission to condition the Western Union-Hughes assignment on the assumption of obligations under their contracts, but the Commission refused to do so, stating that the "[t]he considerable investment PBS and Contel ASC have made in the purchase of Westar transponders, alone, cannot constrain the bargained-for transfer of the Westar system to Hughes."[352]

3.2.13. Administrative and Judicial Reviews

REVIEWS AVAILABLE. Decisions made by the Commission, or by its staff pursuant to delegated authority, are subject to administrative and judicial review. Administrative review may take the form of a reconsideration, which is conducted by the same authority that made the initial decision; or a review, which is performed by a different and higher decision-making authority, sometimes the Commission, itself. Judicial review of Commission decisions is performed by the United States Federal courts of the District of Columbia in Washington, D.C. Administrative review is a condition precedent to judicial review in cases where the decision was made by a Commission staff member pursuant to delegated authority.[353] Reconsideration is not a precondition to judicial review, except where the party seeking judicial review (1) was not a party to the proceeding, or (2) introduces new questions of fact or law.[354]

351. Hughes Acquisition, *supra* note 342.

352. *Id.,* at 6793. In a situation where the buyer does not assume the obligations of seller under transponder sales contracts, as in the case of Hughes and Western Union, the seller will continue to be responsible for all obligations arising under those contracts. The Commission may require that the satellite purchase agreement be so structured as to enable the assignor to carry out its contractual obligations to the transponder owners.

353. 47 U.S.C 155(b)(7) (1988).

RECONSIDERATION. Reconsideration is the least formal type of review process. It provides an opportunity for a party, or any other person whose interests are adversely affected by a decision, to have the same branch, division or bureau that made the decision in the first place, or the Commission, itself, if it made the decision, reexamine its findings and conclusions. Your client must file a "petition for reconsideration" pursuant to Section 405 of the Communications Act [355] and Section 1.106 of the Commission's Rules.[356] The decision-making authority, in its discretion, may grant or deny the petition.

Petitions for reconsideration are very common in satellite-related proceedings. Satellite operators, resellers, users, and other interested parties, often seek to have Commission decisions reversed or modified through reconsideration. For example, in 1986, National Exchange, Inc. (NEX), an entrepreneurial start-up satellite company whose application had been denied by the Commission, sought reconsideration of a decision subjecting it to a newly-codified FCC Rule prescribing financial criteria for licensing of domestic fixed satellites (see Chapter 3.1.1.).[357] For reasons described below, the Commission denied NEX's petition for reconsideration.[358] NEX's principal argument was that the Commission had violated the Administrative Procedure Act[359] by simultaneously adopting and applying the stricter financial qualification requirements to domestic fixed satellite applicants, and that the denial of NEX's satellite applications, therefore, was wrongful. NEX argued that the new financial criteria could not be applied to its application, which was filed prior to the codification of the financial Rules. On the other hand, the Commission contended that the financial Rules were not new, but were merely a codification of existing Commission policy. In 1983, the Commission had, in fact, imposed strict financial requirements on domestic fixed satellite applicants as a matter of policy in order to eliminate speculative applicants and to ensure that valuable orbital space did not remain unused due to the inability of a licensee to finance construction and launch of the satellite (see Chapter 3.1.1.).[360]

In another example, the Commission, in 1983, denied GTE Satellite Corporation's petition for reconsideration of an order that excluded GTE's satellite application from concurrent consideration with a group of other applications due to GTE's late filing. GTE filed its application after the cut-off date established by the Commission.[361] The Commission rejected GTE's principal argument for reconsideration, i.e., that the order was unlawful because it barred applications filed after the cut-off date from being considered with applications with which mutual exclusivity

354. 47 U.S.C. § 405 (1988) and 47 C.F.R. § 1.106(m) (1990).
355. 47 U.S.C. § 405 (1988).
356. 47 C.F.R. § 1.106 (1990).
357. 47 C.F.R. § 25.140 (1990).
358. *National Exchange, Inc.,* 1 F.C.C. Rcd 682 (1986).
359. 5 U.S.C. § 500 (1988).

existed. GTE had invoked *Ashbacker* v. *Federal Communication Commission*[362] in which the Supreme Court held that where two or more radio station applications are mutually exclusive, they are entitled to comparative hearings. Mutual exclusivity exists where the grant of one application precludes the grant of another (see Chapter 3.2.8.). GTE's assertion of mutual exclusivity in this case was based on the fact that the orbital arc suitable for use by U.S. satellite operators was fast becoming saturated, and that orbital locations within a certain portion of the arc particularly suited for its proposed operations might be assigned to other satellite licensees. The Commission denied that an *Ashbacker* type of situation existed because orbital locations would still be available for future applicants, including GTE. Moreover, under established Commission policy, conflicting requests for the same orbital locations do not invoke a right to comparative hearings.[363]

REVIEW. While reconsideration is performed by the same decision-making authority, a review is always conducted by decision makers at a higher level. Accordingly, only decisions taken pursuant to delegated authority are subject to review. Decisions taken by the Commission, itself, are subject to reconsideration, only. A review may be conducted on the Commission's own initiative,[364] or in response to an "application for review" pursuant to Section 5(c) of the Communications Act[365] and Section 1.115 of the Commission's Rules.[366] Any person who is adversely affected by a Commission decision may apply for a review. If the Commission grants an application for review, it may affirm, modify, or set aside the decision.[367] The Commission may deny the application without specifying any reasons therefor.[368] Reviews are less common than reconsiderations, partly because the Commission often will make the initial decision,

---

360. The financial qualification requirements referred to by NEX were codified by the Commission in 1985, 47 C.F.R. § 25.140 (1990), and require domestic fixed satellite applicants to show, at the time of the application, that they are financially qualified to construct, launch and operate the proposed satellite for one year. The purpose of the Rule was to limit the number of domestic fixed satellite applicants at a time when the requests for orbital locations exceeded the number of locations available. Entrepreneurial start-up companies, such as NEX, were unable to meet the financial requirements test, since they could not raise sufficient capital at that early stage of the satellite project. Consequently, their applications were dismissed.
361. *GTE Satellite Corporation*, 93 F.C.C. 2d 832 (1983).
362. 326 U.S. 327 (1945).
363. *GTE Satellite Corporation*, *supra* note 361, at 839, citing *Assignment of Orbital Locations to Space Stations in the Domestic Fixed Satellite Service*, 84 F.C.C. 2d 584, 598 (1981).
364. 47 U.S.C. § 155(d) (1988).
365. 47 U.S.C. § 155(c)(4) (1988); 47 C.F.R. § 1.117 (1990).
366. 47 C.F.R. § 1.115 (1990).
367. 47 U.S.C. § 155(c)(6) (1988).
368. 47 U.S.C. § 155(c)(5) (1988).

itself, if it anticipates that a decision will become controversial.

An example of a situation where an application for a review was filed, again, involves National Exchange, Inc. NEX sought a review of a decision by the FCC Common Carrier Bureau (taken pursuant to delegated authority), denying NEX's motion for separation of rulemaking and adjudicatory proceedings and for expedited relief.[369] In the motion, NEX had sought to separate the rulemaking concerning strict financial standards for domestic fixed satellite applicants and the licensing proceeding to which NEX was a party in order to avoid application of the standards to it. The Commission denied NEX's application for review.[370]

JUDICIAL REVIEW. Judicial review is available to your client when the administrative remedies of review and reconsideration have been exhausted. Any person adversely affected or aggrieved by an FCC action may seek judicial review.[371] FCC decisions are reviewable pursuant to the constraints of Section 402(b) of the Communications Act[372] and selected portions of the Administrative Procedure Act.[373] A dozen or so cases directly involving FCC licensing and regulation of satellites have been brought before the courts. However, numerous court rulings in cases concerning other FCC regulations equally affect satellite operators.

The scope of judicial review is limited. Courts will only consider whether an FCC decision was 1) arbitrary or capricious, 2) in excess of statutory authority, 3) unsupported by sufficient evidence, or 4) contrary to the law.[374] A court will not review whether the Commission's determination pursuant to its mandate (the public interest standard) was prudent. In other words, a court will not decide *de novo* the soundness of the Commission's judgment that a particular action serves the public interest. The

---

369. *National Exchange, Inc.,* FCC Mimeo No. 4971, *released* June 5, 1985.

370. *See Licensing of Space Stations in the Domestic Fixed Satellite Service,* 58 Rad. Reg.2d 1267 (1985), at paras. 29 *et seq.*

371. 5 U.S.C. § 702 (1988). However, actions that are purely discretionary in nature, *e.g.,* failure to take enforcement action, are not reviewable, *MCI v. FCC,* 765 F.2d 1186, 1190 (1985).

372. 47 U.S.C. § 402(b) (1988), pursuant to which, *e.g.,* a satellite company may appeal directly to the United States Court of Appeals if it is: 1) an applicant for a satellite construction permit or operating license whose application has been denied by the Commission; 2) an applicant for modification of a satellite construction permit or operating license whose application has been denied by the Commission; 3) an applicant for authority to transfer, assign, or dispose of a satellite construction permit or operating license, or any right thereunder, whose application has been denied by the Commission; (4) the holder of a satellite construction permit or operating license that has been modified or revoked by the Commission; or (5) a satellite operator whose license has been suspended by the Commission. Any other person who is aggrieved or whose interests are adversely affected by any FCC action or order described in (1)-(4) also may appeal.

373. 5 U.S.C. §§ 551-559 and 701-708 (1988).

374. 5 U.S.C. § 706 (1988).

reason is that the Commission is considered to be in a better position than the courts to determine whether a particular service is likely to benefit the public due to its technical expertise and understanding of the industry it regulates. However, the courts can overrule public interest determinations by the FCC if the decisions violate one of the four categories listed above.

Wold Communications, Inc. v. Federal Communications Commission,[375] provides an example of a court's refusal to review the Commission's public interest determination. Wold challenged the Commission's decision in *Domestic Fixed Satellite Transponder Sales,*[376] which authorized domestic fixed satellite companies to sell transponders. Previously, all satellite companies had operated on a common carrier basis, i.e., holding themselves out for hire on non-discriminatory terms, which afforded resellers like Wold Communications substantial choice among satellite carriers. Concerned that this choice would be severely limited if satellite owners were permitted to sell transponders, Wold Communications attempted to have the Commission's decision overturned. It contended that the Commission had acted "outside its delegated authority,"[377] (in excess of authority) and had "not engage[d] in reasoned decision making" (arbitrary and capricious) when it authorized transponder sales.[378] The court found no merit to Wold's claims, and affirmed *Domestic Fixed Satellite Transponder sales.* The court noted that Wold, in essence, was attacking the Commission's public interest determination, which is outside the scope of judicial review. The court observed that

> Petitioners, in much of their argument, try to tell the court in many words that the FCC's decision is in their view "unwise . . . not likely to succeed in accomplishing what the Commission intended." *National Broadcasting Company v. United States,* 319 U.S. 100, 190, 224 (1943). The only response a reviewing court, mindful of its limited role, should give to arguments thus forecasting failure of the agency's design is that the complainants have selected the wrong forum for such a plea.[379]

In *MCI* v. *Federal Communications Commission,*[380] the court set aside an FCC determination as arbitrary and capricious. MCI challenged the *Sixth Report and Order*[381] in the Commission's Competitive Carrier pro-

375. 735 F.2d 1465 (D.C. Cir. 1984).
376. 90 F.C.C. 2d 1238 (1982).
377. *Wold Communications v. FCC, supra* note 375.
378. *Id.*
379. *Id.*
380. 765 F.2d 1186 (D.C. Cir. 1985). In determining whether an action is arbitrary or capricious, the court will consider the following factors: 1) whether there was a rational nexus between the facts found and the choice made; 2) whether the Commission considered all the relevant factors; and 3) whether there was a reasoned basis for the decision. *MCI v. FCC,* 842 F.2d 1296, 1300 (D.C. Cir. 1988).

ceeding in which the Commission, in a reversal of its own policy, concluded that it would no longer accept tariff filings from companies that had been exempted (forborne) from regulation under Title II of the Communications Act (see Chapter 3.2.3). Domestic fixed satellite operators, including MCI, fell into this category. MCI wished to continue to file tariffs. The court noted that a reversal of Commission policy was not *per se* arbitrary or capricious, but that the change in policy was capricious since it was contrary to the provisions of the Communications Act. According to the court, the Commission did not have the authority under the Act to refuse to accept tariffs filings. Perhaps the reasoning here should have been that the Commission acted in excess of statutory authority.

In *Communications Satellite Corporation* v. *Federal Communications Commission,*[382] the court vacated the Commission's decision in *Teleport International Ltd. and American Satellite Company,*[383] which authorized Teleport International to provide two-way transborder service to Jamaica via a satellite owned by American Satellite Company. The court held that in authorizing this service, the Commission had gone beyond its traditional rationale for so-called transborder satellite authorizations (see Chapter 3.1.4.) and that the Commission's explanations for its conclusions were inadequate and, therefore, failed to satisfy the arbitrary and capricious standard.

In *National Association of Broadcasters* v. *Federal Communications Commission,*[384] the court concluded that the Commission had exceeded its statutory authority by exempting so-called "programmer customers" of direct broadcasting satellite common carriers from broadcast regulation (see Chapter 3.1.2.). The Commission had decided not to impose the statutory restraints normally imposed upon broadcasters.

---

381. *Policy and Rules Concerning Rates for Competitive Common Carrier Services,* 57 Rad. Reg.2d 1391 (1985).
382. 836 F.2d 623 (D.C. Cir. 1988).
383. 2 F.C.C. Rcd 4149 (1987).
384. 740 F.2d 1190 (D.C. Cir. 1984). The Commission corrected this defect in *Subscription Video Services,* 2 F.C.C. Rcd 1001 (1987). This decision was upheld by the court in *National Association of Better Broadcasting v. FCC,* 849 F.2d 665 (D.C. Cir. 1988).

4. Obtain Registration in the International Telecommunication Union (ITU) Master International Frequency Register of Your Client's Frequency Assignment

National authorization to use certain frequencies and to place a satellite in a specific geostationary orbital location, or particular orbital path (discussed in Chapter 3., above), does not protect the satellite operator, your client, from radio interference from the transmissions of foreign satellite operators. Protection of that nature can be obtained through the procedures established by the International Telecommunication Union (ITU or Union), a public international organization based in Geneva, Switzerland, and charged with managing the radio frequency spectrum and registering frequencies used by satellite operators.

The process leading to international protection from radio interference can be complex and time-consuming. Depending upon whether your client intends to launch a geostationary or a non-geostationary satellite system, whether your client's proposed service falls within the fixed or other satellite service categories and whether the proposed satellite system has the potential for causing radio interference to neighboring satellite operations, the process may involve extensive negotiations and take anywhere from ten months to four years. Nonetheless, obtaining international protection from radio interference is essential. Applying the ITU procedures leading to international protection is even obligatory for ITU member States operating or authorizing satellite operations from within their jurisdictions if such operations are capable of causing interference to the satellite or terrestrial operations of another country. Currently, 165 countries are members of the ITU.

All communications with the ITU for purposes of obtaining international frequency protection take place at the State or governmental level. As a private satellite operator your client may not initiate the process through direct contact with the ITU. The national telecommunications administration authorizing your client's satellite operation usually will provide the proper interface with the ITU. In the United States, for example, the Federal Communications Commission serves that function.

4.1. The International Telecommunication Union: Purpose, Function and Structure

ORIGIN AND JURISDICTION. The ITU was founded in 1865 as the International Telegraph Union to promulgate regulations for international telegraphy.[1] In step with subsequent technological advances in telecommunications, the International Telegraph Union gradually assumed jurisdiction over new methods and means of telecommunications, such as telephony and radio broadcasting.[2] In 1932, it became known as the International Telecommunication Union (ITU).[3] The ITU first concerned itself with space communications in 1959.[4]

GOVERNING TREATIES. The ITU's purpose, function and structure are set forth in the International Telecommunication Convention (ITU Convention)[5] and, to some extent, the Administrative Regulations.[6] The ITU Convention is the constituting document of the ITU. The Administra-

---

1. The International Telegraph Union was constituted in 1865 by the International Telegraph Convention. It was a merger of the Austro-German Telegraph Union and West European Telegraph Union. The International Telegraph Union, as well as the International Radiotelegraph Union, was a predecessor to the International Telecommunication Union (ITU). The International Radiotelegraph Union was established in 1906 by the Berlin Radiotelegraph Convention. Both the International Telegraph Convention and the Berlin Radiotelegraph Convention were revised several times until, at a conference in Madrid in 1932, they were merged into the International Telecommunication Convention, which created the ITU. *See* R.L. White & H.M White, THE LAW AND REGULATION OF INTERNATIONAL SPACE COMMUNICATION (1988) [hereinafter cited as White, SPACE COMMUNICATION], at 30-61 (describing the history of the ITU). The International Telecommunication Convention [hereinafter cited as the ITU Convention] has been revised several times. *See infra* note 9 (providing dates and places for such revisions). The ITU is a specialized agency under the aegis of the United Nations. *See* Article 57 of the Charter of the United Nations, *done* June 26, 1945, *entered into force* Oct. 24, 1945, E.A.S. 236, 3 *Bevans* 697 (explaining the meaning of "specialized agency").
2. The International Telegraph Convention was amended in 1903 to include telephone services, and amended again in 1906 to include radio broadcasting.
3. *See supra* note 1 (describing the events leading to the creation of the ITU).
4. *See* Chapter 4.2. and N.M. Matte, *Aerospace Law: Telecommunications Satellites,* 166 ACADEMY OF INT'L L., Extract from Recueil des Cours, at 151, 154 [hereinafter cited as Matte, Extract] (describing the ITU's early involvement with space communications).
5. International Telecommunication Convention, *done* at Nairobi, Kenya, Nov. 6, 1982, *entered into force* Jan. 4, 1984, T.I.A.S. 8572. The ITU Convention was revised at Nice, France, June 1989. This revision has not yet entered into force.

tive Regulations implement and complete the ITU Convention,[7] and are annexed to it.[8] Both legal instruments have treaty status and, accordingly, their provisions are legally binding. They are revised periodically,[9] and revisions are binding only on those ITU Members which have elected to ratify them.[10] Of the Administrative Regulations, the Radio Regulations are especially significant in the context of satellite telecommunications. The Radio Regulations set forth frequencies available for use by specific radio (including satellite) services and contain rules for coordination, registration and operation of radio stations (satellites).

PURPOSES OF THE ITU. The basic thrusts of the ITU are to coordinate and promote the development of telecommunications [11] among nations.[12] Article 4 of the ITU Convention sets forth the purposes of the organization:

> 1. (a) maintain and extend international cooperation . . . for the improvement and rational use of telecommunications of all kinds. . .

---

6. Of the Administrative Regulations, it is the Radio Regulations that pertain to satellite telecommunications. The current Radio Regulations are contained in the *Final Acts,* World Administrative Radio Conference (1979) [hereinafter cited as WARC-79]; *partially revised Final Acts,* Regional Administrative Radio Conference for the Planning of Broadcasting Satellite Service in Region 2 (1983) [hereinafter cited as RARC-83]; *Final Acts,* World Administrative Radio Conference on the Use of the Geostationary-Satellite Orbit and the Planning of Space Services Utilizing It, First Session (1985) [hereinafter cited as WARC-ORB-85] and Second Session (1988) [hereinafter cited as WARC-ORB-88]; and *Final Acts,* World Administrative Radio Conference for Mobile Services (1987) [hereinafter cited as WARC-MOB-87].
7. ITU Convention, art. 42, para. 1 (Nairobi 1982).
8. ITU Radio Regulations, art. 69, No. 5187 (WARC-79).
9. The ITU Convention was revised most recently at an ITU Plenipotentiary Conference at Nice, France, 1989. *See supra* note 5 (providing that this revision is not in force). Previous revisions include those adopted at Nairobi, Kenya, 1982; Torremolinos, Spain, 1973; Montreux, Switzerland, 1965; Geneva, Switzerland, 1959; Buenos Aires, Argentina, 1952; and Atlantic City, United States 1947. The first ITU Convention was adopted at Madrid, Spain, 1932, *see supra* note 1 (describing the history of the ITU). Also, the Radio Regulations are revised periodically at ITU administrative radio conferences. The last *general* revision of the Radio Regulations took place in 1979. *See supra* note 6 (listing subsequent revisions). *See also* Chapter 4.2. (describing plenipotentiary and administrative conferences and the development of Radio Regulations pertaining to satellites).
10. Ratification of the ITU Convention involves acceptance of the Radio Regulations in force at the time of the ratification. ITU Convention, art. 42, para. 1 (Nairobi 1982). In the event of inconsistency between the ITU Convention and the Radio Regulations, the former prevails. *Id.,* art. 41.
11. The term "telecommunication" has been defined by the ITU as "[a]ny transmission, emission or reception of signs, signals, writing, images and sounds or intelligence of any nature by wire, radio, optical or other electromagnetic systems." ITU Radio Regulations, art. 1, No. 4 (WARC-79).

(b) promote the development of technical facilities and their most efficient operation with a view to improving the efficiency of telecommunications services, increasing their usefulness and making them, so far as possible, generally available to the public; [and]

(c) to harmonize the actions of nations in the attainment of those ends.

2. To this end, the [ITU] shall in particular:

(a) effect allocation of radio frequency spectrum and *registration* of radio frequency assignments in order to avoid harmful interference between radio stations of different countries;

(b) coordinate efforts to eliminate harmful interference between radio stations of different countries and to improve the use made of the radio frequency spectrum;

(c) foster international cooperation in the delivery of technical assistance to the developing countries and the creation, development and improvement of telecommunication equipment and networks in developing countries by every means at its disposal . . . ;

(d) coordinate efforts with a view to harmonizing the development of telecommunication facilities, notably those using space techniques, with a view to full advantage being taken of their possibilities; . . . ; [and]

(g) undertake studies, *make regulations*, adopt resolutions, formulate recommendations and opinions, and collect and publish information concerning telecommunication matters.[13]

The purposes set forth in section 2(a) and (b), above, have particular relevance to ITU regulation of satellites as they provide the ITU with authority to 1) *allocate* frequency spectrum to classes of satellite services (see Chapter 4.2., below); 2) establish a regulatory framework for, and *administer the coordination* of, frequencies used by member States in order to avoid radio interference between their operations; and 3) *register* in the Master International Frequency Register satellite frequencies assigned by member States after they have been coordinated (see Chapter 4.3., below). The ITU's authority to adopt regulations, resolutions and recommendations (2(g), above) supports these activities.

---

12. The Preamble of the ITU Convention (Nairobi 1982) provides that

> [w]hile fully recognizing the sovereign right of each country to regulate its telecommunication and having regard to the growing importance of telecommunication for the preservation of peace and the social and economic development of all countries, the plenipotentiaries of the Contracting Governments, with the object of facilitating peaceful relations, international cooperation and economic and social development among peoples by means of efficient telecommunication services have agreed to establish this Convention which is the basic instrument of the International Telecommunication Union.

13. Emphasis added. ITU Convention, art. 4 (Nairobi 1982).

FREQUENCY ALLOCATION. The allocation of frequency spectrum refers to the designation by the ITU of discrete bands, or segments, of the spectrum for use by radio services, such as fixed satellite service,[14] radiodetermination satellite service,[15] broadcasting satellite service,[16] and mobile satellite service.[17] Once a frequency allocation has been adopted, it becomes part of the ITU Table of Frequency Allocations contained in Article 8 of the ITU Radio Regulations,[18] and therefore legally binding on ITU member States that have ratified it. Consequently, as a general rule, all satellite operations authorized by ITU member States must be consistent with the ITU's Table of Frequency Allocations.[19] It is important to note that, while the ITU *allocates* frequencies for satellite services in general, ITU member States *assign* frequencies to specific satellite systems, consistent with the ITU frequency allocations. See Chapter 4.2.

FREQUENCY COORDINATION. Coordination of refers to the process whereby an administration of an ITU member State, which is planning or authorizing a new satellite system, collaborates with administrations of other ITU member States to eliminate harmful interference that might otherwise occur to the existing or planned satellite systems of the latter. The ITU Radio Regulations provide criteria and procedures for such coordina-

---

14. Fixed satellite service is defined as "[a] radiocommunication service between earth stations at given positions, when one or more satellites are used; the given position may be a specified fixed point or any fixed point within specified areas; in some cases this service includes satellite-to-satellite links, which may also be operated in the inter-satellite service; the fixed satellite service may also include feeder links for other space radiocommunication services." ITU Radio Regulations, art. 1, No. 22 (WARC-ORB-88).
15. Radiodetermination satellite service is "[a] radiocommunication service for the purpose of radiodetermination involving the use of one or more space stations." ITU Radio Regulations, art. 1, No. 29 (WARC-79). Radiodetermination is defined as "[t]he determination of the position, velocity and/or other characteristics of an object, or the obtaining of information relating to these parameters, by means of the propagation properties of radio waves." *Id.*, art. 1, No. 10.
16. Broadcasting satellite service is defined as "[a] radiocommunication service in which signals transmitted or retransmitted by space stations are intended for direct reception by the general public. In the broadcasting satellite service 'direct reception' shall encompass both individual and community reception." *Id.*, art. 1, No. 37. The term "space station," as used here, is synonymous with "satellite."
17. Mobile satellite service is "[a] radiocommunication service between mobile earth stations and one or more space stations, or between stations used by this service; or between mobile earth stations by means of one or more space stations." *Id.*, art. 1, No. 27. Depending upon the locations of the Earth stations communicating with the satellite, the Radio Regulations distinguish between land-mobile satellite service, maritime-mobile satellite service, and aeronautical-mobile satellite service. *Id.*, art. 1, Nos. 29, 31, 35.
18. ITU Radio Regulations, art. 8, sec. IV (WARC-79, RARC-83, WARC-ORB-85, WARC-MOB-87 and WARC-MOB-87).

tion. The ITU provides administrative support and acts as a catalyst, but does not become directly involved in the negotiations between or among member States, unless its assistance is specifically requested. See Chapter 4.3.

FREQUENCY REGISTRATION. Registration refers to the process whereby the ITU's International Frequency Registration Board records a frequency assignment in the Master International Frequency Register. As a general rule, a frequency assignment will be recorded if it conforms to the ITU Table of Frequency Allocations and has been successfully coordinated. In some cases, the International Frequency Registration Board may be called upon to determine that harmful interference will not result. The significance of such registration is that it protects the rightful user of the assignment from interference from all subsequently authorized and registered satellite operations. See Chapter 4.3.

ORGANS OF THE ITU. The ITU has seven organs: the Plenipotentiary Conference, the Administrative Conference, the Administrative Council, the General Secretariat, the International Frequency Registration Board (IFRB), the International Radio Consultative Committee (CCIR)[20] and the International Telegraph and Telephone Consultative Committee (CCITT).[21] Of the Administrative Conferences, the Administrative Radio Conferences embrace satellite-related issues.

The Plenipotentiary and Administrative Conferences meet periodically and consist of delegations representing ITU member States. The Administrative Council is composed of representatives of a limited number of member States, and acts on behalf of the Plenipotentiary Conference in the intervals between sessions. The General Secretariat, the IFRB, the CCIR and the CCITT are permanent organs. International civil servants, that is, individuals who in their decision-making owe no employment loyalty to their respective States of nationality, compose the staff of the Secretariat and the IFRB. Representatives of national telecommunications

---

19. ITU Radio Regulations, art. 6, No. 342 (WARC-79). An important exception exists. The Radio Regulations provide that

> [a]dministrations of the Members shall not assign to a station any frequency in derogation of either the Table of Frequency Allocations given in this Chapter or other provisions of these Regulations, except on the express condition that harmful interference shall not be caused to services carried on by stations operating in accordance with the provisions of the Convention and of these Regulations. *Id.*

Furthermore, "footnotes" often appear in the Table of Frequency Allocations denoting exceptions, limitations, or conditions of use by one or more countries. For example, footnote 3787A provides that "[i]n Region 2 in the 11.7-12.1 GHz band, transponders on space stations in the fixed satellite service may be used additionally for transmission in the broadcasting satellite service. . ." provided certain power limitations are observed (in order to avoid interference). *Id.*, art. 8, sec. IV, note 3787A (WARC-79).

20. The acronym is based on the French designation, *Comité consultatif international des radiocommunications.*

21. Again, the acronym is based on the French designation.

administrations and private operating entities designated by member States participate in the CCIR and CCITT.

THE PLENIPOTENTIARY CONFERENCE. The Plenipotentiary Conference is the supreme organ of the ITU.[22] It is composed of delegations of all member States and is convened at regular intervals[23] to determine the general policies of the Union; consider the report by the Administrative Council on the interim activities of the ITU; decide on budgetary and other fiscal matters; elect ITU member States to serve on the Administrative Council; elect the Secretary General; elect members of the IFRB; revise the ITU Convention; conclude or revise agreements between the ITU and other international organizations; and deal with other telecommunications matters as may be necessary.[24] The responsibility to revise the ITU Convention is particularly noteworthy since the Convention is the legal instrument from which the ITU derives its authority.

ADMINISTRATIVE RADIO CONFERENCES. Administrative Radio Conferences are convened periodically[25] to consider specific telecommunications matters,[26] such as frequency allocations, or coordination procedures for particular types of satellite services. Only the items included in the agenda of a particular conference [27] may be discussed at that conference.[28] Administrative Radio Conferences may be global or regional in

22. ITU Convention, art. 5, para. 1 (Nairobi 1982).
23. *Id.*, art. 6, para. 1. ITU. Plenipotentiary Conferences have been convened at approximately eight-year intervals. *See* note 9, *supra* (listing the places and dates of Plenipotentiary Conferences).
24. ITU Convention, art. 6, para. 2 (Nairobi 1982).
25. Administrative Radio Conferences may be convened by a decision of a Plenipotentiary Conference, based on recommendation of a previous Administrative Conference with the approval of the Administrative Council, by a specific proposal of the Administrative Council, or at the request to the Secretary General by at least one-fourth of the Members of the ITU. *Id.*, art. 54, paras. 2, 3. *See* White, SPACE COMMUNICATION, *supra* note 1,
26. ITU Convention, art. 7, para. 2 (Nairobi 1982).
27. The Agenda already has been adopted for the World Administrative Radio Conference for Dealing with Frequency Allocations in Certain Parts of the Spectrum, to be convened in Spain on February 3, 1992. Items that are not on the Agenda cannot be considered at the Conference. *See, however,* ITU Convention, art. 54, para. 4 (providing that the agenda may be changed under certain circumstances). The Agenda was established by the Administrative Council and contained in weekly telegram No. A87, addressed to all ITU Members on June 21, 1990. *See An Inquiry Relating to Preparation for the International Telecommunication Union World Administrative Radio Conference for Dealing with Frequency Allocations in Certain Parts of the Spectrum,* 5 F.C.C. Rcd 6046 (1990), Appendix B (containing the Agenda). *See also* M.L. Smith, INTERNATIONAL REGULATION OF SATELLITE COMMUNICATION (1990) [hereinafter cited as Smith, INTERNATIONAL REGULATION], at 117 (concerning the WARC-ORB-88 Agenda). The Agenda is attached: *See* APPENDIX I.
28. ITU Convention, art. 7, para. 2 (Nairobi 1982).

scope.[29] The agenda of a World Administrative Radio Conference may include a partial or, exceptionally, a complete revision of the Radio Regulations.[30] Only three times since World War II have the Radio Regulations been generally revised, most recently in 1979.[31] The agenda of a Regional Administrative Conference is limited to specific telecommunications questions affecting the region.[32]

Perhaps the most important and often controversial function of the Administrative Radio Conference is the allocation of radio spectrum for different kinds of radio services, including satellite services. This function is important because, without a frequency allocation for a particular service, that service usually cannot be provided in compliance with the Radio Regulations. As a general proposition, national telecommunications administrations only authorize radio operations in frequency bands consistent with ITU frequency allocations.[33] For example, the 4,500-4,990 MHz band has been allocated by the ITU for fixed satellite service. Generally, therefore, this band cannot be used, e.g., for radiodetermination or any other satellite service that is not a fixed satellite service, that is, unless a footnote appears in the ITU Radio Regulations' Table of Frequency Allocations permitting the use of some segment of this band for a particular service other than fixed satellite service in one region, or other specified area, of the world. Frequency allocations may be modified at Administrative Radio Conferences, and ITU member States may propose such modifications.

In the United States, private satellite companies sometimes seek to operate satellite systems in frequency bands allocated by the ITU to satellite services other than those they propose to provide. These companies often request the United States government to propose modifications to frequency allocations at an upcoming Administrative Radio Conference. Frequently, the government agrees. For example, the United States has agreed to request modifications to current frequency allocations at the 1992 World Administrative Radio Conference that would support several private U.S. companies applying to the Federal Communications Commission for permission to provide mobile and radiodetermination satellite

---

29. *Id.*, art. 7, para. 1. The ITU divides the world into three regions: Region 1 includes Europe, Africa, the Middle East, the USSR and Mongolia; Region 2 includes the Americas, the Caribbean and Greenland; and Region 3 includes Asia and the Pacific Basin, except Hawaii. ITU Radio Regulations, art. 8, Nos. 392-395 (WARC-79).
30. ITU Convention, art. 7, para. 3(1) (Nairobi 1982).
31. General revisions of the Radio Regulations took place at World Administrative Conferences at Atlanta, Georgia, in the United States in 1947, and at Geneva, Switzerland in 1959 and 1979. *See* Smith INTERNATIONAL REGULATION, *supra* note 27, at 25 (describing the revisions).
32. ITU Convention, art. 7, para. 3(2) (Nairobi 1982).
33. Exceptions exist. *See supra* note 19 (citing the relevant provision of the Radio Regulations).

services in the 1,610-1,626.5 MHz band via low-Earth orbit, multi-satellite systems. One such company is Motorola Satellite Communications, Inc. of Chandler, Arizona, which is proposing a constellation of seventy-seven satellites ("Iridium") in seven polar orbits for such services. Currently, the 1,610-1,626.5 MHz band is allocated for radiodetermination satellite service, *i.e.*, on a primary basis in the U.S., and on a secondary basis in the rest of the world with a few exceptions. (A service with a secondary allocation cannot cause interference to, or claim protection against interference from, a service with a primary allocation). All the services proposed by Motorola and other companies with similar proposals cannot be provided in the frequency band suggested unless the current allocation is modified. Consequently, the U.S. is proposing that the 1,610-1,626.5 MHz band be allocated co-equally for generic mobile satellite service and radiodetermination satellite service, and that the allocation to the latter service be upgraded to primary status in the world.[34]

THE ADMINISTRATIVE COUNCIL. The Administrative Council is the official agent of the Plenipotentiary Conference, acting on behalf of, and in between, Plenipotentiary Conferences.[35] It is composed of representatives of forty-one ITU member States elected by the Plenipotentiary Conference with due regard to equitable geographical distribution.[36] Each elected Member appoints a person to serve on the Council.[37] The Council's

34. While the United States is influential at administrative radio conferences, its position does not always prevail. Other countries often oppose the U.S. on policy and/or technical grounds. To assert their positions more effectively, countries often form groups and designate chief spokesmen for their positions. For example, at the Administrative Radio Conference for Mobile Services in 1987, the United States proposed a world-wide primary allocation for radiodetermination satellite service in the 1,610 -1626.5 GHz band. A group of European countries formed to oppose this allocation, with the United Kingdom delegation acting as the chief spokesman for the positions of the European countries. A compromise was reached, however, on a secondary allocation for radiodetermination satellite service. U.S. private companies often play an active role during the preparation of an administrative radio conference in trying to persuade foreign governments to support a United States position that will benefit them. For example, in the years prior to the 1987 World Administrative Radio Conference on Mobile Services, Geostar Corporation of Washington, D.C., which had applied to the U.S. Federal Communications Commission for permission to operate three radiodetermination satellites, solicited support from foreign governments for a world-wide allocation for radiodetermination satellite service. Motorola Satellite Communications, Inc. engaged in an effort to garner support at the 1992 World Administrative Radio Conference for a generic mobile satellite allocation in the 1,610-1,626.5 MHz band, which will benefit it.

35. ITU Convention, art. 8, para. 3 (Nairobi 1982). *See* White, SPACE COMMUNICATION *supra* note 1, at 73 (explaining the role of the Administrative Council).

36. ITU Convention, art. 8, para. 1(1) (Nairobi 1982).

37. *Id.*, art. 8, para. 1(2).

responsibilities are to facilitate the implementation of the provisions in the ITU Convention and Radio Regulations;[38] ensure the efficient coordination of the work of the Union and exercise effective fiscal control over the permanent organs;[39] and promote international cooperation, particularly with a view to the needs of developing countries.[40]

THE GENERAL SECRETARIAT. The General Secretariat is the chief administrative organ of the ITU and is located in Geneva, Switzerland. As part of its general administrative tasks, it provides numerous support functions in connection with Plenipotentiary and Administrative Conferences, such as arranging meeting places, collecting proposals from ITU member States and preparing minutes and final reports of the conferences.[41] The General Secretariat is headed by a Secretary-General,[42] who is elected by the Plenipotentiary Conference and is responsible to the Administrative Council for all the administrative and financial aspects of the Union's activities.[43] The Secretary-General also acts as the legal representative of the ITU.[44]

THE IFRB. The IFRB is a committee of five members elected by the Plenipotentiary Conference,[45] owing loyalty to the Union and not their respective countries of nationality,[46] whose primary responsibility is to effect the orderly recording in the Master International Frequency Register of national frequency assignments to geostationary, as well as non-geostationary, satellites.[47] Such recording, *i.e.*, registration, results in international protection from harmful interference from subsequently-registered satellite systems. Recording in the Master International Frequency Register is the culmination of a three-, sometimes two-, step procedure administered by the IFRB, depending upon whether the satellite system at issue is geostationary or non-geostationary (*see* Chapter 4.3.): 1) advance publication (the IFRB publishes information submitted by member States on proposed new satellite systems);[48] 2) coordination (States coordinate their proposed new satellite systems with other proposed and

---

38. *Id.*, art. 8, para. 4(1)
39. *Id.*, art. 8, para. 4(2)
40. *Id.*, art. 8, para. 4(3)
41. *See* White, SPACE COMMUNICATION, *supra* note 1, at 72 (describing the role of the General Secretariat).
42. ITU Convention, art. 9, para. 1 (Nairobi 1982).
43. *Id.*, art. 9, para. 1(3).
44. *Id.*, art. 9, para. 3.
45. *Id.*, art. 10, para. 1. The IFRB members are "custodians of the international public interest." *Id.*, art. 10, para. 2.
46. *Id.*, art. 10, para. 2.
47. *Id.*, art. 10, para. 1. The IFRB effects the recording of frequencies assigned by ITU member States to specific satellite operations in accordance with the procedures set forth in Article 13 of the Radio Regulations. ITU Radio Regulations, art. 13 (WARC-79 and WARC-ORB-88).
48. *See Id.*, art. 11, sec. I (concerning advance publication) and ITU Radio Regulations, art. 10, Nos. 991-1006 (WARC-79) (concerning the IFRB's functions).

existing satellite systems to prevent harmful radio interference);[49] and 3) notification and registration (ITU member States notify the IFRB that they will be bringing into use a satellite system, and the IFRB registers frequency assignments for the satellite systems in the Master International Frequency Register).[50] With respect to non-geostationary satellites, formal coordination procedures do not exist and resolution of potential interference problems takes place only in conjunction with the advance publication process. In light of current proposals by U.S. companies (Chapter 3.1.6.) and one international organization for low-Earth orbit Satellite systems, it is likely that the ITV will adopt coordination procedures also for non-geostationary satellite systems. As an interim solution, the ITU could require compliance with the geostationary coordination procedures to the extent practicable.

"TONGASAT." Recently, the IFRB's role has become somewhat controversial. The controversy erupted over the advance publication by the IFRB of information relating to geostationary positions and frequencies for sixteen satellites for the Kingdom of Tonga, a tiny island in the South Pacific. Tonga is acting on behalf of Friendly Islands Satellite Communications, Ltd. (Tongasat), a company whose Managing Director and driving force is Dr. M.C. Nilson, an American entrepreneur who retired to Tonga. Dr. Nilson is attempting to create an organization[51] that will own and operate a regional satellite system to serve the communications needs of the peoples

---

49. *See* ITU Radio Regulations, art. 11, Sec. II (WARC-79 and WARC-ORB-88) (concerning coordination).

50. *See Id.*, art. 13 (WARC-79 and WARC-ORB-88) (concerning recording) and (ITU Radio Regulations, art. 10, No. 992) (WARC-79) (concerning the IFRB's functions).

51. This organization is referred to by Dr. Nilson as the "International Ownership Body." *See* M.C. Nilson, *The Tongasat Asia-Pacific Regional Communications Satellite System,* Paper Presented at the 13th Pacific Telecommunications Conference, Honolulu, Hawaii (13-16 January, 1991) (describing the Tongasat project). Modeled on INTELSAT, the International Ownership Body will be comprised of "Signatories" of each of the participating countries. Some Signatories will provide the investment funding to construct and launch the initial US$400-600 million satellite system. The investing Signatories will set tariffs charged to all using Signatories. Non-investing and investing Signatories will together set policies of the International Ownership Body. Investing Signatories will hold ownership shares equivalent to the monetary, or in-kind, investment value they contribute to the total capitalization required for each successive generation of the Tongasat satellite system. Tongasat will contribute the IFRB coordinated and registered orbital positions and frequencies in lieu of a monetary contribution. While the International Ownership Body clearly resembles INTELSAT, it differs in at least two important respects: Signatory investments are not tied to the usage of the satellite system and Signatories need not invest in the satellite system to participate in the International Ownership Body. *See* Chapter 5.1. (describing the structure of INTELSAT).

of the Asia-Pacific region.

The International Telecommunications Satellite Organization (INTELSAT), which provides communications satellite services globally, including the Asia-Pacific region (*see* Chapter 5.1.1.), depends upon Pacific geostationary locations in order to continue that service. INTELSAT has claimed that the orbital locations sought by Tonga and Tongasat exceed by far the number realistically needed by Tongasat,[52] and that the company is attempting "to convert the ITU registration process into an opportunity for financial speculation in the geostationary orbit . . . ."[53] INTELSAT was particularly disturbed at overtures made by Dr. Nilson and Tongasat to INTELSAT regarding the lease of orbital locations to the latter, and has rejected outright any such offers. INTELSAT has charged Tongasat with "flagrant abuse of the ITU Radio Regulations."[54] These allegations were contained in a letter dated June 12, 1990, addressed to the members of the IFRB from Dean Burch, then Director General of INTELSAT. Mr. Burch also emphasized the "dangerous precedent" the Tongasat case would set if Tongasat were allowed to pursue its plans unchallenged,[55] and said he believed "the IFRB possesses adequate authority under the Radio Regulations to refuse to recognize the Tongasat filings."[56] Tonga and Tongasat, for their part, have rejected all INTELSAT's allegations. They claim their actions are legitimate and justified by the intent to establish a regional satellite organization.[57]

The dilemma facing the IFRB in reconciling INTELSAT's and Tongasat's positions was that, under a strict "black letter" law interpretation of the Radio Regulations, Tonga's filings to the IFRB on behalf of Tongasat requesting advance publication of orbital locations and frequencies for sixteen satellites are lawful, even though orbital locations are requested in excess of Tongasat's actual needs. Tonga and Tongasat's acts nonetheless may be viewed as a violation of the spirit of the ITU Convention and Radio Regulations and, therefore, a subversion of them. For example, Article 33 of the ITU Convention provides in very general terms that ITU members

---

52. Letter from Dean Burch, Director General, INTELSAT, to Pekka Tarjanne, Secretary General, International Telecommunication Union (June 8, 1990) [hereinafter cited as June 8 Letter], at 2, and Letter from Dean Burch, Director General, INTELSAT, to the Chairman and members of the IFRB (June 12, 1990) [hereinafter cited as June 12 Letter], at 1. The June 12 Letter was officially submitted to the ITU by the United States Federal Communications Commission, which acts on behalf of INTELSAT in ITU matters since only nations can become Members of, and officially interact with, the ITU.
53. June 8 Letter, *supra* note 52, at 1, and June 12 Letter, *supra* note 52, at 1.
54. June 8 Letter, *supra* note 52, at 2.
55. June 12 Letter, *supra* note 52, at 2.
56. *Id.*
57. *See generally* Letter from Sione Kite, Acting Chief Secretary & Acting Secretary to Cabinet, to Pekke Tarjanne, Secretary General, International Telecommunication Union (Aug. 6, 1990) (explaining Tongasat's position).

shall limit their uses of orbit and frequency resources:

> 1. Members shall endeavor to limit the number of frequencies and spectrum space used to the minimum essential to provide in a satisfactory manner the necessary services.
>
> 2. In using frequency bands for space radio services Members shall bear in mind that radio frequencies and the geostationary satellite orbit are limited natural resources and that they must be used efficiently and economically, in conformity with the provisions of the Radio Regulations, so that countries or groups of countries may have equitable access to both, taking into account the special needs of the developing countries and the geographical situation of particular countries.[58]

Yielding to pressure from INTELSAT, the IFRB caused Tongasat to admit that its needs could be satisfied through the use of only three to six orbital locations. Tonga subsequently cancelled advance publication information on the remaining satellite networks that, realistically speaking, never would be established.

CONSULTATIVE COMMITTEES. Of the two Consultative Committees, it is the International Radio Consultative Committee which is particularly relevant to satellite operations. Its task is to study technical and operational issues "relating specifically to radiocommunication without limit of frequency range, and issue recommendations on them . . . ."[59] National telecommunications administrations and recognized private operating entities designated by ITU Member countries are members of the CCIR.[60]

POLITICIZATION ATTEMPTS. The ITU enjoys universal membership and is considered one of the most successful international organizations in the world today. Due to its extremely important and necessary function of coordinating the use of the radio frequencies by its member States, the ITU has escaped to a certain extent the politicization that has plagued, even paralyzed, so many other intergovernmental organizations. Although the organization was victimized in the 1970s and 1980s by North-South and East-West polarization, it has always managed to discharge its duties.

The politicization of the ITU refers, in particular, to the conflict between the needs and desires of the industrialized nations and those of the developing countries, *i.e.*, the "haves" and the "have nots." The developing world has charged the industrialized nations with exploiting orbit and frequency resources entirely for their own benefit without regard to the needs of countries presently unable to afford their own satellites, but which may be able to launch them in the future.

---

58. ITU Convention, art. 33 (Nairobi 1982). *See* M.L. Smith, *Legal and Policy Developments in International Satellite Communication*, XXXIV IISL 342 (1991) (discussing Tongasat in the context of the ITU Radio Regulations)
59. *Id.*, art. 11, para. 1(1)
60. *Id.*, art. 11, para. 2(a), (b).

The conflict is rooted in the so-called "first-come, first-served" approach applied by the ITU to the registration of satellite frequency assignments. Satellite operators, whose frequency assignments have been registered in the Master International Frequency Register, are protected from interference from subsequent new satellite systems. The burden, then, is on the new satellite operator to select technical parameters that do not result in interference to a previously recorded satellite system. Developing countries have claimed that if this recording approach continues to be applied, access to the geostationary orbit and associated frequency spectrum will be preempted by the time they are technically and financially capable of launching satellites. Consequently, they have demanded guarantees of future availability of orbit and spectrum resources. In various ways, the industrialized countries have sought to accommodate them, while also protecting their own interests (see Chapter 4.2.-3.).

The antagonism between the developed and the developing countries has focused to date on the geostationary orbit. It is possible that the Third World resentment, which abated somewhat in the late 1980s and early 1990s, will resurface as the ITU begins to debate the issue of access to non-geostationary orbital paths. No such debate is imminent, but it is perhaps inevitable due to recent announcements by the International Maritime Satellite Organization (INMARSAT) and several private U.S. companies that they plan to launch constellations of multiple satellites in various low-Earth orbits. Applications by these U.S. companies are pending before the United States Federal Communications Commission (see Chapter 3.1.6.). For example, Motorola Satellite Communications, Inc. of Chandler, Arizona, has proposed a seventy-seven satellite constellation ("Iridium"), with eleven satellites in seven circular polar orbits, for mobile voice communications services to and from hand-held, cordless units. Frequency allocations to be used by Iridium and other similar satellite systems will de debated at the 1992 World Administrative Radio Conference.

4.2. History of ITU Administrative Radio Conferences and Related Developments Concerning Satellites

1959 WORLD ADMINISTRATIVE RADIO CONFERENCE. It was not until 1959, two years after the first Soviet Sputnik was launched on October 4, 1957, that the International Telecommunication Union began concerning itself with the allocation of frequencies for space operations. At the World Administrative Radio Conference in 1959, the ITU for the first time defined and allocated frequency bands for "space radiocommunication service."[61] The allocation was prompted by the fact that, during the first two years of space exploration, U.S. and Soviet space missions had caused harmful interference to terrestrial radio stations because no specific frequencies had been set aside for use by space operations. It was recognized at the 1959 World Administrative Radio Conference that the projected increase in space exploration would lead to more interference unless frequency allocations were made to space services.

Since the 1959 World Administrative Radio Conference, eight Administrative Radio Conferences (one regional and seven global) have adopted frequency allocations and regulations for satellite operations. National administrations are currently preparing their positions for the next conference, entitled "World Administrative Radio Conference for Dealing with Frequency Allocations in Certain Parts of the Spectrum," to be held February 3 - March 3, 1992 in Spain.[62] A discussion of the conferences in chronological order follows.

1963 EXTRAORDINARY ADMINISTRATIVE RADIO CONFERENCE. Following the 1959 World Administrative Radio Conference, an Extraordinary Administrative Radio Conference to Allocate Frequency Bands for Space Radio Communication Purposes was convened in 1963.[63] This conference defined and allocated frequencies for "communication satellite service," and defined "broadcasting satellite service."[64] The significance of a particular satellite service definition combined with a frequency allocation was that State/government entities, or authorized private entities, could operate satellite systems providing such service without suffering or causing harmful radio interference. Operations unhampered by interference were essential to the commercialization of satellite communications that was to follow.[65]

The 1963 Extraordinary Administrative Radio Conference laid the foundation for the current regulatory regime governing recording in the

---

61. The allocation to space radiocommunication service was for research purposes only. *See* Matte, Extract, *supra* note 4, at 153-166 (describing ITU administrative radio conferences concerning satellites). The author cites A.G. Haley, SPACE LAW AND GOVERNMENT (1963), at 168-171, and *Space Age Presents Immediate Legal Problems,* I IISL 5 (1958). *See also* White, SPACE COMMUNICATION, *supra* note 1, at 109-265 (providing a fairly comprehensive history of ITU administrative radio conferences concerning satellites); R.L. & H.M. White, *Evolving Principles of Space Communication Regulation,* XXXI IISL 304 (1988) (concerning administrative radio conferences); and Smith, INTERNATIONAL REGULATION, *supra* note 27, at 57-86 (describing the conferences in the context of a WARC-ORB-85 prologue) and, at 87-156 (describing WARC-ORB-85 and WARC-ORB-88).

62. The Agenda for the Conference already has been established. *See supra* note 27 and APPENDIX I. In the United States, preparations for the 1992 Conference are under way at the Federal Communications Commission (FCC) and the National Telecommunication and Information Administration (NTIA). The FCC has conducted a series of inquiries: *An Inquiry Relating to Preparation for the International Telecommunication Union World Administrative Radio Conference for Dealing With Frequency Allocations in Certain Parts of the Spectrum,* Notice of Inquiry, 4 F.C.C. Rcd 8646 (1989); Second Notice of Inquiry, 5 F.C.C. Rcd 6046 (1990); and Supplemental Notice of Inquiry, 6 F.C.C. Rcd 1914 (1991).

63. *See* White, SPACE COMMUNICATION, *supra* note 1, at 119 (setting forth the agenda for this conference).

ITU Master International Frequency Register of frequency assignments for satellites and the process leading to such recording. As previously noted, the significance of recording, or registration, is that it affords the satellite operator international protection from harmful radio interference. The 1963 Conference contemplated a three-step procedure leading to recording of satellite frequency assignments for geostationary satellites, involving 1) submission of information by an administration planning or authorizing the launch and operation of a satellite system for purposes of "advance publication" of the information to administrations of all ITU member States by the IFRB; 2) bilateral coordination with other administrations operating or planning, or whose private entities are operating or planning, satellite or terrestrial radio operations that might suffer interference; and 3) notification to the IFRB of a frequency assignment for purposes of recording in the Master International Frequency Register.[66]

The recording approach adopted at the 1963 Extraordinary Administrative Radio Conference was based on the principle of "first-come, first-served," and essentially was an extension of the recording system in place for terrestrial radio operations, whose foundations were laid at the ITU Plenipotentiary Conference held at Washington, D.C., in 1927.[67] During

---

64. "Communication satellite service" was defined as a space service "between Earth stations, when using active or passive satellites for the exchange of communications of the fixed or mobile service, or between an Earth station and stations on an active satellite for the exchange of communications of the mobile service, with a view to their retransmission to or from stations in the mobile service." *Final Acts,* Extraordinary Administrative Radio Conference to Allocate Frequency Bands for Space Radiocommunication Purposes (1963) [hereinafter cited as *Final Acts,* EARC-63], art. 1. Broadcasting satellite service was defined as a space service "in which signals transmitted or retransmitted by space stations, or transmitted by reflection from objects in orbit around the Earth, are intended for direct reception by the general public." *Id. See* White, SPACE COMMUNICATION, *supra* note 1, at 122 (reciting the definitions). The *Final Acts,* EARC-63 were annexed to the International Telecommunication Convention (Montreux 1965) T.I.A.S. 6267.

65. Institutional frameworks for commercial satellite telecommunication were emerging. INTELSAT was established on an interim basis in 1964 to provide global commercial telecommunications satellite services. *See* Chapter 5.1.1. (describing INTELSAT). The United States had adopted the Communications Satellite Act of 1962, 47 U.S.C. §§701-735 (1988), which created the Communications Satellite Corporation as the U.S.-designated entity for participation in INTELSAT. The first applications by private companies for permission to operate domestic commercial satellite systems were submitted to the United States Federal Communications Commission (FCC) in 1965. *See* Chapter 3.1.1. (describing the FCC's early regulation of satellite communications).

66. Provisions for coordination of satellites were left intentionally vague, while provisions for coordination of Earth stations were more specific. Furthermore, the procedures for the advance publication of satellites were voluntary. *See* White, SPACE COMMUNICATION, *supra* note 1, at 124-128 (describing these procedures).

the 1963 Conference, itself, and during subsequent conferences in the 1970s and 1980s, the perpetuation of the first-come, first-served approach[68] was severely criticized by the developing countries, which perceived it to be unfair since it potentially preempted their access to the geostationary orbit and the radio spectrum allocated for space services.[69]

Based on their fears of orbit and spectrum saturation, the developing nations sought guarantees at the 1963 Conference of future access to these resources. The industrialized nations refused to provide outright guarantees[70] and sought, instead, to accommodate the developing countries through vaguely-worded, non-binding resolutions and recommendations reflecting their concerns. For example, a Recommendation was adopted at the 1963 Conference recognizing that all ITU members "have an interest in and right to an equitable and rational use of the radio frequency bands allocated for space communications,"[71] and recommending that "the utilization and exploitation of the frequency spectrum for space communications be subject to international agreement based on principles of justice and equity permitting the use and sharing of allocated frequency bands in the mutual interests of all nations."[72] This Recommendation represents a trend of attempting to ameliorate the concerns that prevailed throughout the 1970s and 1980s of countries that were technologically incapable of manufacturing and financially unable to purchase their own satellite systems.

1965 PLENIPOTENTIARY CONFERENCE. The 1965 ITU Plenipotentiary Conference at Montreux, Switzerland, convened to revise the ITU Convention,[73] also included extensive debate on space services. Although

---

67. Matte, Extracts, *supra* note 4, citing D.M. Leive, INTERNATIONAL TELECOMMUNICATIONS AND INTERNATIONAL LAW: THE REGULATION OF THE RADIO SPECTRUM (1970), at 72-73.

68. *See* White, SPACE COMMUNICATION, *supra* note 1, at 120 (concerning the debate during the 1963 Conference regarding the legal status of recorded orbital position and frequency assignments).

69. *See* Matte, Extracts, *supra* note 4, at 155 (describing this conflict). Supporting the cause of the developing nations was a United Nations General Assembly Resolution, providing that communications by means of satellite "should be available to nations of the world as soon as practicable on a global and non-discriminatory basis." U.N.G.A. Res. No. 1721 (XVI) (19-61).

70. The developing countries sought to achieve such guarantees through the coordination mechanisms mentioned in the text, above. Led by the U.S., the industrialized countries prevailed in keeping the coordination procedures for satellites intentionally vague in order to prevent situations in which one country would be able to block the satellite system of another country by refusing to agree to the coordination.

71. *Relating to the Utilization of Frequency Bands Allocated to Space Radiocommunication*, ITU Rec. No. 10 A. *Final Acts* EARC-1963, *supra* note 64. *See* Matte, Extracts, *supra* note 4, at 155-6 (reciting Recommendation No. 10 A).

72. *Id.*

73. International Telecommunication Convention (Montreux 1965), T.I.A.S. 6267.

no major change was made in the ITU Convention with respect to space services, resolutions were passed calling for technical cooperation with, and assistance to, developing nations.[74]

1971 WORLD ADMINISTRATIVE RADIO CONFERENCE. Due to an increase in actual and planned space activity,[75] the frequency allocations and provisions for space communications adopted at the 1963 Extraordinary Administrative Radio Conference soon became inadequate. Consequently, a World Administrative Radio Conference for Space Telecommunications was convened in 1971.[76] The Conference defined and allocated spectrum for new space services, and revised and expanded allocations for established satellite services. The category referred to as "communication satellite service" was divided in two: "fixed satellite service" and "mobile satellite service."[77] Each of these services was defined and frequency allocations were made for them. The definition of "broadcasting satellite service" was modified[78] and frequency spectrum was allocated for that service.[79] Moreover, a new service, "Earth exploration satellite service" (remote-sensing satellite service),[80] was first defined at this 1971 Conference and frequency spectrum was allocated to.[81]

Also, the procedures leading to registration of satellite frequency assignments were modified at the 1971 World Administrative Radio Conference for Space Telecommunications. Mandatory procedures were adopted for submission of technical information for purposes of advance

---

74. These resolutions reiterated themes of previous resolutions.
75. By 1971, INTELSAT had launched about one dozen commercial satellites and its membership had increased to include almost half of the ITU member nations. In 1970, a major policy statement was issued by the United States Federal Communications Commission (FCC) stating that the FCC had the power to authorize domestic private commercial communications satellite systems and that the authorization of such systems was in the "public interest," the *touchstone* for FCC licensing of private radio operations. *Establishment of Domestic Communication-Satellite Facilities by Non-Governmental Entities,* 2 F.C.C. 2d 86 (1970). *See* Chapter 3.1.1. (describing this policy decision).
76. The Extraordinary Administrative Radio Conference to Allocate Frequency Bands for Radiocommunication Purposes (1963) [hereinafter cited as EARC-63] had recommended that a subsequent conference be convened. White, SPACE COMMUNICATION, *supra* note 1, at 129.
77. Fixed satellite service was defined as a "radiocommunication service: between Earth stations at specified fixed points when one or more satellites are used; in some cases this service includes satellite to satellite links, which may also be effected in the inter-satellite service; for connection between one or more Earth stations at specified fixed points and satellites used for a service other than the fixed satellite service [for example, the mobile satellite service, broadcasting satellite service, etc.]." *Final Acts,* World Administrative Radio Conference for Space Telecommunications (1971) [hereinafter cited as *Final Acts,* WARC-71], art. 1. The definition is recited in White, SPACE COMMUNICATION, *supra* note 1, at 140.

publication of planned satellite systems.[82] Article 9A of the Radio Regulations[83] now provided that a nation which intends to establish, or whose private entities intend to establish, a satellite system "shall, prior to the coordination procedure . . . send to the International Frequency Registration Board not earlier than five years before the date of bringing into service each satellite network of the planned system, the information listed in Appendix 1B."[84] When the procedure was introduced at the Extraordinary Administrative Radio Conference in 1963, submission of information was voluntary. Furthermore, at the 1971 Conference, the scope of applicability of the coordination procedures was expanded.

Perhaps the most controversial topic at the 1971 Conference concerned broadcasting satellite service. The potential inherent in this technology for beaming satellite television signals across borders to small, individually-owned receiving antennas greatly concerned many socialist and developing countries that perceived the technology as a threat to their own political systems and feared an erosion of the cultural values of their populations. They realized that, if allowed to operate freely, broad-

---

78. The following language was added to the definition of broadcasting satellite service adopted previously at EARC-63, *supra* notes 64 and 76: "In broadcasting satellite service, the term 'direct reception' shall encompass both individual reception and community reception. *Individual reception.* The reception of emissions from a space station in the broadcasting satellite service by simple domestic installations and in particular those possessing small antennas. *Community reception.* The reception of emissions from a space station in the broadcasting satellite service by receiving equipment, which in some cases may be complex and have antennas larger than those used for individual reception, and intended for use: by a group of the general public at one location; or through a distribution system covering a limited area." *Final Acts,* WARC-71, *supra* note 77, art. 1. The definition is recited in White, SPACE COMMUNICATION, *supra* note 1, at 141.
79. *See* White, SPACE COMMUNICATION, *supra* note 1, at 143 (describing these allocations). It should be noted that many of the allocations to space services were made on a shared basis with terrestrial services.
80. Satellite remote-sensing involves obtaining information about the Earth's geography, resources, or atmosphere by collecting electromagnetic radiation reflected or emitted from the object under investigation. Satellite remote-sensing applications include mineral detection, cartography, pollution monitoring, Earth resource management, crop forecasting, urban planning, law enforcement, and more.
81. Frequency allocations to this service were made in the UHF frequency band (300-3000 MHz) and in the SHF frequency band (3-30 GHz) on a shared basis with other services.
82. *Final Acts,* WARC-71, *supra* note 77, art. 9A.
83. *Id.*
84. *Id.* White, SPACE COMMUNICATION, *supra* note 1, at 145. Appendix 1B, entitled "Advance Publication of Information to be Furnished for a Satellite Network," set forth the basic technical information to be provided to the IFRB. *Id.*

casting satellites would serve to expose their populations to ideas, values and life styles from the industrialized West, especially the United States. The governments of these countries realized that such exposure might lead ultimately to their demise and even to the undermining of the philosophical foundations of their societies. To prevent the influx of Western values, certain socialist and developing nations argued that international satellite broadcasting should be subject to *prior consent*, of the receiving country. Western industrialized countries, on the other hand, opposed the notion of prior consent and, instead, favored a free flow of information.

Nonetheless, the socialist and developing countries did obtain a resolution calling for *a priori* planning of the broadcasting satellite service at a future conference.[85] *A priori* planning involves setting aside specific orbital locations and frequencies for each country for its future use, regardless of whether it can be expected realistically to use these resources. In essence, an *a priori* plan serves to guarantee future access. The *a priori* plan contemplated also would limit broadcast coverage areas to national territories[86] and impose power limits on satellite signals. The practical effect of such a plan for the broadcasting satellite service would be to confine broadcast signals (to the extent it is technically feasible) within the boundaries of the nation conducting or authorizing the broadcast.[87]

Further, continuing the trend of accommodating developing countries

---

85. Relating to the Establishment of Agreements and Associated Plans for the Broadcasting Satellite Service, ITU Res. Spa 2-2. *Final Acts*, WARC-71, *supra* note 77.
86. Some spillover, that is, radiation of satellite signals into foreign countries, is inevitable. With present technology, satellite beams cannot be tailored to fit exactly the borders of a country. To deal with this problem, Provision No. 2674 was added to Article 30 of the Radio Regulations, stating that

    > [i]n devising the characteristics of a space station in the broadcasting satellite service, all technical means available shall be used to reduce, to the maximum extent practicable, the radiation over the territory of other countries unless an agreement has been previously reached with such countries.

    ITU Radio Regulations, art. 30, No. 2674 (WARC-79).
87. This is not to say that the ITU adopted a rule of "prior consent." Rather, it resisted dealing with the prior consent/free flow of information issue from a political perspective, and deferred that debate to the United Nations Committee on the Peaceful Uses of Outer Space (COPUOS). The ITU dealt only with the technical aspects of broadcasting satellite service. *See, supra,* note 86 (reciting Provision No. 2674). It is true that the political and technical aspects of the issue cannot be separated entirely. On December 10, 1982, the United Nations General Assembly, upon COPUOS's recommendation, adopted a Resolution calling for "agreements and/or arrangements" to precede the establishment of any international television broadcasting satellite service. U.N.G.A. Res. 37/92 ___ (1982). The Resolution, which was opposed by most of the Western industrialized countries, including the United States, is not legally binding. Nonetheless, it has had a chilling effect on private industry investment in international satellite television broadcasting.

fearing that their access to the geostationary orbit and radio frequencies allocated to space services would be precluded, due to exploitation by the industrialized nations, the 1971 Conference adopted a Resolution providing in relevant part that

> (1) . . . the registration with the ITU of frequency assignments for space radio-communication services and their use should not provide any permanent priority for any individual country or groups of countries and should not create an obstacle to the establishment of space systems by other countries;
>
> (2) . . . accordingly, a country or group of countries having registered with the ITU frequencies for the use by space radio-communications services *should take all practicable measures to realize the possibility of the use of new space systems* by other countries or groups of countries so desiring.[88]

1973 PLENIPOTENTIARY CONFERENCE. Again, continuing the trend of protecting the interests of the developing countries, an ITU Plenipotentiary Conference in Malaga-Torremolinos in 1973 adopted a new Article 33 of the ITU Convention. Article 33, entitled "Rational Use of the Radio Frequency Spectrum and of the Geostationary Orbit," provided in relevant part that

> [i]n using the frequency bands for space radio services Members shall bear in mind that radio frequencies and the geostationary satellite orbit are limited natural resources and that they must be used efficiently and economically, in conformity with the provisions of the Radio Regulations, so that countries or groups of countries may have equitable access to both, in conformity of provisions of the Radio Regulations according to their needs and technical facilities at their disposal.[89]

In calling for efficient and economical use of the geostationary orbit and frequency spectrum, as well as equitable access to both, the provision attempts to balance the needs and interests of the developing nations and those of the industrialized countries. Its call for "equitable access" offers a strong statement in favor of some kind of guarantee of future access for the developing countries to the geostationary orbit and frequency spectrum, while the reference to efficient and economical use indicates that any such guarantee must not translate into a waste of orbit and spectrum resources and preclude their use by countries which have the requisite technology and capital. Article 33 also was significant in the sense that it was legally binding on ITU member nations. Resolutions and recommen-

---

88. Emphasis added. *Relating to the Use by all Countries, With Equal Rights, of Frequency Bands for Space Radio Communication Services.* ITU Res. Spa 2-1. *Final Acts* WARC-71, *supra* note 77. *See* Matte, Extracts, *supra* note 4, at 157-158 (reciting the Resolution).

89. ITU Convention, art. 33, para. 2 (Malaga-Torremolinos 1973).

dations previously adopted were not legally binding.

1977 WORLD ADMINISTRATIVE RADIO CONFERENCE. A concrete step towards implementing the principles enunciated in Article 33 was taken at the World Administrative Radio Conference for the Planning of the Broadcasting Satellite Service in the 12 GHz Band at Geneva in 1977. At this conference, an *a priori* Plan was drawn up for broadcasting satellite service in Europe and Africa (Region I)[90] and in Asia (Region 3)[91] in the 12 GHz frequency band (down-link). (See Chapter 4.3.3.1.). The Plan allotted specific orbital positions and frequencies to each country in these geographical regions,[92] regardless of their current or foreseeable needs.[93] It also determined satellite coverage area, the amount of radiated power necessary and other characteristics.[94] The *a priori* Plan provided the developing countries with the sought-after guarantees that orbital locations and frequency spectrum would be available by the time they were ready to launch their satellite systems.[95] Moreover, such plans, *en practique,* would serve to shield certain socialist and developing countries from unwanted foreign satellite broadcasts. It is important to note that the *a priori* Plan adopted for Regions 1 and 3 is limited in scope and time. It applies only to broadcasting satellite service in the 12 Ghz band (down-link),[96] and its duration is fifteen years.

The United States opposed *a priori* plans, in general, and for the Americas (Region 2), in particular. It viewed the provision of guarantees to developing countries of future access through rigid planning predispositions as wasteful of orbital and spectrum resources.[97] Moreover, since *a priori* plans, as called for in this instance, determine virtually every orbital parameter and, thus, in effect, the technical design of the satellite, they would in the U.S. view serve to stifle technological development and

---

90. The ITU divides the world into three Regions (1-3) for spectrum allocation purposes, *supra* note 29. ITU Radio Regulations, art. 8 (WARC-79). Region 2 includes the Americas, the Caribbean and Greenland. *Id.*
91. *Id.*
92. Broadcasting satellite service is particularly suitable for planning.
93. Specific orbital locations (in degrees longitude) and associated frequencies, *i.e.,* channels, were allotted. The number of channels was dependent upon the size and population of the country. For example, Brunei was allotted two channels, while the Soviet Union was given 65. White, SPACE COMMUNICATION, *supra* note 1, at 159.
94. Such other characteristics included antenna beam width, boresight geographic coordinates, orientation of the ellipse and polarization.
95. Since orbital locations and frequencies are reserved, in the sense that they are predetermined in the Plan, the first-come, first-served principle does not apply here.
96. The Plan governed only transmissions from the satellite to the ground, and not feeder links (Earth-to-space). Feeder links were established at WARC-ORB-88.
97. *See* White, SPACE COMMUNICATION, *supra* note 1, at 164 (discussing how the Plan sacrifices efficiency for equity).

impede technological innovation.[98] At the request of the United States, therefore, the 1977 Conference agreed to defer planning of broadcasting satellite service in the Americas[99] to a Regional Administrative Radio Conference to be convened in 1983.

1979 WORLD ADMINISTRATIVE RADIO CONFERENCE. At the World Administrative Radio Conference in 1979, virtually the entire set of Radio Regulations was up for revision for the first time in twenty years. Since the last revision in 1959, the ITU had witnessed an increase in its membership by over seventy percent. The majority of the new Members were newly-independent nations, thus, strengthening the voice and influence of the Third World. Extensive discussion was devoted at the 1979 Conference to the notion of equitable access to the geostationary orbit and spectrum, and the Conference did pass a number of important resolutions in that regard. Resolution 2 reiterated, in somewhat stronger language, Resolution Spa 2-1 adopted at the 1971 World Administrative Radio Conference for Space Telecommunications, holding that all nations have an equal right to use the limited, natural orbit-spectrum resources.[100]

Moreover, the 1979 Conference resolved to convene a World Administrative Radio Conference no later than 1983 whose purpose would be to "guaranty in practice for all countries equitable access to the geostationary satellite orbit and the frequency bands allocated to space services."[101] It was decided that this Conference would be held in two sessions, the first to decide which space services and frequencies should be planned, and the second to reach agreement on the implementation of the decisions made during the first session. For budgetary reasons, the conferences was delayed and then convened in two sessions held, respectively, in 1985 and 1988.

1982 PLENIPOTENTIARY CONFERENCE. An ITU Plenipotentiary Conference was held at Nairobi, Kenya, in 1982 to revise the ITU Convention. It provided yet another forum for what was becoming a traditional, acrimonious debate between the industrialized and the developing nations. The debate produced an amendment to Article 33 of the ITU Convention. It will be recalled that the Plenipotentiary Conference at Malaga-Torremolinos in 1973 had adopted Article 33, which referred to the geo-

---

98. The U.K., Sweden, France and Germany, among others, have implemented broadcasting satellite operations in accordance with the 1977 Plan.

99. *See, supra* 29 (explaining how the ITU divides the world into three Regions for frequency allocation purposes).

100. *Relating to the Equitable Use by All Countries, With Equal Rights, of the Geostationary Satellite Orbit and of Frequency Bands for Space Radiocommunication Services*, ITU Res. 2 (formerly referred to as Resolution AY). *Final Acts*, WARC-79.

101. *Relating to the Use of the Geostationary Satellite Orbit and to the Planning of Space Services Utilizing It*, ITU Res. 3 (formerly referred to as Resolution BP). *Final Acts*, WARC-79.

stationary orbit and spectrum as "limited natural resources" to be used "efficiently and economically" so that all countries may have "equitable access" to both. New language was added to that provision at the 1982 Plenipotentiary calling for consideration of the "special needs" of the developing countries.[102]

1983 REGIONAL ADMINISTRATIVE RADIO CONFERENCE. Pursuant to a decision taken at the 1979 Conference, a Regional Administrative Radio Conference for the Planning of the Broadcasting Satellite Service in Region 2 was convened in 1983 to adopt an *a priori*-type plan for broadcasting satellite service in the Americas.[103] An agreement was reached by the participating countries on a much less rigid plan than the *a priori* Plan adopted for Europe, Africa and Asia at the World Administrative Radio Conference for Broadcasting Satellites in 1977.[104] While it did set aside specific orbital locations and frequencies for use by countries in the

---

102. The 1973 version of Article 33 used the following language: "According to their needs and the technical facilities at their disposal." The 1982 version substituted "taking into account the special needs of the developing countries and the geographical situation of particular countries." ITU Convention, art. 33 (Nairobi 1982). White, SPACE COMMUNICATION, *supra* note 1, at 189, points out that the 1982 language signalled an important change in the meaning of the principle of equitable access to the orbit and spectrum. While efficiency and economy are still important considerations to the principle of equitable access, states White, "those considerations now must be viewed in light of the explicit recognition that equity explicitly requires, and cannot exist without, consideration of the special needs of the developing countries." *Id.*
103. The conference was entitled "Regional Administrative Radio Conference for the Planning of Broadcasting Satellite Service in the Frequency Band 12.2.-12.7 GHz and Associated Feeder Links in the Frequency Band 17.3-17.8 GHz" (1983).
104. The U.S. was provided eight orbital positions, each with 500 MHz bandwidth (32 channels). Signal strength was a contentious issue at the Conference. The U.S., contemplating direct reception by small privately-owned receiving dishes, favored high signal strength or power flux density value [minus 105 decibel Watts per square meter (dBW/m2)]. The signal strength required is inversely proportional to the size of the receiving antenna. Canada and other countries intending community reception favored lower signal strength. The latter countries prevailed, forcing the United States to register a reservation. *See* ITU Convention, art. 77, para. 16 (Nairobi 1982) (providing that administrations must endeavour to conform to the majority, *i.e.*, strive to reach a consensus, while at the same time allowing for reservation). Specifically, this provision states that

    [a]s a general rule, any delegation whose views are not shared by the remaining delegations shall endeavour, as far as possible, to conform to the opinion of the majority.
    However, if any decision appears to a delegation to be of such a nature as to prevent its government from ratifying the Convention or from approving the revision of the Regulations, the delegation may make reservations, final or provisional, regarding this decision.

region, the 1983 Conference Plan did not set in concrete satellite design and operating characteristics as had the 1977 Plan. It allowed for some individual variations to permit countries to implement technological advances occurring in the period between its adoption and the launch of broadcasting satellite systems. Also, the 1983 Plan was limited in scope and time, involving only the 11.7-12.3 GHz band and associated feeder-links.[105] No broadcasting satellite has been launched in the Americas pursuant to the Plan, although several such satellites have been authorized for operation by the Federal Communications Commission in the United States (see Chapter 3.1.2.). Several satellites serving other parts of the world have been launched elsewhere in the world pursuant to the 1977 Plan, however, and satellite manufacturers and operators have complained about being severely constrained by the design parameters set forth in that Plan.

1985 WORLD ADMINISTRATIVE RADIO CONFERENCE. Also, pursuant to a decision taken at the 1979 Conference, the first session of the World Administrative Radio Conference on the Use of the Geostationary-Satellite Orbit and the Planning of the Space Services Utilizing It was convened at Geneva, August 8 to September 15, 1985 (hereinafter referred to as WARC-ORB-85). The purpose of the WARC-ORB-85 was to "guarantee in practice" that all countries have "equitable access" to the geostationary orbit and frequencies allocated for satellite services. It was recognized that satisfying this objective would require some form of *a priori* planning in certain satellite services and frequency bands. Accordingly, four principal goals of WARC-ORB-85 were to 1) decide which satellite services should be subject to *a priori*-type planning, 2) decide which frequency bands used by these services should be subject to *a priori*-type planning, 3) establish a planning method, including technical parameters, for the selected satellite services and frequency bands and 4) adopt new frequency coordination procedures that would facilitate access to the geostationary orbit by the developing countries with respect to satellite services and frequency bands not selected for planning.[106] Again, the stage was set for a contentious debate between developing and industrialized countries. Initially, the developing countries argued in favor of extensive *a priori* planning of several satellite services and frequency bands. The industrialized nations, led by the United States, wanted to limit planning measures to just a few space services and frequency bands.

A compromise was reached that only the fixed satellite service and, within this service, only certain frequency bands which were not commonly used (the expansion bands)[107] would be subject to allotment planning. This planning approach would result in a much more flexible plan than the *a priori* plans established at the 1977 World Administrative Radio

105. The Plan was incorporated into the Radio Regulations by the *Final Acts*, WARC-ORB-85, Appendix 30.

106. Smith, INTERNATIONAL REGULATION, *supra* note 27, at 87-88.

Conference for Broadcasting Satellites in the 12 GHz Band and at the 1983 Regional Conference. Certain other heavily used, i.e., the "conventional," fixed satellite service frequency bands[108] would be subject to so-called "improved procedures" for coordination of satellite systems. The remaining fixed satellite service bands would be subject neither to allotment planning nor improved procedures.

Improved procedures for coordination (the procedure to be applied to the "conventional" fixed satellite service bands not subject to allotment planning) contemplated "multilateral planning conferences"[109] to solve technical coordination problems between existing and proposed satellite systems in order to facilitate the accommodation of new satellite systems. These multilateral planning conferences would complement the current bilateral approach to coordination. However, the bilateral coordination approach would continue to apply to all other satellite services, except the broadcasting satellite service in the 11.7-12.7 GHz frequency bands, for which plans already had been adopted in 1977 and 1983.[110] See Chapter 4.3.

Eleven planning principles emerged at WARC-ORB-85, which were intended to guide the implementation of the plan and improved procedures at the Second Session of the Conference scheduled for 1988:[111]

1. guarantee of access and equitability;
2. sharing with other services;
3. reservation of resources;
4. technical aspects of special geographical situations;
5. consideration of existing systems;
6. provisions for multi-administration systems;

---

107. The expansion bands were allocated for fixed satellite service at WARC-79 or earlier conferences, but were not generally used by such satellite systems. They include the 4500-4800 MHz (down-link); 300 MHz to be selected from the 6425-7075 MHz band (up-link); 10.70-11.95 GHz (down-link); 11.20-11.45 GHz (down-link); and 12.75-13.25 GHz (up-link). *See generally,* White, SPACE COMMUNICATIONS, *supra* note 1, at 201-232; Smith, INTERNATIONAL REGULATION, *supra* note 27, at 87-116; S.E. Doyle, *Space Law and the Geostationary Orbit: The ITU'S WARC-ORB-85-88 Concluded,* 17 J. SPACE L. 13 (1989); M.L. Smith, *A New Era for the International Regulation of Satellite Communications,* XIV ANNALS OF AIR & SPACE L. 449 (1989); and R.S. Jakhu, *A Legal Analysis of the 1985 ITU Conference Report,* XXIX IISL 103 (1986) (describing the results of WARC-ORB-85).

108. These bands included 3700-4200 MHz; 5850-6425 MHz, 10.95-11.20, 11.70-12.20 GHz (in Region 2), 12.50-12.75 GHz (in Regions 1 and 3), 14.00-14.50 GHz, 18.10-18.30 GHz, 18.30-20.20 GHz and 27.00-30.00 GHz.

109. The concept was not defined until WARC-ORB-88.

110. The Plans dispense with the need for coordination since coordination was effected during the development of the Plans.

111. See White, SPACE COMMUNICATION, *supra* note 1, at 213-216 (elaborating on these principles).

7. flexibility to accommodate unforeseen needs;
8. planning solutions adapted to circumstances;
9. efficiency in orbit and spectrum use;
10. provisions for multi-service and multi-band networks; and
11. administrative costs controlled.

The planning principles were broad and somewhat ambiguous. Most of them were reiterations of themes of existing ITU resolutions, Radio Regulations and the ITU Convention.[112] Of the eleven planning principles, provisions for multi-administration systems were particularly controversial. INTELSAT, supported by many of its member States, had proposed that "special recognition" be granted to multi-administration satellite systems, including the INTELSAT satellite system (see Chapter 5.1.1.), with respect to access to the geostationary orbit. In the end, it was determined not to grant priority treatment to INTELSAT or any other international organization's satellite system.[113] It is important to note that international organizations, such as INTELSAT, cannot be Members of the ITU; only nation States can. Although several international organizations have observer status at ITU conferences, which allows their representatives to be present. In addition, these organizations often have considerable influence over the positions of their member States.

While WARC-ORB-85 did determine which satellite services and frequency bands should be subject to planning or improved procedures, the establishment of implementing mechanisms and procedures was deferred to a Second Session of the Conference. Many important aspects of the plans and procedures also were not addressed. For example, WARC-ORB-85 never defined "multilateral planning conference," which is the central ingredient in the improved procedures adopted for frequency bands in the fixed satellite service not subject to planning. Also left to the Second Session was the task of simplifying the procedures for advance publication, coordination and recording for satellite operations not subject to the planning or improved procedures.

1987 WORLD ADMINISTRATIVE RADIO CONFERENCE. A World Administrative Radio Conference for Mobile Services was held in 1987 primarily to consider frequency allocations for satellites in the context of a global maritime distress and safety system. That conference also was significant, however, in that it for the first time allocated frequencies for radiodetermination satellite service, which paved the way for the commercialization of that service in the United States. Considerable debate also focused on the issue of generic allocations to the mobile satellite service. The United States favored a generic allocation, as opposed to separate allocations to land, maritime and aeronautical mobile satellite services, because of the flexibility that approach would allow commercial

---

112. This observation was made by Smith, INTERNATIONAL REGULATION, *supra* note 27, at 93.

113. *Id.*

operators. The U.S. position was not adopted by the ITU, which led the U.S. to take a reservation. (See Chapter 3.1.5.).

1988 WORLD ADMINISTRATIVE RADIO CONFERENCE. After considerable intersessional activity,[114] the Second Session of the World Administrative Radio Conference on the Use of the Geostationary-Satellite Orbit and the Planning of the Space Services Utilizing It was held at Geneva in 1988 (hereinafter WARC-ORB-88) to implement the results of WARC-ORB-85. The WARC-ORB-88 lasted from August 29 to October 6, 1988, and completed four major tasks specified in the Agenda for the Conference: It 1) established an allotment Plan (i.e., an instrument which is somewhat more flexible than an *a priori* plan, but which still provides some measure of assurance of future access) for the fixed satellite service in the expansion bands, including technical parameters and procedures for establishing satellite systems pursuant to the Plan) (see Chapter 4.3.1.2.), 2) established improved procedures for the fixed satellite service in the conventional bands, 3) simplified the Radio Regulations with regard to advance publication and coordination of frequency assignments for satellite systems, and 4) established feeder links for the broadcasting satellite service in Regions 1 and 3. Decisions made at WARC-ORB-88 involved a partial revision of the Radio Regulations.[115] The revision entered into force March 16, 1990.

Less of the political animosity that had been so prevalent at the preceding administrative radio conferences was present at WARC-ORB-88. The Conference was conducted in a much more business-like manner and, for the most part, the results of the Conference satisfied both the developing and industrialized countries. It remains to be seen whether WARC-ORB-88 in fact represents a turning point and an end to an era in international communications satellite regulation in which a political bickering between the "haves" and the "have-nots," rather than the need for technical efficiency, shaped the agenda. WARC-ORB-88 produced a long sought-after compromise on communications satellite regulation which satisfied the developing countries that their needs and interests were being safeguarded. At the same time, it responded to the requirements of the industrialized nations to continue their intensive use of the geostationary orbit in the conventional bands, pursuant to a stable legal regime allowing for technological advancement while protecting satellite operations from harmful interference.

1989 PLENIPOTENTIARY CONFERENCE. A Plenipotentiary Conference was held in 1989 that revised substantially the ITU Convention (in Nairobi, 1992). The revisions have not yet entered into force because they have not been ratified by the requisite number of ITU member States. Moreover, it is possible that the ITU Convention, as revised in 1989, will not enter into force in its present form. A high-level committee established by the ITU Administrative Council is predicted to recommend fur-

---

114. *Id.*

ther revisions and a limited Plenipotentiary Conference is scheduled for 1992 to consider these recommendations.

1992 WORLD ADMINISTRATIVE RADIO CONFERENCE. As previously noted, the World Administrative Radio Conference for Dealing With Frequency Allocations in Certain Parts of the Spectrum is scheduled to be held in Spain, beginning February 3, 1992. The Agenda for the Conference has been established[116] and includes consideration of frequency allocations *inter alia* for mobile satellite services above and below 1 GHz to be provided by low-Earth orbit satellites, satellite sound broadcasting between 500 MHz and 3,000 MHz, high-definition television (HDTV) broadcasting satellite service and new satellite services above 20 GHz. With respect to allocations to services that may be provided by low-Earth orbit satellite systems, it is important to note that the ITU allocates frequencies to specific radio *services*, and not to *systems*.

---

115. *Final Acts*, ITU World Administrative Radio Conference on the Use of the Geostationary-Satellite Orbit and the Planning of Space Services Utilizing It (1988). Changes were made to Article 1 (terms and definitions), adopting a new definition of "fixed satellite service;" Article 8 (table of frequency allocations), adopting a new provision 839 limiting the use of certain frequency bands in the broadcasting satellite service to national and subregional systems; Article 11 (procedures for advance publication of information on planned satellite systems and coordination of frequency assignments), implementing the results of WARC-ORB-88; Article 12 (notification and recording in the Master International Frequency Register of frequency assignments to terrestrial radiocommunication stations); Article 13 (notification and recording in the Master International Frequency Register of frequency assignments to radio astronomy and space radiocommunication stations); Article 14 (supplementary procedures applicable in cases where a footnote in the table of frequency allocations requires agreement with an administration); Article 15A (coordination, notification and recording of frequency assignments in the fixed satellite service, Earth-to-space, in the 17.3-17.8 GHz band in Region 2), providing feeder links for the broadcasting satellite service; Article 27 (terrestrial radiocommunication services sharing of frequency bands with space radiocommunication services above 1 GHz); Article 28 (space radiocommunication services sharing frequency bands with terrestrial radiocommunication services above 1 GHz); and Article 69 (entry into force of the Radio Regulations). Changes also were made in Appendix 3 (notices relating to space radiocommunication and radio astronomy stations); Appendix 4 (advance publication of information to be furnished for a satellite network); Appendix 28 (method for determining the coordination area around an Earth station in frequency bands between 1 GHz and 40 GHz shared between space and terrestrial radiocommunication services); Appendix 29 (method of calculation if coordination is required between geostationary satellite networks sharing the same frequency band); Appendix 30A (provisions and associated plans for feeder links in the broadcasting satellite service in Regions 1, 2 and 3); and Appendix 30B (provisions and WARC-ORB *a priori* plan for the fixed satellite service).

116. *See supra* note 27 and APPENDIX I (concerning the Agenda).

NATIONAL PREPARATIONS FOR ADMINISTRATIVE CONFERENCES. All ITU administrative radio conferences are preceded by more or less extensive preparations by ITU member States, which have to establish their official positions and unofficial fall-back positions on the various agenda items. Certain countries only have positions on some of the items. The United States typically takes a position on every item on the agenda and submits a comprehensive set of proposals to the conference. The U.S. position is developed jointly by the Federal Communications Commission (FCC), representing the interests of industry, and the National Telecommunications and Information Administration of the Department of Commerce, representing the interests of the Federal government, and is subject to the approval of the Department of State. An extensive inquiry, usually taking place over several years and involving comments from industry and other interest groups, forms the basis of the FCC's positions on the various issues to be debated.[117] ITU members States send delegations of varying sizes to the conferences. While some countries may send only a few delegates, the U.S. delegation normally consists of fifty to sixty individuals, and is made up of representatives from government and industry. If your client is a U.S. company with a vested interest in the outcome of a particular conference, it can participate in conference preparatory activities and request to send a representative on the delegation. The representative may be accepted as a United States delegate if found by the United States Department of State to be adequately qualified and otherwise acceptable to the U.S. Government. Delegates representing private companies must conform their positions to that of the U.S. Government.

4.3. Procedure for Obtaining Registration in the ITU Master International Frequency Register of Your Client's Frequency Assignment

THE NEED FOR REGISTRATION. Registration[118] in the Master International Frequency Register is essential to achieve international recognition of your client's frequency and orbital assignments and to secure protection from harmful radio interference to your client's satellite operation.

Registration denotes that your client's frequency assignment has been recorded by the IFRB in the Master International Frequency Register and is the culmination of a three- and sometimes two-step process, which may involve 1) advance publication by the IFRB of information on a proposed

117. *See e.g. supra* note 62 (discussing the Federal Communications Commission's preparatory procedure for the 1992 Conference).

118. The term "registration" generally is used with reference to a frequency assignment that has been recorded by the IFRB in the Master International Frequency Register.

new satellite system submitted by an ITU member State. 2) coordination between or among ITU member States of the proposed new satellite system with other existing and planned satellite systems to avoid harmful radio interference and 3) notification to the IFRB by the ITU member State sponsoring the proposed new satellite system for purposes of recording in the Master International Frequency Register.[119] In fact, ITU member States planning or sponsoring satellite operations are under a legal obligation to complete the prescribed procedure.[120]

ADVANCE PUBLICATION IN GENERAL. Advance publication refers to the publication by the IFRB in a weekly circular sent to telecommunications administrations or agencies of all ITU member States of certain technical information on a proposed new satellite system. Advance publication takes place after the telecommunications administration planning, or acting on behalf of a private entity planning, a satellite system has supplied the IFRB with the relevant technical information. This information is prescribed by Appendix 4 to the ITU Radio Regulations and includes general characteristics of the satellite network (i.e., one single satellite and one or more typical Earth stations), type of service, operating frequency bands and orbital location. The significance of advance publication is that it puts other administrations and satellite operators on notice that a new system is being planned and alerts all parties to potential interference problems that may need to be resolved.

---

119. Article 11, section I, of the ITU Radio Regulations sets forth procedures for advance publication. Article 11, section II, sets forth procedures for coordination with other geostationary satellite systems. Article 11, section III, provides procedures for coordination with terrestrial radio stations. Article 13 provides procedures for notification and recording. Article 14 provides a supplementary procedure where a footnote in the Table of Frequency Allocations requires an agreement with another administration. Article 15 provides procedures in the event a Plan has been adopted for the particular service to be provided.

120. *See* ITU Radio Regulations, art. 11, No. 1042 (WARC-ORB-88) (providing that administrations planning to operate or authorize new satellite networks "shall" provide information for purposes of advance publication). *See also id.* No. 1060 (providing that administrations proposing or authorizing new satellite systems "shall . . . effect coordination" with administrations concerned). It should be noted that the requirement to effect coordination is a requirement to complete the coordination procedures prescribed in the Radio Regulations, and not an absolute legal obligation to achieve successful coordination. Notification to the IFRB also is required of any frequency assignment to be used for transmission or reception by an Earth station or satellite "1) if the use of the frequency concerned is capable of causing harmful interference to any service of an other administration; or 2) if the frequency is to be used for international radiocommunication; or 3) if it is desired to obtain international recognition of the use of the frequency." ITU Radio Regulations, art. 13, No. 1489-1491 (WARC-79). In practice, notification is always required of frequency assignments for satellites.

COORDINATION IN GENERAL. Coordination refers to the process whereby the administration planning, or acting on behalf of a private entity planning, a new satellite system collaborates with other administrations to eliminate potential radio interference problems. The administration proposing the new satellite system initiates coordination by sending certain technical information to administrations whose own, or sponsored, satellite systems might suffer interference exceeding a threshold value defined by the ITU. Both the administration seeking coordination and the administrations with which coordination is being sought have a shared responsibility to reach agreements on interference issues, even if that requires adjustments in both existing and planned satellite systems. Coordination may be effected through bilateral or multilateral meetings.

The ITU Radio Regulations require that the administration proposing or sponsoring a new satellite system "effect coordination" with other administrations that might be affected. This requirement should be viewed as an obligation to complete the procedures for coordination prescribed in the Radio Regulations rather than an absolute legal duty to achieve successful coordination. Even the Radio Regulations, themselves, recognize that successful coordination may not always be accomplished, and provide for recording in the Master International Frequency Register under certain circumstances where coordination agreements cannot be reached. In practice, administrations usually act in good faith and generally coordination agreements are reached.

NOTIFICATION-RECORDING IN GENERAL. When the proposed satellite system has been advance published and coordinated, where coordination applies, or when an advanced published system cannot be coordinated successfully, the administration planning, or acting on behalf of a private entity planning, the satellite system must notify the IFRB of the technical parameters of the proposed satellite system, the ITU coordination procedures that have been applied and the coordination results achieved. The IFRB examines the notice containing such technical information, focusing 1) on the conformity of the frequency assignment with the ITU Convention and Table of Frequency Allocations; 2) compliance with the coordination procedures prescribed in the Radio Regulations, where they apply; and 3) on the potential for interference in cases where a frequency assignment does not conform to the Table of Frequency Allocations, or where coordination has not been successfully effected. Upon favorable findings, the IFRB will record the frequency assignment to be used by the proposed satellite system. If it is apparent that coordination was being blocked on political grounds, rather than for technical reasons, special provision is made for recording, nonetheless.

THE ITU RADIO REGULATIONS. The criteria and procedures pertaining to advance publication, coordination and notification-recording concerning satellite systems are set forth in Articles 11, 13-15 of the ITU Radio Regulations, which are annexed to the ITU Convention (Nairobi 1982). As noted in Chapter 4.2., the last general revision of the Radio Regulations took place at the World Administrative Radio Conference in 1979. Article 11 and 13-15 of the Radio Regulations subsequently were amended by the Final Acts of subsequent administrative radio conferences, most notably by the *Final Acts* of the World Administrative Radio Conference on the Use of the Geostationary-Satellite Orbit and the Planning of the Space Services Utilizing It, Second Session, 1988. The amendments adopted at the 1988 Conference were substantial. They were intended to simplify the procedures for advance publication and notification, and to facilitate the coordination of proposed new satellite systems.

REQUIREMENTS FOR GEOSTATIONARY SATELLITE SYSTEMS. With the exception of broadcasting satellites and fixed satellites operating in the expansion bands, all geostationary satellite systems are subject to advance publication, coordination and notification pursuant to Articles 11-13 of the Radio Regulations. This is true, regardless of whether the satellite is intended for fixed satellite service (other than in the expansion bands), radiodetermination satellite service, or mobile satellite service, although the technical criteria and procedures sometimes differ from one service to another and occasionally even from one frequency band to another within the same service. Special coordination criteria and procedures have been developed for geostationary satellites because interference problems between the transmissions of such satellites are particularly acute due to the heavy use of the geostationary orbit. The geostationary orbit is an especially attractive location for telecommunications satellites, and careful coordination is necessary of satellite systems located there to prevent harmful interference. Again, the geostationary orbit is a circular orbit in the plane of the Earth's equator 35,687.1 km above the Earth's surface in which the satellites' velocity matches the speed of the Earth's rotation, and in which satellites are stationary with respect to the Earth.

Geostationary satellites in the broadcasting satellite service in the 11.7-12.7 GHz frequency band, and in the fixed satellite service in the so-called expansion bands,[121] are not subject to the three-step procedure of advance publication, coordination and notification outlined, above. Special plans govern these satellite operations, which dispense with the need for the conventional procedures since interference issues were resolved during the development of these plans. See Chapters 4.3.3.1. and 4.3.1.2. describing the plans. With regard to broadcasting satellite service not subject to any plan, ITU Resolution 33 applies, adopted at the 1979 World Administrative Radio Conference, and entitled "Relating to the Bringing into Use Space Stations in the broadcasting satellite Service, Prior to the Entry Into Force of Agreements and Associated Plans for the Broadcasting Satellite Service." This resolution refers to most of the procedures prescribed in Articles 11 and 13 of the Radio Regulations. See Chapter 4.3.3.2.

REQUIREMENTS FOR NON-GEOSTATIONARY SATELLITE SYS-

121. *See* note 123, *infra* (listing the expansion bands).

TEMS. Non-geostationary satellite systems require only advance publication and notification, although some measure of coordination is required as part of the advance publication process. Special coordination criteria and procedures have not been adopted for them for at least three reasons: 1) many non-geostationary satellites in operation today are military satellites, owned by the United States or the Soviet Union, and although the frequencies used by these satellites may be subject to ITU advance publication and recording requirements, the two countries have been able to settle interference issues themselves; 2) non-geostationary scientific satellites, such as those operated by the National Aeronautics and Space Administration and the European Space Agency, are relatively few in number, and frequency coordination has been effected at the space agency level; and 3) commercial non-geostationary satellite operations to date have been extremely limited, including only a few remote-sensing satellites (see Chapter 1.2.).

With the advent of commercial, low-Earth orbit telecommunications satellite systems, such as the multi-satellite systems now being planned by the International Maritime Satellite Organization (INMARSAT) and several private U.S. companies (e.g., Motorola Satellite Communications, Inc. of Chandler, Arizona, is proposing a system of seventy-seven satellites in seven polar orbits), the ITU in the future may have to consider coordination criteria and procedures also for non-geostationary systems. Due to the almost infinite variety of non-geostationary orbital paths, coordination parameters for non-geostationary satellites inevitably will be considerably more complex than those involving geostationary satellites. It will be interesting to see whether the ITU also assumes jurisdiction over orbital paths (physical interference) as an adjunct to its responsibilities with respect to frequency interference. Arguably, the ITU has such jurisdiction.

"FIRST-COME, FIRST-SERVED." As a general rule, recording in the Master International Frequency Register and consequent protection of a satellite operation from harmful radio interference take place on a "first-come, first-served" basis. In other words, when your client's frequency assignment has been recorded, i.e., registered, it is incumbent upon those subsequently seeking to record assignments to coordinate for purposes of avoiding interference to your client's satellite operations. In fact, priority treatment is accorded at an even earlier stage if your client is proposing a geostationary satellite operation. As soon as your client has entered the coordination stage, other administrations proposing or sponsoring new satellites must coordinate with the administration acting on behalf of your client. The first come, first-served rule does not apply when special plans govern, such as in the broadcasting satellite service in the 12GHz band.

ONLY NATIONAL GOVERNMENT AGENCIES CAN DEAL WITH THE ITU. All contact with the ITU for purposes of advance publication, coordination and notification takes place at the governmental level, generally through a national telecommunications administration or agency, such as the Federal Communications Commission in the United States, which acts on behalf of a private satellite company, i.e., your client. As a private company, your client cannot initiate the process leading to advance publication, coordination or recording. Nevertheless, your client may be required to supply the relevant technical information to be submitted to the ITU. For example, in the United States, satellite applicants, permittees, or licensees are required to "provide the [Federal Communications] Commission with all information it requires for the Advance Publication, coordination and notification of frequency assignments pursuant to the international Radio Regulations ...[122]

4.3.1. Geostationary Satellites in the Fixed Satellite Service

With the exception of fixed satellite systems operating in the expansion bands,[123] all fixed satellite systems[124] are subject to the procedures for advance publication, coordination and notification set forth in Articles 11, 13 and 14 of the ITU Radio Regulations.[125] Fixed satellite systems operating in the expansion bands, which are not commonly used today, are subject to an allotment Plan adopted at the World Administrative Radio Conference on the Use of the Geostationary-Satellite Orbit and the Planning of Space Services Utilizing It, Second Session, 1988.[126] See Chapter 4.3.1.2.

The procedures described, below, apply equally to domestic and international fixed satellites (generally referred to as "separate systems" in the United States). Domestic fixed satellites are those intended primarily for communications within a nation's borders, while international fixed satellites are intended for communications between or among countries (see Chapter 3.4.).

4.3.1.1. Fixed Satellite Systems Not Subject to Plan

ADVANCE PUBLICATION. Not earlier than six years, and preferably not later than two years, before the date of bringing your client's satellite network into use, the administration acting on its behalf must send to the IFRB technical information on your client's satellite system as specified in Appendix 4 of the Radio Regulations.[127] The information required under Appendix 4 concerns technical characteristics of the satellite and of one or

---

122. 47 C.F.R. §25.202(c) (1990).
123. The following frequency bands, allocated at WARC-79, are referred to as the expansion bands: 4500-4800 MHz (space-to-Earth); 6725-7025 MHz (Earth-to-space); 10.70-10.95 GHz (space-to-Earth, 11.20-11.45 GHz (space-to-Earth); and 12.75-13.25 GHz (Earth-to-space).
124. *See supra* note 14 (providing the ITU definition of fixed satellite service).
125. *See supra* note 119 (relating the provisions of the Radio Regulations to the procedures for advance publication, coordination and notification).
126. ITU Radio Regulations, art. 11, note 4 (WARC-ORB-88); *cf.* ITU Radio Regulations, Appendix 30B (WARC-ORB-88).
127. ITU Radio Regulations, art. 11, No. 1042 (WARC-ORB-88).

more typical Earth stations to operate with it (the satellite network), including orbital location of the satellite, frequency range, necessary bandwidth, power and modulation characteristics, noise temperature, service area and the satellite system of which the satellite network is part.[128] A satellite system refers to two or more satellites and associated Earth stations, while a satellite network refers to a single satellite and its associated Earth stations. Because of its technical nature, Appendix 4 information should be prepared by an engineer. However, the attorney should package the information and submit it to the appropriate government agency with a transmittal letter and, to the extent possible, make sure that the information is in fact forwarded to the IFRB. Although amendments to the information sent to the IFRB are permitted, they may not be "of such a nature as to significantly change the character of the [satellite network] . . . ."[129]

If your client is a U.S company subject to Federal Communications Commission (FCC) jurisdiction, the FCC generally will forward Appendix 4 information to the IFRB while the application for authorization of your client's satellite system is still pending, provided the FCC is reasonably certain that it will have a requirement for the particular orbital location and frequencies requested (i.e., where the FCC has determined that even if it does not authorize your client's satellite network, it will authorize some satellite network with the same or similar technical parameters). When submitting the information to the IFRB, the FCC uses a neutral designation (such as "USA-Sat 1"), and not your client's name, to indicate that a new satellite system is being planned in the United States.

Within three months of receipt of complete Appendix 4 information the IFRB will publish it in a special section of its weekly circular sent to telecommunications administrations of all ITU member States.[130] It also will advise them by circular telegram indicating the frequency bands and orbital location intended for use by your client's planned satellite network.[131] The telegram and accompanying Appendix 4 information serves to alert all administrations, and through them private satellite operators, whose satellite systems potentially might suffer interference from your client's proposed satellite network.

Administrations that believe your client's proposed satellite network will cause unacceptable interference to satellite systems they are operating, planning, or sponsoring, must send comments to the administration acting on behalf of your client stating the particulars of the interference.[132] Such comments must be sent within four months of the weekly

128. ITU Radio Regulations, Appendix 4 (WARC-ORB-88).

129. ITU Radio Regulations, art. 11, No. 1043 (WARC-ORB-88). If the amended information significantly changes the character of the satellite network, the procedure must be recommenced. *Id.*

130. *Id.*, No. 1044. If the information is incomplete, the IFRB will seek clarification. *Id.*

131. *Id.*

circular.[133] Appendix 29 of the ITU Radio Regulations sets forth the criteria for unacceptable interference.[134] If no comments are received within a four month period, it may be assumed that no administration had any basic objections to your client's planned satellite network.[135]

If the administration acting on behalf of your client receives comments from another administration indicating that unacceptable interference may result from your client's planned satellite operation, the two administrations "shall endeavor to resolve any difficulties that may arise and shall provide any additional information that may be available."[136] The administration acting on behalf of your client shall first explore all possible unilateral means of resolving interference issues without considering adjustments to satellite systems operated or sponsored by other administrations.[137] This may involve design and operating modifications and adjustments to your client's proposed satellite network. If this does not resolve the problem, the other administration may be requested to consider unilateral adjustments to its system. If such unilateral means cannot be found, or are insufficient, your client's administration may resort to bilateral or multilateral meetings and, in exceptional cases, multilateral meetings.[138] If, following this procedure, interference issues still remain unresolved, all the administrations concerned shall make "every possible effort to resolve these difficulties by mutually acceptable adjustments,"[139] which even may include re-location of an operational satellite.

The administration acting on behalf of your client also has a duty to keep the IFRB abreast of the comments it receives from other administrations,[140] as well as on the progress made towards resolving interference issues.[141] The IFRB publishes the information in the weekly circular it sends to all ITU administrations, as well as notifies them by circular telegram that such information is contained in the weekly circular.[142] Fur-

---

132. *Id.*, No. 1047.
133. *Id.*
134. *Id.*, No. 1047A. The administration sending the information on behalf of your client, as well as the administrations receiving the information through the weekly circular, may request the IFRB to assist them in determining whether unacceptable interference will occur. *Id.*, No. 1047A, B.
135. *Id.*, No. 1047.
136. *Id.*, No. 1049.
137. *Id.*, No. 1051.
138. *Id.* If requested by the administration acting on behalf of your client, another administration shall "explore all possible means of meeting the requirements of a requesting administration." ITU Radio Regulations, art. 11, No. 1052 (WARC-79).
139. ITU Radio Regulations, art. 11, No. 1053 (WARC-ORB-88).
140. *Id.*, No. 1956. The IFRB must be informed within four months of the publication of the weekly circular containing the Appendix 4 information. *Id.*
141. *Id.* Such information shall be furnished at intervals not exceeding six months. *Id.*
142. *Id.*

thermore, the IFRB's assistance may be requested in resolving interference difficulties.[143]

The procedures for resolving difficulties at the advance publication stage must not be confused with the subsequent coordination process for geostationary satellites. At the advance publication stage, the purpose is simply to resolve basic incompatibilities, such as when another satellite occupies or is being coordinated for the orbital location sought by your client. By contrast, the subsequent coordination process focuses on more specific frequency usage, and any necessary adjustments made by your client at the coordination stage should not require major satellite design changes, provided basic incompatibilities were resolved at the advance publication stage.

If no comments were received in response to the advance publication, or if interference issues have been resolved, the administration acting on behalf of your client may enter the coordination stage.[144] On the other hand, if the administrations involved have not completed their efforts to resolve interference issues, the commencement of the coordination process shall be deferred by six months.[145] After six months have passed, the administration acting on behalf of your client can proceed to the coordination stage even though interference issues have not been resolved. In other words, agreements with the administrations concerned are not necessary at the advance publication stage. In fact, it is not uncommon that administrations defer to the coordination stage for resolution of interference issues, and merely register potential problems in standard comments at the advance publication stage, typically stating something to the effect that "it is the belief of this administration that harmful interference will occur from the planned satellite operation, and that coordination will be necessary."

The coordination process must be initiated within six years of the advance publication of the information sent to the IFRB initially, or nine years if the permissible three-years extension is sought. Otherwise, the advance publication will be cancelled.[146] This rule prevents administrations from laying claim to orbital locations and frequencies for which they have no immediate or foreseeable need.

COORDINATION. Coordination is the process of resolving interference issues that were not resolved during the advance publication stage. Coordination must be undertaken with "any other administration whose assignment, for a space station on a geostationary satellite or for an Earth station that communicates with a space station on a geostationary satellite, might be affected."[147] Frequency assignments that may be affected are those in the same frequency bands and for the same type of satellite service (or another service to which the particular frequency band has

143. *Id.*, No. 1054.
144. ITU Radio Regulations, art. 11, No. 1058 (WARC-79).
145. *Id.*
146. ITU Radio Regulations, art. 11, No. 1056A (WARC-ORB-88).

been allocated on a shared basis with equal right) as your client's.[148] To be taken into account for coordination purposes, a frequency assignment must have attained a certain level of "ITU status."[149] Naturally, frequency assignments that have been recorded in the Master International Frequency Register must be taken into account.[150] However, assignments also must be taken into account that have been coordinated, while not yet recorded,[151] and that have been advance published, but not yet coordinated, provided the coordination process has been initiated.[152]

Coordination is not necessary, however, in cases where the interference potentially caused to another satellite operation does not exceed a threshold value defined in Appendix 29 to the Radio Regulations.[153] This threshold was raised by the World Administrative Radio Conference on the Use of the Geostationary-Satellite Orbit and the Planning of Space Services Utilizing It, Second Session, in 1988, in order to reduce the need for coordinations.[154] Coordination also is not necessary when an administration proposes to bring into use within the same service area a typical Earth station or an Earth station which would not cause or suffer interference of a level greater than a typical Earth station;[155] or a new Earth station that would not cause or suffer interference of a level greater than an Earth station whose characteristics have previously been published.[156] Exceptions also exist in the event of modifications to a frequency assignment which has been previously coordinated.[157]

The administration acting on behalf of your client must initiate the coordination process by sending to all administrations with which coordi-

---

147. *Id.*, No. 1060. If a frequency assignment is brought into use before such coordination is effected, the advance operation shall in no way afford any priority of the data. *Id.*, No. 1060AA.
148. *Id.*, No. 1061.
149. A frequency assignment shall be taken into account when it is in conformity with the ITU Convention and the Table of Frequency Allocations *and* 1) it has been recorded in the Master International Frequency Register; 2) it has been coordinated; 3) it has been notified to the IFRB without coordination where coordination does not apply; or 4) it is to be taken into account for coordination with effect from the date of receipt by the IFRB of Appendix 3 information, ITU Radio Regulations, art. 11, Nos. 1061-1065 (WARC-79 and WARC-ORB-88).
150. ITU Radio Regulations, art. 11, No. 1063 (WARC-79).
151. ITU Radio Regulations, art. 11, No. 1064 (WARC-ORB-88).
152. *Id.*
153. *Id.*, No. 1067 (WARC-ORB-88). ITU Radio Regulations, Appendix 29 contains a formula for determining whether coordination is necessary.
154. *See* Smith, INTERNATIONAL REGULATION, *supra* note 27, at 176, note 23 (stating that the threshold value was changed from four to six percent and that this change should result in fewer required coordinations)
155. ITU Radio Regulations, art. 11, No. 1066A (WARC-ORB-88)
156. *Id.*, No. 1069
157. ITU Radio Regulations, art. 11, No. 1068 (WARC-79).

nation is necessary the technical information specified in Appendix 3 to the Radio Regulations,[158] with a copy to the IFRB that includes the name(s) of the administrations with which coordination is sought.[159] Administrations that were not included in the mailing, and believe they should have been, can request inclusion in the coordination effort.[160]

The Appendix 3 information required for purposes of the coordination concerns the communications links between your client's satellite and typical Earth station(s) in the proposed satellite network. As illustrated in figure 2, below, the objective of the coordination is to eliminate potential, unacceptable interference that might otherwise result 1) from another satellite to your client's Earth stations, 2) from your client's Earth stations to another satellite, 3) from your client's satellite to another Earth station, 4) from another Earth station to your client's satellite, 5) from your client's Earth stations to terrestrial radio stations in a foreign country, 6) from foreign terrestrial radio stations in a foreign country to your client's Earth stations, 7) from your client's satellite to foreign terrestrial radio stations and 8) from foreign terrestrial radio stations to your client's satellite. Interference between your client's and other Earth stations will not occur and, therefore, is not an issue, as long as different frequency bands are used for up-link and down-link.

Figure 2

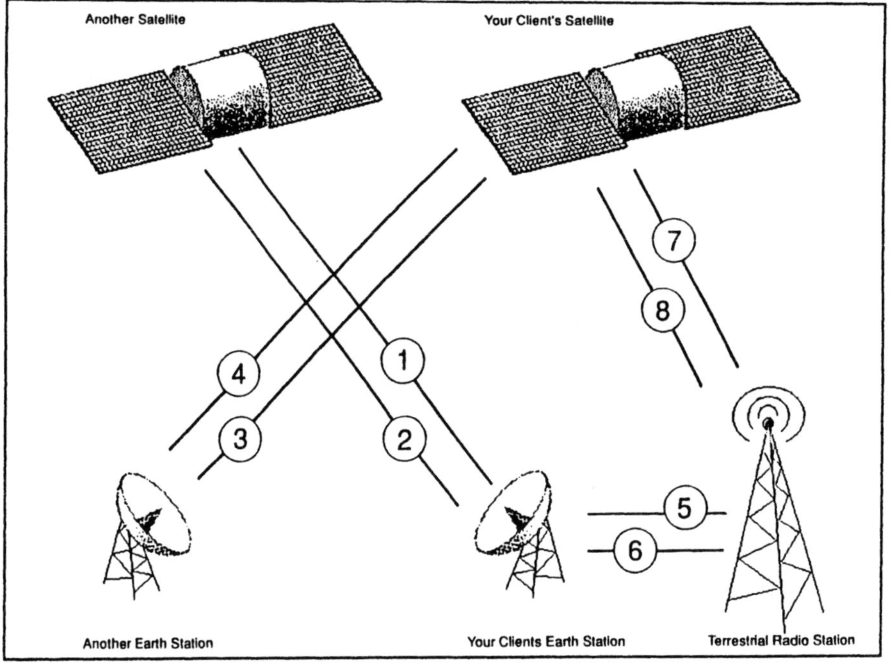

158. ITU Radio Regulations, art. 11, No. 1073 (WARC-ORB-88).
159. *Id.*, No. 1074.
160. ITU Radio Regulations, art. 11, No. 1080 (WARC-79).

Upon receipt of the Appendix 3 information, the IFRB will examine it with respect to conformity with the ITU Convention and the Radio Regulations, particularly the Table of Frequency Allocations.[161] Then, within three months of receiving the information, the IFRB will publish it in a special section of its weekly circular and inform all administrations by circular telegram of the Appendix 3 information.[162]

Administrations receiving Appendix 3 information must acknowledge its receipt, and determine whether unacceptable interference would be caused to their respective radio services.[163] Comments are due within four months of the publication in the weekly circular.[164] An administration that believes it will not cause interference to, or suffer interference from, your client's satellite system must notify the administration acting on behalf of your client.[165] An administration that believes that interference will result, however, and therefore does not automatically agree to coordination of your client's satellite system, shall provide to the administration acting on behalf of your client "the technical details upon which its disagreement is based," and offer suggestions for solutions.[166]

The administration acting on behalf of your client and the other administrations with which coordination is necessary "shall make all possible mutual efforts to overcome the difficulties," that is, to resolve perceived interference problems.[167] In the process, either administration may seek additional information from the other.[168] For the purpose of effecting the coordination, the parties may make use of correspondence, as well as bilateral and multilateral meetings.[169] In exceptional circumstances, they may resort to so-called "multilateral planning meetings" (MPM).[170]

MPMs were adopted by the 1988 World Administrative Radio Conference on the Use of the Geostationary-Satellite Orbit and the Planning of Space Services Utilizing It as a method of accommodating and facilitating access for new satellite systems. They represent a novel coordination approach, and were introduced in response to demands by developing countries for some guarantee of future access to the geostationary orbit and associated frequency bands (see Chapter 4.2.). It was believed that multilateral planning meetings would offer a more effective means of achieving coordination of new satellite networks than the traditional bilat-

---

161. ITU Radio Regulations, art. 11, Nos. 1075-1077 (WARC-ORB-88).
162. *Id.*, No. 1078.
163. ITU Radio Regulations, art. 11, No. 1082 (WARC-79) and Nos. 1083-1084 (WARC-ORB-88).
164. ITU Radio Regulations, art. 11, No. 1084 (WARC-ORB-88).
165. *Id.*
166. *Id.*
167. *Id.*, No. 1085A.
168. *Id.*, No. 1085.
169. *Id.*, No. 1085B.
170. *Id.*, No. 1085C.

eral coordination approach. MPMs do not guarantee access, however.[171]

MPMs are available only in "exceptional cases"[172] if a "major difficulty"[173] is encountered in obtaining coordination of your client's satellite network.[174] Moreover, they apply only to certain frequency bands, i.e., those most commonly used in the fixed satellite service:

3700-4200 MHz
5850-6425 MHz
10.95-11.20 GHz
11.45-11.70 GHz
11.70-12.20 GHz (Region 2, only)
12.50-12.75 GHz (Regions 1 and 3, only)
14.00-14.50 GHz[175]

The results of the MPMs shall be considered as coordination agreements among the participants. The agreements do not include non-participants.[176] The results or agreements are to be communicated to the IFRB.[177]

Regardless of whether MPMs or traditional coordination meetings have taken place, the administration acting on behalf of your client shall, within four months of the weekly circular in which the IFRB published the Appendix 3 information submitted for coordination, inform the IFRB of coordination agreements reached and of progress made with respect to coordination with affected administrations.[178] Such communications shall be made to the IFRB every six months thereafter,[179] in addition to communication on any changes in the published characteristics agreed upon.[180] The administration acting on behalf of your client may request the IFRB to "endeavor to effect" the coordination in cases where coordination is not possible; for example, where the administration with which coordination is sought fails to cooperate (e.g. for political reasons), where there is disagreement as to what constitutes unacceptable interference, or where arranging for multilateral planning meetings or other bilateral or

171. *See* Smith, INTERNATIONAL REGULATION, *supra* note 27, at 160 (pointing out that affected administrations are not even required to participate and that the effectiveness of MPMs is uncertain).
172. ITU Radio Regulations, art. 11, No. 1085C (WARC-ORB-85)
173. *Improved Procedures for Certain Bands in the fixed satellite Service,* ITU Res. COM 6/3, *Final Acts,* WARC-ORB-88 [hereinafter cited as Resolution COM 6/3], Resolves 2.
174. *See generally* ITU Radio Regulations, art. 11, Nos. 1085C and 1085D (WARC-ORB-88) and Resolution COM6/3, *supra* note 173 (describing multilateral planning meetings).
175. ITU Radio Regulations, art. 11, No. 1085C (WARC-ORB-88).
176. Resolution COM 6/3, *supra* note 173, Resolves 6.
177. *Id.,* Resolves 7.
178. ITU Radio Regulations, art. 11, No. 1087 (WARC-ORB-88).
179. *Id.*
180. *Id.,* Nos. 1087A and 1087C.

multilateral meetings poses difficulties.[181]

Depending on the difficulties encountered, the coordination process may take anywhere from four months to several years. For example, if your client plans to locate a satellite in the geostationary orbit two degrees away from an existing or planned foreign satellite operating in the same frequency band, coordination can be quite time-consuming. Generally, the interference potential is greater the closer the spacing between satellites.

Once coordination has been completed, the administration acting on behalf of your client may proceed to the notification stage.[182] Provisions exist for recording of a frequency assignment whose coordination is being blocked for political reasons, rather than on technical grounds. Normally, however, the coordination process is executed in an effective manner and administrations generally act in good faith.

NOTIFICATION AND RECORDING. Notification is the third and final step in the process leading to recording in the Master International Frequency Register and international recognition of your client's frequency assignment. Notification involves the submission to the IFRB of a "notice" containing the information prescribed in Appendix 3 to the Radio Regulations.[183] The administration acting on behalf of your client must submit to the IFRB Appendix 3 information most current and reflecting adjustments made during coordination. The information must reach the IFRB not earlier than three years, and not later than three months, before the date on which your client intends to bring into use its frequency assignment.[184] With respect to Earth stations intended to operate in connection with your client's satellite, only one or more typical Earth stations will need to be notified.[185]

Within forty days of receipt of a complete notice, the IFRB will publish the full particulars in the weekly circular sent to all administrations.[186] Incomplete notices will be returned, and reasons for dismissal set forth.[187]

---

181. *Id.,* Nos. 1088-1093. In response to such a request, the IFRB will take action to ensure the necessary cooperation of other administrations, or otherwise resolve the difficulties. *Id.,* Nos. 1095-1100. If the administration with which coordination is sought simply fails to respond to the IFRB's request for cooperation within certain time limits, that administration has undertaken that no complaint will be made in respect of any harmful interference caused by your client's satellite operations and that its satellite operations will not cause harmful interference to your client's satellite operations. *Id.,* Nos. 1101-1103.
182. Previously, the Radio Regulations (ITU Radio Regulations, art. 11, No. 1105 (WARC-79)) provided that the administration seeking coordination could proceed to the notification stage even if coordination difficulties were unresolved. WARC-ORB-88 suppressed these provisions
183. *Id.,* art. 13, No. 1495.
184. *Id.,* No. 1496.
185. ITU Radio Regulations, art. 13, No. 1494 (WARC-ORB-88).
186. ITU Radio Regulations, art. 13, Nos. 1499 and 1500 (WARC-79).
187. *Id.,* No. 1498.

Complete notices are processed by the IFRB in the order they are received.[188] The IFRB examines the notice with respect to its 1) conformity with the ITU Convention, the Table of Frequency Allocations, and other provisions in the Radio Regulations; 2) compliance with the coordination procedures; and 3) the probability of interference in cases where coordination has not been successfully effected.[189] In making its interference assessment, the IFRB will disregard the effect on an assignment that has been recorded, but which has not in been use for two years or more.[190]

The Radio Regulations stipulate the circumstances under which the IFRB shall record a frequency assignment in the Master International Frequency Register. Your client's frequency assignment will be recorded if it 1) complies with the ITU Convention and Table of Frequency Allocations, and the coordination process has been successfully completed;[191] 2) does not comply with the Table of Frequency Allocations, provided the notice contains a specific reference to Provision No. 342 of the Radio Regulations[192] (Provision No. 342 permits administrations to make frequency assignments not in conformity with the Table of Frequency Allocations on the condition that harmful interference does not result[193]); and 3) has not been successfully coordinated, but otherwise conforms to the ITU Convention and the Table of Frequency Allocations, and its use would not cause harmful interference.[194]

Once your client's assignment has been recorded, it is protected from interference resulting from the use of any subsequently-recorded assignment. Provision No. 1559 of the Radio Regulations states that "[i]f harmful interference is actually caused to the reception of any space radiocommunication station whose frequency assignment has been recorded in the Master Register . . . the station using the latter frequency assignment must . . . immediately eliminate this harmful interference."[195]

4.3.1.2. Fixed Satellite Systems Subject to Plan

THE PLAN AND WHEN IT APPLIES. If your client intends to operate a fixed satellite system in the expansion bands, which are not commonly used frequency bands today, an allotment Plan contained in Appendix 30B of the ITU Radio Regulations[196] applies. The following bands are covered by the Plan:

---

188. *Id.*, No. 1501.
189. *Id.*, Nos. 1502-1512.
190. *Id.*, No. 1513.
191. *Id.*, Nos. 1525-1526.
192. *Id.*, Nos. 1518-1519.
193. *Id.*, art. 6, No. 342. *See supra* note 19 (quoting the provision).
194. *Id.*, art. 13, Nos. 1533 and 1534.
195. *Id.*, No. 1559.

4500-4800 MHz	(space-to-Earth)
6725-7025 MHz	(Earth-to-space)
10.70-10.95 GHz	(space-to-Earth)
11.20-11.45 GHz	(space-to-Earth)
12.75-13.25 GHz	(Earth-to-space)[197]

PURPOSE. The Plan was adopted at the World Administrative Radio Conference on the Use of the Geostationary-Satellite Orbit and the Planning of Space Services Utilizing It, Geneva, 1988, and its stated objective is to "guarantee in practice, for all countries, equitable access to the geostationary-satellite orbit . . . ."[198] The Plan responded to demands by the developing countries that they be provided some guarantee that their geostationary satellite systems will be accommodated when they are able to build or afford to purchase such systems in the future (see Chapter 4.2.).

CONTENTS. The Plan has two components. Part A provides for at least one new allotment, which will translate into one orbital location and associated frequencies for a satellite network for each ITU member State. Part A also recognizes that some member States may need more than one allotment. Part B contains the design and operating characteristics of existing satellite systems in the expansion bands.[199]

An allotment has five components: 1) a nominal orbital position, 2) a bandwidth of 800 MHz (up-link and down-link), 3) a service area for national coverage,[200] 4) generalized characteristics for the satellite network, and 5) a predetermined arc.[201] The predetermined arc concept was introduced to provide more flexibility in the implementation of the Plan. (Compare the Plan adopted by the 1977 World Administrative Radio Conference for the Planning of the Broadcasting Satellite Service in the 12 GHz Band, which allotted specific orbital positions to ITU member States in Regions 1 and 3). "Predetermined arc" refers to a segment of the geostationary orbit about a nominal orbital position, whose size depends on the stage of development of a planned satellite system.[202] The size of the arc decreases as the planned satellite system approaches the operational

196. ITU Radio Regulations, Appendix 30B, entitled "Provisions and Associated Plan for the Fixed Satellite Service in the Frequency Bands 4500-4800 MHz, 6725-7025 MHz, 10.70-10.95 GHz, 11.20-11.45 GHz and 12.75-13.25 GHz" (WARC-ORB-88). The Plan entered into force on 16 March 1990. *See* Smith, INTERNATIONAL REGULATION, *supra* note 27, at 162-181 (describing the Plan).

197. ITU Radio Regulations, Appendix 30B, art. G (WARC-ORB-88).

198. *Id.*, art. R.

199. *See, Id.*, art. F (defining "existing systems").

200. *See Id.*, art. L (concerning subregional satellite systems, *i.e.*, satellite systems created by agreement among neighboring countries intended to provide subregional or domestic service within the geographical area of the countries concerned).

201. *Id.*, art. F.

202. *Id.*, art. J.

stage. At the operational stage, the predetermined arc is zero[203] and the orbital location is fixed.

IMPLEMENTATION PROCEDURES. Appendix 30B of the Radio Regulations, which contains the Plan, also sets forth the procedures for implementing a satellite system pursuant to the Plan.[204] These procedures substitute for advance publication and coordination applicable to fixed satellites in the conventional frequency bands, described in Chapter 4.3.1.1., but refer to the notification-registration procedure normally applied (see Chapter 4.3.1.1.).[205] According to M. Smith, INTERNATIONAL REGULATION OF SATELLITE COMMUNICATION (1990), administrations with existing satellite systems in the expansion bands have a particularly strong obligation to accommodate administrations proposing new systems and seeking to implement their allotments pursuant to Part A of the Plan. An administration may be asked to change orbital location or alter the operating characteristics of the existing system.[206] On the other hand, Smith points out, the administration proposing the new system in accordance with Part A may, itself, be asked to use at least state-of-the-art satellite facilities and Earth station equipment,[207] a measure that facilitates the resolution of potential frequency interference problems with respect to existing systems.

4.3.2. Geostationary Satellites in the Mobile and Radiodetermination Satellite Services

If your client plans to operate a mobile satellite[208] or a radiodetermination satellite[209] system, the procedures for advance publication, coordination and notification-recording set forth in Articles 11 and 13 (and Article 14, depending on the frequency band to be used) of the Radio Regulations,[210] and described for fixed satellites in Chapter 4.3.1.1., apply with only a few exceptions. For example, provisions for multilateral planning meetings, which apply to fixed satellites in exceptional cases where major difficulties are encountered during coordination, do not apply to mobile or radiodetermination satellite systems.

4.3.3. Geostationary Satellites in the Broadcasting Satellite Service

Articles 11 and 13 of the Radio Regulations, which set forth advance

---

203. *Id.*
204. *Id.*, art. L.
205. *Id.*, art. M (providing for the application of Article 13 of the Radio Regulations with some modifications).
206. Smith, INTERNATIONAL REGULATION, *supra* note 27, at 165.
207. *Id.*
208. *See* note 17, *supra* (providing the ITU definition of "mobile satellite service")
209. *See supra* note 15 (providing the ITU definition of "radiodetermination satellite service").
210. *See* note 119, *supra* (explaining the general contents of Articles 11, 13 and 14).

publication, coordination and notification-recording procedures and criteria for other geostationary satellites do not apply directly to broadcasting satellites. In fact, these provisions explicitly exempt broadcasting satellites from their scopes of direct application. Nevertheless, some of the procedural requirements and criteria contained in Articles 11 and 13 apply by reference to broadcasting satellites, as well.

If your client intends to operate a geostationary broadcasting satellite system[211] in the 11.7-12.7 GHz band (down-link), *a priori* plans govern (see Chapter 4.3.3.1.). Other bands allocated to broadcasting satellites have not been planned, and the establishment of broadcasting satellite service in these bands is subject to the procedures set forth in ITU Resolution 33 adopted at the 1979 World Administrative Conference, and entitled "Relating to the Bringing into Use Space Stations in the broadcasting satellite Service, Prior to the Entry Into Force of Agreements and Associated Plans for the Broadcasting Satellite Service." This resolution makes reference to many of the procedural requirements and criteria of Articles 11 and 13 (see Chapter 4.3.3.2.).

4.3.3.1. Broadcasting Satellite Systems Subject to Plan

WHEN PLANS APPLY. If your client intends to operate a broadcasting satellite system in the 11.7-12.7 GHz band (down-link),[212] one of two *a priori* allotment plans and associated provisions apply, depending on which ITU member State is sponsoring the operation. For broadcasting satellite service in ITU Regions 1 (Europe, Africa, the USSR and Mongolia) and 3 (the rest of Asia, Australia and the Southwest Pacific), a relatively rigid allotment plan, adopted at the 1977 World Administration Radio Conference for the Planning of the Broadcasting Satellite Service in the 12 GHz Band (hereinafter WARC-77 Plan), applies.[213] For broadcasting satellite service in Region 2 (the Americas, the Caribbean and Greenland), a more flexible plan adopted at the 1983 Regional Administrative Radio Conference for the Planning of Broadcasting Satellite Service in Region 2 (hereinafter RARC-83 Plan) applies.[214]

THE WARC-77 PLAN. With a duration of fifteen years, the WARC-77 Plan covers the frequency bands of 11.7-12.5 GHz (space-to-Earth) in Region 1 and 11.7-12.2 GHz (space-to-Earth) in Region 3. The Plan desig-

---

211. *See* note 16, *supra* (providing the ITU definition of "broadcasting satellite service").
212. Specifically, these bands are governed by plans: 11.7-12.5 GHz (Region 1), 12.2-12.7 GHz (Region 2) and 11.7-12.2 GHz (Region 3).
213. ITU Radio Regulations, Appendix 30 (WARC-79), entitled "Provisions for All Services and Associated Plan for Broadcasting Satellite Service in Frequency Bands 11.7-12.2 GHz (in Regions 2 and 3) and 11.7-12.5 GHz (in Region 1)."
214. ITU Radio Regulations, Appendix 30 (WARC-ORB-85), entitled "Provisions for All Services and Associated Plan for Broadcasting Satellite Service in Frequency Bands 11.7-12.2 GHz (in Regions 2 and 3) and 11.7-12.5 GHz (in Region 1)."

nated orbital locations and frequencies for each ITU member State in ITU Regions 1 and 3, and specified detailed technical parameters of the satellite system design, based on 1977 state-of-the-art technology. Member states wishing to implement satellite systems pursuant to the WARC-77 Plan, therefore, may not be able to take full advantage of technological advances made since the Plan was adopted. Satellite systems built today are several times more efficient than those models contemplated by the WARC-77 Plan. France, Germany, the United Kingdom (British Satellite Broadcasting Company) and Sweden (with participation also from other Nordic countries) have launched broadcasting satellite systems pursuant to the WARC-77 Plan and have experienced the technical constraints.

The WARC-77 plan provided only for communications in the space-to-Earth direction (down-links). Earth-to-space links (feeder-links) had to be selected outside the Plan, as appropriate. Provisions for feeder links, however, later were made at the World Administrative Radio Conference on the Use of the Geostationary-Satellite Orbit and the Planning of Space Services Utilizing It, Second Session, Geneva, 1988.[215] The bands designated for feeder links for the broadcasting satellite service in Regions 1 and 3 included 14.5-14.8 GHz (Earth-to-space) (only for countries outside Europe) and 17.3-18.1 GHz (Earth-to-space).

RARC-83 PLAN. The RARC-83 Plan is less rigid than the WARC-77 Plan, and provides individual administrations more flexibility in implementing their satellite systems pursuant to the Plan. It also is more spectrum efficient than the WARC-77 Plan, providing for twice as many orbital positions/frequency assignments,[216] while using a smaller segment of the geostationary orbit.[217] The RARC-83 Plan established both down links (space-to-Earth) and feeder links (Earth-to-space), covering the frequency bands of: 12.2-12.7 GHz (space-to-Earth) and 17.3-17.8 GHz (Earth-to-space).[218]

4.3.3.2. Broadcasting Satellite Systems Not Subject to Plan.

If your client intends to operate a geostationary broadcasting satellite system in frequencies other than those covered by a plan, ITU Resolution 33, entitled "Relating to the Bringing into Use Space Stations in the broadcasting satellite Service, Prior to the Entry Into Force of Agreements and Associated Plans for Broadcasting Satellite Service," applies. This resolution must be viewed in light of ITU Resolution 507, entitled "Relating

---

215. ITU Radio Regulations, Appendix 30A (WARC-ORB-88), entitled "Provisions and Associated Plans for Feeder Links for the Broadcasting Satellite Service (11.7-12.5 GHz (in Region 1), 12.2-12.7 GHz in Region 2 and 11.7-12.2 GHz in Region 3) in the Frequency Bands 14.5-14.8 GHz and 17.3-18.1 GHz in Regions 1 and 3, and 17.3-17.8 GHz in Region 2."
216. The number of channels were 2114 versus 984.
217. The orbital segments were 144 degrees versus 237 degrees.
218. *See* ITU Radio Regulations, Appendix 30A (containing feeder links also for Region 2).

to the Establishment of Agreements and Associated Plans for Broadcasting Satellite Service," which calls for planning of all frequency bands allocated to broadcasting satellite service. Resolution 33 was intended to provide procedures and criteria for the establishment of broadcasting satellites pending the adoption of such plans. Both resolutions were adopted in 1979. Resolution 33 refers to many of the provisions of Articles 11 and 13. It is important to note that Resolution 33 does not apply to fixed satellites used for multi-point distribution or broadcasting to individual homes. See Chapter 4.3.1.

4.3.3.3. Additional Restrictions on Broadcasting Satellites

Because many socialist countries, as well as developing nations, perceived broadcasting satellite systems as a potential threat to their ideological and cultural foundations, they insisted in several public and private fora that certain restrictions be placed on the operators of such systems. Governments of these countries believed that, unless restrictions were imposed, U.S. "soap operas," talk shows, news and entertainment programs would be beamed directly into the living rooms of their citizens, thereby eroding fundamental cultural and ideological values espoused by those societies. The ITU, as well as the United Nations Committee on the Peaceful Uses of Outer Space (COPUOS), were called upon to ensure that foreign satellite broadcasts would not reach the population of a given country without that country's prior consent. The United States and several other democratic, industrialized countries opposed a rule of prior consent and, instead, favored free flow of information.

ITU RADIO REGULATIONS. The ITU refused to deal with, and referred to the COPUOS, the issue of prior consent versus free flow of information, claiming that the ITU's purpose was to regulate the technical aspects of satellite communications. However, a compromise provision was adopted by the ITU that, while dealing only with the technical aspects of transborder broadcasting, nevertheless serves to restrict the free flow of information. This provision requires that "[i]n devising the characteristics of a space station in the broadcasting satellite service, all technical means available shall be used to reduce, to the maximum extent practicable, the radiation over the territory of other countries unless an agreement has been previously reached with such countries."[219]

UNITED NATIONS RESOLUTION. In 1982, the United Nations General Assembly adopted a Resolution,formulated by the COPUOS,and entitled "Principles Governing the Use by States of Artificial Earth Satellites for International Direct Television Broadcasting,"[220] which provides for the prior consent of the receiving country. The pertinent provisions provide:

13. A State which intends to establish or authorize the establishment of

---

219. ITU Radio Regulations, art. 30, No. 2647 (WARC-79)

220. *Principles Governing the Use by States of Artificial Earth Satellites for International Direct Television Broadcasting,* U.N.G.A. Res. 37/92, (1982).

an international direct television broadcasting satellite service shall without delay notify the proposed receiving State or States of such intention and shall promptly enter into consultation with any of those States which so requests.

14. An international direct television broadcasting satellite service shall only be established after the conditions set forth in paragraph 13 above have been met and on the basis of *agreements and/or arrangements* in conformity with the relevant instruments of the International Telecommunication Union and in accordance with these principles.[221]

The resolution, which did not gain the favorable votes of the United States and several other non-socialist countries, presumably applies only to broadcasting satellite service in the bands allocated to such service, and not to broadcasting via fixed satellites.[222] Moreover, it applies only to television (and not to radio) satellite broadcasting. Although the resolution is limited in scope and not legally binding, it nevertheless has had a chilling effect on certain commercial satellite broadcasting initiatives. For broadcasting satellite services subject to the WARC-77 Plan or RARC-83 Plan, the additional ITU and U.N. restrictions have only marginal significance, since these services already are severely constrained. The United Nations Resolution quoted above further provides that "[w]ith respect to unavoidable spillover of the radiation of the satellite signal, the relevant instruments of the International Telecommunication Union shall be exclusively applicable."

The European Community is moving in the direction of an "open borders" policy for satellite television signals, which when implemented by the individual member States will allow European governments and private entities authorized by them to broadcast freely across Europe (within the European Community). On 20 November, 1990, the Commission of the European Community adopted a Green Paper, entitled "Toward Europe-Wide Systems and Services," which outlines this policy.[223] Approval by the Council of the European Community is necessary to make the policy

---

221. Emphasis added. *Id.*, Principle J, entitled "Consultations and Agreements Between States." Principle J also states that with regard to "unavoidable overspill of radiation of the satellite signal, the relevant instruments of the International Telecommunication Convention union shall be exclusively applicable." This is a reference to Provision 2647, *supra* note 219.

222. For example, the Luxembourg-based Societe Europeenne des Satellites, which provides broadcasting satellite service in Europe via its Astra fixed satellites, probably is not bound by the Resolution. The company also is not subject to the broadcasting satellite plan for Region 1 (Europe), discussed, above, because it is not operating in the broadcasting satellite service bands. Regardless of the U.N. Resolution, however, some measure of cooperation from the State in which international broadcast signals are being received always will be required since States can otherwise prohibit the import, manufacture, sale or installation of receiving equipment.

legally binding.

4.3.4. Non-Geostationary Satellite Systems

If your client intends to operate a non-geostationary satellite system, the procedural steps necessary to obtain international frequency protection are advance publication and notification-recording, as prescribed in Articles 11 and 13 of the Radio Regulations.[224] The coordination procedure and criteria established specifically for geostationary satellites, and described in Chapter 4.3.1.1., do not apply to non-geostationary satellites, and no separate criteria and procedures have been adopted for them.[225] It is true, however, that certain measures for resolving interference problems are provided in the procedures for advance publication, which apply equally to low-Earth orbit satellites.

Furthermore, an important provision appears in Article 29 of the Radio Regulations with respect to coordination between geostationary and non-geostationary satellite systems in the fixed satellite service, clearly prioritizing the former:

> Non-geostationary [satellites] shall cease or reduce to a negligible level their emissions, and their associated Earth stations shall not transmit to them, whenever there is insufficient angular separation between non-geostationary satellites and geostationary satellites, and whenever there is unacceptable interference to geostationary satellite space systems in the fixed satellite service operating in accordance with these Regulations.[226]

This provision does not apply to mobile and radiodetermination satellite services by low-Earth orbit satellite constellations now being proposed. In order to effect coordination of these systems before the ITU has

---

223. Commission of the European Community, *Toward Europe-Wide Systems and Services, Green Paper on a Common Approach in the Field of Satellite Communications in the European Community,* COM (90) 490 Final, Brussels Nov. 20. 1990.
224. *See* ITU Radio Regulations, art 11, section I (setting forth procedures for advance publication) and *id.*, art 13 (setting forth procedures for notification). It is interesting to note that Appendix 4 to the Radio Regulations, which sets forth the information that an administration must provide to the IFRB for purposes of advance publication, requires that information be provided for each "satellite network." A satellite network is defined as one satellite and associated Earth stations. All of the non-geostationary satellite systems now being proposed contemplate between 20 and 77 satellites. *See* Chapter 3.1.6. (describing some of these satellite systems). In this case, it will be very impractical to provide information separately for every satellite network.
225. Sections II and III of Article 11 set forth procedures for coordination of geostationary satellites. *See supra* note 120 (explaining the general contents of the Articles 11, 13-15 of the Radio Regulations).
226. ITU Radio Regulations, art. 29, No. 2613 (WARC-79).

occasion to establish formal coordination procedures, it may be possible, as an interim measure, to apply, to the extent practicalble, the procedures applicable to geostationary satellites.

The advance publication and notification-recording procedures applicable to non-geostationary satellites are the same as those described for fixed satellites in Chapter 4.3.1.1., with a few exceptions. For example, the administration acting on behalf of your client may submit notification information (Appendix 3) at the same time the advance publication information (Appendix 4) is submitted.[227] Appendix 4 requires that information (for purposes of advance publication) be submitted separately for each "satellite network" making up a satellite system. As will be recalled, a "satellite network" is defined as a satellite with associated Earth stations. With respect to non-geostationary satellite systems consisting of dozens of satellites, this requirement may seem impractical. Furthermore, the criteria for recording of frequency assignments are somewhat different since the geostationary satellite coordination procedures do not apply. If your client's frequency assignment conforms to the ITU Convention, the Table of Frequency Allocations and other provisions of the Radio Regulations, it will be recorded in the Master International Frequency Register.[228] If your client's frequency assignment is not in conformity with the Table of Frequency Allocations and other provisions of the Radio Regulations, it may be recorded nevertheless if the notice contains a reference to Provision No. 342 of the Radio Regulations.[229] This provision allows for frequency assignments in derogation of the Table of Frequency Allocations on the condition that harmful interference will not be caused.[230]

With the advent of multiple low-Earth orbit mobile communications satellite systems now being proposed by INMARSAT, private companies in the United States and organizations in other countries, the ITU may have to adopt low-Earth orbit "traffic rules" in the future, that is, coordination criteria and procedures for *orbital paths* as well as frequencies for these satellites.[231] Clearly, the task of synchronizing the uses of non-geostationary orbital paths is infinitely more complex than regulating the use of the geostationary orbit.[232] Extremely sophisticated computer software

227. ITU Radio Regulations, art. 11, No. 1058D (WARC-ORB-88). The notice shall be considered to be received by the IFRB not earlier than six months after the date of receipt of information for purposes of advanced publication. *Id.*, No. 1058E.
228. ITU Radio Regulations, art. 15, Nos. 1515 and 1516 (WARC-79).
229. *Id*, art. 6, No. 342.
230. *Id.*, art. 13, Nos. 1517 and 1518.
231. *See* R. DalBello, *"Rules of the Road:" Legal Measures to Strengthen the Peaceful Uses of Outer Space*, XXVIII IISL 8 (1985), P.O. Collins & T.W. Williams, *Toward Traffic Systems for Near Earth Space*, XXIX IISL 161 (1986) [hereinafter cited as Collins, Traffic Systems] and P.Q. Collins, *Legal Considerations for Traffic Systems in Near Space*, XXXII IISL 300 (1989) (discussing ways of accommodating multiple satellite systems in low-Earth orbit).

will be necessary to accomplish this task and contributions from technologically advanced countries, such as the United States, Japan and Western Europe, will be essential.

232. There are innumerable, mutually exclusive ways of dividing the low-Earth orbit environment into orbital paths or zones. The difficulty of regulating the low-Earth orbit environment is exacerbated by the fact that non-geostationary "orbits of spacecraft orbiting passively do not remain fixed with respect to the Earth. Nor do they remain fixed with respect to each other, nor with respect to any system of coordinates. Spacecraft orbits . . . evolve through time due to perturbations introduced by the Earth's oblateness, by the influence of other celestial bodies, by the earth's atmosphere, and even by solar radiation . . . . [Moreover,] orbits decay as a result of atmospheric drag." Collins, Traffic Systems, *supra* note 230, at 162. Some measure of station keeping is necessary also in the geostationary orbit, however.

5. Secure Coordination with INTELSAT, INMARSAT and EUTELSAT, as Appropriate, of Your Client's Satellite System

In addition to obtaining national authorization for your client's satellite operations (discussed in Chapter 3.) and registration of its frequency assignment in the International Telecommunication Union's Master International Frequency Register (discussed in Chapter 4.), it is likely that your client's satellite system will have to be coordinated with one or more of three international organizations, i.e., the International Telecommunications Satellite Organization (INTELSAT),[1] the International Maritime Satellite Organization (INMARSAT),[2] and the European Telecommunications Satellite Organization (EUTELSAT).[3] Each of these organizations operates a multi-satellite system, and coordination is required to ensure that their satellite transmissions do not suffer harmful radio interference. Occasionally, coordination also is required to avoid economic harm (adverse business consequences) to these organizations.

Coordination to avoid harmful radio interference is often referred to as "technical" coordination, and coordination to prevent adverse impact on business operations is generally referred to as "economic" coordination. Technical coordination and, depending on the type of service being proposed by your client, economic coordination with INTELSAT, INMARSAT and EUTELSAT, or all three, will be necessary if 1) the State which autho-

1. *See* Agreement Relating to the International Telecommunications Satellite Organization [hereinafter cited as INTELSAT Agreement], *done* Aug. 20, 1971, *entered into force* Feb. 12, 1973, T.I.A.S. 7532, art. XIV (providing for coordination with INTELSAT).
2. *See* Convention on the International Maritime Satellite Organization [hereinafter cited as INMARSAT Convention], *done* Sept. 3, 1976, *entered into force* July 16, 1979, T.I.A.S. 9605, art. VIII (providing for coordination with INMARSAT).
3. *See* Convention Establishing the European Telecommunications Satellite Organization [hereinafter cited as EUTELSAT Convention], *done* July 15, 1982, *entered into force* Sept. 1, 1985, B.G.B.1. 1984 II, at 683, art. XVI (providing for coordination with EUTELSAT).

rized your client's satellite operation is a member of the organization; and 2) the organization provides or intends to provide the kind of services your client has been authorized to provide, or the organization's charter otherwise requires that your client's satellite operation be coordinated.

For example, if your client has been authorized by a European country to provide domestic or international fixed or broadcasting satellite service, and that European country is a Member of INTELSAT, INMARSAT and EUTELSAT, your client's satellite system will have to be coordinated under the Agreement Relating to the International Telecommunications Satellite Organization (INTELSAT Agreement)[4] and the Convention Establishing the European Telecommunications Satellite Organization (EUTELSAT Convention)[5]for any and all of these services.[6] Coordination would not be necessary under the Convention on the International Maritime Satellite Organization (INMARSAT Convention),[7] since INMARSAT does not provide the kinds of services intended by your client, and the INMARSAT Convention does not require their coordination. On the other hand, if your client has been authorized by the same European country to provide *maritime* mobile or radiodetermination satellite service, coordination under the INMARSAT Convention would be required, as well as under the INTELSAT Agreement and EUTELSAT Convention.[8] See Chapter 5.2.

Coordination with INTELSAT, INMARSAT and EUTELSAT must take place before the establishment or use of your client's satellite system. The process may begin as soon as your client has received national authoriza-

---

4. *See supra* note 3 (providing date of entry into force and citation for the EUTELSAT Convention).
5. *See supra* note 3 (providing date of entry into force and citation for the EUTELSAT Convention).
6. Coordination would take place pursuant to the INTELSAT Agreement, art. XIV(c) (with respect to technical coordination of domestic fixed satellite service), art. XIV(d) (with respect to technical and economic harm coordination of international fixed satellite service), and art. XIV(e) (with respect to technical coordination of broadcasting satellite service); and the EUTELSAT Convention, art. XVI(a) (with respect to economic coordination of international fixed satellite service) and art. XVI(b) (with respect to technical coordination of international and domestic fixed and broadcasting satellite services). *See* Chapter 5.2. (explaining the coordination requirements for the various services). It should be noted, however, that the INTELSAT Agreement and EUTELSAT Convention do not use the terms "domestic" or "international" fixed satellite service, *etc. See* Chapter 5.2., below (discussing INTELSAT/EUTELSAT terminology).
7. *See supra* note 2 (providing date of entry into force and citation for the INMARSAT Convention).
8. Article VIII(1) of the INMARSAT Convention requires coordination (technical and economic) if a satellite system separate from INMARSAT's space segment is "intended to meet any or all of the maritime purposes of INMARSAT. . . ."

tion to operate the satellite system, or even before that time if authorization reasonably can be expected. Normally, the technical coordination process goes on in parallel with the procedures for coordination pursuant to the International Telecommunication Union (ITU) Radio Regulations (see Chapter 4.3.). The issues raised in both sets of coordination processes are the same, although the specific procedures differ.

As with the ITU, all communication with INTELSAT, INMARSAT and EUTELSAT for coordination purposes takes place at the governmental level. Typically, the telecommunication administration or agency in the country authorizing your client's satellite operation will provide the appropriate interface with these international satellite organizations. If your client's satellite system is authorized in the United States, the Federal Communications Commission will conduct the coordination on your client's behalf, although the U.S. Department of State becomes involved to ensure that U.S. treay obligations are satisfied. Your client cannot, itself, initiate official coordination discussions with any of these international organizations.

5.1. INTELSAT, INMARSAT and EUTELSAT: Purpose, Function and Structure

WHAT KIND OF INTERNATIONAL ORGANIZATION? INTELSAT, INMARSAT and EUTELSAT essentially have the same basic legal structure. In many respects, they are typical public international organizations: established by treaty and composed of sovereign nations; serving a purpose common to all Member nations; having a legal personalty;[9] and their respective organs providing for the functioning of the organization. However, in the world of international organizations INTELSAT, INMARSAT and EUTELSAT are also quite unique. First, they own[10] and operate satellites and make available satellite capacity on a commercial basis[11] to telecommunications administrations, or designated entities, of Member and non-Member countries. Second, a two-tier system of participation applies to each of these organizations. At one level, States participate in their sovereign capacity and concern themselves with matters affecting them as sovereign nations.[12] At another level, governments, national telecommu-

9. INTELSAT Agreement, art. IV; INMARSAT Convention, art. XXV; and EUTELSAT Convention, art. IV.
10. INTELSAT Agreement, art. V; INMARSAT Convention, art. VI; and EUTELSAT Convention, art. V.
11. INTELSAT Agreement, art. III(a); INMARSAT Convention, art. V(3); and EUTELSAT Convention, art. V(b).
12. States in their sovereign capacities participate in the INTELSAT Assembly of Parties, the INMARSAT Assembly and the EUTELSAT Assembly of Parties. These organs concern themselves with long-term policy and other matters affecting States as sovereign nations. *See* Chapters 5.1.1.-3. (describing the functions of these organs).

nications administrations, or other designated entities, contribute capital to the satellite financing and receive a return on their investments [13] based on the organization's revenues from commercial operations. They also participate in the operational and business aspects of the organizations' activities.[14]

CONSTITUTING AGREEMENT AND OPERATING AGREEMENT. With respect to all three organizations, two separate agreements provide for their foundations, structures, functioning and operations, and establish their two-tier systems of participation. States, in their sovereign capacities, are Parties to the INTELSAT Agreement and the INMARSAT and EUTELSAT Conventions. Governments, Telecommunications administrations, or designated entities, are "Signatories"[15] to the operating agreements for these organizations, that is, the INTELSAT Operating Agreement,[16] the INMARSAT Operating Agreement[17] and the EUTELSAT Operating Agreement.[18]

WEIGHTED VOTING. Another important feature of the three international satellite organizations, which is not uncommon to organizations administering large sums of money contributed by member States, is that

---

13. INTELSAT Agreement, art. V(c); INMARSAT Convention, art. V(2); and EUTELSAT Convention, art. V(d).
14. Governments, telecommunications administrations, or other designated entities (such as the Communications Satellite Corporation of Washington, D.C.), as the case may be, are represented at the INTELSAT Board of Governors and Meeting of Signatories, the INMARSAT Council and the EUTELSAT Board of Signatories. These organs concern themselves with management, financial and operational aspects of the organizations. *See* Chapter 5.1.1.-5.1.3. (describing the functions of these organs).
15. In most cases a national telecommunications administration (PTT), or the operating arm of that administration, is a Signatory. For example, Signatories to INMARSAT include Deutsche Bundespost, PTT Netherland, Swedish Telecommunication Administration and Kokusai Denshin Denwa Company, Ltd., which, until recently, held a monopoly on international telecommunications in Japan. Sometimes the Party to the INTELSAT Agreement or INMARSAT and EUTELSAT conventions also is the Signatory to the organization. Furthermore, the same entity usually serves as the Signatory to INTELSAT, INMARSAT and EUTELSAT. A few countries have designated a private entity to serve as Signatory. For example, the United States created the Communications Satellite Corporation (Comsat), a non governmental entity, in 1962 to be the U.S. participant in the subsequently-formed INTELSAT. Legislation was passed in 1978 allowing Comsat also to assume a Signatory role in INMARSAT. *See* Chapter 3.1.4. (describing the legal framework applicable to Comsat). Comsat's stock is traded publicly.
16. Operating Agreement Relating to the International Telecommunication Satellite Organization [hereinafter cited as INTELSAT Operating Agreement], *done* Aug. 20, 1971, *entered into force* Feb. 12, 1973, T.I.A.S. 7532. *See* INTELSAT Agreement, art. II(b) (providing that States Parties shall sign, or designate a telecommunications entity to sign, the INTELSAT Operating Agreement).

voting is weighted in the management organ, based upon the relative investment shares of the Signatories.[19] This means that the relative influence of States over the organizations' policies and management decisions is determined not only on the basis of sovereign equality among States, but also on the capital investments of their Signatories in the satellites of INTELSAT, INMARSAT and EUTELSAT. Interestingly, States and their Signatories on occasion support divergent positions within a satellite organization. Among other international organizations with weighted voting are the World Bank and the International Monetary Fund.

ONLY THE SPACE SEGMENT. INTELSAT, INMARSAT and EUTELSAT concern themselves only with the space segment of the satellite systems they operate. Signatories (or other persons that are authorized under the domestic laws of the Signatory country), and not the international organizations, own and operate the Earth stations and associated ground networks necessary to communicate via the INTELSAT, INMARSAT and EUTELSAT satellites (see Chapter 3.1.4.). In other words, Signatories and other authorized persons use their own Earth Stations to provide international telecommunications services within their respective countries via the INTELSAT, INMARSAT, or EUTELSAT space segments. Signatories pay utilization charges to the organizations for use of the satellite capacity.[20] Signatories often mark up the prices charged by the international organizations, and sometimes make substantial profits, when offering international telecommunications services to end-users and other telecommunications carriers.

FINANCIAL PRINCIPLES. In the case of all three satellite organizations, the organization, itself, owns or leases the space segment,[21] and the Signatories hold investment shares in the organizations.[22] The investment share of each Signatory in each organization is based on the utilization of

---

17. Operating Agreement on the International Maritime Satellite Organization [hereinafter cited as INMARSAT Operating Agreement], *done* Sept. 3, 1976, *entered into force* July 16, 1979, T.I.A.S. 9605. *See* INMARSAT Convention, art. II(2), (3) (providing that each Party shall sign, or designate a public or private entity within its jurisdiction to sign, the INMARSAT Operating Agreement).
18. Operating Agreement Relating to the Establishment of the European Telecommunications Satellite Organization [hereinafter cited as EUTELSAT Agreement], *done* July 15, 1982, *entered into force* Sept. 1, 1985. B.G.B.1. 1984 II, at 683. *See* EUTELSAT Convention, art. II(b) (providing that each Party shall sign, or designate a public or private telecommunications entity subject to its jurisdiction to sign, the Eutelsat Operating Agreement).
19. INTELSAT Agreement, art. IX(f); INMARSAT Convention, art. XIV(3); and EUTELSAT Convention, art. XI(a). *See also* Chapter 5.1.1.-3. (describing the voting rights at the INTELSAT Board of Governors, the INMARSAT Council and the EUTELSAT Board of Signatories).
20. INTELSAT Agreement, art. V(d), and INTELSAT Operating Agreement, art. 4(c); INMARSAT Operating Agreement, art. 7; EUTELSAT Convention, art. V(e), and EUTELSAT Operating Agreement, art. 8.

the satellites of that organization.[23] Each Signatory contributes to the capital requirements of each organization in proportion to its investment share, and receives capital repayment and compensation for use of the capital,[24] also in proportion to its investment share.[25] The capital requirements of each organization relate to costs in connection with the design, procurement and establishment of the space segments of that organization, as well as operating and administrative costs.[26] Utilization charges paid by Signatories for their use of the space segment[27] contribute to the revenues of the organizations, and the respective Operating Agreements of INTELSAT, INMARSAT and EUTELSAT provide that revenues shall be applied in the following order of priority: 1) meet operating, maintenance and administrative costs of the organization; 2) provide operating funds as their respective management organs may deem necessary; 3) pay the Signatories repayment of capital; 4) to pay a Signatory that has withdrawn from the organization; and 5) pay the Signatories the available balance toward compensation for use of capital.[28] If a Signatory's use of an organization's satellite system is, in effect, identical to its investment share

---

21. INTELSAT Agreement, art. V(a); INMARSAT Convention, art. VI; and EUTELSAT Convention, art. V(a). *See* notes 32, 77 and 118 and accompanying text (describing the space segments of INTELSAT, INMARSAT and EUTELSAT).
22. INTELSAT Agreement, art. V(b), and INTELSAT Operating Agreement, art. 6; INMARSAT Convention, art. V(1), and INMARSAT Operating Agreement, art. 5; EUTELSAT Convention, art. V(c), and EUTELSAT Operating Agreement, art. 6. *See* R.R. Colino, THE INTELSAT DEFINITIVE ARRANGEMENTS: USHERING IN A NEW ERA IN SATELLITE COMMUNICATIONS (1973) [hereinafter cited as Colino, INTELSAT DEFINITIVE], at 27-31 (concerning investment shares in INTELSAT).
23. *Id.* For example, the investment shares of the largest investors in INTELSAT are approximately 24% for the United States, 12% for the United Kingdom, 5% for Japan, 4.4% for France and 3.5% for Germany. The approximate investment shares in INMARSAT in 1990 were 25% for the United States, 13.7% for the United Kingdom, 12% for Norway, 9% for Japan, 5% for France, 4% for the USSR, 2.5% each for The Netherlands and Greece.
24. INTELSAT Agreement, art. III(c), and INTELSAT Operating Agreement, art. 4(a); INMARSAT Convention, art. V(1), and INMARSAT Operating Agreement, art. 3(a); and EUTELSAT Convention, art. V(d), and EUTELSAT Operating Agreement, art. 4(a).
25. INTELSAT Operating Agreement, art. 8(e)(iii), (v), INMARSAT Operating Agreement, art. 8(c), (e), and EUTELSAT Operating Agreement, art. 9(a)(iii), (v).
26. INTELSAT Operating Agreement, art. 4(b), INMARSAT Operating Agreement, art. 3(2), and EUTELSAT Operating Agreement, art. 4(b).
27. INTELSAT Agreement, art. V(d), and INTELSAT Operating Agreement, art. 4(c); INMARSAT Operating Agreement, art. 7; and EUTELSAT Convention, art. V(e); and EUTELSAT Operating Agreement, art. 8.
28. INTELSAT Operating Agreement, art. 8(e); INMARSAT Operating Agreement, art. 8(1); and EUTELSAT Operating Agreement, art. 9(a).

then the only compensation that Signatory might receive would be a component of the charge to non-member States.

The proportional relationship between utilization of the space segment, investment share, capital contribution and capital repayment and compensation that exists with respect to each of the three satellite organizations is illustrated in Figure 3.

Figure 3.

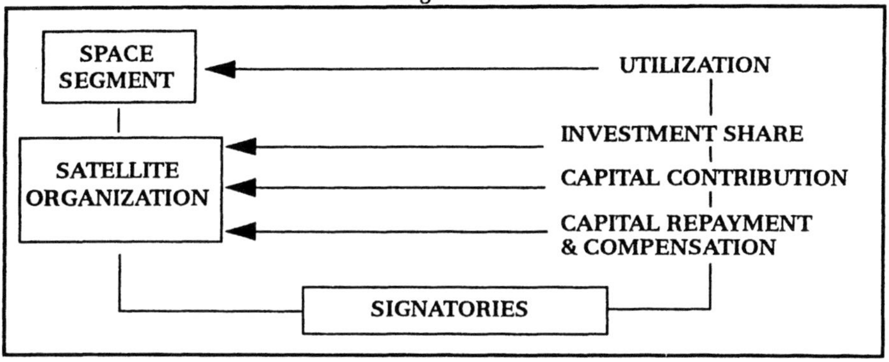

As evidenced by the fact that they pay Signatories the available balance after their revenues have been applied to cover expenses, INTELSAT, INMARSAT and EUTELSAT, while they are organizations involved in commercial activities, they operate on a non-profit basis. The profits associated with international satellite operations refer exclusively to the Signatories's income. In fact, Signatories often make substantial profits. However, it is not the capital compensation from INTELSAT, INMARSAT or EUTELSAT that is the major source of the Signatories' revenues. It is their earnings on international (and occasionally domestic[29]) telecommunication services they provide via the INTELSAT, INMARSAT and EUTELSAT satellites to end-users and carriers in their own countries. Most Signatories, representing national telecommunication administrations (referred to as PTTs), hold a monopoly on the provision of telecommunications services in their respective countries and face no price competition. Consequently, signatories tend to mark up substantially the charges of INTELSAT, INMARSAT and EUTELSAT. In many countries, this practice may not be sustainable much longer. PTTs in all regions of the world are

29. While the basic thrusts of INTELSAT, INMARSAT and EUTELSAT are the provision of international satellite services (INTELSAT Agreement, art. III (a), EUTELSAT Convention, art. III(a), and INMARSAT by the very nature of its service), their respective space segments also may be used for domestic services on an as-available basis, INTELSAT Agreement, art. III(b), (c), and EUTELSAT Convention, art. III(b), (c). The INMARSAT Convention's purpose clause, found in Article 3, does not limit this organization to international services. *See infra* note 37 (describing the use of the INTELSAT space segment for domestic purposes).

facing mounting pressure to relinquish their monopolies. Increasingly, deregulation and privatization of telecommunications equipment and services are occurring. Competition resulting from such developments is bound influence the pricing policies of the Signatories.

5.1.1. INTELSAT

CREATION AND CURRENT OPERATIONS. INTELSAT was established as an interim organization in 1964,[30] and in its current form in 1973.[31] With a membership of 121 States, the Organization now owns and operates a total of fifteen telecommunications satellites at geostationary locations above the Atlantic, Pacific and Indian Oceans. These locations are essential for INTELSAT to provide international, including intercontinental, communications services.[32]

PURPOSE AND SERVICES. INTELSAT's main purpose is to provide for "the design, development, construction, establishment, operation and maintenance of the space segment of the [INTELSAT] global commercial telecommunications satellite system . . . ."[33] Its prime objective is "the provision, on a commercial basis, of the space segment required for interna-

---

30. Agreement Establishing Interim Arrangements for a Global Commercial Communication Satellite System and Special Agreement, *done* Aug. 20, 1964, *entered into force* on the same date. T.I.A.S. 5646.
31. INTELSAT Agreement, *supra* note 1, and INTELSAT Operating Agreement, *supra* note 16. *See* Colino, INTELSAT DEFINITIVE, *supra* note 22 (providing background and explanation on the INTELSAT Agreement and Operating Agreement). *See also* N.M. Matte, AEROSPACE LAW (1977), at 109-117 (offering a description of INTELSAT and comparing it with INTERSPUTNIK, the satellite system used by the former Soviet Union and East Block States).
32. On June 14, 1991, INTELSAT's satellites were located as follows:

Satellite	*Location (degrees East)*	*Region*
INTELSAT V-A (F-13)	307.00	AOR*
INTELSAT V (F-4)	325.50	AOR
INTELSAT VI (F-4)	332.50	AOR
INTELSAT VI (F-2)	335.50	AOR
INTELSAT V (F-6)	341.50	AOR
INTELSAT V-A (F-12)	359.00	AOR
INTELSAT V (F-2)	338.50	AOR
INTELSAT V (F-7)	57.00	IOR**
INTELSAT V-A (F-15)	60.00	IOR
INTELSAT V-A (F-12)	63.00	IOR
INTELSAT V (F-5)	66.00	IOR
INTELSAT V-A (F-10)	174.00	POR***
INTELSAT V (F-3)	177.00	POR
INTELSAT V (F-8)	180.00	POR
INTELSAT V (F-1)	183.00	POR

* AOR means Atlantic Ocean Region.
** IOR means Indian Ocean Region.
*** POR means Pacific Ocean Region.

33. INTELSAT Agreement, art. II(a)

tional public telecommunications services of a high quality and reliability to be available on a non-discriminatory basis to all areas of the world."[34] The satellite services currently provided via the INTELSAT satellites include 1) public-switched telephony, telex, facsimile and data transmission, 2) international television transmission,[35] 3) international private network services,[36] and 4) domestic transponder leases.[37] Of these categories, public-switched services account for about 70% of the traffic via the INTELSAT system.[38]

STRUCTURE OF INTELSAT. INTELSAT has four organs: the Assembly of Parties, the Meeting of Signatories, the Board of Governors and an executive organ responsible to the Board of Governors. The executive organ is headed by a Director General.

THE ASSEMBLY OF PARTIES. The Assembly of Parties is the principal organ of INTELSAT.[39] It is composed of all Parties to the INTELSAT Agreement,[40] and each Party has one vote.[41] The Assembly concerns itself with matters affecting States as sovereign nations.[42] It considers general policy and the long-term objectives of INTELSAT;[43] decides on proposals to amend the INTELSAT Agreement;[44] ensures compliance of INTELSAT's activities with other international agreements;[45] decides on questions concerning the relationship of INTELSAT to States and other international organizations;[46] decides on matters of withdrawal of Parties from INTELSAT;[47] authorizes the use of the INTELSAT space segment for specialized services, such as radiodetermination and broadcasting services, and issues recommendations with regard to the establishment or use by member States of satellites separate from the INTELSAT space seg-

---

34. INTELSAT Agreement, art. III(a). *See* INTELSAT Agreement, art. I(k), and Chapter 5.2.1. (providing definition of "public telecommunications services").
35. INTELSAT's international television transmission must be distinguished from broadcasting, *i.e.*, program distribution for direct reception by the general public, and usually refers to the transmission of video signals between "national gateway" Earth stations operated by Signatories or other licensed facilities operators. These video transmissions then are reformatted and retransmitted by national broadcasting authorities or licensed broadcast stations or cable operators. In the United States and a few other countries, licensed private entities are permitted to receive and transmit video signals via INTELSAT. *See* Chapter 3.1.4. (describing U.S. policy on INTELSAT Earth station ownership).
36. These services refer to international inter- and intra-corporate communications networks. For example, INTELSAT's International Business Service (IBS) features private network two-way data, voice and video communications to and from relatively small Earth stations, which can be located at the customers' premises, or at regional teleports. IBS was introduced in 1983, and currently over 225 Earth stations are employed in this service, and fifty-two countries participate. 3 VIA INTELSAT 1, Feb. 1991. INTELSAT's INTELNET service offers private point-to-multipoint data distribution networks, in which one central "hub" station is used to transmit data via the INTELSAT space segment to tiny receiving-stations, as small as 0.8. meters in diameter.

ment;[48] and exercises any other powers within the purview of the Assembly of Parties pursuant to the INTELSAT A sgreement. Ordinarily, the Assembly of Parties meets once every two years, although extraordinary meetings may be scheduled.[49] For example, on October 30-November 2, 1990, the Assembly held its sixteenth Assembly of Parties meeting at Lisbon, Portugal. Important decisions were taken at this meeting regarding the establishment by member States of separate international satellite systems (see Chapter 5.2.1.).

THE MEETING OF SIGNATORIES. The Meeting of Signatories is composed of all the Signatories,[50] serves the Board of Governors in an advisory capacity, and also has certain decision-making powers primarily in financial and operational matters. Among its specifically enumerated

---

37. These services refer to leases and purchases by member States of INTELSAT transponders for domestic uses. INTELSAT's domestic service offerings began in 1972, and a large number of countries lease or have purchased transponders from INTELSAT to augment their national telecommunications networks for purposes of telephone or television transmissions. Transponder leases are available on a preemptible and a non-preemptible basis, the latter with a higher priority of service. *See* S.L. Gordon, *Meeting Requirements at Home: INTELSAT's Domestic Service Offerings*, 43 J. OF THE BRITISH INTERPLANETARY SOCIETY 341 (1990) (explaining domestic uses of the INTELSAT space segment). Preemptible leases are available at 9 MHz units at C-band in global hemispheric and zone beam transponders and at Ku-band from spot beam transponders. *Id.* These leases are offered for as little as three months and for as long as five years. *Id.* Non-preemptible leases are offered in 18 MHz units for periods of one, five, ten, or fifteen years. *Id.* A diverse group of countries are leasing transponders from INTELSAT, including Algeria, Chile, People's Republic of China, Columbia, Ivory Coast, Denmark, France, India, Libya, Malaysia, Mozambique, New Zealand, Nigeria, Pakistan, Peru, South Africa, Spain, the Sudan, Thailand, the United Kingdom, Venezuela and Zaire. *Id.* The following countries have purchased transponders from INTELSAT under INTELSAT's Planned Domestic Service offering: Argentina, Bolivia, Central African Republic, Chad, Chile, the People's Republic of China, Ethiopia, Gabon, Germany, Iran, Israel, Italy, Japan, Niger, Norway, Portugal, Sweden, Turkey, the United States and Venezuela. *Id.*
38. INTELSAT Annual Report (1989-1990), at 10.
39. INTELSAT Agreement, art. VII(a).
40. *Id.*
41. INTELSAT Agreement, art. VII(f). Matters of substance are decided by a two-thirds majority, and procedural matters by simple majority, of the Parties present and voting. *Id.*
42. *Id.*, art. VII(b).
43. *Id.*
44. *Id.*, art. VII(c)(iii).
45. *Id.*, art. VII(c)(ii).
46. *Id.*, art. VII(c)(ix).
47. *Id.*, art. VII(c)(viii).

functions, the Meeting of Signatories considers and expresses its views to the Board of Governors on the INTELSAT annual report and annual financial statements submitted to it by the Board of Governors;[51] considers and expresses its views regarding reports by the Board of Governors on future INTELSAT programs;[52] decides on recommendations by the Board of Governors concerning an increase in the ceiling with respect to capital contributions to be made to INTELSAT by its Signatories;[53] establishes, upon the recommendation of the Board of Governors, general rules concerning access to the INTELSAT space segment, allotment of INTELSAT space segment capacity and INTELSAT space segment utilization charges;[54] and exercises any other functions coming within its purview pursuant to the INTELSAT Agreement.[55] Ordinarily, the Meeting of Signatories convenes once every year, but extraordinary meetings may be called.[56]

THE BOARD OF GOVERNORS. The Board of Governors consists of representatives of a limited number of Signatories, currently twenty-eight. Governors are elected according to a formula based on investment shares and geographical distribution, as set forth in Article IX of the INTELSAT Agreement.[57] Each Governor's voting participation is "equal to that part of the investment share of the Signatory, or group of Signatories, he represents . . . ."[58] In other words, weighted voting applies to the decisions taken by the Board of Governors. For example, the United States has an investment share of 23.89% and Japan has an investment share of 4.9%. These countries have commensurate voting powers.

The Board of Governors is the management organ of INTELSAT. It is responsible for the design, development, construction, operation and maintenance of the INTELSAT space segment and for implementing

---

48. *Id.*, art. VII(c)(iv), (vii).
49. *Id.*, art. VII(d), (e).
50. *Id.*, art. VIII(a).
51. *Id.*, art. VIII(b)(i).
52. *Id.*, art. VIII(b)(iii).
53. *Id.*, art. VIII(b)(iv).
54. *Id.*, art. VIII(b)(v).
55. *Id.*, art. VIII(b)(xii). Other enumerated powers of the Meeting of Signatories are to express views on proposed amendments to the INTELSAT Agreement and to make decisions concerning amendments to the INTELSAT Operating Agreement, *id.*, art. VIII(b)(ii); make decisions in connection with the withdrawal of a Signatory, *id.*, art. VIII(b)(vi); consider and express its views on complaints submitted to it by a Signatory, *id.*, art. VIII(b)(vii); prepare and present to the Assembly of Parties, and to the individual Parties, reports concerning the implementation of general policies and long-term programs of INTELSAT. *id.*, art. VIII(b)(viii); and approve the use of the INTELSAT space segment between domestic locations separated by natural barriers of such an "exceptional nature" that they impede the establishment of viable wideband terrestrial communications facilities, *id.*, art. VIII(b)(ix).
56. *Id.*, art. VIII(c), (d).

related decisions of the Assembly of Parties.[59] To discharge these responsibilities, the Board has been empowered to adopt necessary policies, plans and programs,[60] as well as procurement procedures, regulations, terms and conditions.[61] Among other functions, the Board also adopts financial policies and statements and approves budgets.[62] It establishes terms and conditions for allotment of space segment capacity[63] and for access to the INTELSAT space segment by telecommunications entities not under the jurisdiction of any party.[64] It also establishes utilization charges for the INTELSAT space segment;[65] adopts criteria and procedures for standard Earth station access to INTELSAT;[66] and approves non-standard Earth stations for access to INTELSAT.[67] Moreover, it appoints and removes the Director General;[68] decides on matters of employment with respect to the executive organ;[69] and expresses its findings with respect to the use by INTELSAT member States of satellite facilities separate from INTELSAT.[70]

THE EXECUTIVE ORGAN. The executive organ is in charge of administrative and operational matters, and is located in the United States in Washington, D.C. It maintains a spacecraft control center, an operations control center, and controls satellite tracking, telemetry and command functions. The Executive Organ also is responsible for the interfaces with the launch providers and satellite manufacturers, and in that connection places personnel in the facilities of the manufacturer during satellite construction. Its chief executive officer and legal representative, the Director General,[71] is appointed[72] by, and is responsible[73] to, the Board of Gover-

---

57. *Id.*, art. IX(a). The Board of Governors shall be composed as follows: 1) one Governor representing each Signatory whose investment share is not less than the minimum investment share of not less than 1.87%; 2) one Governor representing any group of two or more Signatories, not represented in the first group, whose combined investment share is not less than 1.87% and 3) one Governor representing any group of at least five Signatories, not represented in the in the first two groups, from any one of the three regions of the world defined by the International Telecommunication Union (ITU). *Id.*, art. IX(a)(iii). *See* Chapter 4.1. (defining the ITU Regions). However, the number of Governors under this category must not exceed two from each region. *Id.*
58. INTELSAT Agreement, art. IX(f).
59. *Id.*, art. X(a).
60. *Id.*, art. X(a)(i).
61. *Id.*, art. X(a)(ii).
62. *Id.*, art. X(a)(iii).
63. *Id.*, art. X(a)(vii).
64. *Id.*, art. X(a)(xii).
65. *Id.*, art. X(a)(viii).
66. *Id.*, art. X(a)(vi).
67. *Id.*, art. X(a)(xi).
68. *Id.*, art. X(a)(xviii).
69. *Id.*, art. X(a)(xx).
70. *Id.*, art. X(a)(xxv).

nors. The appointment is subject to confirmation by the Assembly of Parties.[74] The Director General performs all duties in accordance with the policies and directives of the Board of Governors.[75]

5.1.2. INMARSAT

CREATION AND CURRENT OPERATIONS. INMARSAT was established in 1979[76] to provide maritime mobile communications and radiodetermination services. With a membership of sixty-four States, INMARSAT now owns and operates two and leases eight additional satellites.[77] More than 16,000 ships, off-shore facilities and aircraft currently are equipped with terminals for the use of the INMARSAT satellite system.

PURPOSE. INMARSAT's purpose is "to make provision for the space segment necessary for improving maritime communications and, as practicable, aeronautical communications, thereby assisting in improving communications for distress and safety of life, communications for air

---

71. *Id.*, art. XI(b)(i).
72. *Id.*, art. XI(b)(iii).
73. *Id.*, art. XI(b)(i).
74. *Id.*, art. XI(b)(iii).
75.
76. INMARSAT Convention, *supra* note 2, and INMARSAT Operating Agreement, *supra* note 17.
77. On July 14, 1991, INMARSAT had launched two of its own satellites (designated "INMARSAT-2" for second generation INMARSAT satellites) and was leasing capacity on eight other satellites, including the European Space Agency's Marecs satellites, Comsat's Marisat satellites and maritime communications subsystems on INTELSAT satellites ("INTELSAT-MCS").

Satellite	*Location (degrees)*	*Region*
Marecs-B2	55.5 W	AOR (W)
Marisat (F-1)*	106.5 W	AOR (W)
INMARSAT-2 (F-2)	15.5 E	AOR (E)
INTELSAT-MCS-B**	18.5 E	AOR (E)
INTELSAT-MCS-A**	63 E	AOR (E)
INMARSAT-2 (F-1)	64.5 E	IOR
Marisat (F-2)*	72.5 E	IOR
INTELSAT-MCS-D	180 E	POR
Marecs-A***	178 E	POR
Marisat (F-3)*	176.5 E	POR

*These satellites are residual-life spares, but their capacity is being leased by American Mobile Satellite Corporation of Washington, D.C., through Comsat, for mobile satellite services in the United States.

** These satellites are residual-life spares.

*** This satellite was retired due to failure in 1991. AOR (W) means Atlantic Ocean Region West. AOR (E) means Atlantic Ocean Region East. IOR means Indian Ocean Region. POR means Pacific Ocean Region.

INMARSAT's satellite system was originally based on three coverage regions. Due to inadequate global coverage, a fourth region, *i.e.*, AOR (W), was added by decision of the INMARSAT Council in 1989.

traffic services, the efficiency and management of ships and aircraft, maritime and aeronautical public correspondence services and radiodetermination capabilities."[78] References to "aeronautical communications" and "air traffic services" were only recently included in INMARSAT's purpose clause. Amendments of the INMARSAT Convention to this effect entered into force on October 13, 1989.[79] An amendment which would allow the Organization to provide land mobile satellite services, as well, was adopted at INMARSAT's Sixth Extraordinary Assembly meeting, January 17-15, 1989. It has not yet entered into force.[80]

SERVICES. INMARSAT provides a range of maritime communications services to ships and off-shore platforms. It also provides limited amounts of aeronautical and, occasionally, land mobile communication and radiodetermination services.[81] INMARSAT's current maritime services are tied to the INMARSAT-A and C Earth stations,[82] manufactured by companies around the world and type-approved and commissioned by INMARSAT.

---

78. INMARSAT Convention, art. III(1).

79. The amendment was adopted in October 1985. *See* W.D. von Noorden, *Space Communications to Aircraft: A New Development in International Space Law,* 15 J. SPACE L. 25 (1987) (discussing the provision of aeronautical mobile satellite services by INMARSAT).

80. The text of INMARSAT's purpose clause has been amended to read as follows:

> The Purpose of the Organization is to make provision for the space segment necessary for improving maritime communications and, as practicable, aeronautical and land mobile communications and communications on waters not part of the marine environment, thereby assisting in improving communications for distress and safety of life, communications for air traffic services, the efficiency and management of transportation by sea, air and on land, maritime, aeronautical and other mobile public correspondence services and radiodetermination capabilities.

The amendment is subject to ratification by Parties to the Convention and subsequent entry into force. *See* W.D. von Noorden & P. Dann, *Land Mobile Satellite Communications: A Further Development in International Space Law,* 17 J. SPACE L. 1 (1989) (discussing the provision of land mobile satellite services by INMARSAT).

81. The INMARSAT space segment is open to use by ships and aircraft of all nations (including non-member States) on conditions established by the Council. INMARSAT Convention, art. VII(a). "Ship" is defined in the INMARSAT Convention to mean "a vessel of any kind operating in the marine environment. It includes *inter alia* hydrofoil boats, air-cushion vehicles, submersibles, floating craft and platforms not permanently moored." *Id.*, art. I(f)

82. Two new INMARSAT terminals, under development and known as INMARSAT B and M, are scheduled for service in 1992-1993. INMARSAT Annual Report (1990), at 12. INMARSAT B is intended for the same types of services as those offered via INMARSAT A Earth stations today but will have an increased range of capabilities. *Id.* Quality and efficiency will also be improved. INMARSAT M will be a low-cost, portable terminal for telephony and low-speed data. *Id.*

INMARSAT-A terminals are used for two-way direct-dial telephone, telex, facsimile and data communications with links via the INMARSAT space segment to the world-wide, public-switched telecommunications network, as well as for instantaneous distress alerting.[83] As of July 1991, 14,772 ships have been equipped with INMARSAT-A terminals,[84] which are less than one meter in diameter. INMARSAT-C terminals are tiny suitcase-sized units used for two-way data message services. This service was inaugurated in 1991.[85] Also, in 1991 INMARSAT began offering aeronautical services on an operational basis. INMARSAT Signatories in several countries have formed consortia offering public correspondence and air traffic control services to their airlines.[86]

STRUCTURE OF INMARSAT. INMARSAT has three organs: the Assembly, the Council, and the Directorate headed by a Director General.[87] The functions of these organs resemble those of the INTELSAT Assembly of Parties, Board of Governors and Executive Organ, discussed in Chapter 5.1.1. The INTELSAT Meeting of Signatories has no counterpart in the INMARSAT organizational structure, although its functions appear to be shared among the other organs.

THE ASSEMBLY. The Assembly is composed of all Parties to the INMARSAT Convention,[88] and each Party has one vote.[89] The Assembly concerns itself primarily with matters affecting the member States in their sovereign capacities. It considers general policy and long-term objectives of the Organization;[90] ensures that INMARSAT's activities are consistent with the INMARSAT Convention, the United Nations Charter and other international agreements binding upon INMARSAT;[91] resolves issues concerning INMARSAT's relationships with States and other interna-

83. INMARSAT Annual Report (1990), at 10. The terminals have been in service since 1982. Transportable versions of the INMARSAT A terminals exist.
84. *Id.*
85. INMARSAT C terminals, to a limited extent, are used also for land mobile communications, for example, by journalists reporting from the Middle East during the 1991 Gulf War.
86. For example, Signatories in the United Kingdom, Norway and Singapore have formed the "Skyphone" service. Similar arrangements exist among the Canadian, French and Australian Signatories, as well as between the U.S. and Japanese Signatories. On September 18, 1990, INMARSAT authorized British Telecom's ground station at Goonhilly, U.K., as the world's first Earth station for commercial aeronautical mobile satellite service. INMARSAT Annual Report (1990), at 14. Such stations have since been authorized for Perth, Australia, Sentosa, Singapore, Eik, Norway, Southbury and Santa Paula, United States, and Yamaguchi, Japan, among other locations. *Id.* As of July, 9, 1991, 28 aircraft were equipped for voice and data communications.
87. INMARSAT Convention, art. IX.
88. *Id.*, art. X(1).
89. *Id.*, art. XI(1).
90. *Id.*, art. XII)1)(a).
91. *Id.*, art. XII(1)(b).

tional organizations;[92] decides on proposals to amend the INMARSAT Convention[93] and termination of membership in the Organization;[94] elects four representatives to the Council with the mandate of ensuring equitable geographical representation;[95] authorizes, on the Council's recommendation, the establishment of additional space segment facilities for radiodetermination, distress, or safety communications;[96] and exercises any other functions conferred upon it by the INMARSAT Convention or INMARSAT Operating Agreement,[97] including expressing its views in the form of a recommendation with respect to technical compatibility and potential economic harm from satellites separate from the INMARSAT system planned by member States.[98] Ordinarily, the Assembly meets once every two years, although extraordinary meetings may be convened.[99]

THE COUNCIL. The Council invites limited participation. Only representatives of twenty-two of INMARSAT's sixty-three Signatories serve on the Council.[100] Representation on the Council is based on investment share and geographical distribution.[101] The Council must attempt to make unanimous decisions, but if it fails to do so, a majority rule applies.[102] Voting is weighted, each representative commanding a voting power equal to the investment share(s) of the Signatory(ies) it represents.[103]

The Council is the management organ of INMARSAT. Its overall duty is to "make provision for the space segment necessary to carry out the purposes of the Organization in the most economic, effective and efficient manner . . . ."[104] To discharge this duty, the Council has been empowered to determine the Organization's requirements for satellite capacity and to adopt the necessary policies, plans and programs to provide for the design, procurement or lease, establishment, operation and maintenance of the INMARSAT space segment,[105] including procurement policies and

---

92. *Id.*, art. XII(1)(f).
93. *Id.*, art. XII(1)(g).
94. *Id.*, art. XII(1)(h).
95. *Id.*, art. XII(1)(e).
96. *Id.*, art. XII(1)(c).
97. *Id.*, art. XII(1)(i).
98. *Id.*, art. VIII(3).
99. *Id.*, art. X(2). For example, an Extraordinary Meeting may be convened in connection with the coordination of satellite systems separate from the INMARSAT space segment to be operated by member States. *Id.*, art. VIII(3).
100. *Id.*, art. XIII(1).
101. Article XIII of the INMARSAT Convention provides a formula for selecting representatives to the Council. Eighteen representatives are appointed, based on the investment shares of Signatories or groups of Signatories they represent. Four representatives of Signatories not otherwise represented are elected by the Assembly, based on equitable geographical representation. *Id.*
102. INMARSAT Convention, art. XIV(2).
103. *Id.*, art. XIV3).
104. *Id.*, art. XV.
105. *Id.*, art. XV(a).

contract terms;[106] adopt criteria and procedures for approval of Earth stations on board ships, aircraft and other structures in the marine environment;[107] adopt financial policies, approve financial regulations and annual budgets, establish charges for use of the INMARSAT space segment and determine investment shares of Signatories;[108] determine arrangements for consultations with bodies recognized by the Council as representing ship owners and aircraft operators concerning their use of the INMARSAT space segment;[109] and exercise any other duties conferred upon it by the INMARSAT Convention or INMARSAT Operating Agreement,[110] including the appointment of the Director General.[111]

THE DIRECTORATE. The Directorate is the executive organ of INMARSAT, that is, the chief administrative organ. It also is in charge of certain operational matters. The operational responsibilities of the Directorate are the same as those listed in Chapter 5.1.1. for the INTELSAT Executive Organ. The Directorate is headquartered in London, England, and is headed by a Director General who is elected by the Council from among candidates proposed by INMARSAT member States.[112] Elected for a six year term,[113] the Director General is the chief executive and legal representative of INMARSAT.[114] The administrative structure of the Directorate and terms of employment of officials and employees are subject to approval by the Council.[115]

5.1.3. EUTELSAT

CREATION AND CURRENT OPERATIONS. EUTELSAT was established in 1977 as an interim organization,[116] and in 1982 as a permanent entity in its present form[117] to provide international satellite telecommunications services within Europe. With a membership of twenty-nine countries, the Organization now operates seven satellites whose locations maximize coverage of the European continent.[118]

PURPOSE AND SERVICES. EUTELSAT's main purpose is to provide for the "design, development, construction, establishment, operation and maintenance of the space segment of the European telecommunication

---

106. *Id.*, art. XV(f).
107. *Id.*, art. XV(c).
108. *Id.*, art. XV(g).
109. *Id.*, art. XV(h).
110. *Id.*, art. XV(j).
111. *Id.*, art. XVI(1).
112. *Id.*, art. XVI(1).
113. *Id.*, art. XVI(2).
114. *Id.*, art. XVI(3).
115. *Id.*, art. XVI(4).
116. Agreement on the Constitution of a Provisional European Telecommunication Satellite Organization (EUTELSAT).,
117. EUTELSAT Convention, *supra* note 3, and EUTELSAT Operating Agreement, *supra* note 18.

satellite system or systems."[119] Its prime objective is to provide international public telecommunications services in Europe.[120] When plans were made for the EUTELSAT satellite system in the late 1970s, the intention was to use it for international telephony and other public-switched services in Europe. With the launch of the first EUTELSAT satellite in 1983, however, it became clear that international television program distribution, rather than telephony, would represent EUTELSAT's principal service component. EUTELSAT leases satellite transponders to its Signatories who use them for international and domestic television program distribution.[121] The Organization also offers private line business services under the label "Satellite Multiservice System."[122] Only a small portion of EUTELSAT's capacity is used for telephony.[123]

STRUCTURE OF EUTELSAT. EUTELSAT has three organs, that is, the Assembly of Parties, the Board of Signatories, and the executive organ headed by a Director General.[124] The functions of these organs resemble those of the INTELSAT Assembly of Parties and the INMARSAT Assembly; the INTELSAT Board of Governors and the INMARSAT Council; and the INTELSAT executive organ and the INMARSAT Directorate, discussed in Chapters 5.1.1. and 5.1.2. As with INMARSAT, EUTELSAT also does not have an organ equivalent to the INTELSAT Meeting of Signatories.

THE ASSEMBLY OF PARTIES. The Assembly of Parties consists of all Parties to the EUTELSAT Convention,[125] and each Party has one vote.[126] The EUTELSAT Assembly of Parties primarily is concerned with matters of interest to States in their sovereign capacities,[127] and among its duties are consideration of general policy and long-term objectives of EUTEL-

118. In December 1991 EUTELSAT's satellites were positioned at the following geostationary orbital locations:

Satellite	*Location (degrees East)*	
EUTELSAT I (F-1)	17.5	(drifting)
EUTELSAT I (F-2)	1	(drifting)
EUTELSAT I (F-3)	LAUNCH FAILURE	
EUTELSAT I (F-4)	7	
EUTELSAT I (F-5)	21.5	
EUTELSAT II (F-1)	13	
EUTELSAT II (F-2)	10	
EUTELSAT II (F-3)	16.5	

119. EUTELSAT Convention, art. III(a).
120. *Id.*
121. *Compare* note 37 (describing INTELSAT's domestic services).
122. *Compare* INTELSAT's IBS and INTELNET services.
123. *Compare* INTELSAT where 70% of the organization's capacity is used for public telephony.
124. EUTELSAT Convention, art. VI.
125. *Id.*, art. VII(a).
126. *Id.*, art. VIII(a). In substantive matters, decisions are taken by two-thirds of the Parties present and voting. *Id.*, art. VIII(b). In procedural matters, decisions are taken by simple majority. *Id.*, art. VIII(c).
127. *Id.*, art. IX(a).

SAT;[128] recommendation to the Board of Signatories on appropriate measures to ensure compatibility of EUTELSAT's activities with other multilateral agreements;[129] authorization, on the recommendation of the Board of Signatories, of the use of the EUTELSAT space segment for purposes other than EUTELSAT's prime objective and of the use by EUTELSAT of satellites separate from the EUTELSAT space segment;[130] deciding on EUTELSAT's relationships with States and other international organizations;[131] deciding on proposals to amend the EUTELSAT Convention;[132] deciding on matters concerning the withdrawal of a Party from, or accession to, EUTELSAT;[133] expressing its views on the use by member States, or their private entities, of satellites separate from the EUTELSAT space segment;[134] and exercising any other function necessary for the performance of EUTELSAT's purpose not expressly attributed to another organ.[135]

THE BOARD OF SIGNATORIES. The Board of Signatories is the management organ of EUTELSAT, and is composed of Board Members, each Member representing one Signatory.[136] Each Signatory has a voting participation equal to its investment share.[137] The Board of Signatories is responsible for "the design, development, construction, establishment, acquisition by purchase or lease, operation and maintenance of the EUTELSAT Space Segment and for any other activities which EUTELSAT is authorized to undertake."[138] To carry out these responsibilities, the Board is empowered to adopt the necessary policies, plans, programs and implementing procedures,[139] and to decide on procurement procedures, regulations and contract terms;[140] adopt financial policies and regulations, approve budgets and annual financial statements, and determine utilization charges for the EUTELSAT space segment;[141] establish terms and conditions for access to,[142] and allotment of,[143] EUTELSAT space segment capacity; adopt criteria and procedures for approval of Earth stations accessing the EUTELSAT space segment;[144] appoint and remove the

128. *Id.*, art. IX(a)(i).
129. *Id.*, art. IX(a)(ii).
130. *Id.*, art. IX(a)(iii).
131. *Id.*, art. IX(a)(vi).
132. *Id.*, art. IX(a)(ix).
133. *Id.*, art. IX(a)(viii), (x).
134. *Id.*, art. IX(a)(v).
135. *Id.*, art. IX(b).
136. *Id.*, art. X(a).
137. *Id.*, art. XI(a).
138. *Id.*, art. XI(a).
139. *Id.*, art. XII(b)(i).
140. *Id.*, art. XII(b)(ii).
141. *Id.*, art. XII(b)(v).
142. *Id.*, art. XII(b)(ix).
143. *Id.*, art. XII(b)(viii).
144. *Id.*, art. XII(b)(vi), (vii).

Director General;[145] settle accounts with those Signatories which are withdrawing from EUTELSAT;[146] decide on amendments to the EUTELSAT Operating Agreement;[147] and provide advice to the Assembly of Parties in certain cases where a member State is planning to establish or use satellite systems separate from the EUTELSAT space segment.[148]

THE EXECUTIVE ORGAN. The Executive Organ is the administrative arm of EUTELSAT and is based in Paris, France. It is also in charge of operational matters equal to those listed in Chapter 5.1.1. for the INTELSAT Executive Organ. Its principal officer is the Director General,[149] who is appointed by the Board of Signatories,[150] subject to the approval of the Assembly of Parties.[151] As the chief executive officer and legal representative of EUTELSAT,[152] the Director General acts under the direction of the Board of Signatories, and is directly responsible to it for the actions and performance of the executive organ.[153] The structure and staff levels of the executive organ, as well as the conditions of employment, are subject to approval by the Board of Signatories.[154]

5.2. Requirements for Coordination With INTELSAT, INMARSAT and EUTELSAT

THE COORDINATION REQUIREMENT IN GENERAL. As mentioned in the introduction to this Chapter, if the country authorizing your client's satellite system is a member of INTELSAT, INMARSAT or EUTELSAT, coordination with one or more of these organizations may be required, depending on the kinds of services your client intends to offer.[155] With

145. *Id.*, art. XII(b)(xvi).
146. *Id.*, art. XII(b)(xv).
147. *Id.*, art. XII(b)(xxiii).
148. *Id.*, art. XII(b)(xiii).
149. *Id.*, art. XIII(a).
150. *Id.*
151. *Id.*
152. *Id.*, art. XIII(d).
153. *Id.*
154. *Id.*, art. XIII(e).
155. Coordination is not required with respect to organizations of which the country authorizing your client's satellite operation is not a Member. For example, the Kingdom of Tonga, a tiny island in the South Pacific, which has authorized Friendly Islands Satellite Communications, Ltd. (Tongasat) to establish a regional communications satellite system in competition with INTELSAT, is not a Member of INTELSAT and, consequently, does not have to coordinate with the organization. *See* Chapter 4.1. (describing Tongasat and its plans, and why Tonga's conduct, nevertheless, caused INTELSAT to be concerned). Furthermore, coordination is not required if a satellite system is intended solely for national security purposes, INTELSAT Agreement, art. XIV(g), INMARSAT Convention, art. VIII(5), and EUTELSAT Convention, art. XVI(c)(ii)

regard to INTELSAT and EUTELSAT, technical coordination is always required, regardless of the type of telecommunications services your client is proposing to provide.[156] The technical coordination requirement is more limited with respect to INMARSAT.[157] Economic coordination is necessary in addition if your client plans to provide the kinds of services which represent the core businesses of any of these organizations.[158] Technical coordination is necessary to ensure that the organizations' planned or existing operations will not suffer harmful radio interference from your client's satellite system ("technical compatibility"[159]). Economic coordination is necessary to ensure that the organizations do not experience "significant economic harm,"[160] i.e., substantial business deprivation, as a result of your client's satellite operation. A third type of coordination is required with respect to INTELSAT to ensure that the use of your client's satellite system does not "prejudice the establishment of direct telecommunication links" through the INTELSAT space segment by all the participants.[161] This rather obscure test was included as a compromise offered by the Japanese delegation during the negotiations of the INTELSAT Agreement and remains a curiosity. Coordination requirements are set forth in Article XIV of the INTELSAT Agreement,[162] Article VIII of the INMARSAT Convention[163] and Article XVI of the EUTELSAT Convention.[164]

WHEN AND HOW TO COORDINATE. As a general rule, coordination should commence as soon as possible after your client has received national authorization to operate a satellite system, or before this time if the country acting on behalf of your client is confident that a satellite system with the same or similar technical parameters as those of your client's satellite system will be established.[165] The United States Federal Commu-

---

156. INTELSAT Agreement, art. XIV(c), (d), (e), and EUTELSAT Convention, art. XVI(b).
157. INMARSAT Convention, art. VIII(1).
158. INTELSAT Agreement, art. XIV(d), INMARSAT Convention, art. VIII(1), and EUTELSAT Convention, art. XVI(a).
159. The term "technical compatibility" is used in reference to technical coordination in the INTELSAT Agreement, art. XIV(c), (d), (e), INMARSAT Convention, art. VIII(a), and EUTELSAT Convention, art. XVI(b).
160. The term "significant economic harm" is used in reference to economic coordination in the INTELSAT Agreement, art. XIV(d), INMARSAT Convention, art. VIII(a), and EUTELSAT Convention, art. XVI(a).
161. INTELSAT Agreement, art. XIV(d). The founders of INTELSAT expressed the desire to achieve "a single global commercial telecommunications satellite system . . . ." INTELSAT Agreement, Preamble, para. 4.
162. *See supra* note 1 (providing title, date of entry into force and citation for the INTELSAT Agreement).
163. *See supra* note 2 (providing title, date of entry into force and citation for the INMARSAT Convention).
164. *See supra* note 3 (providing title, date of entry into force and citation for the EUTELSAT Convention).

nications Commission generally does not institute coordination formally until the particular satellite system has been authorized. As noted previously, your client cannot, itself, initiate the coordination, but must rely on the appropriate governmental authority to do so. However, your client may be asked to supply the necessary technical and, when required, economic information to conduct the coordination. For example, if your client is a United States satellite company authorized by the Federal Communications Commission, "it shall provide the Commission with all information it requires for . . . coordination . . . pursuant to . . . Article XIV of the INTELSAT Agreement."[166] The burden is on the proponent of the proposed new satellite system to show technical compatibility and absence of significant economic harm.[167]

The coordination requirement applies to each kind of service and each telecommunications link because technical compatibility and economic harm necessarily are assessed only with respect to specific services provided to and from specific locations. It is not necessary to coordinate initially all services or communications that potentially may be provided and links that potentially may be activated. Indeed, this may not even be possible or desirable. For example, at an INTELSAT Assembly of Parties Meeting at Lisbon, Portugal, on October 31, 1990, the use of the ASTRA 1B satellite, owned by Societe Europeenne des Satellite of Luxembourg, was coordinated for television and audio services from Luxembourg to Belgium and between Luxembourg and the United Kingdom and Norway.[168] Additional services and communications links for this satellite system may be coordinated later.

ECONOMIC COORDINATION. Economic coordination, or the issue of economic harm, has always been particularly contentious.[169] Since INTELSAT, INMARSAT and EUTELSAT are commercial organizations and their Signatories derive substantial profits from the telecommunica-

---

165. With regard to coordination under Article XIV(d) of the INTELSAT Agreement, the INTELSAT Assembly of Parties at its Sixteenth Meeting in Lisbon, Portugal, 30 Oct.- 2 Nov., 1990 [hereinafter cited as INTELSAT Assembly Meeting 1990] decided to urge all Parties to initiate the technical coordination process as "early as possible in the project development which has the advantage of allowing INTELSAT and the consulting Party or Signatory to consider possible design changes which could ameliorate interference between the two systems." INTELSAT Assembly of Parties Record of Decisions of the Sixteenth Meeting, Lisbon, Portugal (20 Oct.-2 Nov., 1990), INTELSAT Doc. No. AP-16-3E FINAL L/10/90 [hereinafter cited as INTELSAT Sixteenth Assembly Meeting Records], at 22.
166. 47 C.F.R. §25.202(c) (1990).
167. Colino, INTELSAT DEFINITIVE, *supra* note 22, at 94.
168. INTELSAT Sixteenth Assembly Meeting Records, *supra* note 165, at 9.
169. During the negotiations of the INTELSAT Agreement, a divergence of opinion arose with regard to whether *any* economic harm should be considered injurious, or whether some *measurable degree* of economic harm should be required. Colino, INTELSAT DEFINITIVE, *supra* note 22, at 92.

tions services they provide in connection with the satellite operations, the organizations, themselves, as well as the Signatories, have great incentives to prevent the establishment of separate satellite systems that might deprive them of business and revenue. For example, when it became known in 1984 that the United States Government, including the Federal Communications Commission, favored the authorization of private companies to establish satellite systems for international telecommunications services in competition with INTELSAT (see Chapter 3.1.4.), INTELSAT and its Signatories mounted an intensive lobbying campaign to prevent the authorization of the private systems, even before the formal INTELSAT coordination process had begun. While INTELSAT did not succeed in preventing altogether the authorization of separate U.S. private international satellite systems, it effectively influenced the imposition by the Federal Communications Commission of severe operational and service restrictions on these systems, which were designed to protect INTELSAT from economic harm (see Chapter 3.1.4.). Some of these restrictions are now in the process of being lifted.

Over the last few years, INTELSAT, INMARSAT and EUTELSAT have come to realize that the trend is irreversible towards the establishment of additional separate international satellite systems and cannot be halted by political and bureaucratic barriers, such as stringent economic coordination requirements and delaying tactics. Therefore, INTELSAT recently adopted a policy that streamlines and facilitates the economic coordination of separate systems (see Chapter 5.2.1.). It is entirely possible that the economic coordination soon will be no more than a formality with respect to some or all of the satellite organizations.

THE COORDINATION CULMINATES IN A NON-BINDING RECOMMENDATION. It is important to note that neither INTELSAT, INMARSAT nor EUTELSAT can legally block the establishment of your client's satellite system. The organizations express their findings with regard to technical compatibility and economic harm in the form of *recommendations*, which are not legally binding on the member States or their Signatories.[170] However, the establishment or use of your client's satellite system in the face of an unfavorable recommendation most likely would not be permitted by the country authorizing your client's satellite system. In practice,- however, that country will seek to avert a situation from ever occurring that might provoke an unfavorable recommendation. It will attempt to accommodate the organization in question, for example, by placing operational or service constraints on your client, to avoid such a recommendation. With respect to U.S. private separate satellite systems mentioned above, the United States took precisely such steps. See Chapter 3.1.4. The

170. INTELSAT Agreement, art. XIV(c), (d), (e); INMARSAT Convention, art. VIII(2), (3); EUTELSAT Convention, art. XIV(a), (b). Whether INTELSAT should be empowered to make binding determinations or merely advisory recommendations was an issue during the negotiations of the INTELSAT Agreement. Colino, INTELSAT DEFINITIVE, *supra* note 22, at 92-93.

political implications of defying a recommendation of INTELSAT, INMARSAT or EUTELSAT, albeit non-binding, are such that most countries would want to avoid them.

5.2.1. *INTELSAT*

THE COORDINATION REQUIREMENT. Article XIV of the INTELSAT Agreement spells out the coordination requirement with respect to INTELSAT:

> (c) To the extent that any Party or Signatory or person within the jurisdiction of a Party intends to establish, acquire or utilize space segment facilities separate from the INTELSAT space segment facilities to meet its *domestic public telecommunications services* requirements, such Party or Signatory, prior to the establishment, acquisition or utilization of such facilities, shall consult the Board of Governors, which shall express, in the form of recommendations, its findings regarding the technical compatibility of such facilities and their operation with the use of the radio frequency spectrum and orbital space by the existing or planned INTELSAT space segment.
>
> (d) To the extent that any Party or Signatory or person within the jurisdiction of a Party intends individually or jointly to establish, acquire or utilize space segment facilities separate from the INTELSAT space segment facilities to meet its *international public telecommunications services* requirements, such Party or Signatory, prior to the establishment, acquisition or utilization of such facilities, shall furnish all relevant information to and shall consult with the Assembly of Parties, through the Board of Governors, to ensure technical compatibility of such facilities and their operation with the use of the radio frequency spectrum and orbital space by the existing or planned INTELSAT space segment and to avoid significant economic harm to the global system of INTELSAT. Upon such consultation, the Assembly of Parties, taking into account the advice of the Board of Governors, shall express, in the form of recommendations, its findings regarding the considerations set out in this paragraph, and further regarding the assurance that the provision or utilization of such facilities shall not prejudice the establishment of direct telecommunication links through the INTELSAT space segment among all the participants.
>
> (e) To the extent that any Party or Signatory or person within the jurisdiction of a Party intends to establish, acquire or utilize space segment facilities separate from the INTELSAT space segment facilities to meet its *specialized telecommunications services* requirements, domestic or international, such Party or Signatory,

> prior to the establishment, acquisition or utilization of such facilities, shall furnish all relevant information to the Assembly of Parties, through the Board of Governors. The Assembly of Parties, taking into account the advice of the Board of Governors, shall express in the form of recommendations, its findings regarding the technical compatibility of such facilities and their use of the radio frequency spectrum and orbital space by the existing or planned INTELSAT space segment.[171]

Technical coordination with INTELSAT to avoid harmful interference with the organization's existing or planned operations is required for domestic public telecommunications services, international public telecommunications services and specialized telecommunications services, that is, essentially, any kind of telecommunications satellite service[172] your client might be planning to offer, provided the country authorizing the service is a Member of INTELSAT. However, coordination difficulties are posed only when your client plans operations in the frequency bands used or planned for INTELSAT operations.[173] *Economic* coordination is required only if your client is planning to provide international public telecommunications service. Providing such services is INTELSAT's prime objective[174] and these kinds of services consequently represent the core

---

171. Emphasis added. INTELSAT Agreement, art. XIV.
172. The International Telecommunication Union (ITU) defines telecommunication as "any transmission, emission or reception of signs, signals, writing, images and sounds or intelligence of any nature by wire, radio, optical or other electromagnetic systems." ITU *Final Acts,* World Administrative Radio Conference (1979) [hereinafter cited as ITU Radio Regulations], art.1, No. 3. The ITU also defines several classes of satellite services, of which only five have been commercialized: fixed satellite service (domestic and international), broadcasting satellite service, mobile satellite service, radiodetermination satellite service and Earth exploration satellite service (remote sensing). *See infra* notes 180-185 (providing ITU definitions of these services). *See also* Chapter 4.1. (concerning ITU classifications of telecommunications satellite systems and services).
173. In June 1991, the following frequency bands were used by the INTELSAT satellites (listed in *supra* note 32):

Satellite	*Up-link*	*Down-link*
INTELSAT VI	5.890- 6.402 GHz	3.665- 4.117 GHz
	14.042-14.418 GHz	10.992-11.618 GHz
INTELSAT VA	5.967- 6.402 GHz	3.742- 4.117 GHz
	14.042-14.377 GHz	10.992-11.577 GHz
INTELSAT V	5.967- 6.402 GHz	3.742- 4.117 GHz
	14.042-14.377 GHz	10.992-11.577 GHz

Source: INTELSAT Headquarters, External Relations Department.

See also Transmission Characteristics of the INTELSAT System for Use in the Article XIV Coordination Procedure, INTELSAT Doc. No. BG-45-83E (Rev.2), 8 July, 1985 [hereinafter cited as INTELSAT Transmission Characteristics] (providing detailed transmission characteristics of the INTELSAT system).

of the organization's business and revenue base. It was to protect this business that the economic coordination requirement was imposed on INTELSAT member States.

PUBLIC TELECOMMUNICATIONS SERVICES. The term "public telecommunications services" means

> fixed or mobile telecommunications services which can be provided by satellite and which are available for use by the public, such as telephony, telegraphy, telex, facsimile, data transmission, transmission of radio and television programs between approved earth stations having access to the INTELSAT space segment for further transmission to the public, and leased circuits for any of these purposes; but excluding those mobile services . . . which are provided through mobile stations operating directly to a satellite which is designed, in whole or in part, to provide services related to the safety or flight control of aircraft or to aviation or maritime radio navigation.[175]

DOMESTIC VERSUS INTERNATIONAL. Since only international public telecommunications services are subject to economic coordination (see Article XIV(d)), it is important to draw the distinction between domestic and international services. Domestic public telecommunications services are provided within the boundaries of one country, whereas international public telecommunications services are provided between or among two or more countries. Even in cases where a satellite system is established primarily to service the population of one country, but where the satellite operator or user takes advantage of signal "spillover" into a foreign country to provide services also to that country, its services to the foreign country will be considered international public telecommunications services and subject both to technical and economic coordination.[176] It is interesting to note, also, that communications services in coastal areas may be considered international. For example, American Mobile Satellite Corporation of Washington, D.C., which was authorized by the United States Federal Communications Commission in 1989 to provide an unspecified variety of land, aeronautical and maritime mobile satellite services in the United States and coastal areas up to 200 miles off-shore, was required to coordinate under Article XIV(d) of the INTELSAT Agreement for the portion of its services that involved off-shore communications.[177] These communications were considered to be international public telecommunications services. Interestingly, no distinction was made between

---

174. INTELSAT Agreement, art. III(a).

175. *Id.*, art. I(k).

176. *See* Chapter 3.1.4. (discussing the criteria for authorization of "transborder" services by U.S. satellite companies). *See also* C.W. Derrick, *Competition versus Cooperation: The D.C. Circuit Referees the Transborder Policy*, 14 N.C. J. OF INT'L L. AND COMMERCIAL REG. 315 (1989) (discussing U.S. transborder policy)

services within and outside the U.S. territorial sea limit. The Company was required to coordinate the remaining portion of its services under Article XIV(c) and (e) of the INTELSAT Agreement and Article VIII of the INMARSAT Convention.[178]

SPECIALIZED TELECOMMUNICATIONS SERVICES. The term "specialized telecommunications services" means

> telecommunications services which can be provided by satellite, other than those defined in paragraph (k) of this Article, including, but not limited to, radio navigation services, broadcasting satellite services for reception by the general public, space research services, meteorological services, and earth resources services.[179]

PUBLIC VERSUS SPECIALIZED. The distinction between public and specialized services is important in the context of international telecommunications services since only the former are subject to economic coordination (see Article XIV(d)). Essentially, the distinction between public and specialized telecommunications services is characterized by the difference between fixed satellite services[180] and mobile satellite services[181] as defined by the International Telecommunication Union (ITU)

---

177. *See Amendment of Parts 2, 22 and 25 of the Commission's Rules to Allocate Spectrum for and Establish Other Rules and Policies Pertaining to the Use of Radio Frequencies in a Land Mobile Satellite Service for the Provision of Various Common Carrier Services,* Memorandum Opinion, order and Authorization, 4 F.C.C. Rcd 6041 (1989) [hereinafter cited as American Mobile Satellite Corporation Authorization], at 6056-6057 (imposing INTELSAT and INMARSAT coordination requirements on American Mobile Satellite Corporation).
178. *Id.,* at 6057.
179. INTELSAT Agreement, art. I(l).
180. Fixed satellite service is defined as "[a] radiocommunication service between earth stations at given positions, when one or more satellites are used; the given position may be a specified fixed point or any fixed point within specified areas; in some cases this service includes satellite-to-satellite links, which may also be operated in the inter-satellite service; the fixed satellite service may also include feeder links for other space radiocommunication services." ITU Radio Regulations, *supra* note 172, art. 1, No. 22, as amended ITU *Final Acts,* World Administrative Radio Conference on the Use of the Geostationary Satellite Orbit and the Planning of Space Services Utilizing It (Second Sess. 1988).
181. Mobile satellite service is "[a] radiocommunication service between mobile earth stations and one or more space stations, or between stations used by this service; or between mobile earth stations by means of one or more space stations." ITU Radio Regulations, *supra* note 172, art. 1, No. 27. Depending upon the locations of the Earth stations communicating with the satellite, the Radio Regulations distinguish between land-mobile satellite service, maritime-mobile satellite service and aeronautical-mobile satellite service. *Id.,* Nos. 29, 31 and 35.

(Chapter 4.1.), on the one hand, and broadcasting satellite services,[182] radiodetermination satellite services,[183] Earth exploration satellite services[184] and any other telecommunications satellite services, as defined by the ITU,[185] on the other hand. As is true also for the ITU definitions, in practice, the distinctions are not always clear-cut. For example, a satellite operating in the frequency bands allocated by the ITU to fixed satellite service[186] and at power levels characteristic of fixed satellites[187] will be considered to provide public telecommunications service, even if it is used for program distribution to cable operators and individual receiving antennas, i.e., services that resemble satellite broadcasting. For example, Société Européenne des Satellites of Luxembourg uses its ASTRA fixed satellites for television program distribution to cable operators and individual home receivers in the United Kingdom and continental Europe, and its services are coordinated as international public telecommunication services under Article XIV(d) of the INTELSAT Agreement.[188] Further-

---

182. Broadcasting satellite service is defined as "[a] radiocommunication service in which signals transmitted or retransmitted by space stations are intended for direct reception by the general public. In the broadcasting satellite service 'direct reception' shall encompass both individual and community reception." *Id.*, No. 37.

183. Radiodetermination satellite service is "[a] radiocommunication service for the purpose of radiodetermination involving the use of one or more space stations." *Id.*, No. 38. Radiodetermination is defined as "[t]he determination of the position, velocity and/or other characteristics of an object, or the obtaining of information relating to these parameters, by means of the propagation properties of radio waves." *Id.*, No. 10.

184. Earth exploration satellite service is defined as "[a] radio communication service between earth stations and one or more space stations, which may include links between space stations, in which information relating to the characteristics of the Earth and its natural phenomena is obtained from active sensors or passive sensors on earth satellites; similar information is collected from airborne or earth-based platforms; such information may be distributed to earth stations within the system concerned; platform interrogation may be included. This service may also include feeder links necessary for its operation." *Id.*, No. 48.

185. For example, meteorological satellite service, is defined as "[a]n earth exploration satellite service for meteorological purposes." *Id.*, No. 49, *cf.* No. 48. During the negotiations of the INTELSAT Agreement, the controversy concerning "specialized services" primarily related to the scope of INTELSAT's own services rather than to the issue of which services would require economic coordination. Colino, INTELSAT DEFINITIVE, *supra* note 22, at 99.

186. *See* ITU Radio Regulations, *supra* note 172, as amended, art. 8 (containing the Table of Frequency Allocations). *See* Chapter 4.1.-4.2. (providing general background and description of the Table of frequency allocations).

187. Fixed satellites have lower signal power than do broadcasting satellites. Higher power levels are required for direct reception by small Earth stations, which is implied in the definition of broadcasting satellite service, *supra* note 182.

more, the definition of public telecommunications services explicitly exempts aeronautical mobile safety-related services,[189] including air traffic control, and aeronautical and maritime navigation.[190] Consequently, these services are considered specialized telecommunications services. On the other hand, aeronautical mobile public correspondence services are considered public telecommunications services.

Although the definition of "public telecommunications service" requires that these services be "available for use by the public," interconnection with the public-switched network is not a criterion.[191] Intra-corporate or inter-corporate private communications network services, which by definition do not interconnect with the public-switched network (they by-pass), still may be considered public telecommunications services. For example, when the United States Federal Communications Commission authorized several private U.S. companies in 1985 to establish international satellite systems independent of the INTELSAT space segment, it prohibited communications services provided via these systems from interconnecting with the public-switched network. Nevertheless, the services were deemed to be international public telecommunications services and subject both to technical and economic coordination under Article XIV(d) of the INTELSAT Agreement (see Chapter 3.1.4.).

---

188. INTELSAT Sixteenth Assembly Meeting Records, *supra* note 165, at 9.
189. In the aeronautical mobile satellite service, an important distinction exists between safety-related services, including air traffic, on the one hand, control, and non-safety related services, including public (passenger-to-ground) correspondence on the other hand. ITU Radio Regulations, *supra* note 172, art. 50.
190. INTELSAT Agreement, art. I(k).
191. This is evidenced by the fact that INTELSAT member States routinely coordinate such services as international public telecommunications services, and also by the fact that the INTELSAT Assembly of Parties in 1990 developed new procedures and guidelines for coordination of international public telecommunications services explicitly encompassing both public-switched and non-public-switched services. INTELSAT Sixteenth Assembly Meeting Records, *supra* note 165, at 18-23. The INTELSAT Board of Governors has defined service not interconnected with the public-switched network as "communications among a predetermined group of stations rather than among the general universe of public-switched network stations. The key distinction between these services and public switched network services is not necessarily the nature of the facilities that are used to carry communications signals but instead whether such services are accessible only to a predetermined group of users or whether they are available for access by the general public, as in the case of services interconnected with the public switched network." Report of the Board of Governors to the Sixteenth Assembly of Parties on Its Review of Article XIV(d) Non-Technical Consultation Procedures, INTELSAT Doc. No. AP-16-20E L/10/90, 26 Sept., 1990 [hereinafter cited as Report of the Board to the Sixteenth Assembly Meeting], at 21.

A distinction between geostationary and low-Earth orbit satellites appears irrelevant to the definitions of public and specialized telecommunications services. Several private companies have asked the United States Federal Communications Commission for permission to construct and operate low-Earth orbit, multi-satellite systems for mobile and radiodetermination satellite services.[192] Technical coordination of these satellite systems will have to take place under Article XIV(c) and (e), as appropriate. To the extent these satellite systems are used to provide international telecommunications links, as well, economic coordination also is required under Article XIV(d). Depending upon the configuration of the low-Earth orbit satellite system, its capability for satellite-to-satellite links and understandings with foreign telecommunications administrations, terrestrial lines and sub-marine cables may be used instead of satellites, in some cases, for international communications.

COORDINATION PROCEDURE. The specific coordination procedure applicable in any given case depends on whether your client is proposing to provide domestic telecommunications services, international telecommunications services, or specialized telecommunications services. In any event, the initial coordination request may be addressed to the INTELSAT Director General at the Organization's headquarters in Washington, D.C. Again, a government entity must act on your client's behalf. With respect to domestic public telecommunications services, only the Board of Governors becomes involved in the coordination process. The country acting on behalf of your client must "consult with the Board of Governors . . . ," which, upon such consultation, "shall express, in the form of recommendations, its findings regarding the technical compatibility . . . ."[193] In the case of specialized telecommunications services, both the Board of Governors and the Assembly of Parties become involved. The country acting on behalf of your client must "furnish all relevant information to the Assembly of Parties, through the Board of Governors . . . ."[194] The Assembly of Parties, "taking into account the advice of the Board of Governors, shall express, in the form of recommendations, its finding regarding the technical compatibility . . ." of your client's proposed satellite with existing and planned INTELSAT satellites.[195]

If your client is proposing international public telecommunications services, as a general rule, both the Board of Governors and the Assembly of Parties take part in the coordination process. The country acting on behalf of your client "shall furnish all relevant information to and shall consult with the Assembly of Parties, through the Board of Governors, to ensure technical compatibility . . . and to avoid significant economic harm . . ." to INTELSAT.[196] Upon such consultations, "the Assembly of Parties, taking

---

192. *See* Chapter 3.1.6. (describing these companies and services).
193. INTELSAT Agreement, art. XIV(c).
194. *Id.*, art. XIV(e).
195. *Id.*
196. *Id.*, art. XIV(d).

into account the advice of the Board of Governors, shall express, in the form of recommendations, its findings . . . "with regard to technical compatibility and economic harm, as well as with respect to whether the new satellite services will prejudice the establishment of direct links through the INTELSAT system among all its Members."[197]

Due to a large increase in Article XIV(d) coordination requests[198] over the last several years, and also in response to complaints of bureaucratic delays by member States whose public or private entities were trying to coordinate international satellite systems, the INTELSAT Assembly of Parties in 1990 adopted new, streamlined procedures for coordination of satellite systems providing international public satellite services, essentially delegating much of its responsibilities to the Board of Governors.[199]

The procedures distinguish between international public telecommunications services that involve interconnection with the public-switched network and those that do not,[200] and between fixed satellite services and non-fixed satellite services.[201] In the case of services interconnected with the public-switched network, the Board of Governors has been authorized

---

197. *Id.*

198. The following Table indicates the numbers of coordinations accomplished under INTELSAT Agreement, art. XIV(c), (d), (e) from 1973 to 1990:

YEAR	*XIV(c)*	*XIV(d)*	*XIV(e)*	*TOTAL*
1973	7	0	0	7
1974	0	2	2	4
1975	2	0	0	2
1976	3	3	1	7
1977	4	0	0	4
1978	7	2	1	10
1979	3	4	0	7
1980	17	6	7	30*
1981	3	0	0	3
1982	7	31	8	46
1983	24	0	1	25
1984	34	0	0	34
1985	8	87	5	100
1986	5	0	0	5
1987	17	76	22	115
1988	22	15	8	45
1989	65	179	15	259
1990	15	54	6	75**

* An error appears in the Table, with respect to one or more of the figures indicated for 1980.

** Coordinated before 26 Sept., 1990. A large number of satellite networks were coordinated at an Assembly of Parties Meeting later that same year.

Source: Report of the Board to the Sixteenth Assembly Meeting, *supra* note 191, Table No. 1.

199. INTELSAT Sixteenth Assembly Meeting Records, *supra* note 165, at 18-23.

200. *See supra* note 191 (providing a definition of public-switched services).

201. *See supra* note 180 (providing a definition of fixed satellite service).

to make recommendations on behalf of the Assembly of Parties in cases where the communications traffic is forecast at no point to exceed the threshold of one-hundred (100) 64 Kilobits equivalent circuits.[202] In situations where interconnection with the public-switched network will not occur, satellite systems with capacity not exceeding thirty (30) 36 MHz transponders[203] are *ipso facto* considered not to cause economic harm and do not require economic coordination.[204] In these cases, the Board of Governors also makes recommendations with regard to technical compatibility and the issue of prejudice to the establishment of direct links through the INTELSAT space segment.[205] The Board also has been authorized to make recommendations when the proposed international public telecommunications services are non-fixed, i.e. mobile services.[206] Finally, the Board of Governors is authorized to make recommendations in cases of repeated coordinations where only the technical, not the economic, characteristics of a service have changed.[207] In all other cases, the traditional coordination procedures for international public telecommunications services apply as set forth in Article XIV(d) of the INTELSAT Agreement.[208] This also is true if the Board of Governors, in its discretion, declines to issue recommendations.[209] Furthermore, a Party or Signatory may request full Article XIV(d) coordination.[210] The significance of having only the Board of Governors, as opposed to both the Board and the Assembly, involved is that the coordination process can be expedited.

All recommendations referred to, above, whether they are made by the Assembly of Parties or the Board of Governors, shall be made within a period of six months from the date of commencing the coordination procedure.[211] An extraordinary Assembly of Parties meeting may be called for the purpose.[212] As discussed previously, the recommendations are not legally binding.

COORDINATION CRITERIA. While criteria for technical coordination are contained in INTELSAT technical documents[213] and are relatively

202. INTELSAT Sixteenth Assembly Meeting Records, *supra* note 165, Agenda Item No. 9(a), provision Nos. 23(b) with regard to economic harm, and 23(g) with regard to technical compatibility and direct links.
203. Transponders are communications units on board the satellite which receive, amplify and retransmit radio signals.
204. *Id.*, provision No. 23(c).
205. *Id.*, provision No. 23(g).
206. *Id.*, provision No. 23(f).
207. *Id.*, provision No. 23(e).
208. The Board of Governors considered an amendment to Article XIV(d), but concluded that the provision should be contained in its present form, Report of the Board to the Sixteenth Assembly Meeting, *supra* note 191, at 18.
209. INTELSAT Sixteenth Assembly Meeting Records, *supra* note 165, Agenda Item No. 9(a), provision No. 23(i).
210. *Id.*, provision No. 23(j).
211. INTELSAT Agreement, art. XIV(f).
212. *Id.*

uncontroversial, criteria for economic coordination have always been the subject of controversy. Until the new guidelines described above were adopted, an attempt was never made to define "significant economic harm" in discrete, numerical values.[214] Rather, decisions on whether a proposed new satellite system would cause economic harm to INTELSAT were made on a case-by-case basis at the discretion of the Parties and influenced by Signatories with vested interests in the preservation of INTELSAT's financial well-being. The new guidelines represent an improvement in the sense that satellite systems whose services will not involve interconnection with the public-switched network are considered not to cause significant economic harm if they do not exceed a specific capacity threshold, i.e., thirty (30) 36 MHz transponders.[215] If the threshold is exceeded,[216] however, the conventional case-by-case evaluation will be applied to determine whether significant economic harm will result to INTELSAT. The threshold applies to each satellite system operator, not to each satellite or member State.[217] It is the highest level of transponders over the years covered by the coordination that counts.[218] A similar threshold was not adopted with regard to public-switched services. As far as these services are concerned, the only difference instituted by the new guidelines is that the Board of Governors makes the decision in the event traffic interconnected to the public-switched network is estimated not to exceed one-hundred (100) 54 Kilobits equivalent circuits;[219] otherwise, the

---

213. *See* INTELSAT Intersystem Coordination Manual, INTELSAT Doc. No. BG-67-71E R/6/86, 25 June, 1986, Article XIV Intersystem Coordination Procedures (Technical Coordination), INTELSAT Doc. No. BG-28-70E (Rev.1), 14 Dec., 1982; and INTELSAT Guidelines for Intersystem Coordination, INTELSAT Doc. No. BG-43-71E W/9/80, 18 Sept., 1980.

214. *See* Report of the Board to the Sixteenth Assembly Meeting, *supra* note 191, at 7-10 (providing an historic perspective on the application of the economic harm criterion). Traditionally, application of the economic harm criterion involved providing answers to a set of questions designed not to produce a conclusive answer on the issue of significant economic harm, but simply "to provide the information required by the Board and the Assembly of Parties to reach a conclusion on a judgmental, case-by-case basis." *Id.*, at 8. *See* Article XIV(d) Consultation Procedure, INTELSAT Doc. No. BG-64-80E (Rev.1) W/9/85, 6 Sept., 1985 (concerning economic harm coordination guidelines in force since 1985). *See* B.W. Rein, B.L. McDonald, D.E. Adams, C.R. Frank & R.E. Nielsen, *Implementation of a U.S. "Free Entry" Initiative for TransAtlantic Satellite Facilities: Problems, Pitfalls, and Possibilities*, 18 GEO. WASH. J. OF INT"L L. & ECON. 459 (1985) (concerning the debate about licensing of private U.S. trans-Atlantic satellite systems in competition with INTELSAT).

215. INTELSAT Sixteenth Assembly Meeting Records, *supra* note 165, Agenda Item No. 9(a), provision No. 23(c).

216. The Board determines whether the threshold is exceeded. *Id.*, provision No. 23(d).

217. Report of the Board to the Sixteenth Assembly Meeting, *supra* note 191, at 26.

218. *Id.*

Assembly of Parties becomes involved as prescribed in Article XIV(d) of the INTELSAT Agreement.

5.2.2. INMARSAT

THE COORDINATION REQUIREMENT. Article VIII of the INMARSAT Convention sets forth the coordination requirement with respect to INMARSAT:

> (1) A Party shall notify the Organization in the event that it or any person within its jurisdiction intends to make provision for, or initiate the use of, individually or jointly, separate space segment facilities to meet any or all of the *maritime purposes* of the INMARSAT space segment, to ensure technical compatibility and to avoid significant economic harm to the INMARSAT system.
>
> (2) The Council shall express its views in the form of a recommendation of a non-binding nature with respect to technical compatibility and shall provide its views to the Assembly with respect to economic harm.
>
> (3) The Assembly shall express its views in the form of recommendations of a non-binding nature within a period of nine months from the date of commencing the procedures provided for in this Article. An extraordinary meeting of the Assembly may be convened for this purpose.
>
> (4) The notification pursuant to paragraph (1), including the provision of pertinent technical information, and subsequent consultations with the Organization, shall take into account the relevant provisions of the Radio Regulations of the International Telecommunication Union.[220]

Coordination with INMARSAT of your client's satellite system is necessary if the country authorizing your client's service is a Member of INMARSAT and the proposed services "meet any or all of the maritime purposes of the INMARSAT space segment . . . ."[221] These purposes include "improving maritime communications . . . thereby assisting in improving communications for distress and safety of life . . . the efficiency and management of ships . . . maritime . . . public correspondence services and radiodetermination capabilities."[222] Accordingly, three categories of maritime communications services are contemplated for INMARSAT: 1) safety related, 2) fleet management related and 3) passenger-to-shore, shore-to-passenger communications, and 4) maritime radiodetermination

---

219. INTELSAT Sixteenth Assembly Meeting Records, *supra* note 165, Agenda Item No. 9(a), provision No. 23(b).
220. Emphasis added. INMARSAT Convention, art. VIII.
221. *Id.*, art. VIII(1).

(i.e., maritime position-location and navigation).

EXAMPLE. When American Mobile Satellite Corporation of Washington, D.C., was authorized by the United States Federal Communications Commission in 1989 to provide a variety to land, aeronautical and maritime mobile satellite services (see Chapter 3.1.5.), the Company was required to coordinate with INMARSAT for its proposed maritime satellite services, but not its other operations.[223] The Company also was required to coordinate with INTELSAT, as mentioned in Chapter 5.2.1.

COORDINATION PROCEDURES. In situations where the coordination requirement applies, the country acting on behalf of your client must notify the INMARSAT Director General at the Organization's headquarters in London, England, that a new satellite service is being planned.[224] Upon consideration, the Council will express its views in the form of a non-binding recommendation with respect to technical compatibility, and provide its views to the Assembly with respect to economic harm.[225] The Assembly will express its views on economic harm in the form of non-binding recommendations within a period of nine months from the date of commencing the coordination procedure.[226]

---

222. *Id.*, art. III(1). In July 1991, INMARSAT's satellites (leased and owned), listed in *supra* note 77, operated in the following frequency bands:

SATELLITE	*Up-Link*	*Down-link*
	(frequency range*)	
First Generation:	1636.5-1644 MHz	1535-1542.5 MHz
Marecs-B2		
Marisat (F-1)		
Marisat (F-2)		
Marisat (F-3)		
INTELSAT-MCS-A		
INTELSAT-MCS-B		
INTELSAT-MCS-D		
Second Generation:	1631.5-1649.5 MHz	1530-1548 MHz
INMARSAT (F-1)		
INMARSAT (F-2)		
etc. (to be launched)		
Third Generation:	1626.5-1660.5 MHz*	1530-1559 MHz
(under construction)		

* Additional 5 MHz for mobile satellite service will be sought by several administrations at the 1992 ITU World Administrative Radio Conference. Source: Comsat, Washington, D.C.

223. American Mobile Satellite Corporation Authorization, *supra* note 177, at 6057.
224. INMARSAT Convention, art. VIII(1), *cf.* art. VIII(4) (concerning content of the notification).
225. *Id.*, art. VIII(2).
226. *Id.*, art. VIII(3).

5.2.3. EUTELSAT

THE COORDINATION REQUIREMENT. The requirement for coordination with EUTELSAT is set forth in Article XVI of the EUTELSAT Convention:

> (a) Any Party or Signatory which intends, or becomes aware that any person within the jurisdiction of that Party intends, individually or jointly, to establish, acquire or utilize space segment equipment separate from the EUTELSAT Space Segment in order to meet its requirements of *international public telecommunications services* within the EUTELSAT Space Segment service area to provide services in accordance with paragraphs a) and b) of Article III of the Convention, shall, before such establishment, acquisition or utilization, furnish all relevant information to the Assembly of Parties through the Board of Signatories, which shall establish whether there is likely to be any significant economic harm to EUTELSAT. The Board of Signatories shall submit its report and conclusions to the Assembly of Parties. The Assembly of Parties shall give its views within six months from the start of the foregoing procedure. An extraordinary meeting of the Assembly of Parties may be convened for this purpose.
>
> (b) The Board of Signatories shall draft and submit to the Assembly of Parties, as a matter of priority, the guidelines to be considered by any Party or Signatory, which intends, or becomes aware that any person within the jurisdiction of the Party intends, individually or jointly, to establish space segment equipment separate from the EUTELSAT Space Segment in order to meet its requirements for *domestic or international public or specialized telecommunications services* to ensure technical compatibility of such separate equipment and its operation with the use of the radio frequency spectrum and orbital space by an existing or planned EUTELSAT Space Segment.[227]

Technical coordination with EUTELSAT is required if the country authorizing your client's satellite service is a Member of EUTELSAT and the services planned by your client fall within the categories of domestic public telecommunications services, international public telecommunications services, or specialized telecommunications services, which together include any telecommunications satellite service your client might decide to provide.[228] Coordination issues only arise, however, if your client is proposing to use frequency bands utilized by EUTELSAT.[229] Additional economic coordination is required if your client is planning an international public telecommunications satellite service offering *within EUTEL-*

227. Emphasis added. EUTELSAT Convention, art. XVI.
228. *Id.*, art. XVI(b).

SAT's service area.[230] As with INTELSAT and INMARSAT, the economic coordination requirement was imposed to protect EUTELSAT's core business. The definitions of public and specialized telecommunications services[231] are almost identical to those discussed with respect to INTELSAT in Chapter 5.2.1. In the case of EUTELSAT, however, aeronautical safety-related and maritime navigation services are not exempted in the definition of public telecommunications services.

COORDINATION PROCEDURES. The procedures for coordination vary, depending upon whether your client is proposing to provide international public telecommunications services, on the one hand, or domestic public or specialized telecommunication services, on the other. In any event, the country representing your client's interests should address the initial coordination request to the EUTELSAT Director General at the Organization's Headquarters in Paris, France. The request must contain pertinent technical information on the proposed satellite system prepared in consideration of guidelines for technical coordination developed by EUTELSAT. If international public telecommunications service is being proposed, the country acting on behalf of your client should furnish relevant economic information to the Assembly of Parties, through the Board of Signatories. The latter considers whether significant economic harm to EUTELSAT is likely to result, and presents its views to the Assembly of Parties.[232] The Assembly expresses its views in the form of a non-binding recommendation within six months, and may convene an extraordinary meeting for the occasion.[233]

---

229. EUTELSAT satellites (listed in *supra* note 173) currently operate in the following frequency bands:

SATELLITE	*Up-link*	*Down-link*
First Generation:		
EUTELSAT I (F-1)		
EUTELSAT I (F-2)		
EUTELSAT I (F-4)		
EUTELSAT I (F-5)		
Second Generation:	14.0-14.5 GHz	10.95-11.2 GHz 11.47-11.7 GHz 12.5-12.75 GHz*
EUTELSAT II (F-1)		
EUTELSAT II (F-2)		
EUTELSAT II (F-3)		
etc.		

* This band is used for the EUTELSAT Satellite Multiservice System, the Organization's business service. Source: W.L. Morgan, EUTELSAT II: The Newest Regional Ku-band Satellite System is Profiled in Satellite Notebook No. 57, *Satellite Communications,* July 1991, at 32-33.

230. EUTELSAT Convention, art. XVI(a).

231. *Id.,* art. I(k), (l).

232. *Id.,* art. XVI(a).

233. *Id.*

6. Risk Management

While implementing a telecommunications satellite project, your client faces several kinds of risks, including *political* risk (policies, as well as laws, can change rather quickly); *market* risk (the demand for your client's services may be less than expected); *technical* risk (the technology used may not produce the desired results); risk of *damage* to your client's personnel and property, particularly the satellite; and risk of *liability* for injury or damage caused by your client's satellite or personnel.

These risks can be managed. In varying degrees, they can be minimized. For example, selecting a proven technology minimizes the technical risk inherent in your client's venture; sound business planning reduces market and, to some extent, political risks; and launching your client's satellite on a vehicle with a record of successful launchings diminishes the risk of damage to, or loss of, the satellite in the launch phase. Furthermore, risks of damage and liability often can be allocated contractually, or otherwise, to the satellite manufacturer, the launch provider, the customer, the insurance community, or even the government.

CAVEAT. As part of the risk management discussion in Chapter 6.4.-6.5., several satellite purchase and launch agreements are referenced and quoted. Because of the private and often proprietary nature of such agreements, it has not always been possible to reference and quote, if at all, the most up-to-date materials. Both the satellite manufacturing and launch businesses have become fiercely competitive, with manufacturers and launch providers world-wide scrambling for shares of the global commercial satellite market consisting merely of two dozen or so large commercial satellites per year. Consequently, the private parties tend to guard their contracts closely and generally are not willing to disclose or publicize contract terms. Whenever somewhat dated materials are used, however, attempts have been made to point out any discrepancies with respect to current practices.

6.1. Political Risk

CHANGES IN GOVERNMENT, LAWS AND POLICIES. Political risk refers to the possibility of changes in government and government policy that may be adverse to your client's interests, and to changes in laws and regulations that control or affect the implementation of your client's satellite project. In situations where one government is particularly supportive of a satellite project, but where a supporting legal framework for authorizing space projects does not exist, a change in government, or key government personnel, may be fatal to the project, or at minimum pose serious problems. A new government may simply decide that your client's satellite venture is not in the "national interest," or that its implementation must await further studies or legislative initiatives. The situation is even more precarious in cases where the government is not only a regulator, but also a partner, customer, or even a competitor.

Not only changes in government, but also new policies, laws and regulations could jeopardize equally your client's project. Adverse policy and legal changes may go to the heart of your client's business plan, or they may be more of a peripheral nature, such as affecting the taxation of your client's financial backers, or the right to contract with a particular entity for launch services. An example of the latter situation involves a change in U.S. policy concerning commercial satellite launches on the National Aeronautics and Space Administration (NASA) Space Shuttle. Following the *Challenger* accident in 1986, President Ronald Reagan decided that commercial payloads no longer should be flown on the Shuttle unless they require the unique characteristics of the Shuttle, or a Shuttle launch would serve the national security or foreign policy interests of the United States.[1]Several satellite companies that had signed agreements for NASA Shuttle launches were forced to find other launch service providers and, consequently, experienced an expensive slippage in their time-critical plans for operation and marketing. These companies also had to pay considerably higher launch prices compared with the subsidized NASA Shuttle prices. As a result, two companies, whose satellite contracts with NASA could not be honored under the new policy, filed suit against the agency charging it with breach of contract. Contel-ASC of Rockwell,

---

1. *United States Launch Strategy,* National Security Decision Directive 254 (Dec. 27, 1986). The policy was stated in the National Aeronautics and Space Administration Authorization Act, Fiscal Year 1991, P.L. 101-611 §112 (1990). It is interesting to note that while President Reagan's 1986 decision to limit the use of the National Aeronautics and Space Administration (NASA) Space Shuttl, commercial payloads presented problems for satellite companies that had reservations on the Shuttle, it was a blessing to the United States private commercial launch industry. During the years in which NASA engaged in commercial space launch business, private launch companies had been unable to compete effectively due to subsidized Shuttle launch prices offered by NASA.

Maryland filed a $70.1 million suit in September 1989 and Hughes Communications Galaxy, Inc. of El Segundo, California, filed a $288.5 million suit on March 22, 1991.[2]

Another example of a change in government policy and related laws that threatened to pose serious obstacles to the implementation of two satellite projects involves the 1989 enactment by the United States Congress of a law prohibiting the launching of United States-manufactured satellites on the Chinese Long March vehicle.[3] The law, which responded to the Tiananmen Square repression of pro-democracy activists by Chinese authorities, prohibited the issuance of export licenses which are necessary to transport U.S.-made satellites to China for launching. In effect, the law suspended the Memoranda of Understanding signed by the United States and the People's Republic of China that permitted the launching of U.S.-built satellites on the Long March vehicle under certain conditions.[4] The ban potentially affected the Asia Satellite Telecommunications Company of Hong Kong and Aussat, Pty. Ltd. of Sydney, New South Wales, Australia, whose satellites were built by Hughes Aircraft Company of El Segundo, California, and scheduled to be launched on Long March vehicles. Finding alternate, timely and comparably inexpensive launch services would not be possible. However, on December 19, 1989, President George Bush invoked a "national interest" exception contained in the legislation, and launchings of these satellites became possible.[5]

RISK CAN DEPEND ON HOST COUNTRY. Clearly, the political risks involved in implementing a satellite project may vary from one country to the next. In countries where several private sector satellite projects of the same kind previously have been authorized and implemented, and where appropriate regulatory and institutional frameworks already are in place, such as in the United States regarding several types of telecommunications satellites, the political risks can be relatively low. On the other hand, in countries where the governments are unstable, and where no legal framework exists for the authorization and regulation of private satellite projects, the political risk could be substantial.

INDIRECT EFFECT OF POLITICAL RISK. Political risk not only threatens your client's project in a direct sense, it also could undermine your client's project by affecting adversely the interests of potential financial backers and customers. The former are reluctant to invest in or loan

---

2. *See Hughes Sues Government on NASA's Space Shuttle Policy,* SATELLITE WEEK, Apr. 1, 1991, at 2 (providing a brief description of the facts in *Hughes v. NASA*). Orbital Sciences Corporation of Fairfax, Virginia, an entrepreneurial, start-up company in the business of making upper stages for commercial Shuttle payloads, and whose entire business plan was predicated on the assumption that the Shuttle would continue to be used for commercial satellite payloads, was affected more directly by the policy change. It had to redirect its entire business plan.

money to a space project surrounded by political uncertainty, and would-be customers are unlikely to make commitments (e.g. in the form of a transponder purchase or lease) if they perceive the political risks to be unacceptable. It is interesting to note that a critical element in obtaining financing for Spacehab, Inc. of Washington, D.C., was that company's procurement of "political risk" insurance. Spacehab has a contract with NASA whereby the latter will lease space on a pressurized module to be provided by Spacehab for placement in the Shuttle bay. That contract is subject to termination by NASA in the event the United States Congress fails to appropriate the funds needed to pay for the lease. Spacehab procured "political risk" insurance to protect it against such non-appropriation.

MANAGING POLITICAL RISK. Unfortunately, no perfect formula exists for dealing with political risk. Nevertheless, it is important to identify and point out the various risks facing a client's satellite project. At best, your client then will be in a position to prevent or minimize adverse changes in law or policy through effective lobbying or other proper influ-

---

3. Departments of Commerce, Justice, and State, the Judiciary, and Related Agencies Appropriations Act, Fiscal Year 1990, P.L. No. 101-162 §610, 103 Stat. 988, 1938 (1989) [hereinafter cited as Department of Commerce Appropriations Act]. Section 610 provided:

(a) No moneys appropriated by this Act may be used to reinstate, or approve any export license applications for the launch of United States-built satellites on Soviet- or Chinese-built launch vehicles unless the President makes a report under subsection (b) or (c) of this section.

(b) The restriction on the approval of export licenses for United States-built satellites to the People's Republic of China for launch on Chinese-built launch vehicles is terminated if the President makes a report to Congress that:

(i) the Government of the People's Republic of China has made progress on a program of political reform throughout the entire country which includes

(A) lifting of martial law;

(B) halting of executions and other reprisals against individuals for the nonviolent expression of their political beliefs;

(C) release of political prisoners;

(D) increased respect for internationally recognized human rights, including freedoms of expression, the press, assembly, and association; and

(E) permitting a freer flow of information, including an end to the jamming of Voice of America, and greater access for foreign journalists; or

(c) It is in the national interest of the United States.

No prohibition on Chinese launches was included in the Departments of Commerce, Justice and State and the Judiciary, and Related Agencies Appropriations Act, Fiscal Year 1991. *See, however,* Department of Commerce, Justice, and State, the Judiciary and Related Agencies Appropriations Act, Fiscal Year 1992, Pub. L. 102-140§ 608, 105 Stat. 782 (1991) (reintroducing the prohibition on launches of U.S.-made satellites on Chinese Launch vehicles). The prohibition may be waived by the President under certain conditions. Id., §608 (b).

encing of authorities. In certain limited circumstances, insurance may be available. At worst, your client will be prepared to assess alternative options and strategies. In any event, your client should be advised to devise a flexible business plan that can accommodate foreseeable or unexpected, adverse changes in laws and policies. For example, when private U.S. companies first applied to the United States Federal Communications Commission for permission to establish international satellite systems in competition with the International Telecommunications Satellite Organization (INTELSAT), it was uncertain whether these companies, even if authorized, would be permitted to offer services involving interconnection with the public-switched telecommunications network (see Chapters 3.1.4. and 5.2.1.). In managing this regulatory uncertainty, these companies would have been well advised to provide in their business plans for both the eventuality that they would be permitted to provide public-switched services and for the eventuality that they would be authorized only to offer private network services, as was the case in fact.

6.2. Market Risk

EXPLANATION OF MARKET RISK. Market risk refers to the uncertainty regarding the demand for your client's telecommunications satellite services, that is, the risk of greater-than-expected discrepancy between the anticipated or projected market and the actual market. Market risk exists regardless of whether your client caters to an existing market by providing satellite communications services for which there already is a proven need, or attempts to develop a new market. In the former case, the market risk is one of saturation, that is, supply may exceed demand. In this event, your client's services may not be sufficiently subscribed. In the latter case, your client runs the risk that the proposed new market cannot

---

4. Memorandum of Agreement Between the Governments of the United States of America and the Peoples' Republic of China Regarding International Trade in Commercial Launch Vehicles, *done* Jan. 26, 1989; Memorandum of Agreement on Satellite Technology Safeguards Between the Governments of the United States of America and the People's Republic of China, *done* on or about Jan. 26, 1989; and Memorandum of Agreement on Liability for Satellite Launches Between the Governments of the United States of America and the People's Republic of China, *done* on or about Jan. 26, 1989. These memoranda of understanding concerning trade, transfer of technology and liability issues provide the legal framework for launching United States manufactured satellites on the Chinese Long March vehicle. Because China has since adhered to the Convention on Liability for Damage Caused by Space Objects, 1972, the memorandum concerning liability has lost some significance.
5. Department of Commerce Appropriations Act, *supra* note 3, sec. 610(c). On Apr. 7, 1990, a U.S.-built satellite belonging to Asia Satellite Telecommunications Company was successfully launched on the Chinese Long March III vehicle, The Washington Post, Apr. 8, 1990, at A29.

be sufficiently developed or penetrated. In either situation, a risk always exists that a competing technology will exploit your client's target market through less expensive and/or more attractive service offerings.[6]

EXISTING VERSUS NEW MARKETS. In the twenty-five years during which commercial telecommunications satellite systems have been in service, satellite operators have exploited existing communications markets, for example, by augmenting the public-switched telephone networks. They also have developed new markets, such as those for VSAT-networks (private intra-corporate communications networks involving a central hub station, which is connected via satellite to a multitude of tiny transmit and/or receive terminals); program distribution to cable operators; satellite news-gathering; and positioning and paging services. In fact, more than ninety percent of the United States domestic commercial telecommunications satellite capacity today is used to supply these new satellite-developed markets.

Very few private satellite companies have been able to show profits by exploiting existing communications markets, for example, by using satellites for purposes of public telephony. In most situations where satellites have been used for this purpose, losses have occurred, but have been absorbed by a larger operation of which the satellite venture has been only a small component. However, the Communications Satellite Corporation (Comsat) of Washington, D.C., presents an exception. It derives most of its revenues from public telephone transmissions because of that U.S. company's monopoly on *international* communications via the INTELSAT satellite systems, as well as the United States Federal Communications Commission's "loading" policies, which mandate that a certain portion of all U.S. transoceanic telephone transmissions be carried over the INTELSAT satellite system. Comsat earns its revenues from what, in essence, constitutes resale of INTELSAT satellite capacity to U.S. telephone companies and other users.[7]

Private satellite operators have made profit by developing and exploiting new markets such as for USAT networks, program-distribution and newsgathering. Servicing these markets often involves transponder sales

6. For example, Qualcomm, Inc. of San Diego, California, an entrepreneurial, start-up company, is using existing capacity on fixed satellites owned and operated by GTE Spacenet of McLean, Virginia, to provide mobile and radio determination satellite services. Qualcomm proved to be a formidable competitor to Geostar Corporation, which placed expensive and more sophisticated radiodetermination equipment also on GTE Spacenet host satellites, and which planned to build and launch three dedicated radiodetermination satellites in the mid-1990s. Geostar Corporation declared bankruptcy in May 1991.

7. *See* Chapter 3.1.4. (concerning "authorized users" and "direct access"). INTELSAT is not a profit-making organization. All its surplus revenues are paid back to Signatories as return for use of capital. *See* Chapter 5.1. (describing the financial principles governing INTELSAT).

and leases. The transponder sales concept was pioneered by Hughes Communications, Inc. in the early 1980s. (See Chapter 3.2.12.).

TIMING. The timing of market entry is often critical. Your client must be made aware that delays in obtaining regulatory approvals may occur that could distort the timing of the planned service debut. This was the situation for several companies which, in the early 1980s, applied to the Federal Communications Commission for permission to introduce direct broadcasting satellite service in the United States. Authorizations of these companies were delayed for regulatory and other reasons (See Chapter 3.1.2.). In the meantime, a proliferation of cable television systems occurred and, moreover, less expensive, lower-powered satellites were used for broadcasting purposes. Some direct broadcasting satellite companies have argued that, timing being the critical factor, the Federal Communications Commission deprived them of a unique business opportunity.

MANAGING MARKET RISK. Again, no perfect formula exists. Of course, your client should avoid taking unnecessary market risks. Thorough market studies should precede any satellite service, regardless of whether it caters to existing or new markets. Further, flexibility should be built into the business plan to permit your client to take advantage of unexpected market opportunities while, at the same time, allowing it to scale back efforts in market segments that prove to be less penetrable or profitable. For example, Geostar Corporation's target markets changed in the course of its business development. Originally, Geostar proposed to provide satellite position-location services for aircraft, ships, vehicles and individuals. Geostar's marketing efforts soon became targeted almost exclusively at a small sector of the market, namely, the trucking industry, which represented eighty percent of the company's customer base before the Company filed for bankruptcy in May 1991.

6.3. Technical Risk

EXPLANATION OF TECHNICAL RISK. Technical risk particularly refers to the uncertainty inherent in the use of new and innovative technology embodied in the satellite or its launch vehicle, or in Earth stations and associated ground equipment. For example, will the new satellite design or operating concept allow your client to provide the proposed services in a satisfactory manner? Will the new signal compression technique work as promised? Will the innovative program decoders perform? Will the advanced version of the existing launch vehicle deploy your client's satellite safely in the intended orbit?

In the space industry, even the use of proven technology often involves substantial risk. Experience has shown that, due to the complexities of space technology and space operations, spacecraft with track records of successful performance do fail from time-to-time. For example, launch vehicles that have launched successfully a dozen or so satellites suddenly fail for unexpected reasons. See Chapter 8.2. providing a chronology of spacecraft losses and failures.

EXISTING TECHNOLOGY. Unlike some other sectors of the space industry, off-the-shelf and proven technology exists for an array of different telecommunications satellite and launch concepts. In the United States, this technology was first developed in the context of military and scientific space programs, and then later refined and customized by the commercial space industry. Several other countries also have sophisticated, self-sufficient satellite manufacturing capabilities, including the Soviet Union, France, Britain, Germany, Canada, Japan and China. In these countries, the satellite customer can buy the satellite directly from a national manufacturer and, with the exception of Britain and Germany, procure launch services from a national launch company. In countries that do not possess these capabilities, the satellite customer must resort to foreign technology and is then at the mercy of export laws and other restrictions imposed by the manufacturing or launching country(ies).[8]

NEW TECHNOLOGY. Even in countries where relatively sophisticated telecommunications satellite technologies exist, the technological boundaries continue to be challenged. More efficient and sophisticated satellites, and more exotic service concepts, are being introduced constantly. For example, Motorola Satellite Communications, Inc. of Chandler, Arizona, is proposing a low-Earth orbit satellite constellation of seventy-seven satellites in seven polar orbits for global mobile communications to and from hand-held cordless (telephone) units (including interconnection with the public-switched network). The concept has never been exploited and, naturally, involves substantially more technical risk than the proven, traditional undertakings.

MANAGING TECHNICAL RISK. The key to managing technical risk is risk minimization. If your client's business plan can be implemented by relying on existing technology, that is the preferable approach. Regulators, financial backers and customers, alike, are apt to respond more

---

8. U.S. export laws relevant to spacecraft and component parts include the Arms Export Control Act, 22 U.S.C. §§2751-2796 (1988) and its implementing regulations, the International Traffic in Arms Regulations, 22 C.F.R. Parts 121-130 (1990) and the Export Administration Act, 50 U.S.C. §§2401-20 (1988) and its implementing regulations, Export Administration Regulations, 15 C.F.R. §768-99 (1990). Export licenses under the Arms Export Control Act are issued by the Department of State and under the Export Administration Act by the Department of Commerce. Spacecraft and their component parts almost exclusively fall within the scope of the Department of State's jurisdiction. Increasingly, calls are being heard for subjecting certain civilian satellites and their component parts to the jurisdiction of the Department of Commerce whose criteria for granting licenses are different and less stringent, and whose processing is more expedient. *See, e.g.* D. Burnett, *Take Communications Satellites Off Munitions List*, SPACE NEWS, June 17-23, 1991.

favorably if the plan relies essentially on proven technology. If your client's service proposal cannot be implemented by proven technology, it may be advisable to develop a business plan that progresses incrementally, as opposed to one that seeks to implement the ultimate system immediately. Geostar Corporation, for example, authorized in 1986 by the United States Federal Communications Commission to provide a position-location satellite service using three geostationary satellites, opted for a series of interim solutions (i.e., equipment packages on satellites owned and operated by others) to prove its technology, gain experience and establish a customer base. See Chapter 3.1.3.

6.4. Risk of Damage to Your Client's Personnel and Property, Including the Satellite

The implementation of your client's satellite project involves risk of damage or other loss, i.e., death or injury may result to your client's personnel, and loss or damage may result to their property. Loss or damage may result to your client's own property, including the satellite. Moreover your client may suffer loss of revenues and profits as a result of damage and/or delay. Damage may occur at any stage of the satellite project implementation, i.e., during satellite manufacturing, launch activities, or the satellite's operational phase.

Several options exist for managing these risks, and they are discussed in Chapter 6.4.1. and 6.4.2. For example, risk can be reduced by selecting a reliable manufacturer and launch provider. Often, risk can be allocated contractually to the manufacturer, launch company, or even to your client's customers. Insurance procurement is an option when risk cannot be transferred otherwise (see Chapter 8.). As a final solution, it may be appropriate, or unavoidable under certain circumstances, for your client to assume the risk, i.e., self insure.

6.4.1. Dealing With the Manufacturer

In negotiating a satellite purchase contract with the manufacturer, provisions concerning the transfer of risk of damage during manufacturing, as well as the manufacturer's liability for late delivery or malfunction of the satellite in orbit, should be carefully crafted to protect your client's interests. Satellite purchase contracts have become somewhat standardized, particularly in some areas of risk allocation; but there is room for negotiated solutions.

Contractual transfer of risk to the manufacturer often is possible and has an obvious appeal; but it is not without a price. Essentially, the risk protection available to your client is a function of how much it is willing to pay. Your client's success in achieving contractual protection at an affordable price also will depend greatly on its bargaining position. Your client is in a better bargaining position and is likely to obtain more favorable terms if it is a large organization ordering a series of satellites, than if it is a small, entrepreneurial, start-up company procuring, say, two satellites under a deferred payment plan.

MANUFACTURER GENERALLY BEARS RISK UNTIL LAUNCH. Customarily, both title and the risk of physical loss of, or damage to, the satellite pass from the manufacturer to the satellite customer, your client, either at the time of lift-off or at the time of intentional ignition of the launch vehicle first stage engines. Naturally, the manufacturer will want to transfer risk at the earlier point in time, i.e., intentional ignition, thus shifting the risk to the customer of damage to the satellite during an "on-the-pad abort". It is in your client's best interest to have risk transfer occur at lift-off. (See Chapter 8.5.1. concerning inception of coverage under the satellite launch insurance policy). An example of a provision favoring the satellite owner in this respect appears in an INTELSAT contract proposal attached to the Request for Proposal issued by the organization to a potential manufacturer of the INTELSAT VII satellite series (hereinafter INTELSAT VII Contract Proposal). It stipulates that "[t]itle and risk of loss or damage to a Satellite/Spacecraft which is delivered for the purpose of launch shall pass to INTELSAT at lift-off."[9] The contract proposal further provides that "[p]rior to the passing of title pursuant to this Article, any loss or damage to items to be delivered under this contract shall be at the Contractor's risk."[10]

In any event, the manufacturer generally bears the risk of loss or damage during the manufacturing and testing of the satellite, during transportation to the launch site and during the integration of the satellite with the launch vehicle. If the satellite is not scheduled for launching immediately after manufacturing has been completed and is placed in storage by the manufacturer, the manufacturer generally retains title and risk of loss during the storage period. This usually is not true, however, if the customer places the satellite in storage after final acceptance by the customer. In that case, title and risk of loss generally pass to the customer at the time of delivery and acceptance at the manufacturer's premises, or at the storage location. Interestingly enough, however, full responsibility for risk of loss or damage may in some cases revert back to the manufacturer during transportation from the storage site to the launch site, and remain with it until lift-off.

MANUFACTURER CAN INSURE THE RISK. The manufacturer commonly insures against loss of, or damage to, the satellite up to the point of risk transfer to the satellite customer (see Chapter 8.4.). For example, when Ford Aerospace built INSAT 1D for the Government of India's Department of Space, Ford obtained property insurance from Lloyds of London to protect against the risk of loss or physical damage from the

9. Attachment A to INTELSAT RFP No. INTEL-683, Proposed INTELSAT VII Contract Instrument for INTELSAT VII — Spacecraft and Associated Equipment and Services (not dated) [hereinafter cited as INTELSAT VII Contract Proposal], art. XII.B.

10. *Id.*, art. XII.A.

INTELSAT VII.
Provided courtesy Loral Corporation and INTELSAT.

time of unloading of the satellite at the launch site until the moment of launch.[11] In this case, Ford had agreed to bear the risk until launch. Ford's insurance procurement turned out to be prudent risk management on its part. As events turned out, damage was caused to INSAT 1D during its mating withMcDonnell Douglas Corporation's Delta launch vehicle in June 1989 at the Cape Canaveral launch site in Florida. A wire hoist cable of a Dresser one-ton internal overhead bridge crane severed, allowing a 64.5 pound hook and debris shield to fall and impact the satellite.[12] Ford repaired the satellite at a cost of $6 million, and was reimbursed by Lloyds pursuant to the insurance policy. Lloyds subsequently filed a subrogation suit against McDonnell Douglas in the Circuit Court for Brevard county, Florida, to recover the payment, alleging negligence. *Lloyds of London v. McDonnell Douglas Corporation*[13] is still pending.

"TURN-KEY" SYSTEMS. Although satellite purchase contracts traditionally provide for the transfer of title and risk to the customer at or about the time of launch, a few satellite manufacturers in recent years have begun offering so-called "turn-key" systems. The turn-key concept implies that the satellite manufacturer delivers the satellite in an operational condition *in orbit,* and retains title and risk of damage to the satellite until such time. In other words, the manufacturer assumes and thus relieves the satellite customer of the risk of loss of or damage to the satellite also during launching. Typically, in the turn-key deal, the manufacturer undertakes to arrange for and procure launch services, as well. For example, GE Astro Space Division of Princeton, New Jersey, was under contract to manufacture and deliver a "turn-key" system to Nippon Hoso Kyokai (NHK) of Tokyo, Japan, the Japanese national broadcasting organization, when the satellite was destroyed in an Ariane launch failure on February 22, 1990.

The turn-key concept is attractive to the satellite customer because it offers a "package deal" and relieves the customer of having to procure the launch, as well as launch insurance or a launch risk guarantee. Launch risk guarantees now are being offered by some launch companies (see Chapter 6.4.2.). Absent a turnkey arrangement, and unless the satellite owner chooses to self-insure, i.e., assume the risk of loss of or damage to the satellite during launching, the satellite owner will be faced with a launch insurance/risk guarantee premium at a rate currently ranging from 16% to 19% for geostationary telecommunications satellites, depending on the particular launch vehicle and payload. Considering the fact that an average geostationary telecommunications satellite is worth about $90

---

11. Ford Aerospace had purchased a Marine Policy General Provisions, (Cargo) Policy No. C19007B.
12. Lloyds Complaint, Jun. 15, 1990, *Lloyds v. McDonnell Douglas Corporation,* PENDING, at 4. *See infra* note 13 (providing the name of the court).
13. PENDING, District Court for the Middle District of Florida. Removed from Florida Circuit Court, Brevard County, Florida (10th Judicial District) on July 20, 1990.

million and launch services about $80 million, the premium cost is substantial. A launch risk guarantee, if at all available from the launch company, usually is offered at a rate slightly below the insurance market rate.

Although the turn-key system offers a neat solution, it can be a more expensive option. Naturally, the manufacturer will pass on to the customer the cost of launch services and insurance, as well as administrative costs incurred, for example, in connection with negotiations of the launch contract and insurance policy. While your client may have to accept these extra costs as the price of a turn-key system, it must protect itself in the contract in the event of a launch failure. For example, your client should require that it be named an additional insured under any launch insurance policy taken out by the manufacturer. Moreover, it must provide adequately for the refund of progress payments paid up to the time of launch.

If your client cannot negotiate an acceptable turn-key arrangement with the satellite manufacturer (e.g., because it is unwilling to accept the manufacturer's price), it should consider procuring launch insurance in full or in part (see Chapter 8.5.). Self-insurance, or assumption of risk, is suited only for established organizations or corporations that launch a large number of satellites and have substantial reserves to cover any loss that might result. For example, INTELSAT had chosen to self-insure an INTELSAT VI satellite, which failed to reach proper orbit due to a Titan launch failure on March 14, 1990. While INTELSAT could absorb the loss, self-insurance is not a recommended approach for small, entrepreneurial companies whose business survivability depends upon the successful launching of a single satellite.

CONSEQUENTIAL DAMAGES. Even though the manufacturer may bear the risk of direct damage to the satellite during manufacturing, the manufacturer generally will not be liable for incidental and consequential damages suffered by your client if the satellite construction is delayed. Such damages include financial penalties imposed by the launch services provider for a delay in the launch schedule, expenses incurred for storage of the satellite in the event the launch is postponed, and also lost earnings suffered since satellite customers cannot be served. For example, if the satellite is damaged during manufacturing, needed repair work may delay the satellite launch and start of operations by several months, considering that the construction time for an average geostationary telecommunications satellite is about thirty months. Insurance for incidental and consequential damages is available, see Chapter 8.4.

LIQUIDATED DAMAGES. Your client should seek to include in the satellite purchase contract a stipulation of economic penalty in the event the manufacturer does not deliver the satellite on time. In addition to providing an incentive to deliver on time, the penalty, which typically takes the form of liquidated damages,[14] will help offset the losses suffered by your client as a result of late delivery, such as launch delay penalties and lost earnings. The INTELSAT VII Contract Proposal contained the following provision, entitled "Liquidated Damages for Late Delivery:"

> INTELSAT intends to enter into one or more contracts with launch service providers for launch of the Spacecraft/Satellite to be delivered hereunder. Since the launch dates will be established to be consistent with the Spacecraft/ Satellite delivery schedules contained in this Contract, the Contractor and INTELSAT agree that time is of the essence in this Contract, and that delayed delivery of the items required by this contract may cause INTELSAT to incur additional costs, including launch service postponement fees, loss of anticipated revenue, and other damages difficult or impossible to measure. Accordingly, Contractor and INTELSAT agree to liquidated damages for late delivery as provided below, which damages are intended to be compensatory and do not constitute a penalty. In the event any Spacecraft/Satellite and associated Flight Equipment to be delivered hereunder is not delivered on or before the delivery dates specified in this Contract, excluding the number of days of excusable delay, if any, within the meaning of the Article of this Contract entitled *Excusable Delays,* then: (1) until such Spacecraft/Satellite and associated Flight Equipment is delivered, commencing the first day following the specified delivery date, the price for such Spacecraft/Satellite and associated Flight Equipment shall be reduced by TBD . . . for each day, up to a maximum of [*no more than 120 days*]; and (2) if INTELSAT elects to have the Spacecraft/Satellite and associated Flight Equipment delivered to storage pursuant to the Article entitled *Storage of Spacccraft,* Contractor shall provide such storage including necessary refurbishment/retest as provided in Exhibit B, free of charge for a period not to exceed 12 months.[15]

Liquidated damages cannot be relied upon as the sole measure of protecting your client from losses it might otherwise suffer in the way of consequential damage. In addition, your client should attempt to make generous provision for delay in the launch contract, as well in the contracts with customers, in the event the manufacturer does not deliver on time. The provision for launch schedule adjustments contained in a generic General Dynamics Corporation Contract for Launch Services, dated 1987,[16] illustrates the extent to which a launch company may be prepared to accommodate a satellite customer's requests for delay of the launch. Under this provision, the customer may request single or cumulative delay(s) in the launch schedule not exceeding twelve months. If the postponement(s) exceed(s) twelve months, the launch contract shall be subject to renegotiation or termination, unless the delay is "excusable," i.e., occasioned by an act of God or other specified circumstances. The

14. The purpose of liquidated damages is to secure performance, while the purpose of stipulating damages is to fix the amount to be paid in lieu of performance. BLACK'S LAW DICTIONARY 353 (5th ed. 1979).
15. INTELSAT VII Contract Proposal, *supra,* note 9, art. X.A.

provision stipulates that (provided the twelve months test is met) the launch date may be postponed without change to the contract price if (1) the notice of postponement is received at least twenty-four months plus one day prior to the established launch date and (2) the requirements of the U.S. government (which owns the launch sites and facilities) and the maintenance of appropriate clearance times between flights can be met. If both of these conditions cannot be satisfied, the launch postponement carries liquidated damages.[17]

FORCE MAJEURE. *Force majeure* and other exculpatory clauses are common in satellite purchase contracts relieving the manufacturer of responsibility for damage and consequent delay due to circumstances beyond its control. Indeed, such clauses tend to proliferate, and your client should make sure that it is only circumstances *reasonably beyond the control* of the manufacturer that excuse its performance. For example, a labor strike that the manufacturer could have avoided ought to be the risk of the manufacturer, not your client. Moreover, your client should propose language in the contract that requires the manufacturer to take reasonable mitigating measures in the event of *force majeure*. The INTELSAT Contract Proposal attached to the Request for Proposal issued by the organization to a potential manufacturer of the INTELSAT VI satellite series (hereinafter INTELSAT VI Contract Proposal) offers an example of the kind of *force majeure* clause your client can expect to find in a satellite purchase contract:

> Acts of God or of the public enemy, acts of the Government in its sovereign capacity, fires, floods, epidemics, quarantine restrictions, and freight embargoes, which cause failure to perform

---

16. The launch services agreement, entitled "Contract for Launch Services," was attached to a Statement by A.M. Lovelace, Corporate Vice President and General Manager, General Dynamics, Space Systems Division, at a Hearing on the status of the commercial launch industry. *Status of the Commercial Launch Industry Before the Subcommittee on Space, Science, and Applications of the House Committee on Science, Space and Technology* (Sept. 15, 1987). [Hereinafter General Dynamics' Contract for Launch Services is cited as General Dynamics Agreement].
17. General Dynamics Agreement *supra* note 16, art. 3. The Commercial Launch Services Contract Between Martin Marietta Corporation, and International Telecommunications Satellite Organization (INTELSAT) (Aug. 10, 1987) [hereinafter cited as Martin Marietta-INTELSAT Contract], art. 18.2., similarly provides for postponement in the launch date by the customer for up to twelve months without change to the contract price, provided the request for postponement is made before the first day of the twenty-fourth month before the scheduled launch. If postponements are made after this date, liquidated damages are imposed. The contract stipulates that if Martin Marietta and INTELSAT were to agree to postpone the launch beyond twelve months, "fair and reasonable" adjustments in price and/or terms shall be negotiated by the parties.

> hereunder, and in every case are beyond the reasonable control and without fault or negligence of both the Contractor and its subcontractors hereunder shall constitute excusable delay, if notice thereof is given to INTELSAT within twenty (20) days after such event shall have occurred. In the event of delay resulting from any of the above causes, the delivery requirements shall be extended accordingly.[18]

Earthquakes may be of special concern to a satellite customer contracting with a manufacturer located in California,[19] where several earthquakes have occurred in the past and are predicted for the future. While manufacturers generally bear the risk of damage to the satellite due to an earthquake, a resulting delay in the delivery is excusable. To a limited extent, insurance is available for certain *force majeure* events. See Chapter 8.4.

WARRANTIES, INCENTIVE PAYMENTS AND REFUNDS. Of foremost concern to your client is whether the satellite's quality and performance, once the satellite has been delivered to your client, conform with the specifications in the satellite purchase contract. Generally, a manufacturer will agree to bear some responsibility for the satellite's quality and performance beyond the time of delivery. For example, the manufacturer may offer warranties or a clause allowing your client to withhold performance or incentive payments in the event the satellite is determined to be defective. Other remedies are credits and rebates.

A warranty is a statement or representation made by the manufacturer as a part of the satellite purchase contract with reference to the quality or performance of the satellite, and by which the manufacturer undertakes to assure that certain facts are, or shall be, as it then represents them.[20] Warranties often are given separately for each subcomponent of the satellite, such as transponders, solar panels, thrusters, design life and fuel. Breaches of warranties entitle your client to damages.

Often, warranties are provided only while the satellite is on the ground, that is, prior to launching, but may extend beyond this time if such an arrangement can be negotiated. After launch, absent warranties, the customer generally must rely on whatever incentive payment (withholding), credit, rebate or refund arrangement it is able to negotiate. Set forth,

---

18. Attachment A to INTELSAT RFP No. INTEL 153, Proposed INTELSAT VI Contract Instrument for INTELSAT VI — Spacecraft and Associated Equipment and Services (not dated) [hereinafter cited as INTELSAT VI Contract Proposal], art. XIX.
19. For example, Hughes Aircraft Company is located in El Segundo, California, and Space Systems/Loral, formerly Ford Aerospace Company, is located in Palo Alto, California, both of which locations are in close proximity to known geological faults.
20. *See* BLACK'S LAW DICTIONARY 1423 (5th ed. 1979) (providing a model for this definition and citing *Bell v. Menzies,* 110 Ga. App. 436, 138 S.E. 2d 731, 732).

below, is an example of a warranty clause extending only until lift-off, contained in the INTELSAT VII Contract Proposal. The warranty contemplates that delivery and final acceptance of the satellite will take place at some point prior to the transfer of risk, which occurs at lift-off, and addresses itself only to the period beginning with delivery and final acceptance of the satellite until the time of launching. It provides that

> A. Contractor warrants that, notwithstanding prior inspection or acceptance by INTELSAT:
>
> (1) All Deliverable Hardware shall be in good working order and free from all defects in workmanship and materials and shall conform with the requirements of this Contract;
>
> (2) All Deliverable Data shall conform with the requirements of this Contract;
>
> (3) All Services shall be performed in a skillful and workmanlike manner and shall conform with the requirements of this Contract and the highest of professional industrial standards.
>
> B. Promptly after receipt of written notification from INTELSAT that Work is defective or non- conforming, Contractor shall, in accordance with INTELSAT's written instructions, either (1) correct, repair or replace, at INTELSAT's sole option and at Contractor's sole expense, any defective or non-conforming Work so as to comply with the above warranties, or (ii) reimburse INTELSAT for such portion of the price as is equitable.
>
> C. The above warranties shall continue for a period of three (3) years from the date of final acceptance except, however, all corrections, repairs and replacements made pursuant to this Article by Contractor after final acceptance shall be so warranted for a period of three (3) years from the date of acceptance of such corrections, repairs or replacements. The warranties provided in this Article shall not apply to a Spacecraft/Satellite after launch.[21]

In *Public Broadcasting Service v. Hughes Aircraft Company,*[22] Public Broadcasting Service (PBS),[23] a satellite transponder owner, sued Hughes Aircraft (Hughes), the satellite manufacturer, in the United States District

---

21. INTELSAT VII Contract Proposal, *supra* note 9, art. XXXV.A.-C.
22. DISMISSED WITH PREJUDICE Jan. 15, 1992. Case No. 90-0736, U.S. District Court, Central District of California. In a related suit, *Western Union Corporation v. Lexington Insurance Company,* PENDING, Civil Action No. 91-193 (JWB), U.S. District Court, District of New Jersey, Western Union has asked the court for a declaratory judgment that the Company is entitled to recover under Policy WU 456, subscribed to by Lexington Insurance Company, among others, as a result of insufficient fuel on board the WESTAR IV and WESTAR V satellites. *See* Chapter 8.6. (discussing the case).

Court, Central District of California, for breach of express warranty with respect to the satellite's life-time.[24] PBS claimed that Hughes had warranted that the satellite would have a minimum ten-year lifetime, a claim Hughes denied. Current estimates show that the satellite will expire fifteen months before that time. PBS claimed compensatory and consequential damages. The suit was dismissed.

As mentioned previously, the satellite purchase contract may provide for withholding of performance payments, as an alternative to a warranty, in the event the satellite does not operate satisfactorily. This type of provision contemplates that the customer pays for the satellite through a combination of progress payments (during satellite construction) and performance payments (during operation consistent with the specifications in the satellite purchase contract). Failure of the satellite to meet the contract specifications entitles the satellite owner to withhold performance payments otherwise due. For example, the INTELSAT VII Contract Proposal provides that

> 1. The Contractor's entitlement to receive performance payments . . . is dependent on the satisfactory operation of that Spacecraft/Satellite.
>
> 2. For the purpose of performance payments, a Spacecraft/Satellite will be deemed to be in "satisfactory operation" if data available from the Spacecraft/Satellite shows that no conditions exist at any time during a period following injection [into orbit] equal to the longest orbital design lifetime committed to in Exhibit A which affect or may affect adversely the Spacecraft/Satellite operation and it meets all the requirements of Exhibit A. Notwithstanding anything contained in Exhibit A concerning the estimated probability of survival of a spacecraft, or anything relating to the behavior or performance of the Spacecraft/Satellite under failure conditions, the complete Spacecraft/Satellite with one hundred percent (100%) of the [radio frequency] transmission channels in each coverage area must continuously meet all the requirements of Exhibit A without interruption, during the entire [*TBD longest orbital design life committed to in Exhibit A*] lifetime

---

23. PBS had bought four transponders from Western Union Corporation. The satellite purchase contract was entered into between Hughes Aircraft Company and Western Union Corporation, the original owner of the satellite. The satellite was later sold to Hughes Communications Galaxy, Inc., a subsidiary of Hughes Aircraft. The satellite specifications attached to the satellite purchase contract were incorporated by reference in the transponder sales agreement between Western Union and PBS for the purchase of four transponders on the WESTAR IV satellite. *See* note 103 and accompanying text (discussing the suit).
24. PBS also sued under the theories of strict liability, negligence and negligent misrepresentation.

> of the Spacecraft/Satellite in-orbit in order for it to meet the test of satisfactory operation. A defect in a Spacecraft/Satellite that can be satisfactorily corrected by a one-time switch to a redundant unit in the Spacecraft/ Satellite will not be deemed to affect the satisfactory operation of that spacecraft. However, the parties agree that Contractor will pay INTELSAT the daily amount of $ TBD (*an amount equal to 1/30 of the applicable monthly payments in effect at time of defect*) for each day, or portion thereof, that elapses until such defect is corrected.
>
> . . .
>
> 4. Should the Spacecraft/Satellite fail to provide satisfactory operation as defined in this Article, the Contractor will not be entitled to receive performance payments . . . .[25]

In other words, INTELSAT may hold back scheduled performance payments in the event the satellite does not operate in a manner that is consistent with the specifications in the purchase contract. However, the satellite owner is not entitled to hold back payments if the defect can be cured by a one-time switch to a redundant transponder. In that case, the manufacturer agrees to pay the satellite owner the stipulated amount each day until the defect is cured.

LIMITATION CLAUSE. Although your client may negotiate successfully for a warranty or payment withholding arrangement, the manufacturer cannot be expected to assume liability for incidental and consequential damages resulting from satellite malfunction or reduced performance. The remedies associated with warranty and incentive payment clauses usually are limited to the value of the satellite and do not cover lost earnings and liabilities your client may suffer. (For example, your client will nto earn revenues, and its customers may claim against it for revenue losses they have suffered). Indeed, the manufacturer likely will seek to include a limitation clause such as the following:

> THE WARRANTY PROVIDED IN THIS ARTICLE AND THE OBLIGATIONS AND LIABILITIES OF SELLER THEREUNDER ARE EXCLUSIVE AND IN LIEU OF AND BUYER HEREBY WAIVES ALL OTHER REMEDIES, WARRANTIES, GUARANTIES, OR LIABILITIES, EXPRESS OR IMPLIED, ARISING BY LAW OR OTHERWISE, INCLUDING WITHOUT LIMITATION ANY OBLIGATIONS OF THE SELLER WITH RESPECT TO FITNESS, MERCHANTABILITY AND CONSEQUENTIAL DAMAGES.[26]

---

25. INTELSAT VII Contract Proposal, *supra* note 9, art. VIII.A.1., 2., 4.
26. The limitation clause was modeled after one used in an aircraft purchase agreement. Liability limitation clauses very often are printed in capital letters to be particularly conspicuous.

In-orbit insurance is available to protect against expenses and lost earnings that your client might suffer due to satellite in-orbit failures. See Chapter 8.6.

6.4.2. Dealing with the Launch Company

ALLOCATION OF RISK IN GENERAL. Launch contracts offered by the world's major commercial[27] launch companies (see Chapter 7.) have become fairly standardized, particularly in the area of risk allocation.[28] Typically, interparticipant[29] liability (i.e., liability as between the launch company and the satellite owner and their respective contractors and subcontractors involved in launch services for damage to personnel and property) generally is subject to reciprocal waivers of liability. With respect to third party liability, the launch company customarily procures insurance that also protects the satellite owner. In addition, launch contracts often contain warranty disclaimers with regard to the performance of the launch vehicle, as well as other limitation clauses limiting the launch company's liability for consequential damage. The focus of this subchapter is the responsibility for *damage* suffered by the satellite owner (your client) and its contractors and subcontractors. Your client's *liability* to the launch company and its contractors and subcontractors, as well as to third parties, is addressed in Chapter 6.5.2.

WAIVER OF CLAIMS FOR DAMAGE. As indicated, launch companies generally do not assume any risk for damage to your client's satellite or personnel during launch activities. In fact, all major U.S. and foreign launch providers in business today[30] include in their launch agreements cross, or reciprocal, waivers of liability, which essentially require the launch company and the satellite owner,[31] your client, to bear responsibility for damage to their respective property and personnel.[32] Usually, the waivers extend also to the launch company's and your client's contractors and subcontractors involved in launch activities. Consequently, your client, as well as the launch company, will be required to "flow down" the waiver requirement, that is, include waivers in agreements with their respective contractors. These contractors, in turn, must include waivers in agreements with their contractors, and so on. With respect to U.S. private commercial launch contracts, this waiver scheme must be implemented as

27. *See* Chapter 1.2. (discussing the meaning of "commercial" in the context of space activities).
28. Risk allocation provisions refer to the provisions of the launch agreement that determine which party (the launch company or the customer) shall bear the risk of damage, loss or injury sustained 1) by a party, its personnel or its contractors and subcontractors or 2) by third parties.
29. The term "interparticipant," as opposed to "interparty," was chosen because waivers in launch agreements are intended to embrace other participants in the launch activities besides the parties, such as contractors and subcontractors of the parties that are not involved in launch activities, not just the parties, themselves.

a matter of law. Foreign launch providers adhere to this risk sharing formula as a matter of choice.

Even though their launch agreements include waiver provisions, some launch companies now offer satellite launch risk guarantees, essentially launch insurance, for a premium added to the launch price. See Chapter 8.5. In the event of a launch failure, the satellite owner will have recourse under the launch risk guarantee, but not in tort or under the launch contract because of the waiver.

THE ARIANESPACE AGREEMENT. Illustrative of the kind of waiver provision your client can expect to find in a commercial launch contract is a clause appearing in a February 1992 standard draft Arianespace launch agreement (hereinafter Arianespace Agreement), which stipulates that

> [e]ach Party shall bear any and all loss of or damage to property and any bodily harm (including death) and all consequences, whether direct or indirect, of such loss, damage or bodily harm (including death), and/or of a Launch Mission failure and/or of a Satellite Mission failure, which it or its Associates may sustain that arises in any way in connection with this Agreement, or the performance of this Agreement. Each Party irrevocably agrees to a no-fault, no-subrogation, inter-party waiver of liability, and waives the right to make any claims or to initiate any proceedings whether judicial, arbitral, administrative on this account against the other Party or that other Party's Associates for any reason whatsoever.
>
> Each Party agrees to bear the financial and any other conse-

---

30. Major commercial launch providers in business today include Martin Marietta Astronautics Group of Denver, Colorado; McDonnell Douglas Astronautics Company of Huntington Beach, California; General Dynamics Commercial Launch Services, Inc., of San Diego California; and Arianespace of Evry, France. To a limited extent, the Soviet Union, through the government agency Glavkosmos and its marketing agent Space Commerce Corporation of Houston, Texas, People's Republic of China, through Great Wall Industry Corporation, and the U.S. Government, through NASA, also offer commercial launch services. In addition, several small United States start-up companies offer launch services for small payloads (up to about 600 pounds) to low-Earth orbit. See Chapter 7.1. (describing the commercial launch industry).
31. A satellite transponder owner, including a financial institution which has become the owner of transponders as a result of a sale lease-back transaction, also would be precluded from claiming against the launch company.
32. A waiver provision precludes your client from claiming against the launch company for financial loss it may suffer as a result of damage to its satellite or personnel. A reciprocal waiver provision precludes the launch company from claiming against your client, as well, which means that your client cannot be held liable for damage to the launch provider's personnel or property. *See* Chapter 6.5.2.2. (concerning your client's liability to the launch company).

> quences of such loss, damage or bodily harm (including death) and/or of a Launch Mission failure and/or a Satellite Mission failure which it or its Associates may sustain, without recourse against the other party or the other Party's Associates.
>
> In the event that one or more Associates of a Party shall proceed against the other Party and/or that Party's Associates as a result of such loss, damage or bodily harm (including death) and/or Launch Mission failure and/or Satellite Mission failure, the first Party shall indemnify, hold harmless, dispose of any claim, and defend, when not contrary to the governing rules of procedure, the other Party and/or its Associates, as the case may be, from any liability and expense, including attorneys' fees, on account of such loss, damage or bodily harm (including death) and/or Launch Mission failure and/or Satellite Mission failure and shall pay all expenses and satisfy all judgments and awards which may be incurred or rendered against that other Party and/or its Associates.[33]

The term "Associate" is defined in the Arianespace Agreement to include the personnel, as well as contractors and subcontractors, of the launch company and the satellite owner.[34] In other words, the waiver provision requires Arianespace, i.e., the launch company, and its customer, i.e., the satellite owner, to bear responsibility for damage to their respective personnel and property, and precludes each party from claiming against the other party or the other party's contractors or subcontractors. The provision also requires Arianespace to hold the satellite owner harmless from liabilities and expenses resulting from claims by Arianespace's personnel, contractors and subcontractors and, conversely, requires the satellite owner to hold Arianespace harmless from liabilities and expenses resulting from claims by the satellite owner's personnel, contractors and subcontractors.

Further, the Arianespace Agreement provides for the flow-down of the waivers to the parties' respective contractors and subcontractors, whereby the contractors and subcontractors of one party waive their rights to claim against the other party and its contractors and subcontractors in the following fashion:

> Each Party obligates itself to take all necessary and reasonable steps to foreclose claims for loss, damage or bodily harm (including death) by any participant in the launch activity. Each Party shall require its Associate(s) to agree to a no-fault, no-subrogation, inter-party waiver of liability and indemnity for loss, damage or bodily harm (including death) its Associates sustain identical

33. Standard draft Arianespace launch contract, February 1992 [hereinafter cited as Arianespace Agreement], art. 14.1.2.-3.
34. *Id.*, art. 1.

> to the Party's(ies') undertaking under this Article 14 of this Agreement . . . .[35]

UNITED STATES LAW. If your client contracts with a United States launch company for launching of its satellite, a reciprocal waiver provision extending to the parties' contractors and subcontractors will always be included in the launch agreement since the launch company is required to do so under the Commercial Space Launch Act Amendments of 1988 (hereinafter 1988 Amendments).[36] The 1988 Amendments require the launch company (as a condition of the license it is required to obtain from the Department of Transportation's Office of Commercial Space Transportation in order to launch your client's satellite[37]) to enter into reciprocal waivers with its own contractors and subcontractors, as well as with the satellite owner and the satellite owner's contractors and subcontractors, which are involved in launch activities. The purpose of the waiver is to avoid a multitude of claims among participants in launch activities. Specifically, the Act provides that

> [e]ach license issued or transferred under this Act shall require the licensee or transferee to enter into reciprocal waivers of claims with its contractors, subcontractors, and customers, and the contractors and subcontractors of such customers, involved in launch services, under which each party to each such waiver agrees to be responsible for any property damage or loss it sustains or for any personal injury to, death of, or property damage or loss sustained by its own employees resulting from activities carried out under the license.[38]

---

35. *Id.*, art. 14.3.
36. 49 U.S.C. §2615(a)(1)(C) (1988). The 1988 Amendments amended the Commercial Space Launch Act of 1984, 49 U.S.C. §§2601-2623 (1988). Together, the Commercial Space Launch Act of 1934 and its implementing regulations and the 1988 Amendments establish a licensing and regulatory regime for private commercial launch vehicles. The Department of Transportation's Office of Commercial Space Transportation is charged with enforcing this regime. A launch company must obtain a license from the Office of Commercial Space Transportation before a launch can be conducted from within U.S. territory, 49 U.S.C. §2605(a)(1) (1988). As a condition of the license, launch companies must enter into reciprocal waivers of liability with their satellite customers, 49 U.S.C. §2615(a)(1)(C) (1988). These requirements apply even if a U.S. launch company were to launch, *e.g.*, from the high seas, or from foreign territory, unless an agreement exists with a foreign nation whereby that nation exercises jurisdiction, 49 U.S.C. §2605(a)(2), (3)(A), (B) (1988). It should be noted that a foreign launch company does not become subject to United States law by virtue of launching a United States-owned satellite as long a the launch takes place outside U.S. territory.
37. *Id.*
38. 49 U.S.C. §2615(a)(1)(C) (1988).

In this provision, the "licensee" refers to the launch company and "customer" refers to the satellite owner, your client.

Literally, the provision requires the launch company to enter into reciprocal waivers also with the satellite owner's contractors and subcontractors. This is, of course, not the intent. Launch companies cannot reasonably be required to enter into waiver agreements with entities with which they have no direct contractual relationship. Rather, the purpose is to create a comprehensive waiver scheme in which waivers flow down to contractors and subcontractors at every tier. This is accomplished by having both the launch company *and* the satellite owner include waiver provisions not only in the launch contract, but also in contracts they conclude with their respective contractors,in turn, and by having these contractors require their respective contractors to do the same. Consequently, the satellite owner or launch company must include waivers in contracts they might sign, for example, with a manufacturer of a perigee kick motor (designed to boost the satellite into geostationary transfer orbit after deployment by the launch vehicle in a low-Earth "parking" orbit), or with a payload processor.[39] The satellite owner and its contractors and subcontractors are third party beneficiaries under the contracts between the launch company and its contractors and subcontractors, and vice versa.

In the event the launch takes place from a United States Government launch site (currently no private sites exist, although several are being planned), the 1988 Amendments also require that the launch company obtain property insurance in a certain amount, and that for damage exceeding such amount, waivers be entered into between the Secretary of Transportation on behalf of the U.S. Government, its agencies and contractors and subcontractors involved in launch services, and the launch company and its contractors and subcontractors, as well as the launch company's customer (the satellite owner) and its contractors and subcontractors.[40] Here, also, the waiver requirement cannot be taken literally. As far as the launch company is concerned, the provision imposes an obligation to enter into reciprocal waivers with the Government and to include provisions in contracts with the satellite owner and other contractors whereby these parties waive their rights to claim against the U.S. Government, its agencies, *et cetera*, in exchange for assurances that the Government, its agencies, *et cetera*, will refrain from claiming against them.

THE OFFICE OF COMMERCIAL SPACE TRANSPORTATION'S INTERPRETATION. Since 1991, the Department of Transportation's Office of Commercial Space Transportation has required the launch company and its customer, together, to enter into a tri-partite agreement with the United States, represented by the Department of Transportation, whereby each party 1) waives its right to claim against each other party, 2) assumes responsibility for damage it sustains, 3) agrees to extend the waivers to its contractors and subcontractors and 4) agrees to indemnify each of the other parties from loss or liability arising out of claims made by its contractors or subcontractors. This agreement applies to property damage suffered by the parties and to bodily injury and property damage sustained by their employees, resulting from licensed launch activities.

Accordingly, a License Order issued to one U.S. launch company on February 20, 1991 (allowing the company to provide a series of launches on the same type of rocket) provides that

> [the launch company] and each of its customers shall enter into an agreement with the Department of Transportation on behalf of the United States, in the form attached hereto, providing for each party to waive claims it might have and to assume responsibility for property damage it sustains and for bodily injury and property damage sustained by its own employees, resulting from commercial space launch activities carried out under [this license].[41]

---

39. For example, the Astrotech Space Operations, L.P. standard agreement for Payload Processing Services (1991) [hereinafter cited as the Astrotech Agreement], art. 4.3.1., entitled "Inter-Party Waiver of Liability," provides that

> [i]n carrying out this Agreement, Astrotech and Customer will respectively utilize their property and employees in Payload Processing Activity in close proximity to one another and to others. Furthermore, the parties recognize that all participants in Payload Processing Activity are engaged in the common goal of meaningful exploration, exploitation and uses of space. In furtherance of this goal, the parties hereto agree to a no-fault, no-subrogation, inter-party *waiver of liability* pursuant to which each party agrees not to bring a claim in arbitration or otherwise against or sue the other party or other participants (including the U.S. Government) in Payload Processing Activity, and agrees to absorb the financial and any other consequences for Damage it incurs to its own property and employees as a result of participation in Payload Processing Activity, irrespective of whether such Damage is caused by Astrotech, Customer, or other participants in Payload Processing Activity, and regardless of whether such Damage arises through negligence or otherwise. Thus, the parties, by absorbing the consequences of damage to their property and employees without recourse against each other or other participants in Payload Processing Activity, jointly contribute to the common goal of meaningful exploration of space. [Emphasis added].

Article 4.1.2. of the Astrotech Agreement is entitled "Extension of Inter-Party Waiver," and provides that "[t]he parties agree that this common goal will also be advanced through the extension of the inter-party waiver of liability to *other participants* in Payload Processing Activity. Accordingly, the parties agree to extend the waivers as set forth in Section 4.3.1. above to contractors and subcontractors at every tier . . . ." Emphasis added. The waiver provision in the Astrotech Agreement resembles the waiver found in NASA's standard commercial launch agreement, *see infra* notes 41 and 57 (quoting the NASA standard waiver provision). Astrotech operates a payload processing facility located in Titusville, Florida, adjacent to the Cape Canaveral Air Force Station and the NASA Kennedy Space Center. Astrotech may contract for payload processing services with the satellite owner, the launch company, or even the satellite manufacturer, depending on the arrangements among the latter three.

The standard waiver agreement to which this License Order refers, and which is entitled "Agreement for Waiver of Claims and Assumption of Responsibility" (hereinafter Standard Waiver Agreement), provides, in part:

> 2. Waiver and Release of Claims
>
> (a) Licensee hereby waives and releases claims it may have against Customer and the United States, and against their respective Contractors and Subcontractors, for any Property Damage it sustains and for any Bodily Injury or Property Damage sustained by its own employees, resulting from Licensed Launch Activities, regardless of fault.
>
> (b) Customer hereby waives and releases claims it may have against Licensee and the United States, and against their respective Contractors and Subcontractors, for any Property Damage it sustains and for any Bodily Injury or Property Damage sustained by its own employees, resulting from Licensed Launch Activities, regardless of fault.
>
> (c) The United States hereby waives and releases claims it may have against the Licensee and Customer, and against their respective Contractors and Subcontractors, for any Property Damage it sustains, to the extent that claims it would otherwise have for such damage exceed the amount of insurance or demonstration of financial responsibility required under Section 16(a)(1)(B) of the CSLA, and for any Bodily Injury or Property

---

40. 49 U.S.C. §2615(a)(1)(D) (1988), which provides that

> [t]he Secretary [of Transportation], on behalf of the United States, its agencies involved in launch services, and contractors and subcontractors involved in launch services shall enter into reciprocal waivers of claims with the [launch company], its contractors, subcontractors, and customers, and the contractors and subcontractors of such customers, involved in launch services, under which each party to each such waiver agrees to be responsible for any property damage or loss it sustains for any personal injury to, death of, or property damage or loss sustained by its own employees resulting from activities carried out under the license.

The waiver shall apply only to the extent the United States' claim is not covered by insurance the launch company is required to obtain covering damage to Government property. 49 U.S.C. §2615(a)(1)(B) (1988). *See* Chapter 6.5.2.2. (describing the insurance requirement).

41. *See [Launch Company]*, Office of Commercial Space Transportation, License Order No. LLO 91-119, issued Feb. 20, 1991, Order Regarding Financial Responsibility Requirements for Commercial Space Launch Activities, para. 9(a), entitled "Waiver of Claims" (requiring the launch company to enter into a thri-partite waiver agreement among the launch company, its customers and the Department of Transportation, on behalf of the United States).

Damage sustained by its own employees, resulting from Licensed Launch Activities, regardless of fault.

3. Assumption of Responsibility

(a) Licensee and Customer shall each be responsible for any Property Damage it sustains and for any bodily Injury or Property Damage sustained by its own employees, resulting from Licensed Launch Activities, regardless of fault.

(b) The United States shall be responsible for any Property Damage it sustains, to the extent that claims it would otherwise have for such damage exceed the amount of insurance or demonstration of financial responsibility required under Section 16(a)(1)(B) of the CSLA, or for any Bodily Injury or Property Damage sustained by its own employees, resulting from Licensed Launch Activities, regardless of fault.

4. Extension of Assumption and Waiver

(a) Licensee shall extend the waiver and release of claims and the requirement of the assumption of responsibility as set forth in paragraphs 2(a) and 3(a), respectively, to its Contractors and Subcontractors by requiring them to waive and release all claims they may have against Customer and the United States, and against their respective Contractors and Subcontractors, and to agree to be responsible, for any Property Damage they sustain and for any Bodily Injury or Property Damage sustained by their own employees, resulting from Licensed Launch Activities, regardless of fault.

(b) Customer shall extend the waiver and release of claims and the requirement of the assumption of responsibility as set forth in paragraphs 2(b) and 3(b), respectively, to its Contractors and Subcontractors by requiring them to waive and release all claims they may have against Licensee and the United States, and against *their* respective Contractors and Subcontractors, and to agree to be responsible, for any Property Damage they sustain and for any Bodily Injury or Property Damage sustained by their own employees, resulting from Licensed Launch Activities, regardless of fault.

(c) The United States shall extend the requirement of the waiver and release of claims and the assumption of responsibility as set forth in paragraphs 2(c) and 3(b), respectively, to its Contractors and Subcontractors by requiring them to waive and release all claims they may have against Licensee and Customer, and against their respective Contractors and Subcontractors, and to agree to be responsible, for any Property Damage they sustain and for any Bodily Injury or Property Damage sustained by their own

> employees, resulting from Licensed Launch Activities, regardless of fault.[42]

"Licensee" refers to the launch provider and "Customer" to the satellite owner, your client.

The agreement also provides that the launch company, the customer and the United States government (to the extent funds have been appropriated by the Congress) shall indemnify and hold each other harmless from liability, loss or damage arising out of claims the other party's contractors or subcontractors may have for property damage sustained by them and for bodily injury or property damage sustained by their employees, resulting from licensed launch activities. The indemnification extends to the directors, officers, agents, servants, subsidiaries, employees and assignees of the parties, including agencies of the United States government. Waivers, releases, assumptions of responsibility and agreements to indemnify do not apply when damage or injury results from the willful misconduct of the parties, or of their contractors, subcontractors or agents.

PURPOSE OF WAIVER. The purpose of the comprehensive waiver scheme required by the 1988 Amendments as spelled out in the Senate Report accompanying the legislation, is to ensure that each entity participating in launch activities takes responsibility for damage sustained by it or its personnel. The objective is to prevent extensive litigation and the need for each entity involved in launch services to procure insurance in a limited insurance market to protect against potential claims. Specifically, the objectives are "(1) to limit the total universe of claims that might arise as a result of a launch; and (2) to eliminate the necessity for all these parties to obtain property and casualty insurance to protect against these claims."[43] The report emphasizes that the waivers relate only to bodily injury and property damage and are not intended to prevent or encumber the private parties' other contractual rights and obligations.[44]

SCOPE OF THE WAIVER "FLOW DOWN" REQUIREMENT. The precise scope of the waiver requirement with respect to the relationships between the satellite owner (your client) and *its own* contractors, and these contractors and their respective contractors, involved in launch activities, was clarified by the Office of Commercial Space Transportation's Standard Waiver Agreement, quoted above. While the 1988 Amendments do not specifically call for waivers between the customer and its own contractors and subcontractors, it arguably could be interpreted as requiring such waivers, especially in view of the purpose of the Act. This interpretation, however, has not been embraced by the Office of Commercial Space Transportation. Section 4(b) of the Standard Waiver Agreement

42. Emphasis added. *Id.* Standard Waiver Agreement.
43. Commercial Space Launch Act Amendments of 1988, S. Rep. No. 100-593, 100th Cong., 2d Sess. (Oct. 7, 1988) [hereinafter cited as Senate Report], at 14.
44. *Id.*

requires customers of launch companies to extend waivers to its contractors and subcontractors "by requiring them to waive and release all claims they may have against Licensee and the United States and *their* respective Contractors and Subcontractors . . . ."[45] In this passage, "their" can reasonably be interpreted as referring only to the launch company's and the United States' contractors and subcontractors, and not to the satellite owner's own contractors and subcontractors. Interestingly, the waiver clause contained in the standard agreement between NASA and commercial customers launching satellites on the NASA Space Shuttle, and upon which the 1988 Amendments waiver requirement in part was modeled, as well as the NASA regulations adopted in 1991,[46] explicitly exempts from the waiver requirement the relationships between NASA and its own contractors, and the customer and its own contractors.[47]

In *Appalachian Insurance Company v. McDonnell Douglas Corporation*[48] an extended waiver of liability between and among the satellite owner and its contractors and subcontractors was upheld in a subrogation action by the insurers of the satellite owner. The result was reached despite improper flow-down of the extended waiver requirement.

The suit arose out of a malfunction in 1984 of a payload assist module (PAM) intended to boost Western Union's WESTAR VI satellite from low-Earth orbit into geostationary transfer orbit.[49] The PAM was manufactured for Western Union by McDonnell Douglas and its subcontractors, Morton Thiokol and Hitco. The WESTAR satellite was launched successfully to low-Earth orbit by the NASA Space Shuttle on February 3, 1984. However, due to the failure of the PAM, the satellite did not reach geostationary altitude and was left to drift in a useless, low-Earth orbit until it later was retrieved and returned to Earth by the NASA Space Shuttle in November 1984,[50] pursuant to a contract between NASA and WESTAR's insurers. The WESTAR satellite had been considered a total loss and the insurers, including Appalachian Insurance, had paid Western Union pursuant to the insurance policy.

Western Union, to whose rights Appalachian Insurance was subrogated, had contracted separately with NASA for the launching of WESTAR to low-Earth orbit (about 160 miles) on the NASA Space Shuttle and with McDonnell Douglas for the purchase of the PAM to boost the satellite from low-Earth orbit to geostationary altitude. The NASA/Western Union contract contained reciprocal waivers as between NASA and Western Union, and also required Western Union to extend the waiver to

45. Emphasis added. Standard Waiver Agreement, *supra* note 42, sec. 4(b).
46. 14 C.F.R. §1266.103 (1990).
47. *See infra* note 51 (quoting the waiver provision of the standard NASA commercial Space Shuttle agreement).
48. 262 Cal. Rptr. 716, 214 Cal Appl. 3d. I (1989).
49. The PAM, including a perigee kick motor, boosts the satellite to geostationary transfer orbit, and then separates from the satellite. An apogee kick motor built into the satellite helps place the satellite in a circular orbit.

its contractors and subcontractors (such as McDonnell Douglas, Morton Thiokol and Hitco) whereby such contractors and subcontractors would waive their rights to claim against NASA.

The McDonnell Douglas/Western Union agreement implemented this requirement, but did so improperly. The improper implementation of the waiver occurred when Western Union and McDonnell Douglas incorporated, virtually "wholesale," into their agreement the waiver clause contained in the NASA/Western Union agreement.[51] The language of the NASA/Western Union waiver served to obscure the parties' intent with respect to the McDonnell Douglas/Western Union waiver since the NASA/Western Union waiver specifically exempted "claims between the Customer and its contractors and subcontractors . . . ." In the context of

---

50. After retrieval, the satellite, which had become the property of the insurance underwriters, was refurbished by the manufacturer, Hughes Aircraft Company, and later sold to Asia Satellite Telecommunications Company, Ltd. of Hong Kong and successfully relaunched on a Chinese Long March launch vehicle on April 7, 1990. The WESTAR satellite was part of a dual payload launched by the NASA Space Shuttle, the other satellite being the Indonesian Government's PALAPA B-2, whose McDonnell Douglas PAM also had failed, and which also was retrieved by the NASA Space Shuttle. The Agreement Between the United States of America, Represented by the National Aeronautics and Space Administration, and a Group of Insurance Underwriters for the Palapa B-2 Spacecraft, Retrieval and Relaunch (Nov. 2, 1984) provided for the retrieval of PALAPA B-2. Article V.3.b. of that agreement contains an inter-party waiver, by which the Group of Insurance Underwriters and NASA agree to waive the right to claim against the other with respect to damage they suffer during the retrieval effort. The waiver provides in relevant part that

> b. NASA and the Customer (the parties) will respectively utilize their property and employees in STS Operations in close proximity to one another and to others. Furthermore, the parties recognize that all participants in STS Operations are engaged in the common goal of meaningful exploration, exploitation and uses of outer space. In furtherance of this goal, the parties hereto agree to a no-fault, no-subrogation, inter-party waiver of liability pursuant to which each party agrees not to bring a claim against or sue the other party or other customers and agrees to absorb the financial and any other consequences for Damage it incurs to its own property and employees as a result of participation in STS Operations during Protected STS Operations, irrespective of whether such Damage is caused by NASA, the Customer, or other customers participating in STS Operations, and regardless of whether such Damage arises through negligence or otherwise. Thus, the parties, by absorbing the consequences of damage to their property and employees without recourse against each other or other customers participating in STS Operations . . . jointly contribute to the common goal of meaningful exploration of outer space
>
> c. The parties agree that this common goal will also be advanced through extension of the inter- party waiver of liability to other participants in STS Operations. Accordingly, the parties agree to extend the waiver . . . to contractors and subcontractors at every tier of the parties and other customers . . . .

The term "STS Operations" refers to the operations of the NASA Space Shuttle (Space Transportation System).

the NASA/Western Union waiver, the relationships as between Western Union and its contractor, McDonnell Douglas, and subcontractors, Morton Thiokol and Hitco, therefore, were exempted. All the NASA/Western Union waiver required was that McDonnell Douglas, Thiokol and Hitco be precluded from claiming against NASA.

Appalachian argued that the almost identical language, i.e., exempting "claims between Purchaser and its *other* contractors and subcontractors" (emphasis added), incorporated into the McDonnell Douglas/Western Union contract implied that the waiver of liability did not apply to the relationship as between Western Union and McDonnell Douglas, Hitco or Morton Thiokol, and that its suit therefore was permitted. The court disagreed and sustained the McDonnell Douglas/Western Union waiver. The judge pointed to a slight variance in the language of the incorporated waiver (i.e., "other" was added) and to the fact that McDonnell Douglas,

---

51. The waiver provision in the NASA/Western Union Space Shuttle launch agreement provided as follows:

> NASA and the Customer (the parties) will respectively utilize their property and employees in STS Operations in close proximity to one another and to others. Furthermore, the parties recognize that all participants in STS Operations are engaged in the common goal of meaningful exploration, exploitation and uses of outer space. In furtherance of this goal, the parties hereto agree to a no-fault, no-subrogation, inter-party waiver of liability pursuant to which each party agrees not to bring a claim against or sue the other party or other customers and agrees to absorb the financial and any other consequences for Damage it incurs to its own property and employees as a result of participation in STS Operations during Protected STS Operations, irrespective of whether such damage is caused by NASA, the Customer, or other customers participating in STS Operations, and regardless of whether such damage arises through negligence or otherwise. Thus, the parties, by absorbing the consequences of damage to their property and employees without recourse against each other or other customers participating in STS Operations during Protected STS Operations, jointly contribute to the common goal of meaningful exploration of outer space.
>
> The parties agree that this common goal will also be advanced through extension of the inter- party waiver of liability to other participants in STS Operations. Accordingly, the parties agree to extend the waiver as set forth in Subparagraph 3.b. above to contractors and subcontractors at every tier of the Parties and other customers, as third party beneficiaries, whether or not such contractors or subcontractors causing damage bring property or employees to a United States Government Installation or retain title to or other interest in property provided by them to be used, or otherwise involved, in STS Operations. Specifically, the parties intend to protect these contractors and subcontractors from claims, including "products liability" claims, which might otherwise be pursued by the parties, or contractors or subcontractors of the parties, or other customers or contractors or subcontractors of other customers. Moreover, it is the intent of the parties that each will take all necessary and reasonable steps in accordance with Subparagraph 3.e. below to foreclose claims for Damage by any participant in STS Operations during Protected STS Operations under the same conditions and to the same extent as set forth in Subparagraph 3.b. above *except for claims between the Customer and its contractors and subcontractors and claims between the United States Government and its contractors and subcontractors*. (Emphasis added).

Hitco and Morton Thiokol are not "other contractors" in the context of the McDonnell Douglas/Western Union waiver. It should be noted that the McDonnell Douglas/Western Union contract in addition contained a liability disclaimer which protected McDonnell Douglas, but not Hitco and Morton Thiokol.

Figure 4, below, illustrates the contract relationships described, above. "WU" is Western Union, "MDD" is McDonnell Douglas, "MT" is Morton Thiokol, "H" is Hitco and "AI" is Appalachian Insurance.

Figure 4

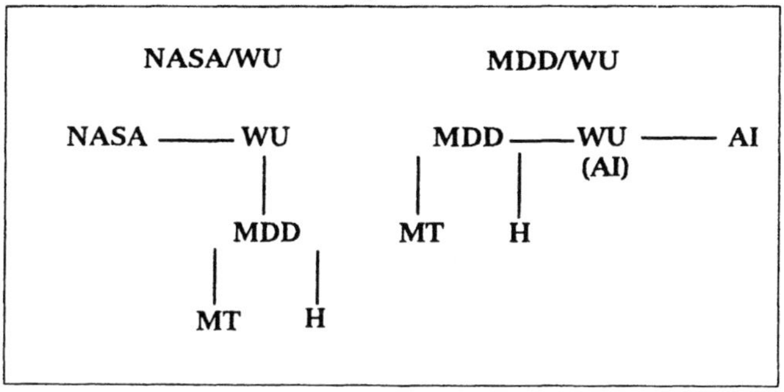

CAN A U.S. LAUNCH COMPANY OFFER LAUNCH RISK GUARANTEES? One might wonder whether the waiver requirement in the 1988 Amendments would preclude a U.S. launch company from offering to assume for a premium the risk of loss or damage to the satellite during launch activities should it wish to do so as a marketing incentive. It appears that such launch risk guarantees are permitted. A significant objective of the 1988 Amendments was to ensure that U.S. launch companies not be placed at a competitive disadvantage *vis à vis* their foreign counterparts. Prohibiting U.S. launch companies from offering incentives to customers provided by their foreign competitors would do just that. Moreover, the assumption of risk on the part of the launch company can be viewed as an insurance deal separate and apart from the liabilities regulated by the waiver requirement. In fact, the waiver should be executed regardless of whether a launch risk guarantee is purchased. If the satellite is lost or damaged, the satellite owner will have recourse under the risk guarantee (compare insurance policy), and not in tort or under the launch contract to the extent the waivers apply. At least one U.S. launch company is offering launch risk guarantees presently, along with a foreign company. In addition, launch price refund/reflight guarantees (see Chapter 7.3.) have been offered by U.S. and foreign companies for quite some time,[52] and do not present an issue with regard to the 1988 Amendments. When launch risk guarantees covering the satellite are offered, they often are offered in conjunction with refund/reflight guarantees (see Chapter 8.5.).

THE MARTIN MARIETTA-INTELSAT CONTRACT. Illustrative of the

kind of waiver provision your client can expect to find in a U.S. launch agreement, consistent with the 1988 Amendments discussed above, is the clause appearing in the Commercial Launch Services Contract Between Martin Marietta Corporation and International Telecommunications Satellite Organization "INTELSAT," dated August 10, 1987 (hereinafter the Martin Marietta-INTELSAT Contract). The fact that the contract was executed before the enactment of the 1988 Amendments has marginal, if any, significance with respect to the waiver provision appearing in this contract. Entitled "Interparty Waiver for Damages Caused to the Person, Goods, or Property of the Parties," Article 17.5. of this Contract provides that

> 17.5.1. Martin Marietta and INTELSAT agree that, with respect to injury to or death of persons involved in, or damage to property used in connection with, Launch Services to be furnished under this Contract, neither Party will make any claim against the other or against the contractors, subcontractors, officers, directors, agents, servants and employees of the other, or any of them, or against any other Titan III launch services buyers, and each party shall bear its own risk of loss with respect to injury to or death of its own employees or damage to its own property howsoever caused.
>
> 17.5.2. INTELSAT and Martin Marietta shall each be responsible for such insurance as they deem necessary to protect their respective property. Any insurance carried in accordance with this paragraph 17.5.2. and any policy taken out in substitution or replacement for any such policy shall provide that the insurers shall waive any rights of subrogation against Martin Marietta, INTELSAT, and the U.S. Government, as the case may be, and their contractors and subcontractors at every tier. Each party shall arrange to have an appropriate certificate issued to the other evidencing any waiver of subrogation required pursuant to this subparagraph 17.5.2.
>
> 17.5.3. INTELSAT shall require its contractors and subcontractors to agree to make no claims against Martin Marietta, the contractors and subcontractors of Martin Marietta, the officers, directors, agents servants and employees of Martin Marietta, or any of them, or against any other Titan III launch services buyers,

52. For example, General Dynamics Agreement, *supra* note 16, art. 1.3., *cf.* art. 8, offers customers the option of a reflight or money-back guarantee, but requires that "the Customer . . . specify, at the time of the Contract execution, whether a refund or a reflight is desired." *See also* Martin Marietta-INTELSAT Contract, *supra* note 17, art. 6, entitled "Reflight/Cash Refund Guarantee" (providing for a new launch or a refund of the launch price should the launch fail).

> with respect to injury to or death of INTELSAT's contractors' or subcontractors' employees involved in, or damage to INTELSAT's contractors' or subcontractors' property used in connection with Launch Services to be furnished under this Contract; further, INTELSAT shall require persons or entities to which INTELSAT has, prior to the completion of the furnishing by Martin Marietta of Launch services for a particular Payload, sold or leased portions of or services on that Payload, to agree not to make claims for damage arising out of the performance of this Contract against Martin Marietta, the contractors and subcontractors of Martin Marietta, the officers, directors, agents, servants and employees of Martin Marietta, or any of them, or against any other Titan III launch service buyers.
>
> 17.5.4. Martin Marietta shall require its contractors, subcontractors and other Titan III launch services buyers to agree to make no claims against INTELSAT, the contractors and subcontractors of INTELSAT, the Signatory members, officers, directors, agents, servants and employees of INTELSAT, or any of them, with respect to injury to or death of such other buyers', or Martin Marietta's contractors' and subcontractors', employees involved in, or damage to such other buyers' or Martin Marietta's contractors' and subcontractors' property used in connection with, Launch Services to be furnished under this Contract.
>
> 17.5.5. Nothing in subparagraphs 17.5.3. and 17.5.4. shall be construed as limiting the rights of Martin Marietta regarding its own contractors and subcontractors or the rights of INTELSAT regarding its own contractors and subcontractors.[53]

With respect to the requirement not to claim against the United States Government, Article 17.3. of the Martin Marietta-INTELSAT Contract, entitled "Release of U.S. Government," provides that

> 17.3. INTELSAT and Martin Marietta hereby waive any cause of action in tort against the U.S. Government, its agents, employees, contractors and subcontractors, to the extent required by the U.S. Government, and agree to furnish appropriate waivers and release as may later be required to implement this paragraph 17.3. in connection with the use of U.S. Government launch facilities, equipment or required launch support services under this Contract and hereby indemnify and hold harmless the U.S. Government from such claims . . . . Except for said indemnity, each Party shall incorporate a similar provision containing the substance of this paragraph 17.3. into contracts with all customers, associated contractors, and subcontractors who participate in activities at [Cape Canaveral Air Force Station or Kennedy Space Center.] [54]

In sum, the waiver scheme set forth, above, includes a cross waiver between Martin Marietta and INTELSAT (subparagraph 17.5.1.); refers the parties to insurance to the extent they desire to protect their respective property, including the INTELSAT satellite, but precludes subrogation suits by the insurers (subparagraph 17.5.2.); requires both INTELSAT and Martin Marietta to "flow down" the waiver requirement to their respective

---

53. Martin Marietta-INTELSAT Contract, *supra* note 17, art. 17.5. A similar provision appears in the Agreement Between the President of India, Represented by the Secretary to the Government of India, Department of Space, and McDonnell Douglas Corporation of the United States of America for Delta 4925 Launch and Associated Services to be Furnished for Spacecraft Insat 1D (Jul. 30, 1987) [hereinafter cited as McDonnell Douglas-India Contract]. Article 4, provides that

> [e]ach Party, vis-a-vis the other, shall bear all damages for bodily harm and all consequences of such bodily harm, whether direct or indirect, which the employees of such Party and its Associates may sustain, that is caused in connection with or by the performance of this Agreement. Each party irrevocably agrees to a no-fault, no-subrogation, inter-party waiver of liability, and waives the right to make any claim or to initiate any judicial proceedings for or with respect to such bodily harm and all consequences of such bodily harm against the other Party or that other Party's Associates for any reason whatsoever. Each party, vis-a-vis the other, agrees to absorb the financial and any other consequences of such bodily harm without recourse against the other Party.
>
> In the event that one or more Associates of a Party shall proceed against the other Party or that Party's Associates as a result of such bodily harm and all consequences of such bodily harm, the first Party shall indemnify, hold harmless, dispose of any claim and defend (when not contrary to the governing rules of procedure) the other Party and its Associates, from any loss, damage, liability or expenses, including attorney's fees, on account of such bodily harm and all consequences of such bodily harm and shall pay all expenses to satisfy all judgments which may be incurred by or rendered against the said indemnities.
>
> Each Party, vis-a-vis the other, shall bear all damage to its own property and that of its Associates and all consequences of such damage, whether direct or indirect, which it and its Associates may sustain, that is caused in connection with or by the performance of this Agreement. Each Party irrevocably agrees to a no-fault, no-subrogation, inter-party waiver of liability, and waives the right to make any claim or to initiate any judicial proceedings for or with respect to such damage against the other Party or that Party's Associates for any reason whatsoever. Each Party, vis-a-vis the other agrees to absorb the financial and any other consequences for damage to its property or to that of its Associates without recourse against the other Party.
>
> In the event that one or more Associates of a Party shall proceed against the other Party or that Party's Associates as a result of such damage to property, the first Party shall indemnify, hold harmless, dispose of any claim and defend (when not contrary to the governing rules of procedure) the other Party and its Associates, from any loss, damage, liability or expenses, including attorney's fees, on account of such damage, and shall pay all expenses and satisfy all judgments which may be incurred by or rendered against the said indemnities.

This waiver provision in the McDonnell Douglas-India Contract resembles that appearing in the Arianespace Agreement, *See supra* note 33, and accompanying text (citing and quoting that provision).

contractors and subcontractors at every tier, requiring these parties not to claim against the other party, its contractors, subcontractors or personnel (subparagraphs 17.5.3. and 17.5.4.), although the flow-down requirement shall not affect the relationships as between each party and its *own* contractors and subcontractors (subparagraph 17.5.5.); and, finally, both INTELSAT and Martin Marietta agree not to claim against the U.S. Government, to require contractors and subcontractors not to claim against the U.S. Government, and to hold harmless the U.S. Government from claims or suits brought against it.

The Martin Marietta-INTELSAT Contract is the subject of litigation,[55] which arose out of a failure by Martin Marietta's Titan III launch vehicle to deliver properly in orbit an INTELSAT VI satellite on March 14, 1990.[56] Due to a wiring problem, the satellite and its attached transfer orbit stage failed to separate from the Titan III second stage, as intended. Consequently, the satellite, the transfer orbit stage (intended to boost the satellite from low-Earth orbit to geostationary altitude) and the Titan III second stage were left in a low-Earth orbit. To avoid reentry into the atmosphere and disintegration of the satellite, INTELSAT subsequently executed a separation maneuver, releasing the satellite from the transfer orbit stage, which remained attached to the Titan III second stage. The Titan III second stage and the transfer orbit stage subsequently reentered the atmosphere and disintegrated. Deprived of its transfer orbit stage, however, the INTELSAT VI satellite, destined for the geostationary orbit, was left to drift in a useless low-Earth orbit without a means to boost it to the higher orbit for which it was intended. An agreement has now been reached between INTELSAT and NASA to "rescue" the satellite. During its April 1992 maiden flight, the Space Shuttle Endeavour is scheduled to rendezvous with the satellite in order for astronauts tol attach a new transfer stage to the satellite.

INTELSAT claimed that the launch failure was due to Martin Marietta's negligence and gross negligence, and that the launch company was guilty of negligent representation and breach of contract.[57] INTELSAT asked for compensatory damages in the amount of "at least $400 million"[58] intended

54. Martin Marietta-INTELSAT Contract, *supra* note 17, art. 17.3.

55. *Martin Marietta Corporation v. INTELSAT,* ON APPEAL, Court of Appeals (Fourth Circuit). The suit was brought by Martin Marietta in the U.S. District Court, District of Maryland, on July 6, 1990. Martin Marietta initiated the litigation with a Complaint for Declaratory Judgment with respect to the validity and enforceability of the waiver provision in the Martin Marietta-INTELSAT Contract, *supra* note 17.

56. *See* INTELSAT Answer and Counterclaim, Aug. 31, 1990, Exhibit C, entitled "Corrective Action Problem Summary" Apr. 17, 1990 (providing an analysis of the incident), *Martin Marietta V. INTELSAT, supra* note 55.

57. INTELSAT Answer and Counterclaim, Aug. 31, 1990, *Martin Marietta v. INELSAT,* supra note 55.

58. *Id.,* at 42.

to cover the value of the satellite, the launch price and lost revenues. Martin Marietta moved to dismiss INTELSAT's claims, arguing that 1) the Martin Marietta-INTELSAT Contract barred recovery, and 2) the 1988 Amendments preempted and prohibited INTELSAT's suit.[59] With regard to the value of the satellite, Martin Marietta invoked subparagraph 17.5.1. of the Martin Marietta-INTELSAT Contract, quoted above, pursuant to which the parties waived the right to claim against each other for property damage "howsoever caused."[60] With regard to the launch price, Martin Marietta referred to an exclusive remedy provision in the Martin Marietta-INTELSAT Contract according to which INTELSAT agreed that a "Replacement Launch" represented INTELSAT's "sole and exclusive remed[y]" and, further, to the fact that INTELSAT had the option of purchasing a launch price cash refund guarantee, which it chose not to exercise.[61] (See Chapter 7.3.) Martin Marietta argued that INTELSAT's claim for lost profits was precluded under subparagraph 17.6. of the Martin Marietta-INTELSAT Contract, which precluded claims for lost profits and other consequential damages (see quote at page 287-289.[62] INTELSAT later conceded that the waiver provision in subparagraph 17.5.1. would prevail, despite negligence, but maintained that the provision was not sustainable in the face of gross negligence.[63] Furthermore, INTELSAT conceded that subparagraph 17.6. precludes recovery for lost revenues.[64]

On April 30, 1991, Judge Marvin J. Garbis of the United States District Court for the District of Maryland granted Martin Marietta's motion to dismiss INTELSAT's claim as to the counts of negligence, gross negligence and negligent misrepresentation, and dismissed the motion with respect to breach of contract.[65] Interestingly, the Judge concluded that the waiver in subparagraph 17.5.1. would prevail, despite gross negligence on the part of Martin Marietta. He stated that while public policy reasons normally prohibit enforcement of contractual waivers of liability in cases involving gross negligence, "in the special context of this case public policy strongly favors enforcement of waivers of all tort claims including those for gross negligence."[66] The only remaining issue, then, concerned the recovery for the price of launch services and, in that connection, Martin Marietta's duties under the contract. The question was whether Martin Marietta's performance fell below an acceptable level, thus, depriving it of its protection under the exculpatory provisions of the contract.

On November 19, 1991, the Judge also disposed of the contract issue, granting Martin Marietta's motion to dismiss with regard to this count, as

59. Martin Marietta Motion to Dismiss Counterclaim, Sep. 19, 1990.
60. *Id.*, at 19.
61. *Id.*, at 18
62. *Id.*, at 19-20.
63. *Martin Marietta Corporation v. INTELSAT*, Memorandum and Order, Apr. 30, 1991, at 19, 763 F. Supp. 1327 (D. Md. May 13, 1991).
64. *Id.*, at 9.
65. *Id.*

well. The Judge found that the exclusive remedy provision in Article 6 of the Martin Marietta-INTELSAT Contract "clearly and unambiguously" bars recovery for the value of launch services. The Judge noted that, INTELSAT was presented with two alternative remedies: 1) it could purchase a reflight/cash refund guarantee before the launch, an option INTELSAT chose not to exercise; or 2) it could purchase a replacement launch in the event of a launch failure. INTELSAT also did not purchase a replacement launch. These were INTELSAT's sole remedies under the contract with respect to the value of the launch services, and the Judge concluded that the contractual limitation of remedies was enforceable

---

66. *Id.*, at 20. It is interesting to note that the Master Contract Between The Space Commerce Corporation and Energetics Satellite Corporation for Spacecraft Launching and Associated Services (not dated) [hereinafter cited as Soviet Launch Agreement], concerning launching of satellites of Energetics Satellite Corporation of Englewood, Colorado, on Soviet launch vehicles from Baikonur Cosmodrome, Kazakh, USSR, specifically makes Space Commerce Corporation of Houston, Texas (which has been engaged by the Soviets to market their launch services in the United States) responsible for its own negligent acts, despite a traditional waiver provision also included in the contract. Article 10.1. of the Soviet Launch Agreement provides that Space Commerce Corporation (SCC) "will be responsible for its negligent acts which cause damage to, or loss of, a spacecraft or other property which has been delivered by User or its contractors into the custody of SCC pursuant to this contract." In addition, a traditional waiver clause in art. 11.3. provides that

> SCC and User agree that, with respect to injury to or death of persons involved in, or damage to property used in connection with, the launch services to be furnished under this contract, neither party will make any claim against the other or against the contractors, subcontractors, officers, directors, agents, servants and employees of the other, or any of them, and each party shall bear its own risk of loss with respect to injury to or death of its own employees or damage to its own property howsoever caused.
>
> SCC and User shall each be responsible for such insurance as they deem necessary to protect their respective property. Any insurance carried in accordance with this subparagraph and any policy taken out in substitution or replacement for any such policy shall prove that the insurer shall waive any rights of subrogation against SCC or User as the case may be, and their contractors and subcontractors at every tier. Each party shall arrange to have an appropriate certificate issued to the other evidencing any waiver of subrogation required pursuant to this subparagraph.
>
> User shall require its contractors and subcontractors to agree to make no claims against SCC . . . .
>
> SCC shall require its contractors and subcontractors and other launch services' buyers to agree not to claim against user . . . .

This provision is remarkably similar to Article 17.5. of the Martin Marietta-INTELSAT Contract, *supra* note 17, and which is quoted in the text. The reference to SCC's responsibility for its own negligence probably was included because the parties realized that the waiver would prevail despite SCC's negligence, and the customer may have wanted additional protection. Energetics Satellite Corporation's satellites have not yet been launched. A policy currently is in effect prohibiting the launching of U.S. satellites on Soviet launch vehicles.

under Maryland law, which applied to the contract. Moreover, the Judge refuted INTELSAT's argument that Martin Marietta's performance under the contract was at a level low enough to constitute a "fundamental breach" of the contract, and that Martin Marietta, therefore, no longer was entitled to the protection of the exclusive remedy provision of the rescinded contract. He ruled that a fundamental breach was not present in this case since "[t]here is absolutely nothing to indicate that Martin Marietta did not attempt to provide [a successful launch] or otherwise fundamentally breached the contract . . . ."[67]

NASA COMMERCIAL LAUNCH CONTRACTS. Although NASA, as a launch service provider, is not subject to the provisions of the 1988 Amendment, it requires that its commercial customers launching satellites on the Space Shuttle enter into cross waivers of liability. In fact, both the Arianespace waiver and the 1988 Amendments were modeled in part upon the waiver provision found in the standard NASA commercial launch agreement drafted after the Space Shuttle became operational in 1982. Regulations applicable to NASA and its commercial Space Shuttle customers stipulate that

> [e]ach Party agrees to a cross waiver of liability pursuant to which each Party waives all claims against any of the entities or persons listed in paragraphs (c)(1)(i) through (c)(1)(iv) of this section based on damage arising out of Protected Space Operations. This cross-waiver shall apply only if the person, entity, or property causing the damage is involved in Protected Space Operations and the person, property, or entity damaged is damaged by virtue of its involvement in Protected Space Operations. The cross-waiver shall apply to any claims for damage, whatever the legal basis for such claims, including but not limited to delict and tort (including negligence of every degree and kind) and contract, against:
>
> [(c)(1)](i) Another Party;
>
> [(c)(1)](ii) A related entity of another Party;
>
> [(c)(1)](iii) Any Party who has signed a NASA agreement that includes a Shuttle flight
>
> [(c)(1)](iv) The employees of any of the entities identified in paragraphs (c)(1)(i) through (c)(1)(iii) of this section.
>
> In addition, each Party shall extend the cross waiver of liability . . . to its own related entities by requiring them, by contract or otherwise, to agree to waive all claims against the entities or persons identified in paragraphs (c)(1)(i) through (c)(1)(iv) of this section.
>
> For avoidance of doubt, this cross-waiver includes a cross-waiver

67. *Martin Marietta v. INTELSAT, supra* note 55, Memorandum and Order, Nov. 19, 1991.

of liability arising from the Convention on International Liability for Damage Caused by Space Objects . . . where the person, entity or property causing the damage is involved in Protected Space Operations and the person, entity, or property damaged is damaged by virtue of its involvement in Protected Space Operations.

Notwithstanding the other provisions of this section, this cross-waiver of liability shall not be applicable to:

(i) Claims between a Party and its own related entity or between its own related entities;

(ii) Claims made by a natural person, his/her estate, survivors, or subrogees for injury or death of such natural person;

(iii) Claims for damage caused by willful misconduct;

(iv) Intellectual property claims;

(v) Contract claims between the Parties based on the express provisions of this Agreement;

(vi) Claims for damage based on the failure of the Parties or their related entities to flow down the cross-waiver . . . .

Related Entity means:

(i) A contractor or a subcontractor of a Party at any tier;

(ii) A user or customer of a Party at any tier; or

(iii) A contractor or subcontractor of a user or customer of a Party at any tier. Contractors and Subcontractors include suppliers of any kind.

Damage means:

(i) Bodily injury to, or other impairment of health of, or death of, any person;

(ii) Damage to, loss of, or loss of use of any property;

(iii) Loss of revenue or profits; or

(iv) Other direct, indirect, or consequential damage;

Payload means any property to be flown on or used on or in the Shuttle; and

Protected Space Operations means all Space Shuttle and payload activities on Earth, in outer space, or in transit between Earth and Outer Space done in implementation of an agreement for Shuttle Launch Services. Protected Space Operations begins at the signature of the agreement and ends when all activities done in implementation of the agreement are completed. It includes, but is not limited to:

(i) Research, design, development, test, manufacture, assembly, integration, operation, or use of: the Space Shuttle, transfer vehicles, payloads, related support equipment, and facilities and services;

(ii) All activities related to ground support, test, training, simulation, or guidance and control equipment and related facilities and services. Protected Space Operations excludes activities on Earth which are conducted on return from space to develop further a payload's product or process for use other than for Shuttle-related activities in implementation of the agreement.[68]

The waiver requirement under the NASA Regulations is somewhat broader than that pursuant to the 1988 Amendements. "Protected Space Operations" encompass more activities and have a longer time duration than "launch activities" (1988 Amendments). Moreover, "Damage" under the NASA Regulatiuons includes loss of revenues. The 1988 Amendments are concerned only with property damage, bodily injury and death.

From the view-point of a commercial satellite operator, the NASA Shuttle launch agreement is not all that significant since NASA is prohibited from launching commercial payloads unless they require the unique attributes of the Shuttle, which commercial satellites normally do not.[69] Another exemption is for satellites or payloads whose launching on the Shuttle is required in the U.S. national security or foreign policy interests,[70] a test a commercial satellite usually will not meet. However, the retrieval of a commercial satellite would, of course, be considered "Shuttle unique," and the above quoted waiver would apply to such a mission.

DISCLAIMER OF WARRANTIES. In a addition to waiver provisions, which essentially exculpate the launch company from liability with respect to damage to the satellite, launch contracts sometimes contain warranty disclaimers with respect to the quality and performance of the launch vehicle, itself. Article 17.6. of the Martin Marietta-INTELSAT Contract provides an example of this type of disclaimer:

---

68. 14 C.F.R. §1266.103 (1990). *See National Aeronautics and Space Administration, Cross-Waiver of Liability,* Notice of Proposed Rulemaking, 55 Fed. Reg. 13912 (1990) (concerning the history of the regulations). The cross waivers shall be broadly construed. 14 C.F.R. §1266.103(a) (1990). *See also* note 51, *supra* (quoting the waiver provision in NASA's standard commercial launch agreement) and 48 C.F.R. §1852.228-72 (1990).

69. National Aeronautics and Space Administration Authorization Act, Fiscal Year 1991, P.L. 101-611 §112 (1990). *See supra* note 1 (providing background for this legislation).

70. *Id.*

> MARTIN MARIETTA HAS NOT MADE NOR DOES MAKE ANY REPRESENTATION OR WARRANTY, WHETHER WRITTEN OR ORAL, EXPRESSED OR IMPLIED, INCLUDING, BUT NOT LIMITED TO ANY WARRANTY OF DESIGN, OPERATION, CONDITION, QUALITY, SUITABILITY OR MERCHANTABILITY OR FITNESS FOR USE OR FOR A PARTICULAR PURPOSE, ABSENCE OF LATENT OR OTHER DEFECTS WHETHER OR NOT DISCOVERABLE, OR EXCEPT AS OTHERWISE PROVIDED IN ARTICLE 6, REFLIGHT/CASH REFUND GUARANTEE IF PURCHASED BY INTELSAT, ANY OTHER WARRANTY WHATSOEVER, EXPRESS OR IMPLIED, WITH RESPECT TO THE TITAN III OR ASSOCIATED EQUIPMENT.[71]

LIMITATION OF LIABILITY. Recognizing the fact that it conceivably may be held liable to the satellite customer, despite waivers and disclaimers, a launch company can be expected to include in the launch agreement a clause limiting further its liability. Such a limitation clause contemplates claims not within the scope of the waiver or disclaimer: For example, those claims relating to negligent handling of proprietary data, third party claims for patent infringement, as well as consequential and incidental damages, including loss of revenues or profits. In most jurisdictions, a limitation clause will not be upheld to protect a party against its own willful misconduct. Set forth, below, is an example of a limitation clause appearing in the Martin Marietta-INTELSAT Contract, which provides that

> Martin Marictta's liability to INTELSAT and to persons claiming by or through INTELSAT, whether or not arising under contract, or in negligence, strict liability, or under any other theory of tort or liability, shall not include any loss of use or loss of profit or revenue or any other indirect, special, incidental or consequential damages. In no event shall Martin Marietta's liability to INTELSAT for any claim arising out of a particular Launch Services exceed the price for that Titan III Launch Services to be paid by INTELSAT as provided in ARTICLE 7, PRICES FOR LAUNCH SERVICES, of this Contract, without any Economic Price Adjustments, provided however that nothing in this paragraph shall affect any right of INTELSAT to a Replacement Launch, a Reflight or a Cash Refund under ARTICLE 6, if purchased by INTELSAT, or obligation by Martin Marietta to INTELSAT under subparagraph 17.2.1.[72]

This provision limits Martin Marietta's liability, whether in tort or under the contract, to the price of launch services but does not in itself constitute a basis for a claim for the launch price. Claims for compensation for the loss of the satellite, as well as for lost revenues and profits, are

---

71. Martin Marietta-INTELSAT Contract, *supra* note 17, art. 17.6.
72. *Id.*

precluded under this provision.

A limitation clause is found in the Arianespace Agreement, as well, limiting the liabilities of Arianespace and the customer in the following fashion:

> Due to the special character of Services, the Parties have agreed that any liability of ARIANESPACE or of Customer arising from the defective, late or non-performance of ARIANESPACE's Services and Customer's technical obligations under this Agreement shall, in all circumstances, including termination of this Agreement, be strictly limited to the liability expressly provided for in this Agreement, to the exclusion of any other remedies or claims for damages and indemnities.[73]

6.5. Risk of Liability for Damage Caused by Your Client's Satellite or Personnel

The implementation of your client's satellite project also involves risk of liability. Your client's satellite or personnel may cause damage and your client may become liable to third parties, as well as to parties with which your client has a direct or indirect contractual relationship, such as the satellite manufacturer, the launch company and the satellite transponder owners and other service takers, and their respective contractors and subcontractors.

The risk of liability can be managed. It can be reduced, for example, by prudent selection of satellite technology, manufacturer and launch company. To some extent, risk can be allocated contractually to the satellite manufacturer (Chapter 6.5.1.), the launch company (Chapter 6.5.2.) and your client's customers (Chapter 6.5.3.). Even national governments under certain circumstances agree to bear certain risks. Insurance provides an option in cases where the risk cannot be reduced or transferred (Chapter 8.). A final solution is self-insurance, i.e., your client assumes the risk.

6.5.1. Dealing With the Manufacturer

Damage for which your client potentially could be held liable may occur during satellite manufacturing, testing and transportation to the launch site, or otherwise during the manufacturer's performance. Such damage may be caused to third parties, as well as to the manufacturer and its contractors, subcontractors and personnel and their property. The satellite owner, your client, should seek to include, and is likely to obtain, in the satellite purchase contract an indemnification and hold harmless clause protecting it from claims by these parties. Such a clause serves to transfer the risk of liability to the manufacturer, a reasonable allocation of

---

73. Arianespace Agreement, *supra* note 33, art. 14.1.1.

risk considering the fact that the satellite is in the manufacturer's care. It is important that the indemnification and hold harmless provision embrace also your client's contractors and subcontractors. A representative clause contained in one satellite purchase agreement provides that

> [t]he [manufacturer] shall indemnify and hold [customer] . . . their officers, agents, servants, employees, subsidiaries, successors and assigns, or any of them, harmless from any and all loss, damage, liability or expense, resulting from damage to all property and injuries, including death, to all persons (natural or juridical), arising from any occurrence caused by an act or omission of the [manufacturer], its Subcontractors, or any of them, and [manufacturer] shall at its sole expense defend any claims, actions, suits and proceedings, whether in law or equity, brought against [customer] . . . their officers, agents, servants, employees, subsidiaries, successors and assigns, or any of them, on account thereof, and shall pay all expenses, including attorney's fees, and satisfy all judgments as may be incurred by or rendered against them, or any of them, in connection therewith, provided [manufacturer] is given prompt notice of any such claim, action suit or proceeding and provided [manufacturer] is given, at [manufacturer's] written request and sole expense such assistance and information as may be reasonably provided by [customer].

As a hypothetical third party liability problem, consider the following situation: The manufacturer contracts with a ground transportation company to transport the satellite from the manufacturer's premises to the launch site. A representative of the satellite owner, your client, is present during loading of the satellite onto a flatbed truck. Inadvertently, a pneumatic wrench required for final assembly of the satellite and mating with the launch vehicle is left on the roof of the truck and, as the truck accelerates to enter the highway, the wrench flies off the roof and hits John Doe's windshield. As a result, John Doe is unable to see, drives off the road, wrecks his car and suffers severe bodily injuries. John Doe is a third party in this incident. Assume that John Doe decides to sue the satellite manufacturer and your client. If the satellite purchase contract contains an indemnification clause in favor of your client, your client is protected.

6.5.2. Dealing With the Launch Company

Damage may occur during launch activities to third parties, to the launch company and its contractors, subcontractors and their personnel, and to the launch site operator. Provisions in launch contracts concerning risk-sharing among some of these parties have become fairly standardized. For example, major launch companies in business today agree to procure third party liability insurance, naming the satellite owner as an additional insured under the policy. Additionally, these companies often can refer to government indemnification for claims exceeding the insured amount. See Chapter 6.5.2.1. Moreover, as discussed in Chapter 6.4.2., these companies also include in their launch contracts reciprocal, or cross, waiver provisions whereby the satellite owner and the launch company waive their rights to claim against each other and each other's contractors and subcontractors. See Chapter 6.5.2.2.

In other words, your client generally will be protected against third party liability through insurance purchased by the launch company and indemnification provided by the launch company's government. Moreover, your client cannot be held liable in tort or pursuant to the launch contract, for damage sustained by other participants in launch activities. These participants include the launch company and its contractors and subcontractors and also your client's contractors and subcontractors to the extent your client has executed waivers with the latter two groups. Waver provisions viewed from the perspective of *damage* to your client, are dealt with in Chapter 6.4.2., above. The risk allocation scheme just outlined applies to U.S. launch contracts as a matter of law.

6.5.2.1. Damage to Third Parties

Consider the following situation: The launch vehicle with your client's satellite on board explodes shortly after lift-off and debris from the explosion is scattered across the territories of your client's country and that of a foreign country, injuring people and damaging property on the ground. Will your client have to pay? Probably not. If your client has contracted with one of the major commercial launch companies in business today, the launch company probably will have purchased third party liability insurance protecting it, as well as your client. Consequently, the insurers will pay. In the event third party claims exceed the insured amount, the national government authorizing or sponsoring the launch company may provide indemnification. (See Chapter 2.8. concerning international liability issues).

THE ARIANESPACE AGREEMENT. If your client buys launch services from Arianespace, that company will procure third party liability insurance, which also will protect your client against third party claims, in the amount of 400 million French Francs (about $65 million). Article 15 of the Arianespace Agreement provides that

> ARIANESPACE shall, for the Launch, take out an occurrence basis type insurance policy at Customer's cost to protect itself and Customer against liability for property and bodily harm which Third Parties may sustain and which are caused by the Combined Space Vehicle or part thereof. In said insurance policy the natural and corporate bodies hereafter shall be named as assured:
>
> 1. The Government of France,
>
> 2. The Centre National d'Etude Spatiale "C.N.E.S." and any state of launch as per Convention of March 29, 1972 related to the international liability for damage caused by spacecraft.

3. The auxiliaries of any kind, whom ARIANESPACE and/or the C.N.E.S. would call for in view of the preparation and execution of the launching operations,

4. The European Space Agency "E.S.A." but only in its capacity as owner of certain facility and/or outfits located in the Centre Spatial Guyanais in Kourou and made available to ARIANESPACE and/or to the C.N.E.S. for the purpose of the preparation and the execution of the launches,

5. The firms, who have participated in the design and/or in the execution and/or who have provided the components of the Launch Vehicle, of its support equipment including propellants and other products either liquid or gaseous necessary for the functioning of the said Launch Vehicle, their contractors subcontractors and suppliers,

6. Customer and Third Party Customer(s) of ARIANESPACE on whose behalf ARIANESPACE executes the launch services as well as their co-contractors and sub-contractors,

7. When they act in the scope of their activities, the Officers and Directors, the legal representatives, the Managing Director, the employees agents as well as the interim staff employed by ARIANESPACE or by the ASSURED mentioned in hereabove Paragraphs from a.1 to a.6 (included).

Said insurance coverage shall come into effect as of the day of the Launch, and shall be maintained for thirty-six (36) months or for so long as all or part of the Combined Space Vehicle remains in orbit, whichever period is shorter.

The insurance policy shall be taken out in the amount of 400,000,000 French Francs . . . .[74]

THE SOVIET COMMERCIAL LAUNCH AGREEMENT. The Master Contract Between the Space Commerce Corporation and Energetics Satellite Corporation for Spacecraft Launching and Associated Services (Soviet Launch Agreement), providing for the launching of Energetics Satellite Corporation's satellites from Baikonur Cosmodrome in Kazakh, USSR, also includes provisions on third party liability insurance and indemnification. It provides that Space Commerce Corporation (SCC) of Houston Texas, which acts as a marketing agent for the Soviet Government, shall obtain third party liability insurance, name the satellite company as an additional insured, and indemnify the satellite company in the event third party claims exceed the insured amount. Article 12 of the agreement provides that

74. Arianespace Agreement, *supra* note 33, art. 15.

> SCC shall procure and maintain third party liability insurance to protect SCC and User against injury, death and property damage caused to third parties, arising out of or resulting from services provided under this contract at STR before, during and/or resulting from the spacecraft while situated at STR before, during and/ or after launch, including but not limited to work performed on or relating to the spacecraft under this contract. Such insurance shall be in an amount as may be required by the U.S. government as a condition of the export license for the spacecraft, or if a non-U.S. spacecraft is launched, then in the amount required by GLAVKOSMOS, provided, however, that if such amount is not commercially available at a reasonable premium in light of prevailing standards in the commercial space launch industry, as determined in good faith by SCC, using its reasonable judgment, such insurance shall be in any lesser amount commercially available at a reasonable premium and acceptable to the government agency referred to in this sentence. Insurance provided pursuant to this subparagraph shall commence upon the arrival of the satellite and User's personnel incident to the satellite launch campaign at STR and shall continue for a term of 90 days after the actual date of launch. Further, SCC shall indemnify and hold User harmless from any and all loss, damage, liability or expense resulting from property damage and bodily harm caused to third parties arising out of the launch or other service provided by SCC to the extent not covered by said insurance, which damage or harm arises out of or in connection with (i) services furnished by SCC under this contract and/or (ii) any satellite, provided that the occurrence giving rise to such damage or harm is during the period commencing on the day of the launch and ending 36 months after the actual date of launch. SCC shall at its sole expense defend any claims . . .
>
> The insurance obtained by SCC pursuant to this article shall name User as an additional insured and shall contain waiver of subrogation rights in favor of User.[75]

"STR" refers to the SCC Test Range, which will be at Baikonur Cosmodrome in Kazakh, USSR. It is interesting to note that under this contract the Soviet Government assumes no risk of liability with respect to the satellite owner. Only Space Commerce Corporation assumes this risk. If presented with an offer of indemnification by a marketing agent without substantial funds, your client may well wonder if the protection is adequate. Currently, launchings of U.S. satellites on Soviet launch vehicles are prohibited as a matter of U.S. government policy, however (see Chapter 7.1.).

---

75. Soviet Launch Agreement, *supra* note 66, art. 12.11.2.

UNITED STATES LAW. If your client contracts with a private U.S. company[76] for launch services, the contract is subject to the risk-sharing arrangements required by the 1988 Amendments.[77] As a condition of the license to launch a vehicle with your client's satellite on board, the launch company must obtain third party liability insurance, or demonstrate financial responsibility sufficient to compensate claims by third parties "for death, bodily injury, or loss of or damage to property resulting from activities carried out under the license in connection with any particular launch."[78] The launch company must name your client and its contractors and subcontractors, as well as the United States Government, as additional insureds.[79] Consequently, your client is protected under this insurance policy for third party damage occurring during launch activities.

The amount of insurance required shall be sufficient to cover the "maximum probable loss" resulting from the launch activities,[80] and is determined by the Secretary of Transportation (the Office of Commercial Space Transportation under delegated authority)[81] on a case-by-case basis as part of the licensing process. The insurance requirement shall not exceed $500 million, or the maximum liability insurance available in the world

---

76. With regard to commercial launches on NASA's Space Shuttle, the National Aeronautics and Space Act of 1958, as amended (NASAct), Section 308, 42 U.S.C. §308 (1988), provides that the amount of insurance shall be agreed upon by NASA and the customer "in view of the insurance available in the world market at a reasonable premium, but is not to exceed $500 million for a single satellite payload." This section was added to the NASAct by the National Aeronautics and Space Administration Authorization Act, Fiscal Year 1980, P.L. 96-48 §6(b), 93 Stat. 348 (1979). Third party claims paid by the customer in excess of the insured amount will be indemnified by the U.S. Government. Section 308(b) of the NASAct, 42 U.S.C. §308(b) (1988), provides that

> [u]nder such regulations and in conformity with this section as the Administrator shall prescribe taking into account the availability, cost and terms of liability insurance, any agreement between the Administration and a user of a space vehicle may provide that the United States will indemnify the user against claims (including reasonable expenses of litigation or settlement) by third parties for death, bodily injury, or loss of or damage to property, resulting from activities carried on in connection with the launch, operations or recovery of the space vehicle, but only to the extent that such claims are not compensated by liability insurance of the user: *Provided*, that such indemnification may be limited to claims resulting from other than the actual negligence or willful misconduct of the user.

Section 308(a) of the NASAct, 42 U.S.C. §308(a) (1988), allows NASA to provide liability insurance to Shuttle users, and provides in part that

> [t]he Administration is authorized on such terms and to the extent it may deem appropriate to provide liability insurance for any user of a space vehicle to compensate for all or a portion of claims by third parties for death, bodily injury, or loss of or damage to property resulting from activities carried on in connection with the launch, operations or recovery of the space vehicle.

77. 49 U.S.C. §2615 (1988). *See supra* note 36 (discussing the regulatory regime applicable to private commercial launch vehicles).

market at reasonable cost, if that is less.[82] So far, insurance requirements have been set at $215 million for Martin Marietta's Titan launches, at $164 million for McDonnell Douglas' Delta launches, and at $10 million for sub-orbital launches. See Chapter 8.7. for further discussion of third party liability insurance.

Up to a certain amount, the United States Government will indemnify the launch company and your client against claims exceeding the insured amount. In other words, if the aggregate of third party claims exceed the insured amount, the United States Government will provide for "the payment . . . of successful claims (including reasonable expenses of litigation or settlement) of a third party against the [launch company], or its contractors, subcontractors, or customers, or the contractors or subcontractors of such customers, resulting from activities carried out pursuant to a license issued or transferred under this Act . . ." in an amount not exceeding $1.5 billion above the insured amount or the amount of demonstrated financial responsibility.[83] The launch company and your client (the "customer"), as well as their contractors and subcontractors involved in the launching, are included in the government indemnification protection.[84] However, the government will not provide for payment of any claim if the damage "has resulted from willful misconduct by the licensee . . . ."[85] Presumably, your client also would not be protected if the launch company were guilty of willful misconduct, although it would have recourse against the launch company.

The purpose of the legislation outlined, above, was to foster and facilitate the growth of the United States private launch industry and the private insurance markets which support it. By establishing a risk allocation scheme involving the private launch industry, the U.S. Government and the insurance community, the legislation strikes a balance among the concerns that the fledgling private launch industry not have to pay exorbitant premiums to insure fully against a worst-case scenario of third party damage; that the government not bear total risk; and that all available insurance capacity not be consumed by only a very few space ventures.

The drafters of the legislation intended the government indemnifica-

---

78. 49 U.S.C. §2615(a)(1)(A) (1988). The notion of the private companies, themselves, assuming risk or obtaining insurance for third party claims was quite novel when it was first introduced in the Commercial Space Launch Act of 1984, 49 U.S.C. §2601-2623 (1988), Nesgos, Risk Allocation, *infra*, note 83, at 3. Previously, these companies had provided launch vehicles under contract with the government, *e.g.* NASA, and obtained indemnification by the government for any liability arising from a failed launch mission.
79. 49 U.S.C. §2615(a)(2) (1988).
80. *Id.* §2615(a)(1)(A).
81. *Id.* The determination is made after consultation with the heads of certain other Federal agencies, including the Secretary of the Air Force and the Administrator of the National Aeronautics and Space Administration. *Id.* .
82. *Id.* §2615(a)(1)(A)).

tion to be transitional. Under current law, the indemnification clause is valid only for a five-year period following the enactment of the 1988 Amendments on November 16, 1988, i.e., to November 16, 1993. Two bills have been introduced in the U.S. House of Representatives aimed at extending that deadline. Congressman Walker's bill, entitled the "Omnibus Space Commercialization Act of 1991" (H.R. 3153), introduced July 31, 1991, would extend the government indemnification to launch companies whose licenses are issued prior to January 1, 2004. A similar provision appears in Congressman Hall's bill of November 21, 1991, entitled the "Commercial Space Competitiveness Act of 1991" (H.R. 3848), calling for government indemnification for launch companies whose licenses are issued prior to January 1, 2000.

THE MARTIN MARIETTA-INTELSAT CONTRACT. Article 17.2. of the Martin Marietta-Intelsat Contract, entitled "Third Party Liability," is illustrative of risk-sharing provisions found in U.S. launch contracts. It provides that

> Martin Marietta shall procure and maintain Third Party liability insurance to protect Martin Marietta and INTELSAT against injury, death and property damage caused to Third Parties, arising out of or resulting from Launch Services provided under this Contract at CCAF or Kennedy Space Center (KSC) and/or after Launch, and/or arising out of or resulting from the Payload while

---

83. *Id.* §2615(b)(1)(A), (B). The government also will pay if the claim is excluded due to an insurance policy exclusion determined by the Secretary of Transportation (Office of Commercial Space Transportation) to be usual for the type of insurance involved, *Id.* §16(b)(1). The Congress considers government support for the commercial launch industry to be temporary. A Report of the Senate Committee on Commerce, Science and Transportation provides:

    > The Government . . . must act as a reliable partner and be willing to provide transitional support to this nascent industry until such time as equitable "rules of the road" are in place and the insurance industry has the capability to accommodate the increased insurance requirements of commercial space activities at reasonable rates.

    Senate Report, *supra* note 43, at 3. The 1988 Amendments also sought to redress a perceived inequality of treatment between emergent U.S. commercial launch operators and foreign competitors since the latter, such as Arianespace and the Soviet Proton and Chinese Long March launch initiatives, are subsidized by governments. *See* P.D. Nesgos, *Recent Developments in Risk Allocation of Concern to the U.S. Commercial Launch Industry and the Insurance Community*, Paper Presented at the Assicurazioni Generali Fifth International Conference on Space Insurance, Rome, Italy (Mar. 2-3, 1989) [hereinafter cited as Nesgos, Risk Allocation], at 6 (making this point and discussing other motivations behind the risk-sharing arrangement set forth in the 1988 Amendments).
84. *Id.* §2615(b)(1).
85. *Id.*

situated at CCAFS or KSC and/or after launch, including but not limited to work performed on or relating to the Payload under this Contract. Such insurance shall be in an amount of U.S. $100 million, combined single limit, or as prescribed by any regulation, directive or order of any United States government agency having authority to regulate commercial launch vehicle transportation, provided that, if such amount is not commercially available at a reasonable premium in light of prevailing standards in the industry as determined by Martin Marietta, using its reasonable judgment, such insurance shall be in any lesser amount commercially available at a reasonable premium and acceptable to the government agency referred to in this sentence. Insurance provided pursuant to this paragraph 17.2.1. shall commence upon the arrival of the Payload and Intelsat's personnel incident to the Payload Launch campaign at CCAFS or KSC, and shall continue for a term of ninety (90) days after the initial date of launch. Further, Martin Marietta shall, either directly or through the U.S. Government, indemnify and hold INTELSAT harmless from any and all loss, damage, liability or expense resulting from property damage and bodily harm caused to Third Parties to the extent not covered by said insurance, which damage or harm arises out of or in connection with (i) Launch Services furnished under this Contract and/or (ii) any Payload, provided that the occurrence giving rise to such damage or harm is during the period commencing on the day of the Launch and ending 36 months after the actual date of Launch. Martin Marietta shall at its sole expense defend any claims, actions, suits and proceedings, whether in law or equity, brought against INTELSAT on account of such damage or harm, and shall pay expenses, including attorney's fees, and satisfy all judgments as may be incurred by or rendered against INTELSAT in connection therewith, provided Martin Marietta is given prompt notice of any such claim, action, suit or proceeding and provided Martin Marietta is given, at Martin Marietta's written request and sole expense, such assistance and information as may be reasonably provided by INTELSAT.

The insurance obtained by Martin Marietta pursuant to paragraph 17.2.1. of this ARTICLE 17 shall name INTELSAT and may name the U.S. Government, and agents, employees, contractors and subcontractors of the U.S. Government, as additional insureds and shall contain a waiver of subrogation rights in favor of any such additional insureds. Martin Marietta shall, at its own expense, submit for INTELSAT's review and approval within 90 days prior to the first day of the Launch Slot a certificate of insurance evidencing the coverage and liability limits required above. The insurance required by paragraph 17.2.2. shall expressly provide that all of the provisions thereof except the limits of liability, shall operate in the same manner as if there were a separate policy with and covering each insured.[86]

It should be noted that the above-quoted provision appears in an agreement dated August 10, 1987, i.e., before the 1988 Amendments were enacted, and that this third party liability clause in a post-1988 launch agreement would vary slightly. For example, under the new law, the Secretary of Transportation (Office of Commercial Space Transportation) determines whether insurance is commercially available at a reasonable premium. The above provision stipulates that Martin Marietta shall make that determination. Furthermore, under current law, a launch company is required to name the U.S. Government as an additional insured. The above provision states that Martin Marietta "may" name the U.S. Government as an additional insured.

WHEN NO INSURANCE OR INDEMNIFICATION IS PROVIDED. In the event your client contracts with a launch company that does not agree to procure third party liability insurance or whose government does not provide indemnification, your client may want to take out insurance. Indeed, your client may be required by the government authorizing the satellite launch and operation to obtain such insurance to protect itself, its contractors and subcontractors, and the government against liability. Your client could be held directly liable under domestic or foreign tort laws,[87] depending upon applicable conflicts of law rules,[88] to private parties who have suffered damage. Furthermore, if damage occurs to persons or property in a foreign country, that country may bring a claim under international law[89] against your client's government. See Chapter 2.8.A foreign State also can sue your client directly pursuant to applicable domestic tort laws.

6.5.2.2. Damage to Participants in Launch Activities

NO LIABILITY TO THE LAUNCH COMPANY AND ITS CONTRACTORS. Generally, your client and its contractors and subcontractors will not be liable to other participants in launch activities, including the launch

---

86. Martin Marietta-INTELSAT Contract, *supra* note 17, art. 17.2.

87. Liability based on negligence or *culpa* will lie in most legal systems. In addition, some civil and common law jurisdictions will impose strict liability on the premise that a satellite launching is an ultrahazardous activity. Where damage has been caused to another spacecraft elsewhere than on the surface of the Earth, liability probably would be fault-based in most jurisdictions on the premise that both parties to the accident/incident are engaged in the space activity. *See* Chapter 2.8. and *infra* note 89 (discussing international liability).

88. A plaintiff usually will seek to apply the laws of the State that provides for the most generous compensation, as well as bring the suit in a forum where a resolution of a dispute can be achieved expeditiously. Since the United States judicial system, comparatively speaking, offers both of these features, the U.S. is likely to be the forum of choice, provided conflicts of law rules permit.

company and its contractors or subcontractors for damage to their personnel and property. Such exculpation from liability of your client and its contractors and subcontractors is a corollary to the exculpation of the launch company and its contractors and subcontractors from liability for damage to your client's satellite and personnel, discussed in Chapter 6.4.2., above. Major commercial launch companies include in their launch contracts reciprocal waiver provisions, whereby the launch company and the satellite owner waive their rights to claim against each other and agree to assume the risk of damage to their personnel and property. These waivers extend to the respective contractors and subcontractors of the parties, as well. The waiver scheme applies to U.S. launch contracts as a matter of law,[90] and to foreign launch companies as a matter of choice.[91] See Chapter 6.4.2. for details on the waivers.

USE OF U.S. GOVERNMENT LAUNCH SITES. If your client is contracting with a U.S. launch company, the launch may take place from a U.S. Government launch site, such as Cape Canaveral Air Force Station in Florida, Vandenberg Air Force Base in California, Wallops Flight Facility in Virginia, or White Sands Missile Range in New Mexico. Several new launch sites are being planned in the U.S. and other countries, but none is yet in operation. It is possible that U.S. launch companies may choose in the future to launch from foreign sites as they become available, and as permitted by law.

---

89. The State that authorized your client's satellite operation, and the one that authorized the launch service provider, if they are not the same, will be jointly liable for damage to third parties pursuant to the Treaty on Principles Governing the Activities of States in the Exploration and Use of Outer Space, Including the Moon and Other Celestial Bodies (Outer Space Treaty) *done* Jan. 7, 1967, *entered into force* Oct. 10, 1967, T.I.A.S. 6347; the Convention on International Liability for Damage Caused by Space Objects (Liability Convention) *done* Mar. 29, 1972, *entered into force* Sept. 1, 1973. T.I.A.S. 7762; and customary international law. When damage is caused on the ground, or to an aircraft in flight, the liability is absolute, Liability Convention, art. II. When damage is caused to a space object elsewhere than on the surface of the Earth, liability is based on fault, Liability Convention, art. III. Countries that have suffered, or whose citizens have suffered, damage and are parties to the Liability Convention have the option of bringing a claim pursuant to, or outside the framework of, the Liability Convention. Private parties cannot, themselves, sue directly under the Convention, and must request a State party to sue on their behalf. Also, Article VII of the Outer Space Treaty imposes liability on a State whose space object causes damage, and Article VI provides that a State shall be internationally responsible for the activities in space of its private (natural and corporate) citizens. *See* Chapter 2.8., above (discussing international liability for private activities in space).
90. 49 U.S.C. §2615(a)(1)(C) (1988).
91. Foreign companies/entities studied for purposes of this book were Arianespace and Glavkosmos, as represented by Space Commerce Corporation of Houston, Texas.

GENERALLY NO LIABILITY TO THE U.S. LAUNCH SITE OPERATOR. In accordance with the 1988 Amendments, the satellite owner is protected from claims by the U.S. Government through a combined insurance and waiver requirement applicable to the launch company and the United States Government. Specifically, the 1988 Amendments require the launch company to obtain liability insurance, or demonstrate financial responsibility, in an amount sufficient to compensate the United States Government for the "maximum probable loss" it might sustain as a result of activities carried out under the launch company's license to launch the satellite.[92] The maximum probable loss is determined by the Secretary of Transportation after consultations with the Administrator of NASA and the Secretary of the United States Air Force.[93] In no event, however, shall the launch company be required to obtain insurance or demonstrate financial responsibility that exceeds $100 million, or the maximum insurance available in the market at a reasonable price.[94] In connection with a launch license issued on February 20, 1991, a major launch company was required to obtain liability insurance for launch site operations in the amount of $70 million. The 1988 Amendments state explicitly that your client also shall be protected under the insurance policy purchased by the launch company.[95] Claims exceeding the insured amount are subject to cross waivers, which the Department of Transportation, acting on behalf of the United States, shall enter into with the launch company, its contractors, subcontractors and customers, and its contractors and subcontractors involved in the launching.[96]

The Department of the Air Force Model Expendable Launch Vehicle Commercialization Agreement, Revision Two, dated May 12, 1989 (hereinafter Air Force Model Agreement), which applies to private launch companies using the Air Force's launch facilities (including Vandenberg Air Force Base, California and Cape Canaveral Air Force Station, Florida), is consistent with the waiver requirement of the 1988 Amendments, despite its somewhat obscure language. Article IV.c., entitled "Liability Responsibility for Paying Claims, and Insurance," provides in relevant part:

> 1. For activities other than those carried out under a DOT launch license, the User shall assume the responsibility of payment for all damage to property of the Government and its contractors and subcontractors arising out of this Agreement, regardless of fault. For activities carried out under a DOT launch license in connection with any particular launch, the User shall assume responsibility for payment for all damage to property of the Government and its contractors and subcontractors arising out of this Agree-

---

92. 49 U.S.C. §2615 (a)(1)(B) (1988).
93. *Id.*
94. *Id.*
95. *Id.* §2615(a)(2).
96. *Id.* §2615(a)(1)(D)).

ment in accordance with the Commercial Space Launch Act as amended.

5. Nothing herein shall alter or affect the requirements for, or the terms of, any reciprocal waivers of claims required in accordance with the Commercial Space Launch Act, as amended. Upon request, the User will provide true copies of all such reciprocal waivers of claims executed by the User and the Government. For activities other than those carried out under a DOT launch license, the Government reserves the right to require execution of such reciprocal waivers of claims, appropriate in the circumstances, as a condition precedent to the Government providing any facilities, property, support or services to the User under this Agreement.[97]

The two paragraphs appear to be contradictory since one imposes liability and the other refers to the requirement of the 1988 Amendments that the U.S. Government waive the right to claim compensation for damage resulting from activities carried out under the launch license. The only logical reading of the two paragraphs together seems to be that for activities that are not carried out pursuant to a launch license, the launch company is liable regardless of fault, but for licensed launch activities, liability is waived (beyond the insured amount). The Air Force Model Agreement currently is being revised, presumably in part to clarify this meaning.

6.5.3. Dealing with the Customer

As the satellite owner, your client may be liable to its customers (such as transponder owners/lessees and other service takers) for breach of contract, or its customer may be entitled to refunds or rebates or to withhold payments, in the event the satellite is unavailable due to delay or destruction, or if it does not perform as specified in the contract with a customer. To limit its liability, your client should seek to make generous provision for delay in the commencement of service; delineate carefully the performance deficiencies that entitle the customer to remedies; as well as include in the contract a *force majeure* clause, a warranty disclaimer and a provision limiting your client's liability in general.

Your client's ability to negotiate favorable liability provisions with its customers is a function of general market conditions, as well as the price at which your client is willing to sell or lease transponders or provide satellite capacity. In a tight transponder market your client is likely to obtain more advantageous terms than if a transponder glut exists. However, your client usually can trade off a lower price for more favorable liability terms. Furthermore, if necessary, your client can purchase in-orbit-life insurance to off-set liability to the customer.

---

97. Department of the Air Force, Model Expendable Launch Vehicle Commercialization Agreement, Revision Two, 12 May, 1989, art. IV.

DELAY. Your client should seek to limit its liability for delay in the commencement of service. Delays may occur as a result of late delivery by the manufacturer and a resulting postponement in the launch, or may be due to adjustments in the launch schedule beyond your client's control, or both. If the delay occurs during manufacturing and the manufacturer pays liquidated damages, these will go to off-set the launch delay penalty, and nothing will remain to pay customers. Often, the liquidated damages are not even sufficient to cover the launch delay penalties. Sometimes launch contracts allow the launch company to delay the launch, say, for safety reasons, without a penalty payment to the satellite owner. Your client should make room for delay in the contracts with its customer and limit its liability for delay. An example of a provision in the contract with a customer protecting the satellite owner from claims for delay in the start of the contracted satellite service provides that the satellite company "shall not be liable for any damages suffered by the customer as a result of any delay in the scheduled service start date."

PERFORMANCE SPECIFICATIONS. Contracts with customers should delineate carefully the kinds of performance deficiencies that give rise to liability. For example, the contract may provide that your client will compensate the customer only in cases where the service is completely unusable to the customer, or where a condition exists which is equivalent of complete unusableness, over a given period of time, say twelve to eighteen consecutive hours, without interruption, after failure notification to the satellite owner. In this case, careful attention must be paid to the definition of "completely unusable." Moreover, the contract should limit damages owing to the customer, for example, to the service charge for the portion of the service that was completely unusable.

If the customer is purchasing or long-term leasing a transponder, the contract should stipulate precisely what kinds of transponder failures give rise to liability. For example, the contract might state that the customer is entitled to compensation or repayment only if the transponder has failed to meet certain performance specifications under certain circumstances for a given period of time. The contract also should address your client's responsibility to provide reserve or spare transponders, and should state that the customer is entitled to a remedy only if your client is unable to furnish a satisfactory substitute transponder. Further, the contract should establish a mutually agreed formula for refund of the transponder purchase/lease price. A transponder sales contract may provide that if the transponder is totally unusable and your client has reimbursed the transponder owner in full, the latter shall transfer all of its right, title and interest in the transponder to your client. In the event the transponder might still have some value for its owner, your client and the transponder owner may want to allow in the contract for the negotiation of a mutually acceptable, reduced price for the transponder.

FORCE MAJEURE. Your client should include in the contracts with its customers a provision that excuses delay and failure of performance due to circumstances beyond your client's control. Typically, such a provision would state that any failure or delay in performance either of the transponder or the satellite owner shall not be considered breach of contract if such failure or delay is due to acts of God, governmental action, receive Earth station sun outage where applicable, or any other action beyond the control of the satellite owner or the transponder owner.

WARRANTIES, REFUNDS, REBATES AND INCENTIVE PAYMENTS. A satellite transponder sales agreement may include warranties, as well as provisions for rebates, refunds and incentive payments in the event of a transponder failure. Often, the transponder sales agreement incorporates by reference the warranties contained in the satellite purchase contract. Ideally, the warranties, rebates, *et cetera,* offered by your client to its customers should not exceed those offered by the manufacturer in the satellite purchase contract, thus allowing your client to off-set liability to its customers by payments from the manufacturer. Your client should disclaim any warranties other than those specifically provided for in the contract with the customer. An example of such a warranty disclaimer might provide that "EXPRESS AND IMPLIED WARRANTIES ARE EXCLUDED AND DISCLAIMED UNLESS OTHERWISE SPECIFICALLY PROVIDED FOR IN THE CONTRACT." The Contract might also expressly state that "THE [SATELLITE OWNER'S] OBLIGATIONS AND THE [TRANSPONDER OWNER'S] REMEDIES ARE EXCLUSIVELY AS SET FORTH IN THE CONTRACT."

In unrelated litigation,[98] Public Broadcasting Service (PBS), the owner of four transponders on the Westar IV satellite, sued Hughes Aircraft Company, the manufacturer of the satellite, for breach of express warranty with respect to the satellite's lifetime. PBS claimed that Hughes Aircraft warranted Westar IV for an operational life of ten years, and that the satellite now is expected to expire fifteen months short of that time. Hughes Aircraft denied that the warranty period is ten years.

PBS purchased the transponders from Western Union Corporation, then the satellite owner, on July 31, 1984. The Spacecraft Performance Specification that was part of the satellite procurement contract between Western Union and Hughes Aircraft was incorporated by reference in the transponder purchase agreement. It would seem that PBS could have sued Western Union under the transponder purchase agreement, but may have elected instead to sue the manufacturer directly, due to the former's financial condition and the fact that Western Union is no longer the owner of the satellite. The WESTAR IV satellite, as well as WESTAR V and a fully constructed, but unlaunched, additional WESTAR satellite, was sold in 1988 to Hughes Communications Galaxy, Inc., a subsidiary of Hughes Aircraft. In the contract between Hughes Communications Galaxy and Western Union, the former assumed some of Western Union's contracts and liabilities, but did not assume the contracts with PBS and other transpon-

---

98. *Public Broadcasting Service v. Hughes Aircraft Company, supra* note 22.

der owners.[99]

LIMITATION OF LIABILITY. Your client should include in the transponder lease, sale, or service contracts with its customers a clause limiting its liability for incidental and consequential damages. Such a clause will preclude a customer's recovery, for example, for lost earnings and profits.

---

99. *See Western Union Corporation*, 3 F.C.C. Rcd 6792 (1988) (providing Federal Communications Commission (FCC) permission to transfer launch and operating authorizations). *See* Chapter 3.2.12. (concerning the transfer of FCC authorizations).

7. Contracting for the Launching of Your Client's Satellite

Launch vehicle options, the timing of launch contract negotiations and the contents of launch contracts are discussed in this Chapter. Launch contracts offered by five major launch companies are analyzed and compared. The comparison reveals a remarkable similarity among the provisions of these agreements. A reader who is interested specifically in the risk allocation provisions of launch contracts should refer to Chapter 6.4.2. and 6.5.2., concerning risk management.

7.1. Launch Vehicle Options

The decade of the 1980s saw the development of a world-wide commercial launch industry, which today allows your client a choice among a variety of launch service providers and vehicles suited for different payload sizes and designs. Prior to the early 1980s, all space launchings were performed either by the Soviet Union or the United States National Aeronautics and Space Administration (NASA). The current stable of commercial launch vehicles, some of which are liquid-fueled and others of which employ solid rocket motors or combinations of the two propellants, include, among others, Arianespace's Ariane vehicles, Martin Marietta's Titan III, General Dynamics' Atlas vehicles, McDonnell Douglas' Delta vehicles, Orbital Sciences' Pegasus, EER Space Systems Corporation's Conestoga and American Rocket Company's Aquila. Launch vehicles whose use is restricted for political or other reasons include NASA's Space Transportation System, i.e., the Space Shuttle, the Soviet Proton and the Chinese Long March.

ARIANESPACE. With a market share of about fifty percent, Arianespace S.A., located South-East of Paris in Evry, France, is the major commercial launch provider in the market today.[1] Its Ariane rocket currently is offered in four different versions (Ariane 1-4). A fifth version, Ariane 5, is under development and will be available in the late 1990s.

Ariane 1, which became operational in 1981, has a lift capacity of 1,800 kg to geostationary transfer orbit.[2] Ariane 2 and Ariane 3 came into oper-

Ariane 4.
Provided courtesy Arianespace.

ation in 1984 and can launch to geostationary transfer orbit payloads of, respectively, 2,200 kg and 2,600 kg. Except for its additional solid propellant strap-on boosters, Ariane 3 is almost identical to Ariane 2. Ariane 4, which became operational in 1988, currently is the most powerful of the Ariane family of vehicles and is capable of lifting from 2,000 kg to 4,200 kg to geostationary transfer orbit, depending on the number of strap-on boosters used. The thrust and the payload capacity of the Ariane 4 were greatly increased over the previous Ariane versions, mainly by lengthening the first rocket stage and increasing the payload fairing considerably.[3] Ariane 2, Ariane 3 and Ariane 4 may be used for single or dual satellite payloads,[4] and for multiple "microsat" or "lightsat" payloads.[5] All Arianespace launches are conducted from a facility at Kourou, French Guiana, South America, a near-equatorial location, which is almost optimal for geostationary satellite launches.[6]

MARTIN MARIETTA. Martin Marietta Astronautics Group of Denver, Colorado, offers its Titan III vehicle for launches of commercial payloads. This vehicle, which is one of a series of vehicles developed by Martin Marietta, can deliver payloads in excess of 14,070 kg to low-Earth orbit.[7]

---

1. Arianespace S.A. was established in 1980 to market launch services, procure Ariane launch vehicles and conduct launches. The company also insures customers' launch risks through a subsidiary called Societe de Reassurance des Risques relatifs aux applications spatiales (S3R). The technology base for the Ariane launch vehicle was (and still is for Ariane 5) developed by the European Space Agency (ESA), a space research organization of thirteen European countries. *See* Chapter 2.8., note 89 (discussing the legal foundation for ESA). Arianespace's shareholders include thirty-six European aerospace and electronics companies, thirteen major banks and the French Centre National d'Etudes Spatiales (CNES). *See* Chapter 1.2., note 44 (providing names of shareholders). Arianespace has set up a U.S. subsidiary, Arianespace, Inc., to market launch services in the United States.
2. Geostationary transfer orbit is a highly elliptical orbit whose apogee reaches the geostationary altitude of about 36,000 km. An "apogee kick motor" built into the satellite will have to be activated to establish a circular orbit.
3. Contractors or subcontractors for production of the Ariane 4 launch vehicle include several of Arianespace's shareholders. For example, Aerospatiale of France, a major shareholder, is the industrial architect for the Ariane 4 launch vehicle, and is responsible for the integration of the first and third stages and for the manufacture of the first stage fuel tanks, among other tasks. Its participation amounts to 20.4% of the total Ariane 4 work-load. Another French shareholder, Matra S.A., is responsible for the Ariane 4 vehicle equipment bay. Contraves A.G. of Switzerland, including other national subcontractors, is responsible for the payload fairing. British Aerospace manufactures the SPELDA (the Ariane dual launch external bearing structure). ERNO GmbH of Germany is responsible for the integration of the second stage, with Aerospatiale, Deutsch, MBB and others serving as subcontractors
4. For example, the Ariane 3 launch vehicle may be used to launch two Delta-class satellites weighing 1200 kg each.

A payload owner-supplied perigee kick motor is required for insertion of the payload into geostationary transfer-orbit, and the Titan III launch vehicle is compatible with a variety of perigee kick motors. As is true for the Ariane launch vehicle, single, dual and multiple payloads can be accommodated on the Titan III, within the weight limitation.

Martin Marietta has been a producer of launch vehicles since the late-1950s, using technology derived from the development of ballistic missiles. The company began commercial operations in the late 1980s. Prior to commercialization of the Titan, Martin Marietta manufactured and sold launch vehicles to NASA and the military, which then operated the launch vehicles, themselves, in their own respective programs. NASA also used the vehicles to launch foreign and commercial payloads.[8] Today, however, Martin Marietta not only builds the Titan vehicles, it also provides launch services for NASA and the military, as well as for commercial U.S. and foreign satellite customers. Martin Marietta's commercial launches are conducted from Cape Canaveral Air Force Station, Florida.[9]

GENERAL DYNAMICS. General Dynamics Commercial Launch Services, Inc. of San Diego, California, provides commercial launch services on a family of four Atlas vehicles: Atlas I, Atlas II, Atlas IIA and Atlas IIAS (the latter of which will be available in 1993). Their payload capacities to geostationary transfer orbit are: 2,245 kg (w/large payload fairing) and 2,335 kg (w/medium payload fairing) for Atlas I; 2675 kg (w/large fairing) and 2,765 kg (w/medium fairing) for Atlas II; 2,810 kg (w/large fairing) and 2,900 kg (w/medium fairing) for Atlas IIA; and 3,490 kg (w/large fairing) and 3,630 kg (w/medium fairing) for Atlas IIAS. Atlas I is an improved version of the Atlas/Centaur flown previously. Atlas II upgrades Atlas I by including increased booster engine thrust and by lengthening of the propellant tanks. Atlas IIA resembles Atlas II, but its performance has been enhanced by an upgraded propulsion system and more sophisticated avionics. Atlas IIAS adds four "Castor IVA" solid rocket motors to the Atlas IIA version. The Atlas vehicle also is based on technology developed for

5. On January 4, 1990, the first vehicle of the modular Ariane 4 version launched the Spot-2 remote-sensing satellite for CNES, as well as six auxiliary UoSat/Microsat satellites. *See* J.M. Lenorovitz, *Seven-Satellite Payload Orbited in First Ariane Mission of 1990,* AW&ST, Jan. 29, 1991, at 26 (describing the payloads). Spot-2 weighed 1,870 kg, and was built by a French prime contractor, Matra, S.A. The UoSats were microsats at 345 X 345 X 600 mm, and weighing 45.5-47.5 kg. Some were equipped with a digital store-and-forward communications transponder and a camera for Earth imaging, among other capabilities. *Id.* The project was a collaborative effort between Amsat North America of Canada and Mitsubishi of Japan, among others. *Id.*
6. Arianespace S.A. headquarters are located at Boulevard de l'Europe, B.P. 177-91006 Evry Cedex, France, and the United States subsidiary, Arianespace, Inc., is located at 700 Thirteenth Street, N.W., Washington, D.C. 20005, U.S.A.
7. Low-Earth orbit here refers to a parking orbit from which the satellite and attached perigee kick motor ascend to geostationary altitude.

the military and, as was the case with Martin Marietta's Titan, the Atlas was commercialized in the late 1980s. Prior to that time, the Atlas launch vehicles were sold to NASA and the Air Force, both of which operated the vehicles. Commercial Atlas launch operations take place from Cape Canaveral Air Force Station, Florida.[10]

---

8. In 1972, President Richard M. Nixon approved NASA's plan to build a fleet of reusable Space Shuttles and directed that the Space Shuttle become this country's primary launch vehicle. He also directed that all expendable launch vehicles then in use, except LTV Corporation's Scout, be phased out of the U.S. Government space program as the Space Shuttle became operational. As contemplated, NASA would use the Space Shuttle for its own scientific payloads, as well as for commercial customers' payloads, and the Department of Defense (DOD) would use the Space Shuttle for military payloads. At the time, both NASA and DOD were relying upon expendable launch vehicles, including Martin Marietta's Titan, General Dynamics' Atlas and McDonnell Douglas's Delta. The Shuttle was first launched in 1981 and was declared operational in 1982. At that time, the phase-out of the expendable launch vehicles began. However, in 1984, the Air Force argued successfully that it needed a complementary back-up capability to the Space Shuttle, and initiated what is now known as the Titan IV program. In the meantime, production lines for the Atlas and Delta were shut down.

   In 1982, President Ronald Reagan initiated a policy of fostering a private sector space transportation industry to launch *commercial* payloads. *See National Space Policy,* Fact Sheet, Office of The White House Press Secretary, 4 July, 1982 (enunciating a clear role for the private sector in space). The policy, as clarified in 1983, was to "endorse and facilitate commercial operations of Expendable Launch Vehicles (ELVs) by the U.S. private sector." Press release, Office of The White House Press Secretary, May 16, 1983. The policy applied both to launch vehicles previously developed for government use, such as Martin Marietta's Titan, and to new space launch systems being developed at the time for commercial applications, such as Space Services' Conestoga. The effort to involve the private sector in the provision of commercial launch services is generally referred to as the "commercialization" of the expendable launch vehicle industry. The policy was codified by the Commercial Space Launch Act of 1984, as amended, 49 U.S.C. § 2601-2623 (1988), which adopted a licensing regime for private launch companies. *See* Chapter 2.4., notes 40-43 and accompanying text (concerning the circumstances leading to the adoption of the Commercial Space Launch Act).

   The Reagan Administration's early attempts to foster a private commercial space launch industry were thwarted, however, by the fact that NASA also was in the "business" of providing launch services, at subsidized prices, thus undermining the private sector competition. A new policy adopted December 27, 1986, in the wake the *Challenger* disaster that occurred January 28, 1986, substantially limited NASA's role in the commercial launch market and has given the rpivate companies a chance to compete. *See United States Launch Strategy, infra* note 12 (limiting the use of the Shuttle to payloads requiring the special characteristics of the Shuttle, or whose launching on the Shuttle would serve the national security or foreign policy interests of the United States, thus, severely limiting NASA's access to commercial payloads).

MCDONNELL DOUGLAS. McDonnell Douglas Astronautics Company of Huntington Beach, California, provides commercial launch services on its Delta II vehicle, which is available in at least two versions: Delta II 6925 and Delta II 7925. The Delta II vehicle can accommodate a wide variety of payloads within the following weight limitations: Delta II 6925 has payload capacity of 1,447 kg to geostationary transfer orbit and 3,983 kg to low-Earth orbit. Delta II 7925 can launch 1,819 kg to geostationary transfer orbit and 5,039 kg to low-Earth orbit. The Delta II is based on the Delta PAM-D, which became operational in 1982. The Delta vehicle was initially developed for NASA in 1960. Commercial Delta launch services began in the late 1980s.[11] Delta launches take place from Cape Canaveral Air Force Station, Florida, and Vandenberg Air Force Base in California.

VEHICLES SUITABLE FOR SMALL PAYLOADS. If your client is planning to launch so-called "microsats" or "lightsats," terms often used for satellites weighing less than 100 kg and 600 kg, respectively, a variety of launch options exist. Your client can request a dual or multiple payload launch on a launch vehicle offered by one of the major launch companies described above, or it can buy single-payload launches from companies offering smaller launch vehicles. These companies include EER Systems Corporation's Space Services Division of Vienna, Virginia.[12] American Rocket Company of Amarillo, California,[13] Microspace International of Herndon, Virginia,[14] and Orbital Sciences Corporation of Fairfax, Vir-

---

9. Martin Marietta Corporation's office responsible for the commercial Titan program is located in Denver, Colorado 80201, U.S.A.
10. General Dynamics Commercial Launch Services, Inc., is located in San Diego, California 92186-5990, U.S.A.
11. McDonnell Douglas Corporation's office in charge of the commercial Delta program is located at 5301 Bolsa Ave. Huntington Beach, California 92647, U.S.A.
12. The launch vehicle offered by Space Services is called Conestoga, and is available in four versions: Conestoga "210-48" with payload capacities of 73 kg to geostationary transfer orbit, 190 kg to 741 km circular 90 degree inclination orbit and 295 kg to 370 km circular 37 degree inclination orbit; Conestoga "310-48" with payload capacities of 113 kg to geostationary transfer orbit, 295 kg to 741 km circular 90 degree inclination orbit and 499 kg to 370 km circular 37 degree inclination orbit; Conestoga "221-48" with payload capacities of 250 kg to geostationary transfer orbit, 410 kg to 741 km circular 90 degree inclination orbit and 680 kg to 370 km circular 37 degree inclination orbit; and Conestoga "421-48B" with payload capacities of 440 kg to geostationary transfer orbit, 712 kg to 741 km circular 90 degree inclination orbit and 1,270 kg to 370 km circular 37 degree inclination orbit. Launches are conducted from Wallops Island, Virginia. Vandenberg Air Force Base is a proposed launch site.
13. American Rocket Company's *Aquila* (Latin for "eagle") launch vehicle has the following payload capacities: 1,135 kg to a 185 km circular polar low-Earth orbit and 1,589 kg to a 185 km 28.5 degree low-Earth orbit. launches take place from Vandenberg Air Force Base, California.

ginia. These four companies primarily have targeted the low-Earth orbit lightsat markets. The latter introduced an innovative launch concept, the Pegasus winged vehicle, which is air-launched from a conventional air transport or bomber-class aircraft. Pegasus was developed in a joint venture between Orbital Sciences Corporation and Hercules Aerospace Corporation of Magna, Utah, and can deliver payloads weighing up to 400 kg. to low-Earth orbit. Its maiden flight occurred on April 5, 1990, when the Pegasus was released for the first time from the wing of a NASA B-52 aircraft flying south over the Pacific Ocean at an altitude of 43,200ft (13.2 km).[15] After falling for five seconds to clear the aircraft, the winged rocket ignited its first stage motor and ascended to place its 423lb (193 kg) payload into a 273 x 370 nautical mile (506 km x 685 km), 94 degree inclination orbit.[16]

NASA. As mentioned previously, the NASA Space Shuttle, a fleet of three reusable orbitors, including Columbia, Discovery and Atlantis, is available for commercial payloads only if they require the unique characteristics of the Shuttle, or if the launch is required in the national security interest or foreign policy interest of the United States.[17] If your client is a private U.S. or foreign company seeking to launch a telecommunications satellite of a conventional size and design for purposes of commercial operations, it is unlikely to meet these tests. The Shuttle can launch payloads of up to 25,000 kg. The maiden flight of the fourth, and last, Shuttle orbiter, Endeavour, is scheduled for 1992.

THE SOVIET UNION. With its Proton launch vehicle, marketed in the United States by Space Commerce Corporation of Houston, Texas, the Soviet Union is a relative newcomer on the commercial launch scene. The Proton vehicle, which has been in operation since 1965, launching scientific and military payloads, has a lift capacity to geostationary transfer-orbit of 2,200 kg and to low-Earth orbit of 4,600 kg. Due to a policy prohibiting U.S.-made satellites from being launched on Soviet launch vehicles,[18] the Proton currently is not an option to United States satellite companies or foreign companies buying satellites from U.S. manufacturers. Commercial Proton launches are conducted from Baikonur Cosmo-

---

14. Microspace International is in the final stages of developing a launch vehicle based on a combination of existing technologies. Strategic partners, or parties otherwise associated with this venture, include Morton Thiokol, Bristol Aerospace and Saab Space. The target market for Microspace International includes payloads of about 200 kg intended for about 650 km polar orbits.
15. M. Mosier, G Harris, B. Richards, D. Rovner & B. Carroll, *Pegasus First Mission Flight Results,* Paper Presented at the Fourth Annual AIAA/Utah State University Conference on Small Satellites, Logan, Utah, 29 Aug., 1990.
16. *Id.*
17. *United States Launch Strategy,* National Security Decision Directive 254, Dec. 27, 1986. The Policy was codified as the National Aeronautics and Space Administration Authorization Act, Fiscal Year 1991, Pub. L. No. 101-106 § 112 (1990).

drome, Kazakh, USSR. A possible launch site at Cape York, Australia, is being explored for Soviet Zenit launch vehicles.[19]

CHINA. Through the Great Wall Industry Corporation, the People's Republic of China offers commercial launch services on its Long March vehicle. The Long March rocket technology was developed by the First Research Academy and Shanghai Astronautics Bureau, and the vehicle is available in at least five versions: Long March 2C, 2E, 3, 3A and 4. Long March 2C and 2E have payload capacities, respectively, of 2,500 kg and 8,800 kg to low-Earth orbit. Long March 3 and 3A have payload capacities, respectively, of 1,400 kg and 2,500 kg to geostationary transfer orbit. Long March 4 can launch 2,500 kg to low-Earth orbit. China offers two launch sites for commercial customers. The Jiuquan Satellite Launch Center, located in the Gobi Desert to the north of Jiuquan in Gansu Province was the first launch center to be constructed in China and is also the largest. The Xichang Satellite Launch Center is located in the city of Xichang, Sichuan Province, in South-East China. Currently, United States law and policy also prohibits the launching of U.S.-made satellites on Chinese vehicles.[20]

JAPAN. A potentially formidable competitor in the future commercial launch market is Rocket System Corporation of Tokyo, Japan, a consortium of twelve industrial companies led by Mitsubishi Heavy Industries Ltd.[21] The consortium plans to market the H-2 launch vehicle, which is now in the late phase of development and scheduled for its first test flight in 1995. The H-2 vehicle is being developed by the National Space Development Agency of Japan and is the first launch vehicle based entirely on Japanese technology. Its predecessors, the N- and H-1 launch vehicles, were developed based on United States technology transferred to the Japanese Government and industries in accordance with a 1960 intergovernmental agreement.[22] The H-2 launch vehicle will have payload capacities of 10,000 kg to a 30 degree inclination low-Earth orbit, and 4,000 kg to geostationary transfer orbit. The H-2 will be launched from a new launch site at Tanegashima, an island in southern Japan, that is 1 km east of the

---

18. This long-standing U.S. policy is likely to change with the political break-up of the Soviet Union. Currently, launch sites exist in Kazahkstan and Russia. It is the launch site in Kazahkstan that has been promoted for commercial operations to the present. Launch vehicles are manufactured mainly in Russia, although the Zenit launch vehicle is manufactured in the Ukraine.
19. A launch site is being proposed at Cape York, Australia, at the northern-most point of the Cape York Peninsula in North-East Australia, on the Pacific coast. The project is being sponsored by the Cape York Space Agency, Pty, Ltd. Soviet Zenit rockets are being considered as the exclusive launch vehicle for use at this site. A division of United Technologies of Hartford, Connecticut, has been invited to take a management role in the project, but the United States Government has conditioned its participation, specifically, its export license, on a pledge by the Soviet Union to forego the launching of Western satellites on Soviet territory among other conditions.

sites used for the N-1, N-2 and H-1 launch vehicles.

7.2. When to Initiate Negotiations with the Launch Company

When the necessary authorizations to launch and operate the satellite have been obtained from the national government (see Chapter 3.) and the satellite design and manufacturer have been selected, your client should approach the launch provider(s) whose vehicles meet the size and design requirements of the satellite, and invite interested launch companies to

---

20. *See* Departments of Commerce, Justice, and the State Judiciary and Related Agencies Appropriations Act, Fiscal Year 1992, Pub. L. 102-140 §608, 105 Stat. 782 (1991) (prohibiting launches on Chinese launch vehicles of U.S.-made satellites). The President may waive the prohibition under certain conditions. *Id.*, §608(b). *President to Renew China's Trade Status,* The Washington Post, May 28, 1991, at A1 (describing President George Bush's address at Yale University in which he announced his decision to block the launching of U.S.-made satellites on Chinese launch vehicles). *See* 50 U.S.C. App. § 2404 (1988) (giving the President the authority to restrict the transfer of certain goods and technologies for national security reasons). The prohibition previously was legislated: Departments of Commerce, Justice, and State, the Judiciary, and Related Agencies Appropriations Act, Fiscal Year 1990, Pub. L. No. 101-162 § 610, 103 Stat. 988, 1938 (1989) [hereinafter cited as Department of Commerce Appropriations Act]. *See* Chapter 6.1., note 3, and accompanying text (quoting Section 610 and describing the circumstances leading to the adopton of the prohibition). No prohibition on Chinese launches was included in the Departments of Commerce, Justice, State and the Judiciary, and Related Agencies Appropriations Act, Fiscal Year 1991. Proposed amendments to the Export Administration Act based on H.R. 4653 and S. 2927, containing such prohibitions, were vetoed by President George Bush in 1990 (for unrelated reasons), and reintroduced the "Omnibus Export Administration Act of 1991," Section 126, based on S. 320. The bill was passed by the Senate and referred to the House of Representatives on February 20, 1991 (H.R. 627). A House version of the bill, H.R. 3489, was introduced on October 2, 1991.
The law, as well as the policy prohibition mentioned above, effectively suspended a series of Memoranda of Understanding between the U.S, and China. *See* Memorandum of Agreement Between the Governments of the United States of America and the People's Republic of China Regarding International Trade in Commercial Launch Vehicles, done at Washington, D.C. January 26, 1989; Memorandum of Agreement on Satellite Technology Safeguards Between the Governments of the United States of America and the People's Republic of China, (1989); and Memorandum of Agreement on Liability for Satellite Launches Between the Governments of the United States of America and the People's Republic of China (1989) (concerning the launching of U.S.-made satellites on the Long March launch vehicle). China has since adhered to the Convention on Liability for Damage Caused by Space Objects, *done* March 29, 1972 and *entered into force* September 1, 1973, T.I.A.S. 7763

submit proposals. Once the proposals have been received, your client should study them and enter into negotiations with the company that offers the most favorable combination of price and terms. The company's launch track record, including success-rate, timeliness and precision, is a consideration, as well, especially if your client is dealing with a small, start-up company. The launch contract usually is executed between six and nine months after the invitation to submit a proposal, and about twenty-four to thirty-six months before launching. The unfolding of events in the case of Martin Marietta and the International Telecommunication Satellite Organization (INTELSAT) is illustrative. On October 10, 1986, INTELSAT contacted Martin Marietta with a request for proposal (RFP) to launch two INTELSAT VI communications satellites. Martin Marietta responded on February 9, 1987, with a proposal to provide launch services on the commercial Titan III vehicle. The parties then entered into negotiations and executed a written launch contract on August 10, 1987, ten months after the RFP was issued and two years before the first satellite was scheduled to be launched.[23] INTELSAT had contracted with Hughes Aircraft for the purchase of the INTELSAT VI satellite series five years prior to initiating the launch procurement, which is somewhat unique.[24] Normally, a commercial launch procurement occurs within a year or so of the satellite purchase. INTELSAT presents a special case in this respect since it usually orders a series of satellites.

It is not uncommon for satellite companies to initiate contact with potential launch providers, even before the governmental satellite authorization has been granted and before a manufacturer has been selected. Satellite size and general design usually will have been determined already at the time the application to build, launch and operate the satellite system is submitted to the appropriate national authority, and the preliminary selection of a launch vehicle may already be possible already at that time. Early selection of a launch company may have tactical advantages. It may serve to convince regulators, financial backers and potential customers that the satellite project is "for real." Another reason for

---

21. Rocket Systems Corporation was incorporated in July 1990.
22. *See* U.S./Japanese Agreement Concerning the Provision by U.S. Industry of Certain Categories of Unclassified Technology and Equipment for the Development of Japanese Q and N Launch Vehicles and Communications and Other Satellites for Peaceful Applications, July 30, 1960, T.I.A.S. 6735 (permitting the transfer of U.S. rocket and satellite technology to Japanese industries and government).
23. The launch period for the first launch was July 30- October 28, 1989, and for the second satellite, December 23, 1989 - March 22, 1990. Commercial Launch Services Contract Between Martin Marietta Corporation and International Telecommunications Organization "INTELSAT" (Aug. 10, 1987), [hereinafter cited as Martin Marietta-INTELSAT Contract], Article 3.1.1.
24. INTELSAT and Hughes Aircraft Company signed the contract for manufacturing the INTELSAT VI series in March 1982.

approaching a launch company at an early stage might be to involve the launch company in the financing of the satellite project. For example, it has been reported that General Dynamics plans to acquire an equity stake in Orion Satellite Corporation of Rockville, Maryland.[25] Orion Satellite Corporation now has received permission from the United States Federal Communications Commission to launch and operate a satellite system for trans-Atlantic communications (see Chapter 3.4.),[26] but the company's negotiations with General Dynamics were initiated before the final governmental authorization was issued. A launch company's motivation for assisting in the satellite financing is, of course, to provide an incentive for the satellite company to select its launch vehicle.

LAUNCH RESERVATION. Launch reservations at an early stage of a satellite project are not uncommon and may be advantageous, but they usually require a considerable, and sometimes non-refundable, downpayment. For example, a General Dynamics Corporation generic Launch Reservation Agreement, dated September 15, 1987,[27] provides that the customer shall pay General Dynamics a deposit of $100,000.00 for each launch reservation made. The reservation entitles the customer to the "right of first refusal for the selected launch quarter reserved." The deposit is refundable. However, in the event another customer offers to make a non-refundable reservation in the same amount for the same launch quarter, the first customer will have fourteen days to confirm its reservation, after which affirmation the initial deposit becomes non-refundable.[28]

7.3. Provisions of the Commercial Launch Contract

Commercial launch contracts generally are fairly extensive documents containing some thirty typed legal-size pages, excluding attachments and

---

25. D. Polsky, *GD Plans Equity Stake in Orion Satellite*, SPACE NEWS, 16 Dec., 1990, at 10.
26. Orion Satellite Corporation was the first private company ever to apply for authority to operate a satellite system for trans-Atlantic communications services in competition with INTELSAT, and the second company to obtain permission to provide such services (Chapter 3.1.4.).
27. Launch Reservation Agreement Between General Dynamics Corporation and [customer] for Commercial Launch Services [hereinafter cited as Launch Reservation]. The agreement was attached to a statement by A.M. Lovelace, Corporate Vice President and General Manager, General Dynamics, Space Systems Division, on the Status of the Commercial Launch Industry, before the House Committee on Science, Space, and Technology, Subcommittee on Space, Science, and Applications. *Status of the Commercial Launch Industry Before Subcommittee on Space, Science, and Applications of the House Committee on Science, Space, and Technology* (Sept. 15, 1987) [hereinafter cited as Lovelace Statement].
28. Launch Reservation, *supra* note 27.

exhibits.[29] They normally have between twenty and forty separate articles describing the parties' rights, duties and responsibilities pertaining to the launch of your client's satellite. A typical launch contract addresses the following items:

- Definitions.
- Launch Services to be Provided
- Completion of Launch Services
- Launch Schedule
- Launch Schedule Adjustments
- Reflight Option
- Replacement Launch
- Remuneration
- Payment for Services
- *Force Majeure*
- Disclaimer of Warranties
- Inter-Participant Waiver of Claims
- Third Party Liability and Insurance
- Treatment of Proprietary Data
- Industrial and Intellectual Property Rights, Including Patents
- Governmental Permits and Approvals
- Limitation of Liability
- Settlement of Disputes/Arbitration
- Termination of the Launch Contract
- General Provisions (Modification, Assignment, Headings, Law Applicable, Entire Agreement, Entry Into Force, *et. cetera*).

Commercial launch contracts offered by major launch providers have become somewhat standardized, not only in terms of the items they address, but also with regard to the actual content of their provisions. Similarities are striking, for example, with respect to risk allocation (discussed in Chapter 6.), launch services provided, launch schedules and

29. Launch and payload specifications and detailed technical descriptions of the responsibilities of each party generally are found in exhibits to the contract and are incorporated by reference.

adjustments, treatment of proprietary data and rights in the other party's patents. Launch agreements sometimes are modeled upon one another and, perhaps in the final analysis, upon the NASA commercial Space Shuttle launch contract developed in the early 1980s when NASA dominated the commercial launch market. Because of the private and often proprietary nature of launch contracts, it has not always been possible to quote or reference the most up-to-date materials. While some of the launch contracts discussed are current, others were executed in the late 1980s and their provisions therefore do not necessarily reflect the current practices of the launch companies involved.

DEFINITIONS. Launch contracts generally contain a set of definitions, usually found either in the beginning or at the end of the contract, or in an annex attached to it.[30] For example, several key terms, such as "Party," "Launch," "Reflight," "Launch services," "Launch period," "Launch slot," "Launch date," "Launch opportunity," "Payload" and "Third Party," are defined in the following contracts: Article 1 of the standard draft Arianespace launch Agreement (February 1992) (hereinafter Arianespace Agreement); Article 1 of the Commercial Launch Services Contract Between Martin Marietta Corporation and the International Telecommunications Satellite Organization "INTELSAT," dated August 10, 1987 (hereinafter Martin Marietta-INTELSAT Contract); Annex 2 to the General Dynamics Corporation generic Contract for Launch Services, dated September 15, 1987 (hereinafter General Dynamics Agreement);[31] and Article 13, i.e., the final provision, of Agreement Between the President of India, Represented by the Secretary to the Government of India, Department of Space, and McDonnell Douglas Corporation, dated July 30, 1987 (hereinafter McDonnell Douglas-India Contract).

The purpose of definitions is to provide a clear reference as to the meaning of certain terms and, in certain cases, also to allow the use of shorter terms in the operative contract provisions without having to explain a term each time it is used. For example, the Arianespace Agreement extends the waiver of liability to the parties' "Associates" (see Chapter 6.4.2.). "Associates" is defined to mean

> any individuals or legal entities, organized under public or private law, who shall act directly or indirectly, on behalf or at the direction of either Party to this Agreement or of the Third Party Customer(s) of ARIANESPACE to fulfil the obligations undertaken by any such Party in this Agreement, or by the Third Party Customer(s) of ARIANESPACE including, by way of example only, the employees of each of the Parties, or of the Third Party Customer(s) of ARIANESPACE, their suppliers and subcontractors.[32]

30. The number of definitions counted in a sample of major launch agreements varied from eight to twenty-eight.
31. The General Dynamics Agreement was attached to the Lovelace Statement, *supra* note 27.

LAUNCH SERVICES TO BE PROVIDED UNDER THE CONTRACT. "Launch services" generally refer to a range of services and associated hardware, including the launch vehicle, itself, which is expendable.[33] For example, the General Dynamics Corporation, *ATLAS Mission Planner's Guide*, describes the commercial launch services provided by that company as "a full launch services package from spacecraft integration through processing, encapsulation, launch operations and verifications of orbit . . . [including]

a. Launch vehicle

b. Launch Operations Services

c. Mission-peculiar equipment design, test and production

d. Technical integration and interface design between the launch vehicle and spacecraft

e. Program interface management

f. A standard set of launch facilities and support provisions

g. Mission-peculiar spacecraft support at [Cape Canaveral Air Force Station]

h. A mission manager

i. Validation of spacecraft separation sequence and orbit."[34]

All the major launch contracts provide a relatively elaborate description of the services to be provided,[35] although detailed technical specifications usually are found in exhibits attached to, and referenced in, the launch contract. For example, Article 1 of the General Dynamics Agreement, entitled "Services to be Provided," stipulates that:

1.1. In consideration of the mutual promises and covenants

---

32. Arianespace Agreement, art. 1.

33. The NASA Space Shuttle (orbiter) is currently the only completely reusable launch vehicle.

34. General Dynamics Corporation, ATLAS Mission Planner's Guide, at 3. Although General Dynamics undertakes to conduct payload processing, this procedure, typically involving final assembly and fueling of the spacecraft, often is contracted out, *e.g.*, to Astrotech Space Operations, L.P., of Silver Spring, Maryland, which conducts payload processing at that company's processing facility in Titusville, Florida. *See* Chapter 3.4.2., note 32 and accompanying text (concerning risk allocation provisions in Astrotech Space Operation's agreement with its customers).

35. Arianespace Agreement, art. 4; Martin Marietta-INTELSAT Contract, art. 2; General Dynamics Agreement, art. 1; McDonnell Douglas-India Contract, art. 1; and Master Contract Between The Space Commerce Corporation and Energetics Satellite Corporation for Spacecraft Launching and Associated Services [hereinafter cited as Soviet Launch Agreement], art. I.

herein contained, the parties hereto agree as follows:

The Contractor shall furnish and the Customer shall accept ___ launch(es), including associated launch services, for the launch of a Customer-furnished Satellite(s) from Cape Canaveral Air Force Station, Florida, United States of America, utilizing an Atlas/Centaur Launch Vehicle as set forth in Annex 1, entitled "Commercial Atlas G/Centaur Launch Services Statement of Work," which is attached hereto and made part hereof.

1.2. The Contractor shall provide launch services as set forth in Annex 1 hereto for the following Satellite(s). The planned launch dates will be as follows.

. . .

1.3. The Contractor shall provide reflight launchings for Customer-furnished Satellite(s) or a refund of the launch costs, in accordance with the provisions of Article 8 of this Contract.[36]

Similar provisions appear in Article 1 of the McDonnell Douglas-India Contract, Article 2 of the Martin Marietta-INTELSAT Contract and Article 4 of the Arianespace Agreement. The latter two provisions add that the launch provider will use its "best efforts" to furnish the launch services as agreed in the launch contract. The Martin Marietta-INTELSAT Contract defines "best efforts" as "diligently working in a good and workman-like manner as a reasonable, prudent manufacturer of launch vehicles and provider of Launch Services."[37] Article 4 of the Arianespace Agreement also stipulates when the launch provider's contract obligation shall be considered to have been completed, stating that "Launch Services . . . are considered to be accomplished by ARIANESPACE once the Launch has taken place since ARIANESPACE has no control over the Launch Vehicle after Launch."[38] A similar statement stipulating the conditions for completion of Martin Marietta's obligations appears in a separate provision in the Martin Marietta-INTELSAT Contract.[39]

It is not unusual that provisions relating to the actual services to be provided appear in several different places of the launch contract. For instance, the Master Contract Between The Space Commerce Corporation and Energetics Satellite Corporation for Spacecraft Launching and Associated Services (1990) (hereinafter Soviet Launch Agreement)[40] offers a fairly elaborate description of launch and associated services to be provided in Article I, entitled "Description of Launch Services to be

36. General Dynamics Agreement, art. 1.
37. Martin Marietta-INTELSAT Contract, art. 2.
38. Arianespace Agreement, art. 4.3.
39. Martin Marietta-INTELSAT Contract, art. 5, providing that Martin Marietta's launch services are completed upon "the intentional ignition of the Titan III solid rocket motors . . . ."

Provided by SCC." SCC refers to Space Commerce Corporation of Houston, Texas, which is the U.S. marketing agent for the Soviet government agency in charge of commercial launch services. Additionally, Article X, entitled "SCC Responsibility for User Property," requires Space Commerce Corporation to "act diligently and exert all reasonable efforts to ensure that employees of SCC and of SCC contractors exercise high standards of care in protecting and preserving property of User or its contractors which has been delivered to SCC pursuant to this contract."[41]

LAUNCH SCHEDULE AND LAUNCH SCHEDULE ADJUSTMENTS. All of the launch contracts compared here contain a launch schedule specifying the window, or time period, within which the launch shall take place.[42] Generally, the contracts specify a launch window of from one to three months, referred to as the "launch period," and provide that the parties shall agree at some future time on a specific launch date. For example, Article 6 of the Arianespace Agreement, entitled "Launch Schedule," provides that

> The Launch of the Satellite shall take place during the following Launch Period:
>
> The Launch Slot within the Launch Period shall be determined by mutual agreement of the Parties no later than twelve (12) months prior to the first day of the Launch Period taking into account the available Launch Opportunities.
>
> The Launch Day within the Launch Slot shall be determined by mutual agreement of the Parties, based on a proposal made by ARIANESPACE, no later than four (4) months prior to the first day of the Launch Slot.
>
> The Launch Window . . . shall be determined by mutual Agreement of the Parties, based on a proposal made by ARIANESPACE, no later than the Final Mission Analysis Review.
>
> In the event that, for any reason whatsoever, the Parties fail to agree upon a Launch Slot within the Launch Period, the Launch Day, or the Launch Window, ARIANESPACE shall determine said Launch Slot, Launch Day, or Launch Window taking into account the available Launch Opportunities, and the requirements and respective interests of Customer and the Third Party Customer(s) of ARIANESPACE.[43]

---

40. Space Commerce Corporation of Houston, Texas, acts as a marketing agent for the Soviet Government with respect to space-related services offered commercially in the United States.
41. Soviet Launch Agreement, art. X.2.
42. Arianespace Agreement, art. 6.; Martin Marietta-INTELSAT Contract, art. 3; General Dynamics Agreement, arts. 1 and 2; McDonnell Douglas-India Contract, art. 3; and Soviet Launch Agreement, art. III.

A similar provision setting forth a launch schedule also appears in Article 3 of the Martin Marietta-INTELSAT Contract, entitled "Schedule for Delivery of Launch Services," although the launch period is three months and the deadlines specified for fixing the launch slot and launch date differ from the Arianespace provision quoted above. Moreover, Article 3 of the McDonnell Douglas-India Contract provides that McDonnell Douglas shall launch the Indian satellite during the Launch Period of March 1, 1989 to April 30, 1989. Article 3 further states that six months prior to the commencement of the Launch Period the parties shall agree to a Scheduled Launch Date within the Launch Period, and that the launch shall take place within seven working days of this Scheduled Launch Date.

Adjustments to the launch schedule, due to postponement by the customer or launch provider, may be addressed in the same provision setting forth the launch schedule, or in a separate provision. For example, the General Dynamics Agreement deals separately with the schedule modifications.[44] So do the Martin Marietta-INTELSAT Contract[45] and the Arianespace Agreement.[46] By contrast, the McDonnell Douglas-India Contract[47] and the Soviet Launch Agreement[48] address scheduling and adjustments in the same provision.

Normally, the parties are given some flexibility for delay in the provision of the payload and launch services. A maximum delay period is often stipulated (e.g., twelve months), and exceeding this period will result in renegotiation of the contract. The timing of the delay also is critical. Provided it does not exceed the maximum delay period, if the delay occurs after a certain date and within, for example, twenty months of the launch period, a delay penalty generally is imposed typically in the form of liquidated damages. On the other hand, if the delay is less than the stipulated delay period resulting in renegotiation of the contract, and occurs prior to the date beyond which a delay penalty applies, the satellite owner incurs no liabilities for not making the payload available as scheduled. See Chapter 6.4.1. for descriptions of launch contract provisions pertaining to late delivery.

REFLIGHT/REFUND OPTION AND REPLACEMENT LAUNCH. Many launch companies offer reflight and even launch price refund options in the event the launch fails. For a premium added to the launch price, a customer can buy a reflight guarantee, which entitles it to a new launch, free of charge, if the launch is unsuccessful; or it can buy a refund guarantee, which entitles it to reimbursement of the launch price. Premium rates now are about 10-12%; usually the premium for a refund guarantee is a few percentage points higher than that for a reflight guarantee. If it elects to

---

43. Arianespace Agreement, art. 6.
44. General Dynamics Agreement, art. 3.
45. Martin Marietta-INTELSAT Contract, art. 18.
46. Arianespace Agreement, art. 10.
47. McDonnell Douglas-India Contract, art. 3.
48. Soviet Launch Agreement, art. III.

purchase a reflight or a refund guarantee, the customer must select one or the other prior to the launch.

Article 8 of the General Dynamics Agreement offers an example of a reflight/refund guarantee. Entitled "Reflight or Refund Option," Article 8 provides the customer with a choice between a reflight or a refund, but requires that the customer's selection be specified in the launch contract. According to the General Dynamics Agreement, reflight/refund is awarded only in the event of a total failure. A Failure Review Board consisting of General Dynamics technical experts and limited customer representation determines whether a total failure has occurred. Also, Article 6 of the Martin Marietta-INTELSAT Contract offers the satellite customer the option of purchasing "Reflight or Cash Refund Guarantees." INTELSAT opted not to purchase either of the guarantees offered by Martin Marietta, an election the Organization certainly must have regretted in light of the launch failure occurring March 14, 1990. INTELSAT nevertheless proceeded to claim the launch price (see Chapter 6.4.2., describing INTELSAT's claim). Some launch companies offer reflight/refund guarantees through separate subsidiaries. For example, on January 1, 1986, Arianespace formed a separate subsidiary, Societe de Reassurance des Risques Relatifs aux Applications Spatiales (S3R), to manage the launch guarantee package available to Ariane users.

A few launch companies now offer satellite launch risk guarantees in conjunction with reflight/refund guarantees. Satellite launch risk guarantees cover the value of the satellite.[49] A combination of reflight/refund and satellite launch risk guarantees was offered by some launch companies in 1991 for premiums ranging from 16.5% to 18%. Offered separately, a reflight or a refund guarantee does not cover the value of the satellite or other payload. Moreover, as discussed at greater length in Chapter 6.4.2., launch contracts generally contain waiver provisions whereby the satellite owner waives its right to claim against the launch company for damage during launching to its property, including the satellite.[50] Launch insurance is available to the satellite owner if the launch company does not offer a satellite launch risk guarantee (See Chapter 8.5.).

A reflight/refund guarantee, which essentially is a form of insurance, must be distinguished from a replacement launch, which may be purchased, albeit on favorable terms, by the customer after a launch failure. No premium is required for a replacement launch, but usually the cus-

---

49. *See* Chapter 6.4.1. (explaining why satellite launch risk guarantees are compatible with the Commercial Space Launch Act Amendments of 1988, 49 U.S.C. § 2615 (1988)).

50. *See also* the Martin Marietta-INTELSAT Contract, art. 6.7. (providing that "[t]he remedies set forth in Article 6 [*i.e.*, reflight and relaunch] shall be the sole and exclusive remedies of Buyer from Martin Marietta in the event of a Titan III mission failure . . ."), and the Arianespace Agreement, art. 13.1, with a reference to a replacement launch, (providing that "[a]ll other rights or claims of the client, whatever their cause or nature, are excluded").

tomer is required to notify the launch company within a stipulated time period after the launch failure of its determination to purchase a replacement launch. It is important to note that the terms "reflight" and "replacement launch" are not used uniformly, and that other terms, such as "relaunch," may replace either of them.

A replacement launch, although it must be purchased, often is available at the same price as the failed launch and subject to a favorable scheduling arrangement. For example, Article 13 of the Arianespace Agreement provides that

> Customer is entitled to request a Replacement Launch from ARIANESPACE in the event that, following the Launch, either the Launch Mission or the Satellite Mission has not been accomplished for any reason whatsoever.
>
> . . .
>
> Customer is entitled to have a Replacement Launch Slot allocated by ARIANESPACE within the ten (10) calender month period following the calender month within which a written Replacement Launch request has been received by ARIANESPACE. The written Replacement Launch Request must . . . have been received by ARIANESPACE no later than the second calender month in which the cause of the failure . . . has been established . . . .[51]

Further, the provision stipulates remuneration and other conditions for the replacement launch.[52]

REMUNERATION AND PAYMENT FOR SERVICES. Launch contracts often have several articles dealing with launch price, terms of payment and economic price adjustment, although the McDonnell Douglas-India Contract and the Soviet Launch Agreement handle all financial matters in one article, entitled "Financial Arrangements". Prices for launch services vary depending upon the size and weight of the payload to be launched and the launch vehicle selected. Approximate price figures for the following launch vehicles (which cater to different payload sizes as described in Chapter 7.1., above) for certain categories of payloads are approximately: US$60-110 million for Arianespace's Ariane III and IV; US$90-120 million for Martin Marietta's Titan III;[53] US$60-80 million for General Dynamics' Atlas; US$45-60 million for McDonnell Douglas' Delta;[54] and about US$10 million for a start-up, entrepreneurial company's low-Earth orbit launch. The Soviets and Chinese have been alleged to subsidize their launch services in order to undercut substantially the launch prices charged by pri-

51. Arianespace Agreement, art. 13.1.1.-3.
52. *Id.*
53. According to Article 7 of the Martin Marietta-INTELSAT Contract, INTELSAT paid $219,960,000.00 for two Intelsat VI launches.
54. Pursuant to the McDonnell Douglas-India Contract, the Government of India paid $44 million for the launch of Insat 1D.

vate commercial launch companies in the West.

Launch contracts normally set forth payment schedules requiring that certain percentages of the purchase price be paid at specific dates prior to the launching, at which time the full price must be paid. A typical payment schedule appears in Article 8 of the Martin Marietta-INTELSAT Contract:

> INTELSAT shall pay the price due under this Contract to Martin Marietta with respect to each firm Titan III to be Launched in accordance with the following schedule:

Payment Due Date	*% Price Due*
At contract effective date	5.0%
33 Mo. prior to Scheduled Launch	5.0%
30 Mo. prior to Scheduled Launch	5.0%
27 Mo. prior to Scheduled Launch	7.5%
24 Mo. prior to Scheduled Launch	7.5%
21 Mo. prior to Scheduled Launch	7.5%
18 Mo. prior to Scheduled Launch	10.0%
15 Mo. prior to Scheduled Launch	10.0%
12 Mo. prior to Scheduled Launch	10.0%
9 Mo. prior to Scheduled Launch	10.0%
6 Mo. prior to Scheduled Launch	10.0%
3 Mo. prior to Scheduled Launch	7.5%
2 Mo. prior to Scheduled Launch	5.0%[55]

Similarly, under Article 5 of the General Dynamics Agreement,

> [t]he Customer will make an Initial Payment for each satellite to be launched as set forth in Article 1, equal to 10% of the Contract Price (less any deposit, if applicable) within thirty (30) days of the last of the following events:
>
> a. The effective date of this contract;
>
> b. The submittal date of the Contractor's invoice in the amount of the Initial Payment; or
>
> c. The passing of that date, which is thirty-six (36) months prior to the launch date of each respective satellite.
>
> The balance of the payments for each satellite launch . . . shall be

55. Martin Marietta-INTELSAT Contract, art. 8.

paid in twelve (12) quarterly payments beginning thirty-three (33) months prior to the launch date with each payment being due the first week of each calendar quarter, and the final payment due at the time of the launch, in accordance with the satellite schedule set forth in Table 5-1.

Table 5-1

Payment Number	*Percent of Launch Service Price*
2	10
3	10
4	10
5	10
6	10
7	10
8	5
9	5
10	5
11	5
12	5
Final Payment	5
	100%

In the event this Contract becomes effective less than thirty-six (36) months ahead of the launch date, the initial payment shall be the cumulative total of the Initial Payment and all Quarterly Payments that would have been made if the Contract had been executed thirty-six (36) months prior to the launch date.[56]

Article 10 of the Arianespace Agreement establishes a penalty for late payment by the customer, requiring it to pay interest "equal to the average ____ increased by three (3) points"[57] during the delay.

While launch contracts generally require payment of the entire launch purchase price by the time of the launch, in certain cases it may be possible to arrange for deferred payment or other favorable treatment from the launch provider. Typically, an entrepreneurial start-up satellite company may seek such treatment, and a launch company may be forthcoming in order to provide an incentive to use its launch vehicle, or if the launch

56. General Dynamics Agreement, art. 5.
57. Arianespace Agreement, art. 10.4.

company has acquired an equity position in the satellite company. Other creative ways of financing satellite launches have been explored. An article appearing in *Space News* on March 6, 1991, entitled "Indonesia Negotiates Launch-for-Oil Deal to Loft Satellite," suggests that Indonesia approached several commercial launch providers for launching of its Palapa B4 in exchange for oil or other raw materials. Such a barter arrangement would be unprecedented in the commercial space industry . . . but interesting and with imaginative possibilities.

Both the Martin Marietta-INTELSAT Contract and General Dynamics Agreement provide formulas for "economic price adjustment" in order to ensure that the Contract Price and Payment Schedule reflect the final price of the Contract.[58] The prices defined in the Martin Marietta-INTELSAT Contract are based on constant year dollars on the effective date of the contract, and the contract provides for appropriate adjustment of each payment stipulated in the agreement.[59]

RISK ALLOCATION. Detailed discussions are provided in Chapter 6.4.-5. of contract clauses pertaining to *force majeure*, interparty liability, warranties, disclaimers and third party liability. Many launch contracts contain *force majeure* clauses, excusing the launch company's failure to perform in certain circumstances beyond its control. Further, major launch providers include in their launch contracts interparty, or rather interparticipant, waivers of liability pursuant to which each participant in the launch activities, including the launch provider and the satellite owner and their respective contractors and subcontractors, agrees to bear the loss it sustains and waives the right to claim against any other participant. Disclaimers of warranty with respect to the performance of the launch vehicle, itself, often are found in launch agreements offered by those launch providers that also are vehicle manufacturers. Liability limitation clauses, generally appearing in launch contracts, serve to limit the launch company's liability for damage not subject to, or within, the scope of the interparty waiver provision, such as the customer's lost profits and other consequential damages and patent infringement claims. With respect to third party liability, the launch provider customarily procures insurance covering this risk, with the satellite owner named as an additional insured under the policy. In addition, the respective national governments of the launch providers often provide indemnification for third party damages damages exceeding the insured amount.

As a general observation, drafters of risk allocation provisions, including waivers of claims and hold-harmless clauses, tend to "overdo" them, presumably out of a fear that a provision may otherwise be deficient and not protect the client sufficiently. Overreaching, overabundance and redundancy often defeat the basic purposes of these provisions, however,

---

58. Martin Marietta-INTELSAT Contract, art. 11, and General Dynamics Agreement, art. 6.
59. Martin Marietta-INTELSAT Contract, art. 11.

and, at least in the United States, the law determining their efficacy is not all that well-settled.

TREATMENT OF PROPRIETARY DATA. For purposes of performance under the launch contract, it will be necessary for one party to disclose [60] to the other party.[61] The disclosing party may want to protect the data from further disclosure to others. Most launch contracts recognize this concern and provide for protection of launch-related proprietary data.[62] The Martin Marietta-INTELSAT Contract defines "proprietary" as pertaining to

> each Party's proprietary, secret and confidential information, data and physical materials, including information originated by, or available only from the disclosing Party and information originated by a Third Party with respect to which the disclosing Party has limited disclosure rights, and which the disclosing Party desires to protect against unrestricted disclosure to others . . . .[63]

The launch contract may require that the proprietary data be marked as such in order to receive confidential treatment.[64]

Normally, the launch contract not only restricts the receiving party's right to disclose proprietary data to individuals within the organization,[65]

---

60. This data typically includes information necessary for purposes of mating the satellite to the launch vehicle, such as information on satellite design, electronic components and stress and heat tolerance.
61. Additional restrictions may apply if the launch provider is a foreign company. Typically, a license to export technical data may have to be obtained. Under United States law, satellite-related technical data is included in the United States Munitions List, Category XVIII, 22 C.F.R. § 121.1 (1990), and subject to export license under the International Traffic in Arms Regulations, 22 C.F.R. § 125 (1990). For purposes of U.S. export regulations, technical data means "(a) Classified information relating to defense articles and defense services; (b) Information covered by an invention secrecy order; [and] (c) Information which is directly related to the design, engineering, development, production, processing, manufacture, use, operation, overhaul, repair, maintenance, modification or reconstruction of defense articles. This includes, for example, information in the form of blueprints, drawings, photographs, plans, instructions, computer software and documentation. This also includes information which advances the state of the art of articles on the U.S. Munitions List. This does not include information concerning general scientific, mathematical or engineering principles." 22 C.F.R.§ 120.21 (1990). The reference to "defense articles" in the definition is a reference to items on the United States Munitions List, which includes satellites
62. Arianespace Agreement, art. 16; Martin Marietta-INTELSAT Contract, arts. 30 and 31; General Dynamics Agreement, art. 21; and Soviet Launch Agreement, art. IX.
63. Martin Marietta-INTELSAT Contract, art. 30.2.
64. Arianespace Agreement, art. 16.5; Martin Marietta-INTELSAT Contract, art. 30.2; General Dynamics Agreement, art. 21.2; and Soviet Launch Agreement, art. IX.2.

but also requires that this party take reasonable precautions to prevent publication or disclosure to others.[66] Generally, the standard of care imposed upon the receiving party is that which the party would take to protect its own property.[67] Failure to meet this standard of care, as well as wrongful intentional disclosure, would render a party liable to the other under contract and/or general tort principles.

Certain categories of information generally are exempt from confidentiality treatment, even in some cases where the information is marked "proprietary." For example, the General Dynamics Agreement provides that

> [t]he aforementioned restrictions [on disclosure] . . . will not apply:
>
> 1. If either party can show that the Proprietary Information received from the other is or becomes generally available through the public domain;
>
> 2. If such Proprietary Information is in a written record in one party's files prior to its receipt from the other party;
>
> 3. If either party at any time lawfully obtains said Proprietary Information from a third party under circumstances permitting its disclosure;
>
> 4. If such Proprietary Information is disclosed with the prior written consent of the other party, provided such disclosure complies in all respects with the terms of such written consent;
>
> 5. Where such Proprietary Information is disclosed more than five (5) years after the date of receipt of the information.[68]

The launch contract also may provide for the return of proprietary data upon the expiration of the contract.

PATENT AND OTHER RIGHTS. Generally, the launch contract provides that neither party to the contract will acquire any rights in the other party's inventions, patents, copyrights, or other intellectual property, or to other proprietary data.[69] Some launch agreements provide for remedies to the party whose rights have been infringed. Article 14 of the Ari-

---

65. Typically, internal disclosure is based upon a "need to know." *See e.g.* General Dynamics Agreement, art. 21.2.c (stating explicitly that disclosure is based on the need to know).

66. Arianespace Agreement, art. 16.3.-5; Martin Marietta-INTELSAT Contract, art. 30.3; General Dynamics Agreement, art. 21.2.c; and Soviet Launch Agreement art. IX.3.

67. *Id.*

68. General Dynamics Agreement, art. 21.2.d.

69. Martin Marietta-INTELSAT Contract, art. 31, and General Dynamics Agreement, art. 24.

anespace Agreement further requires each party to hold the other harmless with respect to injury, cost, or expenditure resulting from infringement of the patent rights or other industrial or intellectual property rights of third parties under certain conditions.[70]

GOVERNMENT PERMITS AND APPROVALS. Often, government authorizations, approvals, or notifications of one form or another are necessary in order to launch a satellite on a particular launch vehicle. For example, a license or authorization must be secured from the national government of the satellite company to place in orbit and operate a privately-owned satellite.[71] Generally, a license or other permit also is required to launch a privately-operated launch vehicle. For example, a United States launch company must obtain a license under the Commercial Space Launch Act of 1984, as amended.[72] Moreover, if a satellite is launched by a foreign launch vehicle, a separate payload approval may be necessary.[73] Furthermore, if the satellite is to be launched from foreign territory, export licenses will be required to transfer the payload and necessary equipment and technical data.[74] Furnishing of data to the United Nations Secretary General, as required under Article IV of the Convention on Registration of Objects Launched into Outer Space[75] (see Chapter 2.5.), also may be addressed in the launch contract.

Usually, the launch contract recognizes that the parties will have to obtain these permits and approvals before the launching can take place and, although each party ultimately is responsible for obtaining its own permits or approvals, requires the parties to cooperate and extend their best efforts in order to obtain them. For example, in the Soviet Launch Agreement, the parties "recognize that approval for furnishing the services contemplated by this contract must be obtained from the U.S. Gov-

---

70. Arianespace Agreement, art. 14.4.
71. *See* Chapter 3.2. (describing the United States Federal Communications Commission's licensing requirements for United States telecommunications satellites). United States telecommunications satellite companies need to obtain construction permits and launch and operating licenses under Sections 301, 308, 309 and 319 of the Communications Act of 1934, as amended, 47 U.S.C. §§ 301, 308, 309, 319 (1988). Remote-sensing satellite operations are subject to a license pursuant to the Land Remote-Sensing Commercialization Act of 1984, 15 U.S.C. §§ 4201-4292 (1988). It is interesting to note that intergovernmental organizations operating satellites, such as INTELSAT, do not require national authorization in the same way a private company would. Decisions of the governing bodies of these organizations substitute for national authorizations as far as the organizations, themselves, are concerned. However, a private party participant in any such organization may require a license. For example, Communications Satellite Corporation (Comsat), which is the United States Signatory to (and "share-holder" in) INTELSAT (Chapter 5.1.) requires permission from the United States Federal Communications Commission to invest in new INTELSAT satellites, as well as to build and operate Earth stations for communications via the INTELSAT system (Chapter 3.1.4.).

ernment in the form of a license to export the spacecraft from the United States to the USSR for launch."[76] The contract calls for Space Commerce Corporation, the U.S. marketing agent which also is party to the agreement, and the customer to "cooperatively extend their best efforts in filing and prosecuting the application for the export license."[77] Similarly, under the Arianespace Agreement, "Customer shall be required to obtain all permits, authorizations, or notices of non-opposition from all national and international public or private authorities having jurisdiction over the Satellite Mission [and] shall also obtain all government permits and authorizations regarding the transfer of the Satellite and its Ancillary Equipment from the country of origin to the Launch Base [in Kourou, French Guiana]."[78] However, the contract also provides that "ARIANESPACE agrees to assist and support Customer and its Associates, free of charge, with any administrative matters related to the importation into French Guiana . . . ."[79]

In some cases the contract explicitly provides for termination at the request of a party in the event the requisite approvals have not been granted. For example, Article 10 of the McDonnell Douglas-India Contract, under which McDonnell Douglas Corporation (MDC) undertakes to provide launch services for the Government of India's Department of Space (DOS), stipulates that

---

72. 49 U.S.C. §§ 2605-2608 (1988). Under Section 6(a)(1) of the Commercial Space Launch Act of 1984, 49 U.S.C. § 2605(a)(1) (1988), "[n]o person shall launch a launch vehicle . . . within the United States, unless authorized by a license issued or transferred under this Act." This requirement applies to U.S., as well as foreign, companies launching from United States territory (no foreign companies are currently launching from U.S. territory). The licensing requirement also applies to U.S. launch companies launching from foreign territory, 49 U.S.C. § 2605(a)(2) (1988). Furthermore, the licensing requirement applies to a foreign launch company controlled by a U.S. person (individual or entity) when launching from the high seas, airspace above the high seas, Antarctica or outer space, unless an agreement exists between the United States and a foreign nation that the latter shall exercise jurisdiction over the launch operation, 49 U.S.C. § 2605(a)(3)(A) (1988). Moreover, a foreign launch company controlled by an individual or entity of the United States launching from the territory of a foreign nation shall not be subject to the licensing requirement under the Act unless an agreement between the United States and that foreign company so provides, 49 U.S.C. § 2505(a)(3)(B) (1988). "Controlling interest" means "ownership of an amount of equity in such entity sufficient to direct the management of the entity, or to void transactions entered into by management. Ownership of at least fifty-one percent of the equity in an entity . . . creates a rebuttable presumption that such interest is controlling," 14 C.F.R. § 401.5 (1988). In the United States, launch licenses are issued by the Department of Transportation's Office of Commercial Space Transportation, and are granted only if the proposed launch is consistent with "the public health and safety, safety of property, and national security interest and foreign policy interest of the United States." 49 U.S.C. § 2606 (1988).

> if MDC's request for approval by the U.S. Government of the sale of launch services to India or for transfer of technical data under this Agreement is denied or not granted within nine (9) months after the Effective Date of this Agreement, DOS may, upon written notice to MDC, terminate this Agreement, in which event MDC shall promptly refund to DOS all payments made by DOS.[80]

The Soviet Launch Agreement provides for suspension of the payments for launch services until an export license has been granted for the U.S.-owned satellite.[81]

TERMINATION OF THE AGREEMENT. Launch contracts normally provide for termination of the launch agreement by the satellite customer, as well as the launch company.[82] Usually, the customer is free to terminate

---

73. For example, if your client is a non-U.S. company and has contracted for a launching by a U.S. launch company, the United States Department of Transportation's Office of Commercial Space Transportation (OCST) exercises some jurisdiction over your client's satellite payload. Section 6(b)(2) of the Commercial Space Launch Act of 1984, as amended, 49 U.S.C. § 2605(b)(2) (1988), provides that "the Secretary [of Transportation, *i.e.*, OCST under delegated authority] may take such actions under this Act as the Secretary deems necessary to prevent the launch of a payload by a license holder under this Act if the Secretary determines that the launch of such payload would jeopardize the public health and safety, safety of property, or any national security interest or foreign policy interest of the United States."
74. *See* note 61, *supra* (concerning export of satellite-related technical data from the United States). Export of U.S.-manufactured satellites and their component parts is subject to the International Traffic in Arms Regulations, 22 C.F.R. §§ 120-130 (1990), since satellites and their component parts are included in the United States Munitions List, Category VIII, entitled "Aircraft, Spacecraft, and Associated Equipment," 22 C.F.R. 121.1.(1988). U.S. export laws are particularly relevant since the majority of the world's commercial telecommunications satellites still are manufactured in that country.

75 *Done* Jan. 14, 1975, *entered into force* Sept. 15, 1976, T.I.A.S. 8480.

75. *Done* Jan. 14, 1975, *entered into force* Sept. 15, 1976, T.I.A.S. 8480.

76. Soviet Launch Agreement, art. XV.1.
77. Id., art. XV.3.
78. Arianespace Agreement art. 17.1.-2. Also, Article 29.1 of the Martin Marietta-INTELSAT Contract provides that "[e]ach party agrees to support the other in obtaining any required permits, licenses and/or approvals.". Under Article 20.1. of the General Dynamics Agreement, "[t]he Customer and the Contractor agree that each party will be responsible for obtaining all licenses, clearances and permits, for taking all actions necessary to carry out their respective obligations under this Contract." Article 20.2. of the General Dynamics Agreement provides that "[t]he Contractor, upon request of the Customer, will provide its best efforts in assisting the Customer in the importation of the Customer-Furnished Satellite and equipment into the U.S."
79. Arianespace Agreement, art. 17.3.
80. "MDC" is McDonnell Douglas Corporation. McDonnell Douglas-India Contract, art. 10.2.

the agreement at any time and for whatever reason, but there is a penalty. Most contracts provide that all launch payments remitted up to the date of the termination, or a large percentage thereof, or of the launch purchase price, remain the property of the launch company and will not be refunded. The launch company generally reserves the right to terminate the agreement if the satellite customer fails to comply with the payment schedule.

SETTLEMENT OF DISPUTES/ARBITRATION. Sometimes, launch contracts provide for settlement of disputes that might arise out of the performance of the launch contract. Arbitration is commonly referred to as a means of dispute resolution.[83] For example, Article 8 of the McDonnell Douglas-India Contract provides that

> [i]n the event of a dispute or difference arising out of or in connection with this Agreement, which cannot be resolved by amicable settlement, the same shall be referred to an Arbitration Tribunal consisting of three members. Either Party shall give notice to the other regarding its decision to refer the matter to arbitration. Within 30 days of such notice, one Arbitrator shall be nominated by each Party and the third Arbitrator shall be nominated by agreement between the Parties to this Agreement. If no such agreement is reached within 60 days of the above mentioned notice, the President of the International Chamber of Commerce shall be requested to nominate a third Arbitrator.[84]

The McDonnell Douglas-India Contract further provides that the third arbitrator shall not be a citizen of the country of either party (here the United States and India), that the arbitration shall be conducted pursuant to the Indian Arbitration Act of 1940, as amended, and that the award, which shall be made by majority decision, shall be final and binding.[85]

GENERAL PROVISIONS. All launch contracts contain a series of general provisions concerning modification, assignment, applicable law, headings and incorporation, usually appearing at the end of the contract. Typically, these provisions will stipulate that modifications to the launch contract can be made only by written agreement between the parties to the contract,[86] and that assignment of rights under the contract without

---

81. Soviet Launch Agreement, art. XV.2.
82. Martin Marietta-INTELSAT Contract, art. 27; General Dynamics Agreement, art. 16; McDonnell Douglas Agreement, art. 6; and Soviet Launch Agreement, art. VII.
83. General Dynamics Agreement, art. 25; McDonnell Douglas-India Contract, art. 8; and Soviet Launch Agreement, art. XIV.
84. McDonnell Douglas-India Contract, art. 8.1.
85. Id., art. 8.2.
86. Arianespace Agreement, art. 20.3; Martin Marietta-INTELSAT Contract, art. 25; General Dynamics Agreement, art. 28; McDonnell Douglas Agreement, art. 12.7; and Soviet Launch Agreement art. XVI.2.

further agreement is prohibited.[87] Launch contracts usually are made subject to the laws of the country or state where the launch company is located. For example, the Arianespace Agreement is subject to French law,[88] while the Martin Marietta and General Dynamics Agreements are governed respectively by the laws of Maryland and California.[89] Exceptions to the general rule include the McDonnell Douglas-India Contract, pursuant to which McDonnell Douglas undertook to launch a satellite for the Government of India with the laws of India being made to apply.[90] Also an exception is the Soviet Launch Agreement for launching of United States satellites on a Soviet launch vehicle, and to which the laws of Colorado in the United States (where the satellite company is located) apply.[91] Furthermore, launch contracts customarily stipulate that the contract with its appendices and exhibits constitutes the "entire agreement," superceding all prior discussions and offers between the parties.[92] Moreover, headings, as used in the launch contracts, are provided merely for the convenience of the reader, and do not prevail over the content of the provisions.[93]

As with all unicultural, multicultural and multinational contracts involving complex relationships and high technology, precise draftsmanship is imperative in order to reduce to an acceptable level the risks of misunderstandings, misinterpretations and false levels of expectancy among or between the parties.

---

87. Arianespace Agreement, art. 20.5; Martin Marietta-INTELSAT Contract, art. 26; General Dynamics Agreement, art. 11; McDonnell Douglas-India Contract, art. 12.2; and Soviet Launch Agreement, art. XVI.6.
88. Arianespace Agreement, art. 21.
89. Martin Marietta-INTELSAT Contract, art. 21, and General Dynamics Agreement, art. 27.
90. McDonnell Douglas-India Contract, art. 11.
91. Soviet Launch Agreement, Art XVI.7.
92. Arianespace Agreement, art. 20.6; Martin Marietta-INTELSAT Contract, art. 37; General Dynamics Agreement, art. 30; McDonnell Douglas-India Contract, art. 12.1; and Soviet Launch Agreement art. XVI.3.
93. Arianespace Agreement, art. 20.4; McDonnell Douglas-India Contract, art. 12.3; and Soviet Launch Agreement, art. XVI.4.

8. Procuring Insurance

Insurance procurement is an important consideration in the implementation of any satellite project. This chapter describes the kinds of space insurance available to the satellite owner, your client (Chapter 8.1.); offers a chronology of space insurance losses (Chapter 8.2.); and explains the interfaces between the satellite owner and the insurance broker, as well as the broker and the space insurance underwriters (Chapter 8.3.). Satellite insurance policies are described and examples are provided of provisions the satellite owner can be expected to find in an insurance policy (Chapter 8.4.-8.7.).

Although the actual insurance procurement may not occur until after a satellite manufacturer and a launch provider have been selected, it is prudent nevertheless for your client to contact a space insurance broker relatively early in the satellite project, that is, at least before signing the satellite purchase and launch contracts. Today's space insurance broker offers a range of risk management services in addition to brokering insurance, and can even assist your client in its evaluation of proposals submitted by the satellite manufacturer and launch provider. Indeed, procuring satellite insurance is not a stand-alone process. Rather, it is closely linked to the satellite and launch procurements. Another reason for selecting a broker at a relatively early stage in the satellite project is to allow for flexibility in the timing of the insurance placement, thereby optimizing the chances of obtaining favorable insurance rates and terms for your client.

8.1. Insurance Options and Providers

FOUR TYPES OF SATELLITE INSURANCE. At least four types of space-related insurance[1] exist, and should be considered by your client to the extent risks of loss or of liability cannot be allocated contractually to the satellite manufacturer or launch company: 1) pre-launch insurance, 2) launch insurance, 3) in-orbit insurance and 4) third party liability insurance. Pre-launch insurance protects against physical damage to the satellite prior to the intentional ignition of the launch vehicle engines, or lift-off, and may cover risk during satellite manufacturing and testing, transportation of the satellite to the launch site, and mating and integration of the satellite to the launch vehicle, or any portion of these activities (see Chapter 8.4.). Launch insurance provides for coverage in the event the satellite is lost or damaged during launching, and typically extends for a period of 120-180 days after the satellite has been successfully deployed in orbit (see Chapter 8.5.). In-orbit insurance provides all-risk coverage indemnifying the satellite owner against partial or total failure of the satellite after it has been declared operational in orbit (see Chapter 8.6.). Third party liability insurance is designed to protect against liability due to loss or damage caused by your client's satellite and personnel or the launch vehicle to third parties, typically, innocent bystanders on the ground (see Chapter 8.7.).

HISTORY OF SPACE INSURANCE. The history of space insurance dates back to 1965, to INTELSAT's first satellite "Early Bird." Insurance was arranged to cover physical damage to the satellite prior to lift-off, i.e., the pre-launch phase, as well as third party liability. The insured amounts were $25 million and $5 million, respectively. No coverage was provided for the launching or in-orbit life of the satellite.

The 1968 failure of INTELSAT III F-1 to attain its intended orbit because of a malfunctioning launch vehicle dramatized the need to insure the launch failure risk, as well.[2] The Communications Satellite Corporation (Comsat), which then served as manager of the INTELSAT satellite system, sought and obtained launch insurance for the remaining satellites in the INTELSAT III series.[3] In these early days, launch insurance policies were written for a series of satellites and generally included one or two

---

1. Insurance can be defined as "[a] contract whereby, for a stipulated consideration, one party undertakes to compensate the other for loss on a specified subject by specified perils [or] [a] contract whereby one undertakes to indemnify another against loss, damage, or liability arising from an unknown or contingent event and is applicable only to some contingency or act to occur in the future." BLACK'S LAW DICTIONARY 721 (5th ed. 1979). In general, insurance may be divided into three categories: life, health and property-casualty (liability). Space insurance falls into the third category, property-casualty, and includes coverage for damage to spacecraft and related property and to persons participating in space-related activities and their property, as well as to third parties and their property damaged by space objects. Insurance often is described as a means by which losses of the few are spread among the many. It has been said that this description is unfitting for space insurance since only a very limited number of space launches have occurred and are occurring.
2. Prior to the INTELSAT III F-1 loss, six launches of commercial geostationary satellites had been conducted, and two satellites had failed to achieve geostationary orbit. Johnson & Higgins, Report on Spacecraft Insurance, 1990 [hereinafter cited as Johnson & Higgins Report], at 1.
3. The coverage obtained was about $4.6 million, which represented Comsat's financial interest. Johnson & Higgins Report, *supra* note 2, at 2.

satellite deductibles. From the mid-1970s on, however, coverage could be obtained for single satellite launches with no deductible. The first satellite in-orbit insurance policy was written for RCA Corporation's SATCOM 1 in 1975.

ATTRACTIONS AND CAVEATS OF SPACE INSURANCE. It is the allure of the large premiums that draws underwriters to space insurance. The attraction is particularly great if the underwriter does not fully appreciate the risk involved in space flight. Moreover, the fact that the premium is large relative to the exposure means that even a few percentage points of commission can translate into significant income for the underwriter if reinsurance is cleverly arranged.[4]

At the same time, the difficulty perceived in evaluating the risks involved in a space venture, a general lack of confidence in spacecraft technology, as well as the fact that losses, when they occur, are so devastating (often in the order of hundreds of millions of dollars), have caused reluctance among underwriters to enter the space insurance market. Evaluation of risk is key to establishing premiums, and is difficult in space business. This is true because, compared to other insured events, relatively few launches have and are taking place, and they may not be sufficient to provide an adequate statistical basis upon which to rely in evaluation of the risk involved in a given space project. Moreover, the technology involved in space operations changes so rapidly that even when a number of launches occur over time with respect to a particular type of vehicle, the specific technology employed today may be different from that used when the same type of vehicle was launched in the 1980s. Consequently, only a relatively small community within the insurance industry is actively involved in providing space insurance.

---

4. In B.G.R. Hughes, *How does Private Enterprise Insure the $200 Million Space Venture*, Paper presented at ABA Forum Committee on Air & Space Law, Lake Buena Vista, Fla. (1st annual forum Feb. 13-15, 1984) [hereinafter cited as Hughes, How Does Private Enterprise Insure], at 11. The author, then Senior Vice President with U.S. Aviation Underwriters, Inc., offered an example of how a small commission can provide significant income to the underwriter if reinsurance is arranged cleverly. Assume that an underwriter writes a risk of $10 million for a premium of 10%, or $1 million. Assume, further, that the broker's commission is 10% of that premium. That is, the broker receives $100,000.00, which means that the underwriter receives a net premium of $900,000.00 for assuming a $10 million risk, *i.e.*, 9%. Assume that the underwriter decides to reinsure 95% of the risk. In other words, the underwriter sells $9.5 million of the risk for a premium of $855,000.00 ($900,000.00 X .95), with a 17.5% reinsurance commission ($149,625.00) to the underwriter. Consequently, the reinsurers receive a net premium of $705,375.00 ($855,000.00 - $149,625.00) for assuming a $9.5 million risk. The underwriter retains a risk of $500,000.00 for a premium of $45,000 ($900,000.00 - $855,000.00) plus the reinsurance commission of $149,625.00. In other words, the underwriter receives $194,625.00 for assuming a risk of $500,000.00, which equals a rate of 38.93%.

THE SPACE INSURANCE MARKET: UNDERWRITERS. While in the very early days of space insurance only a few aviation underwriters in the United States and London would underwrite space ventures, marine and other types of underwriters have subsequently extended the field.[5]Today, major space insurance markets are found in the United States and London. Participants with lesser underwriting capacity are found in France, Germany, Italy, Japan and a few other countries. International Technology Underwriters (INTEC) and U.S. Aviation Insurance Group (USAIG) are major space insurance underwriting managers in the United States.[6] Other U.S. markets with lesser capacity include Southern Marine Aviation Underwriters, American International Underwriters and Extended Reinsurance Group, and the main United Kingdom underwriters are S. Merrett Agencies, C. Rome, M. Marchant and the Ariel Syndicate.[7] Behind the direct underwriters are companies that reinsure part of the risk. In turn, the reinsurers retrocede part of the risk to their retrocessionaires. Consequently, the risk is broken down and dispersed in the world insurance market.

8.2. Chronology of Space Insurance Losses

1977-1979. Although several insurance policies were written,[8] a major insurance claim was not made until 1977 when the European Space Agen-

---

5. The aviation underwriters participating in space insurance in the early days included the London Market, Associated Aviation Underwriters and United States Aviation Underwriters. Marine and other insurance markets began to pursue space insurance aggressively in the early 1980s. Johnson & Higgins Report, *supra* note 2, at 6.
6. Willis Corroon Inspace, Space Risks and Insurance Overview (ed. M.G. Aceto), Nov. 20, 1991 [hereinafter cited as Willis Corroon Insurance Overview], at 10.
7. *Id.* The most prominent space insurance underwriting manager in France is La Reunion Spatiale, which represents a number of important European insurers. *Id.*, at 11. La Caisse Central de Reassurance, a government-owned reinsurance company, is heavily involved in the Arianespace Launch Risk Guarantee program. *Id.* In Germany, Deutsche Luftpool, primarily an aviation insurer, recently has become more involved in the space sector. *Id.* Munich Re participates in Luftpool, but also is a major space underwriter in its own right. *Id.* Assicurazione Generali has dominated the Italian space insurance market since 1977. *Id.*
8. As noted, insurance policies had been written for INTELSAT's Early Bird in 1965. Moreover, Comsat insured (launch insurance) its financial interest in a series of INTELSAT III satellites after 1968, the INTELSAT IV series in 1971 and the INTELSAT IV-A series and Marisat in 1974. In 1975, launch insurance was written for several domestic satellites, including Canada's Anik satellites and satellites owned by India and Indonesia, as well as for the European Space Agency. As noted in the text, the first on-orbit-life insurance policy was also written in 1975.

cy's (ESA) Orbital Test Satellite (OTS) 1 was lost, due to a Delta launch vehicle explosion.[9] Payment on the OTS satellite represented a $29 million depletion of the premium base then established, and caused launch insurance rates to climb approximately one percent to about 8% of the insured value.[10] In 1978, the Japanese Experimental Communications Satellite (ECS) was lost due to a rocket stage separation problem resulting in a $12 million insurance claim, further depleting the premium base.

1979-1984. A catastrophic insurance loss occurred in 1979, when RCA's SATCOM 3 failed to reach geostationary orbit due to an apogee kick motor failure. Underwriters were presented with a claim of $77 million, a sum well in excess of the premiums paid up to that point. This large insured loss brought the loss ratio for space insurance to 200 percent, completely "jolted the market,"[11] and caused underwriters to re-evaluate the space insurance business very carefully.[12] A temporary capacity[13] crisis developed, and speculation was prevalent that insurance premiums would reach as high as 20%. Two subsequent loss-free years, 1980 and 1981, coupled with an infusion of capital from marine and non-marine insurance underwriters, which by then had begun to pursue space insurance aggressively, caused the space insurance market to rebound and insurance capacity to increase. Despite some losses in 1982 and 1983, insurance capacity per launch or per spacecraft increased approximately to $220 million by mid-1983.[14] The 1982 and 1983 losses included India's INSAT 1-A, which failed in orbit in April 1982 after six months of operation, resulting in a claim of about $70 million. ESA's Marecs B was lost the same year, due to a failure of the first operational Ariane launch mission, resulting in a claim of $20 million.[15] Also RCA's SATCOM II suffered tran-

---

9. Insured launch failures had occurred previously, but such losses had been deductible under the policies then in force, and no claim was presented to the underwriters.
10. STAFF OF SENATE COMMITTEE ON COMMERCE, SCIENCE, AND TRANSPORTATION, 99TH CONG., 1ST SESS., REPORT ON INSURANCE AND THE COMMERCIALIZATION OF SPACE (Comm. Print 1986) [hereinafter cited as 1986 Senate Report], at 6, reciting 1 ESA BULL. 67 (1978).
11. Johnson & Higgins Report, *supra* note 2, at 5.
12. The large insurance loss suffered can be attributed to these factors: 1) Launch frequency was too low to assure a healthy flow of premiums, and 2) adherence to the London-based "line slip" approach had prevented many brokers from securing sufficient capacity for their clients and had limited the amount of information available to underwriters on spacecraft risks, leading underwriters to quote artificially low rates. Johnson & Higgins Report, *supra* note 2, at 5-6.
13. Capacity refers to the amount of insurance underwriters are willing to commit for a single event.
14. Johnson & Higgins Report, *supra* note 2, at 6.
15. Marecs-B was insured only for a part of its full value. A meteorological satellite owned by the Italian Government, also destroyed on that Ariane mission, was not insured. 1986 Senate Report, *supra* note 10, at 7.

sponder failures in its seventh year of operation.[16].

1984-1986. The year 1984 turned out to be disastrous for the space insurance industry. First, Indonesia's PALAPA 2-B and Western Union's WESTAR VI failed to reach geostationary orbit due to malfunctioning perigee kick motors, although the two satellites had been deployed successfully from the National Aeronautics and Space Administration (NASA) Space Shuttle.[17] The satellites were insured for $75 million and $105 million each.[18] Later, that same year, INTELSAT V F-9 was lost when an Atlas Centaur rocket failed, resulting in a claim of $102 million.

These losses prompted yet another capacity crisis; only, this time the crisis was to intensify over the next three years. The seriousness of the crisis was evidenced by a substantial increase in insurance rates. For example, insurance rates for NASA Space Shuttle launches increased almost 300 percent, from 5-7% in 1983 to 15-20% in 1984.[19] According to a Report on Spacecraft Insurance, prepared by Johnson & Higgins of New York, "[a]ll underwriting placements were temporarily halted, conservative underwriting philosophies emerged, satellite insurance capacity was significantly reduced, rates skyrocketed, and a new underwriting emphasis was placed on technical analysis of satellite risk."[20] The 1984 insurance crisis was compounded by five satellite and launch failures in 1985 (Canada's ANIK D-2, which was insured for $4.5. million, Hughes' two SYNCOM satellites (IV-3 and IV-4), which were insured for a total of $170 million, GTE Spacenet's SPACENET 3, which was insured for $85 million,

---

16. RCA's claim initially was $29 million, but later was reduced to $9 million. *Id.*, at 9.
17. The NASA Space Shuttle deploys satellites in low-Earth orbit, and the satellites rely on a perigee kick motor attached to the satellite to boost them to geostationary altitude.
18. These satellites were recovered during a subsequent Space Shuttle mission. They were refurbished by Hughes Aircraft, the manufacturer, and re-sold by the insurance companies, which had acquired title to the salvaged satellites after making insurance payments to the satellite owners. In *Appalachian Insurance Company v. McDonnell Douglas Corporation,* 262 Cal. Rptr. 716, 214 Cal. Appl. 3d. 1 (1989), certain companies that had insured Western Union's WESTAR satellite filed a subrogation suit against McDonnell Douglas Corporation and its subcontractors, Hitco and Morton Thiokol, the manufacturers of the malfunctioning payload assist modules. A disclaimer of warranty and a waiver of liability contained in the contract between McDonnell Douglas and Western Union for the provision of the payload assist module for WESTAR served to preclude the insurers' recovery. *See* Chapter 6.4.2., notes 39-41 and accompanying text (discussing the litigation, as well as risk allocation provisions in launch and retrieval contracts).
19. STAFF OF SENATE COMMITTEE ON COMMERCE, SCIENCE, AND TRANSPORTATION, 100TH CONG., 2ND SESS., REPORT ON INSURANCE AND THE COMMERCIAL SPACE LAUNCH INDUSTRY (Comm. Print 1988) [hereinafter cited as 1988 Senate Report], at 9.
20. Johnson & Higgins Report, *supra* note 2, at 6.

and ESA's ECS-3, which was insured for $65 million).[21]

1986-1988. In 1986, the confidence in space insurance business eroded further as faith in space technology diminished significantly. During that year, virtually all major Western launch vehicles failed. On January 28, 1986, the Challenger exploded. The Challenger accident was followed by Titan, Delta and Ariane vehicle failures, all in the first half of the year. Only the Ariane launch was insured,[22] however, including the INTELSAT V F-14 payload for $82 million and third stage of the launch vehicle for $10 million.[23] A radiodetermination package owned by Geostar Corporation on board a GTE satellite valued at $2 million failed in orbit in 1986, as well.[24] Insurance rates soared in response to these losses and the psychological impact of the grounding of almost all Western launch vehicles. In 1987, launch insurance rates were reported to be at an all-time high of 25-30%.

1988-1989. Following the 1986 launch failures, commercial launches were not resumed until 1988. That year, twelve insured satellites generated premiums of about $130 million and losses were in the order of $150 million,[25] which included GTE Spacenet's GSTAR III satellite and India's INSAT 1-C.[26]

1989-1990. The year 1989 created a windfall for satellite insurers. Eleven insured satellites were successfully launched and underwriting premiums exceeded $220 million.[27] Of the twenty-eight satellites launched in the Western world that year, only the European Space Agency's Hipparcos, an astronomical research satellite, suffered a partial failure. A breakeven point for insurers finally was reached in the recovery from the 1984-1987 insurance crisis. Premiums matched total losses paid to that date from the beginning of space insurance, which was about $1.15 billion.[28] Insurance rates dropped to 16.5-17 percent.

1990-1992. On February 22, 1990, an Ariane launch failure caused the loss of two satellites owned respectively by Space Communications Corporation of Tokyo, Japan, and GE Astro, Space Division, of Princeton, New Jersey. GE Astro, the satellite manufacturer, was under contract to Nippon Hoso Kyokai (NHK), the Japanese national broadcasting network,

---

21. *Id.*, Appendix, entitled "Major Satellite Losses to Date."
22. 1988 Senate Report, *supra* note 19, at 7.
23. Johnson & Higgins Report, *supra* note 2, Appendix, entitled "Major Satellite Losses to Date." The Arianespace insurance covered the third stage of the Ariane rocket, *Id.*
24. Johnson & Higgins Report, *supra* note 2, at 7.
25. A. Deering, *Satellite Insurance in 1989*, VIA SATELLITE, March 1990, at 36 [hereinafter cited as Deering, Via Satellite].
26. Johnson & Higgins Report, *supra* note 2, Appendix, entitled "Major Satellite Launches to Date."
27. Deering, Via Satellite, *supra* note 25.
28. R. Jacques, *Windfall Year for Space Insurers May Spark Drop in Rates*, SPACE NEWS, February 18, 1990.

to deliver the satellite in orbit (see discussion of "turn-key" systems, Chapter 6.4.1.). The satellites were insured for $94.3 million and $95.1 million each.[29] An INTELSAT VI satellite worth $150 million, which failed to reach proper orbit when its Titan launch vehicle's second stage did not separate from the satellite payload as intended on March 14, 1990, was uninsured.[30] Another GE Astro/NHK satellite was lost on April 18, 1991, when an Atlas rocket carrying the NHK satellite on board was destroyed by ground command due to an engine failure six minutes after launch from Cape Canaveral, Florida.

8.3. Consulting a Space Insurance Broker

As previously noted, today's satellite insurance broker offers a wide range of risk management services in addition to brokering insurance. For this reason, and also to allow for flexibility in the timing of the insurance placement, it is advisable for your client to consult a broker at an early stage of the satellite project: For example, soon after the regulatory permits and approvals have been secured, but before requests for proposals to build and launch the satellite have been issued. Satellite companies that have launched satellites earlier may have established relationships with brokers, in which case contact often is initiated at an earlier point, for example, in the case of U.S. companies, while applications for satellite authorizations are still pending before the United States Federal Communications Commission.

The broker most often is compensated through a commission, which is negotiated with the underwriters as a certain percentage of the premium, and which usually is received by the broker when the premium is paid by the insured.[31] The commission generally is 5-10% for launch insurance and closer to 20% for other kinds of insurance. A broker may be willing to provide risk management advice throughout the satellite project simply in anticipation of placing insurance and receiving a commission. Sometimes, however, the broker will seek a fee-based consulting contract for risk management services in lieu of a commission, invoicing the insured for the fee plus the net premium (i.e., without a commission).

SPACE INSURANCE BROKERS. Some large brokerage houses have

---

29. J.R. Asker, *Insurance Will Cost More, but Little Movement is Seen to U.S. Launchers*, AW&ST, March 1, 1990, at 21. *See also* D.J. Marcus and S.A. Smith, *Japanese Try to Minimize Damage from Ariane Loss,"* SPACE NEWS, March 11, 1990, at 22 (describing the losses of the satellites and the consequences).
30. *See* E.H. Kolcum, *Separation Failure Places INTELSAT 6 in Useless Orbit,"* AW&ST, March 19, 1990, at 212.
31. The broker sometimes finds itself in the difficult position of having a duty to the satellite owner to obtain insurance at the best possible terms while at the same time receiving a commission from the underwriters. Of course, the higher the premium, the higher the commission.

departments specializing in space insurance. These include Willis Corroon (Willis Corroon Inspace), Johnson & Higgins, Frank B. Hall, Marsh & McLennan, Alexander & Alexander and International Space Brokers in the United States, and Willis Corroon, Leslie Godwin, Crawley Warren, Sedgwick James and C.T. Bowring of Lloyds in London. Willis Corroon, which has main offices both in New York and London, constitutes a merger consummated in 1991 between Corroon & Black Corporation of New York and Willis, Faber & Dumas of London (thereby also creating Willis Corroon Inspace). International Space Brokers, which is based in Rosslyn, Virginia. is a recently formed joint venture between Crawley Warren, Le Blanc de Nicolay Reassurance of Paris, France, and Frank Crystal of New York.

All of these brokers maintain world-wide networks through offices, subsidiaries or affiliates in other countries. Local offices are essential to doing business in foreign countries, although a the broker's London or New York office typically will get involved in brokering the space insurance. For example, Asia Satellite and Telecommunications Company of Hong Kong, a consortium of Cable and Wireless of London, Hutchison Whampoa of Hong Kong and International Trust and Investment Corporation of Beijing, China, consulted Willis, Faber & Dumas directly in London. Large organizations often consult more than one broker initially in order to obtain different perspectives.

THE BROKER'S SERVICES. Although the broker's primary function is to negotiate on behalf of your client optimum terms and pricing for the placement of insurance with underwriters, the broker also provides other services, including assisting your client in analyzing the risks associated with the proposed project; devising strategies for dealing with these risks; and designing an appropriate insurance program.[32] Furthermore, in the event a failure occurs resulting in a loss to your client, the broker will assist your client in pursuing claims against the underwriters.

RISK ASSESSMENT. After having familiarized itself with the proposed satellite project, including your client's objectives and strategies, the broker will assess the risks facing your client. (See Chapter 6. for a general discussion of these risks). Your client's risk profile will depend on the nature of the satellite project and the technologies involved, ownership and financing structures, and risk allocation provisions in the satellite purchase and launch contracts, if such have been consummated, among other factors.

RISK MANAGEMENT. As with the attorney, the broker will offer risk management options and strategies. Based on how risks generally are allocated in the industry, to the extent such a generalization can be made (see Chapter 6.), and your client's particular situation, it will be possible to present your client with a set of options. Those that appear to be more favorable than others will be presented in the form of recommendations.

---

32. Willis Corroon Insurance Overview, *supra* note 6, at 1.

For example, the broker may explain that while satellite manufacturers generally agree to assume the risk of physical damage to the satellite during the pre-launch phase, they generally will not be responsible for consequential damages in the event satellite construction is delayed, such as satellite storage costs, launch delay penalties and lost revenues. (Although, satellite purchase contracts often have stipulations for liquidated damages that may cover a small portion of the consequential damages, see Chapter 6.4.1.). Accordingly, the broker may recommend that your client purchase insurance for consequential damages (see Chapter 8.4.). With regard to the launch phase, your client generally has four options, and the broker will assist in evaluating them. The options are 1) negotiate a "turn-key" arrangement with the manufacturer (i.e., the satellite is delivered in orbit and with the manufacturer bearing the risk of loss or damage also during the launch phase), 2) negotiate a launch risk guarantee with the launch company covering the satellite also (see Chapter 8.5.), 3) purchase launch insurance and 4) self-insure (i.e., your client assumes the risk). Naturally, the broker may be expected to highlight the advantages to your client of being able to control its own terms and price of insurance (option number three).

DESIGNING AN INSURANCE PROGRAM: THE INSURANCE POLICY. When your client has selected options for contractual risk allocation to the satellite manufacturer and launch provider, the broker will design an insurance program that "dovetails with the risk provisions of both the launch service and satellite manufacturing contracts."[33] Assuming your client agrees with the broker's insurance suggestions and program outline, the broker will prepare the insurance policy in collaboration with your client. The attorney then will review the policy and offer its suggestions. There are no standardized printed insurance forms for space insurance (such as exist, e.g., for fire insurance) that are used throughout the space insurance industry. Each space insurance policy is tailor-made, and often is referred to as a "manuscripted policy." However, a space insurance broker often will have a generic policy prepared in-house that may serve at least as a starting point.

It is important to establish the parameters of an insurance program "as early as practicable in order to be prepared to seek the most advantageous timing for placement of coverage in a global market that can change significantly over a span of time [and] it is not uncommon for the most important details of large programs to be pre-arranged as early as three years before the actual inception of coverage . . . ."[34]

---

33. *See* A. Deering, *Launch Insurance Procurement: It's a New Ball Game*, SATELLITE COMMUNICATIONS, June 1990 (hereinafter Deering, Launch Insurance), at 33 (describing the relationship between contractual risk transfer and insurance).
34. Willis Corroon Insurance Overview, *supra* note 6, at 3. Another important benefit of early planning is that it allows for budgeting of insurance expenses at a critical financial planning stage. *Id.*

BROKERING INSURANCE. When the policy has been prepared and the level of coverage (partial or full) and premium rate(s) have been established, the broker will turn to the world insurance market to seek capacity and favorable rates.[35] Your client's collaboration will be necessary for purposes of technical presentations to and consultations with the underwriters. Because the amount of insurance required usually is so large — about $180 million for launch insurance covering physical loss of one average geostationary communications satellite and the value of launch services — no single insurance company has enough capacity to underwrite 100% of the risk. Consequently, the broker must try to accumulate sufficient coverage from several underwriters.[36] Of these, one will be considered the "leader;" the others will be "following insurers," all subscribing to portions of the risk.[37]

So far, the principal underwriters of space insurance have been syndicates in London and the United States. For example, among the underwriting groups that had agreed to insure two satellites lost in an Ariane launch failure on February 22, 1990, owned respectively by Space Communications Corporation of Tokyo, Japan, and GE Astro of Princeton, New Jersey (built for NHK), were International Technology Underwriters, Inc. of Bethesda, Maryland (15%); U.S. Aviation Insurance Group, Inc. of New York; Lloyds Aviation Department of London; Tokyo Marine and Fire Insurance Corporation of Tokyo, Japan; Assicurazione Generali of Trieste,

---

35. World insurance markets primarily include London, Continental Europe and the United States. In the London market, the broker actually will visit the underwriter and present his slip. A.H. Bolton, Luncheon Speech, ABA, Forum Committee for Air & Space Law, Buena Vista, Fla. (1st annual forum Feb. 23-25, 1984) [hereinafter cited as Bolton, Luncheon Speech]. *See* note 36, *infra* (explaining what a "slip" is).

36. In Bolton, Luncheon Speech, *supra* note 35, Bolton, a broker with C.T. Bowring in London, explained the term "underwriter" as follows:

> The term derives from our practice in London where we negotiate a system known as the "slip system," literally using a slip of paper on which is printed all the details of the insurance required. This "slip" will show the name of the assured, his address, the period the insurance is supposed to run, the type of coverage that is required, details of any particular inclusions of risk or exclusions of certain types of exposure, the sum to be insured, whether there are deductibles (amounts to be deducted from the settlement of claim), any standard "market clauses" and conditions, the amount of premium or the rate at which the premium will be charged, and last, but by no means least importantly, the amount of brokerage to be paid to the broker. Each individual underwriter at Lloyd's (and each individual insurance company) will put a stamp upon that slip and along side it write the amount of risk they are prepared to take. . . . The term underwriter therefore comes from the practice of each insurer denoting the share of the risk he is prepared to take by writing his share on the slip under the names and shares of other co-insurers

37. The subscriptions of the various underwriters are added, and the amount for each individual contributor is determined by reducing these shares to a *pro rata* percentage of the amount of the order. Bolton, Luncheon Speech, *supra* note 35.

Italy; and Munich Reinsurance Company of Germany.[38] Reportedly, Japanese insurers provided less than 10% of the total coverage.[39]

INSURANCE CAPACITY. In 1991, insurance capacity (which refers to the amount underwriters are willing to commit for a single launch event, whether it involves a single- or dual-payload, or a spacecraft in orbit) is somewhere between $200-300 million. Given that amount, the broker would be able to obtain full coverage for an average geostationary telecommunications satellite, typically valued at about $90 million and its launch services, which might be valued at $70 million. Moreover, underwriters now are willing to commit themselves up to two years in advance of the insured event. During the capacity crisis of the mid-1980s, some underwriters would not quote rates on programs until ninety days prior to the scheduled launching of the satellite, and the satellite owner at times could not be assured that adequate coverage would be available until a year before the launch.[40] As noted in Chapter 8.2., the space insurance market has been plagued by cyclical downturns and insurance capacity has not always been adequate.[41] Such downturns may recur, again causing a shortage of capacity.

8.4. Pre-Launch Insurance

Pre-launch insurance indemnifies the insured against physical damage to the satellite prior to launch. Consequential damages, such as launch delay penalties or lost revenues, also may be covered. Coverage may even be obtainable for damage and delay resulting from certain *force majeure* perils. Coverage may be purchased for the entire pre-launch period (including satellite manufacturing and testing, transportation to the launch site, payload storage and processing and payload integration with the launch vehicle), or for some portion or phase of this period (e.g., during activities at the launch site). Premium rates range from 0.25-1% of the sum insured per annum.

---

38. D.J. Marcus and S.A. Smith, *Japanese Try to Minimize Damage from Ariane Loss*, SPACE NEWS, March 11, 1990, at 22.
39. *Id.*
40. Deering, Launch Insurance, *supra* note 33, at 33.
41. *See* B. Stockwell and J.M. Eid, *Space Insurance: Friend or Foe*, VIA SATELLITE, March 1990, at 34 (describing fluctuations in space insurance rates and capacity). The authors relate that

> [t]he space insurance market during the past twenty years has been characterized by fluctuating rates and available capacity, resulting from an unstable stream of successes and failures. Initially, optimistic outlooks for new enterprise and high expectations for the performance of space technology applications led underwriters to set insurance rates for space related ventures at artificially low levels. Unfortunately, reliable technology has taken time to develop and market development has been slower than expected. Accidents and failures have occurred over this twenty year period at frequencies and in clusters that were not anticipated, causing underwriters constantly to reevaluate their rating structures, as well as their participation.

PHYSICAL DAMAGE: REPAIR COSTS. Pre-launch insurance covering repair costs in the event of physical damage to the satellite may be purchased by the manufacturer or the satellite customer, depending on the formula for risk-allocation adopted in the satellite procurement contract (see Chapter 6.4.1.). It is quite common for the manufacturer to retain the risk of damage to the satellite until the intentional ignition of the launch vehicle first stage. Therefore, it often purchases pre-launch insurance. In the case of India's INSAT 1D satellite, Ford Aerospace, the manufacturer, agreed to assume full responsibility for physical destruction of the satellite until launch,[42] and purchased property insurance in the form of a Marine Policy General Provisions (Cargo), Policy No. C19007B, insuring all risk of physical loss of or damage to the satellite from the time of unloading the INSAT 1D satellite at the launch site until the time of launch. During loading on to a McDonnell Douglas Delta launch vehicle, INSAT was damaged by a crane hook. Ford repaired the satellite, claimed $6 million for repair costs under the policy, and was reimbursed by its insurance underwriters. The insurers subsequently instituted a subrogation suit against McDonnell Douglas Corporation, alleging that the latter had been negligent in performing the satellite-launch vehicle integration procedure.[43]

In case the manufacturer does not assume the risk, or for some other reason, the satellite customer may want to protect against loss of, or damage to, the satellite in the pre-launch phase. An example of a rather comprehensive pre-launch insurance coverage is provided by the policy insuring Western Union Corporation's WESTAR IV, V and VI satellites, prepared by Alexander & Alexander, October 1, 1981 (hereinafter Western Union Policy). The transit and ground property insurance coverage under that policy encompasses

> [l]oss of or damage of whatever nature and however arising to each WESTAR Spacecraft, Launch Vehicle, Pam-D and all other associated and related equipment and material, complete or incomplete, including (except with respect to a launch vehicle) while in transit.[44]

It is interesting to note that this coverage includes not only the satellite, but also its launch vehicle and the payload assist module (PAM), which

---

42. Ford Aerospace first entered into a contract with the Government of India, Department of Space, on July 21, 1978. On November 8, 1985, the parties entered into a "Second Supplementary Agreement." This agreement was modified by "Contract Notice" dated June 26, 1987, according to which Ford agreed to assume full responsibility for any loss or damage to the satellite until its launch, although it was agreed that title to INSAT 1D would pass to the Government of India, Department of Space, upon final acceptance at a location owned and controlled by Ford Aerospace. Lloyd's Complaint (Aug. 13, 1990), *Lloyd's v. McDonnell Douglas*, PENDING, Case No. 90-10095-CA-D, U.S. District Court for the Middle District of Florida

43. *Lloyds v. McDonnell Douglas, supra* note 42.

was designed to boost the satellite from low-Earth orbit to geostationary altitude.

CONSEQUENTIAL DAMAGE COVERAGE. As noted, insurance can be obtained to cover consequential damages, as well, including launch delay penalties, satellite storage costs, lost revenues and the like, in the event the satellite is damaged prior to launch and not delivered on time. Such insurance usually is purchased by the satellite owner. This is true since, even if the manufacturer agrees to bear the risk of damage to the satellite until launch, it normally does not bear the risk for consequential damages. While a portion of the consequential damages may be off-set through liquidated damages or other penalty levied on the manufacturer, the insurance will cover damages beyond the contractual protection. Moreover, in the event the manufacturer has agreed to provide a "turn-key" satellite system, it may be responsible for on-the-ground storage costs and a launch delay penalty if the satellite is damaged, and it may want to insure, as well.

The Western Union Policy offers an example of coverage protecting the satellite owner against consequential damage at the pre-launch stage. Under that policy, the insurers agreed to pay for

> [e]xtra expense, loss of revenue and increased replacement cost incurred as a result of loss or damage [to the WESTAR Satellites, the Launch Vehicle, the PAM-D and all other associated and related equipment and material];
>
> Payments to the launch supplier for the Launch Vehicle and launch services for which the Named Insured is responsible to the launch supplier under the terms of the applicable launch service agreement, in respect of a delayed or cancelled launch, but only if the delay or cancellation is caused by loss of or damage of whatever nature and however arising to each Westar Spacecraft, Launch Vehicle, PAM-D and all other associated and related equipment and material, complete or incomplete.[45]

FORCE MAJEURE ("ALL RISK") COVERAGE. It is possible, although currently it is not common, to obtain insurance for delay resulting from damage due to certain *force majeure* events, that is, an incident or accident occurring for reasons beyond the control of the satellite manufacturer and satellite owner, typically an act of God. If the satellite manufacturer has included a *force majeure* clause in the satellite purchase

---

44. Western Union Policy No. WU-456, prepared by Alexander & Alexander, Oct. 1, 1981 [hereinafter cited as Western Union Policy], Insuring Agreement, section I, art. 1.A. The policy covered pre-launch (section I), launch (section II) and in-orbit (section III) risks. It should be noted that this policy was drafted a decade ago and does not necessarily reflect the current state of the art in wording of insurance policy provisions.

45. *Id.*, art 1.B., C.

contract, excusing delay in its performance for events beyond its control (see Chapter 6.4.1.), the satellite owner may want to consider *force majeure* insurance.

8.5. Launch Insurance

Launch insurance is intended to indemnify the insured for loss of, or damage to, the satellite during launching, and may cover the value of launch services, as well. It may be possible also to obtain insurance for lost revenues and other expenses due to the launch failure. Launch insurance is available from the insurance community. Increasingly, however, launch providers are offering various types of launch risk guarantees as incentives to potential customers in what has become a fiercely competitive global launch services market. Launch risk guarantees tend to be less comprehensive than conventional insurance, but are sometimes provided at lower rates, which make them particularly attractive.

8.5.1. Indemnification for Loss of, or Damage to, the Satellite

WHEN INSURANCE IS NEEDED. Unless your client is purchasing a "turn-key" satellite system from the manufacturer, or a launch risk guarantee from the launch company, consideration should be given to procuring insurance for the full or partial value of the satellite in the event of loss or damage during launching. Absent a turn-key arrangement with the manufacturer, the risk of loss of, or physical damage to, the satellite normally transfers from the manufacturer to the satellite owner at the time of intentional ignition of the launch vehicle first stage engines. Launch companies customarily require the satellite customer to waive its right to claim against the launch company for damage sustained during launch activities, including loss of or damage to the satellite (see Chapter 6.4.2.). U.S. launch companies are obligated under the Commercial Space Launch Act Amendments of 1988 (1988 Amendments)[46] to enter into such waivers. Recently, however, some U.S. and foreign launch providers began offering launch risk guarantees covering the value also of the satellite. A discussion of compliance of such launch risk guarantees with the provisions of the 1988 Amendments is provided in Chapter 6.4.2.

DURATION. Launch insurance coverage normally begins at lift-off, or the intentional ignition of the launch vehicle engines and remains in effect for a period of 180 days or until successful commissioning of the satellite in orbit. For geostationary satellites, such a post-launch period is intended to cover the satellite's final boost by an apogee-kick motor, or other thrust mechanism, from geostationary transfer orbit to the satellite's assigned location in the geostationary orbit, as well as the deployment of satellite

46. 49 U.S.C. § 2615(a)(1)(C) (1988). *See* Chapter 6.4.2. (describing risk allocation in United States launch contracts and discussing whether the prohibition is absolute).

solar panels and testing of communications equipment. Launch risk guarantees offered by launch companies usually terminate upon separation of the satellite payload from the launch vehicle.

RATES. In 1991, launch insurance rates ranged from 16-20% of the insured value, depending on the satellite and launch vehicle insured. Given a rate, for example, of 17%, and assuming that your client's satellite is valued at $80 million and is insured for its full value, the premium would be $13.6 million. The insured value will be higher if your client chooses to insure also for the value of launch services. (See Chapter 8.5.2.). Launch risk guarantees provided by launch companies and covering the satellite usually are combined with reflight or launch price reimbursement guarantees. In 1991 these combined guarantees were offered to one customer at a flat rate of 16.5% by one launch provider, and at market rate less one percent to another customer by another launch provider. General Dynamics' and Arianespace's guarantee offerings currently are referred to respectively as "Mission Risk Guarantee" and "Combined Risk Management Program."

THE LAUNCH INSURANCE POLICY. No standard launch insurance policy exists. Some generalizations nevertheless are possible. As with other insurance policies, a typical launch insurance policy consists of five parts: 1) declarations, 2) an insuring agreement, 3) definitions, 4) conditions and 5) exclusions. As with any insurance policy, the launch insurance policy constitutes a contract between the insurance underwriters and the insured, and generally is governed by rules of contract law.

DECLARATIONS. Declarations usually include the insured's (your client) name and address, as well as a description of your client's activity (e.g., establishing, maintaining and operating a communications satellite, and providing satellite communications services). Also, generally included among the declarations are the policy period (the period during which the policy is valid, e.g., twelve months); the sum insured; the point at which risk attaches; the point at which risk terminates; and the premium. In cases where the policy combines several different kinds of coverages, e.g., pre-launch, launch and in-orbit, attachment and termination of risk, as well as the premiums for those coverages, may be stipulated in the respective insuring agreements of the policy.

The policy may state that risk attaches at "the opening of the clamps, for purposes of Launch, which anchor the launch vehicle to the launch table," or an equivalent point at which, once the engines have been ignited, the launch vehicle can no longer remain on the launch pad.

Ideally, the attachment of risk under the launch insurance policy should occur at the point in time when the manufacturer's assumption of risk terminates under the satellite purchase contract (see Chapter 6.4.1.). Often the manufacturer's assumption of risk terminates upon the intentional ignition of the launch vehicle engines, thus leaving the satellite owner responsible in the event of a launch abort on the launch pad unless insurance can be obtained from the moment of intentional ignition. However, insurers usually are reluctant to assume additional risk while the launch vehicle is still on the ground.

Risk assumption typically terminates upon the earliest of one of several stipulated events: For example, 1) a specified time and date after attachment of risk (usually 121 or 181 days); 2) when total loss, or constructive total loss, under the policy is agreed for the satellite; 3) when agreed claims under the policy equal the sum insured (i.e., when the claims are paid); or 4) at the end of the policy period. In the event a policy provides that risk attaches at the intentional ignition of the launch vehicle, the policy also may provide for termination of attachment of risk upon termination of ignition of the launch vehicle engines (i.e., aborted launch). In this case, the policy may provide for reinstatement of the coverage in the event of terminated ignition.

Policies sometimes provide for payment of the premium by a relatively large deposit (about 25% of the premium) on or about the date of commencement of the policy period, with the balance due, for example, thirty days before launch. Policies sometimes entitle the insured to call for the return of the premium in the event the launch is delayed for an agreed-upon number of months. In such a case, the policy may remain in force, provided a new launch date can be established within the policy period. The insured generally is entitled to a refund of the premium paid in the event of cancellation of the policy. The policy may be cancelled by mutual agreement, for non-payment by the insured, due to physical destruction of the satellite prior to risk attachment, or because of launch delay exceeding a specified time period.

INSURING AGREEMENT. An insuring agreement stipulates the events, the occurrence of which obligates the insurer to pay or indemnify the insured (your client) in consideration of the premium paid, and subject to the terms, conditions and exclusions of the policy. For example, an insuring agreement in a Sample Satellite Launch Insurance Policy prepared by Willis Corroon Inspace in 1987 (hereinafter Sample Willis Corroon Launch Policy), provides that

> [i]n consideration of payment of the Premium, in reliance upon the statements in the Declarations and in the underwriting information provided to the Insurers, all of which is made part hereof, and subject to all the terms, conditions and exclusions of the Policy, the Insurers agree with the Insured as follows:
>
> To indemnify the Insured, up to the Sum Insured against any Total Loss or Constructive Total Loss or Partial Loss of the Satellite which occurs prior to termination of Risk.[47]

The insuring agreement in the Western Union Policy, Section II, which covers the launch phase, provides that

---

47. Sample Launch Insurance Policy Prepared by Willis Corroon Inspace, 1987 [hereinafter cited as Willis Corroon Sample Launch Policy].

> [i]n consideration of the payment of the premium and in reliance upon the statements in the Declarations, and subject to the terms of this policy, the Underwriters agree with the Named Insured [to pay for]:
>
> A. The failure of a WESTAR Spacecraft to achieve Successful Launch; or
>
> B. Partially Successful Launch.[48]

The Western Union Policy further provides that underwriters will pay

> A. In the event a WESTAR Spacecraft fails to achieve either a Successful Launch or a Partially Successful Launch, or in the event of WESTAR Spacecraft failure, the Agreed Value stated by endorsement for each WESTAR Spacecraft;
>
> B. In the event of a Partially Successful Launch, the amounts of loss calculated as set forth in the Definition of Partially Successful Launch and related definitions.[49]

The agreed values stated by the endorsements for each WESTAR satellite were $90 million for WESTAR IV, and $105 million each for WESTAR V and VI.

Disagreement may arise between the insurer and the insured as to whether an event triggering the insurance payment actually has occurred. In *Hughes Aircraft Company v. Lexington Insurance Company,* [50] which is currently on appeal to the California Court of Appeals, Lexington refused to pay Hughes, the satellite owner, maintaining that a total loss as defined in the policy had not occurred.

The case arose out of the failure of Hughes' Syncom IV-3 satellite to achieve geosynchronous orbit after its deployment by the NASA Space Shuttle on April 13, 1985.[51] Due to a power failure, the satellite's perigee kick motor failed to ignite and the Syncom satellite was left to drift in a useless, low-Earth orbit. [52] Hughes was under contract to the United States Navy to build five and launch four geostationary Syncom satellites on which the Navy would lease capacity.[53] Hughes entered into an arrangement with NASA for a Space Shuttle repair mission to ignite the

---

48. Western Union Policy, *supra* note 44, Insuring Agreement, section II, art. 1.
49. *Id.,* art. 2.
50. Case No. 6-650-805, Los Angeles County Superior Court. ON APPEAL, California Court of Appeal for the Third District. *See* P.D. Bostwick, *Star Wars: A Review of Space Litigation,* Paper presented at the ABA National Institute on Litigation in Aviation, Washington, D.C. (Oct. 10-11, 1991) [hereinafter cited as Bostwick, Star Wars] (discussing the case and other space-related litigation).
51. Bostwick, Star Wars, *supra* note 50, at 16.
52. *Id.*
53. *Id.*

perigee kick motors. Hughes then proposed to the insurers that they advance certain sums to Hughes for the repair mission and pay the remainder of the total loss later.[54] A portion of the amounts paid by the insurers would be returned if the mission was successful.[55] All American and London insurers except Lexington accepted Hughes' plan and paid on the basis of total loss.[56] The repair effort was successfully carried out and the Navy accepted the satellite for service on October 31, 1985.[57]

DEFINITIONS. Definitions of the terms used in the policy are always included. Particularly important are those that define the events that trigger an insurance payment, such as "Total Loss," "Constructive Total Loss" and "Partial Loss." These definitions incorporate other important terms, in turn, such as "Successful Launch," "Actual Satellite Life" and "Satisfactory Operation."[58] In the Sample Willis Corroon Launch Policy, "Total Loss/ Constructive Total Loss" is defined to mean that

> the Satellite, despite the exercise of Due Diligence by the Insured, fails to meet the minimum criteria for achieving Successful Launch, and the Satellite has suffered a failure which cannot be corrected by the use of available onboard components and/or reasonable TT&C modifications, such that the insured, using reasonable business judgment, determines that the failed portion(s) of the Satellite can not be used for its intended commercial communication purposes.[59]

"Successful Launch" is defined in the same policy to mean that

> at the Termination of Risk the Satellite can be used for its intended commercial communication purposes and is capable of achieving and maintaining [certain specified minimum criteria pertaining to]:

---

54. *Id.*, at 17.
55. *Id.*
56. *Id.*
57. *Id.*
58. In the Western Union Policy, "WESTAR Spacecraft Failure" is defined as "[t]he failure of the spacecraft to meet the Performance Specifications to the extent that the cumulative effect is that the spacecraft is unable to perform its intended commercial operations with a minimum of fifteen (15) Operable Transponders, irrespective of transponder ownership." Western Union Policy, *supra* note 44. Definitions, art. N. The same policy defines "Operable Transponder" as "[a]ny transponder on the WESTAR Spacecraft that meets or exceeds the Spacecraft Performance Specifications on an uninterrupted 24 hour day 7 day a week basis." *Id.*, art. G. The Spacecraft Performance Specifications are defined to be those found in the satellite procurement contract between Western Union Corporation and Hughes Aircraft Company, the manufacturer. *Id.*, art. J.
59. Willis Corroon Launch Policy, *supra* note 47, Definitions, art. 15.

(a) Station Acquisition,

(b) Actual Satellite Life . . .,

(c) . . . watts or more in RF power, and

(d) . . . Transponder Years.[60]

"Actual Satellite Life" is defined in that policy to mean

> the remaining span of time, expressed in years, as evidenced 180 days after Launch during which the orbit and attitude control maneuvers necessary to achieve and maintain Satisfactory Operation can be expected to be able to be performed by the Satellite, based on predicted subsystem performance and fuel availability.[61]

"Partial Loss" is defined to mean

> failure of the Satellite to achieve Satisfactory Operation, where such failure does not result in a Total Loss or a Constructive Total Loss.
>
> The indemnity afforded under this Policy for a Partial Loss shall be determined by multiplying the applicable Sum Insured by the following Partial Loss Factor (PLF):
>
> $$PLF = 1 - (\frac{TXP}{12} \times \frac{LF}{9.5})$$
>
> Where
>
> -LF is the Actual Satellite Life expressed in years.
> -LF X 9.5 shall not exceed one (1).
> -TXP is the number of transponders capable of being simultaneously operated in accordance with the Satellite Performance Specifications, but in no event shall exceed 12.
>
> Should the Satellite be declared by the Insured to be a loss of a nature for which the foregoing formula does not apply, and the Satellite is neither a Total Loss or a Constructive Total Loss, the Insured shall show proof of loss to the Insurers and Insured and Insurers shall attempt to agree to a settlement. . . .
>
> The amount of indemnity for Partial Loss shall be the maximum indemnity as described above, except if the Insured has previously been indemnified for a Partial Loss under this Policy or if

60. *Id.*, art. 14.
61. *Id.*, art. 1.

> the Insured simultaneously makes a claim on the Satellite under another clause of this Policy. If either of these exceptions apply, the amount of indemnity for Partial Loss shall be adjusted to eliminate duplicative recovery for loss.[62]

CONDITIONS. General conditions apply to the coverage, imposing certain duties on your client, as well as the insurers. Specifically, your client may be required to act with due diligence to prevent and mitigate damage or loss, and act at all times as if uninsured. Your client may be required to permit inspection by the insurers of its books and records containing information relevant to the insurance coverage.[63] Moreover, the policy may provide that your client warrants that it has not withheld any material information from the insurers concerning deviations from the spacecraft specifications in the satellite purchase contract, and that the policy shall be void if your client has misrepresented or concealed any material fact. Your client also is under a duty to inform the insurers of any material changes in the information already supplied. The insurance policy cannot be assigned without prior written agreement. It normally can be cancelled by either party upon mutual agreement, by the insurers for non-payment of the insurance premium; in the event of loss or damage to the satellite prior to attachment of risk since there is no longer an insurable interest; and by the terms of the agreement in the event of launch delay exceeding a specified time period beyond the scheduled launch date.

Another reason for cancellation by the insurers is when a material change has occurred in the insured satellite after the policy was written. In *INTELSAT v. Lexington Insurance Company,* [64] INTELSAT claimed for the total loss of its INTELSAT VA (F-14) satellite pursuant to a launch insurance policy subscribed to by Lexington.[65] Lexington had refused to pay, contending that the policy had been cancelled because of a material change in the satellite as defined in the policy.[66] Specifically, the INTELSAT V satellite as identified in the policy had been modified into an INTELSAT VA satellite containing an additional international business communications (IBS) payload.[67] Expert testimony presented during trial between July, 28 and August 11, 1988, indicated that adding the IBS payload affected the risk of loss during the launch phase with no more than one-tenth of one percent.[68] Whether that constituted a material change

62. *Id.*, art. 9
63. The policy usually will provide that in the event a loss occurs and a notice of loss is filed with the insurers, additional technical information will have to be provided at the request of the insurers.
64. The case was settled. R.V. Pino, Jr., *Legal Issues Arising from Space Activities,* Paper presented at the Assicurazione Generali Fifth International Conference on Space Insurance, Rome, Italy (March 2-3, 1989).
65. *Id.*
66. *Id.*
67. *Id.*

substantially increasing the risk of loss was an issue for the jury to decide.[69] However, during jury deliberations the parties settled the case, reportedly on terms that were considered favorable to INTELSAT.[70]

Your client must give notice "as soon as possible" to the insurers and file proof of loss in the event of a satellite or transponder failure or other circumstance giving rise to an insurance claim. In this connection, your client may be required to provide pertinent technical information about the satellite and launch vehicle design, fabrication, test and operation. The insurer undertakes to pay the claim, usually within a time period specified in the policy, for example, sixty days. If your client has procured other insurance covering the same satellite for the same event, insurance payment under the policy will be reduced to an amount reflecting the ratio that the sum insured under the policy bears to the whole amount of all valid and collectible insurance. On the other hand, the policy may state that permission is granted for other insurance. It is customary for policies to provide that insurers shall be subrogated to the insured's rights to recover damages. Certain subrogation claims may be precluded, however, simply because the satellite owner has no right. For example, launch agreements commonly preclude claims by the satellite owner in the event of a launch failure (see Chapter 6.4.2.) and sometimes specify that insurers of the satellite may exercise no subrogation rights against the launch company.

Some policies stipulate that the insured may have to return all or part of the payment to the insurers if subsequent events show that the claim should have been reduced or eliminated, for example, if the insured continues to derive revenue from the satellite. In practice, however, it is unlikely that a claim will be paid unless the insurers are absolutely certain that a loss has occurred. In any event, the policy may provide that even though an insurance claim has been paid, your client may use the satellite for scientific, testing or demonstration purposes which do not produce revenue.

The policy may provide for the transfer of title to the insurers at their request and upon payment under the policy following a total loss, or a constructive total loss, of the satellite. An interesting example of title transfer occurred when, after paying on a total loss basis, the insurers gained title to Western Union's WESTAR VI satellite and Indonesia's PALAPA 2B satellite, which were stranded in useless low-Earth orbits when their respective perigee kick motors failed to boost them to geostationary altitudes in February 1984 (see Chapter 6.4.2.).[71] The insurers later

---

68. *Id.*
69. *Id.*
70. *Id.*
71. Litigation ensued with respect to the perigee kick motors. In *Applacian Insurance v. McDonnell Douglas, supra* note 18, the insurers filed a subrogation claim against McDonnell Douglas, the manufacturer of the perigee kick motor. *See* Chapter 6.4.2. (describing the case).

arranged and paid for a NASA recovery mission, which took place in November 1984. The insurers also arranged for satellite refurbishment by Hughes Aircraft, the manufacturer. They later re-sold the satellites. PALAPA 2B was bought back by the government of Indonesia, and WESTAR VI was purchased by Asia Satellite Telecommunications Company, Ltd. of Hong Kong, and re-launched as "ASIA-SAT" on a Chinese Long March vehicle April 7, 1990. It is interesting to note that title transfer to the insurers in the event of payment was not addressed in the original policy. A subsequent agreement providing for transfer of title was concluded immediately before the NASA rescue operation. Reportedly, Indonesia was reluctant to sign at first.

The issues of abandonment and salvage of spacecraft are bound to become more important as additional nations and entities achieve the capabilities to rescue and retrieve satellites (see Chapter 2.7.). Currently, only NASA is in a position to carry out a satellite recovery mission. At such future time as rescue missions become more commonplace, insurers may want to require that satellite owners take certain actions to preclude a situation where the satellite is considered abandoned.

EXCLUSIONS. Exclusions refer to situations or circumstances to which the policy does not apply, and are standardized in property insurance policies today. Your client can expect to find in the policy the following stipulation of exclusions:

> (1) War, hostile or warlike action in time of peace or war, including action in hindering, combating or defending against an actual, impending or expected attack by:
>
> (a) any government or sovereign power (*de jure* or *de facto*),
>
> (b) any authority maintaining or using a military, naval or air force,
>
> (c) a military, naval or air force, or
>
> (d) any agent of any such government, power, authority or force;
>
> (2) Any anti-satellite device, or device employing atomic or nuclear fission and/or fusion, or device employing laser or directed energy beams;
>
> (3) Insurrection, strikes, riots, civil commotion, rebellion, revolution, civil war, usurpation or action taken by a government authority in hindering, combating or defending against such occurrence, whether there has been a declaration of war or not;
>
> (4) Confiscation by order of any government or governmental authority or agent (whether secret or otherwise), or public authority;
>
> (5) Nuclear reaction, nuclear radiation, or radioactive contamina-

tion of any nature, whether such loss or damage be direct or indirect, except for radiation naturally occurring in the space environment;

(6) Electromagnetic or radio frequency interference, except for physical damage to the satellite directly resulting from such interference;

(7) Willful or intentional acts of the insured, or the contractor authorized by the insured to construct and/or operate the satellite, including their legal representatives, designed to cause loss or failure of the satellite, except acts of the range safety officer in carrying out his duties.[72]

In addition, depending on the coverage agreed to in the policy, loss of revenue, extra expenses, incidental and consequential damages and third party liability may be excluded.

8.5.2. Indemnification for the Value of Launch Services, or Reflight/ Refund Guarantee From the Launch Company

As part of a launch insurance package, the satellite owner may wish to include coverage also for the value of the launch services in order to pay for the reflight or simply recover losses in the event of a launch failure. Alternatively, the satellite owner may turn to the launch provider for a launch risk guarantee covering the value of launch services. Major launch companies in business today offer customers the option of purchasing a re-flight or a launch price-refund guarantee (see Chapter 7.3.). If purchased, a reflight or a refund guarantee usually is not the subject of a separate insurance policy, but becomes part of the launch contract in the form of additional provisions. The purchase price for the guarantee option, the "premium," is added to the launch price. Arianespace has provided a re-launch/reimbursement guarantee since 1986 through its subsidiary, Societe de Reassurance des Risques relatifs aux applications spatiales (S3R), and United States private launch companies have been offering these guarantees since they began contracting for commercial launch services in 1987. In November 1991, rates charged by one launch company were about 12% for reimbursement of the launch price and 10% for a reflight.

8.6. In-Orbit Insurance

DESCRIPTION. In-orbit insurance is an all-risk coverage indemnifying the satellite owner, your client, against partial or total failure of the satellite in orbit. Ideally, the coverage should begin upon expiration of the launch insurance, i.e., generally, 180 days after launch, or after the satellite

72. This list of exclusions is standard for the industry.

has been declared operational in orbit. In-orbit coverage usually remains in effect for a year or two and is renewed on an annual basis. A review of the satellite's health will be conducted by the underwriters prior to each renewal in order to assess the risk. As an example of the coverage stipulated in one in-orbit policy, in October 1981, Lexington Insurance Company subscribed to a policy for Western Union Corporation's WESTAR IV, V and VI satellites (Western Union Policy),[73] with a life (in-orbit) coverage beginning at 12:00 A.M. Eastern Standard Time on the 120th day following each launch attempt and terminating at expiration of the policy.[74] WESTAR IV was launched in February 1982. WESTAR V was launched in June 1982, and WESTAR VI was launched in February 1984.[75] The insurance policy expired at 12:00 AM EST October 1, 1984.[76]

PREMIUM RATES. Premium rates are between 1.25% and 3% of the insured value per annum, depending on the health of the satellite. The relatively low rates compared to rates for launch insurance (see Chapter 8.5.) reflect the diminished risk to the satellite's continued successful operation once it has been declared operational in orbit.[77]

SERVICE INTERRUPTION COVERAGE. Satellite in-orbit insurance obtained by the satellite owner must be distinguished from satellite Service Interruption Coverage which may be purchased by your client's customer, such as a transponder owner or lessee. Service interruption insurance is designed to indemnify a transponder owner or lessee for direct and consequential damages, i.e., the value of the transponder and lost revenue, in the event of partial or total transponder failure in orbit.

THE IN-ORBIT INSURANCE POLICY. Again, no standardized in-orbit insurance policy exists, although, as in the case of launch insurance (see Chapter 8.5.), certain generalizations can be made. Satellite in-orbit insurance policies usually consist of at least five parts: 1) declarations, 2) insuring agreement, 3) definitions, 4) conditions and 5) exclusions. Declarations include statements concerning the insured's (your client) name, address and activity; policy period; insured amount; risk attachment and termina-

---

73. Western Union and its insurance broker, Alexander & Alexander, had prepared a co-authored policy for WESTAR IV, V and VI. This manuscript was known as Policy WU-456, and was submitted by Alexander & Alexander and brokers acting in conjunction with it to various underwriters in the world insurance market for subscription. When Lexington subscribed, its Policy issued to Western Union was incorporated by reference into Policy WU-456. Western Union Complaint (Jan. 16, 1991), at 7 and Lexington Answer and Counterclaim (Mar. 12, 1991), at 11-14. *Western Union Corporation v. Lexington,* PENDING. C.A. No. 91-193 (JWB), United States District Court, District of N.J.
74. Western Union Policy, *supra* note 44, Insuring Agreement, section III, art. 3.
75. Western Union Reply to Counterclaim, *Western Union Corporation v. Lexington, supra* note 73 (Apr. 16, 1991), at 7-9.
76. Western Union Policy, *supra* note 44, Declarations, art. 2.
77. *See* Willis Corroon Insurance Overview, *supra* note 6, at 7 (making this point).

tion; and premium rate. The insured amount will vary, depending upon the extent of coverage your client wants. The coverage may include the value of the satellite, as well as lost revenues. Moreover, the policy may stipulate periodic reductions in the insured amount reflecting the depreciation of the satellite's value during the policy period.

INSURING AGREEMENT AND DEFINITIONS. An insuring agreement may provide that, in consideration of the premium paid, in reliance upon the statements provided in the Declarations and the underwriting information provided to the insurers, and subject to the terms, conditions and exclusions of the policy, the insurers agree to pay your client the insured amount in the event of a "total loss/constructive total loss," and to indemnify your client in the event of "partial loss."

Loss may be defined in terms of how the satellite transponders, as well as fuel and power supplies, conform to the satellite performance specifications adopted as a basis for the coverage. The specifications of the satellite purchase contract usually are incorporated by reference in the policy. A Sample Satellite In-Orbit Insurance Policy prepared by Willis Corroon Inspace in 1987 (hereinafter Sample Willis Corroon In-Orbit Policy), defines "Total Loss/Constructive Total Loss" to mean

> physical loss of, or damage, or failure of the Satellite to meet the Satellite Performance Specifications such that the Satellite:
>
> (a) has four (4) or less transponders continuously operating in accordance with the Satellite Performance Specifications, or
>
> (b) the [Partial Loss Factor, see below] meets or exceeds a factor of 0.5.[78]

The same policy defines "Partial Loss" to mean

> the physical loss of, damage to, or failure of the Satellite to function in accordance with the Satellite Performance Specifications and which is not a Total Loss or Constructive Total Loss. The amount of loss payable shall be determined by multiplying the applicable Sum Insured for the Casualty Period by the Partial Loss Factor (PLF).
>
> $$PLF = 1 - \frac{\text{Weighted Actual Cumulative Transponder Life}}{\text{Stated Cumulative Transponder Life}}$$
>
> Where both numerator and denominator are calculated referenced from the same instant of time during the Policy Period.
>
> . . . .[79]

---

78. Sample Satellite In-Orbit Insurance Policy prepared by Willis Corroon Inspace 1987 [hereinafter cited as Willis Coroon Sample In-Orbit Policy], Definitions, art. 10.

In this policy a partial loss becomes a constructive total loss when the satellite is decapacitated by 50% or more.

Below is an example of in-orbit coverage as stipulated in theWestern Union Policy.[80] In that policy, the underwriters agree to pay for

A. WESTAR Spacecraft Failure;

B. Transponder Failure;

C. Insufficient Fuel;

D. Insufficient Power.[81]

The policy further states that the underwriters agree to pay:

> A. In the event of a WESTAR Spacecraft Failure, the Agreed Value stated by endorsement for each WESTAR Spacecraft.
>
> B. In the event of Transponder Failure, the agreed value per Transponder stated by endorsement. There shall be no payment hereunder for transponders not owned by the Named Insured, but this shall not adversely affect payment of the full Agreed Value to the Named Insured in the event of WESTAR Spacecraft Failure.
>
> C. In the event of Insufficient Fuel, the Agreed Value per pound of hydrazine stated by endorsement. Underwriters will pay for loss of hydrazine occurring after the expiration of this policy that results from causes known to exist during the policy period.
>
> D. In the event of Insufficient Power: (i) If the Insufficient Power results in predicted transponder life expectancy that is less than the WESTAR Spacecraft's design life, the amount of loss shall be calculated by the following formula:

---

79. *Id.*, art. 5. "Weighted Actual Cumulative Transponder Life" shall mean
    N ODD + N EVEN, where
    N ODD = the sum of the Actual Transponder Life of each of the five odd numbered Transponders Multiplied by a Weighing factor of 0.095 and
    N EVEN = the sum of the Actual Transponder Life of each of the five even numbered Transponders Multiplied by the Weighing factor of 0.105.
    Id., art. 12. "At any time during the Policy Period, the Stated Cumulative Transponder Life shall mean the product of 10 Transponders multiplied by the period of time, expressed in number of calender years or fraction thereof, counting from any time within the Policy Period until 31st July, 1994." *Id.*, art. 8.
80. The Western Union Policy, *supra* note 44, dates back to 1981, and does not necessarily represent the current state of the art in wording of policy provisions.
81. Western Union Policy, *supra* note 44, Insuring Agreement, section III, art. 1.

X-Y
X Multiplied by: Stated Amount of the WESTAR Spacecraft stated by endorsement
Equals: $Amount of Loss

X = 240 transponder years (life design)

Y = predicted transponder life expectancy (in years)

. . .

(ii) If because of Insufficient Power any transponder which is otherwise an Operable Transponder must be turned off, it shall be considered a Transponder Failure and Underwriters will pay the Agreed Value per transponder stated by endorsement.

Underwriters will pay only the greater of the two loss amounts calculated under (i) and (ii) above.[82]

Endorsements to the policy provide that the Agreed Value of the WESTAR satellites are $90 million for WESTAR IV and $105 million each for WESTAR V and VI; that the Agreed Value of a transponder is $9 million; and that the Agreed Value per pound of hydrazine is $3 million.

Insurance payment for insufficient fuel is at issue in *Western Union Corporation v. Lexington Insurance Company,* [83] which is pending. Western Union, the owner of the WESTAR satellites, sued Lexington, the insurer, for failure to pay under the policy quoted, above. The suit arose out of indications that WESTAR IV and V might fail before the expiration of their expected ten year lifetimes, due to insufficient hydrazine fuel.

As stated in the policy, Lexington agreed to pay Western Union "in the event of Insufficient Fuel, the Agreed value per pound of hydrazine . . . ."[84] "Insufficient Fuel" was defined in the policy as a situation in which "the WESTAR Spacecraft's Reaction Control Subsystem has less than the budgeted amount of hydrazine fuel remaining at the end of the indicated time period as stated by endorsement."[85] The Reaction Control System on the WESTAR satellite, a HS 376 Model manufactured by Hughes Aircraft Company, consists of four thrusters and four tanks containing hydrazine, a liquid propellant fuel.[86] Hydrazine is used to position the satellite in the geostationary orbit and to keep its station on orbit, and is essential to the proper functioning of the satellite.[87]

Lexington had refused to pay, contending among other defenses that

82. *Id.,* art. 2.
83. *See supra* note 73 (providing status of litigation, forum and case number).
84. Western Union Complaint, *supra* note 73, at 7.
85. Lexington Answer and Counterclaim, *supra* note 73, at 16. Western Union was obligated to provide the insurers with a hydrazine budget for WESTAR IV, which was to become an endorsement to Policy WU-456, *Id.,* at 15.
86. Western Union Complaint, *supra* note 73, at 4.
87. *Id.*

there was "no occurrence of insufficient fuel as to WESTAR IV prior the termination of the policy at 12:01 AM EST on October 1, 1984."[88] Western Union argued that, pursuant to the policy, the "[u]nderwriters will pay for loss of hydrazine occurring after the expiration of the policy that results from causes known to exist during the policy period."[89] While it did not become aware of the fuel insufficiency and potential shortened life of WESTAR IV until 1987, i.e., after the policy expired, Western Union claimed that the fuel loss resulted from a cause known to have existed during the policy period.[90] According to a determination made by Western Union and the manufacturer, Hughes Aircraft, the insufficient fuel was caused by "the plume of the jet stream of the fuel hitting a solar panel of the Satellites."[91]

CONDITIONS. Conditions apply to the insurance coverage, that impose certain duties on your client, as well as the insurers. Typically, your client must act with due diligence to prevent or mitigate damages and act at all times as if uninsured. Moreover, your client will be under a duty to provide certain financial and technical information. For example, your client may be required to provide a review of the operating conditions of the satellite, including any anomalies and deviations from performance specifications, before the date of attachment of risk, and always before renewal. Policies sometimes provide that your client warrants that all anomalies and deviations at the inception of the policy period have been disclosed, and that the insurance policy shall be void if your client has misrepresented or concealed any material fact. Your client also is under a duty to inform the insurers of any material changes in the information already supplied. The insurance policy cannot be assigned without prior written agreement, and usually can be cancelled upon mutual agreement or by the insurers for non-payment of the insurance premium by your client.

Your client usually must give notice "as soon as possible" to the insurers, directly or through the insurance broker, and file proof of loss in the event of a satellite or a transponder failure giving rise to an insurance claim. The insurers undertake to pay the claim within a time period usually specified in the policy, e.g., sixty days. If your client has procured other insurance covering the same satellite for the same event, insurance payment under the policy may be reduced (see Chapter 8.5.). Generally, the policy provides that the insurers shall be subrogated to your client's rights to recover damages from, for example, the satellite manufacturer or its subcontractors, and your client is under a duty to cooperate with the insurers in this respect. Some policies provide that the insured shall return all or part of the payment from the insurers if subsequent events show that the claim should have been reduced or eliminated, for example, if the

88. Lexington Answer and Counterclaim, *supra* note 73, at 26.
89. Western Union Complaint, *supra* note 73, at 7.
90. *Id.*, at 9.
91. *Id.*

insured continues to derive revenue from the satellite. Again, this situation is not very practical because the insurers will not pay until they are reasonably certain that a loss has occurred. The policy may provide that even though an insurance claim has been paid, your client may use the satellite for scientific, testing, or demonstration purposes which do not produce revenue. Title to the satellite will transfer to the insurers upon payment of the insurance claim if so stipulated in the policy orn subsequent agreement and the insurers request title transfer.

EXCLUSIONS. Exclusions apply here, as well, and are similar to those found in launch insurance policies listed in Chapter 8.5.1. They typically include war, or war-like, situations, insurrection and strikes, confiscation by order of government, nuclear reaction, electromagnetic interference and willful or intentional act by your client or its contractors. Particularly noteworthy is the exclusion concerning electromagnetic interference, a not uncommon occurrence for which your client, if it is a United States company, has recourse only through the Federal Communications Commission.[92] Revenue loss your client may suffer as a result of a satellite malfunction may also be excluded, depending upon the coverage agreed to under the policy. Third party liability that your client could incur if its satellite causes damage, e.g., to another satellite or to persons and property on the ground, is not covered (see Chapter 8.7., below).

ORBITAL DEBRIS. Orbital debris increasingly will become a concern to insurers, as well as the insured satellite owners. While commercial satellite operations in the geostationary orbit currently are not seriously threatened by orbital debris, the situation may change in the not to distant future, absent comprehensive national and international strategies for addressing the debris problem. The situation in the low-Earth orbit environment already is somewhat precarious. For example, NASA has reported that its Space Shuttle windscreen was damaged by space debris, and on two recent missions, the agency executed collision avoidance maneuvers. Absent effective traffic management and debris mitigation measures, debris could become a threat to low-Earth orbit commercial satellite systems currently being proposed by U.S. private entities (see Chapter 3.1.6.) and the International Maritime Satellite Organization (INMARSAT). Of course, these satellite systems, themselves, will also be debris generators. A report published by the American Institute of Aeronautics and Astronautics in April 1992, entitled "Orbital Debris Mitigation Techniques: Technical, Economic, and Legal Aspects," recommends that certain legal, regulatory and policy actions be taken immediately both at the international and U.S. national level in order to address the debris problem. Before concrete measures are taken to manage the growing debris population in order to keep the risk of impact at an acceptable

---

92. Most interference problems are solved before the satellite is launched, *see* Chapters 3.2. and 4.3. (describing the United States Federal Communications Commission Licensing process and International Telecommunication Union frequency coordination).

level, orbital debris increasingly may have to be factored into the underwriter's evaluation of risk in connection with a particular mission.

8.7. Third Party Liability Insurance

Third-party[93] damage caused by your client's personnel and property, including the satellite, and giving rise to liability, may occur during 1) satellite manufacturing, testing and transportation to the launch site, 2) activities at the launch site, including integration with the launch vehicle, 3) satellite launching, 4) satellite operation in orbit and 5) the satellite's post-operational (debris) phase. For a discussion of your client's liability, see Chapter 6.5., and for a discussion of international liability, see Chapter 2.8.

WHEN INSURANCE IS NEEDED. The risk of third party damage during satellite manufacturing, testing and transportation to the launch site usually is assumed by the manufacturer (see Chapter 6.5.1.), and the satellite owner, your client, does not have to obtain insurance. Furthermore, if your client contracts with a U.S. launch company, the company will have in place launch site insurance, as well as launch insurance, protecting itself, your client, the U.S. government and other private party launch participants against third party claims. (The launch company also will have property insurance to compensate government launch participants for damage to their property). These insurance coverages are required by law. See Chapter 8.7.1., below. If your client contracts with a foreign launch provider, and that company only takes out third party liability insurance for the launch, your client may consider obtaining insurance protecting itself against third party claims during launch site operations.

Third party liability insurance for satellites which have been declared operational in orbit is not common. If your client's satellite is geostationary, the risk of third party damage to the surface of the Earth is virtually non-existent once the satellite has been declared operational. The risk of damage to other geostationary satellites, while present, is not substantial. With very few exceptions (a handful of remote-sensing satellites), all commercial satellite operations to date have been geostationary. However, several low-Earth orbit satellite constellations are now being proposed. If your client is planning a low-Earth orbit satellite system at an altitude where gravity and atmospheric drag could cause the satellite's orbit to decay with a resulting uncontrolled reentry of the satellite into the Earth's atmosphere, the risk of damage on the surface of the Earth is present and

---

93. An innocent bystander is the typical third party. In the context of launch risk allocation, third parties do not necessarily include all parties with which the satellite company, your client, has no contractual relationship. Considering how many commercial launch contracts are structured, the parties that participate in the launch activities will not necessarily be considered third parties even though they are not included in the contract with your client. *See* Chapter 6.5.2. (describing risk allocation for third party damage in the launch contract).

your client may want to consider third party liability insurance. Moreover, as crowding increases in the low-Earth orbit environment, the risk of in-space collisions will increase and your client may want to consider third party liability insurance in the future.

Third party liability insurance for satellites whose lives have expired and which have become non-functional (debris), is not being offered today. At this time, it is unlikely that liability would attach if your client's expired, non-functional spacecraft damaged an operational satellite in space. Under international law (see Chapter 2.8.), as well as under most national legal regimes, the claimant State/satellite owner would have to prove fault. Assuming the fault standard is negligence/*culpa* it would be almost impossible to establish fault given the *current* practice with respect to satellites at end-of-life, the lack of legal requirements for disposal of satellites at end-of-life, the lack of recovery options, and the prohibitive cost of recovery missions. While liability may be unlikely today and in the near future, this will not always be true. As space operations mature, technology evolves, and certain debris disposal methods become standard practice and even legally required, liability will be established and insurance protection will have to be considered.

8.7.1. Insurance Purchased by the Launch Company.

MAJOR LAUNCH COMPANIES PURCHASE INSURANCE. Major launch companies in business today[94] procure third party liability insurance, naming the satellite owner, your client, as an additional insured. In fact, United States launch providers are obligated to do so by the Commercial Space Launch Act Amendments of 1988[95] (the 1988 Amendments), and the insurance shall protect your client's contractors and subcontractors, as well. See Chapter 6.5.2.1. The amounts of coverage purchased by the different launch companies vary. For example, Arianespace takes out insurance in the amount of FF400 million (about $65 million). United States launch companies are bound by determinations of the Office of Commercial Space Transportation[96] regarding the amount of insurance to obtain. Under the 1988 Amendments, this amount shall not exceed $500 million, or the maximum liability insurance available on the world market at a reasonable cost if such insurance is less than $500 million.[97] So far, the insurance amounts prescribed by the Office of Commer-

94. *See* Chapter 7.1. (profiling the major launch companies).

95. 49 U.S.C. § 2615(a)(1)(A) (1988). Alternatively, the launch company can "demonstrate financial responsibility." *Id.* "Any insurance policy obtained . . . shall protect the United States, its agencies, personnel, contractors, and subcontractors, and all contractors, subcontractors and *customers of the licensee or transferee, and all contractors and subcontractors of such customers, involved in providing the launch services* . . . ." 49 U.S.C. § 2615(a)(2) (1988) (emphasis added). "Customer" refers to the satellite owner, your client. The "licensee" or "transferee" refers to the launch company.

cial Space Transportation have been $215 million for a Martin Marietta Titan launch, $164 million for a McDonnell Douglas Delta launch and $10 million dollars for Orbital Sciences. Premium rates for third party liability insurance are about 0.1 percent of the sum insured.[98]

THE DURATION OF THE COVERAGE VARIES. The duration of the third party liability insurance may vary. Depending upon whether your client has purchased the launch from a U.S. or a non-U.S. launch company, the insurance policy purchased by the launch company may provide for risk attachment and termination at different points of the satellite project implementation. U.S. launch companies are required under the 1988 Amendments to purchase third-party liability insurance covering "activities carried out under the license in connection with any particular launch . . . ."[99] The requirement has been interpreted by the Office of Commercial Space Transportation, the agency charged with enforcing the 1988 Amendments, to mean that "[e]ach policy shall provide that coverage shall attach upon commencement of commercial launch activities, and shall remain in force for a period of thirty (30) days following payload insertion into orbit . . . ."[100] In the license order issued to Martin Marietta in February 1990, the agency defined "commercial space activities" as "(i) the launch from the Cape Canaveral Air Force Station (CCAFS) of a Commercial Titan vehicle transporting the INTELSAT VI payload to low earth orbit, to take place not later than September 1990; and (ii) launch site operations at CCAFS associated with the conduct of such launch."[101] The precise event marking the commencement of commercial launch activities

---

96. 49 U.S.C. § 2615(a)(1)(A) (1988), providing that the Secretary of Transportation, after consultation with other agencies (including the Administrator of NASA and the Secretary of the Air Force), shall determine the amount of insurance coverage each launch company applying for a license must purchase. The Office of Commercial Space Transportation acts under delegated authority from the Secretary of Transportation.
97. 49 U.S.C. § 2615(a)(1)(A) (1988).
98. Interestingly enough, although no third party damage from a spacecraft had resulted in an insurance claim, liability insurance rates increased during the space insurance capacity crisis in the mid-1980s from 0.02%.
99. 49 U.S.C. § 2615(b)(1) (1988).
100. *Martin Marietta Commercial Titan, Inc.,* Office of Commercial Space Transportation, License No. 90-013, issued Feb. 15, 1990, Order Regarding Responsibilities for Requirements Under Sections 15(c) and 16 of the Commercial Space Launch Act, at 3. In a more recent launch authorization, the third-party liability insurance requirement was formulated differently, but the requirements to the coverage appear to be the same. *General Dynamics Commercial Launch Services, Inc.,* Office of Commercial Space Transportation, License No. LLO 91-019, Order Regarding Financial Responsibility Requirements for Commercial Launch Activities.
101. *Martin Marietta Corporation,* Office of Commercial Space Transportation License No. 90-013, Order Regarding Commercial Space Activities. at 1, para. 3.

from which the coverage must attach is not specified. However, the logical point for "commencement" of commercial activities is the arrival of the launch operator and its contractors at the launch site. Without such an identifiable logical point for commencement of launch activities, it will be virtually impossible to distinguish which activities would, or would not, relate to the provision of commercial launch services.[102] This reasoning is reflected in the Commercial Launch Services Contract Between Martin Marietta Corporation and the International Telecommunications Satellite Organization "INTELSAT" (hereinafter Martin Marietta-INTELSAT Contract), which provides that third party liability insurance procured by Martin Marietta "shall commence upon the arrival of the Payload and INTELSAT's personnel incident to the Payload Launch campaign at [the launch site.]" [103]

As indicated, under United States law the insurance coverage must be in effect until thirty days following the insertion into orbit of the satellite. It is not the final orbit that is covered. For example, with regard to satellites destined for the geostationary orbit, it is the orbit into which the payload initially is inserted that is critical with respect to the coverage; not the geostationary orbit. The point of insertion into orbit is not the same for all types of launch vehicles. Some vehicles, such as Martin Marietta's Titan, deliver the satellite to a low-Earth circular orbit, while others, such as Arianespace's Ariane launch vehicle, deliver the payload into a highly elliptical geostationary transfer orbit. When a Martin Marietta Titan second stage failed to separate from the INTELSAT VI satellite and its perigee kick motor on March 14, 1990 (see Chapter 6.4.2.), and the satellite was stranded in a useless low-Earth orbit, the insertion into orbit for purposes of the required third party liability insurance, nevertheless, was completed, and the thirty day period began to run.[104] The standard draft Arianespace launch agreement provides that the third-party liability insurance shall remain in effect for thirty-six months or, for the time period during which the payload is attached to the launch vehicle, whichever is shorter. See Chapter 6.5.2.1.

INDEMNIFICATION. It is possible that a third party claim could exceed the insured amount. Who pays for damages in excess of the coverage? Assume that the launch vehicle with your client's satellite on board crashes not far from the launch site causing third party damage. Assume, further, that the launch company has insurance in the amount of $150 mil-

---

102. *See* P.D. Nesgos, *Recent Developments in Risk Allocation of Concern to the U.S. Commercial Launch Industry and the Launch Insurance Community,* Paper presented at Assicurazione Generali Fifth International Conference on Space Insurance, Rome, Italy (Mar. 2-3, 1989) (discussing the time period during which third party liability insurance must be in effect pursuant to the 1988 Amendments).
103. Martin Marietta-INTELSAT Contract, art. 17.2.1 *See* Chapter 6.5.2.
104. *Id.* The Martin Marietta-INTELSAT Contract provides that the coverage shall remain in effect ninety days after the actual launch date. *Id.*

lion protecting your client, but that the aggregate of third party claims amounts to $500 million. In this case, claims of $350 million would not be covered by the insurance.

Governments of launch companies in business today often provide indemnification in the event successful third party claims exceed the insured amount. With respect to the United States government, the 1988 Amendments provide that "the Secretary [of Transportation] shall provide for the payment by the United States of successful claims . . . in excess of the amount of insurance . . . ."[105] The indemnification extends to your client and its contractors and subcontractors, as well as to other launch participants.[106] A cap of $1.5 billion above the insured amount applies to the United States government indemnification.[107] Consequently, responsibility for claims exceeding that amount reverts to the launch company and potentially your client, as well. Moreover, the indemnification does not apply if the third party damage has resulted from willful misconduct by the launch company. Accordingly, your client would also not be protected by government indemnification, but could seek indemnification from the launch company if required to pay a claim.

DURATION OF THE INDEMNIFICATION. Under the 1988 Amendments, government indemnification also applies to claims "resulting from activities carried out pursuant to a license issued or transferred under this Act . . . ."[108] The interpretation with respect to commencement of the insurance requirement is equally relevant here. At present it is unclear whether U.S. Government indemnification extends beyond the period of insurance coverage.

105. 49 U.S.C. § 2615(b)(1) (1988).
106. *Id.*
107. *Id.* § 26(b)(1)(B) (1988).
108. *Id.*, § 26(b)(1) (1988).

Epilogue

Politics, economics, cultures, whole civilizations, and even ideologies and theologies, remain on the cutting edge of change when the catalyst is a vast array of rapidly-evolving technologies. The consequent social tensions among the participating interests are barely, if at all, constrained. Laws and legal regimes are, in effect, mirrors held up against societies and civilizations that reflect attempts at institutionalizing the values underlying those changes. The exploration and commercial exploitation of near and deep space are prime examples of these types of changes resulting from the dynamic tensions created by the evolution of high technology. So, also, do the reflections in the mirror of space law seem to change with alacrity; to be more transitory than institutionalizing in nature. And that, too, is the essence of a daily and pragmatic practice of the space lawyer.

Change, confusion and uncertainty are the reflections in the mirror held up against the immense industry that is the legacy of the former Soviet space program. The newly independent republics have been forced into the strange philosophic constructs and machinations of free market societies in the international arena. The heretofore highly visible and successful space program is expected to be one of the foremost commercial assets of the independent republics, either individually or collectively within the framework of the Commonwealth, as reflected in the December 1991 Minsk Accord. Although the Ukraine is one of two Republics that refused at the outset to sign the twelve-article agreement in Minsk, high technology sales and desperately needed hard currency do seem to go hand-in-glove for the newly elected officials of the republics and representatives of the Commonwealth, but is it a mirage...a fragile straw...a misplaced hope borne of extreme economic frustration? Will the former Soviet space industry be restructured in a fashion that invites significant foreign investment confidence and the development of high quality products to market?

At present, the secretly-nourished and massive space program of the former Soviet Union is straining to reorganize itself amidst economic chaos and extreme political fragmentation. But that does not necessarily mean the vast, complex industry underpinning the space program is gasping its last breaths. It does not even mean that the program has been traumatically crippled. What it does mean, quite simply, is that the program is being readjusted to meet economic and political realities; to take advantage of existing and new economic and social opportunities which, until now, have been closed to the former Soviet space program. Reorganizing and restructuring are integral components of a free market economy. Companies, indeed, entire industries, that do not accomplish these types of business adjustments in a timely fashion, or do not do it well or at all, become non-competitors and, ultimately, non-participants. The governments and industries of the Western World and other countries embracing the economics of free enterprise should be prepared to learn the lessons flowing from the reorganization of the Soviet space program, as well as welcoming it into the international market place arena.

Of course, many former Soviet space projects will be put on hold for short or long durations. The same delays and disappointments occur every day in other countries with space programs, not the least of which is the United States. But the changes taking place in the Commonwealth of Independent States will significantly influence changes in how those other countries and industries do business with respect to the exploration and commercial exploitation of space. This book, as is true for lawyers and businessmen and women who come to use it, will have to respond in a positive, effective, and timely fashion to those changes.

Appendix 1

Agenda for the World Administrative Radio Conference for Dealing with Frequency Allocations in Certain Parts of the Spectrum to be convened in Spain from February 3, 1992

2. THE AGENDA FOR WARC-92 SHALL BE AS FOLLOWS:

   ON THE BASIS OF PROPOSALS BY ADMINISTRATIONS-TAKING INTO ACCOUNT IFRB AND CCIR:

2.1. TO CONSIDER DEFINITIONS FOR CERTAIN NEW SPACE APPLICATIONS AND TO REVIEW THE PROVISIONS OF ARTICLE 1 [of the Radio Regulations]

2.2. TO REVIEW THE PROVISIONS OF ARTICLE 8 . . . WITH A VIEW TO:

2.2.1. THE CONSIDERATION OF POSSIBLE ALLOCATIONS OF FREQUENCY BANDS ABOVE 20 GHZ TO NEW SPACE SERVICES APPLICATIONS;

2.2.2. THE POSSIBLE EXTENSION OF THE FREQUENCY SPECTRUM ALLOCATED EXCLUSIVELY FOR HF BROADCASTING, AS INDICATED IN RECOMMENDATION NO. 511 (HFBC-87);

2.2.3. THE CONSIDERATION OF THE ALLOCATION OF FREQUENCY BANDS TO THE BROADCASTING SATELLITE SERVICE AND THE ASSOCIATED FEEDER LINKS:

   A) FOR BROADCASTING SATELLITE SERVICE (SOUND) IN THE RANGE 500-3,000 MHZ, AS INDICATED IN RESOLUTION 520 (ORB-88), INCLUDING THE ACCOMMODATION OF COMPLEMENTARY TERRESTRIAL SOUND BROADCASTING USES WITHIN THIS ALLOCATION;

(B) FOR RF-BAND HIGH DEFINITION TELEVISION ON A WORLD-WIDE BASIS, AS INDICATED IN RESOLUTION 521 (ORB-88) GIVING CONSIDERATION TO RESULTS OF CCIR STUDIES CARRIED OUT IN ACCORDANCE WITH THIS RESOLUTION;

2.2.4. THE CONSIDERATION OF AN ALLOCATION OF FREQUENCY BANDS TO MOBILE AND MOBILE SATELLITE SERVICES AND ASSOCIATED FEEDER LINKS;

A) IN THE APPROPRIATE RANGE 1-3 GHZ, AS INDICATED IN RESOLUTION NO. 208 (MOB-87);

B) FOR THE DEVELOPMEHT IN THE APPROXIMATE RANGE 1-3 GHZ OF A WORLD-WIDE SYSTEM OF PUBLIC CORRESPONDENCE WITH AIRCRAFT, AS INDICATED IN RECOMMENDATION NO. 408 (MOB-87), OR DESIGNATE FOR THIS USE A BAND ALREADY ALLOCATED TO THE MOBILE SERVICE IN THE SAME RANGE;

C) FOR THE DEVELOPMENT OF THE INTERNATIONAL USE OF THE MOBILE SERVICE FOR FUTURE PUBLIC LAND MOBILE TELECOMMUNICATIONS SYSTEMS, AS INDICATED IN RECOMMENDATION NO. 205 (MOB-87), OR DESIGNATE FOR THIS USE A BAND ALREADY ALLOCATED TO THE MOBILE SERVICE;

D) CONSIDER POSSIBLE ALLOCATIONS OF UP TO 5 MHZ OF A FREQUENCY BAND BELOW 1 GHZ TO LOW-ORBIT SATELLITES ON THE BASIS OF APPROPRIATE SHARING CRITERIA;

2.2.5. THE CONSIDERATION OF THE ALLOCATION OF THE FREQUENCY BAND 14.5-14.8 GHZ TO THE FIXED SATELLITE SERVICE (EARTH-TO-SPACE) WITH DUE REGARD TO ASSIGNMENTS APPEARING IN APPENDIX 30A OF THE RADIO REGULATIONS, AND TO TAKE ACCOUNT SERVICES TO WHICH THESE BANDS CURRENTLY ARE ALLOCATED;

2.2.6. THE EXAMINATION OF THE FREQUENCY BANDS 2025-2110 MHZ AND 2200-2290 MHZ FOR THE SPACE OPERATION AND SPACE RESEARCH SERVICES AS INDICATED IN RECOMMENDATION 716 (ORB-88);

2.2.7. THE CONSIDERATION OF FOOTNOTES RELATING TO THE RADIODETERMINATION SATELLITE SERVICE IN THE FREQUENCY RANGE 1.6-2.5 GHZ WITH THE VIEW TO HARMONIZING THEM AND ALLOWING ADMINIS-

TRATIONS TO REVISE THE STATUS OF THEIR RESPECTIVE ALLOCATIONS TO THIS SERVICE AND TO REVIEW THE SHARING CRITERIA AS INDICATED IN RESOLUTION NO. 709 (MOB-87);

2.2.8. THE EXAMINATION OF FOOTNOTES RR 635 AND 7978;

2.3. TO CONSIDER PROVISIONS OF ARTICLES 55(REV.) AND 56(REV.) OF THE RADIO REGULATIONS WHICH CONCERN THE MANDATORY CARRIAGE ON BOARD SHIPS OF PERSONNEL CERTIFICATED FOR THE ON-BOARD MAINTENANCE OF SHIPBORNE RADIO AND ELECTRONIC EQUIPMENT, AS INDICATED IN RESOLUTION NO. PLEN/8

2.4. TO CONSIDER MINIMUM MODIFICATIONS TO ARTICLE 12 OF THE RADIO REGULATIONS AS A RESULT OF ACTIONS TAKEN WITH REGARD TO APPENDIX 26, AS INDICATED IN RESOLUTION NO. PL-8/2;

2.5. TO CONSIDER APPROPRIATE ACTION, IN LIGHT OF THE DECISION OF THE CONFERENCE RELATING TO DEFINITIONS IN ACCORDANCE WITH RESOLUTIONS PL/10;

2.6. TO MAKE SUCH CONSEQUENTIAL CHANGES AND AMENDMENTS IN THE RADIO REGULATIONS AS MAY BE NECESSITATED BY THE DECISIONS OF THE CONFERENCE;

2.7. TO DEVELOP NEW RECOMMENDATIONS AND RESOLUTIONS IN RELATION TO THE AGENDA OF THE CONFERENCE INCLUDING METEOROLOGICAL AIDS SERVICE IN FREQUENCY BANDS BELOW 1000 MHZ AND SPECIAL ALLOCATIONS TO SPACE SERVICES ABOVE 20 GHZ WHICH WERE NOT PLACED ON THIS AGENDA;

2.8. TO CONSIDER PROBLEMS ASSOCIATED WITH THE USE OF THE FREQUENCY BANDS IN THE RANGE 401-403 MHZ BY METEOROLOGICAL SATELLITE AND EARTH EXPLORATION SATELLITE SERVICES WITH A VIEW TO RECOMMEND THEIR CONSIDERATION BY THE NEXT COMPETENT ADMINISTRATIVE RADIO CONFERENCE;

2.9. TO CONSIDER, REVISE AS NECESSARY, AND TAKE OTHER APPROPRIATE ACTION UPON THE RELEVANT RECOMMENDATIONS AND RESOLUTIONS;

2.9.1. TO SAFEGUARD THE INTERESTS OF SERVICES THAT MAY BE AFFECTED BY CHANGES TO THE TABLE OF FREQUENCY ALLOCATIONS BY ADOPTING APPROPRIATE SHARING CRITERIA WHEN REQUIRED AND TO

ADOPT APPROPRIATE SCHEDULE FOR ENTERING INTO FORCE OF THE DECISIONS ADOPTED BY THE CONFERENCE;

2.9.2. TO REVIEW RESOLUTION NO. 703 IN THE LIGHT OF THE PROCEDURE ADOPTED AT THE XVIITH CCIR PLENARY ASSEMBLY (RESOLUTION PLEN/75) FOR THE APPROVAL OF RECOMMENDATIONS IN THE INTERVAL BETWEEN PLENARY ASSEMBLIES;

2.10. TO IDENTIFY THE FINANCIAL IMPLICATIONS OF THE DECISIONS OF THE CONFERENCE, TAKING INTO ACCOUNT THE UNION'S BUDGETARY PROVISIONS, AND AS NECESSARY TO SUBMIT A STATEMENT THEREON TO THE ADMINISTRATIVE COUNCIL IN ACCORDANCE WITH ARTICLE 80 OF THE INTERNATIONAL TELECOMMUNICATION CONVENTION AND RESOLUTION NO. 48. OF THE PLENIPOTENTIARY CONFERENCE, NAIROBI, 1982.

Biographical Sketch of Pamela L. Meredith

Pamela L. Meredith presently lives in Washington, D.C. She received her law degree from the University of Oslo in Norway and an LL.M. degree from the Institute of Air and Space Law, McGill University in Montreal, Canada, and is a member of the New York Bar.

Since 1987, Ms. Meredith has served as President of Space Consultation & Information, Inc., a space business and regulatory consulting firm. Ms. Meredith also has been an adjunct professor of space law at American University in Washington, D.C., for a number of years. Before 1987, she served as a space law consultant to several Washington, D.C., law firms.

Ms. Meredith participates actively in several professional organizations in the U.S. and internationally. She also is the author of a number of articles and monographs on space law and commerce. She focuses much of her space law efforts on assisting governments and industry in resolving the growing problem of space debris and, toward this end, co-chairs the Orbital Debris Committee of the American Institute of Aeronautics and Astronautics.

Biographical Sketch of George S. Robinson

Dr. George S. Robinson presently lives in Warrenton, Virginia (USA), and is a graduate of Bowdoin College in the State of Maine, where he majored in biochemistry. He holds an LL.B. degree from University of Virginia School of Law, as well as an LL.M. and the first Doctor of Civil Laws Degree awarded by the Graduate Faculty, Institute of Air and Space Law, McGill University in Montreal, Canada. He is admitted to practice in Washington, D.C., Virginia and before the United States Supreme Court.

For the past twenty-three years, Dr. Robinson has served as Assistant and Associate General Counsel of the Smithsonian Institution in Washington, D.C., and before that as legal counsel for the United States Federal Aviation Administration, and as an international relations specialist at the National Aeronautics and Space Administration. He is an active member of a number of professional associations, and is the author of numerous articles and books on space law and business.

Dr. Robinson frequently lectures on topics of space law and business at universities and professional societies in the United States and abroad, and teaches a graduate course at George Mason University in Virginia on the subject of international commercialization of space.

Index